LAWYER'S DESK BOOK

ELEVENTH EDITION

Dana Shilling

PRENTICE HALL

Library of Congress Cataloging-in-Publication Data

Shilling, Dana.
    Lawyer's desk book / c Dana Shilling.—11th ed.
      p. cm.
    Includes index.
    ISBN 0-13-011077-9
    1. Law—United States. 2. Practice of law—United States.

    KF386.L39 2000
    349.73—dc21   99-055711

©2000 by Prentice Hall, Inc.

Printed in the United States of America

10 9 8 7 6 5 4 3 2

This publication is designed to provide accurate and authoritative information in regard to the subject matter covered. It is sold with the understanding that the publisher is not engaged in rendering legal, accounting, or other professional service. If legal advice or other expert assistance is required, the services of a competent professional person should be sought.
—*From the Declaration of Principles jointly adopted by a Committee of the American Bar Association and a Committee of Publishers and Associations*

ISBN 0-13-011077-9

9 780130 110770   90000

ATTENTION: CORPORATIONS AND SCHOOLS
Prentice Hall books are available at quantity discounts with bulk purchase for educational, business, or sales promotional use. For information, please write to: Prentice Hall Special Sales, 240 Frisch Court, Paramus, New Jersey 07652. Please supply: title of book, ISBN, quantity, how the book will be used, date needed.

PRENTICE HALL
Paramus, NJ 07652

On the World Wide Web at http://www.phdirect.com

CONTENTS

Note: Each chapter begins with ¶x01, an introduction.

Part II: Contract and Property Law

Part III: Financial and Credit Law

Part IV: Personal Planning

¶3200 Torts..461

¶3300 Immigration..493

Part V: Tax Issues

¶4100 Personal Income Tax and Tax Planning...515

Part VIII: Law Office Issues

INTRODUCTION

I before e, except after c. Thirty days hath September. The square of the hypotenuse equals the sum of the squares of the other two sides. That's one function of a desk reference for attorneys: a quick summary of basic rules. The other function of a desk reference—and its supplements—is to bring the story up to date by covering statutory developments and case law since the last supplement. This edition deals with events through mid-1999, including the Supreme Court term that ended in June, 1999.

This Eleventh Edition has a new look and is organized differently from the earlier editions. This time, the focus is on problems that the sole practitioner or small-firm attorney will encounter. Topics have been selected on this basis. The topics chosen, and the order in which they are presented, have been changed, in the interests of making this a practical, easy-to-use reference source and guide to statutes, Uniform Law sections, and cases that you may wish to read and cite.

This new edition also reflects new realities. One example is the shift from paper-based legal practice to one where computers are involved in every level and at every stage. Cyberspace creates important legal problems, including jurisdiction, commerce, and trademark issues. On more prosaic *terra firma*, new law continues to be made in traditional areas such as criminal law (especially search and seizure, the death penalty, and appellate practice) and family law (as divorce becomes more widespread and unconventional kinds of families evolve).

The mission of this book is to summarize current legal principles, in the organization that best suits the reader's needs. As the law changes, and as legal research and practice evolve, the *Lawyer's Desk Book* will continue to evolve responsively.

Part I

BUSINESS PLANNING AND LITIGATION

¶100

Organization of the Business Enterprise

[¶101]

For-profit businesses can be organized in many forms. (See ¶170 for not-for-profit organizations, and ¶460.3 for taxation of not-for-profit organizations.) The choice of a form of organization will determine many things about what the business and its participants can and cannot do; who will be subject to liability; how the entity must handle its profits; and how it will be taxed.

The main choices for organizing a business entity are:

- General partnership
- Limited partnership
- Limited liability partnership (LLP) (see ¶110 for a discussion of partnership law and taxation)
- Limited liability company (LLC)
- Subchapter S corporation
- Subchapter C corporation

The basic corporate form is the C corporation, but certain small non-public corporations can make a Subchapter S election, which permits them to become pass-through entities that are taxed more like partnerships than like corporations. (See ¶400 et seq. for a discussion of partnership and corporate taxation.)

There is no central repository of corporate law, although there is a Model Business Corporations Law (MBCL) that state legislators can consult. Many states have adopted the Uniform Partnership Act (UPA), first published in 1914, and the Uniform Limited Partnership Act (ULPA; 1916) or Revised Limited Partnership Act (RULPA). RULPA was broadly adopted in the 1980s and 1990s.

Federal corporate tax was first imposed (albeit at low rates) in 1909; corporate rates did not reach high levels until World War II. Subchapter S was added to the Internal Revenue Code in 1958. The first LLC statute was Wyoming's 1977 law, but the form remained obscure until 1988, when the IRS conceded that LLCs could be taxed as partnerships. All the states allow LLCs, but there is no Uniform Act. Forty-eight states permit LLPs (limited liability partnerships), a hybrid between general and limited partnership.

[¶105] Choosing the Entity

The choice of entity depends on practical[1] and tax factors. It should be noted that the states do not always follow federal tax concepts: not all states have their own version of Subchapter S, for instance, so a corporation that is not federally taxed at the entity level may nevertheless be subject to state taxation.

3

The state and/or municipality may impose property taxes, sales taxes, taxes on income earned inside and/or outside the state, intangible property, stock transfers, etc. State or local taxes on unincorporated business are another possibility. Some areas make an effort to attract and retain businesses (and create jobs) by offering tax incentives.

A business entity that does business in more than one jurisdiction will be obligated to register in the foreign jurisdictions, which will not necessarily have rules as generous as the home state's.

Delaware incorporation is a popular choice, because of that state's historic role in creating innovative corporate law. However, for a small or relatively small or new business, the disadvantages of having to register as a "foreign" corporation in the state in which business is actually being done are likely to outweigh the benefits obtained by any difference between local and Delaware corporation law.

It's possible to change the form of a business' organization, as its needs change; as the ownership group changes due to expulsion, withdrawal, death, or retirement; or to correct mistakes. However, the tax consequences of a change in form can be quite negative, so the best move is to make the correct selection at the outset.

[¶105.1] Franchising

A franchise is a compromise between working as an employee store manager and setting up an entirely independent business. A franchisee is an entrepreneur who invests in one unit of a multi-unit marketing system, and in return for agreeing to abide by the franchise's methods of doing business, is entitled to use the franchise's name, trademark, and business methods in an exclusive territory.

The typical franchise relationship provides training for the franchisee. During the term of the franchise agreement (typically, a term of years, with automatic renewal or options to renew, but with provisions permitting the franchisor to terminate the agreement of franchisees whose performance is deemed substandard), the franchisee makes continuing payments to the franchisor, typically based on sales volume. The franchisor usually imposes quality standards, and may require purchase of essential items from the franchisor itself or acceptable suppliers; the franchise agreement sets out the respective rights and obligations of the franchisor and franchisee.

Although many franchises are quite successful, both for the central operation and most of the franchisees, there is significant potential for economic loss and also exploitation of the franchisee. The Federal Trade Commission has an extensive disclosure rule, found at 16 CFR Part 436, setting out the disclosure obligations that franchisors have to potential franchisees. The required disclosures must be provided in a single prospectus, including the franchisor's balance sheet and income statement, current as of the close of the franchisor's most recent fiscal year.

[¶110] Partnership

A partnership is a business association of two or more co-owners who:

- Carry on a business for profit

- Share profits and losses
- Jointly own and control the firm's capital or property
- Have joint control and management over its business.

Usually, a partnership can consist of any combination of natural persons; other partnerships; corporations; estates and trusts. (See ¶7050.1 for special issues affecting law firm partnerships.) A partnership is not a taxpayer; instead, the partnership files an information return (Form 1065), and the partners pay taxes based on rules summarized in ¶410.

There are several kinds of partnership: general, limited, and limited liability. In a general partnership, all partners have equal liability. Every partner is the agent of every other partner, and has a fiduciary duty to the other partners. Partnerships are obligated to indemnify their partners who make payments, or are subjected to personal liability, for actions in the ordinary and necessary course of partnership business.

Limited partnerships have at least one fully liable general partner, plus one or more limited partners. The limited partners' liability is limited to the amount they have invested in the partnership. Limited partners do not have the power to control management of the partnership, and they are not liable for its debts over and above their investment.

[¶110.1] Organization of a Partnership

A partnership is permitted to use any name that is not deceptive and does not violate trademark or licensing rights of any other business. Many states require registration of partnership names with the Secretary of State, county clerk, or other filing officer. Some states do not permit the name of a deceased person to be included in a partnership name.

Partners can make their contribution to the organization of a partnership in cash, property, or services. In addition to making capital contributions, partners can also lend or rent property to the partnership, and receive loan repayment or rent payments. Loaned or rented property does not become part of the partnership's capital, and is not available to satisfy partnership debts. But property acquired with partnership funds becomes partnership property.

The general rule is that partnerships do not pay interest to partners on their capital contributions. However, the partnership agreement can provide for interest, and might be especially likely to do so if the partnership is subject to regulatory requirements that require large amounts of liquid capital.

[¶110.1.1] Partnership Agreement
The partnership agreement resolves matters such as:

- Initial contributions by partners
- Subsequent capital contributions
- Loans by partners to the partnership
- Duties and responsibilities of each partner

- Percentage share of profits and losses of each partner
- Partnership "draws" (regularly paid amounts)
- Admission of new partners; limitations on transfer of partnership interests
- Withdrawal and expulsion of partners
- Right of partners to withdraw capital
- Payments to estate of deceased partner[2]
- Survival of the partnership after an event that could result in dissolution
- Methods for resolving partnership disputes
- Methods for amending the partnership agreement
- Designation of the Tax Management Partner, who is the partnership's liaison with the IRS.

If the partnership intends to engage in a business requiring a license or permit, the agreement should provide that it does not become effective until the license or permit has been secured.

Unless the agreement is to the contrary, all partners have equal rights in the management and conduct of partnership business. Any limits on the assignability of partnership interests, and the rights and duties of the assignee, also belong in the agreement.

Usually partners are compensated for their work by receiving a share of partnership profits rather than a salary. However, the partnership agreement can provide for salary or other reasonable compensation for services actually performed.

[¶110.2] Dissolution of a Partnership

Dissolution can either be voluntary or mandated by events. A partnership that is created for a specific term dissolves at the end of that term. A partnership at will has no specified duration, and can be terminated at the wish of any partner.

Other dissolution events:

- Death of any partner
- Bankruptcy of the partnership itself, or any partner
- Any event that interferes with a partner's, or the partnership's, carrying on of business (e.g., loss of license)
- Expulsion of a partner under the terms of the partnership agreement.

UPA §31 provides for automatic dissolution of a partnership whenever any partner dies or withdraws, unless the agreement provides for continuation. It is common to provide for continuation, and also to require withdrawing partners to give the partnership or the other partners a right of first refusal on the partnership interest.

The agreement should specify whether the price will be paid in a lump sum (usually preferred by the recipient) or in a series of payments (usually preferred by the partnership). See Code §2703 for criteria the buyout price must satisfy to be accepted by the IRS as the estate tax valuation of the decedent's interest. Broadly speaking, the price must be equivalent to the fair market price that would be received in an arm's length transaction.

The partnership agreement can also provide for the interest of a deceased partner to pass to spouse, children, or other pre-approved successor. In a professional partnership, of course, the successor must also be licensed to practice the profession.

Partnerships are subject to judicial dissolution, if a partner has breached the partnership agreement severely, or is mentally incapacitated or otherwise unable to continue as partner, with the result that maintaining the partnership business is impractical. Judicial dissolution is also available if it becomes impossible to maintain the partnership business at a profit.

When a partnership is dissolved, it can continue doing business until winding-up is completed. The process of winding-up consists of terminating the partnership's business, paying its debts and distributing any remaining assets. Debts owed to non-partner creditors get first priority, followed by loans made by partners to the partnership, then capital contributions made by the partners, and finally distribution of profits to the partners. If the partnership's liabilities exceed its assets, the partners are obligated to make up the shortfall, in proportion to their share of the partnership profits. See UPA §§38 and 40.

[¶110.3] Agency Issues in Partnership

Generally, any partner is an agent of the partnership for the purpose of its business. A partner who acts in the course of the usual business of the partnership will bind the partnership, unless the partner lacks authority to do so, and the other party to the transaction is aware of this fact.

For acts outside the ordinary course of partnership business, a partner can bind the partnership only with authorization from all the other partners. Some very significant transactions (e.g., disposal of partnership goodwill; confession of judgment; submitting a partnership claim to arbitration; assigning partnership property in trust for creditors; any act that would make it impossible to carry out the partnership's business) also require unanimous consent of all partners.

Partners are always entitled to access to the partnership's books and records. They have a duty to account to the partnership for any benefit derived without consent of the other partners. Any partner wrongfully excluded from partnership business has a right to demand a formal accounting.

[¶110.4] Limited Partnership

As noted above, a limited partnership has two tiers of membership: general and limited partners. The general partner(s) are in the same position as partners within a general partnership. The limited partners exchange loss of active management control for limitation of their liability: their maximum liability is the amount invested, plus any mandatory further contributions required by the partnership agreement. Generally speaking, limited partnership interests are assignable. Assignment of a limited partnership interest does not dissolve the partnership, or even make the assignee a partner; it merely gives the assignee a right to receive whatever distributions the partnership would have made to the assignor.

Under the Uniform Limited Partnership Act (ULPA) and Revised Uniform Limited Partnership Act (RULPA), creation of a limited partnership requires both an agreement among the partners, and state registration resulting in issuance of a certificate of limited partnership status. The certificate must be amended whenever new limited partners are admitted.

Limited partnerships can be attractive if the business includes a participant who could not qualify as an S Corporation shareholder; if there are more than 75 participants in the business; if the entity wants to make distributions that are not proportionate to ownership shares (S Corporations are not allowed to make disproportionate distributions); or if the business has losses that can best be used to reduce participants' personal income taxes in limited partnership form.

RULPA provides for dissolution and winding up of a limited partnership according to its certificate; on written consent of all partners; or based on a judicial decree of dissolution. Dissolution also occurs on the withdrawal of a general partner (by death, retirement, or incapacity) unless the certificate gives the remaining general partners the right to continue the business, or unless all partners consent in writing within 90 days of the withdrawal.

[¶110.4.1] Limited Liability Partnerships

The Limited Liability Partnership (LLP) form of organization is usually used by professional firms. It is essentially a type of general partnership, but with some limitations on the personal liability of partners. For example, one LLP partner will not be liable for negligent torts committed by another partner, unless the tortfeasor was under the other partner's direct supervision. Personal liability other than for negligent torts remains unlimited. Formation of an LLP requires filing a certificate with the state.

[¶1 1 5] Professional Corporations

At one time, very few pension and benefit options were available outside large C Corporations. That created a dilemma for doctors, lawyers, accountants, and other professionals. They wanted to be able to create generous benefit plans for their professional firms; they also wanted limitation of liability, but they wanted to practice in a state-authorized form with some of the simplicity and collegiality of partnership.

The solution was the Professional Corporation, or PC. All member-shareholders must be licensed to practice the profession at issue. State law treats the PC as a limited-liability form (although PC shareholders are still fully liable for their own professional negligence and the negligence of those they supervise). Members of a PC are not liable to the PC's trade creditors.

IRC §269A says that a PC will be taxed as a corporation, and will give its members and their employees full access to the range of corporate employee benefits, as long as the corporation acts as a separate entity; performs meaningful business functions; and its principal purpose is some legitimate objective other than avoiding federal income taxation.

[¶120] Subchapter S Corporations

An S Corporation, although it is a corporation (and therefore its stockholders are entitled to limited liability protection), is taxed by and large as a corporation. It is a pass-through entity, and in most instances, there will be no tax at the corporate level (see ¶459.1 for the exceptions). See Code §§311 and 1366-1368, and ¶459 of this volume, for S Corporation taxation.

An S Corporation is allowed to have only one class of stock. It can have only 75 shareholders. All shareholders must be natural persons, estates, some trusts, or tax-exempt entities. Non-resident aliens are not allowed to be S Corporation shareholders. An S Corporation can own stock in a C Corporation, and can own 100% of a subsidiary that is also an S Corporation, but a C Corporation can't own shares in an S Corporation.

An S Corporation that merges into an LLC (discussed in the next paragraph) is subject to capital gains tax on all appreciation in its assets.

[¶125] Limited Liability Companies

The LLC is another hybrid entity. It is governed by state law. Its stockholder-members can elect to have the entity taxed as either a corporation or a partnership; usually they elect partnership treatment. Unlike a partnership, however, LLC stockholder-members are entitled to limited liability. Unlike the stockholders of a C Corporation, they are not subject to double taxation (once at the corporate level, once when dividends are paid).

An LLC's managing member, or any member who participates in operation of the LLC's business for more than 500 hours a year, is subject to self-employment tax on compensation received from the LLC.

[¶130] Business Capitalization

Every business will have some initial group of owners and investors, no matter how the members of this group are characterized for legal purposes. Furthermore, the capital can come in the form of cash, property, and/or services. The contributions can be treated as either a capital investment in the enterprise (equity) or a loan (debt). Equity entitles the contributor to some share of the corporation's profits, but need not be repaid if there are no profits. Debt does have to be repaid.

In some situations, contributions are made by unsophisticated parties who do not insist on a clear statement of the business entity's intentions. Or, there may be documents (even well-drafted ones) that do not conform to IRC principles and will not be effective for tax purposes.

[¶130.1] Debt: Equity Ratios

An entity organized as a corporation has tax incentives to claim that much of its capital comes in the form of debt. A corporation can deduct interest it pays on loans, but can't deduct the dividends it pays to its shareholders. Someone who lends money to a business entity is not taxed on return of the principal (although the interest is taxable income); a corporate stockholder who redeems shares is likely to be taxed on capital gains or dividends.

Code §385(b) prescribes rules to distinguish between business debt and partnership equity or stock ownership. Factors in distinguishing between debt and equity include:

- Presence of a written, unconditional promise to pay
- Due date for the payment (or promise to pay on demand)
- Agreement to pay a determined amount
- Fixed rate of interest
- Question of whether this obligation is preferred or subordinated to other business obligations
- Ratio of debt to equity in capitalization of the corporation
- Whether or not the obligation can be converted to stock
- Whether the so-called debt is proportionate to the so-called lender's stock ownership.

The IRS has the power to re-characterize alleged debt as equity, if this reflects corporate realities. S Corporations are particularly at risk if re-characterization occurs, because the so-called debt might be treated as a second class of stock, thus destroying the S Corporation status.

Code §1361(c)(5)(A) permits a safe harbor for "straight debt": i.e., an unconditional promise to pay a sum certain, payable in money (not property), either on a date certain or on demand. The interest rate of S Corporation straight debt must not be contingent on the corporation's discretion, on its profits, payment of dividends on its common stock, or similar factors that point to equity rather than debt status.

Straight debt must not be convertible (directly or indirectly) into stock or other equity interest in the corporation. Furthermore, the creditor must be an individual who is a U.S. citizen or resident alien, or an estate or trust that is a permissible S Corporation shareholder.

Also see §279, which restricts the corporate interest deduction on some subordinated debt that is convertible or issued with warrants, and that is used to finance corporate acquisitions.

[¶130.2] §351 Transactions

Code §351 says that neither the corporation (C or S) nor a shareholder has gain or loss if: either appreciated or depreciated property is contributed to the corporation, in exchange for shares and nothing else; if the shareholder(s) making the contribution is in control of the corporation right after the contribution.

Control, as defined by §368(c), means ownership of at least 80% of the total combined voting power of all the corporation's voting stock, plus at least 80% of all non-voting shares (measured by number of shares).

If the transaction involves "boot" (something other than shares in the donee corporation), the recipient of the boot has taxable gain: §§351(b), 1001.

If a corporation issues its stock in exchange for services rather than money or property, §351(d) provides that gain or loss can be recognized. The corporation gets to deduct the compensation; the recipient has ordinary income. Also see §83, which says that the recipient is taxable when the stock can be sold or otherwise transferred to someone else, or is no longer subject to a substantial risk of forfeiture.

In a §351 transaction, §358 sets the shareholder's basis for the stock at the basis of the transferred property. A corporation that receives a contribution of securities has the same basis as the transferor had.

[¶135] Organizing a Corporation

The most common business form is the corporation, because it is both a powerful and a flexible form. It provides the advantages of limited liability for shareholders, indefinite existence, centralized management, and free transferability of its stock and other business interests.

The attorney may be involved with the corporation at many levels: assisting in the creation of the corporation; assisting in corporate governance; advising the corporation about legal implications of its business operations; perhaps supervising the Initial Public Offering of the corporation's stock or its merger with or acquisition of (or by) another corporation; or, if necessary, handling a bankruptcy reorganization or dissolution of the corporation.

Apart from federal corporate taxation, bankruptcy, and securities law, most corporate law issues are governed by state law. The corporation must be validly created under the law of one state (usually either Delaware or the corporation's home state). Corporations doing business in additional states will be required to register as foreign corporations.

[¶135.1] Mechanics Of Corporate Formation

State law imposes some fairly minimal requirements for creating a corporation:

- Selecting a corporate name that neither duplicates an existing name nor is deceptively similar
- Naming one or more incorporators (depending on state practice, they may have to be natural persons rather than organizations, and may have to be state residents)
- Filing a Certificate of Incorporation
- Holding an organization meeting
- Electing an initial slate of directors
- Holding the first meeting of the board of directors
- Adopting by-laws
- Getting a taxpayer ID number

11

- Setting up accounts for tax withholding and payment of FICA, FUTA (unemployment), Workers' Compensation, and other amounts relating to employee compensation

Although it is entirely permissible to handle these formalities in a "cookie-cutter" manner, filling in the blanks of standard forms, it is often helpful to custom-tailor the documents in order to anticipate and avoid potential problems of operations and governance.

[¶135.1.1] Reservation of Corporate Name

State laws provide for reserving a corporate name with the Department of State for future use. Typically, the reservation lasts for a short period of time, with one or two extensions permitted; after the last extension, the reservation lapses unless a corporation has been created under that name.

Selection of the corporate name is a difficult problem (and, in fact, there are expensive consulting firms that do nothing but advise on this question). Clearly, the businesses cannot register a name that infringes upon an existing and active corporate name; but a company that wants to do business in many states, or internationally, may discover that its name is valid in the jurisdiction of registration but unavailable elsewhere. (The name may also be innocuous in English but insulting or obscene in other languages!)

The corporate name should not infringe upon an existing trademark, and should not create a risk of confusion (especially a risk of confusion with a "famous" trademark: see ¶1330.1.1). In many instances it is worthwhile to use a corporate name that is itself entitled to trademark protection, although this is not always necessary—especially if the corporation will have many products, which can be trademarked separately. The availability of the corporate name as an Internet domain name is another important issue, which is related but not identical to the trademark question: see ¶7540.

The corporation must designate an office within the state. The Secretary of State is the default agent for service of process on the corporation; most corporations will wish to designate their own agent.

[¶135.2] Certificate/Articles of Incorporation

The Certificate of Incorporation, (called the Articles of Incorporation in some jurisdictions) filed by the incorporator(s) with the Secretary of State, discloses basic information about the corporation. It can also be an important corporate governance document, if the entrepreneurs include optional provisions that determine the way the corporation will be run, e.g.,:

- Grant of preemptive rights (the right to prevent dilution of one's stock ownership by acquiring newly issued shares in the same proportion as one's original ownership)
- Supermajority requirements (requirement of a unanimous, or more than 50%, vote for certain significant corporate actions)
- Limited term for the corporation

- Making stockholders personally liable for corporate debts
- Indemnification of directors and officers for liability to the corporation or its stockholders for fiduciary breaches. (However, indemnification is not available for breaches of the duty of loyalty to the corporation; bad faith; intentional misconduct; knowing violations of the law; improper payment of dividends; or improper receipt of personal benefits.) Indemnification provisions are often handled in the Certificate of Incorporation, rather than by contract or insurance, precisely because it's hard to amend
- Permitting the board of directors (in addition to, or instead of the shareholders) to adopt, amend, and repeal bylaws
- Changing the meeting requirements—e.g., Delaware gives stockholders a statutory right to take action on written consent, without a meeting. This right can only be limited or removed in the corporation's Certificate of Incorporation. In states that do not have a statutory provision allowing shareholder or board meetings by written consent, telephone, or electronically, such powers can probably be created via the Certificate of Incorporation.

[¶135.3] Bylaws

Matters of corporate governance that are not provided by state law, or included in the Certificate of Incorporation, can be enacted in the corporation's bylaws. Usually, bylaws are adopted by either the incorporators or the shareholders at the organization meeting.

However, either state law or the Certificate of Incorporation may provide for adoption of bylaws by the board of directors. In general, bylaws can be amended by shareholder vote (perhaps a supermajority will be required for amendment). Many states allow the directors to amend the bylaws, as long as this is authorized by other bylaws adopted in the Certificate of Incorporation or by the stockholders.

Typical bylaw subjects include:

- Location of the corporate headquarters
- Date of the annual meeting
- How to call a special meeting of stockholders
- How to provide notice to stockholders of annual and special meetings
- Quorum and other factors in the conduct of the meeting
- Record date for the meeting—i.e., the date on which stock ownership entitles a person to vote
- Rules for proxy voting
- Vote required to elect directors and take other measures (e.g., simple majority vs. supermajority)
- Ability of stockholders to act on written consent, without a meeting
- Number and term of directors
- Qualifications for serving as a director
- Rules for holding directors' meetings; whether they must be held in person, or whether the board can take unanimous, super-majority, or majority action in writing, by telephone, or online

- Compensation of directors
- How to remove and replace directors
- Board duties and actions that can be delegated to a committee, such as an investment committee, compensation committee, or due diligence committee to examine possible mergers and acquisitions (Check state law—delegation of certain crucial functions may be barred.)
- Indemnification of directors, officers, and managers; advancement of litigation expenses
- Selection, qualifications, duties, and liabilities of corporate officers
- Removal and replacement of officers
- Regulation of corporate stock, including issuance of certificates; transfer restrictions; record date for determining stock ownership before a meeting; how to replace lost, stolen, or destroyed certificates
- Maintenance of the corporate books and records, such as stock and stock transfer records, and minutes of meetings.

[¶135.4] Registration of Foreign Corporation

A corporation that begins to do business in an additional state, or that has incorporated in Delaware despite having headquarters elsewhere, will be required to file a certificate with the Secretary of State of each state in which it does business as a foreign corporation. The typical certificate discloses:

- Corporate name
- Corporate purposes
- Capitalization (number of authorized shares; classes or series of shares; par value
- Structure of the board of directors (size; qualification of directors; classification of directors; power to adopt and amend bylaws; power to remove directors, fill vacancies, and create new directorships
- Powers reserved to the shareholders

An agent for service of process within the state should be designated.

[¶140] Special Problems Of Close Corporations

Although most of the largest businesses are publicly owned (i.e., their securities are freely traded on exchanges), most businesses are close corporations, whose shares have no public market. A typical pattern is for a company to start up, then "go public": make an Initial Public Offering of its shares.

However, before the IPO, or in the case of companies that have no potential for a public market, a typical set of problems often occurs. In these companies (many of them family-owned), there is a small group of shareholders. Generally speaking, few or no outsiders would be interested in buying corporate shares. However, sometimes competitors of the business are quite interested in purchasing a controlling interest, or enough stock to be a nuisance (by finding out about corporate technological developments or marketing plans, for instance).

A typical pattern develops in small companies: once some of the original founders have retired or died, their families receive gifts of corporate stock, or inherit it from the founders. Soon, there are two groups: an insider group that actually manages the business, and outsiders who are not actively involved in the business. The interests of the two groups are naturally opposed.

Members of the insider group frequently argue that the best use of corporate funds is increasing their own salaries and benefits (which are deductible), and that the corporation should limit its dividend payments and retain capital for future expansion, at least up to the point that the retention is subject to tax penalties (see ¶454). The outsiders, however, have limited or no dividend income, and no ready market for their shares—other than to the insider group, or perhaps to a competitor.

Many states have passed statutes to prevent oppression of minority shareholders in close corporations. For instance, they can be given the right to petition for dissolution of the corporation if the control group is guilty of illegal, fraudulent, or oppressive actions, or if the control group wastes or loots corporate assets or diverts them for non-corporate purposes.

The corporation and its majority shareholders can avoid the dissolution proceeding by buying out the plaintiff(s) at a price and on terms set by the court. The court will set the price based on what a bona fide purchaser would pay for the business as a going concern (not its liquidating value). The value is not necessarily limited by the shareholder agreement.

As a supplement, or in states where there are no statutes, shareholder agreements can be used to cope in advance with governance problems.

[¶145] Shareholder Agreements

Shareholders in close corporations frequently enter into agreements to settle issues of corporate governance, prevent dissension and oppression of minority shareholders, and provide a mechanism for buying out dissidents without involving the courts or dissolving the corporation.

Shareholder agreements are often classified as pooling agreements, proxy agreements, or voting trusts. They are arrangements under which shareholders agree to vote together, or to give their proxies to someone else, who will vote them in a way designed to minimize dissension.

A pooling agreement, also known as a voting agreement, is allowed in most states as long as there is no fraud, vote selling, or oppression of the other shareholders. It obligates the signers to vote in a pre-determined manner in electing directors, amending the corporation's charter and bylaws, etc. A well-drafted agreement will include an enforcement mechanism (such as giving the signer the right to sue non-complying signers for equitable remedies, on the grounds that the signers are at risk of irreparable harm that can't be redressed by money damages if the agreement is breached). Even absent an enforcement mechanism, it's likely that the state court will grant specific performance of the agreement.

A voting trust is an arrangement under which several shareholders place their shares into trust, and the trustee votes the entire block in accordance with the terms of the agreement. A voting trust might be preferred to a voting agreement if, for instance, some of the shareholders are minors or incapacitated persons. A voting trust is more complex than a simple voting agreement, because the trust becomes the legal owner of the shares.

Under a proxy agreement, the parties give another shareholder or a neutral third party the right to vote their shares—either under all circumstances, or only when necessary to prevent deadlock. Corporate proxies are governed by agency law, and the general agency rule is that proxies can always be revoked unless they are coupled with an interest in the corporation or its stock. Some states provide that proxies can become irrevocable if the designated proxy-holder is a party to the voting agreement or voting trust, and the text of the actual proxy says that it's irrevocable.

[¶145.1.1] Checklist for Shareholder Agreements
Typical shareholder agreement provisions include:

- ☐ Size of the board of directors
- ☐ Quorum for the board
- ☐ How officers and directors will be elected
- ☐ How successors will be appointed if a director or officer dies, withdraws, retires, or is removed
- ☐ How often board meetings will be held; who can call one; what can be on the agenda
- ☐ Limitations on the powers and duties of corporate directors and officers
- ☐ Compensation of directors
- ☐ Designation of the corporation's attorneys and accountants
- ☐ Provisions that will require a "supermajority" (i.e., more than the normal majority vote for corporate decisions), e.g.,
  - Amendments to the charter and bylaws
  - Corporate investments, loans, mortgages, or pledges of assets greater than a stated amount
  - Buying or leasing property from, or employing (e.g., as consultants) corporate insiders
  - Changes in the corporation's business purpose
  - Mergers and acquisitions
  - The corporation's repurchase or redemption of its own securities
  - Issuing or offering stock or additional classes or issues of stock
  - Declaration of dividends
- ☐ Arbitration clause
- ☐ Provisions for specific performance of agreement provisions
- ☐ The corporation's undertaking not to reflect transfers on its books if they violate the agreement
- ☐ Covenant of active shareholders not to compete with the corporation
- ☐ Rights of shareholders to inspect books and records

❑ Circumstances justifying termination of the agreement
  • Written consent of all the shareholders
  • Sale of all of the corporation's shares to one stockholder
  • Sale of all or substantially all of the corporate assets
  • Liquidation, dissolution, or bankruptcy of the corporation
  • Initial public offering

Although the general rule of corporate law is that a corporation is managed by its board of directors, some states let the shareholders of a close corporation control the directors' decision-making. However, if this is done, the shareholders and not the directors become liable for errors and omissions.

Check local law. Some shareholder agreement provisions (such as those permitting direct election of officers by shareholders; control of directors' decisions; supermajority requirements) may have to be endorsed on the stock certificate to be fully enforceable.

[¶150] Corporate Stock

The number of shares that the corporation issues at startup has some minor consequences. The filing fee for a Certificate of Incorporation depends on the number and value of shares; franchise tax also is usually calculated based on the number of shares.

Shares can be issued with a par value; their initial purchasers must pay at least that amount. No-par shares can also be issued.

Unless the relevant state statute or the corporation's charter provides to the contrary, all shares of stock have equal voting, dividend, and other rights. Corporations can issue one or more classes of preferred stock, which have greater rights to receive dividends or liquidating distributions than common stock or junior preferred stock.

As long as the corporation is solvent, it can declare and pay dividends. (Dividend payments by insolvent corporations constitute fraudulent conveyances.) Generally, dividends come out of corporate surplus: the corporation's net assets minus its stated capital. Stated capital, in turn, equals the number of shares issued times their par value (or, for no-par shares, the amount allocated to stated capital). Dividends paid out of capital rather than earned surplus must be accompanied by a notice of effect on the corporation's stated capital and surplus.

A corporation can mandate declaration of dividends, but generally one of the most important functions of the board of directors is to decide whether a quarterly dividend will be declared, and how large it will be. As long as the decision is legitimate and not fraudulent, it will be entitled to the protection of the business judgment rule, and courts will not challenge the rationale for the decision.

If the charter permits, the corporation can have classes or series of shares that can be redeemed by the corporation itself: the company buys back its shares out of surplus at any time that it is solvent. The reacquired shares are either canceled by the corporation, becoming authorized but unissued shares that can be re-issued at a later date; or, the corporation itself holds them as treasury shares.

[¶150.1] Transfer Restrictions

Another method for controlling the management of a non-public corporation is to impose transfer restrictions on sales, gifts, pledges, and other transfers of the shares. For instance, transfers to competitors can be forbidden, as can unregistered sales of securities that must be registered to be sold legally, or sales that destroy an S Corporation's eligibility for that status.

The typical form of transfer agreement defines the permitted class of transferees, such as shareholders, their families, and trusts they have established. It is against public policy to impose restrictions that eliminate all possibility of transfer, but reasonable restrictions that serve a valid business purpose are permissible.

The corporation or its shareholders can be given a right of first refusal before a transfer to an outsider will be permitted. A provision calling for repurchase by the corporation when a shareholder dies not only serves the corporation's purposes, but serves the estate planning needs of the shareholders. Another possibility is for the other shareholders to have a right of first refusal, with a right of second refusal for the corporation, on the occurrence of events such as a shareholder's death, insolvency, or permanent disability.

A "drag along" clause, used where an entire company has to be sold at once to make a deal work, allows the minority shareholders to compel the majority shareholders to join in the sale. The corresponding "tag along" structure gives minority shareholders the right to participate in a sale.

The main pricing mechanisms are book value (in which case, the date of calculation is crucial); dollar value mutually agreed by the parties; market price or highest price a bona fide purchaser would offer; and the price set by appraisal.

Be sure to consult local law, because some states provide that a corporation can repurchase its own shares only out of surplus, and cannot buy back shares when it is insolvent or when the repurchase would lead to insolvency. The corporation has to be recapitalized, or raise additional funds, if it has a contractual obligation to repurchase shares.

[¶150.2] Buy-Sell Agreements

Corporate buy-sell agreements overlap with shareholder agreements and voting restrictions, but can serve somewhat different purposes. The agreements safeguard corporate continuity by providing a mechanism for keeping the shares of a retiring, disabled, or deceased member of the management group within the corporation or within the same management group.

There are many ways to structure these agreements. The corporation or the surviving shareholders might be obligated to purchase the shares, and the estate of a deceased shareholder might be obligated to sell. Or, the corporation, and then the surviving shareholders, could be given an option to buy the decedent's shares; the estate is obligated to sell if the option is exercised. Still another variation gives the estate of a deceased stockholder the right to put the stock to either the surviving stockholders or the corporation. Or, there could be no obligation on either side, but if a stockholder or estate wanted to sell, the corporation or survivors might be given a right of first refusal before the stock could be offered to outsiders.

Valuing the shares that will be purchased is a crucial function of the buy-sell agreement. Usually, the agreement sets an initial price, with a schedule for revising the price. Or, the signatories could agree to accept the price set by an outside appraiser. The agreement can also include a valuation formula, based on factors such as the corporate net work, book value, capitalization of profits, or a hybrid method.

It's also crucial for the agreement to set a funding method for the purchase. If the triggering event is a shareholder's death, life insurance is the normal funding mechanism.

If the insurance is owned by the corporation (corporations have a clear insurable interest in the lives of their management, so this is not a problem), the agreement is known as an "entity purchase" agreement. If the other stockholders own the insurance, it's known as a "cross purchase" agreement. Insurance can also be used to fund purchases that are triggered by the disability of a shareholder. However, an agreement used to provide retirement funds and a smooth corporate transition does not involve an insurable event—so either the corporation must have funds available for the purchase, or the other stockholders must use their private funds.

Agreements for purchase of a decedent's shares can also be used to set the estate tax value of the shares. However, for the IRS to accept such valuation, the price must be fixed in the agreement; it must be a fair price that would be acceptable in an arm's-length transaction; and the parties to the agreement, not just their survivors or estates, must be obligated to sell at the fixed price.

[¶152] Employment Agreements

Although, as ¶360.1 discusses, most employees who do not work under a Collective Bargaining Agreement (CBA) are "at-will" employees who do not have a formal contract, it is often a good idea for a business to enter into employment agreements with at least some of its employees. Employment agreements are more likely to be useful for top management or employees with specialized skills who have to be specially recruited, and who are likely to be actively solicited to change jobs.

The employment agreement could be negotiated at the behest of the corporation, which is eager to protect itself and its intellectual property in case the employee wants to leave. Or, the impetus could come from an employee who wants to make sure he or she will be paid for the full contract term even if the contract ends prematurely, or who wants matters such as stock options and bonuses to be promised rather than left to future discretion.

Typical subjects include:

- Duration of the agreement; grounds for termination of employment
- "Golden parachutes"—compensation paid if the employee loses his or her job because of a change in corporate ownership

- Covenants not to compete (which must be reasonable in terms of both duration and geographic scope, and which must not have the effect of preventing the signer from earning a living; protection of the employer's intellectual property is considered a valid motivation)
- Bonuses
- Ownership of patents and other intellectual property developed by the employee
- Renewal of the agreement; usually, such agreements are renewed automatically unless notice is given in time. Renewal is either on the original terms, or on terms to be negotiated in good faith at the time of renewal.

If an employment contract is breached by the employer's unjust firing of the employee, then monetary damages will be awarded, but the court will not order reinstatement. Damages are likely to include back pay (including benefits, raises, fringe benefits, and promotions whose likelihood can be established with reasonable certainty), front pay for the balance of the contract term, minus mitigating amounts earned by the plaintiff by exercising reasonable diligence in finding a new job.

Naturally, no court will order an employee who quits during the term of a contract to go back to work, but the employer will be entitled to consequential damages arising from the breach of contract, such as lost profits and the cost of hiring a replacement. In the alternative, the employer will be entitled to liquidated damages or forfeiture of bonuses the employee would otherwise have received.

[¶160] Corporate Governance

Once a corporation is in operation, it must satisfy certain formal requirements. The board of directors must meet as necessary. Shareholders must meet at least once a year. Important business decisions must be memorialized in resolutions, adopted by the directors and/or shareholders (depending on the subject matter and the structure of the corporation's authorizing documents). Minutes must be taken at meetings, and those minutes must be kept on file for examination by stockholders and regulators. If the company is a "reporting company" under the Securities Exchange Act of '34 (see ¶630), then periodic and annual reports must be submitted to the SEC. Some reports must also be sent to shareholders.

[¶160.1] Annual Meeting

One of the most vital functions of the annual meeting of stockholders is to elect the board of directors. Most stockholders, of course, don't know who the candidates are (and probably don't really care, as long as the stock price holds up and dividends are steady). Therefore, management, and sometimes dissident groups, solicit proxies: they ask shareholders for the right to determine how the shareholders' votes will be applied in the board election. See ¶640 for SEC rules for proxy solicitation in reporting companies.

Ordinarily, each share of stock represents one vote for each director. However, cumulative voting gives the stockholder a total quantum of voting power based on the number of shares times the number of directors to be elected, and stockholders can allocate any part or all of the total to the election of a particular director. For instance, a small stockholder who owns only 500 shares in the corporation, when five directors are elected, might devote all 2500 of his or her votes to a particular candidate. The effect of cumulative voting is to make it easier for small shareholders to have at least some influence on the composition of the board; without it, it would be easy for large shareholders to outvote them.

[¶160.2] Resolutions

Resolutions are the corporate equivalent of the bills passed by a state legislature. In most corporations, both the board and the stockholders vote on and pass resolutions on matters of importance to the operation of the corporation. Typical subjects include hiring major executives; setting up bank accounts; taking loans, lines of credit, and other financing mechanisms; entering into major leases; issuing stock options; creating or modifying employee benefit plans; and declaring dividends.

[¶160.3] Corporate Stock and Dividends

All corporations have to have one class of common stock; they can adopt additional classes of stock as well, with different voting rights and entitlements to dividends. However, Subchapter S corporations are only allowed to have one class of stock (although some differences within the class are permissible). Ordinary common stock has voting rights, but non-voting common stock can be issued.

Preferred stock is preferred in the sense that its holders have a right to receive dividends or liquidating distributions superior to the rights of common stock holders, or the holders of junior classes of preferred stock. The holders of cumulative preferred stock are entitled to make-up payments for quarters in which no dividends were declared, before other stockholders are entitled to receive current dividends.

The corporation's directors decide whether a dividend will be issued,[3] and how large it will be. Usually, this is done on a quarterly basis. (The dividend is "passed" in quarters in which no dividend is declared.) Dividend declaration is subject to the business judgment rule (¶165.3), and if the decision is made legitimately and without fraud, it will not be changed by a court. Dividends can be paid in either cash or stock.

A corporation has the right to declare and pay dividends at any time it is not insolvent—but issuance of dividends by an insolvent corporation is a fraudulent conveyance. It is also generally true that dividends must come out of corporate surplus, defined as the corporation's net assets minus its stated capital. Stated capital, in turn, consists of the number of shares issued times the par value of each; a no-par share is valued at its amount allocated to stated capital. If dividends are paid out of anything other than earned surplus, the corporation must disclose the effect of the declaration on its stated capital and surplus. The resolution declaring a dividend should indicate a record date (a date for determining who is the official owner entitled to receive the dividend) and a date for payment.

[¶160.3.1] Redemption

The corporation's charter can be drafted or amended to authorize classes or series of shares that can be redeemed by the corporation. A corporation authorized to do so can buy or redeem its shares out of surplus at any time it is not insolvent (or does not become insolvent as a direct result of the purchase or redemption). The corporation either cancels the reacquired shares or holds them as treasury shares. Unless the charter forbids it, the shares can be re-issued at a later time.

The effect of redemption is to return more shares and more value to the corporation itself, increasing its ability to borrow. Also, shares that are not held outside the corporation can't be voted contrary to corporate policy, and can't be acquired by a party contemplating a hostile takeover.

[¶160.3.2] Preemptive and Appraisal Rights

The corporate balance of power changes if the board of directors issues a large number of new shares. The effect is to dilute the voting power of the existing shareholders. Preemptive rights give existing shareholders the right to preserve their percentage ownership by purchasing enough of the newly issued shares to retain the same proportion of the total. States differ in the way they treat preemptive rights. In Delaware, for example, these rights exist only if adopted in the corporate charter; in New York, they exist unless they are excluded by the charter.

Appraisal rights are entitlement to get paid in cash for shares in case the corporation undertakes major actions (e.g., merger, consolidation, sale of assets, charter amendments) that the stockholder disapproves of. Before exercising appraisal rights, the stockholder must file a written objection to the action no later than the shareholder meeting at which the action will be voted on, in which he or she demands appraisal rights.

The stockholders surrender their shares, and have no further shareholder rights other than the right to be paid for the shares. The corporation must offer its good faith estimate of the fair market price of the shares. If the surrendering shareholders are unwilling to accept this amount, a court proceeding is required to set the price of the shares.

[¶165] Corporate Directors

Remember, the formal responsibility for management of a corporation rests with its board of directors, so directors have substantial responsibility under corporate law. Failure to meet appropriate standards often results in suit by the corporation, by its stockholders, or by third parties affected by corporate actions. However, as discussed below, it is common for directors to have liability insurance (also see ¶1460.4) and for them to be entitled to be indemnified by the corporation.

[¶165.1] Duties of Directors

The corporation's directors must carry out their duties in good faith, using the degree of care that an ordinary prudent person would use in the same situation. There is a duty of reasonable inquiry; instead of rubber-stamping all proposals from corporate management, they must investigate (although they can place reasonable reliance on data from the corporation's officers, employees, and retained professional experts).

Directors also have a duty of loyalty. They must not put their own private benefit above the needs of the corporation or its stockholders. They cannot compete with the corporation, unless the non-interested directors have been notified and have given their approval.

Directors can't favor one group of stockholders over another; they must abide by the corporate governance instruments (e.g., setting out the rights of preferred stockholders). In some situations, they may have the option of considering the interests of non-stockholder constituencies, such as employees, retirees, suppliers, and the local community.

Outside directors (those not employed by the corporation) must maintain the confidentiality of information they learn about the corporation, its operations, and its intellectual property. Outside directors must be careful to avoid even apparent, and of course actual, conflicts of interest between serving on this board and their other business, government, or outside director responsibilities.

An interested director is one who is involved in a potential corporate transaction: e.g., the corporation wishes to buy equipment from a company owned by one of its outside directors, or wishes to retain the law firm of an attorney-director. Transactions between a corporation and its interested directors are not necessarily void or improper, although the interested director is not allowed to vote on the transaction, and there should be full disclosure and the approval of the other directors. Interested director transactions are permissible only if they are fair to the corporation. Ratification by shareholders may be required: e.g., if the corporation makes a loan to a director.

A corporation's directors who willfully issue improper dividends or violate restrictions on the repurchase or redemption of corporate stock are jointly and severally liable for the wrongdoing. The liable directors are entitled to contribution from the other directors who voted for the improper action.

[¶165.2] Derivative Suits

Theoretically, corporations not only can but should sue directors who have violated their duties. But in many cases, the errant director controls the board, or acted with the connivance of other directors, so a suit by the corporation is not a real possibility.

In response, corporation law gives stockholders the right to bring derivative suits: the stockholder sues on behalf of the corporation, to redress wrongs committed against the corporate entity. Derivative suit judgments or settlements, if any, are paid to the corporation itself, not the derivative plaintiff.

Some improprieties that could justify a derivative suit:

- Improper loans to shareholders
- Negligence about attending or participating in board meetings that permits wrongdoing to flourish
- Improper use of corporate funds in proxy contests
- Failure to detect and prevent antitrust violations
- Improper or imprudent investment of corporate funds
- Failure to detect and prevent embezzlement
- Improper conduct in connection with takeover defense
- Wasting corporate assets.

Before bringing a derivative action, the stockholder must demand that the board itself take action, and the demand must be wrongfully refused. The demand need not be made if there is reasonable doubt that the board is disinterested and independent.

[¶165.3] The Business Judgment Rule

The business judgment rule insulates a corporation's directors against liability if they behave reasonably and exercise appropriate judgment. The business judgment defense is not available if the director has breached the duty of loyalty or due care (e.g., by self-dealing), but it is available and useful in situations where directors acted sensibly and honestly, but made decisions that had bad financial consequences.

The other side of the coin is the doctrine of ultra vires: a corporation follows objectives or enters into transactions that are improper because they are not authorized by state law or the corporation's charter or bylaws. Ultra vires actions can be challenged by stockholders, and the state's Attorney General can seek dissolution of the corporation to prevent further unauthorized actions. However, it is a defense if the stockholders ratify an ultra vires action.

[¶165.4] Indemnification

Given the potential for significant personal liability, many talented individuals might refuse to accept a new corporate job or refuse to serve as outside director. Corporation law allows a corporation to indemnify its directors, officers, and employees against the consequences of their conduct, as long as the individuals were not guilty of deliberate wrongdoing.

The corporate charter can be drafted or amended to rule out monetary liability of directors and officers to the corporation for breaches of fiduciary duty (even those stemming from gross negligence), but not intentional misconduct, self-dealing, breach of the duty of loyalty, or wrongful payment of dividends or repurchase of corporate stock.

An initial distinction must be drawn between conduct undertaken in the scope of employment and that allegedly harmed someone other than the corporation, and conduct alleged to harm the corporation itself. It is much more likely that indemnification will be available in the former situation than in the latter.

Authority for the corporation to indemnify can come from several sources: state corporation law; provisions of the corporate charter and bylaws; private agreements such as employment contracts; and resolutions passed by the board or shareholders.

State laws can furnish either mandatory or permissive indemnification in shareholder or non-shareholder suits or criminal actions. Directors, officers, employees, or agents who prevail in a suit are likely to be entitled to indemnification for their defense costs. Indemnification may also be available for settlements and judgments against the individual. Depending on state law, a corporation may be allowed to indemnify persons who acted in good faith and in a way reasonably believed to be in the best interests of the corporation. State law may also permit the board to advance defense or other expenses to the indemnified person.

"D&O Liability insurance" (see ¶1460.4) covers two types of expenses that might occur: liability incurred by an individual director or officer, and expenses that the corporation incurs when indemnifying such persons. The policy usually covers whatever a party pays for damages, judgments, settlements, costs, charges, or expenses incurred in connection with any proceeding, suit, or action—whether or not indemnification is available under state law.

In this context, a wrongful act is negligence, breach of duty, error, misstatement, omission, etc., charged against a person solely by reason of his or her actions or status as director or officer.

Individuals cannot insure themselves against their own deliberate wrongdoing, and the same principle would probably apply to extreme (but not ordinary) negligence. D&O policies typically exclude acts undertaken for personal profit, such as "short-swing" stock trading; liability arising out of takeover activity; and pollution. It is also typical to exclude indemnification of fines or penalties imposed by law.

The corporation's authority to buy D&O insurance stems from state law and/or the corporate charter and bylaws.

[¶170] Not-for-Profit Organizations

Just as some are born great, some achieve greatness, and some have greatness thrust upon them, some organizations are designed to provide services to the public without making a profit, whereas other organizations are supposed to earn a profit but never manage to do so. A further complicating factor is that some entities, such as schools and hospitals, might be organized and operated as not-for-profits, profit-making businesses, or hybrids.

A not-for-profit organization is created and run for purposes other than pecuniary gain to its founders. Some states allow incorporation of not-for-profit organizations, but they cannot issue stock, and they are not allowed to distribute assets, income, or profits to an ownership group. If there is any incidental profit from operations, it must be devoted to the organization's exempt purpose and not distributed to shareholder equivalents.

Not-for-profit organizations usually (but not always) qualify for federal tax exemption. That is, they are not subject to federal taxation on income that stems from their exempt purpose, although they are subject to tax on any unrelated business income they earn. Further qualifications are required before donors can deduct contributions they make to a charitable organization.

Not-for-profit organizations can operate as either charities (which make grants or provide services directly) or membership organizations. Membership organizations derive their revenue from membership dues, user fees, perhaps commercial revenue, and investment income; charities also get contributions and grants.

[¶170.1] Federal Tax Exemption

The main IRC section governing tax-exempt organizations is §501(c), which allows a federal tax exemption to a charity or membership organization that is organized and operated for a not-for-profit purpose, and both intends and ensures that no benefits inure to private individuals related to the entity. That is, the organization is allowed to pay reasonable salaries, but cannot distribute the equivalent of profits.

No tax is imposed on "exempt function income" such as dues and contributions or funds deriving from activities related to the exempt purpose.

Tax is imposed at corporate rates on Unrelated Business Taxable Income (UBTI)—income from a regularly maintained trade or business that is carried on by the organization, and that does not further the exempt purpose (other than by generating income). Not only is UBTI taxed, but excessive business activities can lead to loss of exempt status. However, the IRS can be fairly generous in interpreting this rule, e.g., allowing museums to operate shops with a wide range of merchandise. Passive income, such as rents, royalties, and interest is not considered UBTI.

Usually (although not always) federal tax-exemption will trigger similar treatment at the state and local level. The organization may also qualify for exemption from the franchise tax on unincorporated business. Charities may also be exempt from sales tax and property tax on both their purchases and sales. In fact, exemption from property tax may be the leading factor in the viability of an organization, or the decision to operate a borderline organization in not-for-profit rather than profit form. See ¶460.3 for further tax information.

[¶170.2] Organization of a Not-for-Profit Corporation

A not-for-profit organization can be an unincorporated association, an inter vivos trust, or a testamentary trust, but most are organized and operated in corporate form. As a general rule, state laws permit not-for-profit corporations to be organized either as membership organizations, with boards of directors elected by the membership, or as non-membership organizations with a self-perpetuating board of directors. Differing classes of membership are usually permitted. Votes can be cast in person or by proxy, and class and cumulative voting are often permitted.

Like a profit-making corporation, a not-for-profit must be formally organized, with one or more incorporators and filing of the Certificate of Incorporation with the Secretary of the state. An organization meeting is held for the initial members or directors to ratify the incorporation and adopt by-laws and elect the slate of officers for the first year. Resolutions are passed dealing with matters such as the corporate seal, its fiscal year, and authority for the initial slate of officers to seek tax-exempt status for the organization. Depending on the organization's exempt mission, it may be necessary to obtain authorization from state regulatory agencies (e.g., for a health care or educational organization).

Not-for-profits that operate in other states will probably have to register as "foreign" not-for-profit organizations, and will be subject to the jurisdiction of the state Attorney General with respect to solicitation of funds.

Many states allow not-for-profits to raise "subventions," which are long-term capital contributions to the organization that pay below-market rates of return. When the organization dissolves, subvention holders have a preference over other members, but are subordinate to the organization's creditors. Ordinary loans from organization members to the organization are also permitted.

[¶170.3] Reporting and Management of the Not-for-Profit

States generally require registered not-for-profit organizations to submit annual financial reports. Organizations that solicit financial contributions must report in greater detail. If a donor earmarks a contribution for a specific purpose, it must be accounted for separately and either used for the designated purpose or for related administrative expenses.

The Financial Accounting Standards Board (FASB)'s SFAS 116 covers reporting of contributions, and SFAS 117 requires financial reporting more or less on the same terms as a for-profit business organization.

Managers of a not-for-profit are subject to the business judgment rule, including their investment decisions. The Uniform Management of Institutional Funds Act authorizes significant discretion, subject to the standard of acting like an ordinary prudent person. Day-to-day operations can be delegated to officers and staff, and financial decisions can be delegated to expert advisers. Not-for-profit managers are entitled to rely on information received from advisers, officers, employees, or specialized committees of the organization, as long as the advisers are chosen with due care; their performance is monitored; and reliance occurs in good faith.

Not-for-profit managers can be sued on behalf of the organization by the state Attorney General; by the organization itself; or derivatively by a director, officer, or member for negligent or self-interested breaches of fiduciary duty. Not-for-profit managers owe an additional duty, to the public, over and above general fiduciary responsibility. A self-interested transaction could have the effect of terminating the organization's not-for-profit status, if it is deemed to constitute inurement for private advantage.

Not-for-profits can indemnify their directors and officers in the Certificate of Incorporation or by-laws, or by subsequent resolution or agreement. State law often provides additional protection (such as a broader scope of indemnification for directors and officers who are volunteers rather than paid professionals). A common pattern is for a non-profit to pay its officers, but for its directors to receive expense reimbursement but no compensation.

[¶170.4] Federal Classification of Tax-Exempt Organizations

Code §501 divides tax-exempt organizations into two main categories ("group entitities" and "charitable entities") and many sub-categories. Group entities, as defined by §501(c)(4)-(8), (10), and (19), are:

- Civic leagues and organizations
- Labor, agricultural, and horticultural organizations
- Business leagues, chambers of commerce, real estate boards, and boards of trade
- Social clubs
- Fraternal organizations
- Veterans' organizations

Group entities receive tax exemption by applying on IRS Form 1024 and paying a user fee with Form 8718. If the IRS approves the application, it issues a letter granting tax-exempt status. Once exempt, the organization must file Form 990 (the equivalent of a tax return) within 4 1/2 months of the close of its tax year.

Charitable entities, as defined by §501(c)(3), are organizations organized for charitable, educational, religious, scientific, literary, or cultural purposes, or for the prevention of cruelty to children or animals. The application for exemption is made on Form 1023, with the user fee paid with Form 8718, and a Form 990 information return must be filed each year. (Private foundations file Form 990 PF.)

Section 501 provides that paying reasonable compensation does not constitute forbidden private inurement, and fund-raisers can be paid a reasonable percentage of the funds they raise.

Limitations are imposed on the political activities of charities, and excessive lobbying or political activity can result in loss of exemption. See §§501(h) and 527.

[¶170.5 Private Foundations and Public Charities

If an exempt organization is a "private foundation" (usually created by a wealthy family to make grants to public charities) rather than a "public charity," it will be subject to additional financial and disclosure regulation.

Under §509(a), a tax-exempt organization is presumed to be a private foundation unless it proves that it is actually a public charity. A public charity can be one which gets its support from the general public (not a single family); serves public functions such as education or health care; is a "supporting organization" for a particular public charity; or gets at least one third of its support from grants, user fees, sales, and charitable activities, and less than one third of its support from investments or UBTI.

[¶170.6 Deductibility of Contributions

Many organizations are tax-exempt, in the sense that they are not liable for income tax, but their donors are not entitled to a tax deduction for contributions. Contributions to a public charity are generally deductible, although a limit is imposed on the income tax (but not estate tax) deductibility of very large charitable contributions.

Section 6115 requires that charities disclose the extent to which contributions over $75, for which the donor receives something (e.g., the right to attend a benefit; concert tickets), are deductible. All contributions over $250 must be documented.

ENDNOTES

1. For instance, depending on the entity selection, an individual who also has some ownership interest in the entity may be either a "partner" who is not entitled to protection of anti-discrimination laws, or an "employee," who is protected.
2. Such payments could represent the withdrawing partner's capital interest; his or her pro rata interest in unrealized receivables and fees; share of potential gain or loss on partnership inventory; or insurance secured by the other partners to make payments to the estate. The partnership agreement should clarify the nature as well as the amount of the payments, especially for tax purposes.
3. Unless the corporation's organizational documents remove the decision from the board's discretion, and require mandatory dividends.

¶200

Commercial Transactions Under the UCC

[¶201]

For many years, the rules of commercial transaction law changed as little as the rules of baseball. Come to think of it, the rules of baseball have made some pretty drastic changes since the inception of the game.

Recently, the speed of innovation in commercial law has picked up drastically. The original Articles 1-9 of the UCC have been altered by two new articles (2A on leasing; 4A on funds transfers), another proposed article that was not adopted (2B on electronic commerce), and serious revisions throughout.

In a sense, "Uniform" is a misnomer, in that states adopt and adapt texts submitted by the National Conference of Commissioners on Uniform State Laws (NCCUSL). It can take several years for an NCCUSL draft to be considered by the states; some UCC provisions are designed with several options from which the states can select; and states may adopt their own variations.

In its present form, the UCC includes:

- Article 1: general principles and definitions
- 2: sales of goods
- 2A: leasing
- 3: commercial paper
- 4: bank deposits and collections
- 4A: funds transfers
- 5: letters of credit
- 6: bulk sales
- 7: documents of title
- 8: ownership and transfer of securities
- 9: secured transactions

The law of commercial transactions cannot be considered in the abstract. Many questions of transactional law will involve contract law: see ¶1000—. Business torts may be alleged (¶3240.4). Products liability questions (¶3260) may arise.

Much of the UCC deals with transactions between "merchants": businesses that presumably are sophisticated and do not require protections that have to be extended to consumers.

[¶205] Sales of Goods

A sale means that the title to goods passes from the seller to the buyer, in exchange for a price. The conceptual and legal problems of an immediate sale, for cash, of goods to a purchaser who takes the goods away then and there are fairly minimal (although if the purchaser is a consumer, there may be warranty and products liability problems to worry about). But this pattern is not very common in "merchant" transactions (i.e., those involving two businesses, not a retailer and a consumer). Both parties tend to have a great deal of paperwork: requests for quotes, bid forms, order forms, contracts of sale, invoices, and the like.

Commercial law has done a fairly good job of sorting out the complexities of paper-based documents exchanged between merchants, especially the "battle of the forms" (¶205.4.1) where each side signs a form purporting to contain the terms of the deal, but the two are inconsistent. An entirely new series of issues is emerging, as "e-commerce" (commerce transacted electronically, especially over the Internet) becomes more common. Now, it is often necessary to decide what a "signature" is in the electronic world; how to determine if parties are who they purport to be; and to make new rules for electronic payments.

The law of sales has to deal with many problems involving risk: who takes the risk if goods are not delivered, are stolen or destroyed, or are damaged in shipping? What happens if the seller's position is that the goods conform to the order, while the buyer alleges defect or non-conformity?

On or off the Internet, the complexities of commercial law multiply as more parties get involved: there may be suppliers involved at various parts of the supply chain; shippers of goods; and, because few merchant transactions are cash-only, various lenders may be involved. Even in a cash transaction, the goods may serve as collateral for loans obtained by the buyer and/or seller.

[¶205.1] Credit Sales

Credit, of course, gives rise to its own set of legal problems, including potential fraud, transactions entered into by parties who have outrun their credit limits, transactions in which the buyer claims that goods were not received or were defective. Furthermore, the parties extending credit will have their own documents such as letters of credit, security agreements, and financing statements. According to the UCC, an agreement for any delay in payment (even if no interest is charged) renders the deal a credit transaction.

A retail installment sales contract (which is typically subject to state Retail Installment Sales Acts, or RISAs, and/or the UCC and the Uniform Consumer Credit Code, or UCCC) involves a down payment plus deferred payments. These payments constitute the cash price which, in conjunction with the finance charge, adds up to the total price. "Commercial paper" means the loan agreements, security agreements, and financing statements generated by retail installment sales. Some dealers (e.g., car and furniture dealers) have their own charge account plans or act as intermediaries to match up buyers with banks that want to make loans that will enable the consumers to buy big-ticket items.

The transaction often becomes an indirect loan, because the seller assigns the retail installment sales agreement to its bank or finance company as security for the money it has borrowed from the bank. Or, the bank or a third party might "discount" the commercial paper: that is, the dealer assigns the sales contracts to the buyer, who pays less than their full face value because of the delay in collection and the risk that not all buyers will pay in full. The bank can aggregate chattel paper from many transactions and use it as security for bonds. If the ultimate obligor is a consumer, the holder of the chattel paper will probably be subject to the same claims and defenses as the seller.

[¶205.2] Sales on Open Account

Sales on open account involve only two parties, both merchants: a buyer and a seller. The buyer issues a purchase order for the goods. The seller investigates the buyer's credit-worthiness (usually by getting a credit report) and, if the result is satisfactory, the seller will send the goods and an invoice. Payment is usually due at the end of that month, or 30 or 60 days after the invoice date or the end of the month in which the invoice was issued. It's common for sellers to offer a discount (e.g., 2% for payment within 10 days) for prompt payment.

The invoice letter of credit is a slightly more elaborate, three-party variation used when the seller requires additional proof of the buyer's credit status. The buyer arranges a line of credit, gives security to its own bank, or arranges for guarantees by credit-worthy individuals or businesses. Given these assurances, the buyer's bank is able to issue a standby letter of credit in favor of the seller. Therefore, when the buyer has issued an order and goods have been shipped, the seller will bill the buyer directly. If the buyer fails to pay, the buyer's bank is willing to pay the seller under the standby letter of credit, because the buyer will either pay the bank or the bank can use the collateral or guarantees.

[¶205.3] Auctions

An auction is a particular kind of sale, where the price of goods is determined by competitive bidding instead of being set in advance. The UCC provision governing auctions is §2-328. A reserve is a minimum price that the buyer must pay; if no bidder offers the reserve or a higher price, the item is withdrawn from the auction. Unless stated to the contrary, all auctions are conducted subject to a reserve, so the owner of the item can terminate the auction even after bidding begins, or can "bid in" (buy the item itself). However, if the original owner manipulates the bidding, §2-328(4) gives the buyer a choice between avoiding the sale and buying the item at the last legitimate bid.

In an auction with a reserve, the bids are offers, and acceptance occurs when the hammer falls. Until the hammer falls, any bid or offer can be revoked. Every higher bid operates as a rejection of the prior bid.

In an auction without a reserve, articles or lots cannot be withdrawn once the auctioneer calls for bids, unless no bid at all is received within a reasonable time: §2-328(3).

[¶205.4] Formation of a Contract

UCC §2-201 holds that contracts for the sale of goods costing $500 or more are enforceable only if they are in writing (the "Statute of Frauds" requirement).

However, the contract can be enforced even if material terms are omitted, imprecisely stated, or incorrectly stated as long as the parties sign the contract and specify the quantity of goods involved. The price, time, place of payment or delivery, or even particular warranties can be left out. But if the quantity of goods is incorrectly stated, then the contract is only enforceable up to the quantity stated in the contract. Once there has been partial performance of the contract, the part already performed is not subject to the Statute of Frauds.

Also see §1-206. A contract for the sale of personal property (rather than goods, securities, or property covered by a security agreement) can only be enforced by lawsuit (or a defense asserted) up to $5,000 unless there is a written contract of sale, signed by the party against whom enforcement is sought, giving the price of the property.

Section 2-201(2) says that an oral contract between two merchants is binding as long as a written confirmation is given after the oral agreement is reached—and if the party who receives the written confirmation lets 10 days elapse after receiving the confirmation without objecting to its contents. Furthermore, an oral agreement can be binding with respect to specially manufactured goods that can't be re-sold in the normal course of the seller's business, as long as the seller made a substantial beginning on the manufacture or committed to buy the supplies needed to manufacture the special goods: §2-201(3)(a).

The "parol evidence" rule applies under UCC §2-202: the written terms cannot be contradicted by evidence of earlier agreements or contemporary oral communications. But a written contract can be explained or supplemented (as distinct from contradicted) by evidence of additional terms consistent with the contract, or by the usual course of dealing or usage of the relevant trade.

When a merchant makes a firm offer to buy or sell goods via a signed agreement, but provides no date for either purchase or sale, UCC §2-205 requires that the offer remain open for a "reasonable" time, not to exceed three months. Offers made by merchants can be accepted by other merchants in any medium and manner reasonable under the circumstances: §2-206. It is no longer required that the acceptance be made in the same medium as the offer.

[¶205.4.1] "Battle of the Forms"

Under the current version of Article 2, a contract is accepted when the recipient accepts it or makes a written confirmation, even if the acceptance includes additional or different terms from the offer (unless the acceptance is conditional on explicit approval of the new terms). If both of the contracting parties are merchants, additional terms are treated as proposed additions to the contract, which become part of the contract unless:

- The addition is a material alteration
- The offer expressly says that additional terms are forbidden, or
- The offeror objects to the additional terms within a reasonable time (§2-207).

These UCC provisions for the "battle of the forms" change pre-UCC laws, which basically required offers either to be rejected, or accepted on their original terms.

[¶205.4.2] May 1999 Revisions

In May, 1999, the American Law Institute approved revisions to Article 2, for submission to the National Conference of Commissioners on Uniform State Laws later in the summer.[1] The "battle of the forms" provisions are divided into several sections. Revised 2-204(b) allows a prompt, definite indication of acceptance to become effective, even if it includes additional or different terms. However, revised 2-203(d) says that if the offer is expressly and conspicuously limited to the proposed terms, there will be no contract if the offeree attempts to modify the terms—unless the parties agree on the modified terms, or their actions show that they both believe a contract has been formed.

The revised version of 2-207(b) governs the terms of a contract that has been formed by a 2-204(b) acceptance. The contract includes all the terms that appear in the documentation of both parties, plus nonstandard terms that both parties agree to (even if they are not recorded), plus standard terms supplied by the one party and assented to by the other, plus "gap-filler" terms and other terms supplied by the UCC.

The revised provision doesn't distinguish between terms suggested by the offeror and those counter-suggested by the offeree. Nor does it matter whether the parties are consumers or merchants.

[¶205.5] Checklist for Drafting a Contract of Sale

Issues to be covered in the contract include:

- ❑ Parties
- ❑ Date
- ❑ Seller's agreement to deliver goods; buyer's agreement to pay
- ❑ Indication of how the offer is to be accepted
- ❑ Description of the goods
- ❑ Quantity of goods (including output terms, reflecting the seller's entire production, and requirements terms, reflecting the buyer's entire needs)
- ❑ Price or mechanism for setting the price
- ❑ Payment terms
- ❑ How, when, and where delivery will be made
- ❑ Buyer's right to inspect the goods
- ❑ Express warranties; disclaimers
- ❑ Remedies for breach
- ❑ Modification and cancellation of contract
- ❑ Assignability[2]
- ❑ Renewal terms
- ❑ Exclusive dealing; scope of territory
- ❑ Liquidated damages clauses

UCC §2-209(1) provides that an agreement modifying a contract doesn't need consideration to be binding, but the Official Code Comment says that any request for modifications must be made in good faith. An agreement between merchants can limit modification or rescission by requiring a signed writing for either. In a merchant/consumer transaction, the consumer must sign a writing supplied by the merchant, which must satisfy the requirements of §2-201.[3]

[¶205.6] Warranties

The UCC has extensive warranty provisions. A warranty is a statement that goods conform to certain properties: for instance, that they conform to a sample item or to a particular description (2-313, -317). Additional statements of fact (not expressions of opinion) or promises made by the seller about the goods become express warranties binding on the seller (2-313). In addition to express warranties stated by a seller, there may be implied warranties that arise out of the relationship between seller and buyer.

Sellers warrant that they are conveying good title, free of security interests or liens that the buyer does not know about: §2-312. Sellers who are merchants of the particular type of goods being sold warrant that their goods are "merchantable" (§2-314), i.e., suitable for ordinary purposes; of fair average quality; fitting the trade's definition of similar goods; adequately packaged and labeled; and in conformity with any representations made on the label.

When the buyer relies on the seller's expertise, and the seller knows the purpose for which the buyer wants the goods, then the seller warrants not only that the goods are merchantable in general, but that they are fit for the buyer's intended use (2-315).

Items can be sold "as is," free of warranties. (But see below for implied warranties that cannot be disclaimed in consumer transactions.) A seller who is permitted to inspect the goods but chooses not to do so will not be entitled to any warranty as to defects that could have been detected by inspection (2-316). Contracts can be drafted to limit remedies for breach of warranty.

Section 2-317 says that, if possible, all express and implied warranties will be construed together and operate cumulatively. If this is not reasonable, the parties' intention governs, interpreted according to the principle that express warranties prevail over inconsistent implied warranties (other than the warranty of fitness); exact or technical specifications prevail over samples, models, or general descriptions; and samples prevail over general descriptions of the merchandise.

[¶205.6.1] Consumer Warranties

UCC 2-318 deals with warranties in the case where a product causes personal injury or property damage. States can choose among three versions of this section. One of them extends the warranty to anyone in the buyer's family, household, or guests who are physically harmed. Another one covers personal injuries to any reasonably foreseeable user of items purchased by an individual. The third alternative also extends the warranty to cover property damage.

If the buyer is a consumer rather than a merchant, federal law requires additional warranty coverage. (See ¶760 for a discussion of the Magnuson-Moss Act, and ¶3260 for warranty implications in products liability litigation.)

[¶205.7] Gap Filler Terms

Under the UCC, there are many circumstances in which a seemingly incomplete document becomes a valid and enforceable contract, because the UCC provides methods for "filling the gaps."

[¶205.7.1] Price Terms

If the contract does not specify a price, UCC §2-305(1) sets the price as a reasonable price at the time of delivery. The methods for setting price in commercial transactions include:

- Cost plus (e.g., overhead and profit)
- Market price: the selling price on an organized exchange
- Price in a trade journal
- Price by leading suppliers
- Price as set by an expert appraiser
- Price to be agreed on later; if the parties fail to agree, §2-305 requires a reasonable price unless the agreement indicates that the parties intended the contract to fail if they do not reach an agreement
- Price set by seller or buyer; §2-305(2) imposes a requirement of good faith
- Escalator clauses: regular adjustments (usually increases) to reflect a standard price index (e.g., Consumer Price Index or Wholesale Price Index promulgated by a government agency or other trusted source)

Under 2-305(4), if the parties do not intend to be bound unless the open price term is supplied, then there is no contract if it is not supplied. In that situation, the buyer must return the goods, or pay the reasonable value of the goods if return is impossible, and the seller has to return any proceeds received.

[¶205.7.2] Quantity Terms

A contract can provide for the sale of a seller's entire output, or a buyer's entire requirement; good faith must be exercised in specifying the size of output or requirement (2-306(1)). In a §2-306 "exclusive dealings" contract, under which a retailer agrees not to carry competing merchandise, the seller must use its best efforts to supply the quantity that the buyer needs, and the buyer must use its best efforts to sell the merchandise.

[¶205.7.3] Delivery Terms

If the contract does not specify a place of delivery, §2-208 sets the place of delivery as the location of the goods where they were identified to the agreement (i.e., allocated to the particular buyer). If the goods are not identified to the agreement when the contract is made, then delivery will be made from the seller's place of business (or home, if he has no place of business) unless otherwise agreed.

Standard commercial abbreviations are often used for delivery terms. The UCC includes these definitions (see, especially, §2-319). FOB stands for Free on Board; FAS stands for Free Along Side (i.e., of a ship or other vessel):

- FOB (Place of Shipment): Unless otherwise agreed, the seller is responsible for shipping the goods and paying for putting the goods in the hands of the shipper. The seller has to notify the buyer of the shipment and deliver the documents of title that will permit the buyer to obtain possession. The buyer has a duty to give the seller proper shipping instructions.
- FOB (Place of Destination): Unless otherwise agreed, the seller has the obligation of paying to transport the goods to the place of destination. The seller is obligated to give the buyer reasonable notification so it can take delivery. The seller must tender delivery at a reasonable time, and keep the goods available for a reasonable time to permit the buyer to take possession.
- FOB (Car or Other Vehicle): In addition to putting the goods in the carrier's possession, the seller has an additional obligation to load them on board the carrier's vehicle.
- FOB (Vessel): The seller must place the goods on board the vessel designated by the buyer. If necessary, the seller must furnish a proper form bill of lading.
- FAS (Vessel): The seller is responsible for delivery (and the cost of delivery) of the goods alongside the vessel designated by the buyer (or on the dock designated in the usual manner for that port). The seller has an obligation to get a receipt, in exchange for which the carrier is obligated to issue a bill of lading.
- CIF (§2-320): The price of the goods includes the cost of the goods plus insurance and freight to the designated destination. The seller is obligated to load the goods, get a receipt showing that freight has been paid or provided for, get a negotiable bill of lading, insure the goods for the buyer's account, and forward all necessary documents to the buyer promptly. If delivery is to be made to the buyer, the buyer has to furnish facilities reasonably suited for accepting the delivery.

  If the agreement calls for delivery to the buyer without moving goods that are in a warehouse or otherwise in the possession of a bailee, the seller has to provide a negotiable document of title or get the bailee to acknowledge the buyer's right to possession of the goods.
- C&F or CF: These terms are equivalent to CIF, except that the price includes only the goods themselves plus freight to the named destination. Insurance is not included.

If the agreement doesn't give a time for delivery, §2-309 uses the standard of commercial reasonableness to require delivery within a reasonable time. A contract of indefinite duration covering successive performances can be terminated at any time by either party on reasonable notice.

Unless the agreement is to the contrary, 2-307 provides that all goods will be shipped in a single delivery, with payment due when the goods are tendered to the buyer. If the agreement or circumstances dictate delivery in lots, the seller can apportion the price and demand payment for each lot as it is delivered. Generally, payment is due under 2-310(a) at the time and place where the buyer is to receive the goods.

Late delivery can be excused if it is due to a contingency whose nonoccurrence was a basic assumption underlying the contract. Good-faith compliance with applicable government regulations also excuses late delivery: §2-615.

Delivery delays are excused under §2-311 and 2-610(a) if performance is suspended because of the buyer's repudiation or the buyer's failure to cooperate as required by the agreement.

When one party is given the right to specify the terms of performance, §2-311, Official Comment (1) says that commercially reasonable specifications made in good faith will be upheld. Agreements that say the buyer will receive an assortment of goods will be interpreted to permit the buyer to determine the assortment, unless the agreement is to the contrary.

[¶205.8] Buyer's Rights

If the buyer has the right to return goods purchased for personal use, the contract is considered a sale on approval. But if the buyer is acquiring goods for resale, the contract is a sale or return (§2-326(1)). The difference is that in a sale on approval, the seller has the obligation of return and the risk of loss. In a sale or return, the obligation of return is on the buyer unless otherwise agreed: §2-327. A "consignment" or "on memorandum" sale is considered a sale or return.

[¶205.8.1] Inspection

The buyer has the right to inspect the goods that are being purchased, when tender of delivery has been made or the goods have been identified to the agreement (§2-513). If payment is required before inspection, then nonconformity of goods does not excuse the buyer unless the nonconformity is so obvious that it can be determined without inspection (§2-512). An agreement to pay against documents may waive the buyer's right to inspection, as does a C.O.D. delivery term (§2-513(3)).

The right of inspection extends to inspection by any reasonable manner, including reasonable testing of the goods. Unreasonable testing (using up an extraordinary quantity of goods in testing; performing unnecessary tests) may be construed as an acceptance. The buyer is responsible for costs of inspection and testing, but if the goods are rejected because they have been found not to conform to the agreement, §2-513(2) allows the buyer to recover the reasonable cost of inspection and testing from the seller.

[¶205.8.2] Rejection

Section 2-602 makes it easier to reject goods than to revoke acceptance. The non-conforming goods must be rejected within a reasonable time. The seller must be notified of rejection. The buyer cannot exercise any ownership rights over rejected goods. A buyer who has physical possession but no security interest in the goods has a duty of reasonable care to hold the goods long enough for the seller to remove them.

The definition of "acceptance" under 2-606 is that the buyer does not reject the goods, after a reasonable opportunity to inspect them; tells the seller that the goods are conforming or will accept them notwithstanding nonconformity; or acts in a manner inconsistent with the seller's ownership of the goods.[4]

The buyer has the right to reject nonconforming goods: see 2-508(1) and 2-601. If the seller tenders delivery or delivers the goods before the contract deadline, and the buyer rejects the goods as nonconforming, the seller can always cure by giving the buyer timely notice and making a conforming delivery within the deadline. The right to cure exists even if the contract says it doesn't.

The "perfect tender" rule of 2-601 covers situations in which the goods or tender of delivery fail to conform to the contract in any way (not necessarily a serious, harmful, or material way). The buyer can either accept all the goods; reject all the goods; or accept any number of commercial units (e.g., crates or cartons) and reject the rest. The perfect tender rule does not apply to installment contracts, and is modified by the seller's right to cure.

After goods have been accepted, 2-608 allows revocation of acceptance within a reasonable time of the discovery of nonconformity. However, the nonconformity must substantially impair the value. Revocation is permitted if the nonconformity was hard to detect before acceptance; the buyer relied on the seller's assurances; or the buyer reasonably believed the nonconformity would be cured, but it was not.

[¶205.9] Seller's Rights

Unless the contract says otherwise, the buyer's tender of payment is a condition to the seller's duty to tender and complete delivery (2-511(1)). The buyer's check is a conditional payment, which is defeated if the check bounces (§2-511(3)). If this occurs, the seller has a right to recover the goods, unless the buyer has transferred them to a good-faith purchaser. The seller can also sue for the price of the goods based either on the dishonored check or on the underlying agreement.

The seller has the right to re-sell goods that were wrongfully rejected by the buyer (2-703(d), -706). The seller is also allowed by §2-703 to withhold delivery, cancel the contract, and sue for the price of the goods or damages for their non-acceptance.

[¶205.10] Passage of Title

Before the UCC, title to goods was the crucial determinant of issues of risk and control; the UCC separates questions of risk (see below) from title, but it is still often important to identify when title has passed from seller to buyer. Note that, under §2-401(4), title revests in the seller by operation of law if the buyer refuses to accept the goods, or withdraws acceptance.

In general, §2-401 provides that title passes to the buyer once the seller has completed its performance by delivering the goods. So if the contract calls for delivery FOB cars at the seller's warehouse, title passes as soon as the goods are placed on the cars at the seller's warehouse. If the agreement calls for the seller to send the goods to the buyer, but doesn't require delivery at the place of destination, title passes to the buyer at the time and place of shipment. If the seller is obligated to deliver the goods to the buyer at the place of destination, title passes to the buyer on delivery.

Title passes at the time and place of delivery of the title document, if delivery is to be made without moving the goods and the seller is required to deliver a document of title (e.g., warehouse receipt). For delivery without moving goods that have already been identified to the agreement and where no document of title is required, title passes to the buyer as soon as the agreement is made.

[¶205.11] Risk of Loss

If possible, the intention of the parties concerning risk of loss will be respected. Also note that if trade custom or usage requires owners to insure work in progress against fire loss, the owner bears the risk of loss unless the agreement is to the contrary. The UCC's general risk rule is that the party best able to bear the loss, or the party who should be expected to bear it, will be at risk for the loss.

Several UCC sections provide risk rules for situations in which the contract does not specify:

- If the seller is required to deliver the goods to the carrier, risk of loss shifts to the buyer as soon as the seller delivers the goods to the carrier (§2-509).
- For goods sold FOB place of shipment, the buyer is at risk of loss as soon as the goods are placed in the hands of the shipper; if sold FOB destination, risk of loss shifts to the buyer at the time and place of delivery or the time and place of tender of delivery to the buyer (§2-319).
- §2-509 provides that, if the seller is obligated to deliver goods to the destination, the risk of loss shifts to the buyer when delivery is tendered to the buyer, who is then able to take possession. The same section provides that, when a merchant seller agrees to deliver goods at the seller's place of business or the present location of the goods, the buyer has risk of loss upon receipt of the goods. But if a non-merchant seller is required to deliver goods to the seller's place of business or the present location of the goods, and the buyer is not a merchant, the buyer does not have risk of loss until tender of delivery.
- For conditional sales, §2-327 provides that goods sold for resale (on sale or return) place the risk of loss during the return on the buyer. But for a sale on approval (goods sold primarily for use of the purchaser), the buyer has the risk of loss as soon as the goods are accepted. The seller is at risk of loss during return of non-accepted goods.
- For nonconforming goods, the risk of loss remains on the seller until the buyer accepts the goods despite their nonconformity, or until the nonconformity is cured: §2-510.
- §2-510 also provides that if the buyer justifiably revokes acceptance, the buyer can treat the risk of loss as having been with the seller to the extent of any deficiency in the seller's insurance coverage.

If, instead, the buyer repudiates the agreement while title to the goods still rests with the seller, the seller can treat the risk of loss as having rested on the buyer for a commercially reasonable time. If the seller's effective insurance coverage is defective, however, the insurance "gap" limits the buyer's liability.

- The risk of loss is generally on the seller if goods identified to the agreement are destroyed, by no fault of the buyer or seller, before risk has shifted to the buyer. But if the goods are totally destroyed, the seller has the right to avoid the agreement. See UCC §2-613. If the destruction is only partial, the buyer has a choice between letting the seller avoid the agreement, and taking the goods at a correspondingly reduced price.

- If the loss was caused by a third party and occurred before the goods were identified to the agreement, §2-722 lets the seller sue the third party. The same section provides that both buyer and seller can sue a third party who is responsible for loss of goods identified to the contract. Any damages recovered go to whomever had the risk of loss at the time it occurred.

Section 2-501 gives the buyer an insurable interest in goods identified to the contract even if they are nonconforming, and even if the buyer has to option to return or reject them. The seller's insurable interest continues as long as it has title or a security interest in the goods.

[¶205.12] Excuse of Performance

UCC §§2-613, -615, -616, and -718 give rules for circumstances under which the seller will be excused from performance under the agreement. This occurs, e.g., when goods identified to the contract that are destroyed before the risk of loss shifts to the buyer, as long as neither party was at fault in the destruction. If there is a total loss, the contract is avoided, and the buyer can get back any downpayment it has made. (In this situation, the seller should have maintained insurance that would compensate.) As noted above, partial destruction or deterioration of the goods gives the buyer a choice between a voided contract or goods accepted at a reduced price.

If performance is rendered commercially impracticable because of a contingency that the buyer and seller relied on not occurring, the seller is excused by §2-615. This is also true if foreign or domestic government regulations prevent performance. If only part of the seller's productive capacity is affected, the UCC requires the seller to allocate the remaining productive capacity among buyers, and to notify each customer of its share of the limited capacity.

The notice triggers the buyer's right to terminate the agreement or accept the allocation of merchandise offered by the seller (if the shortage substantially impairs the value of the contract). Sellers can allocate part of the limited production to regular customers, even if the regular customers do not have explicit contracts.

There is no statutory definition of unconscionability, but §2-302(1) permits a court to decide, as a matter of law, whether an entire contract or any part of it is unconscionable. The court can deny enforcement to the entire contract, strike out the unconscionable portions, or limit application of a clause to prevent an unconscionable result.

[¶205.13] Article 2 Remedies

The general objective of UCC remedies is to put the aggrieved party in the same position as if the breaching party had performed (§1-106(1)).

Liquidated damages clauses are enforceable only on the basis of the anticipated or actual harm from the breach; the difficulty of proving loss; and impracticality of other remedies (§2-718(1)). A clause that sets the liquidated damages too low is unconscionable under §2-302, but one that imposes excessively heavy damages is also void, as a penalty, under §2-718(1).

[¶205.13.1] Sellers' Remedies

The seller's damages for wrongful rejection, repudiation of the contract or revocation of acceptance equal the difference between the market price at the time and place for tender and the unpaid contract price plus incidental damages, reduced by any expenses saved because of the buyer's breach (§2-708). An alternative measure of damages is what the seller would have received from performance: the profits, including reasonable overhead, to be expected from the deal, plus incidental damages and costs incurred because of the breach, reduced by the proceeds of resale.

The seller can recover incidental damages but not consequential ones (§2-710). Incidental damages are direct results of the buyer's breach, such as the cost of stopping delivery, holding the goods after the breach, resale expenses, but not attorneys' fees.

Also see §§2-702, -705 (remedies if the buyer is insolvent). The seller can stop delivery of goods not yet received by the insolvent buyer. The seller can withhold the delivery of goods not yet shipped, and can demand payment in advance even though the contract calls for a credit sale. The seller can also give notice within 10 days of receipt to reclaim the goods. The 10-day limitation is not imposed when the buyer made false representations of solvency within three months of delivery.

[¶205.13.2] Buyers' Remedies

Naturally, Article 2 also provides remedies for buyers. If the seller fails to deliver or repudiates the contract, or if the buyer rightfully rejects the goods or revokes acceptance, then §2-711(1) allows the buyer to cancel the contract and receive a refund of money paid to the seller, subject to the seller's right to cure, which extends until the time for performance has expired (§2-508). Furthermore, the buyer has a security interest in the goods to the extent of payments made and expenses of inspection, care, and transportation (§2-711(3)), so the buyer can hold and resell the goods to satisfy this interest.

"Cover" is the buyer's right under §2-712 to purchase goods elsewhere while receiving damages for the goods affected. It is a form of mitigation of damages. Damages for non-delivery or repudiation by the seller are governed by §2-713. To the extent the buyer has not covered, the damages equal the difference between the

43

market and contract prices, plus incidental and consequential damages (note that sellers are not entitled to consequential damages), minus expenses saved as a result of the breach. In this context, incidental damages involve things done to the goods.

Consequential damages result from the known needs of the buyer that could not have been prevented (by cover or otherwise) and include personal injury and property damage proximately caused by the breach of warranty. Consequential damages can include lost profits, loss of goodwill, and interruption of production.

If the buyer fails to notify the seller that goods are non-conforming, §2-607(3)(a) denies damages to the buyer. The remedy allowed by §2-714 when the buyer does notify equals the value of the goods as warranted minus the value of the nonconforming goods, plus incidental and consequential damages in appropriate cases. The buyer may be able to obtain specific performance, under §2-716(1), if the goods are unique or there are other justifying circumstances. Section 2-717 lets the buyer deduct damages for breach from any amount still due under the contract, but the buyer must notify the seller before doing so (Official Comment (2)).

[¶210] Article 2A: Leases

UCC Article 2A covers leases (arrangements under which the owner receives regular payments in exchange for letting someone else use vehicles, equipment, or other property). Goods leased to consumers are also covered by Chapter 5 of the Truth in Lending Act and the FTC's Regulation M, as long as the lease lasts four months or longer. Leased property worth over $25,000 is immune from these two requirements.

[¶210.1] Consumer Lease Disclosures

The required Article 2A disclosures for consumer leases include:

- Description of the leased property
- The amount to be paid when the lease is signed; status of the payment as refundable security deposit, advance lease payment, credit for trade-in allowance, etc.
- The number of lease payments to be made
- The amount and due date for each payment
- The total of all the scheduled lease payments
- Taxes and official fees for the full term of the lease
- Mandatory charges that are not part of the periodic payments (e.g., delivery, pick-up)
- Extent to which the lessee is required to maintain insurance coverage
- Any express warranties made by the manufacturer and lessor
- Who is responsible for maintenance and servicing of the property. Usually the lessee is responsible, and the lessor is permitted to impose a charge for excess wear and tear, as long as its standards are reasonable
- Any security interest that the lessor obtains in the property of the lessee

- Late payment and default charges
- Whether the lessee has an option to purchase the leased property; if so, when it can be exercised (e.g., only at the end of the lease term; throughout the lease term) and how much the lessee must pay or how the purchase price will be calculated
- Amount of (or method of calculating) charges for default or early termination of the lease; the lessor is forbidden to exact unreasonable charges
- Whether, at the end of the lease, the lessee is required to pay the difference between the estimated value of the property and its actual value.

Disclosures are also required in advertisements for consumer leases. The advertisement must disclose that the transaction is a lease; how large a downpayment is required; and the number and size of the lease payments. The lessee's responsibilities at the end of the lease term must also be disclosed.

[¶215] Article 2B

Legal rules that make sense for shipping a boxcar full of industrial chemicals don't help very much in drafting or interpreting contracts that deal with software or the licensing of information. For one thing, once Company A sells the chemicals to Company B, Company A is no longer able to sell the same chemicals to Company C. Yet a programmer who develops a software program, or a publisher who creates a database or other electronic document, may be able to sell or license the same intangible to dozens, hundreds, or thousands of satisfied customers.

Proposed Article 2B was an attempt by the National Conference of Commissioners on Uniform State Laws to codify the law of software and information leasing.[5] The leading court case on the subject, *ProCD v. Zeidenberg*[6] holds that "shrink-wrap" licenses—printed license terms distributed with commercial software—are enforceable. "Click-wrap" licenses are their Web counterparts: access to some Web sites is limited to people who click "I agree" to a recitation of the site's terms of service. The issue is whether these licenses, which users have no opportunity to negotiate individually, should be enforced or rejected as contracts of adhesion.

The NCCUSL drafting committee decided in November, 1998 to limit the scope of Article 2B to computer-related industries (software and database), specifically excluding entertainment and broadcast media, based on opposition from these industries.

[¶215.1] Uniform Computer Information Transactions Act

In April, 1999, however, the NCCUSL and the American Law Institute announced that they had abandoned attempts to pass Article 2B. Instead, they would shift their attention to developing a uniform law, the Uniform Computer Information Transactions Act (UCITA), for consideration by the states in the fall of 1999.[7] NCCUSL gave its official approval to the UCITA on July 29, 1999.

UCITA covers licensing of information that is communicated electronically (e.g., software and databases), but is not a general licensing statute or a general intellectual property statute. (In fact, the draft has been criticized for creating inconsistent approaches to communications, depending on the medium in which they are made.)

UCITA gives statutory recognition to shrink-wrap and click-wrap (Internet) licenses. Consumer rights are promoted by explicit warranty rules and the right to a refund if the consumer does not find the terms of service for the software acceptable. However, the sellers of software would have the right to disable the software after a license is canceled. The UCITA allows licensors to impose controls on the usage of software; the FTC's position is that the UCITA does not require such controls to be disclosed conspicuously enough.

The value of the UCITA will depend, in part, on the number of states that adopt it, because if it is not widely adopted, information publishers will have to conform to numerous and possibly inconsistent state rules.

[¶220] Commercial Paper

Medieval and Renaissance merchants faced some formidable problems: not only shipping goods under very difficult conditions, but somehow getting paid when currencies were far from standardized, banking was primitive, and even bookkeeping was an exotic novelty. Some of the devices they created still influence the law of "commercial paper"—the devices used to transfer funds from one party to another.

Articles 3, 4, 5, and 7 deal with commercial paper: Article 3 with negotiable instruments, 4 with bank deposits and collections, 5 with letters of credit, and 7 with warehouse receipts.

[¶220.1] Bankers' Acceptances

A banker's acceptance is a "facility": a service offered by a commercial bank. It is a hybrid negotiable instrument, often used in import-export transactions. First, a drawer "utters" (i.e., creates) a draft. The drawee bank accepts the draft (indicates willingness to pay it). In this instance, the bank is really just an intermediary. It creates the acceptance, so the borrower gets credit. The bank generally re-sells the acceptance right away.

[¶220.2] Negotiable Instruments

There are many instances in commercial operation when it is more convenient to satisfy an obligation to other businesses by transferring obligations owed to one's own business. A negotiable instrument is a contract for the payment of money, involving transferable intangible rights in the instrument. An important feature of negotiable instruments is that, in some circumstances, a good faith transferee can actually have greater rights than the transferor.

There are three common types of negotiable instrument: the draft, the check, and the promissory note. Notes have gained prominence because of their role in consumer credit (e.g., car loans). In order to protect consumers, some limits are imposed on the negotiability of consumer notes, and the holder is subject to defenses that could be asserted against the seller (e.g., poor quality or dangerous nature of goods purchased with proceeds of the notes). Even commercial debtors may have causes of action. Since the 1980s, for instance, a "lender liability" cause of action has gained recognition, e.g., when a bank calls demand notes under unfair circumstances.

In order to understand negotiable instruments, it is necessary to understand that "money" is any medium that a seller or service provider is willing to accept, and "payment" is any transfer of "money," usually but not always to pay for goods or services.

Bank deposits are actually debts that the bank owes to its depositors, because the depositors are lending their funds to the bank. When a bank pays a check, it transfers some of its debt from the drawer of the check to the payee. The drawer is the party writing the check; the drawee is the bank or other party expected to pay the check.

A negotiable instrument is an unconditional order or promise to pay a fixed amount of money, with or without interest: §3-104. There are many kinds of negotiable instruments; and a negotiable instrument can be payable either on demand or at a specific time, and either to order (a specified payee) or to bearer (whoever has it).

Section 3-104 further defines a check as a draft that is payable on demand and drawn on a bank. (A money order is considered a check.) A cashier's check is a special check drawn on the payor's own bank; a teller's check is a special check issued by a bank itself (usually in exchange for a cash payment). A traveler's check requires a second signature by its drawer, as a condition of payment. A Certificate of Deposit is a bank's acknowledgment that money has been deposited and will be repaid to the depositor with interest. In effect, it is a note with the bank as maker.

An instrument is negotiated (i.e., transferred or made available for transfer) either by delivery (for bearer paper) or indorsement plus delivery (for order paper). Usually, the indorsement is made on the back of the instrument. Unless the instrument clearly indicates that it is made in some other capacity, any signature will be considered an indorsement (§3-402).

[¶220.3] Promissory Notes

A promissory note (e.g., an installment note or mortgage note) is a written promise to pay a certain sum, either on demand or at a specified future time. In a promissory note, the issuer promises to pay; in contrast, in a bill of exchange (a check or draft), the maker or drawer of the instrument orders a drawee (e.g., a bank) or acceptor to pay.

The note is conditional, and therefore not negotiable, if, for instance, it is expressly conditioned on the carrying out of an executory (future) promise; if the note is subject to or governed by another instrument; or if the note can be paid only from a particular fund. Section 3-109 explains what makes a note payable to order or bearer; §3-110 gives rules for identifying the payee when this is not clear. There is no interest payable on an instrument unless the instrument calls for interest, which can be either fixed or variable (see §3-112), and either antedated or post-dated instruments are permitted by §3-113. Even an incomplete but signed instrument can be given effect (see §3-115), but it has been "altered," and remedies are available under §3-407, if words or numbers are added to an incomplete instrument without the seller's authority.

A negotiable instrument must contain the "words of negotiability": it must say that it is payable to order or bearer. Under §3-109, a note payable to order is payable to the order of a named person; the assigns of a named person; or to his or her order. An instrument is payable to bearer if it is payable to "cash"; if it says it is payable to "bearer"; or if no payee is indicated. An instrument is an order instrument, payable to an identified person, if it is payable, e.g., "to John Smith" or "to John Smith or order."

A bearer instrument becomes an order instrument if the bearer indorses it to a specified person. An order instrument becomes a bearer instrument if the identified payee indorses it but does not name a specific payee. The indorsement rules appear at §3-204–206.

A bearer instrument is payable to anyone who has it and wants to negotiate it. Therefore, if a bearer instrument is lost or stolen, and ends up in the hands of a bona fide purchaser for value, that purchaser is entitled to negotiate it.

[¶220.4] Checks

Both Articles 3 and 4 have to be considered, because a check is a negotiable instrument, but it is also an item which is deposited in a bank and which goes through the collection process.

The UCC permits orders to stop payment of a check that has been issued. Payment can be stopped (via an oral or written stop payment order) at any time before acceptance, certification, or actual payment. An oral order is good for only two weeks, while a written one is valid for six months (§4-403(b)). In practice, even 30-day-old checks are viewed with suspicion, so it is unlikely that a written order would have to be renewed. Payments made contrary to an effective stop order are improper. The bank is liable for damages suffered, although the customer has the burden of proving the amount of loss: §4-403(c).

The effect of certification, as described in §3-411, is to make the bank directly liable on the instrument once it is properly indorsed. The "obligated bank" has to compensate the person entitled to enforce the check, if the bank wrongfully refuses to pay a cashier's or certified check, or stops payment on its teller's check. Damages include expenses and loss of interest stemming from nonpayment. In fact, the obligated bank becomes liable for consequential damages if it still refuses to pay after being notified of circumstances mandating payment.

The drawer can no longer stop payment on the check, no matter who requested the certification. Even if the drawer's signature is forged, the certifying bank will be liable to a holder in due course, on the theory that it knows the drawer's signature and, by certifying, warrants its genuineness.

The states have "bad check laws," making it an offense to issue or negotiate a check that the drawer knows will bounce. Usually, the offense is a misdemeanor, although if the amount involved is large enough, it might be a felony. Intent to defraud is rebuttably presumed from the mere issuance of the check and its subsequent dishonor for lack of funds.

UCC §4-401(a) permits a bank to charge a customer whenever the customer writes a check that creates an overdraft but is otherwise properly payable. The customer remains liable, and the check is good. The bank usually imposes a service charge or treats it as a loan. (This rule does not apply if the customer didn't sign the check and didn't benefit from it.)

[¶220.5] Holders In Due Course

Negotiability is valuable because the owner of commercial paper can gain financial benefit without waiting until the due date of the paper, by exchanging it or selling it to someone else. The new owner of the paper is known as the "holder." The holder of a negotiable instrument takes it subject to all valid claims against it; all contract defenses; and various other defenses.

A holder who qualifies as a "holder in due course" is in a more favorable legal position, because he or she takes the instrument free of claims and defenses (e.g., assignment of a claim) that would be available against another holder. To be a holder in due course, §3-302 provides that the holder must have:

- Taken an instrument that did not appear forged or altered; has no notice of alteration or unauthorized signature of an instrument that looks valid
- Taken the instrument for value
- Taken it in good faith
- Had no notice that it is overdue
- Had no notice of dishonor
- Been unaware of any default, defense or claim against the instrument.

Personal defenses (e.g., failure of consideration; mistake; breach of warranty) cannot be asserted against a holder in due course, but "real" defenses (e.g., forgery; fraud in the inducement; fraud in execution; infancy) remain available. But if the underlying contract has been partially performed, the holder in due course has rights only as against the unperformed part.

Nevertheless, when a negotiable instrument is sold or assigned, consumers may retain certain claims and defenses as a result of the Federal Trade Commission's Trade Regulation Rule (16 CFR Part 433). Under the rule, it is an unfair and deceptive trade practice for a seller who finances or arranges the financing of consumer goods or services to make the consumer's duty to pay independent of the seller's duty to fulfill its obligations.

The FTC requires notice when a seller of goods refers consumers to a creditor. When a seller and lender work together to arrange financing for consumer goods, the loan contract must include the required FTC notice, even if the lender does not pay referral fees to the seller.

Consumer credit contracts must include a clause (in 10-point boldface type) notifying consumers that claims or defenses that could be raised against the seller can also be raised against the holder. UCC §3-106(d) provides that no one can become holder in due course of an instrument subject to such consumer defenses.

[¶230] Article 4: Bank Deposits and Collections

Article 4 covers the relationship between a customer who has a bank account and the bank itself (which is the payor bank for the customer's checks). This relationship is contractual. The customer deposits funds into the bank; the bank agrees to pay the checks written by the customer, and "properly payable" (as defined by §§4-401) but not those that are forged.

The bank has the right to pay valid items and charge them to the customer's account in any order—even if the result is to create an overdraft, leading to "bounced" checks and fees charged to the customer: §4-303(b).

Checks (other than certified checks) become formally stale after six months (§4-404); usually, the bank will ask the customer for permission to pay a check presented after that time.

[¶230.1] The Collection Process

The payee (person to whom the check is payable) indorses the check (adds a signature indicating desire to get value for the check) and brings it to the bank with a deposit ticket. When the deposit is made, the payee's account is credited with the amount of the check, but only provisionally; if the check bounces, the credit will be reversed.

Sometimes a bank's customer will deposit checks in a bank that, coincidentally, is the bank where the drawer of the check has an account. In that case, the depository bank is also the payor bank, and the check is an "on us" item. See §4-105. Otherwise, the check goes through "clearing," the process under which the various banks receive all the checks written on them and deposited with other banks. The purpose of clearing is to settle accounts among the banks as well as to update the accounts of drawers of checks.

Federal laws, including the Expedited Funds Availability Act, 12 USC §4000—and Regulation CC, 12 CFR Part 229, set limits on the maximum time a bank can take before finally (rather than provisionally) crediting the account. The federal rules preempt inconsistent UCC and state-law rules.

When a check is returned to the payor bank, the payor bank must either "finally pay" the check or dishonor (bounce) it (§4-215). The determination depends on whether the check appears to be legitimate, not forged or altered; whether there is a stop-payment order on record; and whether the drawer's account contains sufficient funds to pay the check. UCC §4-214 governs reversing the provisional settlement and charging back the provisional credit if the check is dishonored.

[¶230.2] Properly Payable Items; Forgery; Fraud

Traditionally, banks returned canceled checks to their customers, or provided a monthly or other periodic accounting of items. (The current trend is to make images of the checks available on request, or available online, but not to return the actual checks.) The customer then has a duty to examine the record of statement, and to give the bank prompt notification of any improper items[8]; failure to do so can deprive the customer of remedies against the bank for improper payment of the items: §4-406. But if the customer was negligent and the bank also failed to use ordinary care in paying the item, then the loss is apportioned between the bank and customer: §4-406(e).

It makes a difference when the check was actually written by the customer, but the amount of the check was raised by a dishonest person. In that case, the bank has a right to charge the customer's account for the original amount (§4-401(d)(1)), whereas if either the signature on the check or the indorsement is forged, the check is not properly payable (§4-401(a)), and the bank should not charge the customer's account. The theory is that the bank has the drawer's signature on file, so it can check to see if it appears to be forged (even though it would be grossly impractical to review all signatures).

If it does charge the customer's account, and the customer promptly reviews the canceled checks and notifies the bank of the forgery, the bank must re-credit the customer's account (§4-401).

The customer may become partially liable if its negligence made it easier for the malefactor to forge or alter the check: see §3-406, showing the interrelation between the UCC provisions for commercial paper and those for bank deposits and collections. Furthermore, a check is considered properly payable (as long as the bank acts in good faith and exercises ordinary care) even if the payee is an impostor, or a fictitious party (e.g., a nonexistent company whose existence is asserted under a fraudulent scheme): see §3-404.

Companies are also stuck with the loss if their own employees divert corporate checks for their own benefit, on the theory that corporations have a greater ability to hire honest employees and supervise them than banks have to detect check scams: see §3-405 Official Comment 1.

[¶230.3] Stopping Payment

A check is really the customer's direction to the bank to pay on behalf of the party designated by the customer. The customer (but not the payee or the endorsee) has the right to stop payment on a check by giving the bank reasonable notice (oral or written) of his or her intention: §4-403. The stop payment order lasts for six months, but oral stop-payment orders lose effectiveness after 14 days if they are not reduced to writing in the interim. Of course, the bank must get the order in time to act on it; it's too late once the check has been either paid or certified (§§4-303, -401(c)).

[¶230.4] Wrongful Dishonor

Not only must the bank take steps to pay only checks that are proper, it must take steps to pay *all* checks that are proper, without "wrongfully dishonoring" a properly payable check. See §§4-401(a) and -402(a). Section 402(a) gives the bank the right to dishonor an item that creates an overdraft, unless overdraft protection has been arranged.

Under §4-402(b), a customer who suffers wrongful dishonor of an item is entitled to actual damages, including consequential damages (which could include damages for being arrested or prosecution for check fraud). It is a fact question whether wrongful dishonor of the item was the proximate cause of the customer's damages.

[¶240] Article 4A: Funds Transfers

The adoption of Article 4A required the creation of a completely new system for commercial funds transfers, also known as wholesale wire transfers. However, some important classes of transfers are excluded from the scope of Article 4A, including the consumer funds transfers governed by the Electronic Funds Transfers Act, P.L. 95-630, 15 USC §1693 et seq., and Regulation E, 12 CFR Part 205. Any funds transfer sent by Fedwire is subject to Article 4A, even in states that have not adopted it. Also note that funds a bank receives via funds transfer must be made available for withdrawal not later than the banking day after the banking day on which the funds were received, because of the Expedited Funds Availability Act, 12 USC §4002(a).

Although in general the UCC is interpreted in light of existing principles of law and equity, within Article 4A other principles of law and equity can be applied only to the extent that they do not conflict with Article 4A.[9]

[¶240.1] Payment Orders

Article 4A transfers are made via "payment orders." See 4A-103, -104. A payment order is a written, oral, or electronic order to a receiving bank directing it to pay a fixed or determinable amount of money to a beneficiary, if:

- The sender pays the receiving bank
- The sender transmits instructions directly to the receiving bank, or to an agent, funds transfer system, or communication system for transmission to the receiving bank
- There are no conditions on the order other than the time of payment.

The payment order is issued when it is sent to the receiving bank. The beneficiary is the person to be paid by the beneficiary's bank, which in turn is the bank identified in a payment order by which the beneficiary's account is to be credited. The sender is the person who gives instructions to the receiving bank. An instruction that does not fit into the definition of payment order may create obligations between the parties, but is not subject to Article 4A.[10]

Usually the payment order is sent to the receiving bank through a communications system such as CHIPS or SWIFT. Such a communications system is the sender's agent for the purpose of transmitting the payment order to the bank. Under 4A-206(a), the information sent by the communications system operates as the terms of the sender's payment order. However, this rule does not apply to amounts sent via Federal Reserve System funds transfer systems, and any erroneous processing by the FRB is treated as a 4A-303 erroneous execution of the originating bank's payment order.

4A-104 defines the originator as the sender of the first payment order in a funds transfer. The originator's bank is the receiving bank to which the originator's payment order is issued. An intermediary bank is either a receiving bank other than the originator's or beneficiary's bank. A funds transfer is a series of transactions, beginning with the originator's payment order, engaged in to make payment to a beneficiary, and completed when the beneficiary's bank accepts the payment order for the benefit of the beneficiary.

A receiving bank can encounter obligations, and perhaps liabilities, in several contexts:

- Accepting, amending, or rejecting payment orders (4A-211)
- Executing payment orders (4A-210)
- Making payments.

See 4A-212 for the receiving bank's liability on an unaccepted payment order; 4A-301–305 for its obligations and liabilities with respect to execution of the order, and -402 and -403 for the concerns of the receiving bank.

[¶240.2] Payment Problems

Article 4A deals intensively with the question of what happens if payments are made in the wrong amount or to the wrong person. Under 4A-201, allocation of liability depends on whether a security procedure was in place and was used.

Security procedures are agreed on by customers and receiving banks to verify orders or find errors in transmission. Algorithms and other codes, encryption, and callback procedures are accepted security procedures.

Even unauthorized orders are binding on the customer if the security procedure was commercially reasonable; the bank accepted the order in good faith and pursuant to the procedure; and the bank followed any limitations that the customer imposed on payment orders in the customer's name.

A payment order received by a receiving bank is treated as an authorized order of any identified sender who either authorized it or is responsible for it under agency law (4A-202).

However, if a receiving bank accepts a payment order for which the customer is not liable, the receiving bank may have to refund the amount of the order, plus interest, to the customer. The customer has an obligation to exercise ordinary care to report unauthorized payments to the bank.

The rule of 4A-205 is that if the order is transmitted in accordance with a commercially reasonable security procedure, but nonetheless is sent to the wrong beneficiary, as a duplicate of a legitimate order, or in excess of the amount ordered, the sender is not obligated if the error would have been detected by proper use of the security procedure.

If the recipient is incorrect or the order is duplicated, the sender is not responsible and the receiving bank has a right to recover from the recipient to the extent provided by the law of mistake and restitution. This is also true for an excessive payment to the extent of the excess.[11]

When a payment order is sent to a name, bank account, or other identifier whose beneficiary is nonexistent or unidentifiable, no one becomes the beneficiary, and the order cannot be accepted. The funds transfer cannot be completed, and the funds are returned to sender: 4A-207.[12]

[¶240.3] Acceptance of the Payment Order

A bank that is not the beneficiary's bank "accepts" a payment order when it executes the order (4A-209). This is done by paying the beneficiary; notifying the beneficiary that his or her account will be credited; or that the order is rejected. A payment order is rejected by the receiving bank when it gives oral, electronic, or written notice of rejection to the sender: 4A-210. (It is impossible to prevent acceptance of a payment made by Fedwire.)

4A-405 defines payment as the beneficiary's bank crediting the beneficiary's account; the beneficiary is notified of the right to withdraw the credit (or the bank applies the credit to a debt of the beneficiary or otherwise makes the funds available to the beneficiary). When the receiving bank accepts and executes the payment order, the sender becomes obligated to pay the amount of the payment order to the receiving bank (4A-402(c)).

The sender can amend or cancel a payment order by giving the receiving bank oral, written, or electronic notice: 4A-211. A payment order is deemed canceled by operation of law if it is not accepted by the end of the fifth business day after its execution date or the payment date of the order. This section also provides that even the sender's death or incapacity will not revoke the payment order, unless the receiving bank is aware of the fact and has a reasonable opportunity to act on it before accepting the order.

There is no remedy under 4A-209 or 4A-301 for failure to execute a payment order. The sole remedy is the 4A-402 refund, and that is obtainable only against the prior bank in the chain, not any bank.[13]

Federal Reserve regulations have the force of federal law, and preempt inconsistent 4A provisions; so do Federal Reserve Bank operating circulars, even though they do not have the force of law. See 4A-107.[14]

[¶250] Article 5: Letters of Credit

A letter of credit is part of a multi-party transaction, usually where the parties are too far apart from each other to be able to make an accurate assessment of the risk that the seller will not deliver or will deliver defective goods, or that the buyer will pay late or not at all. The customer (usually the buyer of merchandise, who will need a way to pay once delivery is made) gets its bank to agree to honor drafts on the bank as long as the conditions set out in the letter of credit are met. Letters of credit are irrevocable. (The buyer pays its bank a fee for the service.)

The seller of the merchandise is the beneficiary of the letter of credit. It will be able to draw a draft on the issuer bank by producing a bill of lading and any other required documentation (e.g., import documents; inspection certificates) called for by the letter of credit. In effect, the bank is a mutually trusted third party intermediary. Because both buyer and seller trust the bank, neither has to trust the other.

In Article 5 parlance (as defined by §5-102), an "applicant" gets a letter of credit issued. The "beneficiary" is entitled to have its "documentary presentation" honored by the "issuer" bank. The letter of credit is the issuer bank's undertaking to honor a proper documentary presentation (i.e., the appropriate documents are delivered to prove that payment is due).

Under §5-108, the issuer has a reasonable time, not to exceed seven business days, to review the presentation and honor it if it appears to satisfy the terms and conditions of the letter of credit. If the documents do not appear proper, and unless the applicant made other arrangements, the issuer must dishonor the presentation. The issuer is not responsible for performance of the underlying contract. The rules for identifying and coping with fraudulent or forged documents appear in §5-109; §5-111 provides remedies for wrongful dishonor or repudiation of a letter of credit, subject to the one-year statute of limitations found in §5-115.

When a presentation is honored, the beneficiary warrants, under §5-110, that no forged documents were involved, and drawing on the letter of credit does not violate any agreement between the applicant and the beneficiary, who are typically the buyer and seller, respectively, in a business transaction.

Generally speaking, as a result of §5-112 letters of credit are not transferable, but §5-114 permits the beneficiary to assign the cash, check, or other proceeds paid when the letter of credit is honored.

The various articles of the UCC complement one another; they do not exist in a vacuum. So Article 2 rules must be consulted about the underlying sale. Also see Article 9 for "trust receipts" used by buyers for secured financing of transactions that will be implemented through letters of credit. Letters of credit can also be security when a seller wants to acquire goods from a manufacturer for re-sale to customers.

Note that letters of credit are often used in the international context, so rules and practices of international trade are quite important.[15] Many letter of credit transactions are governed by the International Chamber of Commerce Publication No. 500, "Uniform Customs and Practice for Documentary Credits," and not by Article 5.

[¶260] Article 6: Bulk Sales

Traditionally, Article 6 dealt with "bulk transfers," but the 1989 revision gave states two options. One was repealing the article altogether; the other was to adopt a revised and renamed article.

The problem of bulk sales is one of debtor-creditor relations. Without controls imposed by state law, a desperate creditor might be tempted to sell all of its property and inventory (even those subject to security interests), take the money, and confront creditors with a situation on which there were no remaining goods to seize.

Hence, under the current version of Article 6, the debtor must provide notice in advance to its creditors, at least 45 days before the sale of all or virtually all property. If the creditor group is small, individualized notice is required; if it is large, notice can be made by filing (§6-105).

Even the buyer has obligations under §§6-104 and 6-106(4), which may include distributing the purchase price for the bulk sale merchandise among the claimants named by the seller.

Article 6 applies only to property whose value otherwise available to creditors is at least $10,000; minor transactions are not covered. But neither are very major transactions, exceeding $25 million (§6-103(1).

If a debtor carries out what is in effect a bulk sale without giving the appropriate notice, the sale is not void, and the buyer gets good title to the goods— but §6-107 makes the seller liable to its creditors for any damages that result from failure to comply.

[¶270] Article 7: Documents of Title

This part of the UCC deals with bills of lading, warehouse receipts, delivery orders, and other documents that are used in the process of transporting goods. They prove that the carrier has received the goods and subsequently shipped them, and identify the goods stored in a warehouse. Documents of title are used in bailment relationships—that is, situations in which someone such as a warehouseman has lawful possession of goods that actually are owned by someone else.

The concept of negotiability is important in this context as well as in the context of commercial paper, since deliveries can be made either to order (a designated recipient) or to bearer (whoever presents the appropriate documents). See §7-501.

It is also possible to buy or sell the document and thereby gain rights in the underlying goods. Just as a check or other draft tells a bank or other drawee to give money to a payee, a delivery order instructs a bailee to deliver goods to a purchaser or other deliveree. A negotiable document of title can only be negotiated to a holder, who acquires the document for value, in good faith, and without knowing about any claims or defenses affecting the documents: §7-501. Section 7-502 governs the rights acquired through due negotiation of a document of title.

If the document is not negotiable, naturally it cannot be negotiated, but it can be transferred (§7-504), although the transferee gains only the rights that the transferor had or had actual authority to convey, and the transferor's creditors may have rights superior to those of the transferee.

The warehouseman has an obligation to keep goods covered by a particular warehouse receipt separate from all other goods, except for fungible goods (commodities) that can legitimately be commingled: §7-207.

Although generally a carrier or warehouseman must deliver the goods to the party stipulated in the documents, there are situations under §7-403 in which such delivery is excused. For instance, the seller can direct that delivery be stopped.

If someone else has better title to the goods, delivery can be made to that party (for instance, the goods have been sold in the interim; there is a lien on the goods which gets enforced). If the goods are lost, destroyed, delayed, or damaged under circumstances for which the bailee is not liable, then the bailee is not required to make delivery. This does not, however, relieve the bailee of the duty of ordinary care toward the merchandise, as set out in §7-309. If there are competing claimants for the goods, the bailee doesn't have to deliver them before a reasonable time to determine who has the best claim—or to bring suit for interpleader: §7-603. A court can order delivery of goods, or issuance of a replacement document, on proof of the loss, theft, or destruction of the original document: §7-601.

Sections 7-208 and 7-306 deal with forged and altered documents of title, much as there are rules for forged or altered checks.

Article 7 must be read in conjunction with Article 2's rules on risk of loss and with Article 9's rules for secured transactions.

[¶275] Article 8: Ownership and Transfer of Securities

The original version of Article 8 was created in the 1940s and 1950s, at a time when ownership of securities was usually evidenced by stock certificates, and physical possession of stock certificates was the most relevant measure of ownership.

Article 8 was amended in 1978 to cover situations in which a security is sold without a certificate. But further changes were needed, culminating in a 1994 revision that is the current version of Article 8.

Under current practice, most mutual fund shares are "uncertificated." Stock certificates are still issued for most corporate shares, although it is far more typical for the certificates to be held by clearing corporations.[16] Article 8 covers corporate stock, even if it is not publicly traded: 8-102(a)(15); 8-103(a).

It also covers certain "financial instruments," such as commercial paper and Certificates of Deposit, that are not securities. Part 5 of Article 8, but not the other Parts, applies to stock options that are issued and cleared through the Options Clearing Corporation. But commodity contracts, such as futures contracts and commodity options, do not come under Article 8 because 8-103(f) treats them as neither securities nor financial assets.

Trades are typically made through broker-dealers, and the most significant records are the computer entries in the records of the clearing corporations.

[¶275.1] Transfer of Certificated Securities

The current version of Article 8 copes with the dual system by maintaining rules for transfer of certificated securities. But Part 5 of Article 8 has another set of rules for indirect holdings (the common situation in which an individual owns securities, but a securities intermediary holds the certificates). The central concept of Part 5 is the "security entitlement," defined by 8-102(a)(17) as the rights and property interest of the stockholder in a financial asset.

A security entitlement is acquired, under 8-501, when a securities intermediary credits financial assets to that person's account. The intermediary is required by 8-504 to maintain enough financial assets to satisfy the claims of all entitlement holders. Such assets are held for the entitlement holders, and are not the property of the securities intermediary or subject to the claims of the intermediary's general creditors (8-503).

[¶275.2] Security Interests in Securities

A security interest in securities is created in the same way as any other security interest: i.e., by agreement of a debtor and a secured party (see 9-203). There is no requirement of transfer of the securities or delivery of certificates.

Although a security interest in securities can be perfected in the ordinary way, by filing a financing statement (see ¶280.3), a secured party who has control has priority over a secured party who does not. See §9-116 for automatic perfection of the intermediary's security interest in the financial asset, even if there is no security instrument.

[¶280] Secured Transactions

Article 9 sets out the rights of both debtor and creditor when an extension of credit is made on a secured basis (when personal property is used as collateral).

Security interests include pledges, conditional sales contracts, liens, chattel mortgages, and trust receipts. Article 9 applies to both merchant-to-merchant and consumer transactions, so in addition to Article 9, federal consumer credit laws and/or state consumer protection laws may come into play in a particular transaction.

It is quite common for the same collateral to be subject to more than one security interest, so an important function of Article 9 is to determine priority issues among creditors.

The main discussion involves the existing version of Article 9. See ¶280.7 for a discussion of the revisions proposed in 1998.

[¶280.1] Article 9 Definitions

Within Article 9, the term "consumer goods" applies to those purchased or used primarily for personal, family, or household purposes. "Equipment" refers to goods used or bought primarily for use in business, as well as goods that do not constitute consumer goods, farm products, or inventory. "Inventory" means goods held for sale or lease, or that will be furnished under a service contract. Raw materials and work in progress for eventual business use are also inventory. See §9-106.

Financial instruments may also be covered by Article 9. An "account" is the right to be paid for goods or services rendered. "Chattel paper" is the documentation of a monetary interest that gives rise to a security interest in specific goods (§9-105).

All personal property that does not satisfy the definition of goods, contract rights, negotiable instruments, or accounts falls into the §9-106 definition of "general intangibles."

Based on the agreement between parties (or, sometimes, by operation of law) a "security interest" is created to secure the creditor's right to be paid (for goods) or repaid (for an extension of credit). To become effective, a security interest must "attach."

Creditors interested in securing their rights can take steps to "perfect" the security interest (make it a matter of general record). If more than one security interest attaches to the same goods, the question becomes which one has priority. Generally speaking, priority derives from being the first creditor to file. UCC §9-301 provides that even a possessory interest in collateral (if it is unsecured) can be defeated by an earlier secured interest—even if the possessory interest is later secured.

A "purchase money security interest" (PMSI), which is accorded special priority, is an interest retained by the seller of the collateral; or by a financing agency that advanced money to the seller, and to which chattel paper covering the collateral has been assigned; or benefiting someone who advanced money to the buyer for the purpose of buying the collateral itself. (In other words, if someone puts up collateral to secure credit for another purpose, the creditor is entitled to a lower priority than if the collateral secures the advance of credit used to buy the collateral itself.)

Article 9 is not necessarily the whole story when it comes to the secured transactions of consumer-debtors. Section 9-203(4) makes provision for state consumer protection laws that prevail over inconsistent Article 9 provisions. Creditors may find that federal or state consumer protection laws limit their options. For instance, Article 9 might permit seizure of collateral—but consumer protection laws might limit the creditor's ability to seize without notice and hearing.

[¶280.2] Security Agreement Checklist

Issues to be considered when drafting a security agreement include:

❏ Whether the language reflects the UCC's basic requirements for a security agreement
❏ Nature of the collateral
❏ Whether the collateral is already encumbered by any other security interests (this can be determined by searching the UCC filings under the debtor's name)

- Whether the collateral is in the debtor's possession, or elsewhere
- Whether the debtor's other assets are already subject to liens
- Whether the debtor has been notified of a federal tax lien
- (For corporate debtors) whether appropriate corporate resolutions have been passed to make the agreement effective and enforceable
- If the agreement extends to after-acquired collateral (i.e., collateral acquired after the agreement is in place)
- Whether the collateral consists of consumer goods, inventory, accounts, or general intangibles
- If the goods are likely to be attached to real estate, thus becoming "fixtures," with consequences described at ¶280.5
- If the debtor's spouse or ex-spouse has protectable rights in the collateral
- (In the consumer context) whether Truth in Lending requirements, including disclosure, have been satisfied

The UCC requires that the security agreement be signed by the debtor; the creditor's signature is not mandatory for UCC purposes.

[¶280.3] Perfecting a Security Interest

UCC §9-203 provides that a security interest attaches when the parties agree that it will attach; value has been given (satisfying a pre-existing debt counts as value); the debtor acquires rights in the collateral; and a written security agreement has been created. The security interest is perfected, as described by §9-303, when it has attached and the steps for perfection given in §§9-302 and -304–306 have been completed.

Some security interests are automatically perfected, including a PMSI in consumer goods (other than motor vehicles that have to be registered: §9-302(1)(d)). Otherwise, there are two ways in which a creditor can perfect a security interest. The first is to take possession of the collateral (§9-305). The second, and far more common, method is to file a "financing statement." Depending on the jurisdiction, financing statements must be filed either in a central office for the entire state, or in a county office. See §§9-203, and 9-302.

If the goods are covered by a negotiable document, §9-304(2) holds that while the goods are in the possession of the issuer of the document, the security interest in the goods is perfected by perfecting a security interest in the document.

Many (perhaps most) secured transactions finance inventory, where the normal course of business is that the debtor will sell the inventory and get money for it (proceeds). The secured party has a security interest in identifiable proceeds of the collateral. However, the interest in proceeds remains perfected for only 10 days after the debtor receives the collateral, unless the financing statement that is on file covering the collateral also covers proceeds, or the secured party gets possession within the 10-day period. If the debtor becomes insolvent, the secured party's interest in the proceeds may extend to the debtor's cash and bank accounts, even if the funds can't be identified as cash proceeds of the collateral: §9-306.[17]

[¶280.4] After-Acquired Property and Floating Liens

Generally speaking, the UCC treats after-acquired property clauses as valid. See §9-204. An underlying obligation and/or future advances of credit can be secured by collateral that the debtor acquires after the security agreement is signed. However, after-acquired property clauses can be used in consumer goods security agreements only if the debtor gets rights in the goods within 10 days after the secured party gives value. Consumer "accessions" (9-314), items that are installed or affixed to other consumer goods, can also be the subject of an after-acquired property clause.

A floating lien secures a creditor's interest in collateral that constantly changes: e.g., a store's inventory. The UCC permits floating liens, but does not guarantee that the secured creditor will have priority over all liens that subsequently attach to or are perfected in the same collateral. The floating lien may lose out to a federal tax lien or to a PMSI.

Section 9-204(3) states that there can be a valid security interest in collateral securing amounts that will be advanced in the future, whether or not the advances are made pursuant to prior commitments.

[¶280.5] Priorities Under the UCC

There are two major priority provisions under Article 9 (both of which have been meaningfully altered by the 1998 revisions): §§9-301 and 9-312. Be sure to check your state's adoption of the 1998 revisions to be sure that you are operating under the correct version of the priority rules.

Unless the authorizing statute is to the contrary, §9-310 gives priority to common law or statutory liens for services or materials: for instance, "mechanics'" and "materialmen's" liens.

Section 9-301 holds that an unperfected security interest is subordinate to:

- Persons entitled to priority under UCC §9-312, or the special rules discussed below
- Lien creditors who gain that status before the security interest is perfected
- (For goods, instruments, documents, or chattel paper) an unsecured party who is a transferee in bulk, or a buyer outside the ordinary course of business who gives value and receives delivery of collateral without knowledge of the unperfected security interest
- (For accounts and general intangibles) A transferee who is not a secured party who prevails over an unperfected security interest to the extent that the transferee gives value without knowledge of the security interest, and before it is perfected.

As noted above, PMSIs in consumer goods can be perfected even without filing. For other PMSIs, a 10-day grace period is allowed against creditors and transferees in bulk (§9-301(2)). That is to say, a secured party who files with respect to a PMSI within the 10 days after the debtor gets possession of the collateral has priority over a transferee in bulk or a lien creditor whose lien arose during the period between the attachment of the PMSI and its perfection. The PMSI can take priority over a conflicting security interest under an after-acquired property clause (§9-312).

Not all PMSIs go to the seller of the collateral. Anyone who gives value to enable the debtor to get the collateral can get a PMSI: see §9-107(b)). The best way for the lender to be protected is to pay the seller directly.

In general, a buyer in the ordinary course of business takes the merchandise free of the security interest, even if it has been perfected or the purchaser has actual knowledge of the security interest. A bona fide purchaser for value of consumer goods, who buys the goods for personal, family, or household use, and who has no knowledge of the security interest, takes the goods free of an unfiled security interest: §9-307. Although this was certainly not adopted as such, in the future this may become known as the "eBay provision," because of its obvious applicability to on-line auctions by non-merchants.

Also see §9-307(3): even a buyer outside the ordinary course of business takes free of a security interest that secures future advances made after the secured party had learned that the goods had been purchased, or advanced more than 45 days after the purchase (whichever comes first).

When goods that are subject to a security interest are sold, then returned to the seller, the return places them once again under the prior security interest. This interest is superior to the interest obtained by the assignee of the account created by the sale, but a transferee of chattel paper created by the sale may have a superior security interest: 9-306, -308.

The purchaser of chattel paper or an instrument has priority over prior security interests that were perfected by filing or entitled to temporary perfection without filing. UCC 9-308 provides that such a purchaser also has priority over a security interest in chattel paper that is claimed merely as proceeds of inventory, even with knowledge of the prior interest.

Under 9-309, a holder in due course of a negotiable instrument; a holder to whom a negotiable document of title has been negotiated; or a bona fide purchaser of a security takes priority over an earlier perfected security interest. However, an Article 9 filing does not constitute notice of the security interest to holders or purchasers.

A security interest that attaches to goods before they become fixtures defeats all prior claims in the real estate as well as subsequent claims in the real estate, as long as the security interest in the fixtures is filed before the later real estate claims arise. However, a security interest in goods that attaches after they become fixtures can defeat a subsequent interest in the real estate only if it is filed before the later claims arise.

Section 9-313 also gives priority to the security interest in goods attaching after they become fixtures over prior claimants who have consented in writing to the security interest in the fixtures.

A security interest that attaches to goods before the goods become accessions (attachments to other goods) is superior to prior claims in the goods to which the accessions are attached. A security interest in the accessions is also superior to subsequent claims in the whole goods, as long as it is filed before the later claims arise.

Security interests attaching after the goods have become accessions are superior only to subsequent interests in the whole goods if filed before the subsequent interests arise. Section 9-314 provides that interests in accessions are subject to subsequent advances contracted for under an earlier perfected security interest.

Section 9-315 is concerned with commingled or processed goods. A perfected interest in the goods survives their becoming part of a product or mass, if processing destroys the identity of the goods, or the financing statement covers the product too. If there is more than one interest in the mass or product, their rank is proportionate to their cost contribution to the mass.

[¶280.6] Default

Part 5 of Article 9[18] deals with default by the debtor. The UCC allows the secured party to reduce a claim to judgment, foreclose, or enforce the security interest through judicial proceedings. UCC §9-503 (§9-609 in the 1998 version), taken by itself, lets the secured party take possession of the collateral on default, without judicial process, as long as this can be done without a breach of the peace. Or, the creditor can take steps to make equipment unusable if the debtor defaults.

However, if the debtor is a consumer, there will probably be consumer-protection law limits on "self-help repossession" and other creditors' remedies that do not permit the debtor to get a hearing and assert defenses.

After default, the secured party can sell, lease, or otherwise dispose of the collateral. Section 9-504 (1998: §9-608) requires the proceeds to be applied in this order:

- Reasonable expenses of retaking, holding, and selling the collateral, including reasonable attorneys' fees
- Satisfying the indebtedness secured by the collateral
- Satisfaction of any indebtedness to junior debtors.

If there is any surplus left over, the secured party must account to the debtor for the difference between the amount obtained and the amount secured by the agreement. The debtor remains indebted for any deficiency. The rules are somewhat different if the underlying secured transaction is a sale of chattel paper or contract rights. Unless the agreement provides to the contrary, the debtor is neither entitled to surplus nor liable for deficiencies.

The secured party can dispose of the collateral either publicly or privately, in a commercially reasonable fashion. Notice to the debtor is required unless a perishable commodity, or a commodity for which there is a recognized market, is involved. Those who purchase collateral from a secured party after default take it free and clear of all rights and interests that the debtor may have had—even if the secured party fails to satisfy the UCC requirements or requirements imposed by a judicial proceeding.

[¶280.7] Proposed Revisions to Article 9

At the end of 1998, Revised Article 9 was released, to be considered by state legislatures in early 1999. The National Conference of Commissioners on Uniform State Laws obviously expected the enactment process to take some time, because the revised Article has a delayed effective date of July 1, 2001.

The revised Article 9 is somewhat broader in scope than the original. For instance, the transfer of most rights to collect money from a third party will now come under Article 9, not just the accounts and chattel paper that were always covered. Consignments, sales of promissory notes, commercial (but not consumer) deposit accounts, commercial tort claims, health care financial obligations (such as a patient's right to be reimbursed by a health insurer), and "payment intangibles"—intangibles whose major obligation is the payment of money—are also brought within Article 9's reach.

Therefore, borrowers benefit by being able to use more types of assets as collateral. A transaction is considered a consumer transaction if its primary purpose is personal, family, or household—no matter how much money is involved.

Revised Article 9[19] permits the creation of a security interest even if the underlying note, license, or franchise agreement imposes a penalty for allowing the creation of the interest—or forbids its creation outright. However, in case of default, the restrictive clause will prohibit the secured party from enforcing its security interest.

Debtors have certain basic rights, which they may not waive: e.g., the right to receive an accounting after a default; the right to have the collateral handled lawfully; and remedies against the secured party for failure to satisfy statutory requirements. Nor can a guarantor waive the debtor's access to these basic rights. There is a safe harbor under revised Article 9 if the secured party provides a plain-English notification, a reasonable time in advance, to the debtor of:

- Its intention to sell the collateral
- A description of the collateral involved
- Where and when the sale or other disposition will take place
- Disclosure that the debtor may still owe money after the disposition
- A telephone number the debtor can call to find out how much is owed; contact information to find out how that amount was calculated.

Notice to a commercial debtor is considered reasonable if it is given after default and at least 10 days before the sale. A consumer debtor can claim that even 10 days' notice is unreasonable under the facts of the case.

Under the earlier version, the financing statement was supposed to be filed where the collateral was located; the revised version requires filing where the debtor is located. (Of course, they're often the same!) See §9-501 for the place to file the financing statement. The form of the financing statement is governed by §§9-502–504. Financing statements can be amended as per §9-512, and §9-513 requires a termination statement to be filed when consumer debts are paid off.

Revised Article 9 creates a uniform set of forms which must be accepted nationwide; and any financing statement or amendment that discloses the debtor's name and address MUST be accepted for filing as long as the proper filing fee is paid. "Correction statements" can be filed by those who claim that a filing is erroneous or fraudulent.

These statements do not invalidate an earlier filing, but they do give notice that a challenge is possible. Neither the debtor's nor the secured party's written signature is required—as a transition to an electronic system, where handwritten signatures create problems.

As you would expect, the revised Article 9 copes with the potential for electronic filing. In the future, it is anticipated that a potential creditor will be able to examine all of the Article 9 filings in the nation with a few keystrokes.

ENDNOTES

1. See Gerald T. McLaughlin and Neil B. Cohen, "Revisions for the 'Battle of the Forms,'" *N.Y.L.J.* 6/30/99 p. 3.
2. Under UCC §2-210(1), unless the agreement is to the contrary, either party can delegate its duties, unless the other party has a substantial interest in performance by the original party. §2-210(2) says that (unless the parties agree to the contrary) rights in a contract for the sale of goods can be assigned unless the non-assigning party's duties change materially, its risks increase materially, or its chance of getting return performance diminishes materially. Even if the contract limits assignability, rights that are no longer executory (such as the right to receive payment; damages for breach) can still be assigned.
3. See Official Code Comment (3) to §2-201.
4. In an installment contract, which requires or permits delivery of separate lots, each lot can be separately accepted: §2-612.
5. Drafts of Proposed Article 2B are available at http://www.law.upenn.edu/library/ulc/ulc/htm. Also see various expert practitioners' comments at http://www.2BGuide.com.
6. 86 F.3d 1447 (7th Cir. 1996)
7. See 67 LW 2615 and 68 LW 2069; Brenda Sandburg, "UCC2B is Dead—Long Live UCITA," http://www.lawnewsnet.com/stories/A1807-1999May26.html; and Carlyle C. Ring, H. Lane Kneedler and Gail D. Jaspen, "Uniform Law for Computer Info Transactions is Offered," *National Law Journal* 8/30/99 p. B7.
8. The customer can't make claims against the bank based on unauthorized signatures or alterations of checks more than one year after the statement was issued or the checks were returned to the customer: §4-406(a) and (f). The statute of limitations for having the account re-credited based on an unauthorized endorsement is three years: §4-111.
9. *Community Bank, FSB v. Stevens Financial Corp.*, 966 F.Supp. 775 (N.D. Ind. 1997).

10. See, e.g., *U.S. v. BCCI Holdings (Luxembourg)*, 980 F.Supp. 551 (D.D.C. 1997): a beneficiary bank that has not accepted a payment order doesn't owe anything to the beneficiary, and the beneficiary isn't a creditor of the beneficiary bank.
11. Even if the receiving bank or originating bank has no right of recovery under mistake/restitution principles, it might have a right to subrogation to the beneficiary's right to receive payment from the originator on the underlying, discharged obligation. See Official Comments 2 and 3 to 4A-302. Also see 4A-303 for the definition of "erroneous execution."
12. The beneficiary's bank can pay the party identified by a number in reliance on the number, without checking to see if the name and number identify different parties: 4A-207(b)(1).
13. *Grain Traders, Inc. v. Citibank*, 960 F.Supp. 784 (S.D.N.Y. 1997).
14. The FRB returned the compliment: on November 30, 1990, it adopted Article 4A as Appendix B, Subpart B of 12 CFR Part 210.
15. The Article 5 choice of law rules appear at §5-116.
16. The Depository Trust Company is a trust that acts as a depository for about 600 broker-dealers and banks; its nominee name is the familiar Cede & Company. When trades have been cleared, and accounts have been "netted," (i.e., amounts owned by broker-dealers to other broker-dealers are established), the National Securities Clearing Corporation instructs DTC how to adjust its participants' accounts.
17. The 1998 revisions, discussed in ¶290.7, change the details under this general scheme.
18. Designated as Part 6 in the 1998 revision.
19. Final draft of the revisions: http://www.law.upenn.edu/bll/ulc.ucc9/textcomp.htm. Gerald T. McLaughlin and Neil B. Cohen, "The Impending Changes in Article 9," *N.Y.L.J.* 12/9/98 p. 3; Sandra S. Stern, "How Revisions to UCC Article 9 Will Change Secured Financing," *N.Y.L.J.* 12/8/98 p. 1.

Employer–Employee Relations

[¶301

For most people in the United States, paid employment is a feature of most or all of their adult lives. For most businesses, it will be necessary to have at least some employees during at least part of the business cycle. The relationship between the two covers many areas.

This discussion is organized into three major areas: labor law; compensation and benefits; and employment discrimination. For a fuller discussion of employment-related issues, see this author's *Complete Guide to Human Resources and the Law* (Prentice Hall, 1998, with 1999 Supplement).

[¶310] Labor Law

A body of federal labor law developed in the wake of the Depression and World War II. Today, those laws are still in force, although only about one-seventh of workers are unionized. Labor unions are most powerful in manufacturing, and play a less significant role in service industries. Today's economy is service-based, and manufacturing plays a much smaller role than it did in earlier years.

Most labor law is federal law. The Wagner Act (1935), also known as the National Labor Relations Act (NLRA), established the National Labor Relations Board (NLRB) and cemented the status of labor unions as legitimate bargaining agents.

NLRA §7 gives employees the right to engage in "protected concerted activity": that is, they can act together to form or join a union, present grievances, bargain collectively (negotiate a contract for the whole union), go on strike, and picket.

Federal labor law determines the tactics that can legitimately be used by both management and labor during the certification process (campaign to unionize a workplace). A union can be decertified if it is guilty of misconduct, or if it ceases to represent employee interests. Labor law also determines the process of bargaining for a Collective Bargaining Agreement (CBA) and settling disputes over the interpretation of a CBA.

It also determines when a lawful strike can be called, what tactics are lawful during the strike, the extent to which the employer can hire replacements for strikers, and the extent to which strikers have to be reinstated after a strike ends.

The NLRA, at 29 USC §152, says that the statute governs the rights of "employees,"and that "supervisors" are not included in this classification, so individuals who are classified as supervisors (i.e., need to make independent, individual judgments at work; able to reward or discipline employees; able to resolve employee grievances) or managers (able to set corporate policy) are not entitled to unionize.

The NLRB is empowered to enter a situation if it is a labor dispute (e.g., strike, walkout, picketing, employer refusal to bargain) affecting interstate commerce. When the NLRB issues a complaint or files an unfair labor practices charge, it can petition the District Court to issue a temporary injunction. Permanent injunctions are quite rare in labor law, because most permanent injunctions are forbidden by the Norris-LaGuardia Anti-Injunction Act.

The Labor-Management Relations Act (LMRA) §301(a) gives the District Court jurisdiction over suits for violations of a collective bargaining agreement. The LMRA preempts most state law claims. State laws are preempted in any case in which it is necessary to interpret a collective bargaining agreement, although mere reference to a CBA is not sufficient to invoke preemption.[1] If the CBA includes the common provision for arbitration or a contractual grievance procedure, potential plaintiffs must exhaust their remedies before bringing suit under LMRA §301.

Certain situations have been found not to involve CBA interpretation, and therefore not to trigger LMRA §301 preemption: for instance, retaliatory discharge; discharge of an employee in violation of public policy; claims on implied contracts, such as alleged promises of lifetime employment.

Although LMRA §301 provides that unions can sue and be sued in federal court, they do not automatically have federal jurisdiction; they must show entitlement to use the federal courts just like any other plaintiff.[2]

Because of a 1999 Supreme Court decision, states cannot be sued against their will by public employees who allege violations of federal labor law such as the overtime pay requirements. The analysis of *Alden v. Maine*[3] is that the Constitution protects states that have not waived sovereign immunity against either suit in federal court or suit in state court to enforce federal rights.

[¶310.1] Unfair Labor Practices

An unfair labor practice is a violation of federal labor law by either employer or union. The NLRB has the power to issue "cease and desist" orders when it finds an unfair labor practice. The Board can also extend mandatory orders, e.g., ordering an employer to bargain with a union.

NLRA §8 defines unfair labor practices to include:

- An employer's or union's refusal to engage in collective bargaining
- Employer domination of a union
- Retaliation against employees who file charges with, or testify before, the NLRB
- Discrimination against employees based on union activities or refusal to join a union; discrimination includes refusal to hire, firing, refusal to reinstate, demotion, discrimination in compensation, or in work assignments. (However, if a union security clause (¶310.2.1) is in place, employees can be required to pay union dues, but cannot be forced to join the union.)

- Featherbedding—deliberately inefficient work practices that require an unreasonably large number of workers to be employed
- Some practices in relation to strikes and picketing.

The Labor-Management Relations Act of 1947 (LMRA; also known as the Taft-Hartley Act) extends the NLRB's powers and outlaws certain strikes, including jurisdictional strikes, strikes that serve to maintain unfair labor practices, and secondary boycotts (actions taken against a neutral company to discourage it from dealing with another company with which the union has a dispute). The following union actions are unfair labor practices under the LMRA:

- Restraining or coercing employees who exercise their right to vote against unionization, to choose a representative, or to bargain collectively
- Causing an employer to discriminate against an employee
- Refusing to participate in collective bargaining
- Striking or any other concerted activity undertaken as a boycott or for another improper purpose
- Imposing excessive initiation fees or dues on a union shop
- Featherbedding

[¶310.2] Union Elections

A union that gains "certification" by winning a representation election under the supervision of the NLRB becomes the authorized bargaining agent for the employees in the bargaining unit. The employer is obligated to bargain in good faith with the union.

The campaign begins with a petition for certification, filed by a union or an employee who favors unionization. To be valid, at least 30% of the employees in the bargaining unit must indicate interest in joining a union. If the employer does not oppose holding an election, an election is held on consent. Otherwise, the NLRB is responsible for determining if the representation petition is valid.

The period between filing of a representation petition and an election is known as the "critical period." The NLRB can invalidate the election if either side committed unfair labor practices (e.g., violence; threats; employer's announcement of new benefits to discourage pro-union votes) or otherwise interfered with the conduct of a fair election.

To win, the union needs a majority of the voters, rather than a majority of those eligible to vote. But the election is invalid unless a "representative number" of eligible voters actually voted.

For a period of one year after the election, rival unions are not allowed to seek certification to replace the incumbent union.

In January, 1999, the NLRB first made petition forms for allegations of unfair labor practices in a union election available on the World Wide Web: see http://www.nlrb.gov. (Petition forms for other unfair labor practices were already available.)

[¶310.2.1] Union Security

Closed shops, where no one can be hired without already belonging to the union, are illegal. The NLRA also forbids preferential hiring, where the employer has to hire only union members as long as the union can supply enough qualified applicants.

However, union shops are allowed by the LMRA. In this arrangement, all current employees must be union members. New hires can be required to join the union once they are hired. Agency shops are also allowed: workers must pay initiation fees and union dues, but do not actually have to join the union.

It is not a violation of the union's duty of fair representation for the union to sign a Collective Bargaining Agreement that contains a union security provision that merely echoes the statutory wording.[4]

About a quarter of the states (primarily in the South and West) have adopted "right to work" laws, under which unwilling employees cannot be compelled to join a union or pay dues.

[¶310.3] Collective Bargaining

A collective bargaining agreement (union contract) sets out most of the important work-related issues, including compensation and benefits. Even when a contract is in place, it may be necessary to bargain on the "mandatory" issues described by 29 USC §158(a)(5), and allowable to bargain on "permissible" issues. Mandatory issues are those that materially or significantly affect the terms and conditions of employment, whereas permissible bargaining subjects have a remote or incidental effect.

If bargaining reaches an impasse, when neither side is willing to concede, and neither has any new proposals to submit, the employer can lawfully cease negotiating and implement its own proposals.

When a collective bargaining agreement expires, there is no contract left to be enforced. However, labor law (NLRA §8(a)(5)) requires the employer to maintain the status quo, at least until an impasse is reached.

In a unionized company, the employer is allowed to make unilateral decisions about subjects that are deemed to be management prerogatives, but has to bargain in good faith about other issues. Managerial prerogatives include terminating operations completely; selling an entire business; relocating unit work to a new location; or a partial closing that has business rather than anti-union motivation.

It is an unfair labor practice for an employer to enter into a contract, then disavow it based on doubts about the union's majority status, if the employer already had information justifying the doubts when it entered the contract. In that situation, the employer should have refused to enter into a CBA with a non-representative union, rather than entering into and then seeking to repudiate the contract.[5]

[¶310.4] Labor Arbitration

Arbitration, and other forms of alternative dispute resolution, are becoming more and more common in our society, which is highly litigious but has a court system far too small to meet all demands for dispute resolution. The LMRA is drafted to encourage arbitration. When a union agrees to arbitrate an issue, it more or less agrees not to strike over the issue, and the employer also agrees to avoid unilateral action.

Labor arbitration is divided into two main categories: grievance arbitration or rights arbitration, used to resolve disagreement about interpreting an existing contract; and contract or interest arbitration, used to determine which provisions should be included in a new, renewed, or reopened CBA.

The three 1960 Supreme Court cases known collectively as the *Steelworkers' Trilogy*[6] have determined that if it's not clear whether a company has agreed to arbitrate a particular issue, the issue is deemed arbitrable.

If a CBA contains both an arbitration clause and a no-strike clause, any dispute about the application and interpretation of the CBA is arbitrable unless the contract terms specifically reject arbitration. Arbitrators begin by considering the CBA language, but they can also use the "law of the shop"—practices that have evolved in that particular company. Arbitrators can consider factors such as the effect of a decision on productivity, morale, and workplace atmosphere.

Arbitration begins with a "demand"; usually either the American Arbitration Association or the Federal Mediation and Conciliation Service will be involved in the process. Even if there is no arbitration clause in the CBA, the employer and union can sign a one-time "submission agreement" agreeing to be bound by the arbitration decision in a particular instance.

Once an arbitration award is rendered, it is usually final, binding, and not subject to judicial review by any court.

[¶310.4.1] Arbitrable Issues

The issues that can be arbitrated are quite similar to those that are mandatory bargaining subjects, because arbitration and CBA negotiation are complementary processes. Potentially arbitrable issues include:

- Sale of a business
- Relocation of operations
- Contracting out bargaining unit work
- Temporary shutdowns
- Layoffs
- Choosing employees for reinstatement after a layoff
- Discharge of single employees
- Work schedules and assignments
- Compensation, including overtime pay, incentive pay, bonuses, and severance pay
- Employer's contributions to pension and welfare benefit plans.

[¶310.5] Strikes

The NLRA makes it legal for employees to engage in "protected concerted activities," including organizing, protesting, and going on strike (although without threats, violence, or sabotage). Where a threatened strike imperils national health or safety, the President of the United States has the power to order the U.S. Attorney General to petition the appropriate federal court to enjoin the strike during an 80-day cooling-off period when negotiations can continue.

NLRA §8(b)(4) bans secondary strikes and secondary boycotts—actions taken against one employer to put pressure on a different employer that is engaged in a dispute with the union. Companies subjected to secondary strikes or boycotts can sue for damages under LMRA §303.

Strikes are lawful in three situations:

- Economic disputes with the employer
- Unfair labor practices
- Unreasonably dangerous workplace conditions

If a strike begins as an economic strike, it can be converted to an unfair labor practices strike if the employer acts unfairly or refuses to accept legitimate offers to return to work. The main difference between an economic strike and an unfair labor practices strike is the extent of employees' right to reinstatement after the strike ends.

A sitdown strike (illegal takeover of part or all of the employer's premises) or wildcat strike (called by the rank-and-file without authorization from the union) is illegal, because it is not protected concerted activity as defined by federal labor law.

If the CBA includes a no-strike clause, then an unfair labor practices strike can be lawful, but an economic strike is not protected concerted activity. Therefore, the employer can legitimately fire strikers and deny them reinstatement.

[¶310.5.1] Lockouts

The lockout is the employer's counterpart of a strike; it consists of refusing to let employees come to work. Labor law allows an employer that undertakes a lockout for business reasons to hire replacement workers, but not to use the lockout to permanently contract out work formerly performed by unionized employees. If employees violate a CBA no-strike clause and go on strike, the employer is justified in locking them out.

Lockouts are not permitted if the employer uses them to prevent unionization, or as a means to avoid bargaining with an incumbent union. A lockout is an unfair labor practice if it is inherently destructive of the rights of employees, or if it is undertaken without legitimate economic business justification.

[¶310.5.2] Striker Replacements

During a strike, it is lawful for the employer to hire temporary replacement workers. Under some circumstances, the employer will be able to hire permanent replacements, denying reinstatement to strikers. It may also be permissible to outsource functions previously performed by employees.

Certain circumstances deprive strikers of their employee status, and therefore they are no longer protected under the NLRA and it is not an unfair labor practice to discharge them. People who engage in unlawful strikes (i.e., strikes that are not called by an organized bargaining representative; sitdown strikes; strikes that are not called after a CBA expires, and that are not economic or unfair labor practices strikes) or engage in severe violence lose employee status.

In an economic strike, the employer can hire permanent replacements and keep them on the payroll after the strike ends. However, strikers who have not been replaced are entitled to reinstatement, and it is an unfair labor practice to delay their reinstatement.

If the replacement worker quits or is terminated, the employer must reinstate any former economic striker who makes an unconditional application for reinstatement. The reinstated striker must be treated on a par with nonstrikers and permanent replacements (e.g., benefits and seniority), unless there is valid business justification for treating that worker differently.

If there are no job openings at the time of the application, the employer must reinstate the ex-striker as soon as a job becomes available—unless the ex-striker gets regular and substantially equivalent employment somewhere else, or unless the ex-striker has committed violence or sabotage, or the employer has another good business reason to refuse reinstatement.

A "Laidlaw vacancy," also known as a "genuine job vacancy," occurs if replacement workers cannot reasonably expect to be recalled after being laid off by the employer. In this situation, strikers are entitled to reinstatement.

[¶310.6] The WARN Act

A federal statute, the Worker Adjustment Retraining and Notice Act ("WARN Act," 29 USC §2101), requires large employers to notify employees of events that will result in large-scale job loss. Employers are subject to the law if they have 100 or more full-time employees, or a combination of full-time and part-time employees adding up to the equivalent of 100 people and 4000 weekly work hours.

Before any plant closing (termination, prolonged layoff, serious cutback in work hours) or mass layoff, the employer must give at least 60 days' notice to employees, union, and the federal government.

If the employer fails to give the required notice, each affected employee is entitled to receive up to 60 work days' back pay and benefits. A federal civil penalty of up to $500 per day can also be imposed. Unions can sue for damages on behalf of their employees.

[¶315] Other Statutes Affecting the Employment Relationship

Various other statutes that do not come under the rubric of labor law nevertheless affect the employer-employee relationship, including unemployment insurance programs, workers' compensation, and occupational safety and health laws. See ¶350 below, for anti-discrimination statutes.

[¶315.1] Unemployment Insurance

The states administer an insurance system to provide payments to unemployed workers. Employers pay into the fund. Ex-employees may qualify for benefits depending on various factors, including whether they were involuntarily terminated or quit voluntarily. Employees can qualify for benefits if the employer had good cause to fire them (e.g., tardiness or poor work performance), but not if they were guilty of serious misconduct such as theft. Employees who quit their jobs are not entitled to benefits, unless some wrongful situation operated as a constructive termination.

The employee must have worked at least as long as the "base period" in order to qualify for benefits. The usual base period is the first four of the preceding five calendar quarters. The person seeking unemployment insurance benefits must make a good-faith effort to find another job that is suitable for someone of similar education, training, and experience. Eligibility is terminated by refusal of an offer of suitable work. Benefits are also unavailable in any week in which the claimant receives a pension, annuity, retirement pay, or other payment based on past work history, but not profit-sharing distributions (because those are not compensation for work).

The amount of the benefit is based on the claimant's wages, either the average or the highest wage earned in any calendar quarter of the base period. Calculations are usually based on a 52-week benefit year specific to each claimant, beginning when the claim is filed. Most states provide a maximum benefit period of 26 weeks for the basic benefit. Extensions may be available for weeks 27–39 under the Federal-State Extended Benefits program created by the Employment Security Amendments of 1970. Some states have extended-benefit funds that are completely funded by the state, without federal involvement.

When a person applies for unemployment compensation, his or her last employer is contacted and asked for an explanation of the termination. The employer has a period of time to contest the award of unemployment benefits; after that time passes, the employer has waived the right to protest. The state department that handles unemployment benefits determines whether or not benefits are available. The decision can be appealed to an Administrative Law Judge, an administrative board, and finally in the court system.

Employers are allowed to challenge unemployment insurance claims because the unemployment insurance rate they pay is partially based on the "experience" (the number of claims filed against them).

[¶315.1.1] FUTA Tax

In addition to insurance under the state system, employers must pay a Federal Unemployment Tax Act (FUTA) tax of 6.2% of the first $7,000 of each employee's wages. Any employer who had at least one common-law employee on one day in 20 different weeks, or paid $1,500 or more in wages in any calendar quarter, is subject to FUTA tax.

Unlike FICA (Social Security) tax, FUTA is imposed only on the employer, not both employer and employee. However, most employers qualify for a credit under Code §3302, for state unemployment taxes, so the usual effective rate is only 0.8% of the first $7,000 of wages.

[¶315.2] Workers' Compensation

As a general rule, employees who are injured at work or who suffer work-related illness are not entitled to bring tort suits against their employers. The doctrine of "Workers' Compensation exclusivity" means that their sole means of redress is to receive benefits under the state-run Workers' Compensation system.

The Workers' Compensation (WC) system is funded by employer payments. Depending on state requirements and the employer's option, the funding may take the form of setting aside reserves (self-insurance), purchasing insurance, or making payments into a state fund. Insurance rates depend on the "manual rate" charged for the relevant industry classification, adjusted by the employer's own experience of WC claims.

When an employee claims job-related injury or illness, the claim is heard by a WC tribunal (usually called either a board or a commission) which determines the validity of the claim. If the claim is adjudged valid, the worker is awarded reimbursement of medical expenses, plus weekly income, usually limited to half or two-thirds of the previous wage. Compensation benefits do not begin until a three- to seven-day waiting period has elapsed, to distinguish between minor and serious incidents. However, most states provide retroactive payments back to the original injury or onset date, if the disability continues for a period of time (e.g., over seven weeks).

Most states follow the "agreement system," under which uncontested claims lead to a settlement negotiated by the parties, or by the employee and the employer's WC insurer. Contested cases are decided by the agency administering the system, and appeals rights are granted to both employer and employee.

Benefits are awarded in four categories: permanent total disability; permanent partial disability; temporary total disability (the most common category); and temporary partial disability. There is also a schedule of reimbursement for the so-called "schedule injuries," loss of a finger, toe, arm, eye, or leg. Death benefits are also available to the survivors of persons killed in work-related incidents.

In general, WC is a no-fault system, and negligence by any party is irrelevant. However, in some states, a worker's failure to use safety equipment can reduce (but not eliminate) the benefit.

Most states have statutes penalizing employer retaliation against employees who file WC claims.

Pennsylvania's Workers' Compensation Act requires that, once liability is no longer contested, the employer or its insurer must pay for all reasonable or necessary treatment. However, it is permissible to withhold payment for disputed treatment until an independent third party has performed utilization review. This statute was construed by the Supreme Court in *American Manufacturer Mutual Insurance Co. v. Sullivan.*[7] The *Sullivan* plaintiffs sued state officials, Workers' Compensation insurers, and a self-insured school district, charging that benefits had been withheld without notice, depriving them of a property right.

Their arguments were unsuccessful. The Supreme Court decided that private insurers are not state actors, and therefore their utilization review activities do not raise Due Process issues. Employees do not have a property right until the treatment they seek has been determined to be reasonable and necessary, and therefore there is no right to notice and hearing until that point.

[¶315.3] Occupational Safety and Health

The federal Occupational Safety and Health Act (OSH Act) is enforced by the Occupational Safety and Health Administration (OSHA). OSHA's mandate is to protect employees against unreasonably hazardous workplaces.

All employers must satisfy the "general duty standard" of providing a workplace that is reasonably free of recognized dangers. Other OSHA standards apply to specific situations, especially within the construction industry. OSHA's General Industry Standards cover, e.g., condition of floors in the workplace; number and design of entrances and exits; personal protective equipment; fire prevention and safety; guards on machinery; cutting and welding; proper tool use; and control of electrical and chemical hazards.

The OSH Act gives OSHA the authority to inspect workplaces, order correction of violations, and impose penalties if correction does not occur or is too slow.

The Act also requires employers to record all meaningful workplace injuries and illnesses on the official OSHA-101 Supplementary Record Form (or a comparable in-house or Workers' Compensation form), and to use this information to create annual reports (Form OSHA-200, Log of Occupational Injuries and Illnesses) which must be forwarded to OSHA and disclosed to the workers. The OSH Act covers all employers whose operations affect commerce among the states. There is no minimum number of employees triggering coverage, although certain small-scale or low risk operations are entitled to take advantage of reduced reporting requirements.

The OSH Act imposes requirements for personal protective equipment, lockout/tagout (preventing moving parts of machinery from causing injury), and exposure to hazardous materials. The OSH Act sets Permissible Exposure Limits (PELs) for materials such as asbestos and lead. The PEL is the level of contact that is safe for an employee. The employer must monitor the plant environment to make sure that PELs are not exceeded, to provide appropriate safety equipment, and to train employees in safety. Hazardous materials must be stored properly, and employees must be informed about their presence and trained in the appropriate precautions. The OSH Act also treats excessive noise as a hazardous phenomenon that must be monitored and reported.

Occupational safety enforcement is coordinated between the federal government and the states. States are permitted to draft their own regulatory plans; the plan becomes an "approved state plan" if the federal Department of Labor deems the plan adequately protective of workers' safety. About half the states have approved state plans. In the other states, OSHA has primary responsibility for safety enforcement, but states can regulate issues not covered by the OSH Act, such as furnace and boiler safety.

Inspections of premises are made, either routinely or based on complaints. OSHA can issue citations if hazardous conditions are found during an inspection. In general, employers are given 30 days to abate the violation by correcting the hazardous conditions. There are schedules of monetary penalties, based on factors such as the current number of violations, number found in the past and not corrected, and the actual danger of the violation. In egregious cases, criminal penalties can be imposed. Also see 29 USC §666(e), penalties for willful violations of OSHA standards that result in the death of an employee. Employers are given the right to challenge citations and proposed penalties.[8]

[¶330] Fair Labor Standards Act

The Fair Labor Standards Act (FLSA; 29 USC §§201–219, 251–262) governs wage and hour issues in both the public and private sectors, including the minimum wage (currently $5.15 an hour) and time-and-a-half overtime payments for non-exempt workers.

The FLSA provides a private right of action for employees for unpaid minimum wages and/or overtime, plus liquidated damages, attorneys' fees, and court costs. The Secretary of Labor can also sue for unpaid minimum wages and overtime, which are paid to the employees. Further violations can be enjoined. Willful FLSA violations can be criminal, subject to prosecution by the federal Attorney General's office. Legal and equitable relief can be ordered against employers who retaliate against workers who make FLSA complaints.

[¶330.1] Employee Status

Various benefits are available to, or must be provided to, a company's "employees," so it is often important to distinguish employees from independent contractors, or to determine which company actually employs an individual and therefore is responsible for wage-and-hour compliance.

For instance, a company must pay its share of FICA taxes for its "employees," but independent contractors must pay 100% of their own FICA tax. Whether a benefit plan is discriminatory depends in large part on the percentage of "employees" it covers, and how their benefits compare to those of highly compensated employees (HCEs). Eligibility for participation in pension and welfare benefit plans is usually restricted to employees.

Leased employees—who are formally employed by a company that then leases their services to other companies—may have to be treated as employees of the company where their services are actually performed, if the lease arrangement is long-term rather than limited in duration. See Code §414(n) and cases interpreting it.[9] It is also possible that both leasing company and recipient will be treated as co-employers.

The higher the degree of control the potential employer exercises over a person's working environment and tasks, the more likely that person is to be an employee; the lower the degree of control, the more likely the relationship is to be one between independent contractor and client.

Under the Internal Revenue Code, licensed real estate agents working under written contracts describing them as independent contractors are not employees, but full-time life insurance salespersons, corporate officers, full-time traveling salespersons, and certain delivery drivers are statutory employees.

IRS' IR-96-44, "Independent Contractor or Employee?" sets out a 20-factor test for assessing status, e.g.:

- If the worker is given instructions that must be followed
- If training is provided
- If the services are integrated into the employer's ordinary work or separate
- If the worker works for others at the same time
- If work is performed on the employer's premises or at another location
- If the employer provides tools and materials
- If the worker holds him- or herself out as providing services to the public

Similar tests are used by states, e.g., for unemployment insurance purposes.

Section 530 of the Revenue Act of 1978 permits a safe harbor if the employer, acting reasonably and in good faith, characterized the worker as an independent contractor, based on industry practice or published authority from the IRS itself or the court system. The employer must have treated the individual consistently as an independent contractor (e.g., by filing Form 1099 recording each year's compensation) and must never have treated the individual as an employee. If the safe harbor applies, the IRS will not be able to re-classify the worker as an employee, assess back taxes or penalties, or require payment of back FICA/Medicare taxes.

However, if the safe harbor does not apply, and the IRS determines that certain workers treated as independent contractors were actually employees, at a minimum the employer will have to make up taxes that were not paid. If the employer did not intentionally misclassify workers, and if W-2 and 1099 information returns were properly filed, the penalty will be limited to 1.5% of the employee's wages, plus 20% of unpaid FICA taxes. If information returns were not filed, the penalties are doubled. See ¶330.2.1 for the penalty for failure to collect and remit trust fund taxes.

[¶330.2] Employment Tax Compliance

The employer is required to withhold income taxes from the compensation of common-law employees, based on the amount of wages paid, the worker's marital status, and the number of exemptions claimed on the W-4 (the IRS form used to claim withholding exemptions).

Withholding is done either by the percentage method or the wage bracket method. The percentage method uses tables of withholding allowances and wage rates; the wage bracket method uses tables to compute the withholding per pay period based on wage level, marital status, and the number of exemptions claimed. The official tables are found in IRS Publication 15, Circular E (covering a broad range of employment-related tax compliance issues).

In many instances, withholding is also required from pension payments. (In certain circumstances, the retiring employee is entitled to elect exemption from withholding.) Pension payments in annuity form can follow ordinary withholding procedures, using the number of withholding exemptions claimed by the retiree on Form W-4P.

A lump sum or other non-periodic payment that is eligible for rollover, and that is rolled over (see ¶340.3.1) does not require withholding. Ineligible amounts are subject to withholding; see the instructions for IRS Form 1099-R.

[¶330.2.1] Trust Fund Taxes

FICA (Social Security/Medicare) taxes have two equal components: one paid by the employer, one by the employee. The 1999 rate is 7.65% of compensation for each, consisting of OASDI (Social Security) tax of 6.2% and Medicare tax of 1.45%. OASDI tax is charged only on the first $72,600 of compensation (the "wage base"); Medicare tax is charged on all compensation. If a person has more than one employer during a calendar year, the wage base is applied to compensation from each employer. If this results in over-withholding, the employee must claim a credit for the excess payments.

FICA taxes withheld from employees are "trust fund taxes"; the employer's share of FICA tax and Federal Unemployment Tax Act (FUTA) taxes are a responsibility of the employer, but are not deemed trust fund taxes.

Under Code §6672, a "responsible person" (i.e., responsible for remitting the taxes) is subject to a 100% penalty for willful failure to submit withheld trust fund taxes to the government. Corporate officers, shareholders, and directors can be responsible persons, depending on their level of responsibility within the corporation; even lower-level managers, or bankers or accountants, can become responsible persons if they have actual responsibility for tax remittance.

The penalty cannot be discharged in bankruptcy, and all of the personal assets of the responsible person are subject to this penalty. Under the Taxpayer Bill of Rights 2 (see ¶4390.4), the IRS must give 60 days' advance written notice of intent to impose the penalty (unless collection is in jeopardy).

[¶330.2.2] Routine Tax Compliance

When a new qualified plan is created, it must apply to the IRS for a determination letter, using Form 5300. Form 5310 re-determines qualification when a plan is terminated; Form 5310A is notice to the IRS of plan merger, consolidation, or transfer of assets.

The annual report of a pension plan is filed on the Form 5500 series: the full-length Form 5500, or the 5500-C/R or 5500-EZ for smaller plans with less complex reporting burdens. ERISA §502(c)(2) imposes civil penalties for failure to file the 5500-series form.

Under IRS Announcement 99-37, 1999-15 IRB 9, all applications for a 2 1/2 month extension of time to file Forms 5500, 5500-C/R, or 5500-EZ will be automatically approved if Form 5558 (extension request) is filed on or before the normal due date of the return.

Various forms must be submitted in connection with employee compensation:

- W-2: compensation paid for each employee
- W-3: transmittal form for all W-2 forms for the employer company
- W-4P: employee's election to opt out of withholding, or increase withholding, on pension and annuity payments
- 1096: omnibus transmittal form summing up other transmittal forms submitted by the employer
- 1099-R: reporting of lump sums and periodic distributions
- 941/941E: quarterly returns of federal income tax. Form 941 is used by employers who withheld or paid FICA taxes, 941E by those who did not.
- 5300: excise tax form for failure to meet the minimum funding standard

The ordinary, paper-based method of remitting FICA and Medicare taxes, and forwarding withheld income taxes, is to deposit the funds with a Federal Reserve Bank or other authorized tax depository. Deposits are accompanied by the Federal Tax Deposit (FTD) Coupon, Form 8109. Deposits are made either monthly or once every other week, depending on the amount to be paid. Form 941 accompanies the deposit. Penalties are imposed for late payment or underpayments.

Withholding on pension payments is reported once a year on Form 945, Annual Return of Withheld Federal Income Tax.

Employee compensation for the year is reported on Form W-2. The paper form has six parts: one submitted to the Social Security Administration, one to state or local tax authorities. The employee receives three copies (for filing with the federal and state tax returns, and for the employee's records). The employer retains the sixth copy for its own records.

The EFTPS electronic system of deposit (linked to electronic funds transfer for payments) is being phased in, starting with large employers.

Code §6662 imposes an accuracy-related tax penalty for substantial overstatement of pension liability. It is imposed if the overstatement results in an underpayment of $1,000 or more. Substantial overstatement, carrying a 20% penalty, occurs when the liabilities used to compute the deduction are at least 200% of actual amount; gross overstatement (40% penalty) occurs when the asserted liabilities are at least 400% of the actual amount.

[¶330.3] Routine PBGC Compliance

The Pension Benefit Guaranty Corporation (PBGC) insures part or all of the benefit that employees and retirees would otherwise lose when a defined benefit plan terminates. (The PBGC does not insure defined contribution benefits, because each participant can get his or her individual account balance when the plan terminates.)

Employers must pay a basic premium for PBGC coverage, $19 per participant per year. If the plan is underfunded (lacks funding to satisfy its anticipated obligations), there is an additional premium charge of $9 per $1000 of unfunded vested benefits.

All PBGC-insured plans are required to file Form PBGC-1 each year as a combined annual report and declaration of premium payments. Form 200 must be filed with the PBGC within 10 days of any time at which the company has failed to meet the minimum funding standard by $1 million or more, and no waiver of minimum funding has been granted.

Plan administrators are obligated to report certain unusual events to the PBGC if the events might eventually lead to payment of insurance benefits. The events include the plan's bankruptcy, insolvency, merger, consolidation, or transfer of assets; the sponsoring company's bankruptcy or insolvency; or determination of the plan's non-compliance by a regulatory agency (PBGC, IRS, DOL).

[¶330.4] Compensation Deductions

Code §162 permits a corporation to deduct its ordinary and necessary business expenses, including "reasonable" compensation for services actually rendered. Even very large amounts can be reasonable if they make up for years of underpayment while the business was built up, e.g., a 1999 Sixth Circuit decision approving $4.4 million compensation to a company's president and sole shareholder.[10]

For tax years beginning after 1993, Code §162(m) precludes a public company from deducting any portion of employee compensation (including both salary and benefits) that exceeds $1 million. Qualified retirement benefits are not counted for this purpose. Sales commissions, payments pursuant to a contract in effect on 2/17/93, and performance-based compensation measured by objective goals and approved by a compensation committee of the board of directors, are also excluded.

[¶330.5] Severance Pay

An employer's one-time decision to offer severance benefits to a single individual does not involve ERISA, but a severance pay "plan" (even an informal or unwritten arrangement) is subject to ERISA. A severance pay plan could be either a pension or a welfare benefit plan. Under DOL Reg. §3510.3-2(b) and 29 CFR §2510.3-1(a), the arrangement will not be a pension plan (and will therefore be analyzed under the more liberal requirements for welfare benefit plans) if:

- The recipient is able to seek another job without forfeiting any benefits
- Overall payments are not greater than twice the recipient's compensation for the year immediately preceding the termination
- Payments end within 24 months of termination—or, for a "limited program of terminations," end within 24 months of the time the employee reaches normal retirement age, if that is later.

[¶330.5.1] Parachute Payments

"Parachute" payments are special severance benefits triggered by a hostile takeover or takeover attempt. Usually these are "golden parachutes" that protect the

81

target corporation's top executives, but a few states mandate "tin parachutes" for rank-and-file workers who lose their jobs due to corporate transitions. The theory is that an obligation to make large payments to workers disadvantaged by the transaction will discourage unwanted takeover attempts. A "single-trigger" parachute agreement gives an executive a right to additional compensation whenever the employer company merges or is acquired; a "double-trigger" imposes the additional requirement that the executive be terminated or demoted or otherwise suffer real economic injury.

If a parachute payment is so large that it depletes the corporate treasury, it might be vulnerable to a suit by stockholders charging corporate waste. However, the corporation, and the directors who authorized the arrangement, would probably be able to interpose a business judgment defense (see ¶165.3) on the grounds that the parachute plan defends the corporation against unwanted takeovers, and makes executives more productive by relieving them of economic anxiety.

The Internal Revenue Code (§§280G(b), 4999) imposes a 20% excise tax on "excess" parachute payments. Payments from qualified pension plans; payments made by S Corporations; and payments by non-public corporations that are approved by 75% of the company's stockholders, are exempt from the excise tax.

The payor corporation cannot deduct any portion of a parachute payment that does not constitute reasonable compensation, because such payments are not ordinary and necessary business expenses. An excess payment is any amount that does not represent reasonable compensation for work done either before or after the change in corporate control, and that is more than three times the employee's "base amount." The base amount is the executive's average annual compensation (including bonuses, fringe and pension benefits, and severance pay) for the five years just before the change in corporate control.

[¶330.6] Overtime and Exemption

Under the FLSA, each worker is either salaried and exempt, or an hourly worker entitled to receive time-and-a-half for overtime (more than 40 hours worked in a workweek). Hourly workers are paid for the number of hours actually worked, and are subject to having their wages docked based on variations in quality and quantity of work.[11] Workers are exempt if their primary duties (those that take up 50% or more of the week) are executive, administrative, or professional, or if they are outside salespersons. Overtime pay is not required for retail or service workers whose pay derives 50% or more from commissions, as long as the regular pay rate is at least 150% of the minimum wage.

If an individual is entitled to overtime pay, he or she must receive 150% of the normal pay rate (including commissions) for every hour over 40 worked during a workweek. The workweek is not necessarily Monday–Friday, 9–5: it can be any period of 168 consecutive hours. It is not necessary to pay overtime merely because weekend work is required, or if a particular work day lasts over 8 hours: 29 CFR §778.602(a) requires overtime only if the entire workweek exceeds 40 hours. Overtime must either be paid in cash, on the regular payday for the pay period in which the overtime was worked, or in the form of "comp time" (an hour and a half off for every overtime hour).

A mid-1999 Supreme Court decision, *Alden v. Maine*, 119 S.Ct. 2240 (Sup.Ct. 1999) holds that state governments cannot be sued for violation of federal overtime laws, unless the states have agreed to waive sovereign immunity.

[¶340] Pensions

[¶340.1] Basic Concepts

There are several reasons for dividing employee compensation into current compensation (paid each week, every other week, every month, etc.) and deferred compensation (usually not paid until after the employee has retired, although there may be other ways to access such funds).

For one thing, employees may not save for retirement, so the deferred compensation plan protects them in their later years. For another thing, current compensation is generally taxed in the year it is paid, and high-income persons can face a heavy tax burden. The deferred compensation might be paid in a post-retirement year in which the recipient is in a lower tax bracket, thus saving taxes.

[¶340.1.1] Basic ERISA Concepts

The Internal Revenue Code is critical to analysis of pension plans; so is 1974's Employee Retirement Income and Security Act (ERISA). ERISA establishes detailed rules for "qualified" plans—i.e., plans for whose costs employers are entitled to take a tax deduction. It is also lawful for employers to maintain non-qualified plans, whose costs probably will not be currently deductible.

ERISA also governs welfare benefit plans: plans provided by employers on behalf of employees, but providing fringe benefits rather than post-retirement income.

Certain basic concepts are applicable to both pension and welfare benefit plans. All plans must be operated for the exclusive benefit of plan participants and their beneficiaries, not for the financial benefit of the employer or any private person. This requirement is interpreted to mean that plans cannot cover independent contractors, only common-law employees.

Each type of plan may be subject to a participation requirement (explaining the criteria employees must meet to be eligible for coverage under the plan) and a coverage requirement (at least a certain percentage both of all eligible employees and of employees overall must be covered).

To a certain extent, qualified plans can be more favorable to executives and managers than to rank-and-file employees, but such plans are subject to non-discrimination rules that limit the extent to which highly compensated employees (HCEs) can be favored. Employers can establish non-qualified plans (¶340.2.6) instead of, or in addition to, qualified plans, but non-qualified plans limit the extent to which the employer can take current deductions for plan costs.

ERISA governs the way that qualified plans are set up, the form in which they are administered, which employees are entitled to participate, and how much must be and can be contributed on behalf of each employee. In most instances, ERISA requires plans to be in writing. Plan participants and beneficiaries are entitled to disclosure of the plan's terms and explanations of how it operates, including receiving a Summary Plan Description (SPD), annual reports, and explanation of material changes in the plan.

The management, investment, and distribution of plan assets and plan benefits come under ERISA, and so does the conduct of fiduciaries (trustees and others with responsibility for plan assets). ERISA's tax provisions are administered by the IRS; the labor law provisions come under the control of the Department of Labor. Title I of ERISA covers labor-law issues such as plan structure, fiduciary conduct, and prohibited transactions. Title I, Subtitle B contains many of the most important provisions, including reporting and disclosure; funding standards; fiduciary requirements; and continuation coverage for health insurance. Title II is the tax title.

[¶340.1.2] Defined Benefit Plan Concepts

The traditional pension plan is a defined benefit plan, where the employer's responsibility is to contribute enough each year so that, at retirement, employees will be able to receive a retirement benefit set at a particular number of dollars or defined by a formula (e.g., $x a month for every year worked for the employer). Such plans can be difficult and expensive to administer, and the employer has the investment risk: if the value of the plan's investment declines, the employer will have to contribute more to compensate.

They are also subject to the minimum funding requirement of Code §412; the employer's failure to put enough money into the plan is penalized by excise taxes. Quarterly payments must be made; see §412(m)(1). Underfunding also has to be reported to the PBGC. An employer that fails to fund its plan properly is subject to a lien on all its assets, and the PBGC may become involved in enforcing the lien. However, §4972 also imposes excise taxes on overfunding of qualified plans, so the employer needs skillful actuarial advice on how much to contribute.

[¶340.1.3] Defined Contribution Plan Concepts

Defined contribution plans, that set the employer's responsibility at contributing a certain amount per employee per year, are becoming the dominant form of pension. There are also variants and hybrid plans. Some employers are discontinuing pension plans entirely in favor of 401(k) plans (see ¶340.2.1), funded by elective deferrals of the employees' salaries.

Before the Small Business Job Protection Act of 1996 (SBJPA), employees could be compelled to start receiving their pension payments at the plan's normal retirement age (NRA),[12] even if they continued to work. Current law, however, allows them to defer payment until actual retirement. Furthermore, the plan must continue to make contributions or accrue benefits for the older employee.

[¶340.2] Requirements for Qualified Plans

A qualified plan must meet many requirements; depending on the type of plan, some or all of these must be satisfied:

- The plan must be in writing.
- The formal structure of the plan must be a trust, except for certain plans funded with insurance.
- Participants must be informed about the existence of the plan and how it works.
- The plan must be funded by employer contributions, with or without employee contributions; employee contributions can be either voluntary or mandatory.
- The plan benefits must vest (become non-forfeitable) according to a schedule that is acceptable under Code §411(b).
- Employees must be eligible for plan participation as long as they are 21 years old or older, and have worked for the employer for a year. Part-time employees must be covered if they put in 1000 hours of work for the employer within a 12-month period.
- Defined benefit plans must meet "minimum participation" requirements. On each day of the plan year, the plan must benefit either 50 people, or 40% of the workforce, whichever is less. (Before the Small Business Job Protection Act of 1996, defined contribution plans also had minimum participation requirements, but this is no longer the case.).
- Either a defined benefit or a defined contribution plan must satisfy "minimum coverage" rules found in Code §410(b). Either the plan must cover a reasonable, non-discriminatory classification of employees, or the percentage of rank-and-file employees covered must be at least 70% of the percentage of HCEs covered. The contributions made on behalf of rank-and-file employees (defined contribution plan) or the benefits provided to them (defined benefit plans) must be at least 70% of the ratio for HCEs.
- The employer is not required to consider pre-break service when determining the person's eligibility to participate in the plan if there is a one-year "break in service" (12-month period in which the individual works less than 501 hours for the employer). If the person works between 501 and 1000 hours for the employer in a year, the employee doesn't have to be given "service credit" for the year, but can't be penalized for a "break in service." Furthermore, due to the Retirement Equity Act of 1984, breaks in service caused by parenting obligations usually cannot be penalized.
- Plan amendments generally cannot reduce accrued benefits, even with consent of the employees, although plan sponsors can reserve the right to amend the plan in the future: §411(d)(6). Exceptions are allowed in certain cases of business hardship and for some retroactive amendments adopted shortly after the end of a plan year.

[¶340.2.1] Plan Types

A defined benefit plan is structured to provide a particular level of benefit when the employee retires. The employer relies on actuarial assumptions to fund the plan each year, so that sufficient funds will have been set aside to provide the necessary level of benefits for each covered employee.

The formula uses factors such as age at retirement, number of years of service for the employer, and compensation. Compensation is usually defined as compensation earned in the year of retirement; average compensation over the entire career with the employer; or for several years in which earnings were highest. Most defined benefit plans are non-contributory (i.e., employees do not contribute to their own accounts). However, it is not unlawful for a plan to accept employee contributions, or even to mandate them as a condition of participation. The early 1999 Supreme Court case, *Hughes Aircraft Co. v. Jacobson*[13] deals with a contributory defined benefit plan. A large part of the plan could be traced to employee contributions. The employer suspended its contributions at a time when the plan was operating at a surplus. Hughes also amended the plan to include early retirement benefits and a new benefit structure for new participants, funded by the plan surplus.

The employees sought a share of the plan surplus, but lost. The Supreme Court's reading is that the employer accepts investment risk in a defined benefit plan; if the plan runs at a surplus, it is legitimate for the employer to use that surplus to satisfy other plan obligations, as long as vested benefits are provided according to the plan.

A defined contribution plan (including pension plans, profit-sharing, money purchase, and 401(k) plans) involves a separate account for each employee. The employer's responsibility is to make contributions to each account each year, usually set at a percentage of that year's compensation.

A money purchase plan provides definitely determinable benefits, funded by fixed contributions from the employer. The plan has an allocation formula that sets the amount the employer must contribute, and the amount allocated to each participant's account.

In contrast, a profit-sharing plan has separate formulas for the employer contribution and the allocation to each account. The formula for making the contribution can be set each year, and contributions can be omitted in certain years. Before 1986, contributions to a profit-sharing plan could only be made in years in which the corporation had a profit, but that limitation has been removed.

A 401(k) plan, also known as a CODA (Cash or Deferred Arrangement) takes its basic funding from the employee's own compensation. The employee is allowed to decide how much compensation will be deferred instead of being paid currently in cash, up to a limit of $10,000. The advantage to the employee is not only forced savings, but the fact that increase in the value of the account is not taxed until retirement. Many 401(k) plans call for the employer to match part of the employee's deferral. These plans are subject to non-discrimination requirements; IRS Notice 98-52, 1998-46 IRB 16 includes a non-discrimination safe harbor rule.

In the late 1990s, many major employers converted their pension plans to cash balance form. A cash balance plan is a hybrid plan that is subject to regulation as a defined benefit plan, despite its adoption of certain defined contribution features. The corporation's books carry an individual account for each participant, funded with contributions from the employer, based on a percentage of pay. Because there are individual accounts, the cash balance plan offers more portability than a conventional defined benefit plan. A participant who changes jobs can get a lump sum reflecting the balance in the plan at the time of termination.

Each participant's account accrues interest at a rate specified by the plan; the employer can reduce its contributions if the actual rate of return exceeds the plan rate. The eventual pension that the employee receives reflects two components: the annual benefit credit (a percentage of pay) and the annual interest credit at the specified plan rate.

ERISA and the Code allow employees to be given control over investment of their individual accounts—but this also means that they bear the investment risk, whereas the employer bears the investment risk in a defined benefit plan, and may have to make significant additional contributions to make up for declining investment values.

[¶340.2.2] Non-Discrimination

A qualified plan must not discriminate in favor of HCEs, although a non-qualified plan is permitted to do so. The general rule is that the percentage of compensation allocated to funding pensions for rank-and-file employees must be at least as great as the percentage of HCE's compensation that is allocated toward their pensions.

Like most legal rules, however, this one is subject to certain exceptions. "Permitted disparity," also known as "integration" (with Social Security) allows the employer to reduce the allocation to take FICA taxes and future Social Security benefits into account. Typically, HCEs will have some or a great deal of compensation that is above the Social Security maximum, whereas most or all of the compensation of rank-and-file employees will be subject to FICA taxes, so the practical effect is to allow greater allocation for HCEs without losing plan qualification.

The Code contains special, strict rules for "top-heavy" plans—those that provide 60% or more of benefits to HCEs.

[¶340.2.3] Plan Maximums

Limits are imposed on the greatest amount that a qualified plan can add to a defined contribution account, or contribute toward a defined benefit. First of all, percentage calculations are based only on the first $160,000 of a participant's compensation.

Second, the maximum contribution to a defined contribution plan is $30,000 a year or 25% of compensation, whichever is less. The maximum benefit that can be received under a defined benefit plan is $130,000 a year. See IR-98-63, 10/23/98.

[¶340.2.4] Benefit Accrual

Benefit accrual is the extent to which funds are contributed toward an employee's eventual defined retirement benefit. Vesting (see below) is the extent to which the funds belong absolutely to the employee and cannot be forfeited.

The Code includes three permitted systems of benefit accrual. The objectives are that benefits must accrue in a more or less level fashion, in order to provide the scheduled benefit at normal retirement age.

[¶340.2.5] Vesting

There are two basic vesting schedules for defined benefit plans: five-year cliff vesting, and 3-to-7 graded vesting. Vesting is not an issue for defined contribution plans, because each participant has an individual account, which will be available at retirement, as long as the employer makes the appropriate contributions.

In a plan with cliff vesting, participants are not vested at all for five years—but after five years of plan participation, they are 100% vested as to employer contributions.[14] In a graded plan, there is no vesting for the first three years, then vesting is phased in until it is complete after seven years.

If employees are kept out of plan participation for two years (rather than the normal one year), they must be 100% vested after two years. This combination of deferred participation and faster vesting might be suitable for a company with high employee turnover.

Top-heavy plans (plans that include a high proportion of HCEs) must vest even faster (three-year cliff or six-year graded). The Code vesting requirements are minimums; employers are always allowed to permit faster vesting.

[¶340.2.6] Nonqualified Plans

The employer can establish and maintain nonqualified plans, that do discriminate in favor of top executives or highly compensated employees (HCEs), instead of or as supplements to qualified plans. However, the employer is not entitled to deduct plan costs until the favored employee receives distributions from the plan and includes them in income. See §404.

Code §83 taxes the employee when benefits under the plan are either actually or constructively received. Constructive receipt means that the employee is entitled to receive income, but has deliberately chosen to reject it.[15]

ERISA includes elaborate management requirements for keeping qualified plan funding in trust; these requirements do not apply to nonqualified plans. In fact, some employers do not fund their nonqualified plans in advance. Instead, they use current income to pay plan benefits. If the corporation does reserve funds for paying claims under nonqualified plans, the corporation's general creditors are entitled to make claims against those funds, but not against qualified plan trusts.

There are many forms of nonqualified plans currently in use, such as:

- Supplemental Executive Retirement Plan (SERP), also called an excess-benefit plan, defers amounts greater than those allowed for qualified plans.
- A rabbi trust sets aside assets to pay nonqualified benefits in an irrevocable trust. The employer can't take back the trust assets until all of its deferred compensation obligations are satisfied. However, the funds are subject to the claims of the employer corporation's creditors.
- A secular trust is an irrevocable trust that secures the executive's right to receive the compensation. The assets cannot be reached by the employer corporation's creditors. However, the employee is taxed on the employer contributions to the trust, and sometimes on the income the contributions earn within the trust.
- A top hat plan is an unfunded plan of deferred compensation.

[¶340.3] Distributions from the Plan

The basic method of distributing pension plan benefits is the annuity—a stream of regular payments beginning at retirement. For unmarried employees, the basic payment method is an annuity for the post-retirement lifetime of the employee.

For married employees, the basic payment method is the QJSA (qualified joint and survivor annuity). Payments continue for the lifetime of both spouses, although it is typical for the annuity payment to be reduced when one spouse dies. (The employer can choose to subsidize an unreduced annuity for the survivor.) The plan must also offer a QPSA (qualified pre-retirement survivor annuity) if a married plan participant dies before the annuity begins.

Qualified plans have to offer such annuities; they can choose to offer additional payment choices, such as lump sums. However, a married plan participant needs the written consent of his or her spouse to elect an alternate payment form. (The theory is that employee spouses should not be allowed to deprive their spouses of retirement income without their knowledge and consent.) The consent requirement stems from the Retirement Equity Act of 1984. Final Regulations for notice to participants, and consent by participants and spouses to alternate payment forms, are found in T.D. 8796, 63 FR 70009 (12/18/98).

Although usually a spouse, ex-spouse, child, sibling, or other individual will be named as beneficiary for plan benefits after the death of the employee, a person with a sophisticated plan might direct payment of the benefits into a trust. See 62 FR 67780 (12/30/97) for a Proposed Rule for handling of benefits paid to a trust.

The plan cannot force a participant to "cash out" (accept a lump sum if he or she prefers an annuity payment) unless the balance is very small: $5,000 or less. See T.D. 8794, 63 FR 70335, 12/21/98.

Pension payments cannot be assigned in advance, and creditors can't reach pension payments until each payment has actually been made to a retiree: ERISA §206 and Code §§401(a)(13), 404(a)(2).

There is one significant exception to this rule. A divorce court can order a Qualified Domestic Relations Order (QDRO), Qualified Medical Child Support Order (QMCSO), or both, calling for payments to the non-employee divorcing spouse and/or maintenance of health insurance for the couple's children. Under appropriate circumstances, QDRO payments can even begin before the employee's retirement. The administrator's duty, when receiving an order that purports to be a QDRO, is to see if it satisfies the definition of a QDRO; if it does, the administrator must comply with it.[16]

[¶340.3.1] Withholding and Rollovers

Plan administrators are required to impose mandatory 20% income tax withholding on "designated distributions." This requirement stems from Code §§401(a)(31) and 3405(c). A designated distribution is an amount eligible for a rollover, but not in fact rolled over. All or part of the employee's balance in a qualified retirement plan is rollover-eligible, except:

- Substantially equal periodic payments over the life of the employee or joint lives of employee and spouse
- Annuities for a term of years lasting at least 10 years
- Mandatory distribution of pension payments beginning at age 70 1/2 for officers, directors, and 5% stockholders. (Rank-and-file employees are allowed to defer their first pension payment until they have actually retired, if they choose to work past 70 1/2).

Individuals who are entitled to receive a plan distribution, but who don't want a large sum of taxable cash at that particular time, are allowed to roll over the distribution into an eligible retirement plan: an IRA or another qualified plan.

[¶340.4] Disclosure to Plan Participants

One of ERISA's most important functions is to specify the amount and form of disclosure documents that plans must routinely give their participants and beneficiaries of those participants. Certain documents must be provided routinely; other information must be kept available for inspection by any participant, beneficiary, or representative who requests it.

[¶340.4.1] Summary Plan Description

The central disclosure document is the Summary Plan Description (SPD).[17] It must specify what type of plan it is, circumstances under which benefits can be denied or lost, and the effect of termination of the plan and the disposal of its assets. Plan participants get an SPD when they begin to participate in the plan; plan beneficiaries get an SPD when they start to receive benefits.

The SPD must disclose a "reasonable" procedure for handling claims: i.e., one which describes all claims procedures and their time limits, including how denied claims will be reviewed, and the right of dissatisfied claimants to bring suit under ERISA §502(a).

If the plan is ever amended, an updated SPD, showing changes in the past five years, must be issued every five years (starting from the time the plan first becomes subject to ERISA). An update must be issued every 10 years even if there have been no amendments.

A named fiduciary who did not make the initial determination must perform the review, and the review must take into account all information submitted by the claimant (even if it was not submitted as of the time of the initial claim). Adverse determinations must cite the section of the plan (or its internal rules, guidelines, and protocols) that justifies the denial.

[¶340.4.2] Summary Annual Report

When the plan files its 5500-series form each year, participants must be given a Summary Annual Report (SAR). The SAR gives the plan's basic financial statement, including its expenses; the net value of plan assets; whether the assets increased or decreased in value over the year; and whether the minimum funding standards were satisfied (for defined-benefit plans only).

[¶340.4.3] Disclosure of Changes
The Summary of Material Modifications (SMM) must be given to plan participants, and submitted to the Department of Labor, whenever the plan is modified significantly..

Participants, beneficiaries, and unions are also entitled to notice if the plan is amended in a way that significantly reduces the rate at which benefits will accrue in the future. In December, 1998, the IRS issued T.D. 8795, Final Regulations published at 63 FR 68678 (12/14/98), and effective for amendments adopted on or after December 12, 1998. The notice must contain the text of the plan amendment and its effective date. Notice must be given after the amendment is adopted, and least 15 days before its effective date.

In addition to notices that must be given to all participants and beneficiaries, the plan is obligated to provide certain individual notices, such as notices to employees leaving the company's employ when they are entitled to vested benefits; when a claim is denied; before a person receives a plan distribution that could be rolled over into an IRA or another qualified plan to save taxes; and an explanation of QJSA and QPSA benefits and Qualified Domestic Relations Orders (QDROs).

[¶340.5] Fiduciary Duty

The trustees of an ERISA plan, as well as their investment advisors and others to whom they delegate responsibilities, are fiduciaries as to the plan, its participants, and their beneficiaries. Fiduciaries have an obligation to administer the plan for the sole benefit of participants and beneficiaries. They also have a common-law duty of loyalty that impels them to provide complete, accurate information rather than partial or fragmentary information to beneficiaries. If silence could be harmful, fiduciaries have a duty to disclose even information that was not specifically requested.[18]

Plan fiduciaries have an obligation to disclose proposals for improvements in the plan (e.g., early retirement incentives) as soon as the proposals are under serious consideration.[19]

If there is more than one plan fiduciary, they are jointly and severally liable.

[¶340.6] Termination of a Pension Plan

Although pension plans are supposed to have an indefinite duration, sometimes the sponsoring company goes out of business or merges with another company. The plan itself might be terminated, even though the sponsor company is still operational. Sometimes the PBGC has authority to get a court order terminating a badly managed plan.

Generally speaking, when a plan is terminated or partially terminated, all accrued benefits must vest immediately, even benefits that would not be vested yet under normal circumstances. This rule is imposed to reduce employers' incentive to terminate pension plans for financial reasons.

Plans can be terminated either voluntarily, at the option of the plan sponsor, or involuntarily, if the plan is shut down for improper operations.

The case of *Hughes Aircraft v. Jacobson*, 119 S.Ct. 755 (Sup.Ct. 1999) involves plan termination as well as plan surplus issues. The company suspended its plan contributions at a time when the plan had a surplus, and created a new, noncontributory plan for new participants. The participants in the existing plan alleged that the plan had been terminated or, in the alternative, that they were entitled to demand involuntary termination of the plan.

The Supreme Court refused to treat the changes as the equivalent of termination, and refused to recognize either a standard or a distress termination in a situation in which the plan continued to provide benefits and to accumulate funds to make payments in the future.

See 63 FR 48376 (9/9/98) for amendments to 29 CFR §2520-102-3(1), the SPD requirements for disclosure of plan termination options. If the plan includes any provisions that allow the sponsor or other party to terminate the plan or eliminate some or all plan benefits, participants must be informed of the circumstances under which benefits can be altered or terminated.

[¶340.6.1] Standard, Distress, and Involuntary Terminations

A standard termination, as described by ERISA §4041, is used by plans that have enough assets to pay the level of benefits guaranteed by PBGC insurance (see below). A standard termination requires prior notice (60-90 days before termination) to participants, beneficiaries, and alternate payees under QDROs (see ¶3020.4) that the plan will be terminated. A contact person must be identified so questions about termination can be answered.

The plan files Form 500 (Standard Termination Notice) with the PBGC, and participants and beneficiaries must be notified again, this time of what their benefits will be, factors used to calculate the benefits, and how payment will be made. The plan administrator gets a certificate from an actuary and submits the certificate to the PBGC.

The PBGC has the right to review the plan and can object to improper terminations. If the PBGC doesn't object, the plan will be terminated and its assets will be distributed.

Plans that do not have the assets to satisfy their liabilities can apply to the PBGC for permission to do a "distress" termination. The plan must prove financial hardship—e.g., bankruptcy or insolvency, or the sponsor corporation's need to terminate the plan in order to pay its debts and stay in operation. PBGC Form 601 is the request for a distress termination. Participants and beneficiaries must also be notified.

ERISA §4042 gives the PBGC the right to force an involuntary termination, supervised by a trustee appointed by the District Court, if the plan can't pay benefits when they are due; the plan hasn't satisfied its minimum funding requirements; inappropriate distributions have been made to major stockholders of the corporation; or termination is needed to keep the plan's liabilities from increasing unreasonably.

The PBGC has an obligation to seek involuntary termination if the plan doesn't have enough assets to pay current benefits that are already due (as opposed to being able to continue paying benefits as they fall due), or the plan has applied for a distress termination but is too short of funds to pay the guaranteed benefits. Although the automatic stay (¶2160) halts most forms of litigation, the PBGC has the power to apply for involuntary termination even against a company that has filed for bankruptcy protection or is the subject of an involuntary petition.

IRS Form 5310 is used to seek an IRS determination letter about the status of the trust associated with the pension plan.

[¶340.6.2] PBGC's Role

The Pension Benefit Guaranty Corporation (PBGC) supervises termination of defined benefit plans and, if necessary, takes over payment of the insured portion of employees' pensions. (The termination of a defined contribution plan is much simpler—each employee just gets his or her own account balance, so federal supervision is not required.) When the PBGC has to pay benefits, it looks to the employer for reimbursement if the plan terminates when the company's assets are insufficient to pay benefits. Liability is capped at 70% of the employer's net worth, or 75% of the unfunded guaranteed benefit.

The PBGC covers "basic benefits": a monthly annuity for the life of the participant of the terminated pension plan, starting at age 65. ERISA §4022(a) sets the maximum guaranteed benefit; the 1999 level is $3051.40 a month (at age 65).

[¶340.7] Early Retirement

Although in most cases it is unlawful to discharge employees or force them to resign merely on account of age (as long as they are capable of adequate job performance), in fact there are many reasons why employees leave the work force well before normal retirement age. Sometimes early retirement is motivated by poor health; sometimes it is a personal choice; and sometimes the employer offers incentives to leave the workforce early.

The Older Workers Benefit Protection Act (OWBPA) governs early retirement incentives. Voluntary incentives are permissible. Employers can provide subsidies in the form of dollar amounts, extra benefits, or percentage increases. Early retirees can be treated as if they retired at a later age, if this will increase their pension benefits.

[¶340.7.1] Retiree Health Benefits

Some employers permit their employees to retain coverage under the EGHP, even after they have retired; others provide health benefits as a separate retirement benefit, perhaps as an incentive for early retirement.

However, it should be noted that retiree health benefits (like all welfare benefits) do not vest. Therefore, it is lawful for an employer that retains the right to amend, modify, or terminate health benefits to cut back on retiree health benefits (e.g., by requiring an employee contribution to a previously non-contributory plan) or eliminate the benefits entirely. However, in some circumstances, an employer's promise to retain benefits at a particular level will create promissory estoppel, and the employer will not be able to change the benefit.[20]

Employer group health plans are required to cover over-65 active employees on equal terms with younger employees: either the cost per employee must be the same no matter what the employee's age, or equal benefits must be offered to all. Age Discrimination in Employment Act §3(f)(2) creates a safe harbor under the ADEA and the Older Workers Benefit Protection Act if the employer abides by the terms of a bona fide employee benefit plan.

[¶343] Individual Retirement Accounts (IRAS)

An IRA is a personal account, established by a person or couple in their own behalf, funded with their contributions. Anyone with earned income, or whose spouse has earned income, can establish an IRA. Once an IRA is established, it is not necessary to make contributions in any year, and the owner has discretion to contribute less than the maximum permitted contribution, although amounts in excess of the permitted contribution will be subject to an excise tax penalty if they are not removed from the account. It is also permissible for an individual to have several IRA accounts, as long as the contribution to all accounts in any year does not exceed the maximum.

Since 1997, IRAs have been divided into two main categories: back-loaded (Roth) and conventional. The theory is that taxpayers can accumulate funds within an IRA, without paying tax on the appreciation in the value of the account while the account remains intact in accumulation status. However, even though appreciation is not taxable, it should not be reported as tax-exempt interest on the tax return.

Taxpayers are also allowed to contribute up to $500 per year per child, until the child reaches age 18, to an "education IRA." Appreciation on education IRA accounts is not taxed during the accumulation phase, and withdrawals can be made from the account tax-free up to the amount of the child's college tuition for that year.

Contributions made to a conventional IRA may be deductible, up to limits ($2,000 per person, $4,000 per married couple, regardless of whether or not they are both employed); the extent of deductibility depends on the account holder's income and participation in an employer's qualified pension plan. Because the IRA is supposed to be a retirement account, taxpayers will be subject to an excise tax penalty if they make withdrawals before they reach age 59 1/2, unless the withdrawals fall into a permitted hardship category.

A conventional IRA is not supposed to be a primary estate planning tool either, so Minimum Distribution Requirement (MDR) rules apply. That is, another excise tax penalty is imposed if the taxpayer **fails** to begin withdrawals from the IRA by April 1 of the year following the year in which he or she reaches age 70 1/2.

The tax is imposed on the difference between the required minimum withdrawal, calculated based on the account owner's life expectancy, or adjusted joint expectancies of owner and beneficiary, and the actual withdrawal. There is no penalty for excessive withdrawals: a taxpayer can withdraw up to the entire balance in any year. However, amounts withdrawn from a conventional IRA constitute taxable ordinary income.

In contrast, contributions to a Roth IRA (which are subject to the same $2,000/$4,000 limit as conventional IRA contributions) are never tax-deductible. Thus, this form of retirement investing may be attractive to a high-income person who would not be entitled to a conventional IRA deduction.

In 2005 and later years, amounts that have remained within a Roth IRA for five years or more will be able to be withdrawn tax-free. Nor are Roth IRAs subject to MDRs, so a person who has adequate retirement income may choose to retain funds within the Roth IRA so that they can be transmitted to heirs.

[¶343.1] IRA Deductibility

As noted above, the general maximum contribution to an IRA is $2,000. A married couple filing jointly can each contribute $2,000 to their IRAs, even if one is a homemaker who does not work outside the home. (The deduction is reduced for certain very low-income couples.) However, deductibility of the IRA contribution phases down based on income. Couples filing jointly and reporting over $160,000 AGI cannot take IRA deductions; the deduction is reduced when AGI is between $150,000 and $160,000.

If neither spouse is covered by an employer's qualified pension plan, then the full amount can be deducted. One spouse's coverage under a qualified plan will not affect the deductibility of IRA contributions made by the other spouse, who is not covered.

A person who **is** covered by an employer's qualified plan will not be entitled to an IRA deduction if he or she is married and files a separate return. In this circumstance, a single person's or head of household's IRA deduction will be reduced if his or her modified AGI exceeds $30,000 and will be eliminated at modified AGI of $40,000. A married person filing jointly, or a qualifying widow or widower, has the deduction reduced at modified AGI of $50,000 and eliminated at $60,000, if he or she is also covered by an employer plan.

[¶343.2] Employment-Related IRAs

In small companies, or companies where the management is unwilling to offer conventional pension plans, Simplified Employee Pension (SEP) and Savings Incentive Match Plan for Employees (SIMPLE) are IRA-type plans that are initiated by the employer, not the individual employees.

In a SEP plan, the employer makes contributions to employees' IRAs, pursuant to a non-discriminatory written plan. The employee can make the maximum IRA contribution to his or her account, and the employer makes additional contributions (which do not disqualify the employee contributions). The employer can contribute up to the defined-contribution plan limit. The employee can exclude from income the employer's contribution up to $30,000 in contributions or 15% of the employee's compensation—whichever is less.

In a SIMPLE plan (available only in companies with 100 or fewer employees), the employer uses the employees' IRAs as a funding vehicle. The employer contributes up to $6,000 per employee per year, either by contributing 2% or more of the employee's compensation, or by matching the employee's contribution to his or her own IRA in an amount of at least 3% of that employee's compensation.

[¶345] Health Benefit Plans

Employee group health plans (EGHPs) and fringe benefit plans are another important element in employee compensation. To an increasing extent, health benefits are being offered in the form of managed care, discussed in ¶1470.2; see ¶1470 for a discussion of health insurance in general.

Employers are not required to offer any health or fringe benefits at all, but if benefits are offered, certain requirements (e.g., non-discrimination) are imposed. ERISA considers health and other fringe benefits to be "welfare benefits," not pension benefits. Therefore, the detailed rules governing pension plans are not applicable, and the benefits are not subject to vesting.

Most EGHPs are insured—that is, the employer purchases policies from an insurance company, and care is rendered under those policies. At one time, employers usually paid the entire premium; over time, a trend has emerged to require employees to pay an ever-increasing share of the premium. Employees also have copayment responsibilities, including deductibles (an amount they must pay before there is any coverage under the plan) and coinsurance (a percentage of the cost of each covered service that the employee is responsible for).

Some plans are self-insured. Instead of paying premiums for an insurance policy, the employer sets aside an equivalent sum of money that is invested and used to pay employee health claims. See ¶1470.1 for a discussion of indemnity health insurance, and ¶1470.2 for managed care.

[¶345.1] ERISA Preemption

For the past decade or so, most cases involving EGHPs had to be tried in federal court because ERISA preempts state laws that "relate to" employee benefit plans covered by ERISA Title I, including health insurance welfare benefit plans. However, state laws are not preempted if the case involves insurance rather than plan benefits.

The traditional analysis is that ERISA preempts state laws if the employee seeks benefits or protests a benefit denial under the plan, because construction of the plan language is required. In contrast, ERISA does not preempt state law in medical malpractice cases or cases challenging the quality of care, although in many such cases, the plaintiff would be able to proceed against the allegedly negligent doctor or hospital, but not against the managed care plan, on the theory that the managed care plan has not provided the care and is not responsible for its quality.

These traditional concepts are eroding. It is very likely that Congress will pass bills extending the appeal rights of HMO patients in late 1999 or early 2000; see the Supplement for details.

[¶345.2] EGHP Tax Issues

The main tax sections covering EGHPs are §§104–106, explaining plans of "Accident and Health Insurance" (A&H). A properly structured A&H plan permits the employer to deduct the costs of the plan, and does not create taxable income for the participating employee.

If the employee pays for the A&H plan, or if benefits paid by the plan can be traced back to employer contributions that were already taxed to the employee, §104 provides that payments from the plan are not gross income for employees who receive them.

Code §105 makes amounts received from an A&H plan taxable if they are paid directly by the employer, or come from employer contributions that were not already taxed. But the employee might be eligible for an offsetting medical expense deduction under §213.

Section 106 states that employees do not have gross income if their employers provide A&H insurance.

[¶345.3] Medical Expense Reimbursement Plans

A medical expense reimbursement plan is a plan that covers employees (although not necessarily all employees). If the plan is a welfare benefit plan for ERISA purposes, it must be in writing; otherwise, the plan can be an informal arrangement, as long as the employees receive reasonable notice of the plan's existence and how it operates.

The typical plan is self-insured and provides direct reimbursement to employees of medical expenses up to a certain amount per year. For tax purposes, the critical question is whether the plan shifts risk to a third party (an insurer, or anyone other than the employer or employee). A plan can get administrative services from an insurance company and still be considered self-insured if the employer retains the risk.

Code §105(h) requires self-insured medical expense reimbursement plans to satisfy coverage and non-discrimination tests. At least 70% of employees must be eligible for coverage, and at least 80% of the eligible employees, and 70% of all employees, must actually be covered by the plan. The plan is not required to cover employees under 25 years old, part-time or seasonal employees, employees of under three years' tenure, or those covered by a collective bargaining agreement.

The non-discrimination requirement demands that benefits for HCEs and their dependents must also be provided for rank-and-file employees. The plan can impose a dollar maximum on benefits, but the maximum cannot be defined as a percentage of compensation, because that would provide an unfair advantage to HCEs.

[¶345.4] Medical Savings Accounts (MSAs)

Internal Revenue Code §220 deals with Medical Savings Accounts (MSAs). The MSA is somewhat similar to an IRA. Qualified individuals can take a tax deduction for their contributions, and amounts remain tax-free as long as they stay in the account. MSA accounts are coordinated with "high-deductible" health plans. Funds withdrawn from an MSA are not tax-deductible when used to pay medical expenses (because a deduction has already been taken). Funds withdrawn for other purposes are taxable income and also subject to a 15% excise tax.

[¶345.5] 401(h) Plans

A 401(h) plan is a pension or annuity plan that also provides incidental health benefits (for sickness, accident, hospitalization, medical expenses) for retirees. The health-related benefits must be subordinated to the retirement benefits. All incidental benefits (health plus insurance) must not cost more than 25% of the employer's total contributions to a defined benefit plan.

401(h) plans must maintain separate accounts for retiree health benefits and pension benefits. The employer must make separate, reasonable, and ascertainable contributions to fund the health plans.

[¶345.6] Claims Procedures

ERISA §503 requires all employee benefit plans to give adequate written notice of claims denial. Participants whose claims have been denied must be given a reasonable opportunity to have a plan fiduciary review the denial.

In September, 1998, the Pension and Welfare Benefits Administration (PWBA) proposed a rule for claims procedure (covering both pension and health plans), published at 63 FR 48390 (9/9/98). The Proposed Rule, which has been vociferously opposed by health industry and employer groups, requires faster notice of claims denial (especially for claims involving urgent care) and a lengthier appeal period for employees.

[¶345.7] Mandates

Certain federal and state laws impose mandates on health plans. The Veterans' Affairs, Housing and Urban Development and Independent Agencies Appropriation Act, P.L. 104-204, requires EGHPs with 50 or more employees to grant parity between benefits for physical and mental illness.[21]

That is, if the plan does not impose lifetime or annual benefits on medical/surgical benefits, limits cannot be imposed on mental health benefits. Most plans do have limits; in this case, the statute requires the same limit to be applied to both kinds of benefits. Unless renewed, the statute will expire on September 30, 2001.

The mental health parity requirement does not mandate addition of mental health benefits to a plan that does not provide them. Substance abuse treatment is not covered. The plan can have different deductibles, coinsurance amounts, or number of days or visits of coverage for physical and mental ailments, as long as the overall plan limit is the same. Plans are exempt from the statute if parity would raise the cost of the plan by 1% or more.

The Newborns' and Mothers' Health Protection Act of 1996, P.L. 104-204, and the Taxpayer Relief Act of 1997, P.L. 105-35, generally require group health plans to cover a hospital stay after childbirth of at least 48 hours (at least 96 hours for a Cesarean section). This requirement applies to both self-insured and insured EGHPs, whatever their number of employees; state laws that require a longer hospital stay are not preempted. Interim rules (63 FR 57,545) and proposed rules (63 FR 57,565) for implementation were published on October 27, 1998.

The Women's Health and Cancer Rights Act of 1998, P.L. 105-277 (10/21/98) requires EGHPs that cover mastectomy to cover reconstructive breast surgery that the mastectomy patient wants and that has been prescribed by the attending physician. The statute is effective for plan years beginning on or after October 21, 1998.

[¶345.8] Dental Plans

Dental plans provide coverage of tooth and gum treatment. Most of them are fee-for-service plans, although managed care forms such as HMOs and PPOs are becoming more common. Most dental plans have a schedule of covered procedures and the payments for each procedure, defined either as a dollar amount or a percentage. Usually, the lower the cost of the procedure, the higher the percentage of coverage, so employees generally have a high copayment responsibility for the more expensive procedures.

Dental plans are subject to the COBRA continuation coverage requirements (¶345.11).

[¶345.9] Family Benefits

Some employers choose to offer coverage under their plans for the spouses and dependent children of the covered employees. It is common to require employees to pay for dependent coverage, or to pay more for dependent coverage than for their own.

As ¶3020.4 discusses, Qualified Domestic Relations Orders (QDROs) are used to direct distribution of pension benefits to an ex-spouse. QDROs have a counterpart, the Qualified Medical Child Support Order (QMCSO), issued to EGHPs to prevent children from losing health coverage when their parents divorce. QMCSOs identify children entitled to coverage. In many instances, the employee-parent has an obligation to make payments to the plan to maintain coverage for the children.

Some companies choose to provide coverage for the "domestic partners"—unmarried cohabitants—of employees. An interesting twist: in mid-1999, the Southern District of New York ruled[22] that it is not discriminatory to offer domestic partner coverage to same-sex couples but deny it to heterosexual couples.

The employer's rationale, as upheld by the court, was that heterosexual couples have the option of getting married if they wish to secure benefits, whereas same-sex couples do not.[23]

[¶345.10] The Family and Medical Leave Act

The Family and Medical Leave Act (FMLA), 29 USC §2601, requires employers to provide up to 12 weeks' unpaid leave in each "leave year." FMLA leave is available to employees who are sick, or who need to care for a newly born or adopted child or for a sick family member (spouse, child, parent, or step-parent, but not sibling or parent-in-law). To qualify for leave, the employee must have worked at least 1250 hours for the same employer in the previous year (e.g., new hires are not eligible). A leave year is a 12-month period; it can be a calendar year, plan year, or year since the employee's last exercise of FMLA rights. The 12-week limitation is applied per year, not per illness. Employers are subject to the FMLA if they have 50 or more employees in each working day in each of 20 or more workweeks in a leave year.

Although the leave is unpaid, and seniority and additional benefits do not accrue during FMLA leave, the employee cannot be deprived of benefits that accrued prior to leave. Health care coverage must be maintained. When the employee returns from leave, he or she must either be reinstated in the former job, or offered another job with equivalent conditions, benefits, and pension rights.[24]

FMLA leave does not have to be taken in a block: employees can take intermittent leave (e.g., every Tuesday afternoon to receive chemotherapy) as long as it does not add up to more than 12 weeks per leave year.

If the leave is taken for non-emergency purposes (e.g., to care for a person after a scheduled operation) the employer can require 30 days' advance notice of the time the leave is expected to begin.

29 USC §2612 defines damages for violations of the FMLA as lost compensation or the cost of providing health care for the person requiring care, if no compensation was lost. Jury trials are permitted in FMLA cases.[25] The *McDonnell-Douglas* analysis does not apply to FMLA cases. Instead, the plaintiff must prove, by a preponderance of the evidence, that he or she was discharged in violation of FMLA rights.[26] The statute of limitations is two years, or three years for a willful violation.

The IRS published a Final Rule at 64 FR 5160 (2/3/99) explaining the interaction of the FMLA with the "continuation coverage" requirements of the Comprehensive Omnibus Budget Reconciliation Act, discussed immediately below.

[¶345.11] COBRA Continuation Coverage

The loss of employment-related coverage can be financially quite severe for an individual or family. Therefore, the Comprehensive Omnibus Budget Reconciliation Act, Code §4980B, gives a "qualified beneficiary" the right to a certain number of months of "continuation coverage"; the number of months depends on the "qualifying event." COBRA regulations first proposed in 1987 were at last finalized in 1999: see 64 FR 5160 (2/3/99).

Employers are subject to COBRA if they maintain an EGHP (either an insured or self-insured plan), and if they have 20 or more employees on the average working day.

[¶345.11.1] Qualifying Events

A former employee or the ex-employee's spouse and dependents have the right to take over payment of the group policy premium (plus an administrative fee that is not permitted to exceed 2% of the premium[27]) and continue coverage under the EGHP. Qualifying events include termination (other than for gross misconduct), resignation, layoff, retirement, or the employer corporation's filing for Chapter 11 bankruptcy.

After a divorce, after an ex-employee dies, or when an ex-employee becomes eligible for Medicare, the ex-employee's spouse and dependents have their own rights to continuation coverage. Ex-employee's children also have continuation coverage rights once they lose their coverage as "dependents" under the EGHP; this usually occurs at age 19, if they are not full-time students.

The right to continuation coverage is not limited to common-law employees; partners, self-employed people who are plan participants, and eligible independent contractors covered by an EGHP also have COBRA rights.

The basic duration of COBRA coverage is 18 months. However, if the employee is totally disabled at the time of termination, the ex-employee and family members are entitled to 29 months' coverage,[28] but for the 11 months that follow the regular 18-month period, the employer is allowed to charge 150% rather than 102% of the basic premium. Spouse and dependents of an ex-employee who has become Medicare-eligible are entitled to 36 months of continuation coverage.

[¶345.11.2] COBRA Notice

Employees are entitled to a written notice, as defined by Code §4980B(f)(6)(A) and ERISA §606, as soon as they become eligible for continuation coverage. The notice must explain COBRA rights, including duration of continuation coverage, how to make the election, and events that permit termination of continuation coverage (e.g., the employee gets another job and becomes entitled to coverage under another EGHP). Qualified beneficiaries must be given a period of at least 60 days to elect continuation coverage.

Failure to abide by COBRA requirements can subject an employer to a penalty of up to $100 per day per beneficiary (with a family maximum of $200/day), with an aggregate maximum of $500,000 or 10% of the costs paid or incurred for the EGHP in the previous year (whichever is less). The employer also loses the tax deduction for the health plan, because a non-COBRA-compliant plan does not give rise to "ordinary and necessary business expenses" deductible under §162. There is also a private right of action on behalf of anyone wrongfully deprived of COBRA continuation coverage rights.

An employer can terminate COBRA coverage if the employee gains access to other coverage after making a COBRA election, but COBRA eligibility cannot be terminated on the basis of access to coverage prior to the election.[29]

[¶345.12] Health Insurance Portability Under HIPAA

The Health Insurance Portability and Accessibility Act of 1996 (HIPAA), also known as the Kennedy-Kassebaum Act, adds a new Chapter 100, §§9801-9806, to the Internal Revenue Code, providing health insurance portability when workers change jobs.

Work done after 7/1/96 can give rise to "creditable coverage" that can be transferred between EGHPs. However, creditable coverage terminates if the individual has gone for 63 or more days without some form of coverage (from an EGHP, individually purchased policies, Medicare, or Medicaid)—an incentive to maintain COBRA continuation coverage to prevent a lapse in coverage.

It is unlawful under HIPAA for a plan to condition eligibility or ongoing coverage on an employee's or dependents' health status, claims experience, medical history, insurability, or disability. Nor can employees be charged higher premiums or copayments based on their health status.

HIPAA also limits the use of preexisting condition limitations (i.e., denials of illnesses beginning prior to plan coverage). The second plan cannot use a more stringent definition of preexisting condition than the mental or physical condition for which medical advice, diagnosis, care, or treatment was sought during the six months before enrollment in the second plan. The maximum duration of preexisting condition limitations is 12 months from initial plan eligibility.

Preexisting condition limitations cannot be imposed on pregnancy, and usually are barred with respect to employees' newly born or adopted children.

Health plans that fail to comply with HIPAA are subject to penalties: $100 per person per day of noncompliance, up to a maximum of the lesser of $500,000 or 10% of the EGHP's costs for the preceding year. Small employers (2–50 employees) are exempt from penalties that are traceable to insurer error or misconduct. But if a plan is found to be out of compliance with HIPAA after it has received notice of income tax examination, a mandatory tax of $2,500 or the tax that would otherwise be imposed, whichever is less, is imposed and cannot be waived.

HIPAA also makes it harder for insurers to turn down applications for coverage, especially applications for small (2–50 person) group plans.

[¶345.13] Disability Plans

Inability to work due to injury or illness is addressed by both the private and public sectors: the private sector, by disability insurance and self-insured plans offered by employers; the public sector, by providing Social Security disability benefits for persons who are permanently and totally disabled.

Private-sector plans can cover either short- or long-term disability; the usual dividing line is to call a disability "short-term" if it lasts either less than six months or less than a year. Long-term disability coverage begins when short-term coverage is exhausted, and lasts either for a period of years (e.g., five years) or until the individual reaches 65 and presumably would be eligible for pension and/or Social Security benefits even without a disability. Typically, the plan replaces only part of income, such as 70% of pre-disability income, and the benefits are reduced by government benefits and tort damages.

An "own occupation" plan defines a person as disabled if he or she can no longer perform the work tasks of the pre-disability occupation. An "any occupation" definition makes benefits available only if the employee is unable to work at all, or unable to do any work suitable for his or her education and training.

For ERISA purposes, most disability plans are welfare benefit plans, subject to disclosure, filing, and fiduciary requirements (see ¶348) However, some are top-hat plans limited to executives, so they have more limited disclosure obligations. See 63 FR 48389—(9/9/98) for a Proposed Rule reducing the length of time in which plans must grant or deny disability claims.

Code § 106 excludes from income coverage received under an employment-related accident and health insurance plan. Either premiums paid by the employer for disability insurance or the value of coverage under a self-insured disability plan will satisfy this requirement. If and when the employee receives disability benefits, they are included in gross income to the extent that they come from previously-excluded employer contributions. Direct payments by the employer are also included in gross income. But payments made for permanent loss of a body part, or loss of use of a body part, or for disfigurement are not included in gross income, if they are computed without regard to absence from work.

[¶346] Non-Health Fringe Benefits

Especially for small, start-up, or otherwise cash-poor companies, fringe benefits can be an important element in compensation. They can also be used as a motivational device to improve employee performance.

Code §6039D sets out the reporting requirements for fringe benefit plans. The employer must provide information about, e.g., its total number of employees; number of employees eligible to participate; number actually participating; percentage of HCEs participating; total cost of the plan for the year. If the plan includes any taxable fringe benefits, the employer can either add their value to the regular wages for a payroll period, or withhold federal income tax at the 28% flat rate used for supplemental wages.

The treatment of the employer's contributions to welfare benefit plans is almost opposite to that of contributions to pension plans. In the pension context, the Code and ERISA make sure that the employer's contributions are adequate. But for fringe benefits, §§419 and 419A specify a maximum funding level for welfare benefit trusts, and excessively large trusts lose their tax-exempt status. The employer's tax deduction for maintaining a welfare benefit trust is limited to the "qualified cost" of the plan for the year: the direct cost of funding benefits, plus additional amounts permitted by §419A.

ERISA defines a welfare benefit plan as a plan created by a corporation and administered to provide participants who are common-law employees and their beneficiaries with benefits such as:

- Health care and medical benefits
- Accident insurance
- Disability benefits
- Supplemental unemployment benefits
- Vacation pay
- Day care centers
- Prepaid legal services

[¶346.1] Stock Options

Stock options permit employees to buy shares of the employer company's stock, on terms set out in the agreement. Naturally, the expectation is that the value of the stock will increase significantly, so employees will gain a windfall by exercising stock options, purchasing stock, and eventually re-selling it on the open market. Stock option plans can be structured in many ways; the choice of form, and the facts at the time of grant, exercise, and re-sale, will determine the tax consequences of the transaction.

It is very common for the employee to have a put obligation: i.e., to be required to sell the stock back to the corporation when employment terminates, at book value, a set price/earnings ratio, or other price defined by the contract.

A stock bonus plan is similar to a profit sharing plan for tax and ERISA purposes, but the distributions are made in the employer's common stock rather than in cash. In this instance, if the stock is not readily traded on an established market, the put option serves to protect employees by entitling them to have shares repurchased by the corporation.

An Employee Stock Ownership Plan (ESOP) is a stock bonus plan or a hybrid stock bonus/money purchase plan. Such plans invest primarily in the employer's common stock. A KSOP is a 401(k) plan structured as a stock bonus plan investing in employer stock. An HSOP is an ESOP combined with a 401(h) retiree health plan (see above): the plan borrows funds to buy employer securities. As the securities are allocated to employees' benefit plan accounts, they fund retiree health benefits for the participants.

[¶346.1.1] ISOs and NQSOs

See Code §422 for the tax-favored category of Incentive Stock Options (ISOs). An ISO plan does not have to be non-discriminatory, but favorable tax consequences are available to the employee only if the shares are retained for at least one year from the exercise of the option (i.e., actual purchase of the shares) or two years from the grant of the option (i.e., the first date at which shares could be purchased).

Section 422 requires ISO plans to state the aggregate number of shares that can be optioned, and which employees are qualified to buy them. ISO plans must be approved by the corporation's shareholders. Options can be granted only during a period of ten years after adoption of the plan (although further plans can be adopted later).

ISOs must have an option price equal to or greater than the fair market value of the stock at the time the option is granted; they can't be issued at a bargain price. No employee can have an aggregate fair market value of stock greater than $100,000 (measured as of the grant of the option) in the first calendar year for which the options are exercisable. Any amount over $100,000 is denied ISO treatment.

The employee has no taxable income when ISOs are granted or exercised, but does have taxable capital gain or loss on disposition of stock acquired under an ISO. Nor can the employer deduct the cost of providing the plan. If the employee disposes of ISO shares within two years of the grant of the option, or one year of its exercise, the gain or loss is ordinary, not capital.

Nonqualified Stock Options (NQSOs) are stock options that fail to satisfy the §422 tests for ISOs. There is no tax effect when an NQSO is issued, as long as the option itself is not actively traded and does not have a readily ascertainable market value. When the option is exercised, the employee has taxable income equal to the FMV of the stock less the consideration paid for the option.

But if the stock is not transferable and subject to a substantial risk of forfeiture, then the income is not taxed until the condition lapses, at which time the gain is calculated based on the FMV as of that time. The FMV at the time of exercise, minus the price of the option, is a preference item for Alternative Minimum Tax purposes.

[¶346.1.2] Tax Issues Under §83

Code §83 governs stock options, and also other transfers of property in exchange for performance of services. The person who performs the services has ordinary income when rights in the property become transferable or are no longer subject to a substantial risk of forfeiture. (A substantial risk of forfeiture includes the right to the stock being conditioned on the continuing employment of the worker in the same company.) The income equals the FMV of the property minus any payments made by the employee.

Options are taxed as soon as they are granted if they are freely tradable with an independent market value. Otherwise, there is no taxable event until the option is exercised. The employee is taxed once again (probably at capital gains rates) when he or she sells the stock received under the option plan.

The employer can deduct the amount of compensation that the employee includes in income under §83, as long as the compensation is reasonable. The deduction is taken in the employer's taxable year that includes the year in which the employee includes the sum in income.

[¶346.2] Life Insurance Fringe Benefits

There are several Code provisions dealing with life insurance in the employment context. If the employer pays the premiums and the proceeds go to the employee's designated beneficiary (as opposed to "key-person" insurance payable to the corporation itself), the employee has taxable income, and the employer can deduct the cost of providing the insurance, as long as it is an ordinary and necessary business expense. See Reg. §1.1035-1.

Code §101 prevents the proceeds from being taxed to the beneficiary. The employee benefits, despite the taxable status, because of the ability to get significant insurance coverage at low cost.

Such insurance plans are not required to be non-discriminatory, so they can legitimately be limited to higher-paid employees, or employees whom the employer particularly wishes to motivate.

The employee does not have taxable income on account of receiving group-term life insurance coverage, as defined by §79, up to $50,000 in coverage. If a particular employee's coverage is greater, he or she does have taxable income, measured by the Uniform Premium Table found in the IRS Regulations.

Group-term life plans (unlike other plans under which the employer pays for insurance) generally must cover at least 10 employees, and must either be available to all full-time employees with at least three years' tenure, or be available to groups of employees defined in a way that does not allow selection, exclusion, or amount of coverage to be set on the basis of personal characteristics.

The Regs. prescribe non-discrimination tests for §79 plans. If the plan is discriminatory, then key employees must include the full cost of coverage in taxable income.

A split-dollar plan is a method of financing insurance. Employer and employee enter into an agreement. Usually, the employer contributes an amount each year equivalent to the increase in the policy's cash value over the year. When the employee dies, the employer either is reimbursed for the premiums paid or receives a portion of the proceeds equivalent to cash value. The employee's beneficiary gets the balance of the proceeds.

[¶346.3] Cafeteria Plans

A cafeteria plan, as governed by §125, is a "menu" of benefits from which employees can select the ones they prefer; to a certain extent, they can substitute cash for benefits. The plan itself must be in writing, and must provide at least a choice between cash and one taxable and one non-taxable benefit. The cafeteria plan can include a 401(k) (Cash or Deferred Arrangement) component, but no other deferred compensation.

Cafeteria plans can include (*means a non-taxable benefit):

- *Accident and health plans
- *Group-term life insurance, not limited by the $50,000 that can be received tax-free
- *Disability coverage
- *Dependent care assistance
- *Vacation days
- Benefits that are not otherwise qualified because they discriminate in favor of the highly compensated

- Group automobile insurance or other benefits paid for with the employee's after-tax dollars
- *Medical expense reimbursement

Cafeteria plans must be non-discriminatory. Benefits for HCEs must not be greater than 25% of the total benefits for the year. The election between cash and benefits must be made before the plan year begins, and can be changed only based on changes in family status, not employee preference.

[¶346.4] Education Assistance

Code §127 governs the tax treatment of educational assistance supplied by employers to employees and received tax-free. Qualified employer education assistance includes up to $5,250 a year for tuition, fees, and related expenses (but not room and board or transportation) for undergraduate-level courses. Employees always have taxable income if their employers pay for graduate-level courses.

Tax-qualified educational assistance plans must be written plans, disclosed to employees. Education benefits cannot be included in a cafeteria plan. The plan must be non-discriminatory, and at least 95% of the benefits must go to rank-and-file employees. The employer must submit an information return to the IRS each year, explaining the provisions of the plan.

[¶346.5] Dependent-Related Plans

Dependent care assistance plans, under §129, can either be structured as direct payments by the employer for care of employees' dependents, or payments by employees that are reimbursed by the employer. The employer must explain to employees that the plan exists and how it works. It is not required that the employer fund the plan in advance.

Dependent care expenses that can be covered under §129 are household services and other costs that permit a person to accept paid employment. Eligible dependents are children under 15 or spouses or other dependent relatives who are physically or mentally incapable of caring for themselves.

Dependent care assistance is not taxable, subject to somewhat restrictive conditions. The plan's dependent care payment cannot exceed the employee's compensation. The employee has taxable income if the §129 benefits exceed the income of the employee's spouse, unless that spouse is a full-time student or disabled. The employer contribution that can be excluded from income pursuant to §129 is also subject to dollar limitations: $5,000 per employee, or $2,500 per employee who is married filing separately.

Dependent care assistance plans are required to be non-discriminatory: i.e., not more than 25% of contributions to the plan or benefits received under the plan can go to shareholders, owners of 5% or more of the company's stock, or their families. The average benefits for rank-and-file employees must be at least 55% of the average benefits to HCEs. If the plan fails the non-discrimination tests, HCEs (but not rank-and-file employees) will have taxable income as a result of the plan.

[¶346.5.1] Adoption Assistance

For years after 1996, employers can establish a written adoption assistance program, pursuant to §137, providing benefits of up to $5,000 in total (not just in a single year) for "qualified adoption expenses"—$6,000 if the adoptee has special needs.

Qualified adoption expenses include adoption agency fees, attorneys' fees, and court costs. The plan must be non-discriminatory: not more than 5% of the benefits can go to HCEs and stockholders. The employer must notify employees about the plan, but is not obligated to pre-fund it.

In general, the employee does not have taxable income as a result of the adoption assistance, but individuals may have some taxable income if their AGI exceeds $75,000, and adoption assistance is fully taxable to persons with AGI over $115,000.

[¶346.6] Miscellaneous Fringe Benefits

Code §132 provides that employees do not have taxable income from certain minor fringe benefits that the employer provides to all employees in a non-discriminatory fashion. This category includes employee discounts; subsidized cafeterias that benefit the employer by shortening employees' meal breaks; some moving expense reimbursement; and transportation fringe benefits such as parking spaces and van pools.

Also see §119, excluding from gross income meals and lodging that are furnished on the business premises for the convenience of the employer.

[¶348] ERISA Enforcement

ERISA imposes numerous and detailed requirements on plan sponsors and plan fiduciaries and administrators. The overriding objective is operating the plan only for the benefit of its participants and their beneficiaries, and making sure that benefits are provided in accordance with the terms of the plan. ERISA compliance requires regular reporting, plus reporting of unusual events as they occur. It also requires notification to plan participants and beneficiaries.

[¶348.1] Fiduciary Duty under ERISA

Naturally, a plan's trustees are fiduciaries and thus have fiduciary duty to the plan and the people covered by it. Other classes of people are also ERISA fiduciaries, including those who are paid by the plan to give investment advice; those with any authority (even if not discretionary) over management and disposition of plan assets[30]; those with any discretionary authority or control over plan management; and those with discretion or authority over day-to-day administration of the plan.

ERISA fiduciaries have four basic duties:

(1)   Loyalty

(2)   Prudence (behaving with the care, skill, and diligence that a hypothetical prudent person familiar with the plan would use)

(3)   Compliance with the plan's governing instrument and other relevant legal documents. There is also a clear fiduciary duty to provide copies of mandated plan documents, such as the Summary Plan Description and Summary of Material Modifications.

(4)   Keeping informed of the performance of the other fiduciaries.

In general, fiduciaries have a duty to diversify the plan's investment portfolio unless it is prudent *not* to diversify.

A fiduciary who is guilty of a breach of duty is personally liable to the plan and must make reimbursement for any loss in value of the plan assets caused by the violation. See ERISA §409 for the fiduciary's obligation to disgorge any improper personal profits deriving from breach of fiduciary duty. The plan can get a court order removing a fiduciary who has breached his or her duty. See ERISA §409 for suit by the plan against the fiduciary, and §502(a)(3) for suits by participants and beneficiaries. ERISA §502(i) governs civil penalties imposed by the Department of Labor on fiduciaries—or non-fiduciaries who knowingly participate in a fiduciary violation.

A plan cannot contain language that limits the fiduciary's liability for breach of fiduciary duty: ERISA §410. The employer (as distinct from the plan) is allowed to indemnify the fiduciary or buy insurance covering the fiduciary. The fiduciary can also buy liability insurance personally.

[¶348.2] Prohibited Transactions

Because interested parties cannot be expected to be objective, ERISA bans certain types of transactions between plans and "parties in interest"[31] and "disqualified persons"—even if in fact the transaction is fair.

Prohibited transactions include buying, selling, or leasing property to or from a plan insider; extending credit; performing services; making payments to a fiduciary; conflicts of interest by a fiduciary. The IRS imposes an excise tax on prohibited transactions (Code §4975), and the Department of Labor also imposes similar penalties on non-qualified plans (see ERISA §502(i). A disqualified person who engages in a prohibited transaction is subject to the excise tax even if he, she, or it did not know that the transaction was prohibited.

ERISA §408 exempts certain classes of prohibited transactions from sanction[32]; the DOL and the IRS have the right to exempt particular transactions on request of the intended parties to the transaction. An exemption will be granted only if the proposed exemption serves the best interests of plan participants and beneficiaries and protects their rights.

[¶348.3] ERISA Lawsuits

Plan participants and beneficiaries, the DOL, and other fiduciaries have a broad range of causes of action under ERISA §502. Section 502(a)(1)(B) lets participants and beneficiaries (but no one else) sue to recover benefits due under the terms of the plan, to enforce rights under the terms of the plan, or to clarify rights to future benefits under the plan.

The sponsor corporation acts as a plan fiduciary when it gives out information about benefit security, and therefore a deliberate falsehood can be punished as a breach of fiduciary duty.[33]

Any participant, beneficiary, or the DOL can sue under §502(a)(2) based on an allegation of breach of fiduciary duty under ERISA §409. Injunctions or equitable relief ordering specific performance of the terms of the plan are available to the DOL, participants, beneficiaries, or other fiduciaries under ERISA §§502(a)(3) and (a)(5).[34] Monetary penalties are imposed for each day of failure to supply mandated information: see §502(a)(1)(A).

The Department of Labor is empowered to bring suit under §502(a)(6) to collect the excise tax on prohibited transactions, and the DOL is not only allowed to, but obligated to, impose civil penalties under §502(l) for certain fiduciary violations (including non-fiduciaries who participate in the violation).

Both civil and criminal penalties are imposed under ERISA §510 for interference with ERISA rights. The typical example is firing an employee to prevent benefits from accruing,[35] but all forms of adverse job action (suspension, discipline, discrimination) are forbidden. Force, fraud, or violence to restrain, coerce, or intimidate a participant or beneficiary to prevent exercise of ERISA rights is a crime: ERISA §511.

An employer that is delinquent in making contributions to fund its plans can be sued under ERISA §515.

[¶350] Employment Discrimination

In a perfect world, all employers would focus only on each applicant or employee as an individual, and would never be influenced by prejudices. In our own very imperfect world, federal and state laws forbid discrimination on the basis of suspect classifications such as age, sex, race, nationality, and disability, in all of the "terms and conditions of employment," including hiring; compensation; working conditions; and discipline and dismissal.

Major federal statutes in this regard are Title VII of the Civil Rights Act of 1964 (as amended), and the Equal Pay Act. (Sexual harassment is covered under Title VII as a form of sex discrimination.)

The Americans with Disabilities Act (ADA) requires employers to make "reasonable accommodation" to the needs of applicants and employees who are "qualified individuals with disabilities." Both of the phrases in quotation marks have been quite controversial, and have given rise to significant litigation. Much of the conflict was resolved by the Supreme Court in a series of unpopular mid-1999 decisions, holding that the determination of whether an individual is "disabled" is made after mitigating measures have been taken: e.g., a person with extremely limited uncorrected vision, but with fairly normal vision with eyeglasses or contact lenses.[36]

Employees are entitled to a working environment free of sexual or racial harassment, and this has been an important area of regulation and litigation in recent years. It is also unlawful for employers to retaliate against employees who make charges under anti-discrimination laws.

[¶350.1] Employment Discrimination Charges and Litigation

Depending on the type of claim and the circumstances, charges of employment discrimination can be based on "disparate treatment" (unfair treatment of a suspect classification) and/or "disparate impact" (facially neutral practices that have a disproportionately negative effect on a suspect classification). The selection of a theory affects issues such as statute of limitations, burden of proof, and potential remedies.

Under *St. Mary's Honor Center v. Hicks*, 509 U.S. 502 (Sup.Ct. 1993), the discrimination case plaintiff always has the "ultimate burden of persuasion." Thus, a plaintiff who fails to offer enough evidence can lose a discrimination case, even if the judge or jury (whichever is the trier of facts for the case) does not believe the employer's explanation of its conduct.

If an employee is fired or quits, and subsequently brings a discrimination charge, the employer can investigate the employee's conduct during work. Evidence of conduct during employment that is acquired after employment ended is admissible at trial of the discrimination charge.[37] Such "after-acquired evidence" will not give rise to summary judgment, but can be used to limit the remedies available to the plaintiff.

[¶350.2] Discrimination in Hiring Practices

To avoid discrimination, employers should review their recruitment practices. If recruitment is limited to a particular neighborhood, or to the family and friends of current workers, it is likely that any past patterns of discrimination will be repeated. Recruitment among the general population, including outreach efforts to find qualified applicants from groups not part of the traditional workforce, is more likely to survive a challenge.

Pre-employment inquiries should be made uniformly of all applicants—e.g., it is improper to ask female applicants with children if they are able to undertake a significant amount of business travel, if male applicants with children are not asked the same question. In fact, information about marital and family status is not relevant until and unless a person has been hired and is about to be enrolled in a health plan, so such questions should not be asked until the company is ready to extend a job offer.

For companies (e.g., manufacturers) that are federal contractors, EEOC regulations at 41 CFR Part 60 require job applications to invite Vietnam veterans, disabled veterans, and persons with disabilities to identify themselves, because federal contractors have affirmative action responsibilities in these regards.

[¶350.2.1] Pre-Employment Testing

It's legitimate for employers to assess the relevant job-related skills of job applicants. However, written tests can have a disparate impact on some groups whose members have suffered educational disadvantage. It is discriminatory to give pre-employment tests **only** to members of minority groups, but the Civil Rights Act of 1991 makes it equally unacceptable to have a lower passing grade for minority-group members, or to grade their test scores on a curve.

Pre-employment testing should measure the applicant's ability to perform specific tasks that will be used in the job, not to categorize applicants in the abstract.[38] *Albemarle v. Moody*,[39] permits a test that has a disproportionate impact on a minority group, as long as the test has been validated by testing professionals and the test actually predicts important elements of work behavior.

[¶350.2.2] Disability

If a qualified person with a disability is hired, or a current employee becomes disabled, the ADA requires the employer to provide reasonable accommodation to the disability (see ¶354). However, current interpretations of the ADA forbid certain pre-employment inquiries about health status as discriminatory: e.g., whether the applicant has been treated for certain diseases; whether he or she has ever been hospitalized; prescription drug history. It is improper to ask if there are any health reasons that prevent the applicant from doing the job applied for, but permissible to restrict the inquiry to specific job functions (lift 25 pounds; work rotating shifts; drive a tractor-trailer) and ability to perform them with or without accommodation.

Other questions can legitimately be asked—but only after the employer has extended a conditional job offer (i.e., may be willing to employ the applicant).

It is not permissible to ask a job applicant about past receipt of Workers' Compensation benefits, but if a conditional job offer is made, the employer can ask about past injuries that may require reasonable accommodation.

[¶350.2.3] Immigration Issues

See ¶3300 et seq. for a discussion of U.S. immigration law in general. The Immigration Reform and Control Act of 1986 (IRCA), 8 U.S.C. §1324a, requires employers to verify the employment status of all newly hired persons. The employer must employ only a U.S. citizen or a non-citizen holding a visa that permits him or her to work in the United States (i.e., not a tourist).

See P.L. 105-277, the American Competitiveness and Workforce Improvement Act, increasing the number of H1-B non-immigrant visas that can be issued for temporary employment of foreign professionals, but also requiring measures to prevent replacement of U.S. workers with H1-B visa holders.

The newly hired person must submit a Form I-9 within three days of being hired, documenting his or her immigration employment status. Civil and criminal penalties can be imposed on employers who hire persons who are not eligible to work in the United States. Penalties are also imposed for document fraud on the part of either employer or job applicant.

[¶350.2.4] Credit Reporting in the Hiring Process

¶2030 discusses fair credit reporting in the context of granting or denying credit. Credit reports are also sought by potential employers checking up on job applicants. The Fair Credit Reporting Act, 15 USC §1681a et seq., as amended (effective 9/30/97) by the Consumer Credit Reporting Reform Act of 1996, P.L. 104-208, governs the use of credit reports and investigative credit reports.

An FCRA provision, 15 USC §1681b(3)(B), specifically permits requesting a credit report for employment purposes ("evaluating a consumer for employment, promotion, reassignment or retention as an employee"). If the report results in an adverse action, the employer is required to give the consumer oral, written, or electronic notice of the adverse action, including information about how to review the file and correct errors. The employer must also furnish any credit reporting agency it uses with a statement that the employer complies with federal law about the use of credit reports by employers.

A credit report is a written or oral communication from a consumer reporting agency dealing with a consumer's creditworthiness, character, reputation, lifestyle, or personal characteristics.

An investigative credit report is based on personal interviews with persons who claim to have information about the consumer. Employers must give job applicants a written disclosure statement, and obtain their written consent, before requesting either kind of report about the job applicant. Further written disclosure mailed no later than three days after requesting an investigative report is mandatory, informing the applicant that the report covers matters such as character and conduct.

[¶351] Title VII

Title VII of the Civil Rights Act of 1964, 42 USC §2000e, forbids discrimination in the terms and conditions of employment. Job applications; interviews; hiring; retention; promotion; compensation; benefits; and dismissal are all treated as terms and conditions of employment. Retaliation against employees who exercise their Title VII rights, or participate in an investigation or proceeding, is also unlawful.[40]

Only employers[41] with 15 or more employees are covered by Title VII.[42] The forbidden grounds of discrimination are race, color, religion, sex, pregnancy, and national origin. Sexual orientation discrimination is not forbidden by federal law, although a number of state and local anti-discrimination laws do forbid it.[43]

The "reasonable accommodation" concept, central to the Americans with Disabilities Act, also applies to making reasonable accommodations to employees' religious practices, such as allowing them to use vacation or personal days for religious observance and accommodating religious dress in the workplace.

Title VII bars both disparate treatment discrimination (overt intentional classifications that advantage certain groups and disadvantage others) and disparate impact discrimination (facially neutral practices that have a disproportionately unfavorable impact on certain groups, e.g., minimum height requirements that limit the employment of women and certain non-Caucasian groups). Usually, disparate treatment cases are proved with direct or indirect evidence of explicit discrimination. Disparate impact cases usually involve introduction of statistics, but statistics are not necessarily persuasive, especially in the case of a small, unrepresentative sample.

The basic Title VII case is a three-step process. The plaintiff establishes a prima facie case by introducing facts suggestive of discrimination. Next, the employer is permitted to rebut the charge, by proving legitimate non-discriminatory reasons or business necessity for the conduct. Finally, the plaintiff is permitted to show pretextuality—that the employer's stated explanation is merely a pretext for discrimination.

In a disparate impact case in which the employer asserts a business necessity defense, the plaintiff can prevail by showing that the employer refused to adopt a non-discriminatory alternative practice that would have satisfied its business needs.

Where there are many factors behind a workplace decision and the plaintiff challenges more than one criterion, the plaintiff must be able to prove disparate impact of each criterion.

A "mixed-motive" case is somewhat different: in such cases, the employer has several motivations behind a decision, some lawful and some discriminatory. The plaintiff can win by showing the influence of the discriminatory motive; it is not necessary to show that there were no legitimate motivations for the decision. But if the employer would have acted in the same way even without the discriminatory motive, the plaintiff's remedies will be reduced: §107(b) of the Civil Rights Act of 1991 limits relief in mixed-motive cases to injunctive and declaratory relief, but not damages.

In many instances, employees seek to bring their cases in state court, believing that they will get a faster resolution, more sympathetic juries, and access to additional remedies (e.g., emotional distress damages and punitive damages). It is often possible for the employer to get the case removed to federal court, for instance if the issue is preempted by a federal law such as ERISA.

[¶351.1] Title VII Remedies

Some discrimination claims are breach of contract claims, but most of them are tort claims. In contract cases, the remedy is to put the plaintiff in the position that would have been obtained if the contract had been fulfilled, probably lost earnings and fringe benefits, perhaps out-of-pocket expenses of mitigating damages by finding another job.

Title VII tort damages are drawn from reinstatement, back pay (including fringe benefits; limited to two years), front pay from the end of the trial, lost earnings, medical expenses, pain and anguish, attorneys' fees, and emotional distress. Further discrimination can be enjoined: see 42 USC §2000e-5(g).

The District of Columbia Circuit ruled that punitive damages are never available in Title VII cases absent egregious conduct by the employer. The Supreme Court relaxed that standard somewhat in *Kolstad v. American Dental Ass'n*, 119 S.Ct. 2118 (6/22/99), finding that punitive damages can be ordered even if the employer's conduct is not egregious. However, the employer will not be liable for punitive damages on the basis of conduct by a manager that violates the employer's good-faith effort to provide a workplace that is compliant with the requirements of federal law.

The Civil Rights Act of 1991, P.L. 102-166 (CRA '91) caps the total damages that can be received by any successful Title VII plaintiff, including punitive damages and most compensatory damages (but not medical bills and other monetary losses incurred before the trial as a result of discrimination). The cap depends on the employer corporation's size, not the seriousness of the discrimination charges.

Companies with fewer than 15 employees are exempt from Title VII, so the smallest unit for CRA '91 purposes is the company with 15–100 employees; the damage cap is $50,000. It is $100,000 for companies with 101–200 employees, $200,000 for 201–500 employees, and $300,000 if the company has more than 500 workers.

Clearly, breach of contract damages are taxable income for the plaintiff, because they replace earned income that would have been taxable. Tort damages received for "personal injury" are tax-free. However, a 1992 Supreme Court decision[44] characterizes Title VII damages as taxable income, because they are not sufficiently similar to bodily injury damages in traditional tort cases.

The Small Business Job Protection Act of 1996 amended Code §104(a)(2) to provide that, effective August 21, 1996, damages received for physical illness and other "personal [i.e., bodily] physical injuries" will be tax-free. Damages for emotional distress are taxable except to the extent of medical expenses for treatment of emotional distress.

[¶351.1.2] Exemptions from Discrimination Laws

A neutral, bona fide seniority system that does not manifest discriminatory intent is permissible, even if it provides different terms or conditions of employment for employees with differing seniority—and even if the effect of the system is to maintain past discrimination. See 42 USC §2000e-2(h).

Employers are not guilty of discrimination if their conduct is justified by a Bona Fide Occupational Qualification (BFOQ). For instance, authenticity might dictate hiring a male rather than a female for a role in a film. Privacy might dictate hiring a female rather than a male as a dressing room attendant. Public safety might require a pilot or police officer to be young enough to have youthful reflexes. However, the BFOQ defense is not accepted in cases of alleged racial discrimination.

A business necessity defense is also possible if alleged discriminatory conduct is needed to maintain safety and efficiency.

[¶351.1.3] The Civil War Acts

The Civil Rights Act of 1866, 42 USC §1981, gives all citizens the same employment and contractual rights as "white citizens." It covers employers of all sizes; the 15-employee limit of Title VII is not applicable, and at-will employees can sue under §1981.[45] It is not necessary to exhaust administrative remedies before bringing a §1981 suit, and there is no limitation on the amount of compensatory and punitive damages that can be awarded.

The Civil Rights Act of 1991 generally requires race discrimination claimants to proceed under §1981 before accessing Title VII. Title VII compensatory and punitive damages are not available to persons who can receive such damages under §1981.

[¶351.2] Sex Discrimination

Discrimination on account of sex is unlawful under Title VII. In addition, Executive Order 11246 forbids sex discrimination by government contractors and subcontractors; violators can be barred from doing business with the federal government.

Under a 1983 Supreme Court decision,[46] it constitutes sex discrimination for an employer to provide more benefits for male employees and their spouses than for female employees and their spouses.

The Pregnancy Discrimination Act (PDA; 42 USC §2000e(k)) bars discrimination on the basis of pregnancy or related conditions. A common misunderstanding is that the PDA requires employers to treat pregnancy as a disability. What the act really does is to require any pregnancy-related disability to be covered by employer plans to the same extent as other non-work-related disability.

The PDA does not require an employer to add health care coverage if it would not otherwise provide it. However, if health care coverage is provided, pregnancy-related conditions must be covered on terms of equality with non-pregnancy-related conditions.

The Equal Pay Act, 29 USC §206 (EPA) is a statute outside Title VII that forbids sex discrimination in compensation. It covers employers of two or more (versus 15 or more for Title VII coverage). Discrimination is forbidden in salary or other compensation on the basis of sex, if the jobs require equal skill, effort, and responsibility and are performed under similar working conditions. Therefore, the EPA does not cover "comparable worth" allegations that women are being underpaid as compared to men who perform different jobs of allegedly lesser value.

[¶352] Sexual Harassment

Sexual harassment is the subjection of an employee to unwanted sexual contact, solicitation, or innuendoes. It is considered a form of sex discrimination that violates Title VII. Both quid pro quo harassment (employee is either threatened with detrimental consequences for not providing sexual access, or offered job benefits for providing it) and hostile environment harassment[47] are actionable.

Harassment of an individual is actionable whether the harasser is of the opposite sex or the same sex, and either males or females can bring sexual harassment claims.[48] In the view of the EEOC, conduct is unwanted if the employee did not solicit or initiate it, and he or she finds the conduct undesirable or offensive.

Most sexual harassment cases involve harassment allegedly committed by a supervisor, although in some cases, conduct by a co-employee or a customer (e.g., a bar patron who harasses a cocktail waitress) is actionable. In virtually all instances, the proper defendant is the employer corporation; the individual harasser generally cannot be sued.

In 1999,[49] the Supreme Court resolved questions of what the employer can do to free itself of liability in harassment cases. If the employment action had adverse effect on the harassment victim, the employer is absolutely liable. If there was no adverse employment effect, the employer is liable unless it maintained proper anti-harassment and grievance policies.

Obviously, employers must create, promulgate, and enforce an anti-harassment policy, and must have a complaint mechanism that allows employees to assert harassment claims (and to someone other than the direct supervisor, if he or she is the alleged harasser).

If the investigation reveals that the claim is well-founded, some action must be taken that is not punitive to the victim of harassment. Depending on circumstances, it could include firing the harasser; subjecting the harasser to a lesser degree of discipline; transferring either the harasser or victim to prevent further contact; or other appropriate response.

For the EEOC's interpretation of an employer's duties in the post-Faragher/Ellerth environment, see "Enforcement Guidance: Vicarious Employer Liability for Unlawful Harassment by Supervisors," http://www.eeoc.gov/docs/harassment.html.

[¶353] ADEA

The Age Discrimination in Employment Act, 29 USC §621—, generally protects individuals over 40 from age-based job discrimination. Employers are subject to the ADEA if they have 20 or more employees.

The ADEA covers discrimination in hiring, firing, and terms and conditions of employment, including benefits. A 1989 Supreme Court case, *Public Employees Retirement System of Ohio v. Betts*[50] held that the ADEA does not cover employee benefits, but in 1990, Congress passed the Older Workers Benefit Protection Act (OWBPA) to make it clear that benefit discrimination does indeed come under the ambit of the ADEA. The OWBPA allows employers to reduce severance benefits by sums such as retiree health benefits; supplemental unemployment insurance benefits; and additional pension benefits provided as early retirement incentives.

[¶353.1] ADEA Exclusions

To a limited extent, a Bona Fide Occupational Qualification (BFOQ) defense can be raised to an ADEA charge: if, for instance, a police officer or firefighter has to be under 40 to have the physical fitness needed for the job.

Reasonable Factors Other than Age (RFOAs) can also provide an ADEA defense, if the employer can prove that it used objective, uniformly applied, job-related criteria to make the decision that is being attacked as age-based.

A related business necessity defense is available: for instance, if older employees were being discharged or laid off because their salaries were higher than those of potential younger replacements. 29 USC §623(f)(2) creates an ADEA exception for actions taken in compliance with a bona fide seniority system or employee benefit plan. However, this defense cannot be used to justify failure to hire or involuntary retirement.

Mandatory retirement is permissible in the case of persons who have reached age 70, and who were bona fide executives or held a high policy-making position at least two years before the forced retirement, as long as they were entitled to immediate nonforfeitable annual retirement benefits of $44,000 a year or more. EEOC Guidelines at 29 CFR §1625.12(d) define executives and policy-makers.

Tenured university professors can also be required to retire on the basis of age, under the Higher Education Amendments of 1998, H.R. 6 (10/7/98).

[¶353.2] Proof of the ADEA Case

Although most discrimination charges involve immutable characteristics, such as race and sex, age discrimination cases present some philosophical questions because of the inevitability of human aging.

The basic prima facie ADEA case is:

- The plaintiff belongs to the protected group (persons over 40)
- The plaintiff was qualified for the job he or she held or applied for
- Adverse action was taken on account of age
- (In appropriate cases) the plaintiff was replaced by one or more other employees.

A 1993 Supreme Court case[51] makes it possible to win an ADEA case based on proof of improper age-related motives for discharge, even if the replacement employee is over 40.

A number of ADEA cases really allege "age-plus" rather than simple age discrimination. That is, the plaintiff charges that he or she has been fired because lengthy employment and a good track record have made the employee's salary high enough so that the company can save money by replacing the employee with a lower-paid neophyte. *Hazen Paper Co. v. Biggins*, 507 U.S. 604 (Sup.Ct. 1993) requires the plaintiff to prove that age itself, not just age-related factors such as long tenure, influenced the employer's conduct.

[¶353.3] ADEA Releases

The Older Workers Benefit Protection Act permits exiting employees to release their ADEA claims, as long as the waiver is knowing and voluntary. A valid release must:

- Refer specifically to ADEA claims
- Give the employee at least 21 days to consider (at least 45 days, if a group of employees is being terminated at one time)
- Give the employee at least seven days after signing to withdraw the release

- Inform employees that the release is a legal document, and that they can get legal counsel before signing it.

See 29 CFR Part 1625 for the EEOC policy on waivers under the OWBPA. A Final Rule on ADEA waivers was published at 63 FR 30624 on June 5, 1998. The employee who signs a valid waiver must receive additional valuable consideration for signing that would not be available without waiving ADEA claims.

An employee who wishes to bring suit notwithstanding having signed a release is not required to "tender back" (return) the consideration received for the release as a precondition of bringing suit: *Oubre v. Entergy Operations, Inc.*, 522 U.S. 422 (Sup.Ct. 1998).[52]

[¶354] ADA

The Americans with Disabilities Act of 1990 (42 USC §12101) covers public accommodations discrimination, but this discussion deals with disability discrimination in employment, employment-related practices, and terms and conditions of employment (including benefits). Employers (but not individuals[53]) are liable under the ADA if they discriminate against a qualified individual with a disability.

Disability is a physical or mental impairment that substantially limits at least one life activity[54]; the ADA is triggered by a person's being perceived as disabled even if in fact no disability exists. Determination of disability is made after mitigating factors (e.g., medication, assistive devices, eyeglasses or contact lenses) are applied.[55]

Reasonable accommodation can include making the workplace accessible, changing work schedules, modifying or purchasing new equipment, or reassigning the disabled individual to a vacant position. It is not necessary to create a new job, fire or demote another employee, or provide any accommodation that is an undue hardship to the employer. The EEOC's position has been set out in a major document. "Enforcement Guidance: Reasonable Accommodation and Undue Hardship Under the Americans with Disabilities Act.[56]

A qualified individual with a disability is one who has the experience and education, and is otherwise able to perform the essential functions of the job, either with or without reasonable accommodations made by the employer. It is unlawful to discriminate against now-sober persons who used to abuse alcohol or drugs, but current substance abuse is not a disability for ADA purposes.

Mixed-motive ADA cases (i.e., disability discrimination was one factor among others leading to termination) and hostile environment ADA cases can be brought.[57]

Employers are not permitted to ask job applicants about their disability or health status. However, once the employer is willing to extend a conditional job offer, it can lawfully ask applicants about their ability to perform the essential job functions, and ask about accommodations that may be required.

After hiring, the employer is permitted to make inquiries and require a medical examination based on objective evidence of a medical condition that limits the employee's ability to perform essential job functions, or that makes him or her a safety threat.

The ADA is jointly enforced by the EEOC and the Department of Labor. ADA procedures, timing requirements, and remedies are similar to those for Title VII. In the Ninth Circuit, the ADA plaintiff's prima facie case includes proof of the existence of an available job that he or she could perform with reasonable accommodation. The EEOC's position is that employers have a duty to engage in an interactive process with employees to develop reasonable accommodations, but failure to do so is not a separate cause of action under the ADA.[58]

Employers are permitted to make benefit plan determinations consistent with sound underwriting principles, unless the determinations are a subterfuge to avoid ADA compliance. It is not lawful to refuse to hire, or to fire, a person because of the effect his or her disability will have on the cost of the group health plan. Preexisting condition limitations are permissible.

Applying for SSDI benefits is not necessarily inconsistent with making an ADA claim, given that SSDI focuses on inability to work, and the ADA permits consideration of ability to work with reasonable accommodation. The plaintiff is entitled to explain the discrepancy between claiming disability and claiming to be able to work with reasonable accommodation.[59]

[¶355] Litigation Issues in Discrimination Suits

An individual who believes that he or she has suffered workplace discrimination must exhaust administrative remedies. The employee who charges employment discrimination must file a charge either with the EEOC or with the state or local anti-discrimination agency. If the employee starts with an EEOC filing, the federal agency generally "defers" to the state or local agency (see 29 CFR §1601.74)—i.e., it forwards the paperwork to the other agency, giving it 60 days to resolve the complaint.

The EEOC has a dual role. Not only does it investigate allegations and seek to conciliate (bring employer and employee to a compromise that satisfies both), it has independent power to investigate and bring suits as a plaintiff. Furthermore, there is no statute of limitations for EEOC suits.

If the EEOC can't settle a charge informally, it determines whether or not there is reasonable cause to believe that the employee's charge is well-founded. See 29 CFR §1601.24(a) for criteria for this "reasonable cause" determination. If the EEOC determines that reasonable cause is not present, the agency informs the charging party of its decision. If the employee still intends to sue, he or she must get a "right to sue" letter in a Title VII or ADA case (but this is not required in an Equal Pay Act or ADEA case). The potential plaintiff is then required to file suit within 90 days of receiving the right to sue letter, or the claim will be waived.

Title VII and ADA charges must be filed with the EEOC within 180 days of the alleged act of discrimination (or the last in a series of alleged discriminatory acts) if there is no "deferral" agency involved, or within 300 days of the alleged discrimination and 30 days of the time the deferral agency terminates processing of the charge.

ADEA charges follow a similar trajectory, although some states are "referral" states that have work-sharing agreements under which charges are sent to the EEOC; others are "deferral"states where the EEOC gives the state 60 days to process the charge. However, ADEA suits can be brought as soon as administrative proceedings are completed, and there is no requirement of a "right to sue" letter. The would-be ADEA plaintiff must bring suit within 90 days of the time the EEOC either makes a ruling or dismisses the charge.

Generally, the various time limits are strictly enforced. However, tolling of the statute of limitations is permitted in a narrow class of cases, including deception by the employer that prevented timely filing; timely filing in the wrong court; timely filing of a defective pleading; and the employer's failure to post the required EEOC notices that explain employees' rights.

In many instances, defendant employers will take the position that litigation of discrimination claims is inappropriate, because the claimant is covered by a Collective Bargaining Agreement or an individual employment contract that contains an arbitration clause. Under *Wright v. Universal Maritime Service Corp.*,[60] a CBA must be specific as to which statutory discrimination claims must be arbitrated. A general requirement of arbitration rather than litigation is not enforceable.[61]

[¶355.1] EEO Records

Companies with 100 or more employees are required to file an annual report, the Employer Information Report (EEO-1) with the EEOC by September 30 of each year. This report is a simple two-page form tracking the composition of the workforce. The most current report must be filed at headquarters or at every company unit required to file.

Records of application forms, requests for accommodation, and other employment-related data must be retained for one year (running from the later of collecting the data or taking personnel action). 29 CFR §1602.14 requires that all records of a personnel action that becomes the subject of a discrimination charge must be retained until the case is over, or the statute of limitations has run on the charge.

[¶360] Wrongful Termination

Some employees work under union contracts that contain disciplinary and grievance procedures outlining steps that must be followed to discipline or fire an employee for cause. Other employees have negotiated individualized contracts specifying their tenure, circumstances under which they can be fired, and circumstances under which their compensation must be continued even if their services are dispensed with.

Most workers, however, are "at-will" employees. Their employment is conceptualized as continuing at the will of the employer, and they can be fired with or without cause if the employer wants to cut the payroll or is dissatisfied in some way with the employee. An at-will employee can be fired for good cause, or for no cause at all—but not for an unlawful cause.

As the preceding discussion shows, various groups are entitled to civil rights protection, and refusing to hire a person, firing that person, discriminating in working conditions, or otherwise disfavoring a person in employment because of membership in such a group is illegal.

As a general rule, "statutory" claims (claims arising out of a civil rights suit; Family and Medical Leave Act claims) must be brought under those statutes, which will usually mean following the EEOC procedure and perhaps eventually suing in federal court.

However, if the allegation does not involve job action in violation of federal law, or if the employer is too small to be covered by the federal law, then the employee, would-be employee, or ex-employee may be able to sue in state court, under a state anti-discrimination law, for breach of express or implied contract, or under a tort theory.

The advantage of suing in state court is that cumbersome EEOC procedures need not be followed (although the state law may have its own cumbersome requirements). The time to get to trial may be much shorter in the state system, and additional remedies such as punitive damages and damages for emotional distress may be available in state courts when they would not be available under federal civil rights law.

There are two broad categories under which wrongful termination suits are usually brought:

* Implied contract theories
* Public policy theories

[¶360.1] Implied Contract Theories

Implied contract theories take the position that the employer's words or actions, or those of its agents, create a contract under which the employee cannot be fired without good cause and without due process.

One stream of cases involves employee handbooks. These handbooks often contain language about "lifetime employment" or "no one will be fired without good cause." However, the handbooks also usually contain a conspicuous express statement that the employee handbooks are not contractual in nature, and do not constitute an employment contract; the employees continue to work at will. Although there are some cases treating employee handbooks as contracts, and thus requiring employers to go through the full grievance and discipline procedure stated in the handbook before firing an employee, handbook provisions will usually not be treated as contracts of employment.

Another stream of cases uses a promissory estoppel theory.[62] A person who is induced to leave an existing job, and perhaps move to a new city, sell one home and buy another, etc., may be treated as entitled to a promise of indefinite or at least several years' tenure, if he or she acts in reliance on the offer of the new job.

In some cases, the Statute of Frauds acts as a bar, on the theory that a contract lasting more than a year must be in writing to be enforceable; yet courts determined to find for the plaintiff will also find that the Statute of Frauds problem is solved by treating the contract as one that could be ended in less than a year by the employee's death or disability.

[¶360.2] Public Policy Theories

These theories state that it is improper to terminate an employee for lawful or even laudable behavior. For example, it is unlawful to fire an employee for serving jury duty or carrying out a military reserve or National Guard commitment, or with the motive of preventing the employee from qualifying for ERISA-protected benefits. Retaliation for filing a Workers' Compensation claim may also be treated as contrary to public policy.

A very significant public policy theory involves "whistleblowers": individuals who report corporate wrongdoing, or participate in investigations. Many states have whistleblower statutes protecting the employment rights of such persons. However, recent cases tend to treat whistleblower protection quite narrowly, and local case law should always be consulted before bringing suit.

The recent Supreme Court case of *Haddle v. Garrison*[63] holds that an allegation that an at-will employee was fired for cooperating with a criminal investigation of the employer (here, for Medicare fraud) states a cause of action under 42 USC §1985(2), because an injury to person or property has occurred.

In late 1998, the Fifth Circuit allowed an at-will employee to sue under 42 USC §1981 (ban on racial discrimination in the making of contracts).[64]

ENDNOTES

1. *Lividas v. Bradshaw*, 512 U.S. 107 (Sup.Ct. 1994). *Textron v. UAAIW,* 523 U.S. 653 (Sup.Ct. 1998) holds that an allegation that an employer violated a collective bargaining agreement presents a federal question, but allegations that the employer defrauded the union into signing a contract and promising not to strike by promising not to subcontract out work, were not governed by LMRA §301 and did not present federal questions.
2. *K.V. Mart Co. v. United Food & Commercial Workers*, 67 LW 1635 (9th Cir. 4/14/99).
3. 119 S.Ct. 2240 (Sup.Ct. 1999).
4. *Marquez v. Screen Actors Guild*, 119 S.Ct. 292 (Sup.Ct. 1998).
5. *Auciello Iron Works Inc. v. NLRB*, 517 U.S. 781 (Sup.Ct. 1996).
6. Reported beginning at 363 U.S. 564.
7. 119 S.Ct. 977 (Sup.Ct. 1999).
8. It is not double jeopardy to impose administrative penalties on an employer that has already been convicted of criminal OSHA violations, because the administrative penalties are purely civil and do not carry the possibility of imprisonment: *S.A. Healy Co. v. OSHRC*, 138 F.3d 686 (7th Cir. 1998).
9. The EEOC's guidance on leased employees is published at http://www.eeoc.gov/press/12-8-97.html. *Bronk v. Mountain States Telephone & Telegraph Inc.*, 98-1 USTC ¶50,316 (10th Cir. 1998) finds it lawful to draft a plan to exclude leased employees, even those who are common-law em-

ployees, on the grounds that the Code and ERISA merely require leased employees to be treated as employees, not necessarily that they be offered plan participation. In contrast, the Ninth Circuit's decisions in *Vizcaino v. Microsoft*, 97 F.3d 1187 (9th Cir. 1995), *aff'd* 120 F.3d 1006 (9th Cir. 1997) and #98-71388, 99-35013 entitle individuals who had long-term assignments at Microsoft through temporary agencies, who Microsoft claimed were independent contractors, to participate in Microsoft stock purchase plans.

10. *Alpha Medical, Inc.*, 83 AFTR2d ¶99-697 (6th Cir. 4/19/99).

11. However, the mere possibility of salary reductions for disciplinary infractions does not make an otherwise salaried worker a non-exempt hourly worker: *Auer v. Robbins*, 519 U.S. 452 (Sup.Ct.1997).

12. Most plans have an NRA of 65, but the plan can set the NRA below 65 if this is customary for the company or its industry. If the NRA is below 55, §415(b) requires reduction of the maximum pension payable under the plan. In a plan with an NRA over 65, or one which does not specify the NRA, each participant's NRA is the later of his or her 65th birthday or fifth anniversary of plan participation.

13. 119 S.Ct. 755 (Sup.Ct. 1999).

14. In a plan that requires, or even accepts, employee contributions, employees must always be 100% vested in their own contributions.

15. See T.D.s 8814 and 8815 for the FICA/FUTA status of nonqualified deferred compensation.

16. If the employee/ex-spouse objects to the terms of the order, he or she must litigate with the non-employee/ex-spouse in state court, but the plan administrator has no liability for complying with the QDRO: *Blue v. UAL Corp.*, 160 F.3d 383 (7th Cir. 1998).

17. Proposed amendments to the SPD requirements for pension plans were published by the Pension and Welfare Benefits Administration (PWBA) at 63 FR 48376 (9/9/98).

18. *Krohn v. Huron Memorial Hospital*, 67 LW 1619 (6th Cir. 4/1/99).

19. *Fischer v. Philadelphia Electric Co.*, 96 F.3d 1533 (3rd Cir. 1996); *McAuley v. IBM Corp.*, 67 LW 1480 (6th Cir. 1/22/99).

20. See, e.g., *Diehl v. Twin Disk Inc.*, 65 LW 2472 (7th Cir. 12/12/96).

21. Interim regulations were published by the DOL and IRS at 62 FR 66931 (12/22/97).

22. *Foray v. Bell Atlantic*, *N.Y.L.J.* 6/14/99 p. 31 Col. 4 (S.D.N.Y.)

23. The unavailability of marriage for same-sex couples was also cited in *Tanner v. Oregon Health Sciences University*, 971 P.2d 435 (Ore. App. 1998), justifying class treatment for unmarried same-sex couples. The Oregon Constitution forbids discrimination on the basis of sexual orientation, so discrimination against the class violated the state Constitution and was not a permissible distinction on the basis of marital status.

24. But see *Tardie v. Rehab. Hospital of Rhode Island*, 67 LW 1521 (1st Cir. 2/24/99): reinstatement is not required if the employee is no longer able to

perform the essential functions of the job, and the FMLA (unlike the ADA) does not impose a requirement of reasonable accommodation on employers.

25. *Frizzell v. Southwest Motor Freight*, 154 F.3d 641 (6th Cir. 1998).

26. *Diaz v. Fort Wayne Foundry Corp.*, 131 F.3d 711 (7th Cir. 1997).

27. For a self-insured plan, the ex-employee is charged a "premium" that represents a reasonable estimate, based on reasonable actuarial assumptions, of the cost of providing health coverage for a similarly-situated person.

28. An IRS Notice of Proposed Rulemaking, published at 63 FR 708 (1/7/98), intended to harmonize COBRA with HIPAA and the Small Business Job Protection Act, explains the implications of the extension of coverage to 29 months.

29. *Geissal v. Moore Medical Corp.*, 524 U.S.574 (Sup.Ct. 1998).

30. Note that, under *John Hancock Mutual Life Ins. v. Harris Trust*, 510 U.S. 86 (Sup.Ct. 1993), assets held in an insurer's general account, not guaranteed by the insurer, are plan assets subject to the fiduciary requirements of ERISA.

31. ERISA §3(14) defines a party in interest as fiduciaries, plan employees, plan service providers, their relatives, employers, unions whose members are covered by the plan, employees, officers, and directors of the plan, and other groups.

32. For instance, loans to parties in interest where the plan gives all participants and beneficiaries approximately equal access to loans; paying reasonable compensation to a party in interest for services actually rendered to the plan; buying insurance from an insurance company related to the plan sponsor; investing more than 10% of plan assets in the securities of the employer.

33. *Varity Corp. v. Howe*, 116 S.Ct. 1065 (Sup.Ct. 1996).

34. But see *Mertens v. Hewitt Associates*, 508 U.S. 248 (Sup.Ct. 1993): §502(a)(3) remedies are not available against a non-fiduciary who allegedly knowingly assisted a fiduciary to breach fiduciary duty.

35. The benefits need not be vested, or even of a type subject to vesting, so improprieties relating to welfare benefit rather than pension plans are covered: *Inter-Modal Rail Employees v. Atchison, Topeka & Santa Fe RR*, #96-491, 65 LW 4319 (Sup.Ct. 4/12/97). However, in this context, ERISA preempts state-court suits for wrongful termination, and all claims of benefit-related firing or retaliation must be brought in federal court: *Ingersoll-Rand v. McClendon*, 498 U.S. 133 (Sup.Ct. 1990).

36. *Sutton v. UAL*, 119 S.Ct.2139; *Murphy v. UPS*, 119 S.Ct. 2133; *Albertsons v. Kirkingburg*, 119 S.Ct.2162, all 6/22/99.

37. *McKennon v. Nashville Banner Pub. Co.*, 513 U.S. 352 (Sup.Ct. 1995).

38. *Griggs v. Duke Power Co.*, 401 U.S. 424 (1971).

39. 422 US 407 (Sup.Ct.1975).

40. A former employee is an "employee" entitled to bring a retaliation action: *Robinson v. Shell Oil Co.*, 519 U.S. 337 (Sup.Ct. 1997).

41. Most of the Circuits have already ruled that Title VII liability is limited to employer companies, not individuals. See the cases cited in *Lissau v. Southern Food Service*, 159 F.3d 177 (4th Cir. 1998).

42. The calculation includes everyone on the payroll—including part-time employees: *Walters v. Metropolitan Educational Enterprises*, 519 U.S. 202 (Sup.Ct. 1997).
43. A recent District Court case, *Quinn v. Nassau County Police Department*, #97-3310 (E.D.N.Y. 7/2/99), finds that sexual orientation discrimination creating a hostile work environment is unconstitutional under the Equal Protection clause. See Daniel Wise, "Discrimination Against Gays & Lesbians Violates Constitution," http://www.lawnewsnet.com/stories/A3066-1999Jul2.html.
44. *U.S. v. Burke*, 504 U.S. 229 (Sup.Ct. 1992). This is also true of Age Discrimination in Employment Act damages: *Comm'r of Internal Revenue v. Schleier*, 515 U.S. 323 (Sup.Ct. 1995).
45. *Fadeyi v. Planned Parenthood*, 160 F.3d 1048 (5th Cir. 1998); *Spriggs v. Diamond Auto Glass*, 165 F.3d 1015 (4th Cir. 1999).
46. *Newport News Shipbuilding v. EEOC*, 462 U.S. 669 (Sup.Ct. 1983).
47. This cause of action was first recognized by the Supreme Court in *Meritor Savings Bank v. Vinson*, 477 U.S. 57 (Sup.Ct. 1986).
48. Same-sex harassment cognizable: *Oncale v. Sundown Offshore Services Inc.*, 523 U.S. 45 (Sup.Ct. 1998).
49. *Burlington Industries, Inc. v. Ellerth*, 118 S.Ct. 2365 (Sup.Ct. 1998); *Faragher v. City of Boca Raton*, 118 S.Ct. 2275 (Sup.Ct. 1998).
50. 492 U.S. 158 (Sup.Ct. 1989).
51. *O'Connor v. Consolidated Coin Caterers Corp.*, 517 U.S. 308 (Sup.Ct. 1997).
52. The EEOC's proposed regulations to implement *Oubre* are found at 64 FR 19952 (4/23/99) and http://www.eeoc.gov/regs/tender.html. A Question and Answer sheet about the proposal appears at http://www.eeoc.gov/regs/quanda.html.
53. *Mason v. Stallings*, 82 F.3d 1007 (11th Cir. 1996).
54. Being HIV-positive is a disability because it limits the major life activity of reproduction: *Bragdon v. Abbott*, 524 U.S. 624 (Sup.Ct. 1998).
55. *Sutton v. UAL*, 119 S.Ct. 2139; *Murphy v. UPS*, 119 S.Ct. 2133; *Albertsons v. Kirkingburg* 119 S.Ct. 2162 (6/22/99).
56. Available at http://www.eeoc.gov/docs/accom.html.
57. Mixed motive: *McNely v. Ocala Star-Banner Corp.*, 99 F.3d 1068 (11th Cir. 1996); hostile environment: *Hendler v. Intellicom U.S.A. Inc.*, #95-CV-2490 (E.D.N.Y. 5/97).
58. *Barnett v. U.S. Air*, 157 F.3d 744 (9th Cir. 1998).
59. *Cleveland v. Policy Management Ass'n*, 119 S.Ct. 1597 (Sup.Ct. 5/24/99).
60. 67 LW 4013 (Sup.Ct. 11/16/98).
61. Also see *Albertson's v. United Food & Commercial Workers*, 157 F.3d 758 (9th Cir. 1998): an employment contract between a company and a single worker can require arbitration of FMLA claims, but a CBA covering an entire bargaining unit cannot.
62. See, e.g., *Kidder v. American South Bank*, 639 So.2d 1361 (Ala. 1994); *National Security Insurance Co. v. Donaldson*, 664 So.2d 871 (Ala. 1995);

Choate v. TRW, Inc. 14 F.3d 74 (D.C. Cir. 1994); *Pickell v. Arizona Components Co.*, 1997 Westlaw 27173 (Colo. 1/27/97).

63. 119 S.Ct. 489 (Sup.Ct. 1998).
64. *Fadeyi v. Planned Parenthood*, 160 F.3d 1048 (5th Cir. 1998).

¶400

Business Taxes

Note: When this book went to press, both Houses of Congress had passed H.R. 2488, the Taxpayer Refund and Relief Act of 1999, but the President had indicated his intention to veto it. The bill includes significant reductions in business taxes, so it is likely that even a compromise version will make significant changes favorable to the business community.

[¶401]

Business taxation is divided into two broad categories: taxation of the partnership and its partners (because the partnership is a pass-through[1] entity, the salient issue becomes how much tax the partners will have to pay on account of partnership items), and taxation of the corporation. Both the corporation and its stockholders are subject to taxation.

Although having two sets of books is often a sign of dishonesty, it is quite legitimate to maintain tax records that use different accounting conventions than other business records. To reduce taxes, corporations will probably want to take the largest permissible deductions, as early as possible—yet they will also want to report large and increasing earnings, which suggests taking as few deductions as possible and taking them over a longer period of time.

Also see the discussion of at-risk rules and passive activities at ¶410.7. Although these concepts primarily arise in personal income tax, personal service corporations and some closely held C Corporations are also subject to these rules.

[¶410] Partnership Taxation

Partnership taxation is governed by Subchapter K of the Code. For tax purposes, a partnership is a business entity involving two or more members that chose, or defaulted to, partnership status under the "check-the-box" regulations, and is not compulsorily taxed as a corporation.

Business entities are given broad discretion to determine how they will be taxed (as long as they conform to the minimum requirements for the form they have chosen). Reg. §301.7701-3 allows a newly formed general partnership that has at least two partners to elect to be taxed as either a partnership or a corporation. If no election is made, the entity will be taxed as a partnership.

A limited liability company (LLC) is a state-regulated business entity that, if not required to be taxed as a corporation under those "check the box" regulations, can elect either partnership or corporate taxation. Once again, if there is no election, the LLC will be taxed as a partnership. Whichever tax structure it chooses, its participants will still have limited liability.

129

See ¶110.4 for the distinction between general and limited partners. Prop.Reg. §1.1402(a)-2(h) says a person is a limited partner and not a general partner unless:

- He or she is personally liable for partnership debts or claims against the partnership by reason of being a partner
- State law gives him/her the authority to contract on behalf of the partnership
- He or she spends more than 500 hours per year on the partnership's trade or business.

Prop. Reg. §1.1402(a)-2(h) also governs LLCs. P.L. 105-34 §935, (8/5/97), imposed a moratorium on further Regulations defining "limited partner" under §1402(a)(13). (Section 1402 deals with net earnings from self-employment, a category where allocation of partnership items has obvious relevance.)

A partnership is a pass-through entity for tax purposes: income is taxed at the partner rather than the entity level. Because an S Corporation is also a pass-through entity, many businesses will have to decide which form to operate in. A partnership, unlike an S Corporation, can have any number of partners, with no limitation on their identity. A partnership can make special allocations of profit, loss, and credits among the partners. A partner's basis in his or her partnership interest includes his or her share of partnership liabilities.

Section 6031 requires partnerships to file Form 1065 as an information return reporting gross income and deductions for the tax year. (Filing is not required for any period before the partnership received its first taxable income or had deductible expenses, or any year in which the partnership does not carry on business within the United States and has no U.S.-source income.)

The due date of Form 1065 is the fifteenth day of the fourth month after the close of the partnership's tax year: §6072(a). Each partner (or nominee for a partnership) must receive a copy of Schedule K-1, Form 1065, disclosing that partner's share of partnership items.

Under §§771-777, an "electing large partnership" having at least 100 members can adopt a simplified reporting system, reducing the number of items that must be reported to partners. Most items of income, deduction, credit, and loss can be calculated at the partnership level if this election is made; net amounts are passed through to the partners. Audit requirements for electing large partnerships are also streamlined by §§6240-6255.

For purposes of the Social Security self-employment tax, a general partner is taxed on his or her distributive share of the partnership's income and losses (even if not distributed), plus his or her entitlement to guaranteed payments (i.e., payments for services, or for use of capital, that are not based on partnership income). See Reg. §1.1402(a)-1(a)(2). A limited partner is taxed only on guaranteed payments for services rendered: Prop.Reg. §1.1402(a)-2(d)(g).

A partnership can receive an automatic three-month extension of the time to file the partnership return via Form 8736; the IRS can respond to a request on Form 8800 for a longer, discretionary extension. The fact that a partnership gets an extension does not extend the individual partners' time to file their individual tax returns.

However, to prevent abuse of the partnership form, the §701 "anti-abuse" Regulations give the IRS power for income tax (but not for other taxes) to recast transactions to achieve an "appropriate" result when partnerships are formed or availed of to reduce partners' tax liability in a manner inconsistent with Subchapter K.

[¶410.1] Partnership Tax Year

Unless it makes an election or can satisfy the IRS that there is a business purpose for a different year, §706(b) sets the partnership's tax year as:

- The majority interest tax year (the tax year of one or more of the partners holding an aggregate interest of 50% or more)
- If there is none, the tax year of all of its 5% or more partners (i.e., calendar year if they're natural persons)
- If they don't have the same tax year, the tax year that results in the smallest amount of deferral
- If all else fails, calendar year.

Section 444 permits a partnership to elect a different tax year, as long as it is not abusive. The deferral period of the year elected (i.e., the number of months from the beginning of the elected tax year to the following December 31) cannot exceed three months. The election is made on Form 8716.

[¶410.2] Tax Issues in Creation of a Partnership

A partner's contributions to the partnership are generally tax-free under §721 (no gain or loss recognized to either the partner or the partnership), unless, e.g., the transaction was entered into in an individual capacity, not when acting as a partner; or if the partnership assumes the partner's indebtedness. There is no taxable gain or loss to either the partnership or the partner if appreciated or depreciated property is transferred to a partnership solely in exchange for a partnership interest.

Furthermore, if a partner receives a capital interest in the partnership in exchange for services, the partner has taxable compensation income. If a partner receives an interest in partnership profits in exchange for services, he or she has compensation income only if the stream of income from the partnership assets is substantially certain and predictable (or if the partner disposes of the interest within two years of acquiring it).

The partnership has the same basis in the contributed assets as the contributing partner had, plus any gain the contributing partner had to recognize under §721(b): §723.The partnership's holding period (used to distinguish short-term from long-term items) includes the partner's holding period (§1223(2)).[2]

The basis of a partnership interest acquired by a tax-free contribution of money and/or property is defined by §722 as the total of contributed cash plus the adjusted basis of contributed property. The partner's basis in encumbered property is reduced by the amount of indebtedness that the other partners assume. The basis of a capital interest acquired for services is the value of the capital interest.

Once the partnership is underway, the partner's basis must be adjusted in various ways as prescribed by §§705 and 732(c). Basis is increased, e.g., by further contributions; by an increase in the partner's share of partnership liabilities; and by his or her distributive share of partnership income.

Under §733, the partner's basis is reduced (but not below zero) by any part of the interest that has been sold; by money and property distributed to the partner in a non-liquidating distribution from the partnership[3]; by the partner's distributive share of partnership losses; and by any decrease in his or her share of partnership liabilities.

Within the partnership, entitlement to income (or responsibility for liabilities) may be quite different for different partners. The basic rule of §704 is that the partnership agreement determines the allocation of items among the partners. If there is no partnership agreement, or if a purported agreement lacks substantial economic effect, allocation for tax purposes will follow the comparative size of the partners' interests in the partnership.

Reg. §1.704-1 is a safe harbor for partnership agreements. As long as the agreement allocates distributive shares of partnership items among partners in a way that has substantial economic effect, the IRS will abide by the shares set out in the agreement. But if the safe harbor is not used, or the IRS believes that the agreement fails to satisfy its tests, then §704 gives the IRS the right to allocate items among partners in accordance with their true interests in the partnership.

The safe harbor requires the partnership to establish a capital account for each partner, tracking contributions to and distributions out of capital. Income, deduction, loss, and credit items must in fact be allocated in accordance with the agreement.

[¶410.3] Partnership Tax Management

Unlike an S Corporation, which is taxed on some limited items of income (see ¶460.1), a partnership is a pure conduit. Under §701, only the partners are liable for taxes on partnership income. Partners receive their share of the partnership's income and deductions. The partnership files Form 1065, an information return, disclosing each partner's distributive share of the tax items.

The partners are required to include their distributive shares (including guaranteed payments of salary and interest) of partnership items on their own tax returns. The items are included in the partner's return for his or her tax year in which the partnership's tax year ends (§706; this provision is required because most partners are individuals, who have a calendar tax year, whereas partnerships often have fiscal years). They must treat the tax items consistently with the partnership's treatment of the items. Section 6222(a) obligates them to file Form 8082 to disclose and explain any inconsistent treatment.

Also see §6621, providing that the treatment of partnership items on a partner's individual return can be changed only by unified proceedings at the partnership level. Additions to tax and penalties are also determined at the partnership level.

"Guaranteed payments" (see §707(c)) are made to partners who have contributed services or capital. The payments are made without regard to partnership income—for instance, a payment defined as 10% of profits does not satisfy the definition of guaranteed payment. Guaranteed payments are taxed to the partner as salary or interest payments, not as partnership distributions. The partnership can deduct the payments (in arriving at partners' distributive shares) only if the payment would be deductible if made to a non-partner employee or lender.

When the partnership is operating at a loss, a partner's deduction for partnership losses cannot exceed his or her basis in the partnership interest: §704(d). Depending on the nature of the partnership's business and the individual partner's role within it, a partner's loss may also be limited by the at-risk and passive activity rules (see ¶410.7).

Section 707(b)(1) disallows a loss deduction on sales or exchanges involving a partnership and the owner of a 50% or greater interest in its capital or profits, and between two partnerships in which the same persons own 50% or more of the capital or profit interests. However, if the transferee of the partnership property later re-sells the same property at a gain, the gain is taxed only to the extent that it exceeds the previously disallowed loss.

Under §731(b), the partnership (subject to certain exceptions under §736 and 751) has neither gain nor loss on either ordinary or liquidating distributions to partners. Section 731(a)(1) requires the partner to recognize gain only if the distribution exceeds the partner's adjusted basis in the partnership interest. The partner recognizes loss under §731(a)(2) if his or her adjusted basis exceeds the money, receivables, and inventory received in a liquidation of the partner's interest in the partnership.

[¶410.3] Tax Matters Partner

Every partnership must have a Tax Matters Partner (TMP): see Code §6231(a)(7). The partnership can designate any of its general partners to act as TMP. If the partnership fails to make a designation, the general partner with the largest profits interest automatically becomes the TMP; if two general partners hold equal interests, the one whose name comes first in alphabetical order becomes the TMP.

If, for some reason, that selection procedure is impractical, the IRS has statutory authority to designate any partner (even one who does not become a general partner until after the designation) for this role. Before the IRS makes a designation, however, it will notify the partnership, giving it 30 days to make its own selection of TMP.

Instead of dealing with all of the partners, the IRS deals primarily with the TMP, who represents the other partners and the partnership. IRS notices and orders are sent to the TMP, and the TMP represents the partnership at audits and in litigation. The TMP has the power to petition the Tax Court to readjust partnership items determined by the IRS: §6226.

Code §6223(g) gives the TMP the duty of informing the other partners of the progress of tax negotiations, hearings, and litigation. Any partner has the right, under §6224, to participate in IRS administrative proceedings that determine the tax treatment of items at the partnership level, because the partner's own tax position could be affected.

[¶410.4] Taxation of Disposition of Partnership Interests

The partner's basis computation is also affected by §732, which sets the basis of property received in liquidation of a partnership interest at the partner's adjusted basis for the interest minus funds distributed in the same transaction, with adjustments prescribed in §732(a) and (c)-(e). Section 733 provides that a partner's adjusted basis in the partnership interest is reduced by the value of distributed money and property, but not below $0.

For property that is not received in a liquidation, the basis is carried over from the partnership's basis in the same property, but cannot exceed the partner's adjusted basis in the interest minus cash received in the transaction. TRA '97 sets the rules for allocating basis adjustment in assets distributed to the partner.

When a partner sells a partnership interest, or the interest is liquidated, the partner's gain or loss is usually capital, because §741 treats the transaction as a capital transaction rather than a sale of a proportionate interest in each of the partnership assets. Reference should be made, however, to §751, which may require some of the gain or loss to be treated as ordinary in nature (if, for instance, it derives from the partnership's unrealized receivables or inventory[4]).

In general, sale of the partnership interest has no effect on the partnership's tax position, but it can elect under §754 to step up its basis in the relevant assets to reflect the gain recognized by the selling partner.

If all the partners sell their shares, the status of the transaction as either a sale of assets or a sale of partnership interests depends on whether mere assets were sold, or whether the partnership itself was sold as a going business.

[¶410.4.1] Payments to Retiring Partners

The first question is how much of the payment received represents payment for capital assets, and how much represents the retiring partner's share of partnership income.

Payments received on liquidation of an interest (e.g., when a partner retires, or payments to the estate of a deceased partner) are treated as guaranteed payments or income distributions to the extent that they exceed the value of the partner's interest in the partnership property.

When payments are made to a retiring partner, or to the estate of a deceased partner, each element of the payment must be analyzed to determine whether it is capital gain or ordinary income. The characterization depends on whether it can be traced to a share of the fair market value of partnership assets; an interest in unrealized receivables; or under an agreement with the other partners that has the same effect as an insurance policy.

Under §736, distributions for interests in partnership property are taxed as if they had been made by an ongoing partnership, and therefore will be capital gains unless they are disproportionate distributions or distributions deriving from substantially appreciated inventory. Distributions not made for interests in partnership property are taxed either as distributive shares of partnership income, or as guaranteed payments.

[¶410.5] Tax Consequences of Termination

For partnership tax years beginning after 1997, §706(c)(2) provides that the partnership's tax year is closed with respect to any partner when the partner's entire interest in the partnership terminates: e.g., he or she dies, retires, or transfers his or her entire partnership interest. Partnership items for that short tax year go into the partner's final income tax return.

For tax purposes, a partnership generally will not terminate until its operations discontinue (i.e., no part of its operation is carried on by any partner), or until 50% or more of the total interests in the partnership are sold or exchanged within a 12-month period. As ¶110.2 shows, local law may force the termination of a partnership whenever any partner departs (the partnership or this life), so once again tax treatment differs from substantive regulation of business.

[¶410.6] Family Partnerships

The family partnership is sometimes used as a financial management and estate planning device, to coordinate lifetime and post-death shifts in asset ownership within the family.

Code §704(e) provides that if capital is not a material income-producing factor for the partnership, a family member will be recognized as a partner only if he or she contributes substantial services to the partnership. However, if capital is a material income-producing factor, then intrafamily gifts of capital interests are permissible. A minor can be a partner in a family partnership on two conditions: if the child has a guardian; or if the child, although legally a minor, is in fact competent to manage property.

[¶410.7] Publicly Traded Partnerships

As a general rule, partnership interests are not very liquid, because of the risk of unlimited liability and the lack of perpetual continuity. However, there are some instances in which partnership interests, especially limited partnership interests, are offered to the public. Code §7704 provides that a publicly-traded partnership (including one described as a master limited partnership) will be taxed as a corporation, notwithstanding its description as a partnership, unless at least 90% of its gross income derives from qualifying passive-type income. Qualifying income includes, e.g, interest; dividends; rent; and gain from the disposition of real property: §7704(d).

[¶410.8] Special Rules for Real Estate Partnerships

It is common for real estate to be owned and operated by multi-level partnerships, with a few general partners and a larger number of investor limited partners. Under prior law, real estate investment often operated as a tax shelter. However, current law combines a small number of comparatively low tax brackets with crack-down efforts on perceived abusive tax shelters.

Under the §465 "at-risk" rules, a taxpayer's loss deduction in connection with an investment is limited to the amount at risk in the transaction. Therefore, for instance, it is no longer possible to claim losses on property purchased with non-recourse obligations. The at-risk rules apply to most business activities that are not carried on by widely-held corporations, so obviously they are of concern in calculating partners' taxes, and especially those of limited partners. (Losses that cannot be currently deducted because of the at-risk rules can be carried over to other tax years, so the deduction is not necessarily entirely lost.)

The maximum loss that a partner can deduct is either the partner's basis or the amount the partner has at risk in partnership activities, whichever is lower. However, certain nonrecourse financing in real estate transactions will not be subject to the at-risk rule.

Individuals (including partners), personal service corporations, and closely held C corporations are subject to the "passive loss" limitations of §469. Taxpayers who do not "materially participate" in the business activity can only use net losses and credits from passive activities to offset income from other passive activities. The losses and credits cannot be claimed against salary or portfolio income.

An exception is made for individuals who actively participate in real estate activities and whose gross income does not exceed $150,000. Certain rental real estate losses can be used to reduce nonpassive income, notwithstanding the basic §469 rule. When the individual's entire interest in the passive activity is disposed of in a fully taxable transaction, any unused passive losses can be used to offset either passive or nonpassive income.

In this context, material participation means regular, continuous and substantial involvement in the activity, so limited partners don't qualify.

[¶450] Corporate Tax

[¶450.1] Tax Rates

Certain businesses operated in forms similar to corporations, and even certain corporations, are not subject to corporate tax at all. Limited liability companies (¶125) are taxed as partnerships (see above for issues of partnership taxation). Subchapter S corporations are also "pass-through" entities that are not taxed at the corporate level. Subchapter C corporations ("C corporations"), however, are subject to corporate tax.

"Qualified personal service corporations" as defined by §448(d)(2) are required by §11(b)(2) to pay a flat rate of 35% of their taxable income. A personal service corporation, (PSC) is a C Corporation whose principal activity is the rendition of personal services (such as performing arts, law, health care, and consulting) which are substantially performed by one or more employee-owners. Such personal services are the corporation's principal activity if more than 50% of the company's payroll is allocable to the personal services. The services are substantially performed by stockholder-employees if 20% or more of the compensation cost for personal services is attributable to them.[5]

Other domestic corporations are taxed at graduated rates. Theoretically, there are only four corporate brackets, but the effect of "surtax" is to create additional brackets for practical purposes. Corporate tax rates are:

15% of the first $50,000 of taxable income
$7500 + 25% of TI between $50,000 and $75,000
$13,750 + 34% of TI $75,000-$100,000
$22,250 + 39% of TI $100,000-$335,000
$113,900 + 34% of TI $335,000-$10,000,000
$3,400,000 + 35% of TI $10,000,000-$15,000,000
$5,150,000 + 38% of TI $15,000,000-$18,333,333
35% on any additional TI.

Corporate capital gains, unlike the capital gains of individuals, are not taxed at preferential rates. However, the capital/ordinary asset distinction remains meaningful to corporations, because corporate capital losses are deductible only to the extent of capital gains, and §§1211(a) and 1212(a) allow some carry-forwards and carry-backs.

[¶450.2] Corporate Tax Compliance

The basic corporate income tax return is Form 1120. The short-form 1120A can be filed by a corporation whose ownership is concentrated and whose gross receipts, total income, and total assets are all under $500,000. Personal holding companies must file Schedule PH with their returns, and Subchapter S corporations file an information return (because they are not generally separate taxpayers) on Form 1120S. The Sub S corporation must show actual and constructive distributions to the shareholder on the 1120S, and must disclose this information to the shareholders on or before the filing date of the 1120S. Corporate returns must be signed by an authorized officer, such as President, treasurer, or controller.

The due date for a Form 1120 or 1120A is March 15 for calendar-year corporations, or the fifteenth day of the third month after the end of a fiscal-year corporation's tax year. The tax must be paid in full by the original due date for the return: §6151(a). A corporation that expects a net operating loss (NOL) in the current year can file Form 1138 (see §6164) to get an extension on filing the preceding year's tax return, so that the current-year NOL can be carried back without needing to file a return followed by an amended return.

Form 7004 provides an automatic extension of six months of any corporation's time to file its income tax return, but this form does not extend the time to pay. An extension of time to pay the tax of up to six months can be granted to corporations that file Form 1127 and demonstrate undue hardship if forced to pay the tax on time. See §6161(a). Form 1127 must be filed no later than the due date of the return. Unlike income taxes, employment taxes must be filed on time. The IRS will not grant an extension: Reg. §31.6162(a)(1)-1.

Transition is underway from a paper-based to an electronic filing system, but it has been a bumpy road. Several extensions have been granted for smaller corporations to start electronic payments. A Proposed Rule, 64 FR 13940 (3/23/99) suggests raising the threshold for mandatory electronic payment from $50,000 to $200,000 as of January 1, 2000. Most small businesses would be relieved of penalties for filing on paper instead of electronically, as long as they make timely filings.

Corporations that do not file electronically must mail their tax payments at least two days before the due date, with the Form 8109 deposit coupon attached. The payment must be remitted to a Federal Reserve Bank or IRS-authorized commercial bank.

Corporations must file tax returns even in years in which they have no taxable income (§6012(a)(2)), and §6020 empowers the IRS to file a required return for a corporation that was required to, but failed to do so. However, a shell corporation that has a charter but no business activity can be excused from filing, under Reg. §1.6012-2(a)(2), if it submits a statement to the local District Director to the effect that it has not yet perfected its organization; does not transact business; and has received no income from any source.

Even after a corporation terminates its business and dissolves, retaining no assets, it must make a return for the part of the year it was still in existence. This return is due on the fifteenth day of the third month after the dissolution and liquidation. If any cash at all is retained, returns are due until all the cash has been distributed.

[¶450.2.1] Corporate Estimated Tax

The general rule is that the corporation must pay 100% of the current year's tax (ordinary income tax plus AMT, minus allowable credits) in its four estimated tax installments. However, certain corporations (including small businesses with taxable income under $1 million a year) can escape penalty if their estimated tax payments equal at least 100% of the previous year's tax liability: §6655.

Form 8109 is used for corporate estimated tax payments. Installments are due on the fifteenth day of the fourth, sixth, ninth, and twelfth month of the corporation's fiscal year. The general rule is that each installment must be accompanied by at least 25% of the income tax liability for the year. However, §6655 allows the corporation to take advantage of rules for "annualized income installments" or "adjusted seasonal installments," which permit eligible taxpayers to lower their estimated tax payments somewhat.

Corporate as well as individual taxpayers use Form 2220 to calculate and remit the underpayment penalty. The §6655 penalty is waived if a corporate taxpayer owes less than $500, or if the failure to pay one or more required installments was the result of a Chapter 11 filing.

If the estimated tax payments exceed the actual tax liability for the year, the corporation can file on Form 4466 for an expedited (not over 45 days) refund, as long as the overpayment is not only at least $500 but also at least 10% of the tax for the year. The appropriate time to file the form, as prescribed by §6425, is after the tax year has ended but before the 16th day of the third month after the end of the year; in any case, before the tax return for the year has been filed. However, if the corporation claims an excessive refund, interest (at the rate the IRS charges for underpayments) on the excessive refund is treated as an addition to tax.

[¶450.2.2] AMT

The Alternative Minimum Tax is imposed by §55 to prevent taxpayers entitled to significant deductions and credits from escaping federal taxation altogether. Taxable corporations, individuals, and complex trusts are subject to AMT, but partnerships, S Corporations, and grantor trusts are not. The corporate AMT rate set by §55(b)(1)(B) is 20% of a tax base including various adjustments and preference items excluded from the calculation of ordinary corporate taxes. The calculation involves Adjusted Current Earnings, a concept related to the accounting concept of Earnings & Profits (E&P).

The Taxpayer Relief Act of 1997 and technical corrections added by the Internal Revenue Service Restructuring & Reform Act of 1998 amend §55(e): small corporations are exempt from AMT for tax years beginning after 1997. For this purpose, a small corporation is one that has gross receipts under $5 million for each of three years beginning after 12/31/93, and ending before tax year for which AMT exemption is sought.

Once small corporation status is established, the corporation remains AMT-exempt as long as its average gross receipts for the three years prior to the current tax year do not exceed $7.5 million. Furthermore, all corporations are generally treated as AMT-exempt for their first year of existence, no matter what their receipts are.

A non-exempt corporation may nevertheless be free from AMT, based on the §55(d)(2) exemption of $40,000.

Although individuals pay either the regular tax or the AMT, whichever is greater, corporations that are subject to the AMT must pay both the regular tax and any AMT they are subject to. However, in the tax year after a year in which AMT was payable, the corporate taxpayer is entitled to a "minimum tax credit" (§53) against regular tax. Form 8827 is used to claim the credit.

[¶450.2.3] Tax Year

The general rule of §441 is that a taxpayer's tax year is the year (calendar or fiscal) on which it keeps its books. Taxpayers that do not keep books, or that do not have an annual accounting period, or whose annual accounting period does not qualify as a fiscal year, must have a calendar tax year. (A fiscal year is a 12-month period that ends on the last day of any month other than December.) Other taxpayers can choose between a calendar and a fiscal year; IRS permission is not needed to adopt any year that is permissible. The taxpayer must adopt its first tax year on or before the date for filing the return for that year, including any extensions obtained.

Unless it makes an election (e.g., to retain the business year in effect before the corporation became an S Corporation), an S Corporation must have a "permitted year." The permitted year is defined by §1378 as either a calendar year or an accounting year adopted for business purposes acceptable to the IRS.

Section 441 provides that a personal service corporation also must have a calendar year unless it makes a fiscal year election[6] or proves the business purpose of the fiscal year to the IRS. Under §444, the election cannot result in a deferral of more than three months.

Once an accounting period has been adopted, §442 and its Regulations allow certain changes to be made automatically, without approval by the IRS. All other changes do require advance approval from the IRS, which is solicited by filing Form 1128. The IRS will grant the request only if the taxpayer not only shows a substantial business purpose for the change, but agrees to meet any terms and conditions mandated by the IRS to prevent substantial distortion of the taxpayer's income. Furthermore, under §442, once a change in accounting period is approved, the IRS will not approve another request for a change until ten years have elapsed.

[¶450.2.4] Taxpayer's Accounting Method

The accounting method that the taxpayer adopts determines, for instance, the amount of income, gain, loss, deduction, or credit that the taxpayer claims, and when it realizes or recognizes income and other items. Various methods and hybrids are permissible, in various circumstances, but the principle of the Code is that whatever method is chosen must clearly reflect the taxpayer's income and must be used consistently. The major Code sections governing accounting methods are §§446 and 448.

The two major accounting methods are cash and accrual. A taxpayer that does not have inventory (e.g., a PSC) must always use the cash method. However, businesses for which the production, purchase, and/or sale of merchandise is an income-producing factor (obviously, a category that includes most businesses) must use the accrual method unless the IRS permits a change in accounting method.

Furthermore, a C Corporation that is not a PSC, or a partnership that has a C Corporation as a partner, is not permitted to use the cash method (even if it would otherwise be allowed) if its annual gross receipts for the past three years averaged more than $5 million. (For entities that have not yet been in existence for three years, the entire period of existence is the measuring factor.)[7] See §448(b)(3), (c)(1).

Cash-method taxpayers include in gross income all cash or property actually or constructively received during the tax year. (Most cash-method taxpayers will also have a calendar year, although it is not absolutely impossible for a cash-method taxpayer to have a fiscal year.)

An item of income is constructively received if receiving or deferring the item is wholly within the taxpayer's control, and is subject to the taxpayer's unconditional demand for payment. Cash-method taxpayers take deductions in the year money and/or property is paid or transferred. Under the cash method, it is irrelevant when income is actually earned or expenses are actually incurred.

In contrast, under the accrual method, income is reported in the year the **right** to receive the income becomes fixed: all the events entitling the taxpayer to receive the income have occurred, and the amount of the income can be determined with reasonable accuracy. By the same token, a deduction is permitted when all events creating the taxpayer's obligation to pay a reasonably determinable amount have occurred.

If the taxpayer knows from experience that payment will not be received for certain services, §448(d)(5) permits the taxpayer not to accrue such income, unless the taxpayer imposes a late payment penalty or interest in conjunction with those services. An accrual-method taxpayer can deduct all properly accrued expenses, whether or not the expense has actually been paid.

When the right to receive income is contingent, the taxpayer doesn't have to accrue the income until the event occurs. Income must be recognized when the taxpayer is the plaintiff in a suit; the defendant concedes liability; and the taxpayer can accurately estimate the recovery. On the other hand, if the defendant does not concede liability, income accrues when the litigation concludes or is settled.

Generally speaking, an accrual-basis taxpayer who is paid in advance for services to be performed later must report the income in the year it is received (irrespective of the time of performance of the services). However, the taxpayer can elect (using Form 3115[8]) to defer the income over the period for performing the services, if the agreement with the recipient of the services calls for completion by the end of the following year. But if the agreement does not stipulate the schedule for performance, or if services can be performed more than one year after the year of initial payment, deferral is not permissible.

[¶450.2.5] Inventory Valuation

Inventory is usually valued by one of two methods: either its cost, or the cost of the market value of the item, whichever is lower (§471). Section 471 requires taxpayers to use the method prescribed by the Secretary of the Treasury as the clearest reflection of income, and which satisfies the best accounting practices of the relevant trade or business. The "lower of cost or market" calculation is performed for each item; the taxpayer is not permitted to compare the total cost of all inventory items to their aggregate value. Once an inventory method is adopted, the taxpayer must maintain consistency.

The cost of goods on hand at the start of the accounting period must be equal to their value in the closing inventory for the previous accounting period. The cost of purchased goods is their invoice price, minus any trade or other discounts, but plus shipping and other charges necessary for the buyer to take possession of the goods.

For a taxpayer who produces goods, cost equals the opening inventory plus the cost of supplies and raw materials used in the manufacturing process; direct labor costs (both regular and overtime); and certain indirect costs.

If inventory is actually unsaleable, as a result of, e.g., damage, imperfection, or changes in style (and is not merely slow-moving), the taxpayer can "write it down" for tax purposes: value it at its selling price minus the direct costs of disposition.

The normal state of inventory is constant fluctuation, as some items are sold or used in manufacturing, and others are acquired. Therefore, it is necessary for the taxpayer to adopt a method of tracking inventory items. The basic method is FIFO (First In, First Out): the assumption is that items are disposed of in the order they were purchased. In many instances, that means that lower-priced items are deemed to have been used first, with more potential taxable income for the taxpayer.

Certain taxpayers can elect the §472 LIFO (Last In, First Out[9]) method by filing Form 970 with the return for the tax year in which this method is initially adopted. Once made, the LIFO election applies to all subsequent years unless the IRS authorizes a change back (§472(e)).

LIFO taxpayers assume that their most recently purchased or produced items are the first to be sold. The general rule of §472(b) is that the LIFO election is available only to taxpayers who value their inventory at cost (not the lower of cost or market). Under §472(c), taxpayers who use LIFO for tax purposes are also obligated to use the system for credit purposes and in reports issued to partners and stockholders. (In other words, if the business insists on using a system that depresses its taxable income, it must equally depress the results reported to stockholders and analysts.)

[¶450.3] Employment Tax Withholding

Companies must withhold income taxes from the "wages" paid to "employees" (§§3401, 3402). In many instances, companies will wish to avoid the compliance burden—and the individuals performing services will prefer to be treated as independent contractors whose compensation is not subject to withholding.

The issue is even more salient when it comes to FICA (Social Security) taxes because employer and employee are each required to pay 7.2% percent of employee compensation up to $72,600, plus a Medicare tax of 1.45% each on all compensation. Independent contractors are responsible for 100% of the FICA tax.

However, it is not a matter of private contract whether or not a person who performs services is an employee or an independent contractor. The basic test is whether the payor for the services controls both what is done and how the work is to be done. The IRS rules include a "20-factor test" (see ¶330.1). Some of these factors imply that the person performing the services is an employee (whether the payor sets working hours; whether the payor trains the person providing the services); others imply that the person performing the services is an independent contractor (e.g., his or her services are made available to the public; his or her investment in office space, equipment, advertising).

Employee status also has other implications: see, e.g., ¶340 for the determination of who is entitled to coverage under a company's pension and fringe benefit plans. Whether a pension or welfare benefit plan is discriminatory depends on the number and percentage of "employees" it covers. Coverage under various anti-discrimination laws (¶350) is also pegged to the number of "employees," so mis-characterization of employees as independent contractors can have unintended consequences outside the tax arena.

For individuals who are, indeed, employees, the employer performs income tax withholding on the gross wage, before FICA, pensions, union dues, and other items are deducted. The Code, at §3402(b) and (c), authorizes two methods of calculating the amount to be withheld: the wage bracket method, under which the employer refers to officially published tables; and the percentage method, involving separate computations.

Code §3405(c) imposes a requirement of 20% withholding on distributions from pension plans that are eligible to be rolled over (to another qualified plan or to an IRA) but which are not, in fact, rolled over. Required distributions under §401(a)(9) (generally, distributions to owner-employees who have reached age 70 1/2 but have not yet retired) are exempt from this requirement. So are annuity payments and other periodic payments made for life; for the joint life of the employee and designated beneficiary; or for a term of years lasting at least 10 years. Even if the employee is theoretically subject to the 20% withholding requirement, he or she can opt out by filing Form W-4P.

Section 3405(a) also requires withholding on periodic payments, based on the number of withholding exemptions claimed on Form W-4. If there is no W-4 on file, withholding is done as if the employee were married with three exemptions. 10% withholding is required on non-periodic distributions (e.g., lump sums) unless the employee files a W-4P to prevent withholding. Form 945 is used by the employer to report the total of its withholding on all nonpayroll amounts. Form 945 is due on January 31 of the year after the year of the payments, or on February 10 if all amounts were deposited in a timely fashion: §31.6071(a)-1(a)(1).

At the time of hiring, new employees are supposed to fill out a W-4 withholding analysis certificate, indicating the number of withholding exemptions (reflecting the number of the employee's dependents and other factors, such as holding another job, that affect withholding): §3402.

Employees are exempt from withholding if they had no income tax liability in the previous tax year, and certify on the W-4 that they do not expect any tax liability this year (e.g., low-wage casual workers; workers entitled to Earned Income, child tax, and other credits that wipe out tax liability). The employer is required to file Form 941, a quarterly statement reflecting withholding performed in the quarter just ended. Due dates for the 941 are April 30, July 31, October 31, and January 31. It's permissible for the employer to file the 941 up to 10 days later, as long as the taxes were deposited on a timely basis. Depending on the amount of employment taxes incurred in the previous year , Reg. §31.6032-1(a) requires the employer to make either monthly or semi-weekly tax deposits. Furthermore, if the employer fails to collect, account for, or deposit income or employment taxes, §7512 gives the IRS the power to order the employer to make its deposits to a special trust account.

In addition to its reporting obligations to the IRS, the employer has obligations to its employees. It must furnish the employees with the appropriate number of copies of the W-2 form (depending on whether the employees are subject to local as well as federal and state income tax) no later than January 31 following the year in which the wages were paid.

See ¶450.2 for a discussion of electronic filing of tax reports and electronic paying of tax liabilities.

[¶451] Income Items

The corporation's potentially taxable income is made up of a number of items, each of which can generate its own problems of interpretation.

[¶451.1] Corporate E&P and Dividends

A corporation must calculate its earnings and profits (E&P) both for rendering accounting reports and in preparing its tax returns. However, the E&P calculation will not necessarily be the same for both purposes.

The general rule of §316 is that a distribution made by a corporation to its shareholders is a dividend, and will be taxable to the shareholders. However, this is true only if the distribution comes from current or accumulated E&P. Taxpayers include amounts they receive as dividends (as defined by §316) in their gross income. Other distributions are applied to reduce the taxpayer's adjusted basis in the stock, and any non-dividend distributions over and above the taxpayer's basis are taxed as capital gains. See §312 for the effect of distributions of various kinds of property (e.g., appreciated; encumbered) on the corporation's E&P.[10]

[¶451.2] Installment Sales and Long-Term Contracts

A taxpayer who is not actually a dealer in the type of property involved, who sells property under an agreement calling for at least one payment in a year after the year of sale, generally reports gain (but not loss) from the transaction under §453's installment sale rules. (Installment sale characterization applies unless the taxpayer opts out (§453(d)); but this method cannot be used for sales of securities traded on an established market.)

Under the installment method, the taxpayer reports the gain element of each payment as it is received, rather than "bunching up" all the gain on the transaction in the year of the sale. The gain for each year, as reported on Form 6252, consists of the installment payments received in that year, times the gross profit ratio. The gross profit ratio equals the gross profit already or to be realized, divided by the total contract price.

A related concept, the long-term contract, is governed by §460. The basic rule for a contract for manufacture, building, installation or construction of property that is not completed in the tax year in which the contract was entered into is that the "percentage of completion" method is used to report income. (The actual time to completion, not whether the taxpayer reasonably expected completion within one tax year, is determinative.)

In practice, the percentage of completion method is used most often for construction contracts, because §460(f)(2) provides that the method is used for manufacturing contracts only if the item to be manufactured is unique (not of a type normally included in the taxpayer's inventory) or fabrication normally takes more than 12 months.

Contracts for construction of personal residences do not have to use the percentage of completion method: see §460(c)(5),(6). Nor is this method required for fairly short contracts (an original estimate of completion within two years of the contract date) of small contractors (average annual receipts for the past three years not more than $10 million; §460(e)(2)(B)).

If, however, the percentage of completion method is required, the taxpayer's gross income for a particular tax year includes the total expected revenue from the contract times the cumulative percentage completed by the end of the tax year, minus cumulative contract revenue already included in prior tax years. The percentage of completion is determined by the ratio between costs allocated to the contract and incurred in the current tax year and estimated total contract costs. (A deductible loss could occur in a year in which the estimated contract costs increase.)

The taxpayer can also elect a modified percentage of completion method. The taxpayer can elect not to recognize income under the contract, and not to take into account any costs allocable to the contract in any tax year in which less than 10% of the estimated total costs are incurred.

[¶451.3] Damages

The general rule (also applicable to individual tax returns) is that punitive damages are taxable income for the recipient. A business has ordinary income from damages or settlements for claims of injury to the business that causes lost profits. Amounts received from business interruption insurance also constitute taxable income.

[¶452] Business Deductions

Once a corporation's income is computed, it becomes necessary to determine what deductions are permissible, and in what tax year.

The key section here is §162, which permits a deduction of a business' "ordinary and necessary" expenses. This category includes reasonable compensation paid to employees, but not bribes or other illegal payments, costs of influencing legislation, or excessive remuneration to employees.

[¶452.1] Start-Up Expenses

As a general rule, a newly organized corporation cannot deduct its costs of organization, such as legal fees and state-imposed registration charges. Sections 248 permits the corporation to treat organization expenses as deferred expenses, deducted over a period of at least 60 months from the start of operations.

Code §195 allows a newly organized corporation to make an election, on Form 4562, to deduct "start-up expenses" for tax purposes (even if the expenses have to be capitalized for accounting purposes). The deduction is taken over a period of 60 or more months, beginning in the first month of active business. The deductions that qualify include consultants, advertising, hiring and training employees, and other costs that must be incurred before the company is open for business. The very substantial costs of issuing stock do not qualify. (If the business doesn't make the election, it must capitalize the expenses and can't amortize them, much less deduct them currently.)

The difference between the two sections is that organizational expenses create the corporation itself; start-up expenses are expenses that make it possible for the corporation to produce its product or services, and thus open for business.

[¶452.2] Compensation Deductions

The basic rule is that a corporation can deduct reasonable compensation (including pensions and benefits and severance pay) for personal services actually rendered to the business. However, a public corporation is not permitted to deduct more than $1 million a year for its CEO and its four other highest-paid officers: §162(m). It's not illegal to make higher payments; the excess merely becomes non-deductible by the corporation.

Nor are "excess parachute payments" deductible. A parachute payment is a guarantee to top executives (defined as the business owner, officer, shareholders, and highly compensated employees) that they will not suffer financially if they lose their jobs in a corporate takeover. An excess parachute payment is defined as a payment, contingent on change in corporate ownership, that is more than three times the "base amount." The base amount is roughly equivalent to the parachute recipient's average gross income for the preceding five years. Again, deductibility, not legality, is at issue. See §280G.

An employer can deduct contributions made to a welfare benefit fund (a plan providing non-pension employee benefits such as a health plan), but not in excess of the qualified cost of the welfare benefit plan: §419. Reg. §1.162-10(a) defines some of the deductible welfare benefit costs.

The general rule is that the employer is not entitled to a compensation deduction for stock transferred under a statutory stock option or ESOP plan, unless the employee disposes of the stock prematurely and recognizes income: §421.

Under Reg. §1.162-7(b)(1), amounts claimed as compensation might be recharacterized by the IRS as dividends (i.e., taxable to the recipient, but not deductible by the corporation) if they are proportionate to the recipient's stockholdings, and appear suspicious because they do not reflect the reasonable value of the services performed by the recipient.

[¶452.3] Rentals and Related Expenses

Rent on property used in trade, business, professionals, or production of income is deductible under §162(a)(3), but personal-use rent is not deductible. However, renting property from related parties (e.g., family members or stockholders) will be scrutinized. Any excessive portion of the rent will not be deductible, and may be treated as a dividend.

The cost of acquiring a lease is not deductible; Reg. §1.162-11(a) requires it to be amortized over the unexpired period of the lease. The lessor's costs of leasing property (as well as a lessee's costs of subleasing property) are also amortized, ratably over the term of the lease.

It is often important to distinguish between rent (of property that the renter does NOT intend to buy) and a conditional sales contract. Payments under the conditional sales contract are not deductible as rent (although it may be possible to capitalize them based on the useful life of the property). Whether a lease with option to buy is a sale depends on factors such as the amount required to purchase the property after the lease term; and whether "rent" payments are applied to create equity. Problems of characterization may also arise under a sale-leaseback arrangement (A sells a property to B, but A continues to occupy the property, paying rent to B).

[¶452.4] Net Operating Loss (NOL) Deductions

If a corporation's deductions (calculated for this purpose with certain modifications from ordinary tax principles) exceed its gross income for the year, the corporation has a Net Operating Loss (NOL) as governed by §172. The corporation has a choice of how to treat this loss for tax purposes. It can be carried back to past years (thus resulting in a tax refund) or forward (to reduce the tax for future years).

The general rule of §172(b)(1), instituted by TRA '97, is that NOLs can be carried back for two years, forward for 20. (The pre-TRA rules, effective for tax years beginning before 8/6/97, called for carrying NOLs back three years, forward for 15.) However, a farming corporation, or a small business with average gross receipts under $5 million a year, can carry its casualty, theft, and disaster losses back for three years even post-TRA '97: §172(b)(1)(F). Under special §172(f) provisions, product liability losses can be carried back ten years or forward 20 years.

The taxpayer can also make an irrevocable election, under §172(b)(3), to carry all NOLs forward and waive all carrybacks.

[¶452.5] R&E Expenditures

A taxpayer can deduct (i.e., treat as expenses not chargeable to the capital account) research and experimental expenditures currently. However, a corporation that takes a current deduction must do so for all R&E expenditures not only of that year but of later years unless the IRS permits a change. Section 59(c)(1) gives all taxpayers (including partners and S Corporation shareholders) the option to deduct all or part of their R&E spending ratably over ten years.

Otherwise, R&E spending that is not chargeable to depreciable or depletable property can either be deducted currently, capitalized, or elected on Form 4562 as deferred expenses. Form 4562 expenditures are taken ratably over a period that does not exceed 60 months: §174(b). This is a likely area for Congress to grant tax relief.

[¶452.6] Corporate Charitable Deduction

Section 170(b)(2) allows a corporation to deduct up to 10% of its taxable income (measured without regard to charitable contributions, dividends received, and carrybacks for Net Operating Losses and capital losses) each year for contributions made to one or more charitable organizations recognized by the IRS as qualified to receive deductible contributions. Contributions are not necessarily deductible just because they are made to an organization that is tax-exempt as to its own income. Contributions in excess of the limit can be carried forward for five years under §170(d)(2).

Code §170(e) contains special, more generous rules for C Corporation do-nations of materials used for the ill, needy, or for infants (e.g., a drug company con-tributes inventory); contributions of computer equipment to schools (this provision is scheduled to expire in 2000); or scientific property donated to an institution of higher education or a tax-exempt organization.

[¶452.7] Other Corporate Deductions

The treatment of business bad debts under §166 is somewhat different from the treatment of non-business bad debts. A business can deduct debts that are par-tially or wholly worthless, and it is an ordinary rather than a capital loss. The de-duction is taken in the year the debt becomes worthless. To be deductible, a partially worthless debt must be only partially recoverable; it must not be evidenced by a security; and it must be charged off on the corporate books during the tax year.

A corporation's legal expenses are currently deductible unless they are cap-ital expenditures, or expenses of acquiring, perfecting, or defending title to prop-erty: Reg. §1.212-1(k).

Insurance premiums that constitute business expenses are probably de-ductible. Insuring business property is a deductible expense. However, if a cor-poration chooses to self-insure (i.e., maintain reserves for possible future payments) instead of buying insurance, the reserves are not deductible.

Life insurance on the lives of employees that is an employee benefit (see ¶346.2) is generally deductible. However, if the corporate taxpayer itself is the beneficiary (e.g., key-man insurance on the corporation's top officers), the pre-miums are not deductible.

Penalties or fines imposed for violating a law (including the tax laws) are non-deductible: §162(f). But in the case of civil litigation rather than criminal charges, judgments or settlements that the taxpayer has to pay that are directly connected with the taxpayer's business are deductible.

[¶453] Treatment of Capital Expenditures

Unlike a current expense, which relates only to the current year of corporate op-erations, a capital expenditure has anticipated benefits that last more than one year. Capital expenses can be expenses of building, buying, improving, adding value, or extending the useful life of corporate property.

Although in some instances an entire capital expenditure can be "expensed" (deducted in a single year as permitted by §179), the basic rule of §263 is that capital expenditures will have to be "recovered" over time (i.e., amortized, de-preciated, or depleted over a period of years)—even if in fact the corporation spent all the money in a single year.

A corporation's depreciation deductions are reported on Form 4562. Land is not depreciable, because it is not subject to wear and tear or obsolescence. Other real and personal property is defined as depreciable by §167 if it is:

- Used in the corporation's trade or business, or held for the production of income
- Has an exhaustible useful life that can be determined
- Is not inventory, stock in trade, or held as an investment.

Section 263 provides that capital expenditures are not deductible. This category includes amounts paid for new buildings, restoring property, or permanent improvements that increase the value of property. Amounts that qualify as R&E spending or §179 costs are not treated as capital expenditures.

If the property that is acquired or constructed will serve as inventory, then its cost is included in the corporate cost of inventory. Non-inventory property, however, generally has to be capitalized or amortized. Code §263A's uniform capitalization system mandates corporations[11] to include the "allocable costs" of inventory property in the calculation of the value of the inventory. The allocable cost of all other property must be capitalized. Allocable costs are direct costs of property, and certain indirect costs (e.g., taxes). However, sales and marketing expenses and research and experimentation expenses are excluded from the category of "allocable costs." Section 263A includes methods for allocating labor costs and capitalizing interest.

The Taxpayer Relief Act of 1997 created a new 15-year amortization provision (enacted as §197) for certain intangibles acquired by the taxpayer, most of them entertainment-related (e.g., films and videocassettes). Intangibles created by the taxpayer don't qualify.

The treatment of computer software is extremely complex, and depends on factors such as whether the taxpayer created or merely acquired the software, and whether it is an off-the-shelf, generally available product or customized by or for the corporation's individual needs.

Some taxes and carrying charges that could otherwise be deducted currently or amortized can, if the corporation so elects, be capitalized under §266. The effect is that, if the property is depreciable, the deduction is deferred until the later years in the depreciation schedule; otherwise (e.g., for unimproved real estate), the effect of capitalization is to increase the basis and therefore reduce the eventual capital gain when the property is sold.

Natural resources, such as timber, oil, gas, and minerals in the ground, are treated under "depletion" rather than depreciation rules (§§612-614). Most depletion is measured using the "cost depletion" method, but the more generous "percentage depletion" (a percentage of the gross income of the corporation taking the deduction) is permitted for mining and some oil and gas well interests.

As for another environmental question—cleanup costs—for the period 8/5/97-12/31/2000, corporations can elect to take a current deduction for certain environmental cleanup expenses that would otherwise require capitalization. Section 198 provides that the cost must be paid or incurred to control or abate environmental hazards at a contaminated site. Generally, the expenses of acquiring property that turns out to be contaminated are not entitled to the §198 election, although some of the depreciation claimed on the property can be assigned to environmental clean-up.

If the property does not qualify for §198 treatment, or the taxpayer does not make the election, cleanup expenses have to be capitalized to the extent that they improve the property, increase its value, or extend useful life. As opposed to contaminated property acquired and then remediated by the taxpayer, if the taxpayer is actually responsible for the contamination, the cost of restoring the property to clean condition is deductible because it does not increase the value of the property.

[¶453.1] MACRS System

Congress has taken many approaches to capitalization of business-related costs. Before 1987, the Accelerated Cost Recovery System (ACRS) was in force, and indeed certain businesses still have assets in use that continue to be subject to ACRS rules.

Depreciation begins when property is placed in service—a determination that is governed by Tax Code conventions, not the actual date of first use. These conventions may reduce the amount of deductible depreciation if, for instance, a piece of machinery is treated as if it had been in use for only half a year, so only a half measure of depreciation is allowable in that year. Depreciation ends when the property is retired from service; when it is sold; or when the cost or other basis has been fully recovered—whichever comes first.

Under MACRS, recovery property (depreciable tangible property used in a trade or business, or for the production of income) is depreciated by a prescribed method over its recovery period, which in turn depends on the kind of asset it is. MACRS classes call for depreciation over 3, 5, 7, 10, 15, or 20 years. A longer depreciation period, 27.5 years, is called for for residential real estate, and an even longer 39-year period applies to nonresidential real estate placed in service after May 12, 1993.

The taxpayer can elect to use straight-line depreciation (i.e., the same percentage is used to calculate depreciation throughout the whole recovery period). The Alternative Depreciation System (ADS), more or less a straight-line depreciation method with a longer recovery period, is optional for some assets and mandated for others. Real property must be depreciated on a straight-line basis in any case. Depreciation elections are made in the year the property is placed in service (§168(b)(5)) and are irrevocable.

If the business use of property drops below 50% level, depreciation must be recaptured. In other words, the taxpayer must give back tax benefits that were obtained on the basis of a business use of the property that is no longer applicable. Form 4797 is used to report the recapture amount, which equals the expense deduction taken minus the MACRS depreciation that would have been allowed.

Recapture of depreciation is governed by §§1245 and 1250. If business policy calls for getting rid of an asset that has not yet reached the end of its depreciation schedule (so recapture would be necessary on sale), recapture can be avoided by making a tax-free exchange for other property; keeping the property in use until the end of the depreciation schedule; or retaining the property but borrowing against its value (a tactic that is especially practical in the case of buildings). This, too, is an area where Congress is likely to grant relief.

[¶453.2] Amortization

Intangible assets, movies, videos, and master sound recordings are not depreciable under MACRS; instead, they are subject to amortization.

Section 197 governs the amortization of goodwill; going concern value; market share; customer lists; franchises, trademarks, and trade names; and patent, copyrights, formulas, processes, and designs.But §197(c) says that interests in a partnership or corporation; computer software available to the general public; or patents and copyrights acquired in any transaction other than acquisition of the assets of a business are not §197 intangibles.

In addition, §167 provides that non-MACRS property that is not subject to §197 is to be depreciated over its "useful life." Computer software is to be depreciated on a straight-line basis over 36 months.

[¶453.3] Basis of Corporate Property

Under §1012, the determination of basis of corporate property begins with the cost of the property, deemed to include liabilities the property is subject to, even if the corporation did not assume them in purchasing the property. A cash basis corporation's basis in accounts receivable is zero. The basis of intangibles such as patents, copyrights, goodwill, and covenants not to compete is what was paid for them.

Basis is then adjusted by adding capital expenditures relating to the property, but basis is not increased by items that can be deducted as expenses (e.g., carrying charges) unless they were capitalized rather than deducted. Basis is reduced by depreciation, cost recovery, and amortization deductions taken with respect to the property(§1016). A corporation's basis in property acquired from its shareholders as contributions to capital equals the shareholder's basis, plus any gain the shareholder recognized on the transfer: §362(a)(2).

If corporations merge or are acquired, basis considerations come into play both for the acquiror and for the target. If the transaction is structured as a tax-free reorganization (see ¶459.3), the acquiror's basis in property received in the transaction equals the target company's basis in that property plus gain to the target. The exception is a transfer of securities in the target corporation: this basis rule obtains only if the securities were acquired in exchange for securities of the acquiring company (§362(b)).

[¶453.4] Gain and Loss on Dispositions of Property

A taxpayer has gain on property if the cash received for the property, plus the fair market value of non-cash property received, exceeds the property's adjusted basis (its cost plus improvements, but minus depreciation: §1011). If the buyer pays or assumes any of the seller's indebtedness on the property, then this amount is added to the amount received. The amount of the mortgage on encumbered property is considered part of the sales price, even if the seller is not personally liable for the mortgage debt, and whether or not the buyer assumes the mortgage. See §1001.

A cash basis seller reports the gain of a profitable transaction in the year of actual or constructive receipt of the sale proceeds; cash-basis losses are reported in the year the transaction is completed by a fixed, identifiable event. An accrual basis seller reports either gain or loss in the year of the completion of the sale, when there is an unqualified right to receive the purchase price. In any transaction involving stock, the trade date (the date the sale was entered into) and not the settlement date is what counts.

Under §1032, a corporation has neither gain nor loss when it sells or exchanges its own stock for cash or property, or when a warrant or option to buy or sell its stock lapses.

The computation of tax on corporate capital gains is significantly simpler than the routine individual taxpayers must follow (¶4130). The general rule is that the corporation must include all of its capital gains, net of all capital losses, in taxable income. A corporation can deduct capital losses, but only to the extent of its capital gains. Losses can be carried back three years and forward five years; but a carried-over capital loss is treated as short- rather than long-term. See §1211.

Gain must be recognized, but losses cannot be, in sales and exchanges between "related taxpayers" as defined by §267. See §267(b). Related taxpayers include a corporation and a taxpayer owning 50% or more of the corporation's stock; a corporation controlled by a trust or the trust's grantor and a fiduciary; two or more corporations within a controlled group of corporations; a corporation and a partnership, if the same persons own 50% or more of the value of each; two S corporations meeting that criterion; or an S Corporation and a C Corporation each controlled by the same persons.

[¶454] Accumulated Earnings Tax

A corporation cannot deduct the dividends that it pays to its shareholders, even though the dividends are taxed to the shareholders who receive them. Therefore, corporations (especially closely held corporations) have some incentive to retain money within the corporation instead of paying it out as dividends.

Code §§531–537 are designed to reduce this incentive, by imposing an "accumulated earnings tax" of 39.6% of accumulated taxable income, imposed over and above all other taxes due for the year. The corporation has the burden of proof of demonstrating that earnings were retained for a reasonable business purpose (e.g., having funds available to buy new equipment or hire additional personnel or redeem corporate stock) and not to permit shareholders to avoid tax. See §537.

[¶454.1] Personal Holding Companies

A tax at the same rate (39.6%), also in addition to other taxes due, is imposed on undistributed Personal Holding Company (PHC) income that is not subject to the accumulated earnings tax. A PHC, as governed by §§541–547, is a company at least 60% of whose AGI for the year consists of PHC income, and at least 50% of whose outstanding stock (at any time during the second half of the taxable year) is held by one to five stockholders. PHC income, in turn, consists of AGI from sources such as personal service income, interest, dividends, rent, and royalties, rather than manufacturing or wholesale or retail sales of goods and services.

[¶455] Business Tax Credits

The general business credit allowed under §38 is the total of various incentive credits, including the investment credit, the disabled access credit (limited to small businesses that make their premises accessible), and the low-income housing credit.

The §38 credit allowed in any particular year equals the current year's credit, plus carryforwards and carrybacks to that year, subject to limitations based on the corporation's "net income tax." Net income tax is the regular tax, plus Alternative Minimum Tax, minus certain credits.

In general, for years after 1997, the general business credit can be carried back one year and forward 20 years.

Corporations that are subject to foreign taxes can claim a dollar-for-dollar tax credit under §901. However, it is not mandatory that the credit be used: §§27 and 164 give the taxpayer a choice each year between deducting the taxes and claiming them as a credit.

[¶456] Effect of Thin Capitalization

In general, as ¶130.1 shows, the organizers of a corporation have broad latitude in determining whether to issue common stock, preferred stock, or debt securities, as well as broad latitude in deciding the proportion of each in the corporation's capital structure.

However, the Code in some ways favors debt capitalization over equity, because a corporation is entitled to deduct the cost of its debt service but is not entitled to deduct the dividends it pays to its stockholders. The way a corporation characterizes its securities when they are issued is binding on the corporation and the holders of the securities—but not necessary on the IRS (§385(c)).

If a corporation is capitalized too "thinly" (i.e., too much debt to equity), the IRS has the power to treat certain securities as equity rather than as debt, and correspondingly deny "interest" deductions. The factors include the debt:equity ratio, the business purpose or economic reality behind the transaction, whether securities are convertible, presence or absence of a fixed maturity date, subordination of the securities, and holders' rights.

[¶457] Controlled and Affiliated Groups

Groups of related corporations may be treated as controlled groups under §1561, with the result that even if they file separate tax returns, the brackets will be applied to the aggregated taxable income of the entire group (in other words, the benefit of the lower tax brackets will apply only once, not once per corporation). Furthermore, the entire group is entitled to only one accumulated earnings tax credit and one AMT exemption. Section 1563 defines two kinds of controlled group: the parent-subsidiary and the brother-sister.

In a parent-subsidiary controlled group, the parent corporation owns at least 80% of the voting power in at least one corporation in the ownership chain. Each corporation within the chain (other than the parent) has at least 80% of its voting power owned by one or more corporations in the chain.

In a brother-sister group, at least 80% of the voting power of each corporation is owned by one to five individuals, estates, or trusts; and these persons own 50% or more of the voting power of each corporation within the group.

Treatment as a controlled group is somewhat undesirable (in that it tends to increase taxes), but Code §§1501–1505 allow the creation of an "affiliated group," a move that can have positive tax consequences. The corporations can make an election (generally irrevocable) to file a consolidated return, based on connection of their stock ownership through a common parent corporation.

A group, for instance, might choose to do this if taxes can be saved if there are significant intragroup payments of dividends (which are 100% deductible when issued within a group), or if one group member has operating losses that would serve to offset operating profits elsewhere in the group. See the Regulations for §1502 for allocation of tax items within the group.

The parent corporation must own 80% of the voting power and 80% of the total value of the stock of at least one corporation within the group. One or more corporations within the group must own at least 80% of the stock in the other corporations in the group (not the parent).

The consolidated return for the group is filed by the parent corporation, on Form 1120. For the first year of the election, it must be accompanied by Form 851 (affiliation schedule) and Form 1122 (consent from each corporation within the group).

[¶458] Reorganizations and Related Transactions

The Code provides for many tax-free or partially tax-free transactions between corporations, or between a corporation and its shareholders. This category includes A-G reorganizations; incorporation; transfers of property to a controlled corporation; and redemption of a corporation's own stock.

The concept of "boot"—consideration other than corporate stock—is significant in such transactions. Sometimes the receipt of boot will disqualify the transaction from tax-free status; sometimes the boot itself will bear unfavorable tax consequences, but the underlying transaction will be tax-free.

[¶458.1] §351 Transfers and Distributions

When a business incorporates, or when a transfer of property is made by a party to a corporation it controls, the transfer is generally tax-free, and no gain or loss is recognized. (This section cannot be used for transfers in bankruptcy, receivership, or foreclosure.) The transferred property can be cash; tangible property; or intangible personal property (but not the transferor's services to the transferee corporation, or indebtedness of the transferee corporation that is not evidenced by a security).

To qualify for §351 treatment, the transfer must be made to a corporation, solely in exchange for that corporation's stock (but not rights, warrants, or options or certain preferred stock). Immediately after the transfer, the transferor(s) must control the transferee corporation. Control means owning at least 80% of the transferee corporation's voting stock and at least 80% of all other classes of stock. A transaction can satisfy §351 if certain transferors receive voting stock while others get non-voting preferred shares, as long as the 80% requirements are met overall.

In transactions that would qualify under §351 except that boot is received, no transferor can recognize loss as a result of the transaction. However, gain is recognized, up to the amount of the boot (defined as the amount of cash plus the FMV of boot property). The transferred property retains its characterization as ordinary income property (e.g., inventory) or capital assets, so this determines whether the transferor's gain is capital or ordinary.

Section 357 provides that a transfer remains tax-free if the transferred property was encumbered (subject to liabilities), but the liabilities constitute boot if the transferor had a tax avoidance motivation, or if there was no business purpose for having the transferee assume the liabilities. If the assumed liabilities exceed the transferor's adjusted basis, the excess constitutes gain.

Under Section 311, a corporation can recognize gain but not loss when it distributes property to shareholders other than in the course of liquidation. A corporation never has either gain or loss on distribution of its own stock or stock rights. If a non-liquidating distribution of appreciated property is made, the corporation has gain to the same extent as if it had sold the property to the stockholders receiving it, at its fair market value as of the time of the distribution: §311(b).

[¶458.2] Redemptions

Transfer of stock from a stockholder to the issuing corporation is often treated as the corporation's "redemption" of those shares (whether the corporation cancels the stock, retires it, retains it as treasury stock, or does anything else with it: §317(b)).

If the transaction falls under the §302 redemption provisions, the distribution from the corporation is treated as payment for the stock in a sale or exchange, so the stockholder is likely to have capital gain because the stock will probably be a capital asset in the hands of the taxpayer. See §318 for attribution rules, under which one taxpayer will be deemed to own shares belonging to another, related taxpayer such as a family member or a trust, S Corporation, partnership, or C Corporation that the taxpayer controls.

Four kinds of transactions are treated as redemptions, and therefore as payment for stock, under 302(b):

- A redemption that is "substantially disproportionate" as to the shareholder

- Complete redemption of all of the shareholder's shares (if he or she owns both common and preferred shares, all shares of both types must be redeemed)
- A redemption that is not essentially equivalent to a dividend
- Redemption of the stock of a non-corporate shareholder, as part of a partial liquidation of the corporation whose shares are involved.

Similar rules apply under §303 to redemption of the shares of a decedent, with the proceeds used to pay death taxes.

As you would expect, each type of redemption has its own rules, which are laid out in §302(b). For the redemption to be substantially disproportionate, two tests must be met. After the redemption, the stockholder must own less than half of the corporation's voting stock. Furthermore, the percentage of the voting stock and common stock now held must be less than 80% of the level held before the redemption.

A redemption does not have the effect of a dividend as long as it causes a meaningful reduction in the stockholder's proportionate interest in the corporation. If the shareholder owned over 50% of the voting power before the redemption, reduction to a minority level will probably be treated as meaningful. For someone who held a substantial minority interest prior to the redemption, the reduction will be meaningful if it increases the number of other shareholders' collaboration needed in order to control the corporation. Any redemption in a low percentage minority interest will probably be considered meaningful.

A redemption in conjunction with a partial liquidation must go to a non-corporate shareholder; must not be dividend-equivalent (from the corporation's viewpoint, not the stockholder's); and must be made pursuant to a plan, in the year the plan was adopted or the following year. See §302(e).

Estate-tax-oriented redemptions of a decedent's shares that are included in his or her gross estate are permitted up to the total federal and state death taxes imposed on the estate (including interest), plus deductible funeral and administration expenses. Section 303(a) imposes three tests. The redeemed stock must constitute at least 35% of the adjusted gross estate,[12] and the redemption distribution must occur after the decedent's death, but no later than three years and 90 days after the filing of the estate tax return. Furthermore, the shareholder must have the burden of taxes or expenses, and payment of death taxes, funeral and administration expenses, reduces his interest.

Also see §304, which deals with the situation in which a shareholder owns stock in two related controlled corporations, and sells stock in the issuer corporation to the acquirer corporation for cash or property. If the corporations are part of a brother-sister controlled group, the transaction is a redemption by the acquirer corporation. If the issuer corporation is the parent corporation of the acquirer corporation, then the transaction is treated as a redemption by the issuer corporation.

[¶458.3] Corporate Reorganizations

The underlying theory under the Internal Revenue Code's treatment of reorganizations is that a qualifying reorganization will have no tax consequences, because the same underlying investment is merely being transmuted in form. All qualified reorganizations share several characteristics, as laid out in §§356 and 368:

- The transaction must have a business purpose; it must not be solely tax-motivated[13]
- There must be a "plan" of reorganization (and copies of the plan have to be filed with the returns of the corporations participating in the plan)
- The stock to be exchanged must come from a corporation that is a party to the reorganization or, in certain circumstances, the parent corporation of a party
- There must be continuity of interest: i.e., after the reorganization, the target shareholders must still have a significant proprietary stake in the reorganized corporation(s). In most instances, this requires that much of the consideration for the transaction must be in the form of the stock of the acquiring corporation (or, perhaps, its parent corporation)
- There must be continuity of enterprise: the acquiring corporation must continue to carry out the acquired corporation's historic business, or use a significant portion of the acquired corporation's historic business assets in business.

[¶458.3.1] Classification of Tax-Free Reorganizations

Tax-free reorganizations are described as types A through G. The letters are subsections of §368(a)(1). A "triangular" transaction, permitted in types A, B, and G, involves the stock of the acquiring corporation's parent corporation rather than that of the acquiring corporation itself.

A Type A reorganization is a merger or consolidation carried out under federal law or the laws of a state. In a B reorganization, the acquiring corporation gets stock in the target corporation in exchange for nothing but voting stock in the acquiring corporation, and the acquiror is in control of the target following the reorganization.

In a C reorganization, substantially all the properties of the target corporation are acquired for voting stock of the acquiring corporation. The statute and Regulations do not explicitly define "substantially all," but there is case law to the effect that 68% is not sufficient. The IRS will only issue a favorable advance ruling if the target transfers at least 90% of the fair market value of its net assets and 70% of its gross assets. The target corporation must liquidate (distribute everything received, and all its other properties, to its shareholders) unless the IRS waives the distribution requirement. A C reorganization can involve "boot" (consideration other than voting stock of the acquiring corporation), but at least 80% of the value of all of the target's properties must be exchanged for voting stock of the acquiring corporation.

Unlike a "stock for stock" C reorganization, a D reorganization involves the transfer of some or all of the target company's assets to another corporation, with the result that right after the transfer, the transferor and/or its shareholders control the transferee corporation. Furthermore, the transferor either distributes all of its assets (including the stock of the transferee corporation) to its shareholders in a liquidation that is part of a plan of reorganization, or distributes the transferee corporation's stock in a tax-free spin-off, split-off, or split-up under §354-356. If a complex transaction fits the rules for both a C and a D reorganization, §368(a)(2) says that it will be treated as a D reorganization.

A type E reorganization involves only one corporation, which undergoes a change in capital structure, such as exchanging old bonds for new ones, making changes in stock to conform to charter amendments, or exchanging one class of common stock for another. A type F reorganization is a change in identity, form, or place of organization of just one corporation. A type G reorganization is a corporation's transfer of part or all of its assets to another corporation under a court-approved plan of bankruptcy, receivership, or foreclosure, with the securities of the transferred corporation distributed in a transaction that satisfies §§354, 355, or 356.

[¶458.3.2] Corporate-Level Effects

For most reorganization transactions, "control" is defined as 80% of combined voting power plus 80% of the total shares of each class of non-voting stock, but different rules, involving 50% ownership, apply to D reorganizations.

As a result of §354, no gain or loss is recognized when the holder of stock or securities receives stock and nothing else under a plan of reorganization. Nonrecognition also applies when stock in a company that is a party to the reorganization is exchanged for other securities whose face amount does not exceed the face amount of surrendered securities. For D and G reorganizations to operate as nonrecognition transactions, the transferee corporation must get substantially all of the transferor corporation's assets, and the transferor must make a full distribution.

Section 356(a)(1) provides that if any boot is received, then all of the recipient's gain on the exchange is recognized, and is taxed up to the amount of the boot. It will be taxed as an ordinary dividend to the extent that the exchange has the same effect as the declaration of a dividend; any balance will be taxed as gain from the exchange of property.

At the corporate level, §361 says that a corporation involved in a reorganization has no gain or loss on the exchange of its property solely for stock and/or securities of another corporation involved in the reorganization. If the corporation (rather than the stockholders) receives boot, then gain is recognized on the exchange, but only up to the extent of boot that is not distributed to stockholders. Distribution of appreciated property to stockholders may require recognition of gain.

The acquiring corporation can make an irrevocable election, under §338, to treat the purchase of a target corporation's stock as if it were a purchase of assets, if it is possible and desirable to step up the basis of the target's assets. This might occur where the target has significant losses that can offset the acquiror's gains; if the target owns a great deal of depreciated property; or if major depreciation and amortization deductions are available. (If this is done, the target and the selling shareholders may have to recognize gain, because the target is taxed as if it had sold all its assets at fair market value.) The election is made by the acquiring corporation, on Form 8023-A, which is due the fifteenth day of the ninth month after the month of the acquisition.

Note that owning §306 stock, which is issued in connection with a reorganization (or as a stock dividend) will usually give rise to ordinary income rather than capital gains when the holder sells it or it is redeemed. Also see §355, which governs spin-offs, split-offs, and split-ups, which are tax-free methods of dividing a corporation into two or more corporations so that the stockholders of the former corporation continue to own the new corporations, although not necessarily in the same proportions.

[¶458.4] Corporate Liquidations

Liquidation, as governed by §§331–336, is a corporation's process of dissolving completely and distributing all assets to its shareholders. The corporation can have taxable gain or loss when the property is sold or distributed in connection with the liquidation. Usually, the shareholders will have capital gain or loss on the distribution, on the theory that they receive full payment in exchange for their stock, measured by comparing the cash and fair market value of property received to their basis in the stock.

However, if the corporation is a "collapsible" corporation as defined by §341 (i.e., one created specifically to be liquidated to take advantage of tax benefits stemming from ordinary income assets such as inventory), anyone who owns 5% or more of the shares will be denied capital gains treatment on liquidation to the extent that the gains are attributable to ordinary income assets.

[¶459] Special Corporations

The discussion above involves the conventional, C Corporation. The Internal Revenue Code includes rules for taxation of various other kinds of corporations; generally, these rules are more favorable to taxpayers than the C Corporation rules, provided that stringent qualifications are satisfied.

[¶459.1] Subchapter S Corporations

The ordinary, or C corporation, is a taxpayer separate and apart from its stockholders. The corporation itself must calculate its income, deductions, credits, and other items, and must prepare a tax return and make corresponding payments. The dividends paid to stockholders then become taxable income for the stockholders.

This double taxation is resented by most taxpayers, and the Code has responded by permitting certain small corporations to operate under Subchapter S of the Code, §1361–1379. These "S corporations," somewhat like partnerships, are "pass-through" entities. That is, there is little or no taxation at the entity level.[14] Instead, tax items are passed through to partners and S corporation shareholders, and are taxed at that level.

All corporations are C corporations unless a valid Subchapter S election is in place.

[¶460.1.1] Criteria for S Corporation Election

To make the election, a corporation (or unincorporated entity taxed as a corporation) §1361 requires that it must:

- Be a U.S. entity
- Be eligible to make the election (e.g., insurance companies are not allowed to elect Sub S)
- Not have more than 75 shareholders (but a husband and wife are counted as a single shareholder)
- All shareholders must be individuals, decedents' estates, bankruptcy estates, trusts permitted to own S Corp. stock, 501(c)(3) tax-exempt organizations, or 401(a) qualified plan trusts
- Not have any non-resident alien shareholders
- Have only one class of stock.

Initially, the eligibility of trusts to own Sub S shares was quite limited, but it has been expanded over time, and now many classes of trusts are permitted by §1361(c)(2) to own Sub S shares. Grantor trusts, §678 trusts (in which someone other than the grantor is treated as substantial owner of the Sub S stock), testamentary trusts (for two years after they are funded after the testator's demise), Electing Small Business Trusts (§1361(e)), and Qualified Subchapter S Trusts (§1361(d)) are all permissible shareholders. A voting trust (see ¶145) is also a permissible shareholder, but each trust beneficiary counts toward the limit of 75.

[¶460.1.2] Single Class of Stock

Although an S Corporation can have only one class of stock, this is not necessarily a severe limitation. As defined by §1361(c)(4), a corporation has only one class of stock when no shares have been issued as a second class (e.g., an S Corporation cannot issue both preferred and common shares), and all stockholders have equal rights on the dissolution or liquidation of the corporation. Differential voting rights (including voting and non-voting common) are permissible.

Agreements that affect the transferability of the corporation's shares (such as buy-sells, redemption agreements, and transfer restrictions) do not create a second class of stock as long as they set a stock price reasonably close to FMV, and they are not intended to evade §1361.

An option, warrant, or similar security, however, might constitute a second class of stock if it is issued at a price significantly below the fair market value of the shares and is therefore substantially certain to be exercised. Because of §1361(c)(5), straight debt is not a second class of stock unless it is actually treated as equity under general tax principles, and is used to evade the reach of §1361.

[¶460.1.3] Procedure for S Corporation Election

The rule of §1362 is that the S election is made on Form 2553, which must be signed by an authorized corporate officer, and must evidence consent of all the shareholders.

The election can be made in one tax year for the following tax year, or until the 15th day of the third month of the year for which the election is supposed to take effect.

The IRS has the power, under §1362(a)(5) to waive invalidity in an election, or to treat a late election as if it had been timely made (or even to treat a corporation as an S Corporation when no election was filed at all).

[¶460.1.4] Tax Treatment of S Corporation Stockholders

Once the election is effective, §1366 provides that the S Corporation allocates items of income, loss, deduction, and credit for each day in the tax year on a pro rata basis among the individuals and entities who were shareholders on that day. A separate allocation to each shareholder is required whenever such treatment could affect the shareholder's own tax liability.

The shareholder takes the items into account in the shareholder's tax year that includes the last day of the S Corporation's tax year. (This provision is necessary because most S Corporation shareholders are individuals with calendar years, whereas fiscal years are very common for S Corporations.)

The amount of a distribution from an S Corporation to its shareholder is defined by §§301(c) and 1368(a) as the sum of cash and the fair market value (as of the time of the distribution) of any property distributed.

If the S Corporation did not have earnings and profits (E&P) as of the time of the distribution, the amount of the distribution reduces the shareholder's basis. If the distribution exceeds the shareholder's basis, then it is deemed payment for the stock and therefore will probably constitute capital gain for the shareholder.

If the corporation did have E&P as of the time of distribution, then §1368 prescribes a complex series of calculations based on the corporation's Accumulated Adjustment Account.

Deductions, capital losses, and Net Operating Losses are passed through and deducted by the shareholders, but §1366(d)(1) limits the deduction to the shareholder's adjusted basis in the stock, adjusted for increases (attributable to the stockholder's share of S Corporation income) and decreases (for non-dividend distributions and debts of the corporation to the shareholder). The shareholder's basis cannot be reduced below zero (§1367), but carryovers are permitted for items that cannot be currently deducted.

Code §6037(c) requires S Corporation shareholders to treat tax items consistently with the way they were reported by the S Corporation on its 1120S information return. Taxpayers who treat items inconsistently are obligated to file Form 6037 to notify the IRS of the discrepancy.

[¶460.1.5] Termination of S Corporation Status

The S Corporation election can be revoked on consent of the holders of a majority of the corporation's issued and outstanding stock (including any non-voting stock). Yet another possibility is involuntary termination of the election by the IRS, if and when the company ceases to qualify as an S Corporation (e.g., it has more than 75 stockholders, or any ineligible stockholders) or if the corporation began as a C Corporation, accumulated E&P as a C Corporation, converted to Subchapter S status, and derived 25% or more of its income from passive sources for three consecutive years. See §1362(d)(2).

For revocations and terminations occurring in 1997 and later years, §1362(g) provides that five years must elapse before the corporation again elects Sub S status, unless the IRS permits an earlier election.

[¶460.2] Other Special Corporations

Two sections of the Code provide favorable treatment for the shareholders of small businesses. Under §1202, a shareholder who received stock in the original issue of stock by a "qualified small business," and who received the stock in exchange for money, services to the corporation, or property other than corporate stock, and who holds the stock for at least five years before selling it, can exclude 50% of gain from taxable income.

A shareholder who sells certain small business stock covered by §1244 can treat any gain as capital gain, but is entitled to treat any loss as an ordinary loss.

[¶460.3] Tax-Exempt Organizations

Although the bulk of business activities are conducted by for-profit corporations (or at least corporations intended to earn a profit, whatever actually happens), hundreds of thousands of organizations, ranging from small groups with limited activities to quasi-businesses with thousands of employees and millions of dollars in annual turnover, are operated as not-for-profit organizations.

There are two aspects of not-for-profit organization operation under the Internal Revenue Code. The first is whether the organization is an "exempt" organization in the sense that it is exempt from corporate tax on its own activities (other than income-earning business activities that are not related to the organization's exempt purpose).

The other is whether it is a "donative" non-profit: that is, whether contributors are entitled to donate contributions they make to the organization. (Note that, as discussed at ¶4150.8, an individual's donations to all charities are limited by the individual's "contribution base," but estates are entitled to an unlimited charitable deduction.)

Application for non-profit status is made on Form 1023 for 501(c)(3) organizations, Form 1024 for other kinds of tax-exempt organization.

[¶460.3.1] Categories of Tax-Exempt Organizations

Once an organization is established as a tax-exempt organization, the next level of inquiry is whether it renders its services broadly and is under public or widely disseminated management. If so, it will be considered a "public charity." But an exempt organization whose aims are narrower, and/or which is dominated by a single family or company, may be treated as a "private foundation" and subjected to stricter tax requirements.

The Code recognizes many types of exempt organization, including:

- §501(c)(3) organizations, the best-known type; organizations with religious, charitable, scientific, literary, educational, or similar purposes
- 501(c)(4) non-profit civic organizations for social welfare
- 501(c)(5) labor, agricultural, and horticultural organizations
- 501(c)(6) chambers of commerce, business leagues, boards of trade
- 501(c)(7) social clubs.

In order to qualify as a §501(c)(3) organization, an applicant must be organized and operated for its stated exempt purpose. No part of its net earnings can inure to private individuals. (This requirement prohibits profit-sharing, but not payment of reasonable salaries.) The organization can have members, but cannot have shareholders.

"Action organizations" devoted to propaganda, lobbying, and influencing legislation are not entitled to §501(c)(3) characterization. (Charitable organizations that want to do substantial lobbying generally create a related organization that is not qualified under §501(c)(3), and which solicits contributions that are not tax-deductible.)

A 501(c)(3) organization can lose its non-profit status if it engages in excessive lobbying, unless it qualifies under §501(h) to make a revocable election on Form 5768 to spend permissible amounts on lobbying without sacrificing not-for-profit status. A two-tier excise tax is imposed on excessive political expenditures by §4955. Code §7409 gives the IRS power to apply for an injunction against flagrant political activity by a tax-exempt organization.

If an organization is, in effect, an ordinary profit-making business, it will be taxed on all its income—even if the income goes directly to an exempt organization, unless it qualifies as a §502 "feeder" organization. A feeder organization is exempt if it is controlled by, and provides services solely for, a single exempt organization or group of related exempt organizations.

[¶460.3.2] UBTI

The annual tax return for non-profits is Form 990. If the organization has Unrelated Business Taxable Income (UBTI) as defined by §§511–512, that income must be reported on Form 990-T.

UBTI is income deriving from a trade or business that the organization regularly carries out (even if it does so on a seasonal basis) that provides funding for the organization but is not otherwise related to the exempt purpose. However, if an activity is entirely carried out by volunteers, it will not generate UBTI.

UBTI is business income, not investment income: dividends, interest, rent, and royalties received by a not-for-profit organization are not taxed as UBTI.

[¶460.3.3] Private Foundations

All 501(c)(3) organizations are presumed to be private foundations, unless they notify the IRS of their public charity status on Form 1023 within 15 months of the end of the first month in which the charity has been organized. (Churches and organizations with annual gross receipts under $5,000 are exempt.)

A private foundation is a non-profit that is not a "50% charity" (one eligible to receive contributions of a large part of a donor's income), is not publicly supported, or is controlled by "disqualified persons" who have too close a relationship to the organization.

Private foundations are subject to a number of excise taxes, imposed by §§4940-4945, that do not apply to other charitable organizations:

- Tax on net investment income
- Tax on self-dealing with closely related persons such as family members of the person who set up the foundation or major contributors
- Tax on a non-operating foundation's failure to distribute its net income
- Tax on investments that place the charitable purpose in jeopardy
- Tax on propaganda and political activities.

The private foundation income tax return is the Form 990-PF, an information return due on the fifteenth day of the fifth month after the close of the foundation's tax year.

ENDNOTES

1. The Internal Revenue Code uses the barbaric spelling "pass-thru."
2. Regulations have been proposed, at §1.1223-3 (8/9/99) as to the partner's holding period in his, her, or its partnership interest.
3. A partner who receives a liquidating distribution has capital gain only to the extent that cash received exceeds the partner's adjusted basis in the partnership interest. Loss is recognized on liquidation of the partner's entire interest if the distribution is limited to cash, inventory, and unrealized receivables.
4. The Taxpayer Relief Act of 1997 eliminated the prior-law requirement that only substantially appreciated inventory counted in this context.
5. Note that, under §269A(a), the IRS can reallocate income, deductions, credits, and other tax items between the corporation and its owner-employee or -employees, if the PSC is "availed of principally" for tax avoidance in that it gives a 10% owner-employee significant tax benefits that would otherwise be unavailable.
6. Form 1128, "Application for Change in Accounting Period."
7. To the extent that a tax-exempt trust has unrelated business taxable income (UBTI), §448(d)(6) requires it to be treated as a C Corporation.
8. Form 3115 is also used to apply for a change in accounting method. See §446(e), and also see §481 for adjustments the IRS may mandate so that the change in accounting method will not distort the taxpayer's taxable income.
9. Additional refinements such as "simplified dollar value LIFO" are explicated at §474(a). Section 474(c) defines an eligible small business as one with average annual gross receipts under $5 million for the preceding three years.

10. The amount of depreciation used to calculate E&P is lower than the amount allowable in computing taxable income in general.
11. Corporations are exempt if their annual gross receipts for the preceding three years averaged less than $10 million, with respect to personal property acquired for resale: §263A(b)(2)(B).
12. The stock of two or more corporations can be aggregated, if at least 20% of the stock of each corporation is included in the decedent's estate.
13. IRS has the power, under §269, to disallow deductions and credits if control of a corporation, or that corporation's assets, is acquired principally to avoid tax by making use of the deductions and credits. Also see §382 and 384, limiting the extent to which an acquired corporation's built-in gains can be used to offset the acquiring corporation's losses, and to which the acquired corporation's excess credits and net capital losses can be used. "Trafficking" in NOLs is forbidden.
14. However, S Corporations are subject to tax on their built-in gains; their net capital gains, their excess passive income; and on investment credit that must be recaptured from the time after the creation of the corporation but prior to its Sub S election. See §§1363(d)(1), 1374, and 1375(a).

¶500

Mergers and Acquisitions

[¶501]

In the 1980s, the law governing mergers and acquisitions, especially hostile takeovers, was one of the most volatile and eagerly followed areas of the law. It became quiescent in the 1990s, until the emergence of commercial activity on the Internet lead to a rash of initial public offerings—and a high degree of concentration as failing companies merged or stronger companies acquired their weaker competitors. Thus, at the end of the 1990s, M&A law once again became a hot topic.

A merger or acquisition involves extremely complex legal problems, and involves the attorney in considerations other than those of statute and regulation. The structure of the deal will depend on many practical factors, involve much uncertainty (e.g., movements of stock prices, which affect the amount to be received in the deal), and call for extreme diplomacy, because the interests of the buyer and seller are often starkly opposed. Because M&A transactions involve a great deal of money, tax factors are significant—but the attorney's tax advice will often be brushed aside, because measures that save taxes (e.g., structuring the deal to speed up write-offs and preserve carry-overs) are not in the surviving company's best interests in the stock market, which relies on large and increasing earnings.

When a new company achieves a certain amount of success, but needs further capital to expand, it's natural to think of carrying out an Initial Public Offering (IPO)—"going public." However, not every corporation is suitable for going public, and IPOs are very dependent on market conditions. For some companies, merging with a peer or being acquired by a larger company can provide an even better "exit strategy" for the company's founders than going public, because they receive cash and/or shares in a more established company. After an IPO, the original stockholders are subject to certain restrictions on their ability to sell their shares.

As soon as a corporation becomes public, and its shares can be freely purchased by anyone, the corporation becomes a potential target for a hostile takeover or "greenmail" (i.e., a person who doesn't actually want to take over the corporation to run it threatens a takeover, hoping to be paid to go away). See ¶520 for a discussion of "poison pills" and other measures that a company can take to protect itself against hostile takeovers.

If one or both corporations involved is very large, or if the market in which they operate is so small that eliminating a competitor could have a major effect on competition, antitrust issues may arise. See ¶840 for a discussion of approval under the Hart-Scott-Rodino Act, and other antitrust implications.

[¶510] Types of Transaction

Various kinds of transactions involving either aggregation or disaggregation of companies can be carried out. The particular structure that is chosen determines what kind of agreements can be made; who has to approve them (e.g., the Boards of Directors of all corporations involved; all the shareholders; a plurality or majority of shareholders); whether tax will be due for the year of the transaction; and the future tax status of the surviving corporation(s).

Seven kinds of transactions can be engaged in tax-free: Types A, B, and C reorganizations; spin-off, split-off, or split-up; recapitalization; change in identity or form; or transfer of assets from a bankrupt corporation to another corporation. If the transaction fails to fit into one of these categories, it will be taxable, and all realized gain or loss must be recognized. See ¶459.3 for taxation of reorganizations.

One of the most significant issues is whether the merged or acquired corporation will sell its assets, or will sell its stock. It is also very significant what consideration the surviving/acquiring corporation will furnish: all cash, all shares of its own stock, or somewhere in between. The buyer has a natural interest in deriving as much of the consideration as possible from shares of its own stock rather than cash, but a rise in stock prices can make an acquisition more expensive than originally planned.

The price of the transaction can be fixed and determined in advance; or it might be contingent on various things; or it may be subject to an obligation to make continuing payments, which in turn may be contingent on earnings, profits, or other factors.

For tax purposes, a statutory merger (one that satisfies state law) is known as a Type A reorganization. Type B is a stock-for-stock transaction; Type C involves exchange of one corporation's stock for another corporation's assets.

[¶510.1] Sale of Assets

A corporation can sell all or part of its assets to another corporation; and a potential buyer can acquire certain assets while rejecting others. The buyer is entitled to step up the basis in the acquired assets to reflect fair market value as of the acquisition.

The stockholders of the seller corporation must approve the transaction, but the buyer corporation doesn't have to obtain approval from its own shareholders. In many cases, the seller will need permission from lenders and other major creditors, because loan and sale contracts often require permission before the buyer/debtor sells its assets or otherwise engages in transactions out of the ordinary course of business.

However, a sale of assets is more expensive (because schedules of assets have to be prepared, and each asset has to be valued) and takes longer to consummate than a sale of stock. It may also be disfavored by the seller, because it is subject to double taxation. Dissenting stockholders in the selling corporation may have appraisal rights: i.e., the right to have their shares bought back by the selling corporation.

[¶510.2] Sale of Stock

Most transactions are carried out as either a merger or consolidation (in which both constituent companies dissolve and are replaced by a surviving company); a stock-for-stock sale, in which the selling company surrenders its own stock in return for stock of the buying company; or a deal in which the acquiring company buys the selling company's stock. It should be noted that, in a stock deal, the buyer company assumes all of the liabilities of the seller company—a result that is not necessarily obtained in an asset sale.

The selling company's stockholders must consent to the transaction; in many situations, the buyer company's stockholders must also consent. Appraisal rights may be available to dissenting stockholders.

Although a sale of stock can be structured to be tax-free, the selling corporation does not get a step up in basis for the assets that come along with the stock, unless the deal satisfies Code §338.

[¶510.3] The Due Diligence Process

Before entering into a major transaction, a corporation must engage in "due diligence"—a complete examination of all facets of the potential deal. Failure to engage in due diligence can subject the corporation, and perhaps its officers, to liability to its own stockholders.

If due diligence is not performed, the acquiring corporation may find that it is a successor that has assumed some of the acquired corporation's obligations (such as its union contracts) or liabilities (such as environmental liability; products liability; unpaid taxes and penalties).

The due diligence process requires asking the other corporation for detailed information about its customers, work force, products, hard assets, intellectual property and other intangible assets, and financial condition. Moreover, all such contentions must be verified, not merely accepted on trust.

Financial due diligence issues include:

- Are the figures audited, and has the company received a clean opinion from its auditor?
- What are the profit margins on the various product lines?
- Are each operation's sales and general expenses modest or oversized?
- Are each operation's accounting assumptions conservative or aggressive, and what can be done to harmonize discrepancies?
- What is the capital structure (debt vs. equity) of each, and how much working capital does each have?
- What are the business and strategic plans for each?
- What are the sales forecasts and budgets for each?

- What deferred compensation and employee benefit plans does each maintain, and will the new entity adopt the more or the less generous plan structure?
- How reliable are the internal controls within each organization?

Corporate due diligence must also be performed, determining what provisions appear in the corporation's charter and bylaws; what resolutions have been passed; whether the corporation is a subsidiary or has subsidiaries; and how the securities are held.

It must be determined whether the deal could involve antitrust or other regulatory problems. The tax implications of various potential deal structures must be considered, and an important part of the negotiation will be choosing structures favorable to the negotiating entity.

[¶510.4] Documents and Drafting

The due diligence process (see ¶510.3) requires each corporation to learn a great deal about the other. This process nearly always involves disclosure of valuable confidential and proprietary information. To prevent misuse of this information (especially if the negotiations fail and the transaction is never consummated), M&A transactions nearly always begin with signing of a non-disclosure agreement (NDA) by both parties. Each agrees not to disclose or otherwise make use of confidential information acquired during negotiations.

Any merger or acquisition transaction will involve an extremely lengthy and detailed agreement. In some transactions, the agreement is precedent by a Letter of Intent (LOI). The LOI is somewhat like a "binder" in a real estate deal, and has some of the same drawbacks. Although it is not a full-scale, formal contract, it can make it difficult to re-negotiate points that have already been conceded. Furthermore, if the acquiring company is a public company, securities law may require it to disclose to the public when negotiations are underway.

[¶510.4.1] Letter of Intent
The Letter of Intent includes:

- Non-disclosure provisions (unless an NDA is already in place)
- Preliminary pricing data
- A "no-shop" provision, also known as a "lock-up," which prevents the potential seller from seeking a higher offer elsewhere
- The seller's covenant to continue doing business normally during the negotiations, and not to divest assets or otherwise decrease its value
- Allocation of expenses of the transaction between the parties
- Provision for a breakup fee—an amount to be paid in case the transaction is not consummated.

Probably the majority of transactions proceed directly from negotiations to the purchase contract. The contract spells out all of the terms of the deal, including contingencies that will permit the deal to be modified or either side to back away from the deal. An important function is to make sure that all material facts are disclosed, so that a disappointed deal party will not be able to assert that the other party is liable for non-disclosure.

[¶510.4.2] Contract of Sale
The contract of sale includes:

- Conditions for closing the deal (e.g., approval by lenders and stockholders)
- Final pricing structure, e.g., $X in cash and Y shares of stock in the buyer corporation, to be paid pursuant to a particular schedule; or exchange of X shares of the seller corporation's stock for every Y shares of the buyer corporation's
- Representations and warranties by the party; most of these relate to the seller rather than the buyer
- Agreements about how the business will be maintained until the closing
- Reciprocal indemnification of the parties
- Other documents attached as schedules or appendices (e.g., financial statements; union contracts; long-term business contracts).

[¶510.5] Effect of Accounting Issues

For accounting purposes, in an asset-purchase deal, the buyer values the acquired assets and liabilities at their fair market value. When assets are written up to reflect the increase in market value since their acquisition, the amount of the write-up must be depreciated. Goodwill (the difference between the actual purchase price and the aggregate FMV of the assets) must be amortized over a period of years.

This is one of the areas in which tax accounting diverges from general accounting. For tax purposes, the taxpayer usually wants as many deductions as possible, and wants to take those deductions in a single year or over a short period of time. But for general accounting purposes, the corporation usually wants to show high earnings, and does not want depreciation and amortization to continue to depress earnings for many years at a time.

[¶520] Defensive Measures

For both selfish reasons and because of a genuine belief that the corporation's current ownership and policies serve the best interests of the stockholders, it's understandable that entrenched management will tend to oppose unsolicited takeover attempts. In some instances, a corporation can attempt to protect itself against hostile takeovers by adopting Articles of Incorporation provisions or bylaws that discourage takeover attempts.

Depending on the nature of the corporation, how its stock is held, the terms of the proposed takeover, and the success of the current management, the stockholders may be grateful for these protective measures—or may deem them to be an abusive attempt by incompetent managers to protect their own jobs at the expense of stockholder interests.

Given the role of Delaware as the home of so many major corporations, the leading case law on hostile takeovers comes from the Delaware courts, especially its Court of Chancery.

[¶520.1] The Business Judgment Rule

Although the business judgment rule applies to all corporate actions, it is perhaps most often evoked in the M&A context. Corporate directors are not personally liable for their business decisions if they act in good faith, on sufficient information, and as they reasonably believe is in the best interests of the corporation's shareholders. Business decisions are presumed to satisfy this rule if all three tests are satisfied, and if there has been no fraud, bad faith, or self-dealing. However, if the presumption is unavailable, then the directors must prove that their actions were fair.[1]

In the tender offer context, the business judgment rule will apply, subject to additional scrutiny. (Heightened scrutiny is applied because of the potential conflict of interest between directors who want to retain their power, and stockholders the valuation of whose shares might increase under another regime.)

The basic test of *Unocal v. Mesa Petroleum*,[2] is that directors who adopt defensive measures against a takeover must have acted on a reasonable belief that the takeover threatened corporate policy and effectiveness. The defensive measures must have been reasonable in the context of the actual threat. Furthermore, all decisions by directors must have been made based on complete information about the situation; hasty and ill-informed decisions are likely to result in personal liability for the directors.[3]

The board must get complete information about all available offers. Once it becomes inevitable that the corporation's control will shift (whether the corporation itself initiated the sale process or the takeover attempt was unsolicited), or that it will be broken up, the board of directors have a fiduciary obligation to "auction" the company in a way resulting in the greatest possible value to shareholders.[4] However, a "just say no" strategy is permissible if an unsolicited takeover bid is deemed by the board to violate the corporate culture or otherwise harm the shareholders.[5]

[¶520.2] Poison Pills and Other Devices

Various provisions can be adopted by a corporation to make itself a less attractive target for a hostile takeover. However, the obligation of the corporation's board of directors is to act in the best interest of stockholders, which can include auctioning off the company to the highest bidder once the company is "in play" (a potential takeover target). Defensive measures must not be "draconian," "coercive," or "preclusive": i.e., they may operate to make the eventual transaction more beneficial to stockholders, but may not operate to prevent any transaction at all under any circumstances.[6]

[¶520.2.1] Lock-Ups

A "lock-up" is an arrangement under which a potential acquiror (typically, a "white knight" favored by the current management) takes an option or has the right to acquire major corporate assets or blocks of the target corporation's stock. Lock-ups are not illegal, but they are invalid if adopted to favor one potential bidder and prevent other potential bidders from engaging in the auction required by *Revlon*. Granting a lock-up can breach the directors' duty of loyalty if it is adopted for a self-interested or other improper purpose.

The target corporation can lawfully offer break-up or engagement fees to compensate a white knight for its expenses of a contest for control, as long as the effect is to increase the competitiveness of the auction, rather than precluding a vigorous bidding contest.[7]

[¶520.2.2] Shareholder Rights Plans

A shareholder rights plan, often known as a "poison pill," is a plan to discourage hostile takeovers while encouraging friendly offers. A legitimate shareholder rights plan must not have the purpose or effect of discouraging proxy contests or fair offers for acquisition of the entire company.

The poison pill works by giving the pre-takeover shareholders the right to buy stock in the target (or, sometimes, the potential acquiror) at a deep discount, if certain business combinations occur or if a specified percentage of the target's stock is acquired. The effect is to dilute the interest already acquired by the acquiror.

Under appropriate circumstances[8] adoption of a poison pill can be a permissible defensive measure that satisfies the business judgment rule. However, a plan that makes it impossible to undertake any hostile takeover is invalid, because it entrenches existing management even if this is not in the best interests of the shareholders.[9]

A "dead hand" plan can only be redeemed by the board of directors that adopted the plan, or their designated successors, or limits the ability of successor boards to redeem the plan. The Delaware courts have found this device invalid, because corporate directors must be able to operate with complete freedom on legitimate topics of corporate governance, and one set of directors cannot be given powers greater than those of successor directors.[10]

Pennsylvania has a statute that says that an acquiror of "control shares" (three defined ranges of voting power, beginning at 20%) can't vote these shares until the shareholders approve a tender offer. However, a would-be acquiror can continue to vote shares until it reaches the 20% ownership limit.[11]

[¶530] Securities Law Implications

In some instances, it will be possible to do a "street sweep": acquire enough securities on the open market to gain control. Generally, however, a hostile takeover will be structured either as a proxy contest or a tender offer. The proxy contest is a method of gaining voting control over a corporation by getting existing stockholders to give the contestant the right to vote their shares. A tender offer solicits stockholders to sell their shares.

A proxy statement that includes a discussion of the history of the merger is culpably incomplete if it fails to mention a rejected bid that was higher than the successful bid.[12]

[¶530.1] Tender Offers

If a target's board of directors is hostile to the possibility of merger or acquisition, the buyer often responds by making a tender offer directly to the shareholders: i.e., offering to purchase shares that they "tender," or make available.

The Williams Act, '34 Act §§13–14, is designed to protect target shareholders from raiders. Like most securities statutes, it is disclosure-oriented. Notification must be filed with the SEC of the buyer's background, identity, residence, and citizenship; the purpose of the stock purchase; source and amount of funds used to buy the shares; the number acquired; and disclosure of any contracts, arrangements, or understandings about the target company's securities. The SEC's Tender Offer Statement is Schedule 14D-1.

Tender offers must be kept open for at least 20 business days, plus at least 10 business days after a change in the amount of securities sought or the price offered for them, so target stockholders will have a chance to review the disclosure materials provided to them.

[¶540] M&A Antitrust Issues

Clayton Act §7 allows the federal government to block any acquisition that has the effect of lessening competition substantially or creating a monopoly. The determination depends on factors such as the market share of buyer and seller and the market dominance that would be gained by a proposed merger. The FTC can issue a preliminary injunction against a proposed merger, under FTC Act §13(b), pending the resolution of Clayton Act §7 charges.

Note that *Cargill v. Monfort*,[13] holds that a business cannot bring a Clayton Act case challenging a merger of two competitors on the basis of an alleged "cost-price squeeze" from the merged companies. In the Supreme Court's analysis, any such price reductions would be laudable price competition, not violative anti-competitive conduct.

Since 1976, the Clayton Act has also contained §7A, added by the Hart-Scott-Rodino Antitrust Improvements Act of 1976. Companies that desire a merger must give the government specified information about the transaction, and must abide by a waiting period that gives the FTC time to assess potential antitrust impact. The waiting period is 30 days, reduced to 15 days for a cash tender offer.

Both the acquiring and acquired companies must file pre-merger notification if three conditions are all present:

(1)   Either one is engaged in interstate commerce or in any activity affecting interstate commerce. (If either company is listed on a stock exchange, stock exchange requirements may also have to be satisfied.)

(2)   The acquiring company has $100 million in annual net sales or total assets and the acquired company has $10 million in total assets or net sales, or vice versa.
(3)   The acquiror would have at least 15% of the acquired company's stock, or would own over $15 million of combined stock and assets of the acquired company.

On April 8, 1997, the Department of Justice and the FTC promulgated revised guidelines for analyzing horizontal mergers (i.e., those between competitors; vertical mergers are between companies at different levels of the supply chain): see 65 LW 2678. On March 11, 1998, the FTC, DOJ, and the National Association of [state] Attorneys General agreed on a protocol for coordinating federal and state investigations of mergers. The protocol is available at http://www.ftc.gov/os/9803/mergerco.op.htm.

[¶550] Transaction Tax Issues

The Tax Court required[14] a bank to capitalize costs, such as investigative costs and legal fees, incurred before deciding to implement a merger. The costs had to be capitalized, and could not be deducted currently as costs related to expanding an ongoing business. Capitalization is required because of the connection to a transaction with significant long-term benefits. However, if the merger had been abandoned rather than consummated, the costs would have been deductible.

Under Advance Revenue Ruling 99-23, 1999-20 IRB 3, expenses incurred in an attempt to acquire a particular business are not start-up expenses, and therefore cannot be amortized over 60 months using Code § 195. Costs incurred after deciding which business to acquire must be capitalized, even if they are incurred before the acquiror enters into a contractual relationship with the acquiree.

ENDNOTES

1. See *Aronson v. Lewis*, 473 A.2d 805 (Del. 1984); *Cede & Co. v. Technicolor*, 634 A.2d 345 (Del. 1993).
2. 493 A.2d 946 (Del.Sup. 1985).
3. See, e.g., *Smith v. Van Gorkom*, 488 A.2d 858 (Del. 1985).
4. *Revlon, Inc. v. MacAndrews & Forbes Holdings, Inc.*, 506 A.2d 173 (Del. 1986).
5. *Paramount Communications, Inc. v. Time, Inc.*, 571 A.2d 1140 (Del.Supr. 1989).
6. For instance, see *Unitrin, Inc. v. American General Corp.*, 651 A.2d 1361 (Del. 1995); *Moore Corp. Ltd. v. Wallace Computer Services*, 907 F.Supp. 1545 (D.Del. 1995).
7. *Samjens Partners I v. Burlington Industries Inc.*, 663 F.Supp. 614 (S.D.N.Y. 1987); *CRTF Corp. v. Federated Department Stores, Inc.*, 683 F.Supp. 422 (S.D.N.Y. 1988); *Brazen v. Bell Atlantic Corp.*, 695 A.2d 43 (Del. 1997).

8. *Moran v. Household International, Inc.*, 490 A.2d 1059 (Del.Ch. 1985), *aff'd* 500 A.2d 1346 (Del. 1985).
9. *City Capital Associates Limited Partnership v. Interco Inc.*, 551 A.2d 787 (Del.Ch. 1988); *Grand Metropolitan PLC v. Pillsbury Co.*, 1988-1989 CCH Fed.Sec.L.Rep. ¶94,104 (Del.Ch. 12/16/88).
10. *Carmody v. Toll Brothers Inc.* C.A. No. 15983 (Del.Ch. 7/24/98); *Quickturn Design Systems, Inc. v. Shapiro*, No. 511, 1998 (Del.Supr. 12/31/98).
11. *AMP Inc. v. Allied Signal Corp.*, 67 LW 1543 (3rd Cir. 2/18/99).
12. *Arnold v. Society for Savings Bancorp Inc.*, 650 A.2d 1270 (Del.Sup. 1994). Later proceedings in the same case, 678 A.2d 533 (Del.Sup. 1996) hold that the merging corporations are not vicariously liable for one corporation's director's breach of the duty to make full disclosures in the proxy statement.
13. 479 U.S. 104 (Sup.Ct. 1986).
14. *Norwest Corp.*, 112 T.C. No. 8 (1999).

Securities Regulation

[¶601]

Securities such as stocks and bonds are a vital part of the U.S. economy. Corporations that have been operating privately can raise capital by making an initial public offering of securities (IPO). Once it is public, a corporation can make further (secondary) offerings of stock,[1] and can offer its bonds to investors. However, the vast majority of securities trading occurs on secondary markets: persons and institutions who own securities sell them to someone else, with no direct involvement by the company that issued the securities. In recent years, securities trading on-line (using the Internet) has undergone explosive growth, creating both practical and regulatory problems (see ¶695).

Securities are regulated both by the federal government and by the states (Blue Sky Laws). The federal government allows states to supplement, but not contradict, federal law-making in this area. Most securities laws focus on disclosure, not quality. That is, the law forbids deception and manipulation, and specifies the amount and form of information that must be disclosed to potential buyers and to stockholders.

However, the fact that a security is registered does not constitute a government endorsement of the current or potential future value of the security. The objective of securities regulation is to provide a continuous flow of information about the business entity whose securities are being traded, with extra disclosure when a decision is required (e.g., proxy voting).

Because of the risk of manipulative and deceptive practices, all securities laws have general antifraud provisions, covering manipulation of stock prices, misstatements by corporate management, and trading by insiders based on non-public information.

''The two major federal securities regulation statutes are the Securities Act ("'33 Act" ; 15 USC §77a; the regulations appear in 17 CFR Part 230) and the Securities and Exchange Act ('34 Act; 15 USC §78, regulations at 17 CFR Part 240), but they have been supplemented by many other statutes. In recent years, the focus has been on limiting securities fraud suits that are perceived by Congress as invalid and as limiting the development of the economy: see ¶¶690, 692.

The '33 Act (¶610, below) regulates public offerings of securities. It prohibits offers and sales of securities that aren't registered with SEC unless they qualify for an exemption from registration. This statute also prohibits fraudulent or deceptive practices in the offering or sale of securities.

The secondary (post-IPO) market is regulated by the '34 Act (¶630 below). It imposes disclosure requirements for public corporations, bans manipulative or deceptive devices; and sets limits on margin transactions. It gives the SEC authority to supervise exchanges and clearinghouses. Broker-dealers have to be registered with, and regulated by, the SEC.

Currently, the Glass-Steagall Act of 1933 forbids banks to deal in securities, other than government bonds (although repeal measures have been introduced in Congress several times, and have a good chance of succeeding). The Glass-Steagall Act was a Depression-era measure motivated by the belief that unwise securities dealings by banks caused bank failures and losses to depositors, but legislative attitudes have changed in the interim.

Federal law also regulates the activities of brokerage and investment advisory firms. A dealer is a firm that buys and sells securities for its own account, hoping to resell them at a profit. A broker transacts on behalf of a customer. Securities firms typically operate as broker-dealers, carrying out both functions. A market maker is a firm that buys and sells a particular security in order to maintain a liquid market.

The Investment Company Act of 1940 (¶660) gives the SEC regulatory authority over public companies (e.g., mutual funds) investing and trading in securities. The SEC has the power to regulate the management of investment companies; their capital structure; and their transactions with related parties such as directors, officers, and affiliates.

The Investment Advisers Act of 1940 (¶670) imposes requirements for the registration and regulation of investment advisors similar to, but looser than, regulation of broker-dealers.

Although speculation is inherently risky, investors are entitled to be protected against fraud (as distinct from inevitable market risk). The Securities Investor Protection Act of 1970 established the Securities Investor Protection Corporation (SIPC), which supervises the liquidation of securities firms and pays off claims from their investors.

[¶605] What Is a Security?

To be subject to securities regulation, a financial instrument must first be defined as a security. Stock issued for investment purposes is clearly a security. In *Landreth Timber Co. v. Landreth*,[2] the Supreme Court rejected the argument that the sale of a business, by transfer of all of its outstanding stock, should not be considered a sale of securities. Some of the characteristics of stock identified in this case are:

- The right to receive dividends out of corporate profits
- Negotiability
- Ability to be pledged or hypothecated
- Voting rights
- Potential for appreciation in value

Although they are securities, bonds are covered by the Trust Indentures Act rather than by the '33 and '34 Acts. As for notes, they're securities unless they bear a "strong family resemblance" to an accepted exception such as home mortgages and commercial lending. The analysis[3] requires a look at:

- The motivation of lenders and borrowers
- Whether the notes are traded for investment
- Whether a reasonable member of the public would consider the instrument an investment
- If it's already regulated in a way that makes it unnecessary to apply securities laws

Life insurance policies, annuities, and CDs are exempt from the '33 Act registration provisions, but not from the anti-fraud provisions. However, variable annuities are securities.[4]

Puts, calls, and options are definitely securities, but contracts for future delivery of commodities are regulated by the Commodity Futures Trading Commission (CFTC), not the SEC. The Eleventh Circuit has held that trading of Treasury bond futures is subject to commodities rather than securities regulation.[5]

The factors in characterizing an unusual or hybrid investment include whether there is an investment in a common enterprise and expectation of profits from the efforts of a promoter or third party. For instance, limited partnership interests generally are securities, but general partnership interests are not, because general partners' profit expectations come from their own participation in the enterprise.

Certain securities are subject to general anti-fraud and civil liability provisions, but are not subject to registration and disclosure requirements:

- Obligations issued, guaranteed by US, state, or local government ('33 Act §3(a)(2))
- ('33 Act only) Securities issued by banks and savings & loan institutions; bankruptcy certificates; insurance policies and annuity contracts (§3(a)(2)); notes arising out of current transactions with maturity under 9 months (§3(a)(3)) (Exchange Act §3(a)(10) excludes *all* notes with maturities under 9 months)
- ('33 Act) §3(a)(9), (10) securities issued in exchange for other securities
- §3(a)(11) intrastate offerings
- §3(b) small (not exceeding $5 million) offerings

[¶610] The '33 Act and its Registration Process

The '33 Act provides that (unless an exemption is available), unregistered securities cannot be sold in interstate commerce. Once registration has occurred, the security can only be sold if it is accompanied by a prospectus that discloses the mandated information about the security. '33 Act §2(a)(10) defines a prospectus as any communication that offers a security for sale or confirms a sale, but a communication is not a prospectus if it is delivered with a prospectus or merely identifies the price of the security and where orders can be executed.[6]

There is a private right of action if materially false statements are made (or material facts are omitted) in a registration statement or in connection with the sale of a security (§11). Remedies under the '33 Act are available only to purchasers. The '34 Act has remedies for sellers as well. In addition, the SEC can sue in federal court if the '33 Act or its rules are violated.

As noted above, the focus of the '33 Act is disclosure, not regulation of the quality of proposed IPOs. (The theory is that the investment banking firms that underwrite the issues will distinguish between high- and low-quality proposals, and will refuse to participate in the latter.)

Major provisions of the '33 Act include:

- §§3, 4: types of securities and transactions exempt from registration requirement
- §5: forbidding the offer or sale of an unregistered security unless it is entitled to an exemption ("jumping the gun")
- §§6, 8: procedure for registration
- §7: information to be disclosed in the registration process; Schedule A is a disclosure checklist
- §8A: SEC cease and desist proceedings
- §10: information required in the prospectus
- §11: civil liability for misstatement or omission in a registration statement
- §12(1): civil liability for offers or sales that violate §5
- §12(2): liability for misstatements or omissions in any offer or sale of registered, unregistered, or exempt securities
- §16: limitations on class actions; see ¶690.2
- §17: fraudulent or deceitful practices in connection with any interstate offer or sale of securities (registered or not)
- §18: limits on state regulation; see ¶620
- §19: SEC powers
- §20: prosecution of, and injunctions against, securities offenders.

[¶610.1] Registration Statement

If registration is required, it is performed by filing a registration statement. A '33 Act registration statement covers only the particular securities that are offered, for the purposes of the offering described in the statement (§6(a)). (In contrast, the '34 Act covers entire classes of securities.) The registration statements consists of a prospectus, which must be furnished to every purchaser, and information and exhibits that are filed with the SEC and made available to the public at the SEC office, but do not have to be given to every purchaser.

Section 6(a) requires the issuer to sign the registration statement; everyone who signs the registration statement is subject to liability under §11(a)(1) for false or misleading statements.

The basic, long-form registration form is Form S-1, although in some circumstances, the SB-1 or SB-2, a briefer, less detailed form can be used. Form S-2, limited to companies that have been reporting under the '34 Act for at least three years, lets the issuer meet its burden of disclosure by including its latest annual report in the registration statement and prospectus, and incorporating its latest SEC annual report (Form 10-K) by reference.

Form S-3 also incorporates by reference information that is already circulating in the public markets. A company that has been a '34 Act reporting company for at least 12 months can use this form to register secondary offerings of senior securities, or new offerings of equity securities if the market value of publicly held voting stock is at least $75 million.

Regulation S-B provides forms that small business issuers can use for disclosure and reporting under both Acts. (See ¶610.2 for small offering exemptions that can be used to raise limited amounts of capital bypassing the laborious and expensive registration process.)

Form SB-1 is a streamlined disclosure document that gives the registrant a choice between traditional "narrative" disclosure and the question-and-answer format of Regulation A (see ¶610.2.4). It can be used by a company qualifying under Rule 405 to issue up to $10 million in securities sold for cash in any 12-month period. The full-scale S-1 filing requires compliance with financial reporting requirements set out in Regulation S-X, whereas the SB-1 financial statements merely have to conform to Generally Accepted Accounting Principles.

The SB-2 can be used for an offering of any size made by a small business issuer qualifying under Rule 405. Form S-4 is used for mergers and acquisitions; S-8 by Employee Stock Ownership Plans (ESOPs); and S-11 by real estate companies.

[¶610.1.1] The Registration Process

Regulation C, Rules 400–498 under the '33 Act, details how to register an issue of securities, and gives the general form for registration statements and prospectuses. It should be read in conjunction with Regulation S-T, 17 CFR Part 232, the rules for electronic filings. Most registrants will be required to file documents (e.g., registration statements, proxy materials) in electronic rather than paper form, unless a hardship exemption is available or unless confidential data is involved.

Securities Act §8(a) provides that registered securities can be sold to the public as soon as the registration statement becomes "effective." (Earlier sales are considered "gun-jumping" and are banned by §5(c).) Unless the SEC delays or suspends effectiveness, this occurs 20 days after filing. The effective date can be accelerated by the SEC to a period of less than 20 days; see Rule 461. Each time the prospectus is amended, another 20-day period starts to run. Even if the SEC doesn't require any amendments, at least one amendment will usually be required: the actual price at which the securities will first be issued.

However, Rule 430A permits information about the price of the offering and terms of underwriting to be left out of the registration statement at the time it becomes effective, as long as the information is provided in a final prospectus filed under Rule 424 or Rule 497. If, however, the final prospectus is not filed within 15 days of the effective date, a post-effective amendment will be required. Rule 434 permits supplementing the preliminary prospectus with a "term sheet" containing additional information about the offering.

In theory, section 8(b) permits the SEC to issue a "refusal order" denying effectiveness to any statement that, on its face, is "incomplete or inaccurate in any material respect." A §8(d) "stop order" suspends the effectiveness of a registration statement that is found to omit or misstate a material fact. In practice, however, the SEC never issues refusal orders, and few stop orders are issued. Instead, "deficiency letters," also known as "letters of comment," are issued, refusing acceleration. Given that the issuer and underwriter usually want to sell the stock as soon as the price of the offering has been determined, denial of acceleration is a powerful sanction.

The traditional underwriting process (which is being altered to some extent by the Internet; see ¶695) involves one or more investment banks as underwriter. The underwriter buys securities from the issuer and distributes them to investors.

In firm commitment underwriting, the underwriters are principals in the deal. They buy the securities from the issuer and/or stockholders of the issuer, resell the securities to dealers, who sell them to the public. Usually, the offering is made at a fixed price, and the dealers agree to offer the securities at the price stated in the prospectus.

Underwriters who are more dubious about an issue's prospects may insist on a best-efforts underwriting, in which they sell as many shares as they can, in exchange for a commission, but are not required to pay the issuer for the entire offering.

Underwriters are liable under §11 for false or misleading statements in the registration statement, unless their sole interest in the deal consists of distributing the securities in exchange for a commission.

[¶610.1.2] Timing Requirements

The timing requirements of '33 Act §5 divide the process into five parts: the pre-filing stage; the filing date; the waiting period, until the SEC permits the offer to become effective; the effective date; and the post-effective period. No offers to sell the securities can be made before the registration statement is filed. No actual sales can be made before the effective date. Once effectiveness occurs, securities cannot be sold without delivery of a prospectus, and the prospectus must conform to the statutory requirements.

During the waiting period (which begins when the registration statement is filed, and ends when it become effective), offers to buy are permitted, but the securities cannot be sold. During this time, only two kinds of written materials (and their electronic counterparts) are allowed: "red herrings" (preliminary prospectuses,[7] so-called because of the warning statement in red type on the cover) and tombstone ads (simple statements that securities can be purchased subsequent to review of the prospectus).

Unusual publicity about the issuer's business, or even its industry, may be deemed an offer. On the other hand, reporting companies have an obligation of continuing disclosure, so '33 Act Rule 135 lets the issuer put out a press release or notice of offering in bare-bones terms, balancing the obligation to communicate with the investing public against the duty to refrain from providing incomplete or inaccurate information.

Although companies "going public" for the first time must use the cumbersome IPO process, a company that is already public can use the Rule 415 "shelf registration" procedure. An offering of securities can be registered and distributed at a later time, or can be registered and distributed in several installments, with pricing based on current market conditions.

Effective in 1997, the SEC requires prospectuses to be in plain English: see Securities Act Release No. 7497 (1/22/98) for guidelines. On and after 10/1/98, registration statements must also be in plain English.

Rule 421 defines plain English to mean:

* Understandable language
* Use of tables or bullet lists to make information easier to access
* Use of common words instead of technical jargon
* Organizing the material with headings and subheadings.

[¶610.2] Exemptions from Registration

The full registration process is cumbersome, expensive, and not really appropriate in certain circumstances—as Congress recognizes by enacting registration exemptions. Securities can be offered without registration based on the characteristics of the securities themselves; the nature of the issue or issuer; or because the securities are marketed in a way that does not create a risk that naïve purchasers will acquire the securities without adequate disclosure. The exemptions overlap, and often the potential issuer will be able to structure the offering to fit one of several exemptions. In most instances, the anti-fraud rules will continue to apply, even though registration is not required.

Short-term commercial paper (with a term under nine months) can be issued without registration, under '33 Act §3(a)(3), 15 USC §77c(a)(3). Section 3(a)(8) exempts the sale of insurance policies and annuity contracts by sellers subject to state insurance or banking regulation.

[¶610.2.1] Sale-Based Exemptions

Because the purpose of the '33 Act is to regulate issuers and underwriters, §4(4) exempts brokerage transactions on customers' orders that do not involve an issuer, underwriter, or dealer. This exemption removes the huge "secondary" market (sales by one investor to another) from the '33 Act.

Section 4(2) makes "nonpublic" offerings exempt. In a typical §4(2) "private placement," all the offerees are either institutional investors or sophisticated private individuals, so there is no need to protect the public via the registration process.[8] A private placement may not be advertised to the public, but a brokerage firm handling a private placement is permitted to communicate to its customers who are sophisticated investors. It is permissible to qualify an offering under both §4(2) and Regulation D (Securities Act Rules 501–508); it is not necessary to decide before the offering which exemption it will satisfy.

[¶610.2.2] Intrastate Offerings

Federal law does not apply to strictly intrastate offerings, so they are exempt from registration under §3(a)(11). (See below for a discussion of state Blue Sky Laws, which do govern intrastate offerings.) It should be noted that many companies doing business in other states prefer to incorporate in Delaware, but doing so prevents use of the intrastate offering exemption. The intrastate-offering exemption is lost entirely (not reduced proportionately) if any of the offerees or purchasers of the securities reside outside the state.

Rule 147 provides a safe harbor for intrastate offerings,[9] but does not permit resales outside the state for at least nine months after the completion of the intrastate offering.

[¶610.2.3] Issue-Based Exemptions

Under §3(b) of the '33 Act, the SEC can exempt issues of up to $5 million. Under §4(6), issues of up to $5 million can be sold to accredited investors, as long as there is no public solicitation or advertising, and as long as the issuer notifies the SEC that it is relying on this exemption. An accredited investor is a person or institution who is able to assess the value of an offering, and does not need the protection of the normal disclosure rules, based on "such factors as financial sophistication, net worth, knowledge, and experience in financial matters, or amount of assets under management."

[¶610.2.4] Regulation A

Regulation A, 17 CFR §230.251-263, is the most widely used of the §3(b) exemptions. The issuer can issue a total of $5 million a year, and does not have to aggregate Regulation A offerings with Rule 504 or 505 offerings. Of that $5 million, up to $1.5 million can come from sales of the securities by affiliates of the issuer.

Although Regulation A securities can lawfully be sold without full-scale registration, the issuer has to go through a "mini-registration" process including disclosure and a prospectus-like "preliminary offering circular" that must be given to offerees and purchasers. See Rule 255 for the disclosure requirements.

If the issuer is in a state whose Blue Sky law requires registration, but permits "registration by coordination" between state and federal regulators, Regulation A will be a poor choice. Regulation A is denied to "bad boys": if either the corporation or an officer, director, or major stockholder has ever been found culpable of disclosure violations, Regulation A will be unavailable.

[¶610.2.5] Rule 701

Rule 701 allows up to $1 million in securities to be issued in a 12-month period (possibly higher, depending on the corporation's assets and prior stock issues; disclosure requirements are higher if the issuer sells over $5 million in securities under Rule 701), in connection with employment contracts or written compensation plans. There can be any number of offerees and any number of purchasers among the issuer's employees, management, and their family members who get the securities as gifts from insiders or pursuant to divorce-related court orders. Rule 701 securities are restricted securities, but their restricted status terminates 90 days after the issuer becomes a '34 Act reporting company.

[¶610.2.6] Regulation D

Regulation D is another method of issuing securities without registration. It authorizes three registration exemptions:

(1) Rule 504 exempts "small offerings." It can be used to offer up to $1 million in securities a year, by "small issuers"—companies that are not "reporting companies" under the '34 Act (see below) and are not investment companies. There is no restriction on the number of purchasers, and purchasers do not have to meet suitability tests.

General advertising or solicitation for Rule 504 securities is not permitted, unless the activities are limited to (a) state(s) whose Blue Sky Laws require pre-sale delivery of a disclosure document (and the document is provided as required); if disclosure documents from one state are provided in all states; or if the securities satisfy a state-law requirement allowing advertising as long as all sales are limited to accredited investors. In states that do not require disclosure documents, Rule 504 sales may not exceed $500,000.

(2) Rule 505 exempts offerings of up to $5 million per year.[10] The offering can be made to any number of accredited investors, and up to 35 "other purchasers." A corporation counts as a single purchaser. So does each client of an investment advisor or broker, so this exemption cannot be used to distribute securities widely among a broker's clients. What counts is the number of offerees, not the number of purchasers, so it's quite possible that the maximum permissible number of offerees will be solicited, but few or none will choose to acquire the securities.

(3) Rule 506 permits offering and sale of any amount of securities to a group of any number of accredited investors, plus not more than 35 investors qualified by "knowledge and experience in financial matters," provided either by the investors themselves or their purchaser representatives. The issuer must check the credentials of all purchasers, though not necessarily of all offerees. If all offerees are accredited investors, then it is not necessary to provide a disclosure document in a Rule 506 offering.

An "accredited investor," as defined by Rule 501, is an institutional investor; private business development company; tax-exempt organization with more than $5 million in assets; corporation or partnership with assets over $5 million (but not an entity formed specifically to acquire the security); trusts with assets over $5 million and a sophisticated adviser; and entities wholly owned by accredited investors.

Natural persons count as accredited investors if they are officers, directors, or general partners of the issuer, or if their net worth is high enough. The net-worth standard is $1 million (for a person, or a married couple). A person can also become an accredited investor by satisfying an income test: earning at least $200,000 a year ($300,000 for a married couple) for the past two years, with the income level expected to continue.

A company that is already a "reporting company" under the '34 Act cannot use Rule 504 for later offerings of securities, although it can use Rule 505 or 506, and in fact can use its '34 Act reports to satisfy the disclosure requirements under these rules.

There is no specific information disclosure requirement for Rule 504 offerings, although compliance with the antifraud rules may make it necessary to disclose the issue's financial background. Rule 505 and 506 offerings are covered by Rule 502, which mandates financial and non-financial disclosure, in amounts depending on the size of the offering and the issuer's status as a reporting or non-reporting company.

Form D itself is filed with the SEC, within 15 days after the exempt securities have begun to be sold. It informs the agency of the issuer's identity and management; describes the exempt securities and their offering price; explains how the proceeds will be used. If the issue is otherwise complying, failure to file the form with the SEC will not remove the exemption from the securities, but could preclude the issuer from using Regulation D for later offerings.

[¶610.2.7] The "Aircraft Carrier" Proposals

The National Securities Markets Improvement Act of 1996 empowers the SEC to create new conditional or unconditional exemptions from any securities law provision, as long as the exemption fits the public interest and protects investors.

The suggestion was taken up in November, 1998. The SEC's position is that it would prefer more companies to make registered offerings, and fewer to engage in private placements. Proposals nicknamed the "Aircraft Carrier" release (because of the immensity of the document) would make registration easier and more flexible by scrapping the existing registration forms in favor of Forms A, B, and C.

If adopted, the Aircraft Carrier release would also make it easier for issuers to communicate with potential purchasers without going through a full-scale registration, by allowing broader dissemination of "factual business communications" (information about the issuer and its business—but forward-looking statements would not come under this safe harbor).

Under the proposal, Form A would be a default form used for all offerings not eligible for Forms B and C. The smaller, newer issuers would be subject to review when they made a Form A filing, whereas more established issuers would have more control over and more options for their Form A filings.

Form B, for use by seasoned issuers, would become effective on the date designated by the issuer, without pre-effective review by the SEC staff. Other issuers could also use Form B in a way similar to the current Rule 144A—possibly without the limitation to qualified institutional buyers. Form C would cover business combinations and exchange offers; SEC review would be required.

Hybrid private placement/registered offerings would be permissible under the proposal. Revised Rule 152 would permit switching from one form to another, depending on market conditions and the response to an offering.

[¶610.3] Steps in a Registered Offering

Usually, the company and its managing underwriter begin the process by signing a letter of intent. The issuer's securities counsel begin to draft the registration statement. The attorney(s) for the managing underwriter and other members of the managing syndicate start to draft the full-scale underwriting agreements, covering the relationship among the underwriters, designating a lead underwriter, and also covering the relationship between underwriters and issuer.

The underwriters agree on the number of shares to be purchased and the price to the syndicate. The syndicate also enters into agreements with dealers, governing the discount at which the dealers can purchase securities. Although underwriting agreements between underwriter and issuer are negotiated and drafted early in the process, they are not actually signed until the effective date of the prospectus.

In the early stages, the issuer undertakes any necessary corporate steps, such as passing resolutions and getting authorizations.

A draft registration statement is filed with the SEC. The agency has 30 days to comment on the statement, and usually takes full advantage of this option.

The underwriters and dealers use preliminary prospectuses to build interest in the impending issue.

The draft registration statement is amended to prepare for effectiveness, based on the SEC comments, and to fill in previously unavailable terms.

The underwriters make the final decision to defer or pursue the offering and set the offering price. However, a price amendment is often filed with the SEC on the effective date of the prospectus. Rule 424 requires a final prospectus to be filed after effectiveness.

When trading opens, the securities are priced by the underwriter, but the expectation is that the price of the stock will rise much higher, creating opportunities for quick profits for those who received shares of stock that they could re-sell on the first day or first few days of trading. The issuer receives only the initial price and does not benefit directly by the price run-up (although it can benefit indirectly by being perceived as issuing a "hot" stock). From the issuer's point of view, the difference between the trading price and the issue price is thought of as "leaving money on the table."

Underwriters' compensation is typically about 7% of the offering price.

It is also typical for the underwriting agreement to impose restrictions on resale of IPO stock by corporate insiders, usually for six months. The purpose is to maintain the stock price for the first few months; large sales by insiders would tend to depress the price. (Frequently, the price of a stock does fall as soon as the restrictions are removed and large blocks enter the market.)

[¶610.4] Resale of Securities

Once a security is registered, any holder can easily find a buyer on the open market. As a worst-case scenario, the broker-dealer that is the "market maker" will purchase the security and hold it until another buyer is found. But the picture is more complex for securities that have been issued in a private placement and are exempt from registration.

Section 4(1) of the '33 Act covers transactions by persons other than the issuer of the securities, underwriters, or dealers—typically, corporate insiders or purchasers under a private placement or Rule 506. For §4(1) purposes, an affiliate has the direct or indirect power to control the policies and direction of the corporation's management, even if the power is never actually exercised.

Restricted securities are acquired either directly or indirectly from the issuer without a public offering, via Rules 144A, 504, 505, or 506. Resales are forbidden for a period of time, unless the securities are registered or unless the conditions for one of the exemptions are present. However, Rule 504 securities are not restricted if the issue was registered under a state law that calls for disclosure, or if the issue comes under a state law allowing general solicitation and offering to accredited investors and no one else.

[¶620] Blue Sky Laws: State Securities Regulation

Even before the '33 Act, states had laws to prevent securities fraud and induce disclosure in connection with securities sales. The states regulate the issue of securities, and may require a registration process even for securities that do not require federal regulation. Typically, however, the "Blue Sky" process is less difficult and expensive than federal registration.

In contrast to SEC regulation, which centers around disclosure, some states do practice "merit regulation," and can deny approval to an issue that is believed to be financially unsound (or whose issuer is believed to be financially unsound). But most states follow the federal model, limiting the registration process to disclosure. About three-quarters of the states permit "registration by coordination," in which federal registration is also operative at the state level. The Uniform Securities Act, adopted by most states, permits registration by coordination, qualification (full-scale disclosure) or notification (a simplified procedure for established companies that already have publicly traded securities).

The states also license broker-dealers and investment advisers, and offer remedies to investors injured by the conduct of issuers or brokers. When Blue Sky laws are violated, the buyer may be entitled to rescission of the transaction; the issuer may be able to rescind all purchases of a violative issue, with adequate disclosure of the nature of the violations.

The National Securities Markets Improvement Act of 1996 limited the state role in securities regulation, by preempting state regulation of mutual funds as well as state registration of securities listed on the American or New York Stock Exchanges or participating in the NASDAQ system: '33 Act §18.

[¶630] The Securities Exchange Act

The Securities Exchange Act of '34 (the '34 Act), unlike the '33 Act, deals with securities after they have been released onto the market. The '34 Act penalizes manipulation, especially fraud, in the market for post-IPO securities, and limits trading by insiders (e.g., corporate officers). The '34 Act includes criminal penalties for violations; the '33 Act does not.

The '34 Act controls the activities of "reporting companies": those that must report to the SEC because of they have issued securities that are registered on an exchange, or registered for over-the-counter (OTC) trading under Exchange Act §12.

The '33 Act requires registration of securities sold in a particular offering or transaction. The '34 Act works differently; it requires registration of classes of securities. The basic registration forms are Form 10, 10 S-B (for small business), and 8-A for companies already reporting under '34 Act §13 or 15(d). See '34 Act §13, requiring quarterly reports (Form 10-Q) and annual reports (10-K) to the SEC, plus Form 8-K disclosure of material transactions and events such as acquiring or divesting major assets or changing auditors.

Regulation S-K (17 CFR Part 339) contains the general disclosure rules; small businesses may be entitled to the less cumbersome Regulation S-B disclosure format. In addition to disclosures that must be made to the SEC, stockholders are entitled to annual reports and proxy statements in appropriate statutory form.

An important feature of the 10-K and 10-Q reports is the "MD&A" (management discussion and analysis) of the corporation's financial condition, for instance trends and events likely to influence the company's financial affairs and results.

The general rule is that all filings must be made electronically, becoming part of the SEC's EDGAR (Electronic Data Gathering, Analysis & Retrieval) database, although hardship exceptions can be granted for companies unable to file electronically. See Regulation S-T, especially the EDGAR Filer Manual (17 CFR §232.301) for instructions.

Under '34 Act §13(d) and (g), any individual who is beneficial owner of 5% or more of a reporting company's securities must file a statement with the SEC disclosing the size of his or her holdings.

Section 16 of the '34 Act places limitations on the reporting company's directors, officers, and 10% shareholders. They are not allowed to sell the corporation's stock short. They must file reports with the SEC disclosing their holdings and transactions in the issuer's securities. Section 16(b) permits the issuer itself, or any shareholder suing on the issuer's behalf, to force the insider to disgorge the "short-swing" profits earned by buying and then selling, or selling and then buying, the issuer's stock without the mandatory six-month holding period. In general, short-swing profits are forbidden even if no inside information was used, but SEC Rule 16b-3 exempts many employee benefit plan transactions from the short-swing rule.[11]

[¶630.1] Anti-Fraud Rules

An important function of the Exchange Act is to penalize securities fraud and manipulation, and offer remedies to those injured. Exchange Act §9 forbids manipulative practices in trading the securities of any reporting company that is listed on a national exchange. Victims can recover the difference between the security's actual value and the price as affected by manipulation. Recovery can also include costs and attorneys' fees.

Perhaps the central section of the Exchange Act is §10(b), which forbids any deception or omission of material fact in securities transactions. This section applies even if the issuer is not a reporting company and its shares are not listed on an exchange. It prohibits "any manipulative or deceptive device or contrivance in contravention of such rules and regulations as the commission [i.e., the SEC] may prescribe as necessary or appropriate in the public interest or for the protection of investors."

The traditional "fraud on the market theory," espoused by *Basic, Inc. v. Levinson*, 485 U.S. 224 (Sup.Ct. 1988) is that there is a presumption that securities in which plaintiffs invested were based on the integrity of the stock price set by the market, and therefore they indirectly relied on any misstatement that affected the stock price.

According to the Second Circuit, benefit-of-the-bargain damages are not available under '33 Act §11, but are available under '34 Act §10 if they can be established with reasonable certainty.[12]

[¶630.1.1] 10(b) Rules

The SEC has promulgated many rules under 10(b). Exchange Act rules are found in 17 CFR and are numbered, e.g., Reg. §240.10b-1, etc.

- Rule 10b-1 forbids market manipulation, even if the securities are exempt from registration
- 10b-3 forbids broker-dealers to manipulate or deceive with regard to municipal securities or securities not listed on an exchange
- 10b-5 forbids material misstatements and omissions; it has been the focus of a great deal of litigation as to its scope
- 10b-10 imposes requirements for confirmation of transactions
- 10b-17 requires announcement of events such as dividends and stock split either to be made pursuant to the rules of an exchange, or to be disclosed to the National Association of Securities Dealers (NASD) at least ten days before the record date.

There is no private right of action for aiding and abetting a §10(b) violation: *Central Bank of Denver v. First Interstate Bank of Denver*, 511 U.S. 164 (Sup.Ct. 1994).[13]

[¶630.1.2] Other Anti-Fraud Rules

Section 12(2) of the '33 Act bars material misrepresentation or omission of material fact in a prospectus or oral communication. The Supreme Court limits this to public offerings made by an issuer or controlling shareholder.[14]

Section 18(a) of the '34 Act imposes liability on anyone responsible for material misstatements or omissions in any document filed with the SEC under the '34 Act. Investors who read and rely on such documents have a private right of action. Officers and directors of the reporting company are personally liable, unless they acted in good faith and without knowledge that the statements were false and misleading.

Exchange Act §14(a) makes a knowingly false statement of reasons, opinions, or beliefs in a proxy statement actionable. Mere proof of disbelief or undisclosed belief or motivation is not a source of liability unless the statement also expressly or impliedly stated something false or misleading about its subject matter. There is no implied private right of action under §14(a) for a shareholder whose vote is not required to authorize a transaction, because the shareholder has no damages.

[¶630.1.3] Litigation Issues

Successful securities fraud plaintiffs can recover their "actual damages," which are defined as the market-adjusted value of their losses due to fraud.

The question of statute of limitations is a complex one. Traditionally, securities fraud statutes of limitations were borrowed from state law. The 1991 Supreme Court case *Lampf Pleva Lipkind Prupis & Pettigrow v. Gilbertson*,[15] sets the statute of limitations at one year from discovery of the fraud, and three years from its occurrence, which had the effect of barring a significant number of potential suits.

Congress enacted §27A of the '34 Act to overturn *Lampf Pleva*, but the Supreme Court found this statute unconstitutional, in that it violates the separation of powers doctrine by requiring the federal courts to re-open final judgments entered before the enactment of §27A.[16]

In recent years, courts have denied private rights of action in various contexts, e.g.,

- Injunction under '34 Act §13(a), so shareholders cannot compel a corporation and its officers to file quarterly and annual reports[17]
- Membership in the American Stock Exchange or other self-regulatory organization (SRO), so SROs can't be sued for money damages for wrongful denial of a membership application[18]
- Conspiracy to fraudulently buy or sell securities through a Ponzi scheme.[19]

[¶630.2] Insider Trading

Corporate insiders get early access to information about the corporation's future plans (e.g., mergers; acquisitions; earnings; new products). This information would permit them to speculate unfairly and manipulate the market, to the injury of public investors, so insider trading is illegal. Although there is no statutory definition of "insider trading," there is legislation and case law on the subject. Insider trading can be summed up as the purchase or sale of securities by insiders who gain access to material information that is not available to the public.

The misappropriation theory[20] holds that merely having information creates a duty to respect the confidentiality of that information, even if the securities being traded are not issued by the client or employer of the person possessing the information.[21]

Material information[22] is information that a reasonable shareholder would consider important in making a decision about a stock: for instance, earnings, dividends, new products or contracts, major litigation developments, major changes in the corporation's financial condition.

Insider fiduciaries, such as corporate officers and directors, are clearly barred from insider trading.[23] Outsiders, such as underwriters, lawyers working on a securities transaction, printers, or others who get non-public information in the course of a confidential business relationship are also barred from trading.[24] An insider who gives investment tips to a non-insider, and the "tippee," can also be liable, but tipping liability requires an intent to get direct or indirect personal gain from disclosing the information.

Insider traders can be liable under '34 Act §21(d)(3) for a civil penalty, payable to the U.S. Treasury of up to $500,000. (There are three tiers of penalties, graded by level of culpability.) Administrative sanctions are also available against anyone who fails to submit a report required by either the '34 Act or the Williams Act (see ¶650), which governs mergers and acquisitions. "Controlling persons" (employers of individuals who engage in illegal insider trading) who knew of the violation, or who recklessly disregarded the likelihood of insider trading and failed to prevent it, are liable. '34 Act §15(f), and a parallel provision in §204A of the Investment Advisers Act, require corporations to maintain written policies to prevent misuse of material nonpublic information.

"Contemporaneous traders" who trade at the same time as insiders, but without access to the material information) have a private right of action under '34 Act §20A.

Rule 14e-3 bars insider trading during an existing or planned tender offer, even in the absence of fiduciary duty to stockholders.

[¶630.3] Regulation of Broker-Dealers

Exchange Act §15(a) requires broker-dealers to register with the SEC unless their activities are purely intrastate and do not involve any facility of a national securities exchange. Section 15(b)(7) gives the SEC power to impose standards for broker-dealers' operational and financial competence. Rule 15c1-7 forbids "churning" (recommendations to buy or sell motivated by the broker's desire to enhance commissions rather than increase the value of the customer's account). Rule 10b-6 requires disclosure of the cost of margin transactions (those in which securities are purchased on credit).

The federal securities laws are interpreted based on the "shingle theory": that, by hanging out a shingle, the broker holds himself or herself out as an expert either in investment in general or in the securities of a particular issuer. Therefore, a high standard of care will be required when the broker makes representations and recommends investments. The recommendation implies that the broker has enough information to form an opinion about the merits of the security.

Broker-dealers are organized into self-regulatory organizations (SROs). The SROs have their own rules about suitability and knowing the customer. It is unethical for brokers to recommend investments that do not meet known needs of the client.

Transactions in foreign currency options that occur over the counter, rather than on a regulated exchange or board of trade, are exempt from the Commodity Exchange Act, and are not subject to regulation by the CFTC.[25]

A number of SEC rules have been promulgated under '34 Act §15(c), which prohibits manipulative, deceptive, or fraudulent acts or practices by broker-dealers:

- Rule 15c1-2 (§240.15c1-2) is another ban on fraud and misrepresentation
- 15c2-5 requires broker-dealers who control or are controlled by an issuer to disclose the relationship before entering into a customer's transaction. Rule 15c1-6 requires disclosure of their extent of participation or interest in a distribution

- 15c1-8 forbids sales "at the market" unless the broker-dealer has a reasonable belief that a general market exists
- 15c2-7 forbids fictitious market quotations, and impels disclosure of the identity of the broker-dealer placing each quote
- 15c2-8 makes it a deceptive act or practice to fail to deliver a prospectus that is required by the '33 Act.

Brokerage agreements typically include arbitration clauses, so most broker-client disputes are arbitrated rather than litigated. *Shearson-American Express v. McMahon*,[26] compels enforcement of the arbitration clause when the client asserts a §10(b) claim. Arbitration was already compelled[27] for pendent state-law claims (e.g., claims under the state's Blue Sky Laws) against a broker, even if arbitration would lead to bifurcated proceedings in more than one forum.[28]

[¶640] Proxy Regulation

In many instances, corporate decision-making (e.g., election of the board of directors; approval of mergers or other extraordinary transactions) will require a vote by stockholders. Very few stockholders are willing to turn up at corporate annual meetings, so the actual voting process is conducted by getting stockholders to sign proxies allowing someone else to cast their votes.

In addition to the proxy regulation imposed by federal securities laws, the proxy process is also subject to state corporate law and to the principles set out in the corporation's own articles of incorporation and by-laws (see ¶135).

[¶640.1] Form and Content of Proxies

The Exchange Act governs disclosure and other aspects of the proxy process: e.g., Exchange Act Regulation 14A (17 CFR §240.14a-1 et seq.), Rules 14a-4 and 14a-5, and Schedule 14A set out the content and form of the proxy statement. Proxy materials have to be filed with the SEC (Rule 14a-6). The purpose of Schedule 14A is to ensure that the proxy materials as a whole will provide enough information for a reasonably prudent shareholder to make intelligent decisions about candidates and proposals.

Rule 14a-3 requires all stockholders to get an annual report, and prescribes the form for the report. Rule 14a-4 sets the form of the proxy, and requires that it indicate whether it is being solicited on behalf of management or someone else. Rule 14a-5 requires additional information to be disclosed. Rule 14a-7 sets out the circumstances under which a shareholder is entitled to get a complete shareholder list, for use in soliciting proxies for a dissent slate or in support of a stockholder proposal. Rule 14a-9 forbids false and misleading statements in proxy statements.

It is becoming increasingly common for companies to use voice mail and the Internet for proxy solicitation. Proxy materials can be posted on the company's own Web site, or the site maintained by the proxy solicitation firm. Proxy materials should be retained on line at least until the meeting has been held and the votes have been tallied.[29]

[¶640.2] Shareholder Proposals

Rule 14a-8 gives stockholders a limited right to insist that their own proposals be included in the proxy statement so that other shareholders can vote on the proposal. The right is limited because, under corporate law, many issues (including the conduct of ordinary business operations) are under the control of the Board of Directors and corporate management, and therefore are not appropriate for a shareholder vote. The corporation can omit a stockholder proposal that deals with a personal grievance and does not offer benefits to the shareholders in general.

Exchange Act Release No. 39093 (9/18/97) makes it easier for shareholders to get proposals into the proxy statement, but also makes it easier for companies to reject repeat proposals that have already been submitted to, and rejected by, the stockholders.

Also see Exchange Act Release No. 40018, 5/21/98, holding that employment-related shareholder proposals dealing with social policy issues are not automatically excludable as within the discretion of management. Release 40018 also requires an "override" procedure for including proposals that have attracted significant shareholder interest.

If a shareholder proposal is included in the proxy materials, the company has the right to make a statement in opposition, but the proponent of the proposal must then be given 30 days notice before the mailing of the proxy statement, to reply. If the company deems the proposal to be inappropriate for inclusion in a proxy statement, it must notify the SEC and give the proponent 80 days' notice before the definitive proxy statement is filed with the SEC. It is often wise, in controversial cases, for the company to get a "no action" letter from the SEC if it wants to omit a proposal.

[¶650] Tender Offer Disclosure (Williams Act)

In addition to proxy solicitation by management (to elect its chosen slate to the board of directors), proxy solicitation is also used in attempts to take over the corporation. If enough shareholders give their proxies, the party seeking the takeover can elect a majority, or at least a substantial plurality, of the board of directors, and thus control or at least influence board decisions.

An alternative takeover method is the acquisition of enough shares to dominate the board of directors. Parties seeking control make a "tender offer": i.e., they invite stockholders to tender (turn over) their shares.

Each takeover method has its advantages and disadvantages. A proxy contest is much less expensive, because there is no need to actually purchase shares. On the other hand, a tender offer leaves the offeror in the position of owning securities, which can appreciate in value.

The Williams Act requires that a tender offer made by a third party (rather than an issuer seeking to re-acquire its own stock[30]) must be kept open for at least 20 business days from the time the offering materials are filed with the SEC and given to shareholders (Rule 14e-1). The bidder must either pay promptly for the tendered shares, or return them after withdrawing the tender offer. Furthermore, because of Rule 10b-13, as long as the offer is open, the bidder can only buy shares pursuant to the tender offer, not on the open market.

Schedule 14D-1, the tender offer statement, must be filed with the SEC, the exchanges, and the target company: see Rule 14d-3(a). Communications to the target shareholders are controlled by Rules 14d-2, -3 and -4. Rule 14e-4 forbids "short tenders" (tendering of stock not currently owned, unless the tenderer has an option on the stock).

If the percentage of the company's securities sought in the tender offer goes up or down, or if the offering price changes, the offer must be kept open for an additional 10 business days. While the offer is open, Rule 14d-7 mandates that stockholders must have the right to withdraw shares that they have tendered.

The target company is given 10 days, by Rule 14e-2, to inform its stockholders of its position with regard to the tender offer (including "none"). A "stop, look and listen" letter is permitted—i.e., the target company can suggest that stockholders refrain from tendering until the target company's board of directors makes a recommendation.

Perhaps the most significant section of the Williams Act is Exchange Act §13(d), which imposes the requirement of filing Schedule 13D to disclose purchases of the target company's stock in a tender offer. The acquiror must disclose its identity and background; its relationship to the issuer of the stock; how much was paid; the source of funds for the payment; and the reason for the acquisition, as soon as it reaches 5% ownership of the target's stock. (Other Williams Act forms include the Schedules 13E and G, 14D, 14D-1 disclosure by bidders as to the bidder's purpose in making a tender offer, and the 14D-9 filed by targets informing the SEC of their recommendations as to tender offers.) "Beneficial owners" of tendered stock must file, but parties with purely ministerial responsibilities don't have to.

Exchange Act §14(e) forbids material misstatements and omissions and fraudulent, deceptive, or manipulative acts or practices in connection with a tender offer. However, under *Schreiber v. Burlington Northern, Inc.*,[31] a §14(e) action cannot be maintained unless the defendant committed misrepresentation or nondisclosure.

At one time, bidders attempting a hostile takeover of a corporation could put pressure on target shareholders by making discretionary tender offers that favored those who surrendered their securities earliest. However, the "all-holders" rule now requires equal access to the tender offer for all holders of the target securities (Rule 14d-10), and everyone who tenders must get the same price.

On October 15, 1998, the SEC approved for publication reform proposals for business combinations (tender offers and mergers). Under current rules, there are more limitations on tender offers where the offeror proposes to pay in stock than on those where cash is offered.

The proposal (see 67 LW 2238) would place cash and stock tender offers on an equal footing. The proposal also calls for a new Regulation M-A for disclosure of business combination, including Schedule TO for third party tender offers. A term sheet in plain English would be mandatory for cash tender offers, cash mergers, and transactions in which a public company "goes private." The SEC also proposed rule changes that would allow large, seasoned issuers to design their own, simplified disclosure documents and would reduce the "quiet period" during which companies are not permitted to comment on impending stock issues.

[¶660] The Investment Companies Act of 1940

This statute, 15 USC §80a-1 through 80a-52, protects investors who entrust their funds to mutual funds and other investment companies in order to obtain expert management and portfolio diversification. It regulates the capital structure of investment companies and determines who can serve on an investment company Board of Directors. Convicted criminals and persons who have been detected in prior securities law violations are barred from responsible positions in investment companies.

All investment companies that do not qualify for an exemption must register with the SEC on Form N-8A. Investment companies must file their sales literature with the SEC within 10 days of issuance. Fees paid to the company's own investment advisers must be disclosed. The Investment Companies Act protects investors against conflicts of interest on the part of investment companies and strengthens the anti-fraud and private remedies provisions of the '33 and '34 Acts. One powerful sanction is that contracts of non-registered, non-exempt investment companies are unenforceable.

Companies subject to the Act are classified into three groups: unit investment trusts; companies that issue face-amount certificates; and management companies. Management companies, e.g., mutual funds, are the largest category, subdivided into open-end or closed-end, diversified or non-diversified.

The Investment Companies Act does not apply to broker-dealers, banks, insurance companies, savings and loan institutions or small loan companies, because they are already regulated. Pension plans and not-for-profit voting trusts are also exempt.

[¶670] Investment Advisers Act Of 1940

"Investment advisers"—persons who receive compensation for advising others "as to the value of securities or as to the advisability of investing in, purchasing or selling securities"—are regulated by 15 USC §80b-1 et seq. However, a number of professional groups are excluded from the definition: advisers who work solely for insurance companies; banks; lawyers, accountants, engineers, and teachers rendering incidental advice to their clients; broker-dealers providing incidental advisory service; and bona fide news media including general-circulation financial publications.

The question of investment newsletters is a difficult one. The public must be protected, but so must First Amendment rights of commercial speech. The Supreme Court's view of the proper balance[32] is that an investment newsletter providing investment advice that is not tailored to the specific needs of individual clients is not an investment adviser.

Persons falling within the definition of investment adviser are required to register with the SEC on Form ADV. They must provide periodic disclosure to the SEC on ADV-5 reports. Much of that information must be given to clients and prospective clients. They are subject to minimum fair dealing requirements and can be penalized for fraudulent or deceptive practices. However, the SEC has the power to prescribe standards of qualifications and competence for broker-dealers, but not for investment advisers. Investment advisers are subject to SEC monetary penalties, imposed through administrative proceedings or civil suits, and even criminal penalties.

[¶680] SEC Enforcement

In addition to formally promulgated regulations, the SEC makes its policies known in various forms. SEC Releases are statements distributed to interested parties. No-action letters are responses to private inquiries, so called because SEC says it will "take no action" with regard to proposals that do not violate any laws.

If the SEC does believe that laws have been violated, its actions will depend on the nature of the perceived violation and who has committed it:

- Against a broker-dealer or registered investment advisor, the SEC can bring a proceeding to revoke/suspend registration or take intermediate disciplinary action. Initial findings are made by an ALJ, with the final decision coming from the SEC
- Against issuers registering under '33 Act, the SEC can seek to suspend the effectiveness of the registration statement
- Against anyone: a cease-and-desist order forbidding further violations
- Administrative proceedings seeking disgorgement orders and/or fines
- Suits in District Court for injunction against future violations
- Referral to the Department of Justice for prosecution of egregious criminal violation of securities laws.

According to the Second Circuit, it does not constitute double jeopardy to require a securities offender to disgorge profits and pay a civil fine for a securities fraud for which he had already been convicted and ordered to pay restitution, because the disgorgement and fine were not criminal in nature and were not ordered for punitive purposes.[33]

[¶690] Limits On Securities Litigation

In the 1980s and 1990s, many fraud cases were filed by disgruntled investors. Concerns were raised that "professional plaintiffs" would file what were essentially strike suits in order to collect judgments or force parties with little or no culpability to settle. Congress passed legislation, in 1995 and 1998, to deter improper securities litigation.

[¶690.1] Private Securities Litigation Reform Act (PSLR)

The Private Securities Litigation Reform Act of 1995, P.L. 104-67, was vetoed by President Clinton on December 19, 1995, but was re-passed over his veto on December 22, 1995. The PSLR adds a new §27, "private securities litigation," to the '33 Act and also amends §21 of the '34 Act.

The objective of the PSLR is to discourage frivolous securities litigation. However, Congress acknowledges that securities fraud does in fact occur, and the PSLR strengthens the audit requirements by requiring accountants to examine corporate books for signs of fraud. Suspicious phenomena must be reported to corporate management; if management refuses to take action, whistle-blowing is required.

Many pre-PSLR cases arose when stockholders claimed that they lost money by relying on corporate predictions. The PSLR includes safe harbor provisions for oral or written forward-looking statements, such as earnings projections that do not pan out. To qualify for the safe harbor, the statement must be issued in conjunction with "meaningful cautionary statements," specific discussion of factors that could prevent the predictions from coming true. This safe harbor is a statutory exemption of the "bespeaks caution" doctrine adopted by at least five Circuits: i.e., that alleged omissions or misrepresentations become immaterial, as a matter of law, if they are accompanied by adequate cautionary language.

There is no duty to update forward-looking statements, so there would be no liability if a corporate officer truthfully announced that a new pharmaceutical had performed well in lab tests—but did not issue a later statement after side effects were discovered.

The safe harbor is not available in IPO registration statements or sales of penny stock; in financial statements prepared in accordance with GAAP; in connection with tender offers; in §13(d) statements disclosing beneficial ownership; or in connection with an offering of a partnership, limited liability company, or direct participation program.

Most of the PSLR deals with class actions rather than individual actions.[34] Congress was worried about the prevalence of "professional plaintiffs," who purchased a few shares of stock merely to be able to sue the issuer, and were not representative of long-range investors. Under the PSLR, the party with the greatest financial interest in the proposed relief is rebuttably presumed to be the "most adequate plaintiff" who must lead the class action.[35]

No one can act as lead plaintiff more often than five times in a three-year period. The lead plaintiff is entitled only to a pro rata share of the judgment, not a "bounty" for bringing the case. The most adequate plaintiff's selection of counsel for the class requires approval of the court hearing the class action; the Southern District of Florida suggests that the choice should be made by sealed bid auction among interested law firms.[36]

The PSLR increases the pleading obligation on the plaintiff. For each statement alleged to be misleading, the plaintiff must give the reason(s) why the statement is misleading. For allegations made on information and belief, the information on which the belief is formed must be plead. Facts giving rise to a strong inference that the defendant acted with the requisite state of mind must be specifically alleged.

If there are multiple defendants, their liability is proportionate, not joint and several, because Congress was concerned about the possibility of deep-pocket defendants being forced to settle cases in which they had little or no culpability, simply to avert joint and several liability on a massive judgment.

Oral or written "forward-looking statements" may qualify for safe-harbor protection under the PSLR. Such statements are not actionable unless they are material. Statements are not actionable if they are accompanied by "meaningful cautionary statements" about the factors that could prevent the predictions from being met. To prevail, the plaintiff must be able to prove that the maker of the statement had actual knowledge that it was false or misleading, not merely foolishly optimistic or inaccurate.

For statements made by a corporation or other entity, the standard is whether the statement was made by or with the approval of an executive officer of the entity who knew it was false or misleading.[37] The safe harbor is not available to issuers who were convicted or subjected to a decree involving a securities law violation in the three years before the statement was made.

There is no duty to update forward-looking statements, even if they were appropriate in light of conditions that have changed since the statement was made.

PSLR plaintiffs must prove "loss causation" by demonstrating that their damages were caused by the misstatements or omissions alleged in the complaint, rather than by market conditions. Pleading standards are also tightened up: fraud plaintiffs must specify each statement alleged to be misleading, give reasons why it is misleading, and provide facts that give rise to a strong inference that the defendant's state of mind was fraudulent.[38]

The one-year/three-year statute of limitations deriving from *Lampf Pleva* is retained under the PSLR.[39]

The PSLR clarifies that there is no express private right of action against aiders or abettors of a securities law violation. (As noted above, *Central Bank of Denver* holds that there is no private right of action under 10b-5 for aiding and abetting.) The PSLR rules out securities fraud as a predicate offense for civil RICO claims.[40] No one—not even the SEC—can bring a conspiracy case against a trader who allegedly participated in a market manipulation scheme.[41]

If there are multiple defendants in a PSLR suit, the jury instructions must call for a determination of the percentage of responsibility of each defendant, including those who settle, and a determination as to whether each defendant knowingly committed securities fraud. Defendants whose violation was not knowing can be held liable only for the portion of damages attributable to their percentage of responsibility. In a §12(2) action, if a defendant shows that all or part of the decline in the value of the stock was not caused by the alleged misstatement or omission, then damages will not be available for that part of the loss.

Discovery is stayed pending the ruling on a motion to dismiss, unless exceptional circumstances (e.g., terminal illness of a vital witness) are present. Since a motion to dismiss is filed in nearly every case, the practical result is that the plaintiff will not be able to obtain discovery during the interim period.

Within 20 days of filing the complaint, the filing plaintiff must notify class members using a wire service or "widely circulated business publication." According to the legislative history, e-mail or other electronic notice methods are acceptable.

If the court deems a securities suit to be abusive, Rule 11 sanctions can be imposed (see ¶7040) and the plaintiff class can be ordered to pay the defendant's attorneys' fees. The plaintiff class (or their attorneys) can be required to provide undertakings for payment of the attorneys' fees. If the plaintiff class prevails, its attorneys' fee award is limited to a reasonable percentage of the damages and prejudgment interest actually paid to the plaintiffs. Funds disgorged under an SEC administrative action or suit do not affect attorneys' fees, because they are not considered part of the fund created under the securities class action.

[¶690.2] Securities Litigation Uniform Standards Act

The PSLR has been supplemented by further legislation, the Securities Litigation Uniform Standards Act of 1998 (11/3/98).[42] The 1998 law enacts a new '33 Act §16, and a new '34 Act §28(f) with identical language:

"No covered class action based upon the statutory or common law of any state or subdivision thereof may be maintained in any State or Federal Court by any private party alleging" misstatement or omission of material fact, or certain manipulative or deceptive conduct. In other words, this does not just bar class actions in state court, but eliminates state-law causes of action as pendent claims in a federal case. It is not yet clear if contractual causes of action (e.g., borrowing or merger transactions) are preempted; Congress probably wanted to be comprehensive.

A covered class action involves 50 or more claimants and relates to the purchase or sale of a covered security—i.e., one that is listed or authorized for listing on the NYSE, American Stock Exchange, or NASDAQ.

Thus, IPOs are covered only if they were authorized for listing at the time of the alleged unlawful act. However, if a company issues any covered securities, any of its other securities that are of equal or senior status to those securities (e.g., preferred stock of a company whose common stock is listed) are also considered covered, even if they are not publicly traded.

Individual claims are not preempted unless they can be aggregated and analyzed as a constructive class action involving more than 50 persons seeking damages. This provision can be used strategically by a defendant who is sued by an individual, but then seeks consolidation of claims for discovery purposes, or who attempts to prevent "stock drop" cases (allegations that the fall in price of a security can be blamed on corporate misrepresentations) from being brought in state court.

It has been held that '34 Act §6, which requires exchanges to register with the SEC, does not imply a private right of action by an investor against exchange members who break the exchange rules, or against the exchange itself for failure to enforce the rules, or by a company that was delisted by NASDAQ allegedly in violation of its own rules.[43]

[¶692] Other Recent Legislation

The Securities Enforcement Remedies and Penny Stock Reform Act, P.L. 101-249; the Market Reform Act P.L. 101-432, and the Securities Act Amendments (P.L. 101-550) expand SEC enforcement powers and add new remedies.

P.L. 101-249 adds remedies such as cease and desist orders against securities violation; disgorgement and civil penalties; and the SEC's ability to petition the federal courts for civil money penalties over and above disgorgement. The agency can also seek an injunction preventing a person found guilty of fraud offenses from service as an officer or director of a reporting company. The SEC's enforcement powers with respect to penny stocks (low-priced issues) are also strengthened.

P.L. 101-432 amends the Exchange Act to extend the SEC's powers to prevent market crashes by extending emergency powers and adding tools to combat market volatility. P.L. 101-550 gives the SEC greater power to work with foreign governments against international securities fraud. It also increases mutual fund shareholders' access to information and speeds up the schedule for delivering proxy materials.

P.L. 104-290, the National Securities Markets Improvement Act of 1996, adds a new category of private investment companies exempt from registration. The objective is to give venture capital firms better access to money that can be used to fund start-ups. This statute also authorizes the SEC to set standards for a single nationwide marketplace for the mutual fund industry.

[¶695] Securities Activities on the Internet

In the nineteenth century, securities trading was a decorous activity, largely carried on by institutions, during "bankers' hours," and subject to fixed commissions. Today, securities ownership is much more broadly distributed (millions of individuals either have a portfolio or control investment of their pension accounts). International trading is a factor.

The widespread availability of connections to the World Wide Web has changed almost every aspect of the securities market. For one thing, a tremendous number of individual investors are participating in the market, especially for technology companies and especially for IPOs rather than secondary market trading in established issues. "Day trading"—short-term speculation rather than long-term investment—is much more common. Because commissions have been deregulated, there is extensive price competition.

Because the amount of information (valuable or otherwise) that is readily available has increased exponentially, and because computerized communications make it easy to place trades, markets are extremely volatile. Soon, trading will be available 24 hours a day year-round—and not necessarily involving conventional stock exchanges, either.[44]

[¶695.1] Disclosure

Traditionally, securities disclosure revolved around personal or mail delivery of printed materials (prospectuses, proxy statements, etc.). Before an IPO, selected institutional and qualified investors might be invited to a "road show," or could have telephone "conference calls," at which the new issue was discussed or analysts discussed the business prospects of an issuing company.

Under current regulatory policy, much of this information can be placed on the Internet, although it may be necessary to take steps (such as requiring a password) to limit access to the information to high-net-worth accredited investors. Posting of the information may also be subject to time limits. SEC releases treat the use of electronic media as at least an equal alternative to publishing on paper.

There is tremendous demand for current price quotations, and many services offer these quotations on-line (with or without an explicit fee). It is very simple to post disclosure information on a company's Web site instead of printing and mailing the information, and doing so saves a great deal of money (not to mention landfill space). It is more complex, but not impossible, to use the Web for road shows and conference calls (although here the issue arises of making sure that only qualified investors see the material).

In the last few years, the SEC has responded by permitting more and more securities functions to be handled on-line. An increasing amount of order processing is handled entirely electronically; disclosure can be done on-line as long as the same information is disclosed electronically, in the same format, as in conventional printed materials (although a hypertext summary of the prospectus, and links to other corporate materials such as the annual report, are permitted) and there is evidence that the investor actually received the information. When a company makes disclosures in electronic form, investors and potential investors must still be given the option of receiving paper documents if they prefer.[45] Companies that seek an interpretive letter or no-action letter from the SEC can make their request by e-mail (cfletters@sec.gov).

In early 1998, the Third Circuit ruled[46] that there were triable issues of fact under §10(b), precluding summary judgment. In this view, it is not necessarily adequate for brokers to rely on NASDAQ's National Best Bid and Offer Price system when looking for the best price for executing customer orders; it may be necessary to check on-line sources of price information.

[¶695.2] Control of Fraud

Unfortunately, ease of communications also makes it easier to commit fraud, because a larger (and perhaps less cautious) audience is exposed to the fraudulent statements. (Many ignorant novices also lose money online by trading based on nonfraudulent, although idiotic, information posted by other ignorant novices.) The SEC maintains a fraud reporting hotline at http://www.sec.gov/consumer/cyberf.htm.

As a typical example, on October 28, 1998, the SEC announced 23 separate actions against fraud in e-mail, on-line newsletters, message boards, and Web sites promoting very small stocks. For instance, some newsletters failed to disclose payments they received to promote stocks.[47]

A May, 1998 no-action letter[48] permits a broker-dealer, acting as distributor for a mutual fund, to accept credit cards for buying shares in the fund on the Internet. If successful, this could lead to a general acceptance of using credit cards to buy mutual fund shares.

As discussed at ¶7575, Year 2000 (Y2K) issues have significant legal repercussions that will take until well into the twenty-first century to resolve. SEC Releases Nos. 33-7609 and 33-7558[49] express the SEC's position on stock issuers' obligations to disclose Y2K problems.

ENDNOTES

1. A "double-barreled" offering involves both primary elements (the issuer sells stock to the public) and secondary elements (shareholders sell stock).
2. 471 U.S. 681 (Sup.Ct.1985).
3. Under *Reves v. Ernst & Young*, 494 U.S. 56 (Sup.Ct. 1990).
4. *SEC v. Variable Annuity Life*, 359 U.S. 65 (Sup.Ct. 1959); *SEC v. United Benefit*, 387 U.S. 202 (Sup.Ct. 1967).
5. *Messer v. E.F. Hutton Co.*, 847 F.2d 673 (11th Cir. 1988).
6. Section 2 has provisions dealing with the full statutory prospectus (§10(a)); the preliminary prospectus, also known as the "red herring" and summary prospectus (§10(b)); the "tombstone ad" (§2(10)(b) and Rule 134); the ad is called a tombstone because it merely states bare facts about the transaction and does not include copy to motivate sales; and supplemental sales literature (§2(10)(a)).
7. Governed by Rule 430. Also see Rule 431 for the summary prospectus, which can be used post-effectiveness in some cases. After the registration statement becomes effective, §§5(a)(2) and 5(b)(2) require delivery of securities to buyers to be preceded by or accompanied by a copy of the final prospectus. Dealers are subject to prospectus requirements if they sell any securities registered during the previous 90 days (40 days for issuers who have already registered an issue of securities): §4(3), no matter how often the shares have changed hands since the IPO. If the securities are listed on a stock exchange or on NASDAQ, the additional prospectus requirement is reduced to 25 days.
8. The classical test under *SEC v. Ralston Purina*, 346 U.S. 119 (Sup.Ct. 1953) is the ability of offerees to "fend for themselves."
9. The issuer is a state resident, is headquartered in the state, and does business within the state; it is organized under the laws of that state and gets 80% of its gross revenues and assets from that state. Furthermore, 80% of the net proceeds of the offering are applied to in-state operations. All offerees live or have their principal office within the state.
10. The $5 million limit is applied to the 12-month period prior to the current Rule 505 offering, and covers the aggregate of all securities sold under Rules

504 and 505, plus any Regulation A securities and any securities that should have been but were not registered.

11. A §16(b) plaintiff is not deprived of standing by a merger that gives the plaintiff stock in the issuer's new corporate parent: *Gollust v. Mendell*, 501 U.S. 115 (Sup.Ct. 1991).

12. *McMahan & Co. v. Wherehouse Entertainment*, 65 F.3d 1044 (2nd Cir. 1995).

13. See *Klein v. Boyd*, 66 LW 1508 (3rd Cir. 2/12/98), which holds that attorneys cannot be held liable for aiding and abetting a RICO violation. However, even if investors were not aware of a law firm's role in drafting fraudulent offering documents, the firm is still primarily liable under 10(b) and 10b-5 if the firm is the author of the misleading statements, and its lawyers knew or should have known that investors would rely on the documents.

14. *Gustafson v. Alloyd Co.*, 513 U.S. 561 (Sup.Ct. 1995).

15. 501 U.S. 350 (Sup.Ct. 1991).

16. See *Plaut v. Spendthrift Farm*, 514 U.S. 211 (Sup.Ct. 1995).

17. *Gray v. Furia Organization Inc.*, 896 F.Supp. 144 (S.D.N.Y. 1995).

18. *Feins v. American Stock Exchange Inc.*, 81 F.3d 1215 (2nd Cir. 1996).

19. *Dinsmore v. Squadron, Ellenoff, Plesent, Sheinfeld & Sorkin*, 135 F.3d 837 (2nd Cir. 1998).

20. Set out in *U.S. v. O'Hagan*, 521 U.S. 642 (Sup.Ct. 1997).

21. *SEC v. Adler*, 137 F.3d 1325 (11th Cir. 1998) says that the defendant has to use, not merely possess, material non-public information to be guilty of insider trading, but possession of information at the time of a trade gives rise to a rebuttable inference that the information was "used."

22. As defined by *TSC Industries, Inc. v. Northway*, 426 U.S. 438 (Sup.Ct. 1976).

23. *Chiarella v. U.S.*, 445 U.S. 222 (Sup.Ct. 1980).

24. *Dirks v. SEC*, 463 U.S. 646 (Sup.Ct. 1983).

25. *Dunn v. CFTC*, 519 U.S. 465 (Sup.Ct. 1997).

26. 482 U.S. 220 (Sup.Ct. 1987).

27. *Dean Witter Reynolds Inc. v. Byrd*, 470 U.S. 213 (Sup.Ct. 1985).

28. *Iowa Grain Co. v. Brown*, 67 LW 1580 (7th Cir. 3/23/99) involves an arbitration agreement that did not cover multi-party proceedings. The result was that investors who filed a class action did not waive their right to arbitrate securities claims by filing a class action.

29. See Bonnie J. Roe, "The Use of Electronic Media in Proxy Solicitations and the 'Electronic' Shareholders Meeting," 32 *Review of Securities & Commodities Regulation* 49 (3/10/99).

30. If the offeror tries to repurchase securities to frustrate a tender offer, Rule 13e-1 requires the issuer to disclose the purchases to the SEC.

31. 472 U.S. 1 (Sup.Ct. 1985).

32. *Lowe v. SEC*, 472 U.S. 181 (Sup.Ct. 1985).

33. *SEC v. Palmisano*, 66 LW 1509 (2nd Cir. 2/4/98).

34. Also see *Matsushita Electric Industrial Co. v. Epstein*, #94-1809, 116 S.Ct. 873 (Sup.Ct. 1996), requiring the federal courts to give full faith and cred-

it to a Delaware court's release of '34 Act class action claims, with respect to parties who failed to either object or opt out.

35. There can be more than one lead: see *Cephalon Securities Litigation*, CCH Fed.Sec.L.Rep. ¶99,313 (E.D. Pa. 8/27/96).

36. *Sherleigh Associates LLC v. Windmere-Durable Holdings Inc.*, 67 LW 1556 (S.D. Fla. 3/9/99).

37. A statement is not material, and therefore cannot give rise to liability, if investors have access to other documents that suggest caution. For instance, warnings in a registration statement can immunize a press release: *Grossman v. Novell Inc.*, 120 F.3d 1112 (10th Cir. 1997).

38. To the Southern District of New York, recklessness can constitute scienter for PSLR purposes, but no strong inference can be derived from mere pleading of motive and opportunity: *In re Baesa Securities Litigation*, 969 F.Supp. 238 (S.D.N.Y. 1997). The Northern District of Illinois reads the PSLR to require the plaintiff to plead motive and opportunity to commit fraud, or circumstantial evidence of conscious misbehavior or recklessness: *Rehm v. Eagle Finance Corp.*, 954 F.Supp. 1246 (N.D. Ill. 1997). The plaintiff's allegation—that the corporation's losses were vastly understated as compared with GAAP accounting—was deemed adequately pleaded.

39. The one-year statute of limitations begins when the plaintiff knew, or would have known with reasonable diligence, that the defendant knowingly made a false representation: *Law v. Medco Research*, 113 F.3d 781 (7th Cir. 1997). *Bernstein v. Misk*, 948 F.Supp. 228 (E.D.N.Y. 1997) holds that a fraud action was time-barred because the promoter's conduct raised "red flags" that would have impelled a reasonable investor to investigate.

40. The bar on securities fraud as a civil RICO predicate is not retroactive, so a plaintiff who had pending claims when the PSLR was enacted can pursue the claims: *Mathews v. Kidder, Peabody & Co.*,161 F.3d 156 (3rd Cir. 1998).

41. *SEC v. U.S. Environmental Inc.*, 897 F.Supp. 117 (S.D.N.Y. 1995).

42. See John C. Coffee Jr., "A Primer on Uniform Standards Act," *N.Y.L.J.* 12/17/98 p. 3 col. 1.

43. *Sparta Surgical Corp. v. NASD*, 159 F.3d 1209 (9th Cir. 1998); *Spicer v. Chicago Board of Options Exchange Inc.*, 977 F.2d 255 (7th Cir. 1992).

44. See Exchange Act Release No. 40760 (12/8/98) for SEC rules regulating Alternative Trading Systems (ATS), defined as a system other than a self-regulatory organization that brings together the purchasers and sellers of securities, or otherwise acts like a stock exchange.

45. See Securities Act Release No. 7233/Exchange Act Release No. 36345 (10/6/95). Also see Securities Act Release No. 7299/Exchange Act Release No. 37182 (5/9/96) for online activities of broker-dealers and investment advisers and Sec. Act Release No. 7289 (also 5/9/96) allowing electronic media to use any reasonable means of stressing information that must be printed in red ink or boldface type in its paper version. Exchange Act Release 7516 (3/23/98) explains the SEC's approach to materials that are online and

offshore (originate outside the United States): an issue has not been made in the United States, for registration purposes, if the offeror takes adequate measures to prevent participation by U.S. persons.

46. *Newton v. Merrill Lynch*, 115 F.3d 1127 (3rd Cir. 1998).
47. Fraud actions: see 67 LW 2250.
48. *Technology Funding Services Corporation*, 5/20/98; see 66 LW 2758.
49. 67 LW 2300.

Where UDAP punitive damages are available, the injured consumer can recover the punitive component from each defendant contributing to the consumer's damages.[11]

[¶720.2] Automobile-Related Claims

The status of the automobile as an expensive, necessary, dangerous item, containing many hard-to-understand and even harder-to-fix components, opens the way for many areas of potential consumer abuse.

The sale of an automobile often involves multiple fees, and less-scrupulous dealers may reduce the type size and list their fees near the government-imposed fees and taxes to deceive consumers into believing that the amounts are government-mandated. It is deceptive to fail to disclose fees that are not optional; all fees that are part of the Truth in Lending finance charge must be disclosed as such.

Excessive fees can be unconscionable. It is also improper to add more fees after a price has been agreed on, because that's a unilateral modification of the contract. If the seller drafts the purchase agreement reflecting the price that the customer agreed to pay, but includes a higher amount in the credit documents, there is a TIL violation, because the overbilling is treated as a finance charge that has not been properly disclosed.[12]

Collusion by unscrupulous dealers to charge the same excessive fees could be a treble-damage antitrust violation. Also note that it violates the Fair Credit Reporting Act for an automobile dealer to get a credit report about a person who is shopping for a car, but has not actually applied for credit.

Other areas in which abuses have been identified:

- Kickbacks to dealers from lenders to whom auto loans are steered
- "Spot delivery" violations, in which the seller offers a price for "delivery on the spot," then subsequently tells the buyer that the deal was not approved, and the buyer must either surrender the car or pay a higher price, higher fees, or higher rates. The buyer is often rendered more vulnerable by a false representation that the traded-in vehicle has already been sold (a practice nicknamed "unhorsing")
- Odometer fraud
- Inflation of the trade-in price offered for the buyer's current vehicle, paired with even greater inflation of the price of the vehicle the dealer wants to sell.

Under the relevant UDAP, auto repair shops may be required to disclose their method for calculating labor costs, and the major provisions of the warranties they offer. The consumer is entitled to receive either a written warranty or a statement that work is done on a no-warranty basis.

[¶750] Other State Consumer Protection Laws

All of the states have at least some consumer protection laws, and some have numerous enactments and an active enforcement program. In recent years, many states have passed or amended laws dealing with issues such as collection agency operations; identity theft (misappropriation of personal identification information, usually for fraudulent purposes), regulation of loan brokerage, and limitations on charges that can be imposed on returned checks.

Retail Installment Sale Acts (RISAs) regulate credit transactions, setting maximum and minimum finance charges and delinquency charges. Some states have general RISAs, others limit coverage to motor vehicles; a third group of RISAs covers all merchandise except motor vehicles.

States also deal with weights and measures; unit pricing and disclosure of prices; consumer product safety; financial supervision of health clubs (e.g., escrow requirements); and set plain English requirements for consumer contracts.

State interest and usury laws set maximum legal rates of interest: the legal rate, the contract rate (agreed on by the parties), the corporate rate, and the judgment rate (imposed on court judgments between the date they were handed down and the date of actual payment). As a general rule, state regulation of interest rates on first mortgages on residences is preempted by federal law, the Depository Institutions Deregulation and Monetary Control Act, P.L. 96-221. However, about a quarter of the states exercised their right to override federal preemption.[13]

States set limits on wage assignments (made voluntarily by a debtor) and garnishments (court-ordered anticipation of future wages), although the Fair Labor Standards Act at 29 USC §206(a)(1), preserving at least a minimum amount of salary from garnishment, supersedes state laws that are less protective of the worker. But if the debt comes from taxes, alimony, or child support, larger garnishments are permitted.

Some regulation of credit insurance (insurance purchased by a consumer to satisfy the consumer's obligations if he or she dies or becomes disabled before the obligation is fully paid) is also universal among the states. Some states simply permit credit insurance to be sold within the state; others regulate who can issue it, the amount that can be issued, premiums that can be charged, the debtors' rights, and state-imposed penalties for violations.

[¶750.1] The U3C

The Uniform Consumer Credit Code (U3C) is the state-law counterpart to the federal Truth in Lending laws. The U3C's subject matter includes retail installment sales, consumer credit, small loans, and bans on usury, if the purchase was made primarily for personal, family, household, or agricultural purposes, where the amount of consumer credit is $25,000 or less.

Only ten states have adopted the U3C: Colorado, Idaho, Indiana, Iowa, Kansas, Maine, Oklahoma, South Carolina, Utah, and Wyoming.

The U3C is a comprehensive statute designed to replace other state statutes dealing with retail installment sales, revolving credit, home solicitation sales, home improvement sales and loans, and truth in lending. The purpose of the U3C is to restrict creditor abuses and further debtors' rights, especially through administrative enforcement by the state.

Creditors are permitted to repossess collateral when a debtor defaults. States impose statutory requirements on repossession, such as filing an affidavit of enti-

panies at different levels of distribution). Horizontal agreements are deemed to present a greater threat to competition than vertical ones.

Restraint of trade occurs when an agreement has anticompetitive effects that outweigh its pro-competitive benefits. Depending on the circumstances, analysis involves either a presumption of per se illegality or the "rule of reason" (see below); the inquiry is essentially the same in either case, according to *National Society of Professional Engineers v. U.S.*, 435 U.S. 679 (Sup.Ct. 1978).

Per se illegality is a conclusive presumption that manifestly anticompetitive conduct (such as "naked" anticompetitive agreements for which no plausible efficiency arguments can be made) has the effect of restraining trade. Horizontal price-fixing, horizontal divisions of the market, and horizontal group boycotts or concerted refusals to deal are all per se illegal.

Two kinds of vertical agreements are illegal per se: resale price maintenance and some "tying" agreements. Resale price maintenance is setting a minimum price at which the buyer can re-sell an item. Suggested retail prices are permissible, as long as there is no attempt to enforce them against unwilling purchasers.

As a result of *State Oil Co. v. Khan*, 522 U.S. 3 (Sup.Ct. 1997), agreements that set a **maximum** resale price are not per se illegal. *USA Petroleum, Inc. v. ARCO*, 495 U.S. 328 (Sup.Ct. 1990) holds that a competitor does not have standing to sue to challenge vertical maximum price fixing.

A tying agreement involves the sale of two distinct products. The customer cannot purchase the "tying" product it wants without also buying the "tied" product. Whether a tying agreement is per se illegal depends on factors such as how substantial an amount of commerce is involved, and whether the seller has enough market power to create an anticompetitive effect in the market for the tied product.

Vertical agreements that are not per se illegal[5] are analyzed according to the rule of reason. That is, the Sherman Act has not been violated if, given the facts prevailing in the particular industry, the business conditions before and after imposition of the restraint, and the proven and projected future effects of the restraint, the restraint was a reasonable one.

The analysis involves identifying the relevant market (by product and in geographic terms) and discovering whether the defendant had market power: the ability to raise prices above the competitive level. Absent market power, the agreement will probably not be anticompetitive. An additional layer of complexity was added in mid-1999 by *California Dental Association v. FTC*.[6] The Supreme Court disapproved the use of "quick look" analysis (a truncated application of the rule of reason). According to the Supreme Court, the reasonableness of a restraint (in this case, advertising restrictions imposed on members of a non-profit dental association) should be analyzed on a continuum, not restricted to three categories (per se illegal; quick look; rule of reason).

The National Association of Attorneys General has promulgated Vertical Restraints Guidelines (NAAG Guidelines; last revised March, 1995) for analyzing tying, price restraints, and non-price restraints. The NAAG maintains a multistate task force to investigate, settle, or litigate vertical cases involving more than one state.

If the plaintiff proves market power, the defendant can rebut with evidence of the pro-competitive benefits of the agreement, such as providing operating efficiencies; making more products available to consumers; or increasing output. The plaintiff can show that the asserted benefits are mere pretexts and do not really exist, or that they could be achieved in a less restrictive fashion.

[¶810.2] Sherman Act §2

Sherman Act §2 forbids monopolization, defined as possession of monopoly power, plus willful acquisition or maintenance of monopoly power by predatory tactics. Having a better product (or good luck) is not considered predation.

Predatory tactics include refusals to deal with competitors without legitimate business justification (or citing a pretextual explanation); denying competitors access to an essential facility that cannot be duplicated; or predatory pricing (below reasonable cost measures).

Monopoly power is roughly equivalent to market power—the ability to control prices—with the additional element of being able to exclude competition.

Section 2 also forbids attempted monopolization and conspiracy to monopolize. The elements of attempted monopolization are:

* Predatory conduct
* Specific intent to monopolize, shown either by direct evidence or inferred from anticompetitive conduct
* Dangerous probability of success of the attempt, shown by a market share above 50%[7]

The elements of conspiracy to monopolize are:

* Existence of a combination or conspiracy
* Overt acts (not necessarily illegal) in furtherance of the conspiracy
* Specific intent to monopolize

[¶810.2.1] Predatory Pricing

Predatory pricing is a somewhat nebulous concept; one good formulation is deliberate sacrifice of current revenues with the objective of driving rivals out of business, followed by raising prices to monopoly levels once competition is eliminated.[8] However, the Circuits differ as to how costs should be calculated, and even which costs should be considered fixed and which are variable.

To be predatory, prices must be maintained long enough to drive rivals out of the market; an introductory low price for a product is not considered predatory. Also see Robinson-Patman Act §2(b), 15 USC §15(b), which permits good-faith price reductions to meet competition, even if the reduced price is below cost.

Furthermore, recent Supreme Court cases seem to indicate that injury to competition occurs only if the defendant is in a position to recoup the losses it sustains through predatory pricing, and recoupment is not very plausible in a market that is highly diffuse and competitive, where entry barriers are low, or both.

Many e-commerce sites feature below-cost prices for products in an effort to build traffic; it will be interesting to see how this affects predatory pricing analysis.

[¶820] The Clayton Act

The Sherman Act is generalized, condemning any practice that has certain forbidden effects on commerce. The Clayton Act is more particularized, forbidding specific acts and practices engaged in by parties engaged in interstate commerce.

Clayton Act §2 bans discriminatory pricing by a seller, if the effect is anticompetitive; forbids price discrimination that is induced, or even knowingly received, by a buyer; bans discrimination in allowances for services or facilities; and also forbids certain brokerage payments and discounts.

Section 3 makes it illegal to have an agreement, arrangement, or condition whose effect is to keep a product's buyer or lessee from using or dealing in products that compete with that product. Tying agreements and exclusive dealing agreements are covered. Section 3 applies only if the limitations on dealing tend to create a monopoly or have the effect of substantially limiting competition.

Section 7, discussed in ¶840, below, forbids certain mergers and certain acquisitions of stock or assets. Section 8 places stringent limits on "interlocking directorates": i.e., corporate boards that share directors or officers.

[¶830] The Robinson-Patman Act

The Robinson-Patman Act, which includes provisions amending the Clayton Act, concentrates on price discrimination by the seller (15 USC §13(a); "primary-line injury") and its counterpart, solicitation or acceptance of price discrimination by the favored buyer (15 USC §13(f); "secondary-line injury"[9]). The Act is violated only if the effect of price discrimination is to substantially lessen competition; tend to create a monopoly in any line of commerce; or injure, destroy, or prevent competition with any person.

The FTC used to bring a fairly large number of Robinson-Patman Act cases, but these are now quite rare. Twenty-two states have laws forbidding price discrimination, so in these states, the Attorney General may take a role in enforcement of price fairness. There is also a private right of action under §§4 and 16 of the Robinson-Patman Act (15 USC §§15, 26).

Certain Robinson-Patman Act violations are criminal: for instance, territorial price discrimination implemented in order to destroy competition or eliminate a competitor; charging unreasonably low prices for the same reasons; or discrimination in granting discounts, rebates, or allowances. (15 USC §13a, which is not the same as 13(a)). The criminal provisions are not considered an "antitrust law" as defined by the Clayton Act, so there is no private right of action for damages or injunctive relief.

[¶830.1] Price Discrimination

The prima facie case for price discrimination by a seller, with respect to purchase of commodities[10] of like grade and quality, is:

- A seller engaged in interstate commerce
- Discriminates in the course of commerce
- Actual sales are made; offers don't count
- At least one transaction crosses a state line; interstate "effect" is insufficient
- Differentiation in price or related terms of sale (such as credit and freight allowances).

Goods having physical differences that affect marketability are not of "like grade and quality," so they can legitimately have different prices. But labeling, or factors that affect consumer acceptability, are irrelevant under the Robinson-Patman Act.

Competitive bidding situations are excluded from the Robinson-Patman Act; it is not a violation to beat a competitor's price: *Great Atlantic & Pacific Tea Co. v. FTC.*[11]

The Robinson-Patman Act does not require suppliers to offer discounts based on their customers' functions as wholesalers or retailers within the supply chain. However, any discounts that are offered must have a reasonable relationship to the value of those services to the supplier, or the customer's actual cost of performing the function: *Texaco, Inc. v. Hasbrouck.*[12]

A price differential is legitimated by 15 USC §13(a) if it reflects an allowance for differences in the cost of manufacture, sale, or delivery resulting from different quantities or methods of delivery. A good-faith defense is also available if prices were changed to equal (but not to undercut) what the seller believed was a competitor's price: see *A&P v. FTC,* above.

[¶840] Antitrust Aspects of Mergers

The Federal Trade Commission and/or Department of Justice may have to be notified, and may exercise or attempt to exercise the power to enjoin a large-scale merger that could have a significant effect on competition (e.g., creating a very large, affluent entity that knocks out competitors and creates barriers to entry of new firms).

Clayton Act §7 forbids any "person" (not necessarily a corporation) from acquiring the stock or assets of another person if the acquisition may have the effect of substantially lessening competition, or may tend to create a monopoly in any line of commerce, in any section of the country. Clayton Act §7 applies to horizontal (among competitors), vertical (among members of the supply chain), and conglomerate (among unrelated companies) mergers. However, being acquired by another person (even on consent) is not penalized by §7.

Clayton Act §7A[13] imposes a requirement that parties planning a large-scale merger must notify the Department of Justice or the FTC at least 30 days in advance. The notice, of course, gives the agencies a chance to assess the competitive effect of the transaction and, if necessary, seek an injunction. If the agencies need more information, the waiting period can be extended by an additional 20 days, running from the time the additional information is received (plus, of course, any time the potential merger parties take to compile and submit the information). FTC regulations may impose additional advance notification requirements based on the industry involved (e.g., food distribution).

Transactions involving small companies are exempt. So are transactions in which the acquiror ends up with less than 15% or less than $15 million worth of the target's voting securities or assets. Also exempt are, e.g., acquiring real or personal property in the ordinary course of business; additional acquisitions of control by a party that already owns at least 50% of the target's outstanding voting securities; pure investment transactions of less than 10% of a company's outstanding voting securities; and acquisitions that do not increase the acquiror's percentage ownership of the target. The DOJ and FTC have the power to exempt any party or transaction that is not deemed likely to violate the antitrust laws.

However, if a manufacturing acquiror or target that has total net sales or total assets over $10 million (or any other acquiror or target has total assets over $10 million, irrespective of sales) intends a transaction with annual net sales or total assets over $100 million, notification is required. Both parties in a non-exempt transaction must file a report form. The filing fee is $45,000.

For large-scale tender offers, the would-be acquiror is required to file premerger notification; the target is not obligated. The standard waiting period for a tender offer is only 15 days, which can be extended 10 days if more information is sought by the federal enforcement agencies.

On March 11, 1998, the DOJ, FTC, and National Association of Attorneys General issued a protocol[14] for conduct of joint federal and state investigations of mergers, with the special objective of protecting confidential information. The state Attorneys General will get access to information provided in response to the Hart-Scott-Rodino process or civil investigative demands. The protocol also contains checklists for coordination of federal and state investigations, settlement negotiations, and release of information to the media.

The FTC and DOJ have issued several statements about health care mergers, most recently "Statements of Antitrust Enforcement Policy in Health Care," 8/28/96.[15] This statement authorizes various kinds of provider networks. The agencies view sharing of financial and other risks within a network as efficiencies and therefore pro-competitive. Provider networks that include competitors can even have a joint pricing schedule, as long as they share substantial financial risks.

[¶850] Standing and Antitrust Injury

Any plaintiff—within or outside the antitrust context—must have standing to be able to bring and maintain a suit. According to *Associate General Contractors v. California State Council of Carpenters*, 459 U.S. 519 (Sup.Ct. 1983), factors in antitrust standing include:

- Whether the plaintiff was an intended victim of the harm

- Causal connection between an antitrust violation and harm to the plaintiff
- Whether the plaintiff is a consumer or a competitor of the alleged miscreant
- Whether the plaintiff's damage is provable or speculative
- Directness of the injury
- Presence or absence of other, more appropriate plaintiffs

Furthermore, to succeed, an antitrust plaintiff[16] must demonstrate both injury to competition and personal antitrust injury. Under *Brunswick Corp. v. Pueblo Bowl-o-Mat*,[17] treble damages are unavailable without proof of antitrust injury, and *Cargill, Inc. v. Monfort of Colorado, Inc.*[18] requires antitrust injury for a private party to get injunctive relief.

Antitrust injury is the kind of injury the antitrust laws were enacted to prevent and punish. The injury must flow from the anticompetitive implications of the challenged process.[19]

In a Clayton Act §4 private suit, antitrust injury is present only if the disfavored customer's ability to compete is impaired[20]; A favored buyer's ability to attract customers away from disfavored buyers can constitute injury to competition.[21]

Also note that the "disaggregation rule" is often applied in antitrust cases. That is, if the plaintiff charges several, discrete unlawful acts or practices, the damages cannot be proved in the aggregate. The plaintiff must prove the damages flowing from each separate area of anticompetitive conduct. This rule is applied by courts that feel that aggregate damages might be too speculative.

ENDNOTES

1. The McCarran-Ferguson Act, 15 USC §1011-15.
2. Clayton Act §6, 15 USC §17, and the Norris-LaGuardia Act, 29 USC §101.
3. So-called because it derives from *Eastern Railroad Presidents' Association v. Noerr Motor Freight*, 365 U.S. 127 (Sup.Ct. 1961) and *United Mine Workers v. Pennington*, 381 U.S. 657 (Sup.Ct. 1965).
4. *Copperweld Corp. v. Independence Tube Corp.*, 467 U.S. 752 (Sup.Ct. 1984).
5. According to *Continental TV Inc. v. GTE Sylvania* ("*Sylvania*") 433 U.S. 36 (Sup.Ct. 1977), vertical assignments of territories are considered fundamentally pro-competitive, and therefore are analyzed under the rule of reason rather than being considered per se illegal.
6. #97-1625, 1999-1 CCH Trade Cases ¶72,529, 1999 Westlaw 320796 (5/24/99).
7. See *Spectrum Sports, Inc. v. McQuillan*, 506 U.S. 447 (Sup.Ct. 1993).
8. See, e.g., *AD/SAT v. Associated Press*, 920 F.Supp. 1301 (S.D.N.Y. 1996).
9. Liability for secondary-line injury is derivative—there must have been a preceding primary line injury—and defenses such as meeting competition and cost justification apply to both primary and secondary line injury.
10. The Robinson-Patman Act covers only sales and purchases of tangible commodities, not real estate or intangibles.
11. 440 U.S. 69 (Sup.Ct. 1979).

12. 496 U.S. 543 (Sup.Ct. 1990).
13. Enacted by the Hart/Scott/Rodino Antitrust Improvements Act of 1976, so this procedure is sometimes described as Hart/Scott/Rodino or HSR.
14. See http://www.ftc.gov/os/9803/mergerco.op.htm or 66 LW 2565.
15. Discussed at 65 LW 2157.
16. Either a private plaintiff or the government, suing in its proprietary capacity, for Clayton Act §4 monetary relief or Clayton Act §16 equitable relief.
17. 429 U.S. 477 (Sup.Ct. 1977).
18. 479 U.S. 104 (Sup.Ct. 1986).
19. *Atlantic Richfield Co. v. USA Petroleum Co.*, 495 U.S. 328 (Sup.Ct. 1990).
20. *J. Truett Payne Inc. v. Chrysler*, 451 U.S. 557 (Sup.Ct. 1981).
21. *Falls City Industries Inc. v. Vanco Beverage, Inc.*, 460 U.S. 428 (Sup.Ct. 1983).

Part II

CONTRACT AND PROPERTY LAW

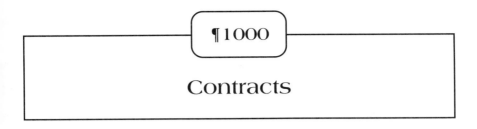

¶1000

Contracts

[¶1001]

A contract is simply a legally enforceable promise, either made by one side (a unilateral contract) or, much more commonly, reciprocal promises made by two sides in exchange for one another (a bilateral contract). All parties to all contracts have a duty of good faith and fair dealing in the performance and enforcement of contracts: see Restatement (2nd) of Contracts §205.

In most circumstances, an oral contract will theoretically be valid, although it will be difficult to prove the terms of the contract unless there is a document to consult. (Certain types of transactions, such as real estate transactions and contracts that, by their nature, take more than one year to perform, fall under the Statute of Frauds—-see ¶1015—and therefore are invalid unless the contract is expressed in writing.)

Contract law usually deals with express contracts (intended by both sides to be contracts), although sometimes a contract will be implied in the interests of justice. The legal system makes a promise enforceable if valid consideration was received for it: if the person receiving the promise relied on the promise in a financially disadvantageous way ("detrimental reliance"), or if the promise is made enforceable by a statute.

[¶1005] Contract Requisites

To create a contract, the parties must bargain to set the terms; there must be an offer; and there must be acceptance of the offer.

[¶1005.1] Required Terms

In a bargained-for contract, both parties must manifest their intention to be bound, and they must arrive at an agreement that is specific and definite enough for the court system to enforce. It's not necessary that every term be spelled out—only that a court can determine what the parties intended and hold them to it. The requirement of definiteness applies to the contract itself, not to the offer.

The degree of definiteness required depends on the type of contract, with the highest level reached, e.g., in the case of a real estate contract for which specific performance (a court requirement that a party conform to the contract) is requested. Specific performance will be granted only if the contract outlines all of its material terms with certainty and definiteness.

The material terms are the parties; the price; and the subject matter. Although the time for performance is important, the court is likely to read in a requirement of performance within a reasonable time, thus satisfying the requirement. Whether a contract term is material also depends on the circumstances. For instance, interest rates are likely to be material—but only if the contract calls for a series of payments over time.

The Uniform Commercial Code (UCC) makes provisions for "gap-fillers": information added to an incomplete contract to make it enforceable. See ¶205.7.

[¶1005.2] Consideration

To create an enforceable contract, there must also be consideration—i.e., each side must receive something of value, as in the situation where one party sells goods that are purchased by the other party.[1] The return promise or performance can come from someone other than the original promisee, or go to a third party other than the original promisor. However, there is no consideration if only an illusory promise is made. Contracts require especially close scrutiny if they are conditional on an event within the control of the promisor.

Legally adequate consideration can be quite disproportionate to the benefits received or expected under the contract. The adequacy of the consideration may be relevant to the availability of some remedies or defenses, but not to whether there was a contract in the first place.

An oral contract can serve as consideration if the obligor of a promise that is unenforceable under the Statute of Frauds signs a written memorandum.

A promise to perform a legal duty that already exists under a binding contract is not consideration to support the other party's promise to undertake additional duties. However, if one party is already in breach, an additional promise to carry out the contract and not sue might be binding.

The law of contracts is, in large measure, state law. There are few federal statutes that affect contract law. However, in many situations, the determination of a contract question will require reference to the Uniform Commercial Code (UCC; see the Commercial Transactions chapter), especially if one or both parties is a merchant (dealer in the kind of property covered by the contract).

[¶1005.3] Unilateral and Bilateral Contracts

Most business contracts are bilateral: each party promises to act or refrain in a particular way, in return for the other party's promise to act or refrain in a particular way. If a promise is made solely in return for the offeree's act or forbearance from action, the contract is unilateral, because the offeror is the only side to be bound. The offeree hasn't promised anything, and therefore can't be sued for non-performance.

Under both the Uniform Commercial Code and the Restatement (2nd) of Contracts, an offer that reasonably expresses a desire for a return promise is an offer to create a bilateral contract, and a contract results when the offeree accepts. However, an offer that expresses a desire for performance, but does not request a return promise, is an offer for a unilateral contract. The contract is created (and the offeror becomes bound) when the offeree performs as requested. If it is not clear whether the offer is bilateral or unilateral, the offeree can accept in any way it chooses.

[¶1005.4] Severable Obligations

A contract might provide for several items of performance and return performance that can be analyzed as separate and severable: for instance, a landlord might contract with a tree surgeon to remove a tree from one location for $300 and another, more obstinate, tree somewhere else for $500. The obligations can be treated as severable if:

- The same number of actions must be taken by each party
- Each party's performance can be divided into parts, and the value of the parts is not inter-dependent
- Performance of each task by each party is done in exchange for the corresponding task from the other party (e.g., x number of tasks versus x number of payments).

The significance of severability is that the breaching party is liable for damages for any part(s) of the contract that is or are breached. Nevertheless, the breaching party retains the right to perform (or sue under) severable parts of the contract that are not breached.

[¶1005.5] Third Party Beneficiaries

A contract can be enforced by someone other than the original parties. A third party beneficiary can enforce the contract, but only if the original principal parties intended the third party to have enforceable legal rights. (A third party who is not intended to have enforceable rights is known as an incidental beneficiary; an example might be a homeowner whose home becomes more valuable when a golf course is constructed nearby, although this was not the intention of the golf course architect or the owner of the property.)

A third party beneficiary is subject to any defenses that the promisor is entitled to assert, other than defenses arising out of a transaction between the third party beneficiary and the promisee under the original contract.

[¶1010] Offer and Acceptance

Rules have evolved to determine when a valid offer has been made, and when it has been accepted (or only made the subject of further negotiations) by the offeree.

[¶1010.1] The Offer

An offer is proof of willingness to be bound, definite enough so that a reasonable person would think that making a promise or carrying out a requested act would result in a contract. The element of definiteness is what distinguishes an offer from preliminary negotiations that have not resulted in a contract. The objective actions that a party communicates have more significance than the party's subjective intent.

The general rule is that offers are made to a specific party, and are not assignable. One exception is the "option contract," under which the offeree has provided consideration so that the offer will not be revoked, and therefore is allowed to assign the promise. Offers do not become effective until they are communicated to the offeree.

If an offer contains a time limit, the offer terminates at that time, and any attempt to accept after the time limit is considered a counter-offer, not an acceptance, and a counter-offer is treated as an implied rejection that terminates the offer.

Silence or failure to respond is generally not considered acceptance of an offer, although it might act as such as part of a continued series of dealings between two parties. The common-law rule is that a person who receives goods knowing that they are for sale accepts the goods, and becomes obligated to pay for them, by keeping the goods. However, there are statutes that alter this rule: state consumer protection statutes, for instance, may treat unsolicited merchandise sent by merchants to consumers as gifts to the consumers.

Similarly, when services are offered in the expectation of compensation, the accepting party will be liable for the stated value of the services, or their reasonable value if none is stated, if the circumstances provided a reasonable opportunity to reject them.

Furthermore, if the offeree unconditionally rejects the offer, it is considered terminated for contract-law purposes, and cannot be revived by the offeree's decision that it should have been accepted after all. Once again, the rejection becomes effective when it is received by the offeror. (In practice, the offeror will probably be glad to renew the offer, as long as no one else has purchased the offered item(s) in the interim.)

The offeror generally has the power to revoke an offer at any time until someone accepts it. The exceptions are option contracts (the offeree has paid for the privilege of non-revocability); situations in which the offeree detrimentally relied on the offer staying open; the UCC or another statute makes the offer irrevocable; or the contract is unilateral, and the offeree has already begun its performance. In all other circumstances, the offeror can revoke the offer, even if the offeror represented that it would remain open for a particular period of time. Circumstances that would induce a reasonable offeree to believe that the offer was revoked will result in revocation; but if the offeree accepts the offer before learning of those circumstances, then a contract is created.

Under contract law, the offeror is treated as master of the offer, and therefore is able to specify not only the terms of the future deal but the means for acceptance, which is effective as soon as it is sent if the offeree uses the means specified by the offeror; it does not become effective until it is received if the offeree does not use the specified method.[2] An advertisement is probably not an offer, because the advertiser does not know who sees the advertisement, and steps (beyond merely seeing the advertisement) must be taken to create a contract.

[¶1010.2] Acceptance and Counter-Offer

Under contract law, an acceptance must be unconditional and must conform completely to the terms of the offer. A so-called acceptance that contains additional or different terms really isn't an acceptance at all; it is a counter-offer. The party that made the original offer can create a contract by accepting the counter-offer. If the offeree agrees to be bound by the offeror's terms, but merely suggests (and doesn't insist on) a change, that is an acceptance. (See ¶205.4.1 for the UCC rule, found at 2-207(1).)

[¶1010.3] Conditions

Frequently, one party's contract performance is conditional on performance by the other party. In fact, both performances might be conditional—in which case, as a practical matter, someone will have to break the deadlock! Restatement (2nd) of Contracts defines a condition as an event that is not certain to occur, and which either must occur or an excuse must be granted, before return performance under the contract is due.

Conditions can be used either offensively (suit for breach of promise) or defensively (against a charge of nonperformance). Conditions can be expressed in the contract, implied under the contract (for instance, someone will have to let the plumbers onto the premises before the plumbing system can be upgraded), or constructive (imposed by the court to achieve a fair result).

The traditional rule of law is that an express condition must be fully and literally satisfied before the other party's duty arises, but this often provides results that are so harsh that courts look for escape clauses, because forfeitures are disfavored.

For instance, if a construction contract has an express condition that the obligation to pay for building a $1 million house depends on total compliance with the plans and specifications, the traditional rule would deprive the builder of any payment if the wrong handles were used on the kitchen cabinets, unless he rebuilt the entire house. A modern court would be far more likely to order that the owner pay the contract price, less the cash value of the departures from the standard (and the departures might have no monetary value).

Modern contract doctrine, as expressed in Restatement (2nd) of Contracts §241, is that failure to meet conditions should be analyzed according to:

- The extent to which the injured party is deprived of reasonably expected benefits
- The extent to which those lost benefits can be compensated
- The extent to which the breaching party would be forced to forfeit by strict enforcement
- Breaching party's ability to cure
- Whether the breaching party acted in good faith and dealt fairly; there can never be substantial performance if the breaching party knowingly and willfully departed from the contract requirements.

However, if the express condition for payment is the approval of a third person (for instance, certification by an inspector), the condition probably will be literally enforced if this can be done without imposing a forfeiture. The court probably will not look behind the honest judgment of a third party who was designated by the contracting parties.

[¶1010.3.1] Excuse of Conditions
A condition can be legally excused if:

- A party attempts to tender payment or other performance in a way that complies with the contract, but the tender is refused by the other party
- A prior condition fails
- The other party engages in anticipatory repudiation: i.e., announces that it will not go through with the contract
- Compliance is impossible (e.g., the subject matter of the contract has been destroyed)
- It is evident that it is extremely unlikely that the other party will be able to perform, especially if the unlikelihood is the result of that other party's own actions
- The other party agrees not to insist on the occurrence of a condition that is not material to the contract. (If the condition is material, then a contract modification is necessary to waive it.) Waiver of a condition becomes irrevocable if the beneficiary of the waiver reasonably relied on it to the point that it is no longer reasonable to reinstate the waived term.

Although a technical distinction can be drawn between a condition precedent (precedent, that is, to the other party's performance) and a condition subsequent (which removes an existing duty of performance instead of giving rise to a duty), they are enforced similarly. In fact, a condition subsequent can be considered a way of breaking up a contract into a series of payments, with the condition precedent for each being that the condition subsequent has **not** occurred.

[¶1015] Statute of Frauds

The Statute of Frauds, a traditional English principle adopted in U.S. law, bars enforceability of long-term oral contracts. As a general rule, a contract that cannot be fully performed within one year will be enforceable only if it is in writing. The criterion is whether the terms of the contract actually preclude performance within one year (for instance, a requirement of delivering a summary of the news of the past month, for 15 months). So many contracts that appear to come within the Statute of Frauds, such as a three-year fire insurance policy, are actually exempt (because, in this example, the house could burn down in the first year).

The public policy purpose is to maintain an evidentiary function; a cautionary function (it is hoped that contracting parties will be deterred from unrealistic representations if there will be a written memorandum); and a channeling function (standardizing transactions and encouraging precision in important agreements).

The Statute of Frauds also applies to sale of real property and real estate interests; leases and brokerage agreements with a duration of one year or more; suretyship and guaranty; and promises to pay time-barred debts or debts that have been discharged in bankruptcy.

The Uniform Commercial Code has its own Statute of Frauds requirements, such as §2-201 (requiring a writing for a sale of goods worth $500 or more); §8-319 (contracts for the sale of securities); and §9-203(1)(a) (agreements about security interests in personal property or fixtures).

The Statute of Frauds is satisfied by a signed[3] writing that reasonably identifies the subject matter of the contract; indicates that a contract has been made; and defines the unperformed portion of the contract with reasonable certainty: Restatement (2nd) of Contracts §131.

For this purpose, the necessary writing can consist of several documents, including unsigned documents that are clearly related to the transaction. Testimony can also be used to establish the contents of a lost writing.

[¶1015.1] Reliance

Detrimental reliance on a promise can create a contract by promissory estoppel: i.e., the party that did not rely detrimentally is estopped from denying the existence of enforceable obligations.

Detriment, for legal purposes, is broader than the concept of harm. It constitutes doing something one was not previously obligated to do, or refraining from something legally permissible. Therefore, there is no detriment in performing a duty that was already in existence.

The Restatement (2nd) of Contracts §87(2) provides that if an offeror makes an offer that is reasonably expected to induce substantial action or forbearance, and if the offeree does act or forbear, then the offer becomes a binding option contract to the extent needed to prevent injustice.

[¶1020] Contract Interpretation

If there have been two or more inconsistent expressions of intent, the latest one controls the earlier ones (because it shows the most contemporary intention of the party). If the offer is made on a printed form, but the parties add hand-written terms, the hand-written terms will control because they express later and more personal intention.

The prior course of dealing between the parties, and usages prevailing in the relevant trade or community will also be consulted. (For instance, trade custom may determine the standard quantity of a commodity to be packaged and sold as a unit.) What emerges in performance may be enough to make a contract enforceable even though, without the course of performance, it would have been too vague to enforce.

According to the Restatement (2nd) of Contract §203, an interpretation that makes the contract's terms reasonable, lawful, and effective will be preferred to an interpretation that will result in invalidation. The express terms of the contract will be given more weight than the usages of the trade or prior course of dealing; specific terms are more influential in interpretation than general language.

Section 202 provides that words and conduct will be interpreted in light of all relevant circumstances. If the parties' principal objective in entering into the contract is known, it will be given great weight. Any writing is interpreted as a whole, and all of the writings relevant to a particular transaction are interpreted together.

The legal system understands that, in the interests of saving time, many transactions will involve standardized "contracts of adhesion" such as forms, where there is little or no opportunity for individual negotiation. Although contracts of adhesion are not per se unconscionable, they will be interpreted against the party that drafted the form.

[¶1020.1] The Parol Evidence Rule

The parol evidence rule, which is actually a substantive principle of contract law, not just an evidentiary rule, says that if the parties have expressed their agreement in a completely integrated writing, neither can introduce evidence of extrinsic agreements that were prior to or contemporaneous with the contract for the purpose of adding new terms or modifying the existing terms. However, evidence can be offered of subsequent agreements, such as contract modifications. Although "parol" implies spoken words, parol evidence is anything (including other writings) that is extrinsic to the contract that is being construed.

A partial integration is a writing that is final but is not complete. Extrinsic evidence of prior or contemporaneous intentions can be introduced either for terms that are consistent with the writing and are supported by separate consideration, or terms that might "naturally" have been omitted from the contract by parties who are similarly situated to the actual parties. A document that appears to constitute a complete contract will probably be treated as one, especially if it has a "zipper" (integration) clause identifying the document as the complete agreement between the parties.

The parol evidence rule only applies to evidence that is being introduced in order to modify the contract. Extrinsic evidence is perfectly proper to prove contract defenses, such as misrepresentation, mistake, duress, and unconscionability.

Although evidence of trade usage or the course of dealings between the parties cannot be introduced to contradict a written contract, such evidence can be used to supply consistent additional terms or interpret the language of the underlying contract. The performance history of the contract can be used to prove waiver or modification of the contract.

Testimony can be introduced about specific statements and agreements as to the parties' intention about the meaning of terms in the contract only if the contract is ambiguous (i.e., even by applying the usual interpretive methods, the court is unable to construe the contract language).

[¶1030] Contract Drafting Checklist

Certain basic elements must be found in most, if not all, contracts:

❏ Identification of the document as a contract of a particular type
❏ Identification of the parties. If there are multiple parties on one or both sides of the contract, whether their responsibilities are individual or joint and several
❏ Subject matter of the contract, including definitions of terms
❏ Consideration, including issues such as fees, late charges, points, and currency risk (if the consideration is not entirely payable in U.S. dollars)
❏ Representations and warranties. Typically, in a business contract both buyer and seller represent and warrant that they are corporations in good standing, and that the corporation is authorized to enter into the transaction and has obtained any necessary resolutions. The seller represents and warrants that it has title to goods, that there are no pending lawsuits or intellectual property issues to prevent the transaction, that its financial statements are accurate and in proper form, and either that there is no finder's or brokerage fee due on the transaction, or that arrangements have been made for paying it.
❏ Allocation of risk of loss, including when risk shifts to the buyer, and any requirements for maintaining insurance
❏ Conditions on the transaction, e.g., regulatory approval; availability of imported merchandise in adequate amount and quality
❏ What constitutes adequate performance under the contract
❏ Term of the contract; dates for performance
❏ Boilerplate provisions, such as choice of law (which state's law will govern interpretation of the contract); severability of invalid provisions and enforceability of the rest of the contract; and integration (the "zipper clause" stating that the contract represents the entire agreement of the parties and cannot be altered by parol evidence)
❏ Signatures.

[¶1030.1] Merchant Contracts

If the contract covers a sale of goods between merchants, typical terms will include:

❏ Description of the goods
❏ Price and method of payment
❏ Warranties and limitations of warranties
❏ Risk allocation
❏ Conditions that will excuse sale or alterations of the terms (for instance, increases in the costs of materials or labor)
❏ When, where, and by what method the goods will be delivered
❏ Installation and maintenance provisions
❏ Assignability of the contract.

See ¶700— for a discussion of consumer protection, and 2010 for disclosure and other requirements in consumer credit contracts.

[¶1030.2] Employment Contracts

Typical provisions in employment contracts:

❑ When employment will begin
❑ Nature of duties; who the newly hired person will report to; title the newly hired person will hold
❑ Signing bonus
❑ Regular pay
❑ Conditions for paying other bonuses
❑ Stock options and limitation on sale of the issuer company's stock
❑ Fringe benefits
❑ Ownership of intellectual property developed by the employee during employment
❑ Conditions under which employment can be terminated, possibly including continuing payment of compensation after premature termination
❑ Agreement not to compete with the employer after leaving the employment covered by the contract; agreement not to solicit the employer's customers or employees after employment ends.

[¶1030.3] Contract Formalities

Traditional language, such as "recitals" ("Whereas, East Wind Realty owns a property located at 2209 Elm Plaza, an offer to purchase said property having been made by Kludgeonics Electronic Corp. and having been accepted...") and "testimonium clauses" (e.g., "In witness hereof, the parties have executed this agreement on the 29th day of March 2000") are not really necessary, as long as the contract fully expresses all necessary elements of the agreement between the parties.

The best case, of course, is either for the parties to draft a contract specifically for their relationship, or for a form contract to be used and all the blank spaces to be completed in accordance with the agreement between the parties. (Where it is intended that a portion of the preprinted form be inoperative, the best practice is to strike it out or draw a line through the blanks, indicating that the parties were aware of the provision but did not find it applicable to their agreement.)

If blank spaces are left when the contract is signed, the question then becomes whether the contract is valid as it stands (probably yes, if all material terms are completed) and whether one party can fill in the blanks (yes, if the party has express authority to do so, or if authority can be implied on the basis of the agreement).

Under current law, "signature" usually means a hand-written signature, although a few states already have statutes authorizing digital signatures for purely electronic documents. A corporation does business through its human staff, so the proper signature is the typed corporate name, "by" a named person who signs the contract personally. The person's corporate status should be given: for instance, "Bigcorp by Steven Anderson, President."

If any other documents are incorporated by reference, it makes sense to attach a copy of the document to the contract into which they are incorporated.

Deeds and other documents affecting real property (e.g., tax deeds and mortgages) may have to be recorded; check the local requirements. UCC filings (see ¶200 et.seq.) may be advisable to protect the rights of the secured party under a security agreement.

[¶1040] Assignment and Delegation

Although the phrase "assignment of a contract" is often used, in fact what is assigned is a right under a contract—for instance, one party does work under a contract, but payment goes to a creditor of that party. If rights are embodied in a tangible object (for example, a season ticket for sporting events), the object itself must be transferred before the assignee can enforce the right.

The obligor under a contract has a valid objection to an assignment only if the duty is materially changed; if the risk of not getting return performance is materially increased; or the value of performance under the contract is significantly reduced.

Contract law recognizes that assigning rights under a contract is an accepted financing device.[4] Therefore, a contract clause that limits assignments will be strictly construed. An outright ban on assignment is often construed to mean that rights can be assigned but duties can't be delegated. "Rights shall not be assigned" is considered a promise not to assign, with the result that the assignment is effective, but the obligor can sue the assignor for breach of the promise. A provision that "attempted assignment is null and void" is usually applied only for the benefit of the obligor, who can refuse to deal with the assignee. The assignment remains valid as between the assignor and the assignee, and between the assignor and its creditors or subsequent assignees.

[¶1040.1] Revocable and Irrevocable Assignments

Ordinarily, assignments are revocable at the will of the assignor. Assignments are also deemed revoked by:

- Subsequent assignment of the same right
- The assignor's demand for performance from the obligor
- The assignor's death, bankruptcy, or loss of capacity

However, certain circumstances will render an assignment irrevocable:

- The assignee provides consideration for the assignment. An assignor who receives value for an assignment warrants that the underlying right exists, and that it is not subject to any defenses other than those disclosed by the assignor. The assignor also warrants that he, she, or it is not aware of any factor impairing the value of the right, and will not do anything in the future to impair its value
- The underlying rights are represented by an object or document which has been delivered to the assignee

- The assignee has changed position in reasonable reliance on the assignment
- The assignee has either been paid by the obligor or has obtained a judgment against the obligor, or has a contract with the obligor that modifies the underlying obligation.

[¶1040.2] Delegation of Duties

Duties of performance under a contract can't really be transferred. Duties can be delegated, but the original party is still responsible for the performance. When the promisee party agrees to release the original promisor and accept the delegate instead, a novation has occurred, not just a delegation. Novation requires consent of the original parties and the new substitute party. There must have been an existing previous obligation, intent to waive the duties under the old agreement, and creation of a new, valid, enforceable contract.

Duties can be delegated (to someone with the appropriate skills and experience) unless they are inherently personal. Painting a portrait is personal, because the purchaser wants it to be done by a particular artist, but painting a barn is not, as long as the barn is adequately weatherproofed. A duty to pay money or supply fungible goods or ordinary services is not personal.

[¶1050] Quasi-Contract

Quasi-contract is the obligation to prevent unjust enrichment by making restitution in exchange for benefits that were obtained without a contract. For example, a seller who is overpaid would be required to return the excess. When goods or services are supplied with the expectation of compensation, and it is reasonable to assume that the recipient would have expected to pay for them, the court may recognize a quasi-contractual right of recovery for the reasonable value of the goods, or the reasonable rate that would be included in a contract for services.

Quasi-contract is invoked in situations such as:

- Benefits conferred by mistake
- Necessaries
- Aid rendered in an emergency
- Work done under an oral or other contract that is unenforceable because of the Statute of Frauds
- Discharge of another party's duty (e.g., a tenant pays the real estate taxes on a property to prevent foreclosure).

[¶1060] Contract Remedies

When one party has breached the contract, and the non-breaching party sues and proves its case, the question for the court becomes what remedies should be awarded. Depending on the circumstances, the proper remedy might be to put the innocent party in the position it would have been in if the contract had been fully performed—or the status quo if the contract had never been signed in the first place. There are several major approaches to contract remedies: rescission (cancellation of the contract) and money damages to reflect expectation, reliance, and restitution interests.

Damages awarded in a contract action must be reasonable, foreseeable, and quantifiable with a reasonable degree of certainty. General damages are the type of damages that are the natural and probable result of breaching a particular type of contract. The defendant is deemed to have anticipated such damages to occur, so the plaintiff will not be required to prove foreseeability. Special (also known as consequential) damages arise out of the facts of the case, and can be recovered only if the defendant could have anticipated them at the outset of the contract. Emotional distress is usually not considered foreseeable in the contract context,[5] and therefore such damages are seldom awarded in contract cases.

Non-breaching parties are subject to a duty to mitigate; they can't recover whatever damages could have been avoided by reasonable effort and without undertaking unreasonable risks. For instance, consequential damages will not be awarded for nondelivery of merchandise that could readily have been purchased from other sources.

It is unusual for specific performance (forcing a breaching or unwilling party to perform a contract) to be ordered, because in most instances the plaintiff can be adequately compensated with money damages, and money damages do not impose a heavy burden on the court to supervise performance. However, specific performance might indeed be ordered in the case of unique property (e.g., a portrait), and each parcel of real estate is considered unique. Because specific performance is a descendant of old equity-court remedies, it will not be ordered unless the court determines that the contract was fair and equitable, as of the time it was made.

The Uniform Commercial Code has its own remedy rules, involving concepts such as rightful rejection of goods and having defective goods repaired or replaced; see ¶200 et seq.

[¶1060.1] Expectation

Analysts think of the "expectation interest" as a basic part of entering into a contract. A person who has not received the benefit of the bargain as expected is entitled to money damages for breach of contract. The calculation of damages begins with the expected profits that would have accrued if the contract had been performed. The initial sum is reduced by sums saved by not having to perform under the contract. In other words, the non-breaching party receives the benefits that would have come from full performance of the contract as expected.

Where the performance is incomplete rather than defective, the measure of expectation damages is the cost of completing the contract, not the reduction in value attributable to incomplete performance.

[¶1060.2] Reliance

In certain situations, it is clear that the defendant has breached the contract, causing damage to the plaintiff, but the amount of expectation damages cannot be established.

The damages for the non-breaching party are the expenses or losses incurred in reasonable reliance on the contract (e.g., a homeowner contracts to have his home remodeled, and buys tiles, wallpaper, and roofing material to be used by the contractor). The purpose of the remedy is to return the non-breaching party to his or her pre-contract status quo.

Reliance damages will not be awarded if they exceed expectation damages.

[¶1060.3] Restitution

The purpose of a restitution remedy is to make the defendant give up the benefits obtained by entering into and breaching a contract. Unlike expectation and reliance remedies, the restitution remedy looks at what the breaching party gained and not what the non-breaching party lost or failed to receive.

Restitution damages do not even require proof of the existence of a contract. They can be recovered in quasi-contract (¶1050) cases and some tort cases (for instance, intellectual property licensing cases). Constructive trust, equitable lien, accounting for profits, subrogation, indemnity, and contribution are all restitutionary remedies.

[¶1060.4] Rescission

Rescission can be voluntary—both parties agree to rescind the old contract and substitute a similar new contract, such as one with lower prices reflecting a change in market conditions, or ordered as a remedy.

[¶1060.5] Quantum Meruit

This phrase, which is Latin for "what he deserves," is a remedy involving recovery of benefits conferred on someone else. Traditionally, a party who breached a contract after part performance would not be entitled to receive quantum meruit damages for the part of the contract actually performed. Current practice does not entirely rule out quantum meruit damages for a breaching party: see, e.g., UCC §2-718(2).

[¶1060.6] Liquidated Damages

Liquidated damages are either a sum of money agreed on in advance, or other remedies (such as a commitment to make repairs) also agreed on in advance.

They are most appropriate if, based on the facts available at the time of contracting, the parties agree that it would be difficult or impossible to quantify damages in case of breach. In fact, a minority of jurisdictions will not enforce a liquidated damages clause without proof that damages could not be reliably ascertained after the breach. On the other hand, a party's attempt to restrict its exposure by negotiating an unreasonably small amount of liquidated damages will probably be enforceable unless the clause is unconscionable.

Liquidated damages are unenforceable if they constitute a penalty.[6] Damages for delay are more likely to be upheld if the amount increases as the delay continues, rather than a single flat sum irrespective of the duration of the delay.

[¶1060.7] Punitive Damages

A defendant who engages in fraudulent, malicious, oppressive or otherwise reprehensible conduct in connection with a contract might be required to pay punitive damages, measured by the defendant's capacity to pay rather than by quantifiable damage to the plaintiff. However, punitive damages are quite rare in the contractual context, although the defendant's conduct might be tortious as well as constituting a breach.

[¶1065] Excuse of Performance

Under most circumstances, a party who guessed wrong or made an incorrect prediction will be required to abide by its contract obligations—or face penalties for breach—even if performance turns out to be more difficult or more expensive than anticipated. However, performance will certainly be excused if performance becomes impossible: an art dealer will not be required to deliver a Rembrandt painting that was destroyed in a fire after being sold but before delivery, for instance.

The more difficult question is when performance will be excused when it is merely impracticable, not absolutely impossible. The defense of impracticability requires four elements:

* An event (such as a natural disaster) has occurred to make performance impracticable, at least as contemplated; related higher costs are not enough to excuse performance, but hugely higher costs might be
* The event is not the fault of the party seeking to be excused
* The event is one whose non-occurrence was a basic assumption underlying the contract. In contrast, a party who enters into a futures contract can be presumed to know that prices will fluctuate, since that's the rationale for futures contracts
* The party seeking excuse did not agree to assume the risk of what actually occurred, either in express contract language, or by assenting to a list of conditions other than the one that actually occurred.

The doctrine of economic frustration covers the situation in which post-contract events make performance, even though it is perfectly possible, useless to one party. Just after Prohibition was declared, for instance, breweries had plenty of beer, but their tavern customers couldn't use it (well, not legally, anyway).

Restatement (2nd) of Contracts §265 permits discharge of future duties under a contract if the party is not at fault and the principal purpose motivating the contract is frustrated by an event whose non-occurrence was a basic assumption underlying the contract. (Discharge is not permitted if the contract contains language to the contrary.) However, even if discharge is granted, the other party may be entitled to restitution of benefits already provided under the contract, or reliance damages to compensate for having changed position in reliance on the contract.

[¶1070] Defenses

A party accused of breach of contract may be able to stave off the accusations by proving that no valid contract was ever formed; that the defendant's conduct did not in fact breach the contract; or that a defense is available.

[¶1070.1] Incapacity

Contracts may become either voidable or absolutely void if entered into by parties lacking contractual capacity. However, the promise of incapacitated persons still constitutes consideration, so they can enforce contracts that cannot be enforced against them. Contracts are voidable rather than void if the incapacity is only partial.

Minors' contracts, except for contracts for necessities (such as food and medical care) are voidable (by themselves or their guardians), once the minor reaches adult age, unless the minor chooses to reaffirm them after becoming an adult. If the contract is disaffirmed, the legal effect is to revest the contract property in its original owner. In many instances, this is a practical impossibility, because the property has been consumed, destroyed, or transferred to someone else. Some jurisdictions require the minor to reimburse the other party for such losses.

For adults, where the question is impairment by reason of developmental disability, mental illness, or aging-related deterioration, the standard of contractual capacity is fairly low: the ability to understand the nature of the transaction and its implications. A distinction may be drawn between impaired persons who lack cognitive capacity (such contracts could be treated as voidable whether or not the other party knew or could have known about the impairment) and those who suffer mental illness that impairs their motivational control (contracts probably voidable only if the other party knew or should have known of the illness).

Another approach some jurisdictions take is to allow contracts to be avoided on the grounds of incapacity if the status quo can be restored, even if there was no reason for the other party to know of the condition.

The burden of proof is on the party seeking to avoid the contract. Rescission will be available if the contract is still executory, but unless the other party took advantage of an impaired person, the right of avoidance may be limited to the part of the contract that has not already been performed.

In addition to the potential for avoidance of the contract, mental impairment might be relevant to claims of undue influence.

[¶1070.2] Duress and Related Concepts

A contract is obtained by duress if a significant threat of unlawful harm or economic loss is applied to motivate the contract. A threat to act in a legal manner (e.g., to bring suit or publicize someone else's conduct), even if the consequences of doing so would be very serious, does not constitute duress.

Contracts can also be avoided if they have illegal subject matter (e.g., assassinations; drug deals); if they violate public policy (e.g., racially restrictive covenants in property deeds); and if they are unconscionable (so unfair that the legal system will not become involved in their enforcement).

Furthermore, an exculpatory contract term is not enforceable if it has the effect of relieving a party from liability for harm that is intentionally inflicted on others, or that results from reckless conduct.

[¶1070.3] Undue Influence

Duress is severe enough to overbear the will. Undue influence is related but less severe. Undue influence consists of taking advantage of someone else's mental state or personal characteristics to prevent free choice and induce that person to enter into an unfair contract. The person's immaturity, illness, bereavement, lack of sophistication, etc., has the effect of limiting the ability to make valid decisions.

Undue influence can also be asserted in the context of a fiduciary relationship, where the non-fiduciary naturally relies on the fiduciary's judgment. In such situations, unfair contracts can be set aside, even if there was no conscious abuse of the relationship on the fiduciary's part.

[¶1070.4] Misrepresentation

Misrepresentation is an assertion that is not in accordance with the true state of facts. Concealment of negative facts also constitutes misrepresentation; so does failure to disclose but only if there is a duty to disclose (e.g., imposed by a statute; implied as part of a fiduciary relationship; needed to correct a previous assertion that was accurate when made but has been rendered inaccurate by subsequent events). There may also be a duty to disclose in situations where the potential discloser is aware that the other party is operating under a mistake.

The doctrine of "fraud in the factum" says that there is no contract if alleged consent is obtained by misrepresentation—e.g., the individual did not think that the document he or she signed was a contract. The difference between no contract, in the case of fraud in the factum, and a voidable contract, in the case of misrepresentation where the innocent party knew that a contract was created, becomes significant if a bona fide purchaser for value enters the situation.

Contracts can be avoided for misrepresentation only if the misrepresentation was material, fraudulent, or both. A misrepresentation is material in general if it would be likely to induce a reasonable person to enter into the contract. In a particular situation, a misrepresentation can be material if it was known to operate as an inducement to a particular person (a fanatical electric train collector or fervent Greek patriot, for instance). Even an innocent or negligent material misrepresentation can justify avoidance of a contract.

A representation is fraudulent if it is made with the intention of inducing reliance, and it was either known to be false or the maker of the representation lacked sufficient facts to be aware of whether it was true or false. An opinion can be a misrepresentation, but only if the speaker believes the assertion to be false.

The party seeking to avoid the contract must have relied on it (it must have contributed significantly to the decision to enter into the contract). Either that party must have had pecuniary detriment, or must not have received the expected bargain. Furthermore, reliance must have been reasonable, as judged from the viewpoint of a person in that party's situation. Reliance on a pure statement of opinion is not justified. In general, statements of future intentions cannot be relied upon, because people can change their minds.

[¶1070.5] Mistake of Fact

Mistake of law usually does not offer a contract defense, because everyone is presumed to know the law (however distant that assumption is from real life).

On the other hand, a significant enough mistake of fact operates as a defense, because it prevents a contract from being formed at all (e.g., mistake about the identity of the parties). An offer that is the product of a mistake is not an effective offer and cannot create a contract. Nor is there a contract if communications are exchanged that include materially different meanings, and neither side has reason to know what the other party meant. The classic case involves two ships named *"Peerless"* that were shipping cargo at the same time.

A fundamental unilateral error that the other party knows about could operate as a defense; so could a misunderstanding about the contract terms that cannot be resolved by a court's interpretation of the contract.

A mistake of fact involves present factual matters in existence at the time the contract was created. A mistaken prediction of what will happen (e.g., the price of wheat six months in the future) does not qualify as a mistake of fact. Furthermore, since the principle is that contracts are made to be performed rather than avoided, relief on the basis of mistake of fact is the exception, not the rule.

Under Restatement (2nd) of Contracts §152, a mutual mistake that is material to the agreed-on exchange of performance allows avoidance of the contract by the adversely affected party, unless that party bore the risk of mistake on such issues. (A unilateral mistake actually induced by representations of the other party might give rise to a defense of misrepresentation.) The facts must have existed when the contract was signed.

A party who assumes the risk of mistake with regard to the accuracy of facts has no defense if the facts are wrong. This might occur in a futures contract, which reflects assumptions about future price trends, or if the contract itself reflects the assumption, such as a construction contract reciting that the contractor has tested the soil conditions.

ENDNOTES

1. But see UCC §2-209(1), allowing a good faith modification of a contract without new consideration.
2. The UCC rule is a little different: §2-206 says that, unless the language of the offer or the circumstances are to the contrary, an offer invites acceptance by any reasonable medium or manner.

X for life, and then to Y" or "To X for the life of Y, and then to Z." The holder of the life estate can transfer his or her rights to someone else, but the transferee's rights end when the transferor (or the named life) dies.

[¶1110.2] Future Interests

Future interests are divided into three main categories, each of which has sub-categories, depending on criteria such as whether they belong to the grantor or another party; whether they are vested or contingent (i.e., certain to happen, or may possibly happen, respectively); and what event is necessary to trigger them.

- Reversionary interests are vested interests retained by the grantor, e.g., the right to re-possess the property after a fee simple determinable has ended, or the right to take steps to terminate a fee simple on condition subsequent when the specified event has occurred. A reversion is what the grantor retains after transferring only part of his or her interest in the property. The reversion itself is a property right that can be given away, sold, or devised in a will.
- Remainder interests are future interests given, sold, or left by the grantor to someone else. Remainder interests are created at the same time as a present interest: i.e., the property goes to Alice Ames for 25 years, with a remainder to Bob Blake. A remainder can be contingent (e.g., a remainder to all of the grantor's grandchildren who are alive in 2013), and can terminate when a specified event occurs.
- Executory interests are future interests transferred by the grantor to someone else, and which have the effect of eliminating the grantor's retained interest in the property or dispossessing someone else.

Note that, for gift tax purposes, a gift of a present interest can qualify for the annual exclusion, but a gift of a future interest cannot: see ¶3130.

[¶1110.3] Rule Against Perpetuities

This rule exists to frustrate attempts to tie up property forever, without its ever becoming freely transferable. The rule provides that property interests must vest (if they ever do) no later than 21 years (plus nine months for gestation of a conceived but unborn heir) after the life of a person who was already alive when the interest was created.

In other words, it is not possible to set up a non-charitable trust that will last forever, or to tie up land ownership forever. (The Rule Against Perpetuities doesn't apply to charitable trusts.)

Some states have adopted the Uniform Statutory Rule Against Perpetuities, which says that a non-vested interest that actually does either vest or fail within 90 years of creation is valid. In the other states, the common-law "wait and see" doctrine applies: instead of declaring an interest invalid at the outset, the decision is deferred until actual events make it possible to determine if vesting has occurred. The doctrine of *cy pres* (as close as possible) permits reformation of documents so that it becomes clear whether or not the interest will vest in time.

[¶1115] Shared Ownership

There are various situations in which property has more than one owner concurrently. The most common forms of shared ownership are joint tenancy with right of survivorship (JWROS) and tenancy in common. There are also forms of tenancy limited to married couples: community property, and a special JWROS form, tenancy by the entireties.

Tenancy in common can be created by deed, by will, or when there is no will and property is inherited by intestate succession.

Tenants in common are equally entitled to possess the property, although they may own different shares in it. Tenants in common can sell, give away, or devise their ownership shares without consent of the other tenant(s) in common. The cotenants can agree to partition the property, or partition can be ordered by a court.

In contrast, when one joint tenant with right of survivorship dies, his or her ownership share passes automatically, by operation of law, to the surviving joint tenant(s), each of whom now has a larger percentage ownership. (If there is only one, he or she has 100% ownership.) A JWROS tenancy cannot be created by intestate succession, only by deed or by will. JWROS requires four conditions:

- Cotenants must acquire their interests in the property at the same time
- They must have acquired their interests under the same deed or other instrument, or because of the same act of adverse possession
- They must have the same interest in the property
- Each must be entitled to possess the whole property

Although any joint tenant can sever the joint tenancy, thus eliminating the right of survivorship, and although any joint tenant can compel partition, an attempt to sell or give away a JWROS interest makes the buyer or donee a tenant in common with the other joint tenants. (The acquiror does not become a joint tenant because the interests were created at different times; if the intention is to create a new joint tenancy, the old one must be severed and a new one created respecting the "four unities.")

Tenancy by the entireties is a marital joint tenancy that offers additional protection from claims of creditors.

Community property is a legal fiction that a married couple's property is held not by the spouses as individuals, but the marital "community." As ¶3020.3 shows, it may be necessary to distinguish between the separate property of the spouses, and community property. Generally speaking, anything acquired prior to the marriage is separate; anything acquired during the marriage is community; and the community property states have taken various approaches to, for instance, income earned during marriage on separate property. Spouses may also be able to alter the state community property rules by pre- or post-nuptial agreement, and make interspousal gifts that turn community into separate property.

When the spouses divorce, each spouse takes back his or her separate property (if any), and the community property is divided. Spouses in community property states can devise their separate property, but community property passes automatically by operation of law.

The basic contemporary rule (which has been altered by some state statutes) is that if a conveyance does not indicate the form in which multiple owners will hold the property, it will be presumed to be a tenancy in common. (This is a change from the traditional presumption of JWROS.) Evidence can be produced to rebut the presumption. Some of the state statutes presume that a conveyance to a married couple is intended to make them joint tenants or tenants by the entireties.

[¶1120] Real Estate Transactions

Some houses are "FISBOs"—For Sale By Owner—with no involvement of a real estate broker. However, most residential sales, and nearly all commercial sales, involve a real estate broker.

Many problems arise because of the multiplicity of documents that can be used in the course of a real estate transaction, and potential for misunderstanding of each document. A common sticking point is the use of a "binder" or pre-contract; before there is a closing or even a contract of sale, the potential buyer decides not to buy, or the potential seller gets a better offer, and it then becomes necessary to decide whether the binder is indeed an enforceable contract or merely an agreement to agree.

Generally speaking, the contract of sale will obligate the seller to convey good marketable title at the time of the closing. Therefore, the seller must use the pre-closing period to remove any encumbrances from the chain of title, and cure any defects (e.g., unrecorded conveyances) in the chain of title. Failure to do so permits the buyer to sue for breach of contract. Most buyers will also have title insurance which will compensate them if good title is not delivered.

If the seller breaches the contract, the buyer may be entitled to specific performance; because real property is unique, a damage award would not necessarily fully compensate the buyer. The buyer can, however, sue for damages, especially if specific performance is unavailable (e.g., the house has burned down). The buyer can also obtain rescission of the contract and return of the deposit. State law usually requires that the deposit be placed in escrow until the closing.

Few courts would order specific performance by a breaching buyer; it is more likely that the buyer would be ordered to pay damages that compensate the seller for the loss of the bargain. If rescission is obtained in this situation, the seller would be entitled to keep the down payment. A common-sense rule is to make sure that the deposit is large enough to cover the broker's commission, expense of title search, and to compensate for the additional time needed to find another buyer if the first buyer defaults.

Contracts of sale are often drafted subject to "contingencies," the most common being the potential buyer's ability to obtain mortgage financing on satisfactory terms before the closing. A purchase money mortgage (PMM) is provided by the seller rather than by a lending institution: i.e., instead of the buyer paying the full price at closing, the buyer pays part of the price, then makes continuing payments to the seller. It is common for the PMM to be a second mortgage, with the first mortgage conventionally financed by a lender.

The lender may also be willing to have the buyer "assume" the seller's mortgage—i.e., instead of the seller paying off the mortgage balance at closing, the lender merely transfers the mortgage obligation to the buyer. Loans that are backed by the Federal Housing Administration (FHA) or Veterans' Administration (VA) can always be assumed by the buyer at the rate of interest paid by the seller.

Another problem is the interpretation of the "listing agreement" between the seller and the broker. In agency terms, the broker is the agent of the seller; it is also possible for buyers to hire a broker to act as their agent. A state license is required to act as broker, and brokers are considered fiduciaries.

Disputes often arise as to whether or not a particular broker is actually the procuring cause of a sale, and therefore entitled to a commission—a problem that will become more acute as listing properties for sale on the Internet becomes more common. If the buyer is willing to consummate the transaction and the seller is not, the seller may be liable for the broker's fee, because the broker produced a suitable willing buyer.

Local practice determines the respective roles of attorneys, brokers, and title insurance agents; often, the transaction is handled and the closing held with very little attorney involvement. However, non-lawyers should be careful to avoid overstepping the bounds and engaging in unauthorized practice of law.

[¶1120.1] Elements Of Contract Of Sale For Residential Property

Apart from the practical value of stipulating every feature of a deal involving large amounts of money, contracts for the sale of real estate are subject to the Statute of Frauds, and are not enforceable without a writing.

- Parties and their addresses
- If seller is married, spouse joins in the conveyance
- Description of property
  buildings
  structures
  improvements
  personal property included with the sale—e.g., appliances that are not fixtures; custom-made draperies
  fixtures
- Type of deed granted
  encumbrances, e.g., zoning laws, existing party walls, taxes, liens, easements, restrictions
- Plans of the property
- If the seller must provide a survey at his/her own expense; when the survey must be delivered; how long the buyer has to raise survey-based objections.

As an alternative, the contract can provide that the property is delivered subject to local zoning and setback ordinances (and that the seller is not aware
of any violation of those ordinances); that the contract is subject to the state
of facts that would be shown by an accurate survey; and subject to any
recorded covenants or restrictions that do not render title unmarketable
- Representations and warranties; warranties are usually implied that the seller will deliver marketable title, and that the property will be habitable. An
  express warranty that the buyer's intended use does not violate the zoning
  ordinance is common.
     Environmental, related problems—radon, brownfields, lead paint, LUSTs
     (leaking underground storage tanks), smoke detectors, termites
- Seller agrees to deliver any necessary instruments so the buyer can get
  Certificate of Title
- Purchase price
     Deposit already in escrow; conditions of escrow
     Payable at closing
     Adjustments to be made at closing—e.g., taxes, water bills, oil in tank
- Time for performance and delivery of deed; conditions excusing performance
- Condition of premises warranted when Buyer takes title; or extension to
  perfect title and get premises in shape; refund in case of failure—unless
  Buyer elects to proceed with title as-is
- Seller has fully performed when Buyer accepts title
- Buyer who defaults has to forfeit deposit
- Insurance (e.g., fire) Seller has to maintain until delivery of title
- Seller's obligation to pay broker's fee

For multi-family residential properties, it's important to determine whether the
property will be delivered vacant (with no tenants residing there) or subject to existing leases. The buyer should ascertain rather than assume that all of the rental
apartments are lawful and have a Certificate of Occupancy.

The buyer must ascertain if there are any pending landlord-tenant actions;
if the tenants' apartments are habitable; if any repairs are required; what the rent
roll is; and if there are any rent control or rent stabilization laws in effect and if
the sitting tenants are entitled to any special protection against eviction (e.g., if they
are aged or handicapped).

[¶1120.2] The Closing Process

Local custom varies widely as to what formalities occur in order to "close"
the real estate deal. The fundamental transaction is the exchange of the purchase
price for the deed to the property. Unless the buyer is in a position to pay all cash,
mortgage or other financing has to be obtained. At the closing, the buyer signs the
mortgage documents and the seller signs and transfers the deed—or these steps
have already been taken, and only representatives rather than the principals themselves appear at the closing. Both the mortgage and the deed should be recorded
as soon as possible post-closing.

Prior to the closing, the buyer's down payment is held in escrow. Depending on local practice, the escrow agent might be the seller's lawyer, a title company representative, or a loan officer at the institution issuing the mortgage.

To satisfy the Statute of Frauds, and to be eligible for official recordation, a property deed must:

- Be written;
- Be signed by the grantor;
- Indicate a present (not future) transfer of ownership;
- Describe the property accurately.

A "general warranty deed" promises that the grantor has never impaired the title, and neither has any prior owner. A "specialty warranty deed" promises that the grantor has never impaired the title, but makes no warranties as to anyone else. A quitclaim deed simply transfers the grantor's title, whatever that may be worth and whatever claims may exist against it.

A seller who agrees to deliver "marketable title" promises that the title is not encumbered by mortgages or anything else affecting the value or use of the property. This is the most common contract requirement. If the seller promises to deliver marketable record title, then the state of title and the chain of ownership must be provable by deed records. Where the contract is silent, a promise to convey marketable title will probably be implied.

Traditionally, property deeds are recorded in large books that are summarized in an index of grantors and grantees, and title is searched in order to trace a chain (and also to see if any co-owners have granted interests in the property inconsistent with the potential purchaser's ownership rights). The immense task of transferring these records to computer is being undertaken—naturally, it's much easier to click the mouse a few times than to look through huge, dusty volumes. In a state with a "marketable title" act, it is only necessary to establish the chain of title for a certain period of time (e.g., 20 years), not back to the time of the earliest records.

If competing claims of title are asserted, the states have various approaches to settling the priority. A "race" statute (referring to the "race to the courthouse") means that the first person who records the deed wins. A "race-notice" statute means that the first person to record the deed wins, unless he or she actually is aware of someone else who has been granted the same property. A "notice" statute makes an unrecorded deed invalid against a bona fide purchaser who has done a title search but does not have notice of the competing claim.

Sellers who take back a purchase-money mortgage should also record this mortgage.

[¶1120.2.1] Title Insurance

Cautious buyers protect themselves by purchasing title insurance. The buyer pays the premium (usually as part of the closing costs). The policy is delivered at closing, after title company attorneys have had a chance to search the title (consult records that demonstrate ownership). If the title proves to be defective, the buyer can collect insurance proceeds as well as carry out the underlying remedy of suing the buyer for breach of the warranty that marketable title will be delivered.

Buyers sometimes protect themselves by hiring an attorney who drafts an opinion letter as to the state of title, including any defects or encumbrances. If anything goes wrong, the buyer may have the additional remedy of suing the lawyer if the letter of opinion was inaccurate.

[¶1120.3] RESPA

The lending institutions involved in real estate purchases can impose quite a few fees, which in the aggregate can become substantial. A federal law, the Real Estate Settlement Procedure Act of 1974 (RESPA) requires advance disclosure of the nature and extent of these fees in connection with "federally related" first mortgages on one- to four-family properties.

A federally related mortgage is made, insured, guaranteed, or supplemented by the federal Department of Housing and Urban Development (HUD); is made in connection with a federal housing program; or will be re-sold by the lender to the Federal National Mortgage Association (FNMA, nicknamed "Fannie Mae"), Government National Mortgage Association (GNMA, "Ginnie Mae"), Federal Home Loan Mortgage Corporation (FHMLC, "Freddie Mac"), or to a financial institution that will sell the mortgage in turn to FHMLC.

Certain transactions are exempt from RESPA, e.g., refinancing, home improvement loans, construction loans, loans to construct a building on land the builder already owns, and loans to purchase more than 25 acres.

If the transaction is subject to RESPA, the lender must mail a copy of the official HUD guide to settlement costs to every loan applicant not later than three days after receipt of the application. The official guide explains the services involved in the settlement process and the fee structure for them.

Also within three days of receipt of the application, the lender must disclose the lender's good faith estimate of the settlement costs. HUD requires the estimates to "bear a reasonable relationship to the charge a borrower is likely to be required to pay at settlement, and must be based upon experience in the locality or area in which the mortgaged property is located."

Lenders who require borrowers to use (and pay for) the services of a particular title company, insurer, or attorney must disclose whether or not these service providers have a business relationship with the lender, and their fees must be included in the estimate. It is unlawful (and buyers can recover three times the charge for title insurance) for a seller of real estate that will be financed by a federally related mortgage to directly or indirectly condition the sale on the buyer's purchase of title insurance from a particular company. RESPA forbids kickbacks and fee splitting (payments to persons who did not earn a portion of the fee). However, payments under multiple listing services, or agreements between real estate agents and brokers, are exempt from this provision.

In addition to its disclosure requirements, RESPA limits the amount that buyers can be required to place in escrow accounts toward their real estate taxes and insurance. The maximum deposit that lenders can require is the amount due and payable at the time of the settlement, plus one-twelfth of the estimated total real estate taxes and insurance for the first post-closing year.

If the mortgage is an adjustable-rate mortgage with a term of a year or more, Regulation Z (the Truth in Lending implementing regulation) requires the creditor to provide the buyer with the official *Consumer Handbook on Adjustable-Rate Mortgages*, or another publication with comparable content.

At the closing, the person conducting the closing of a federally related mortgage loan must complete HUD Form 1, the Uniform Settlement Statement, itemizing all charges paid by either buyer or seller at the closing. (Charges that are paid "outside the closing" by agreement need not be included.) Neither the lender nor the borrower can lawfully be charged a fee for preparing the RESPA statement.

If there is no formal closing, or neither the borrower nor the borrower's agent attends the closing, the lender's obligation is to deliver a completed settlement statement to the buyer as soon as possible after the transaction closes.

Where the seller assumes all the settlement-related expenses, or the total the buyer must pay at settlement is a fixed amount that was disclosed at the time of the loan application, it is not necessary to provide HUD Form 1.

At the time of consummation of the loan, the lender must provide a Truth in Lending statement disclosing the annual percentage rate (effective interest rate) for the mortgage. The borrower can also request this information at the time the loan application is made.

[¶1130] Property Taxes

Taxes on commercial and residential property are an important source of income for states and municipalities, used to finance projects such as public works and schools. Although rebates and exemptions are often available (e.g., to induce a large employer to either settle there or refrain from moving away), the basic rule is that property taxes are imposed at a rate multiplied by the assessed value of the property.

Taxpayers who believe the assessment on their property is excessive can petition for reduction of the assessment. The process generally begins with a formal protest and application for correction addressed to the taxing authority. A denial can be reviewed in court. The three main grounds for reducing an assessment are:

- Overvaluation (higher than the full and fair market value of the property)
- Inequality (disproportionate to the valuation of comparable properties in the same area)
- Illegality (irregular manner of imposing the tax, or including exempt realty in the assessment)

Review of the assessor's report may disclose factual errors that can be corrected to the advantage of the property owner. For income-producing property, the history of recent past income and expenses is highly relevant to market value. Expert testimony (about what constitutes a comparable property, and the market value and assessments of "comps"; about the condition of the building or its reproduction cost)is critical to the assessment appeal.

[¶ 1 140] Landlord-Tenant Law

A residential or commercial lease is a contract governing the tenant's occupancy of the premises for a certain period of time. At the end of the lease, the landlord re-takes occupancy. The lease itself is subject to the Statute of Frauds—i.e., if the term is a year or more, it will not be enforceable without a writing.

A tenancy for a term of years begins and ends on specified dates, at which time the lease terminates. Notice is not required to terminate the lease in accordance with its terms. In contrast, a tenancy at will continues as long as both parties want it to. It can be terminated by either without prior notice.

A periodic tenancy (year-to-year, month-to-month, etc.) lasts the specified period of time, and is automatically renewed when each cycle ends, unless either landlord or tenant gives timely written notice of termination. Notice is timely if it arrives by the last day of the month or other period before the period when the tenancy is supposed to end.

Although there are some exceptions, leases for more than a year are subject to the Statute of Frauds, and therefore must be written to be enforceable. However, state laws to protect tenants often provide that a landlord who fails to sign and deliver a lease that has been signed by the tenant will be bound by the lease as if it had been properly executed.

It is not uncommon for tenants to "hold over"—i.e., simply fail to vacate the premises at the end of the lease term. The landlord can either attempt to evict the tenant (which can be very difficult, especially in cities with low vacancy rates where the landlord-tenant judge or hearing officer is likely to feel sympathetic toward the tenant) or accept the tenant as a periodic "tenant at sufferance."

The Uniform Residential Landlord and Tenant Act allows the landlord either to accept the holdover tenant as a month-to-month tenant, or to sue for eviction. The landlord can obtain damages of up to three months' rent or three times the actual damages (whichever is greater), plus attorneys' fees, if the tenant willfully held over the property in bad faith.

The basic rule is that either landlord or tenant can assign or transfer his or her interest. However, if the lease limits the tenant's ability to transfer, such restrictions will be enforceable and strictly construed. An "assignment" covers all of the tenant's interest in the remaining term of the lease; a "sublease" is for less than the entire term. A lease that forbids "subleases" will not prevent the tenant from making an enforceable assignment. It is common for lease provisions to be drafted so that the landlord must not unreasonably refuse consent to assignment or sublease.

It is typical in both residential and commercial leases for the tenant to make a deposit which the landlord can use if the tenant ceases to pay rent, damages the premises, or otherwise defaults on the lease. For tax purposes, the deposit remains the property of the tenant until and unless the landlord is entitled to take the funds on the tenant's default.

Many states have laws limiting the size of security deposits that can be charged on residential leases. The landlord may also have an obligation to pay interest to the tenant when the security deposit is returned at the end of the lease, and/or keep the security deposits in special accounts that are not subject to the claims of the landlord's creditors.

A few cities impose some degree of control over residential rents, by limiting the rent that can be charged to a new tenant and rent increases when tenants renew their leases. However, apartments may become "decontrolled" when a new tenant moves in, or newly constructed buildings may be exempt from rent control. Rent control ordinances, if properly promulgated, are not unconstitutional "takings",[1] but rent control ordinances are inconsistent with the current legal climate, and are likely to be restricted or repealed in the future.

[¶1140.1] Commercial Leases

The commercial lease contains certain features absent from the residential lease—and lacks certain other features (such as pro-tenant protections intended to prevent homelessness, that are not relevant in the commercial context).

Commercial leases frequently give the tenant the option to renew the lease, either indefinitely or a certain number of times, as well as an option to purchase the building on stated terms.

The square footage of a residential apartment is usually not very controversial, but highly varying methods are used to calculate the size of a commercial property, possibly including storage areas, common areas, and staircases and elevators. It is common for commercial leases to require payment of taxes and/or utility charges by the tenant, or for the stated rent to increase automatically based on these factors or reflecting actual increases. Tenants may be obligated to pay maintenance and service charges (cleaning, snow removal, etc.), or else either to pay the landlord for the items or subcontract out their performance.

Commercial leases often last for many years, or even for decades, so it is critical to include a mechanism for adjusting the rent (from the landlord's perspective) and controlling rent increases (from the tenant's). A "step-up" lease gradually increases the rent at stated intervals. An "escalator" lease is the most common long-term office lease form. The tenant's basic rent is fixed, but the tenant is also obligated to pay a stated percentage of real estate taxes, insurance, and non-structural repairs. The rent could be adjusted based on changes in the cost of living or other objective index.

A net lease requires the tenant to pay not only a fixed base rental but all property-related costs, including taxes and assessments, heating and air conditioning, routine maintenance, and repairs. (Such a lease is "net" because the landlord receives a net figure with no need to pay related costs.)

A percentage rental, often used in shopping center leases or long-term (over three year) store leases, starts with a fixed base amount for rent but is adjusted by a percentage of sales the store makes. Of course, the definition of "sales" or "net sales" subject to the percentage is crucial, and handling of factors such as phone, mail, and on-line orders, returns, and shipping and handling charges must be built into the definition. The tenant should be required to maintain books and records showing the sales and any permissible deduction from sales, and the landlord should be given the right to audit the books.

A commercial tenant's needs frequently change over time, resulting in a need for more or less space. The adjustments are often handled by options within the lease. A cancellation option gives the tenant the right to give notice at designated times to reduce the amount of rented space (usually with a penalty payable to the landlord). The additional space option gives the tenant the right to give notice to rent additional space in the same building, or another building owned by the landlord. Advance permission to sublease is another possibility.

Other issues that may arise in the commercial lease: environmental premises liability (see ¶1250) and compliance with the public accommodations requirements of the Americans With Disabilities Act (¶354).

If the lease involves space in a building that is under construction or under renovation, the lease must resolve issues of liability if the premises are not ready for occupation on time, if changes are made from the blueprints and specifications included with the lease, or if changes are made to suit the tenant's requirements. In the latter case it must be determined who is liable for expense and damages, and whether the changes must be left in place after the tenancy terminates, or whether the tenant is permitted or required to remove them and restore the premises to their original condition.

The commercial lease also governs the availability of storage space, parking spaces, loading facilities, and the availability of elevators, heating, water, and air conditioning outside normal business hours. To an increasing extent, provision of phone lines and Internet connections will become a critical part of the lease obligation.

[¶1140.2] Lease Interpretation

Ambiguous terms in a lease—like ambiguous insurance policy provisions—are usually construed against the party who drafted the document. Another principle is that leases are interpreted in the way that is least restrictive to the tenant's lawful use of the property.

In case of "superseding illegality" (i.e., the tenant takes the property for a use that was legal when the lease was signed, but which later becomes illegal, and the lease restricts the use to the one illegal one) the tenant will generally have the right to terminate the lease. However, if the tenant's use of the premises is not restricted, the tenant probably will not have the right to terminate the lease even if, in practical terms, the tenant does not obtain the intended results. A tenant who could have, but did not get, a zoning variance that would permit the use is not entitled to remedies because of the zoning law. The tenant has the risk of failing to get the zoning variance.

The doctrine of "commercial frustration" covers the situation in which a government act makes the premises less valuable for a commercial purpose, but does not out-and-out ban the intended use. If the government act was not reasonably foreseeable when the lease was signed; the landlord knew how the tenant intended to use the premises; and the commercial value of the premises is eliminated or catastrophically reduced, the tenant may be able to terminate the lease. However, some jurisdictions require the tenant to continue to pay rent despite commercial frustration.

At common law, any changes to the premises made by the tenant constituted "waste," so the tenant was obligated to remove them and surrender the property in its original condition when the lease terminated. This was true even of changes that enhanced the value of the property. Current law usually does not treat changes as waste unless the property's value is seriously impaired.

[¶1140.3] Landlord's Remedies

The tenant's obligation to pay rent is an important part of the lease relationship. If the tenant fails to pay rent, the landlord can sue to recover the unpaid amount (although the tenant may be able to assert a defense that poor conditions justify such a withholding).

Usually, the lease gives the landlord the right to sue for possession of the premises if the rent is unpaid—i.e., to evict the tenant. Evictions of "holdover" tenants—those who do not leave at the expiration of the lease term—are also permitted. Most states forbid self-help eviction (i.e., the landlord removes the tenant's property—or the tenant—by force and locks up the premises). Instead, the landlord must bring eviction proceedings, usually known as "summary proceedings" because they are handled in a relatively expedited fashion. The landlord must give the tenant "notice to quit" explaining why eviction is justified. Then the landlord and tenant get a hearing shortly after the notice is issued, generally in a special landlord-tenant court or court part.

An "acceleration" clause makes all rent for the balance of the term due immediately as soon as the tenant stops paying rent, or otherwise seriously breaches the lease.

It's much easier for the landlord to sue for the entire balance of the rent than to have to bring multiple suits based on multiple non-payments. However, the landlord has to choose: either accelerate the rent obligation or terminate the lease and re-take the premises, but not both.

The tenant must be given notice and a reasonable amount of time to cure before acceleration is imposed. Furthermore, for a long-term lease, the court may award the landlord only the present value of the future rent obligation, not the sum itself.

If the tenant stops paying rent and moves out, the landlord can't—but doesn't need to—bring an eviction proceeding, because the premises are already vacant. The landlord can terminate the lease and find another tenant; keep the premises vacant and sue the tenant as unpaid rent falls due; or find another tenant, and apply that tenant's rent to the abandoning tenant's liability.

The landlord is only entitled to rent arrears if it accepts the surrender of the premises and terminates the lease.

The Restatement (2nd) of Property §12.1 does not obligate the landlord to mitigate damages by finding another tenant, so the landlord can keep the premises vacant and sue for future rent as each payment falls due. However, several states (and the Uniform Residential Landlord-Tenant Act) reject this position, and do require the landlord to mitigate damages if possible.

[¶1140.3.1] Fixtures

When personal property is permanently attached to a structure, it becomes a fixture: for instance, cabinets or appliances built into a kitchen wall. The common-law rule was that any fixtures added by tenants to the premises automatically became the landlord's property. Most American states consider the fixtures to be the property of the tenant unless the tenant gave objective indication of intention (e.g., difficulty of removing fixtures without severe damage to premises) to make the fixtures part of the property that would remain at the termination of the lease.

Trade fixtures (used in business) are analyzed somewhat differently. According to the Restatement (2nd) of Property §12.2(4), tenants are allowed to remove trade fixtures on or before the termination date of the lease, but they are responsible for repairing any damage caused by removal (e.g., holes in the wall). Trade fixtures that remain in place when the lease ends become property of the landlord.

[¶1140.4] Tenant's Remedies

Although a tenant has no duty to take possession of the leased premises, the landlord has a duty to deliver actual possession of the premises on the first day of the lease term. The tenant's remedies, if the landlord fails to do so, are either to rescind the lease and sue for actual damages, or confirm the lease, move in as soon as possible, and sue for actual damages for the time when possession was denied.

Leases imply a covenant of quiet enjoyment: that the tenant can maintain use and enjoyment of the premises without disturbance from the landlord or anyone who claims title from the landlord or title superior to the landlord's.

Actual eviction occurs when the tenant is physically expelled from the premises or excluded from possession of the premises. Wrongful eviction by the landlord or someone with title superior to the landlord's allows the tenant to terminate the lease, sue for damages, or remain in possession but without paying rent. If the landlord's breach of the covenant of quiet enjoyment prevents the tenant from using part of the premises, this will be considered a partial actual eviction.

Constructive eviction is action or failure to act by the landlord that results in the tenant being deprived of use and enjoyment of the leased premises to a substantial extent. This argument is often raised by tenants who claim that the landlord failed to make repairs or provide essential services. The tenant must notify the landlord of the condition, and give the landlord a reasonable opportunity to repair, before asserting constructive eviction. Some statutes and case law require the tenant to vacate the premises, but the Restatment (2nd), bearing in mind the difficulty of finding affordable housing, does not impose this requirement.

A tenant subjected to wrongful eviction has the options of staying on the premises and withholding rent; terminating the lease; and suing for damages. (The Restatement (2nd) of Property does not allow tenants to remain and withhold rent after a partial eviction.)

The traditional common law rule was that tenants took the property as is, with whatever patent or latent defects were present. Current law usually implies a warranty of habitability in residential leases (less commonly in commercial leases, which can and sometimes do place the duty to repair on the tenant). Commercial leases may be interpreted under an implied warranty of "suitability" for the intended commercial purpose.

This implied warranty obligates the landlord to deliver premises in a habitable condition at the beginning of the term, and to maintain habitability throughout the lease (e.g., by performing necessary repairs). The general rule is that the warranty of habitability cannot be waived. The landlord must be given notice of the defect and reasonable opportunity to repair it before breach of warranty is asserted.

Depending on local law, the warranty might be breached if the local housing code is violated; if the premises are unsafe; if there are latent defects that would not be detected by reasonable inspection prior to signing the lease; or if a reasonable person would not deem the premises to be habitable. The tenant's remedies for breach of warranty of habitability can be:

- Damages (including punitive damages and damages for infliction of emotional distress)
- Specific performance (ordering the landlord to provide a habitable apartment)
- Rescission of the lease (requiring the tenant to move out)
- Reformation of the lease (e.g., a period of free or reduced rent).

It is a defense against eviction if the tenant can prove that the landlord's motivation is retaliation against the tenant for the tenant's assertion of a breach of the warranty of habitability.

At common law, landlords were not liable for personal injuries suffered on the leased premises. Today, a significant amount of statutory and case law alters that result, especially if the common areas (rather than individual leased premises that tenants might be expected to repair) contain defects; if the injury is due to a latent defect; or if the landlord did make repairs but did so negligently, leading to injury. Under the law of premises liability, the landlord's liability for criminal acts on the premises is limited, but the landlord may be liable if security on premises is inadequate and/or the landlord is on notice of foreseeable risk of criminal activity.

[¶1140.5] Fair Housing Laws

Some degree of protection against housing discrimination has been in place since 1866, when 42 USC §1982 was enacted, giving all citizens the same rights as "white citizens" to "inherit, purchase, lease, sell, hold, and convey real and personal property." More than a century later, housing discrimination was still rampant, leading to the passage of the Fair Housing Act, which is part of Title VII (42 USC §3601—).

The Fair Housing Act makes it illegal to discriminate on the basis of race, color, religion, sex, having children in the family (but not marital status), national origin, or handicap, either by disparate treatment or disparate impact. FHA violations include:

- Refusal to sell or rent a dwelling
- Discriminating in the terms or conditions of housing sale or rental; refusing to permit a handicapped person to make reasonable modifications to a housing unit
- Discriminatory advertising
- False representations: i.e., telling a black applicant that the apartment is rented, while subsequently showing it to a white applicant
- "Blockbusting": inducing sales or rentals by claiming that members of a disfavored group are about to move in to the area.

Single-family dwellings, owner-occupied dwellings of up to four units, private clubs, and housing projects for the elderly are exempt from the Fair Housing Act.

In addition to the federal law, most states and many localities have their own fair housing laws.

Constitutional arguments often fail in the fair housing context, because the Equal Protection Clause requires state action—at least state action in letting the courts enforce private restrictive covenants such as those barring persons of a particular race or religion from purchasing property[2] and that involve intentional discrimination, not just disparate impact.[3]

[¶1150] Condominiums and Cooperatives

For much of human history, people lived in single-family dwellings, whether huts or palaces. Urbanization, and the invention of the elevator, made large multi-family dwellings more feasible. In high-cost urban areas, few families can afford to buy single-family homes, so the demand for ownership is often satisfied by purchase of a condominium unit or shares in a cooperative apartment complex.

The major distinction between the two ownership forms is that the purchaser acquires ownership of the unit itself in a condominium, plus the right to use the common areas (also known as common elements) such as lobby and any recreational facilities. A condominium is real property, on which real estate taxes are separately assessed, and which can be separately financed by an individual mortgage. Unit owners will be assessed charges for maintenance of the common areas. The condominium operates under a "declaration" or "master deed" and is managed by a homeowner's association (sometimes referred to as the unit owners' association or property owners' association).

A co-op "purchaser" actually acquires personal property in the form of shares in a cooperative corporation. The corporation exercises a significant degree of control over operations, including who will be allowed to purchase the shares. The entire project has a single mortgage (buyers get personal loans to finance their share purchases) and a single real estate tax bill. Maintenance charges cover mortgage financing and real estate taxes as well as the upkeep of shared areas.

Creation of a condominium requires the owner or developer of the property to record the declaration, including a description of the physical layout of the project and the Articles of Incorporation and bylaws that will govern its operation.

Many states require a registration process similar to that required for a "Blue Sky" stock issue. The offering plan for the condominium may have to be submitted to the city or state Attorney General for review. A preliminary "red herring" prospectus for the sale of condominium interests or co-op shares may have to be prepared and submitted for approval.

Conversion of an existing project to condominium or co-op form may require an agreement by a certain percentage (e.g., 15%) of the tenants that they will buy their apartments or shares before the regulatory authorities will approve the conversion. Usually tenants who agree to buy their apartments during a short time frame, such as 90 days, are entitled to a lower, insider's price; other people who buy later, or after the conversion, have to pay a higher outsider's price for the unit or shares.

State and local law determine whether a developer who engages in a conversion has the right to evict non-purchasing tenants. Tenants may be given the option of remaining as rent-paying tenants after the conversion; or the landlord may be able to sell the occupied apartments to an investor who hopes to be able to re-sell the apartment when the current tenant moves out or dies. There may be a special provision protecting low-income, senior citizen, or disabled tenants from eviction during a conversion, or requiring the developer to provide relocation assistance.

[¶1155] Real Estate Investment Trusts (REITs)

A REIT, a form that has been in existence since 1960 (and has had several peaks and troughs of popularity since then), is a structure for real estate investment and for raising funds for real estate development. In essence, it is a mutual fund that invests in real property rather than securities. Tax treatment is governed by IRC §§856 and 857.

REITs can be pass-through entities (i.e., items are passed through to participants, with no tax at the entity level[4]) if all of these criteria are met:

- There are at least 100 shareholders
- Most of the entity's income derives from qualifying rents and interest. That is, at least 75% of income must come from real estate activities, and at least an additional 20% must come either from real estate activities or other passive sources; active trade or business income outside the real estate context must be 5% or less
- The majority of the entity's assets must be real estate and/or mortgages secured by real estate
- At least 95% of annual income must be distributed to shareholders
- Certain services performed for tenants of property owned by the entity must be performed by independent third-party professionals.

REIT distributions are either ordinary income or capital gains to the shareholders, in the year of receipt. They are ordinary income up to the extent of REIT earnings and profits. Shareholders are taxed only on actual distributions, but REITs are not permitted to pass through losses.

A REIT is treated as a domestic corporation for federal income tax purposes, although there is generally no tax at the entity level. It files an annual return on Form 1120-REIT.

REITs can be organized as C Corporations, in which case investors' equity interests are in the form of shares of stock, or as a trust, in which case investors receive common shares of beneficial interests. REIT ownership interests are "securities" for purposes of the '33 Act (see ¶610), and are usually registered on Form S-11.

[¶1160] Easements and Covenants

Under some circumstances, someone other than the owner may be permitted to exercise certain rights over the owner's property, without affecting the ownership of the land. For instance, a person whose property is surrounded by someone else's property may be granted an easement to use a driveway to leave his own property and connect with the public road. The presumption is that easements are attached to the land and automatically belong to a person acquiring the land; some easements are personal, however, and are not transferred unless there is an express transfer.

Easements can either be positive (such as right to do something) or negative (forbidding the property owner to do something that would work to the disadvantage of the person holding the easement). They usually require a writing signed by the owner of the land affected by the easement. However, easements may be implied in cases of strict necessity, or where usage has continued for a long period of time without protest.

A real covenant is a similar device, but it is contractual, usually expressed in a deed. It, too, can be either positive (affirmative covenants) or negative (restrictive covenants). The covenant "runs with the land," so it stays in place when ownership changes. A suit for specific performance can be brought with respect to either an easement or a real covenant; the practical difference is that money damages can be awarded for breach of a covenant but not of an easement.

[¶1170] Land Use Planning

At common law, ownership of land implied the right to use the land in any way the owner desired. Present-day law, however, makes the owner's unfettered use of land subject to the police power to protect public health and safety, including the power to determine how many and what kinds of structures can be built and operated in a particular area.

Most zoning laws are state laws that delegate the actual power to prescribe land use to cities or other units of local government. They are so-called because the area is divided into zones, some of which are purely residential, others commercial, agricultural, industrial, or mixed-use. Under appropriate circumstances, the locality can even condemn land (take it over, with compensation to the owner).

[¶1170.1] Zoning

The locality develops a master land-use plan which is embodied in zoning ordinances. A zoning ordinance can be challenged, and invalidated, if it fails to comply with the plan, and if the required notice procedures are not observed. Zoning ordinances are also vulnerable to challenges based on due process, equal protection, takings, or if they have the effect (even if not the purpose) of excluding members of a suspect classification (generally a race or nationality group) from the area.

A variance is an administrative grant (usually issued by a Board of Adjustment) that allows a use contrary to the zoning ordinance. If it is anticipated that non-authorized uses will have some justification, the zoning ordinance may provide for special permits allowing such uses. Non-conforming uses that predate the zoning ordinance are likely to be grandfathered in.

Zoning can impose content-neutral regulation even if a First Amendment defense is raised, if the zoning ordinance serves a substantial governmental interest (e.g., requiring adult entertainment enterprises to be located at least 1,000 feet away from residential zones, dwellings, schools, and churches).[5] Commercial speech regulation in billboards and other outdoor advertising is acceptable if these rules are narrowly tailored and do not restrict the content of the advertiser's proposed commercial speech.[6]

It is improper to have a zoning ordinance that explicitly discriminates on the basis of race or nationality. However, in general a zoning ordinance can impose restrictions (such as minimum lot size) that have a disproportionately negative effect on low-income minority groups,[7] although disparate impact of this type may be covered by Fair Housing laws.

Several states (e.g., New Jersey, California, Oregon, Florida, and Washington) require zoning ordinances to take into account the need for affordable housing.

According to the Supreme Court, the right of a family to live together is a fundamental right that cannot be impaired by zoning ordinances; no such fundamental right exists for unrelated persons to live together. Thus, a zoning ordinance that bans communes or even roommate relationships can be Constitutional. But a home for the mentally disabled cannot be zoned based on neighbors' fears or prejudices about the mentally ill.[8]

[¶1170.1.1] "Takings"

Except as discussed below, when land is condemned, governments are not allowed to seize or "take" privately owned land. The Fifth Amendment requires just compensation if public property is taken by the federal or a state government for public purposes. A valid zoning ordinance is not considered a "taking,"[9] but a zoning ordinance that removes all viable uses for the property will constitute a taking,[10] which can lead to invalidation of the ordinance. The owner who has suffered damages as a result of an inappropriate zoning ordinance may be able to recover those damages from the municipality.[11]

[¶1170.2] Condemnation and Eminent Domain

The police power of the state government includes acquiring land by eminent domain, if the acquisition is necessary for the public good and the land is used for public purposes.

The acquisition requires appropriate notice and compensation at a fair rate (a rate that leaves the former owner in no worse position than if condemnation had never occurred). Generally speaking, this will be fair market value, reflecting the highest and best use for the property rather than its actual use. Objective standards, rather than any additional personal value the property has to the owner, will govern.[12]

When business property is condemned, in general the government only has to pay for the land, not lost business goodwill—unless there is some reason why it is impossible for the business to relocate.

A lessee who has a long-term lease at below fair market rental may be entitled to part of the condemnation proceeds, since the lessee loses economic benefits because of the condemnation. Some states call for payment of the full proceeds to the lessor, making it up to the lessee to recover a fair share.

Inverse condemnation, also known as regulatory taking, occurs when there has been no physical seizure of the property, but government actions impair the use of the property. The property has been "taken" if the state regulation does not advance a legitimate state interest or, even if the objective is legitimate, the effect is to deprive the owner of all economically viable uses.

Reduction in value of the property is a factor, but by itself does not constitute a taking. The more that the government action interferes with the reasonable expectation of investors in the property, the more likely it is that a taking will be found.[13]

Any physical invasion of property, even a trivial one, will be considered a taking: e.g., a state law requiring building owners to provide physical access to cable companies to install cables and boxes.[14]

More recent cases deal with the question of trade-offs (individual applies for permit or variance, and is told that it will be issued conditional on the applicant doing something for the public benefit). At least rough proportionality is required between the cost or other inconvenience to the applicant and the public benefit supposedly obtained.[15]

[¶1170.3] Nuisance

The way that a property owner behaves with respect to the property can have unreasonably negative consequences for others, constituting a private and/or public nuisance. (See ¶1210.3 for discussion of nuisance and trespass in the environmental context.)

At times, the same conduct may constitute both trespass and nuisance, but the traditional distinction drawn between the two torts is that trespass is an interference with a property owner's possessory interest in the property.

Nuisance, in contrast, interferes substantially and unreasonably with the right to use and quiet enjoyment of the property (although rights to view, or light and air unobstructed by other buildings, are not protectable by suit for nuisance). Trespass generally requires a physical entrance onto the property, so intangible entrances such as pollution and noise are more likely to constitute nuisance. By and large, either trespass or nuisance liability requires intentional rather than negligent acts.

If nuisance is proved, injunction is the traditional remedy, although modern practice allows damages to be awarded if the use that constitutes the nuisance has enough social utility to make an injunction inappropriate.

[¶1180] Mortgages and Foreclosure

A mortgage is a written document proving a security interest in real property. The mortgagor is an owner or potential owner of property who needs financing for the property. The mortgagee is a bank or other lender (e.g., the seller of the property; a private investor) who advances the financing, receiving in turn a security interest in the property. On default, the mortgagee is entitled to foreclose, and if there is a balance still outstanding after the foreclosure, the mortgagee can get a deficiency judgment enforceable against the borrower's other assets.

A deed of trust is a variant used in some localities. The mortgagor conveys the property to a trustee, in trust for the mortgagee; the property is conveyed back to the property owner when the balance is paid in full. If the property owner/borrower defaults, the lender exercises its power of sale rather than foreclosing on the mortgage.

Most mortgages are "amortizing mortgages": the borrower agrees to make a series of payments, each consisting of interest and principal, until the entire amount has been paid off. There may be a larger "balloon payment" due at the end of the term.

Some states conceptualize mortgages under the "title theory": that is, the mortgagee has the title to the property, but allows the mortgagor to use the property until the mortgage is satisfied, at which point title returns to the mortgagor. But this is the minority view. Most states follow the "lien theory," which gives the mortgagee a lien on the property until the loan is paid off.

There can be more than one mortgage on a property. The first mortgage is known as the senior or primary mortgage; subsequent mortgages are junior or secondary mortgages. Mortgage priority depends on the date of recordation, not the size of the debt or even the intentions of the parties.

[¶1180.1] Construction Financing

The lender on a conventional residential or commercial mortgage is at least able to inspect the property, estimate its value, and determine the creditworthiness of the mortgagor. Construction financing is riskier, because the funds are needed to build the project in the first place—and a variety of factors can delay completion of the project (and its potential to earn income that can be used to

Bailment contracts are permitted to limit the bailee's liability for losses, as long as the bailor accepts the conditions, and as long as the bailee does not try to limits its liability for willful actions or gross negligence.

[¶1190.3] Accessions

Work done on property, or other goods added, can increase the value of property. "Accessions" are the additional goods and/or services. The general rule is that the owner of the underlying goods is entitled to the accessions if someone else's work results in only a slight increase in the value of the property. However, the worker may be entitled to ownership if the accessions significantly increase its value.

If underlying property is significantly changed by adding goods of several owners, the finished "third good" probably becomes the property of the owner of the underlying goods that were altered.

[¶1190.4] Joint Accounts

Joint bank and brokerage accounts create some difficult problems, especially for divorce and estate planning. A "true" joint account is intended to belong to both (or all, if there are more than two) depositors, whereas a "convenience" joint account is often used by a disabled person who wants someone else to be able to perform banking transactions, but who remains the owner of the funds in the account at all times.

Generally, a true joint account will be a JWROS account, so it will pass by operation of law to the surviving joint tenant(s) on the death of the first joint tenant to die. Thus it should not be possible for the first joint tenant to dispose of the account balance by will. A convenience joint account will be the property of the owner, and therefore can be bequeathed. However, state law may impose different rules. The most important factor is usually the signature card signed when the account was created, indicating whether or not survivorship is present.

The POD (payable on death) and Totten trust accounts are related forms, similar but not identical to the convenience joint account. Ownership remains at all times in the depositor, but the signature card indicates who should receive the account proceeds at the time of the depositor's death.

A bank is always justified in paying account proceeds (up to and including 100% of the balance) to any joint tenant, even a non-depositing one. However, a joint tenant who withdraws more than a proportionate share can be required to account to the other joint tenant.

ENDNOTES

1. *Pennell v. City of San Jose*, 485 U.S. 1 (Sup.Ct. 1988).
2. *Shelley v. Kraemer*, 334 U.S. 1 (Sup.Ct. 1948); *Barrows v. Jackson*, 346 U.S. 249 (Sup.Ct. 1953).
3. *Arlington Heights v. Metropolitan Housing Development Corp.*, 429 U.S. 252 (Sup.Ct. 1977).

4. But see §857(b), imposing entity-level taxes on, e.g., violation of the income tests or receipt of income from prohibited transactions.
5. *City of Renton v. Playtime Theatres, Inc.*, 475 U.S. 41 (Sup.Ct. 1986).
6. *City of Ladue v. Gilleo*, 512 U.S. 43 (Sup.Ct. 1994).
7. *Village of Arlington Heights v. Metropolitan Housing Development Corp.*, 429 U.S. 252 (Sup.Ct. 1977).
8. *Moore v. City of East Cleveland*, 431 U.S. 494 (Sup.Ct. 1977) [grandmother and grandsons are a "single family"]; *Belle Terre v. Boraas*, 416 U.S. 1 (Sup.Ct. 1974) [unrelated persons]; *Cleburne v. Cleburne Living Center*, 473 U.S. 432 (Sup.Ct. 1985) [mentally disabled persons].
9. *Euclid v. Ambler Realty Co.*, 272 U.S. 365 (Sup.Ct. 1926).
10. *Lucas v. South Carolina Coastal Council*, 505 U.S. 1003 (Sup.Ct. 1992).
11. *First English Evangelical Lutheran Church v. County of Los Angeles*, 482 U.S. 304 (Sup. Ct. 1987).
12. See, e.g., *U.S. v. 564.54 Acres of Land*, 441 U.S. 506 (Sup.Ct. 1979).
13. *Penn Central Transportation Co. v. New York City*, 438 U.S. 104 (Sup.Ct. 1978) [re landmark restrictions on alteration of appearance of property]; *Agins v. Tiburon*, 447 U.S. 255 (Sup.Ct. 1980); *Keystone Bituminous Coal Ass'n v. DeBenedictis*, 480 U.S. 470 (Sup.Ct. 1987).
14. *Loretto v. Teleprompter Manhattan CATV Corp.*, 458 U.S. 419 (Sup.Ct. 1982).
15. *Nollan v. California Coastal Commission*, 483 U.S. 825 (Sup.Ct. 1987); *Dolan v. City of Tigard*, 512 U.S. 374 (Sup.Ct. 1994).
16. Qualified acquisition indebtedness incurred prior to October 13, 1987 is grandfathered in; its interest is deductible even if the indebtedness exceeds $1 million.

Environmental Law

[¶1201]

The regulation of the environment is primarily a federal function, for various reasons. Interstate commerce is obviously heavily involved, and contaminated air and water as well as escaped toxic substances can end up quite far from the place of contamination or release. The implications for public safety and health are immense, and there is value in nationwide uniformity. However, this is not an area of complete federal preemption, and the states are permitted to play a role—particularly if they choose to adopt standards more protective than the federal requirements.

The various federal statutes give the Environmental Protection Agency (EPA) broad powers to detect and punish violations of environmental statutes. In flagrant instances, criminal as well as civil penalties can be imposed on polluting corporations—and on individuals responsible for pollution. In addition, most of the statutes authorize citizen suits.

Note: for coverage of environmental liability under liability and other insurance policies, see ¶1460.2.2.

¶1205 Federal Environmental Laws

Since the issue came to public note in the 1970s, Congress has passed numerous federal environmental laws dealing with various forms of pollution and the proper disposition of potentially hazardous wastes:

- The Clean Air Act, 42 USC §7404, as amended by P.L. 101-549
- The Clean Water Act (formally known as the Federal Water Pollution Control Act), 33 USC §1365
- The Comprehensive Environmental Response, Compensation and Liability Act (CERCLA, or "Superfund"): 42 USC §9659
- Emergency Planning and Community Right to Know Act, 42 USC §11046
- Resource Conservation and Recovery Act (RCRA), 42 USC §6901—
- Safe Drinking Water Act, 42 USC §300j-8, reauthorized in 1996 by P.L. 104-182
- Toxic Substances Control Act, 14 USC §2619
- Asbestos Hazard Emergency Response Act of 1986, TSCA Title III, P.L. 99-579, 20 USC §4011—
- Oil Pollution Act of 1990, 33 USC §2701—
- Hazardous Materials Transportation Authorization Act, 49 USC §5101, including rules for safe packaging of hazardous materials
- Land Disposal Flexibility Act of 1996, P.L. 104-119

In addition to federal and state public enforcement, most environmental statutes permit citizen suits by private plaintiffs. (Unlike a toxic tort suit seeking compensation for personal injuries or property damage, a citizen suit seeks correction of pollution and the payment of fines into the public treasury.)

Most of the federal environmental statutes carry the potential for criminal charges against polluting corporations and/or individuals within the corporation responsible for environmental harm. Note that the federal sentencing guidelines for corporations do not apply to environmental offenses.

In 1995, the EPA issued an announcement, "Voluntary Environmental Self-Policing and Self-Disclosure Interim Policy Statement," 60 FR 16875 (3/31/95), announcing a policy under which criminal charges might be averted if a company voluntarily corrects and reports violations, although fines and even criminal charges may still be filed in particularly egregious cases.

[¶1210] CERCLA

CERCLA, enacted in 1980, provides funds and enforcement power to clean up "brownfields" (contaminated sites) and respond to spills of dangerous substances. See ¶1240, below, for a discussion of RCRA, which regulates active hazardous waste sites; CERCLA deals with cleanups of sites already contaminated, as well as current reporting of releases of potentially hazardous materials. CERCLA has been a very active area of litigation, because a very wide range of potential defendants can be involved, and because CERCLA deals with conditions that may have been created many years before the enforcement efforts.

One reason CERCLA has been controversial is the number of enforcement avenues (i.e., potential ways in which a property owner or company involved with a site can become liable). CERLCA §106(a), 42 USC §9606, gives the Environmental Protection Agency (EPA) power to obtain a court order to abate a condition of imminent and substantial danger to the public because of an actual or threatened release of a hazardous substance from a facility. CERCLA §106(a) orders can compel investigation and remediation by private parties at waste disposal sites.

Another possibility is for the EPA to perform a response action, then sue the responsible parties for cost recovery. The EPA is the arm of the federal government empowered to "respond" to the presence of forbidden substances at a site, giving rise to "response costs." The definition of response costs is broad enough to encompass the federal government's costs of overseeing a cleanup performed by a private party.[1]

Under CERCLA §104(e), the EPA has the power to enter facilities and take samples, as well as to secure information and documents from site owners. The EPA does a preliminary assessment of the site, based on all available information. The next step is a field assessment of the conditions. The Hazard Ranking System of 40 CFR Part 300, Appendix A gives each site a score; high-scoring sites are placed on the National Priorities List (NPL) of sites for which federal CERCLA funds can be appropriated for cleanup.

EPA performs an RI/FS (Remediation Investigation/Feasibility Study) at the site to determine the best way of cleaning it up. The agency notifies potentially re-

but the Supreme Court did not provide guidance as to what would constitute adequate compensation in this situation.

The owners of land abutting the site of a major oil spill must prove physical encroachment on their property as a prerequisite to a negligence or private nuisance claim based on fear of future health damages or reduction in the value of their property.[23] (See 42 USC §§9614(a), 9652(d): federal laws do not preempt common-law public nuisance actions.)

Selling contaminated property "as is" transfers environmental liability to the buyer only if the deed explicitly provides for this. Requiring transfer of a fee simple, subject to environmental regulations, is not sufficient to shift liability to the buyer.[24]

Absent fiduciary duty, a seller does not have to disclose defects in the property to potential buyers. Therefore, a bank had no duty to warn condominium purchasers of nearby toxic waste contamination, especially since the condominiums themselves showed no apparent damage.[25]

The seller of an asbestos-containing building does not become liable under CERCLA merely because a subsequent purchaser removes the asbestos. The ex-owner is not an "arranger" because the sale of the building was not a disposal of hazardous materials; the seller could not reasonably foresee that agents of the buyer would create a hazardous condition by mishandling the asbestos removal.[26]

Whether CERCLA and RCRA claims made by the buyer of contaminated property can be discharged by the seller's bankruptcy depends on whether the relief ordered could be converted into a right to payment (a monetary obligation). Environmental claims will not be discharged if the buyer did not have enough information to impose liability on the seller before the bankruptcy was confirmed.[27]

[¶1220] The Clean Water Act

In 1972, one of the first federal anti-pollution laws, the Federal Water Pollution Control Act, was passed. In 1977, it was renamed the Clean Water Act. It consists of five elements:

(1) Water quality standards
(2) A program for issuing discharge permits
(3) Industry standards for maximum permissible levels of effluent discharge
(4) Provisions about chemical and oil spills
(5) Grants and loans for building public water treatment facilities.

The CWA gives states broad authority to protect not only water quality, but also the quantity of water flowing into streams and rivers. A state can mandate a minimum water flow needed to protect fish in a river, and supervision of hydroelectric projects can extend to wildlife protection as well as water quality.

Under CWA §311 (33 USC §1321), it is unlawful to discharge RQs (reportable quantities) of hazardous substances into or upon surface waters or shorelines. RQs are set in 40 CFR Part 117, and the EPA's list of which substances are deemed hazardous for this purpose appears at 40 CFR §116.4.

The National Pollutant Discharge Elimination System (NPDES) requires permits before discharging any pollutant into water. Permits can be issued for ocean discharges only if the issuing authority determines that the planned discharge will not degrade the environment unreasonably. At first, the CWA called for the EPA to issue the permits, but states have been given the option to take over the process, and nearly all of them have done so.

The NPDES permit establishes "performance levels" that the discharger is expected to meet. If the standards are not met, the discharger is required to make a prompt report.

The Safe Drinking Water Act, initially passed in 1974 and amended in 1986 and 1988, is designed to protect water quality. The EPA sets national standards for contaminants in drinking water. The EPA also advises states on the protection of single-source aquifers (underground sources of drinking water). Lead-free materials must be used in all water systems and water coolers. The SDWA attempts to control use of underground injection as a means of waste disposal. In states where underground well injection could endanger drinking water, 40 CFR Parts 124 and 144-148 require the state to have an EPA-approved injection control program.

Forty-eight states have adopted standards "no less stringent" than the federal standards and have "adequate" enforcement procedures. Therefore, they have been granted primary enforcement authority for their public water systems.

If an RQ discharge occurs (unauthorized discharge of an impermissibly large—and hence Reportable—quantity of a hazardous substance), the person in charge of the facility where the discharge occurred must telephone the Coast Guard National Response Center immediately. Failure to report is penalized by a fine of up to $10,000 and/or a year's imprisonment.

Willful failure to report can be penalized by up to $250,000. An additional penalty of up to $5,000 a day can be imposed on the owner/operator or person in charge of the facility for each day the discharge continues (even if it is reported), and they can be made to pay the government's cleanup costs resulting from the discharge.

The Third Circuit has ruled[28] that environmentalist groups and their members do not have standing to sue for violations of a CWA discharge permit unless they can show that they use waters that are harmed or at serious risk of harm because of the violation.

In a CWA civil penalty action, jury trial is available.[29] Citizen suits can be brought under CWA §505 against the discharger, or against the EPA for failure to enforce the law. However, at least one continuing violation must exist to support a citizen suit for violation of the NPDES permit system. The suit cannot be premised merely on past violations, although the plaintiff need only show a reasonable likelihood of continuing violations, as of the time the suit is filed. The suit is not mooted if there are no further violations after the filing.[30]

According to the Eleventh Circuit, post-filing compliance moots a claim for injunctive relief, but civil penalties that were appropriate at the time the suit was filed can still be assessed.[31]

The CWA contains criminal sanctions, §309(c) (2). To convict a corporate officer, the prosecution must show that the officer knew the nature of his or her acts and performed them intentionally, but it is not necessary to prove knowledge that the conduct was illegal. Conviction of a CWA felony requires proof that the defendant acted knowingly with respect to each element of the offense.[32]

[¶1230] The Clean Air Act

The Clean Air Act is divided into four titles, dealing with stationary sources of pollution; mobile sources of pollution (e.g., vehicles); the definitions and standards used in judicial review; and acid deposition control (reduction of the emission of nitrogen and sulfur oxides; control of truck emissions). The EPA and the states share responsibility for defining and preserving air quality.

The EPA has a duty, under CAA §108, to issue a list of pollutants emitted from numerous or diverse sources, and which can reasonably be expected to endanger public health or welfare. The EPA must set a National Ambient Air Quality Standard (NAAQS) for each (CAA §109). All substances that endanger the public health must be placed on the list. Neither cost nor technical feasibility of eliminating the hazard can be considered in compiling the list.

A "PSD area" is one whose air quality is better than the national standards require. A "nonattainment area" fails to comply with the standards. In nonattainment areas, new or modified sources of pollution are required to meet additional anti-pollution requirements, based on technological feasibility. (See 42 USC §§7470-7479.) Owners of "major emitting facilities" in PSD areas must get a permit before building a new facility or substantially modifying an existing facility.

CAA §110 requires each state to have a State Implementation Plan (SIP). Either the state drafts an SIP that is adequate to meet the NAAQS, or the EPA imposes one. SIPs can include provisions more stringent than the federal standards, if this is necessary to attain the national standards for air quality. The Federal Highway Administration has a duty to promulgate guidelines so that federal highways will satisfy approved SIPs for ambient air quality: see 23 USC §109(j).

The Clean Air Act Amendments of 1990, P.L. 101-549, broaden EPA enforcement powers. Title III of the statute embodies a comprehensive plan for reducing the amount of nearly 200 toxic air pollutants emitted into the atmosphere, especially those resulting from the combustion of solid waste. Title IV adds regulatory powers to limit "acid deposition." Title V creates a system of operating permits similar to the NPDES program. The enforcement title, VII, adds more criminal violations and increases the number of felony violations (e.g., emission of hazardous air pollutants creating an imminent risk of death or serious injury).

The CAA requires prompt notification to the EPA whenever an asbestos-containing structure is renovated. But, because the statute is not clear as to whether failure to notify is a one-time violation or a violation that continues until abated, only the penalty for a single-day violation can be imposed.[33]

Violations of the CAA are subject to administrative, civil, and criminal enforcement. Under 42 USC §7413, when the CAA is violated, the EPA can:

- Obtain an administrative compliance order
- Impose penalties of up to $25,000 per day of violation

- Bring a federal civil suit for temporary and/or permanent injunctive relief, with or without civil penalties of up to $25,000 a day
- Seek criminal penalties of one to 15 years' imprisonment. Criminal penalties are imposed, e.g., for knowing violation of a SIP permit; knowingly making a false material statement or omitting material facts in CAA reports; or knowing or even negligent release of hazardous pollutants.

[¶1240] Resource Conservation and Recovery Act

RCRA, as amended by the Hazardous and Solid Waste Amendments of 1984, imposes complete control over generation, transport, and disposal of "active" waste. "Solid waste" means all discarded material other than household refuse and industrial discharges that are otherwise subject to permit requirements; see RCRA Subtitle D, 42 USC §§6941-6949a and 40 CFR Parts 240-257. RCRA forbids states to permit the creation of additional open waste dumps and requires states to schedule closing or upgrades to existing open dumps.

"Hazardous waste" is solid waste which is a health risk because of its quantity, concentration, or nature (physical, chemical or infectious). (See 40 CFR parts 264 and 266.)

Generators and transporters are required to handle waste properly, and to report to the EPA on what they have done. RCRA also regulates "TSD" (treatment, storage, and disposal) facilities, which operate subject to permits issued by the EPA: 40 CFR Parts 264 and 265. The statute gives the EPA broad authority to inspect operations that generate hazardous waste.

A RCRA permit is not required if a facility accepts and burns only non-hazardous waste, but a Clean Air Act permit will be required for the emissions of such a facility, and the permit will have more stringent provisions if it is issued in a non-attainment area (one in which air quality standards are not met).

RCRA's "cradle to grave" tracking system requires everyone who transports hazardous waste to have an EPA registration number. Waste generators are obligated to package and label waste properly. Before shipment, they must confirm that the TSD facility is willing to accept the waste, and has the capacity to handle it properly. The generator has to fill out a four-part "manifest" that can be used to track the progress and eventual disposition of the waste.

Under 42 USC §6973(a), the EPA can sue to enjoin the disposal of any waste (even if it is not hazardous) that may present an imminent and substantial danger to health or the environment. Anyone who contributed to the threat can be ordered to take any action necessary to abate the hazard. A fine of up to $5,000 a day can be imposed for non-compliance with the EPA order.

There is no RCRA statutory requirement for reporting spills, but EPA regulations at 40 CFR §264.51 do require TSD facilities that handle hazardous waste to create a contingency plan and designate an emergency coordinator to notify the community if a spill, fire, or explosion at the facility endangers the community.

A 1988 RCRA amendment, the Medical Waste Tracking Act (P.L. 100-582), enacted at 42 USC §§6903 and 6992, covers New York, New Jersey, Connecticut, the area contiguous to the Great Lakes, and any other state or geographic region that

ception for reproduction, display, and performance of works in the last 20 years of their copyright term—i.e., the newly-added extension—if it is impossible to obtain the works commercially at a reasonable price.)

[¶1310.6] Digital Millennium Copyright Act

The Digital Millennium Copyright Act (DMCA; P.L. 105-304 (10/28/98)) is another late-1998 copyright statute.[11] It implements two copyright treaties ("the World Intellectual Property Organization [WIPO] Copyright Treaty and the Performances and Phonograms Treaty") and updates the Berne Convention (international law of copyright protection) for new technology. A phonogram is a sound recording, and the corresponding treaty deals with protection of sound recordings distributed over computer networks in digital form.

Because of DMCA, new Chapter 12 of the Copyright Act provides for digital "watermarking" of copyrighted material, by affixing electronic files containing information about the proprietorship of the material. It is a crime to remove or alter the watermarking information without permission, or to sell technology for circumventing the watermarking process. Certain exceptions are allowed, such as security testing and reverse engineering; broadcasters can make short-term copies (for instance, creating a CD with multiple music selections, for convenience in on-line broadcasting).

The DMCA also absolves Internet Service Providers and other on-line "broadcasters" of liability for direct contributory, or vicarious copyright infringement in situations in which they serve as a conduit for infringement by routing, caching, storing, or linking copyrighted material without consent of the proprietor, but have no editorial involvement with the material. To qualify under this safe harbor, service providers must create, publicize, and enforce a policy of removing material from the service as soon as they become aware of infringement, and must designate an agent to whom infringements can be reported.[12]

Other DMCA provisions deal with compulsory licensing of music for Internet transmission of music, with accompanying royalty provisions, and distance education and academic fair use.

[¶1310.7] Fair Use

There are various situations in which undoubted use of copyrighted materials, without the consent of the copyright proprietor, will be permitted. The "fair use" exception is set out in 17 USC §107. For instance, a limited amount of material can be quoted, e.g., in a scholarly article or book review, in order to further the argument of the article or give review readers a chance to form their own opinion of the work. Reproduction for criticism, comment, news reporting, teaching, scholarship, or research is deemed to be permissible fair use.

However, the amount of "taking" of the copyrighted work must not be excessive relative to the purpose of the alleged fair-use work and the market for the original product and authorized derivative works.[13]

The factors involved in distinguishing fair use from infringement include:

- Purpose and character of the use
- Nature of the copyrighted work
- Amount used in relation to the copyrighted work as a whole
- Effect of the use on the potential market for the product.[14]

Parody is a sub-type of fair use. Of course, at least some elements of the parodied work must be duplicated for the audience to recognize that a parody is involved; see *Campbell v. Acuff-Rose Music, Inc.*, 510 U.S. 569 (Sup.Ct. 1993).

[¶1310.8] Other Defenses to Infringement Charges

Remember, only specific expressions of ideas and not the ideas themselves can be copyrighted. It is a defense to infringement that the defendant, rather than infringing on a copyrighted work, made use of a common body of materials on which both expressions drew. This is sometimes referred to as a the "scene a faire" (obligatory scene) doctrine. That is, the mere fact that two detective stories each involve a scene in which the detective calls the suspects together and explains which one is guilty does not mean that the second to be published or filmed plagiarizes the earlier one. This is a fundamental element (or cliché) of the genre, which can be used by many authors.

[¶1310.9] Registration and Notice

Copyrights are registered by filing a form with the Copyright Office, and depositing copies of the work with the Copyright Office and the Library of Congress.[15]

For works published after 3/1/89, according to the Berne Convention Implementation Act, P.L. 100-568, copyright protection does not require that published copies carry a copyright notice. Nevertheless, copyright notice is useful, to identify the owner and show date of publication, and it eliminates the possible defense of innocent infringement.

[¶1310.10] Remedies and Copyright Litigation

17 USC §501(b) gives the legal or beneficial owner of an exclusive right the ability to sue for infringement of that particular right, occurring during ownership of that right.[16] There are two elements in an infringement case: proof of ownership of a right in a valid copyright; and direct or circumstantial proof of copying. Circumstantial proof can exist through proof of access and substantial similarity of expression. (Similarity of ideas is not enough, because the ideas are not copyrightable.)

[¶1310.10.1] Injunction

The availability of preliminary injunction in an infringement case depends on the normal factors: the likelihood that the plaintiff will succeed on the merits;

the risk of irreparable harm; the presence or absence of serious questions on the merits of the case; and the balance of hardships between the parties. See 17 USC §502(a). Irreparable injury will be presumed on proof of reasonable likelihood of success on the merits, or presentation of a prima facie case of infringement.

17 USC §502(b) permits a permanent injunction to issue against future infringement nationwide, but only if the plaintiff proves a probability or threat of continued infringement. Infringing copies can also be impounded and destroyed.

[¶1310.10.2] Money Damages

The plaintiff in an infringement case can recover either actual damages (e.g., lost profits) or statutory damages as prescribed by 17 USC §504. Statutory damages can range from $500 to $20,000 "as the Court considers just."

In March, 1998, the Supreme Court held that there is no statutory right to a jury trial in a Copyright Act §504(c) case, in which the copyright owner seeks statutory damages,[17] because the statute refers to what the "Court" will do. Nevertheless, a jury trial is available under the Seventh Amendment on all of the issues pertinent to the §504(c) award, including the amount of damages, because historical precedents support the jury's role in setting damages. Punitive damages are not available in infringement cases.[18]

Also note that statutory damages are not available unless the copyright in the allegedly infringed work was registered before the alleged infringement occurred; §412 also denies an award of attorneys' fees against an infringer of an unregistered copyright.[19] A published work is entitled to a three-month grace period, even if the infringement occurred pre-registration, as long as the copyright was registered within three months of first publication.

[¶1310.10.3] Willful Infringement

Criminal penalties can also be imposed, under 17 USC §506(a) and 18 USC §2319. Criminal infringement is willful infringement undertaken for purposes of commercial advantage or private financial gain. It can be penalized by up to a year's imprisonment and/or a $25,000 fine; higher penalties are imposed for certain motion picture and sound recording infringements.

These provisions are supplemented by The No Electronic Theft Act of 1997, P.L. 105-147, which imposes penalties for willful copyright infringement, especially in the electronic arena. This statute clarifies that it is not necessary that a defendant receive commercial gain from infringement for the infringement to be punishable. This Act imposes criminal penalties of up to six years, depending on the number of works improperly reproduced, their value, and whether it is a first or repeat offense.

[¶1310.11] Technology and Copyright

Although the holders of copyrights in films claimed that the sale of videocassette recorders to the public constituted contributory infringement, the Supreme Court squelched that argument in 1984.[20] To the Supreme Court, VCRs were used primarily for "time-shifting" (recording a broadcast program for viewing at a more convenient time), thus increasing the viewing audience. The Court did not believe that viewing rented videocassettes impaired the commercial value of film copyrights or created likelihood of future harm.

When a new technology is introduced, the question arises as to how it will affect broadly drafted contracts already in force. One theory is that a grant of "all rights" will cover new technologies; another is that it applies only to new technologies that reasonably fall within the medium described in the license.[21]

The ideas themselves in a computer program are not copyrightable, but the program itself can be protected as a literary work if it embodies an expression of ideas. Under 1980 amendments to 17 USC §101, a computer program can be copyrighted if it's a set of statements or instructions enabling a computer to perform the operations intended by the user. Creating an archival copy or limited modified copy of the program can be fair use. But loading copyrighted software into a computer's random access memory (RAM) is a copyright infringement, in that it creates a tangible, fixed unauthorized copy[22] of the program.

If a software licensee allows an unauthorized third party to use a licensed, copyrighted computer program, the copyright holder is entitled to bring state law breach of license claims; the issues involved are not limited to, or preempted by, federal copyright law.[23]

[¶1330] Trademarks and Trade Names

Although a patent is an authorized monopoly, with the result that the patented product will have limited sources (only the patent holder and its assignees and licensees), most goods and services are available from many sources.

Trademarks and trade names identify the source of goods (and servicemarks perform the same function for services), permitting sellers to develop a brand name and image that will encourage purchasers to select their products rather than competing products. A trademark is usually associated with a specific product. A tradename is representative of the business' established reputation and goodwill.

The federal government has preempted patent and copyright regulation, but the states have a major role in trademark regulation. Furthermore, the regulation of trademarks overlaps with prohibitions on unfair competition and other business improprieties.

Given the growing internationalization of trade, other countries also have a role to play. P.L. 105-330, enacted 10/30/98, implements the 1994 Trademark Law Treaty and makes small changes needed to harmonize the Lanham Act (the U.S. trademark statute) with world practice.[24]

[¶1330.1] The Lanham Act

The federal trademark statute is the Lanham Act, 15 USC Chapter 22, which has been amended many times.

The Lanham Act definition of a trademark is "any word, name, symbol, or device, or any combination thereof, adopted and used by a manufacturer or mer-

Once a mark is adopted, it should be used consistently, including pictorial elements such as color, use of symbols, type face used for the name, and relationship between the name and the pictorial elements. Protests should be made whenever the brand name is used as a generic description for a kind of product: e.g., "Snorple® brand furnish-sifters are a product of the Vreeble Corporation; please respect the trademark and do not use "Snorple" as a term for all furnish-sifters." (One advantage of the World Wide Web is that it's easy to find sites that refer to a particular product, and see who is using the name in what context.)

[¶1340] Trade Secrets

Many businesses have processes, products, or combinations of the two that are not patentable (or that the company deems would not be beneficial to patent). Although there is no specific federal statute extending trade secret protection in line with copyright, trademark, and patent protection, various state laws extend the common-law protection of trade secrets. Forty-one states (but not including New York, a major commercial center) have adopted the Uniform Trade Secrets Act (UTSA).

A trade secret is a formula, pattern, program, device, method, technique, or collection of information used in business in order to obtain competitive advantage. A corporation's strategic or marketing plans; its customer lists (if not generally known or easily derived from public sources)[29]; its databases and computer programs, product specifications, recipes, and employee manuals, might all constitute trade secrets.

The subject matter of the trade secret must be kept secret, not disclosed, and the owner must take reasonable steps to maintain secrecy. Matters of public knowledge, or that are well-known within an industry, don't qualify for trade-secret status. The Uniform Trade Secret Act requires that keeping the information secret must have actual or potential independent economic value.

However, unlike patent or copyright protection, there is no requirement of novelty, creativity, non-obviousness, or originality for trade secret protection. In some ways, trade secret protection is broader than other forms of intellectual property rights. Patents are available only for processes, machinery, manufactures, or compositions of matter. There are no corresponding limitations on trade secrets. Trade secret protection is simple and inexpensive: no searches have to be made, and registration is not required.

The UTSA imposes liability only if misappropriation has occurred—that is, either acquisition of someone else's trade secret by improper means, or use or disclosure of trade secrets acquired improperly or in violation of a duty of confidentiality. Improper means include theft, bribery, and industrial espionage. However, independent invention, reverse engineering, licensing, and discovery from observing public domain processes are legitimate means that do not create UTSA liability.

The Restatement (3rd) of Unfair Competition gives a trade secret owner a claim for mere improper acquisition of a trade secret, even if the acquiror does not use it.

Suit can be brought (especially for an injunction rather than damages) as soon as disclosure of the trade secret is threatened, because trade secret protection is lost as soon as the information becomes generally known.[30] The grant of injunction would probably be limited to the time before the material would become known anyway.

The statute of limitations for a UTSA action is three years from the time the owner of the trade secret discovers, or reasonably should have discovered, the misappropriation of the trade secret.

Monetary damages (instead of or in addition to injunction) might be measured by the loss to the owner of the trade secrets (such as lost profits or the cost of developing the trade secret); the misappropriator's gain (including savings due to increased efficiency); or a reasonable royalty that might have been charged if the trade secret had been licensed instead of appropriated. In very serious cases, punitive damages might be allowed.

[¶1340.1] Protecting Secrecy

There are no exceptions to the UTSA rule that trade secret protection requires the owner to safeguard the confidentiality of the material. Appropriate security steps include:

- Drafting a written security manual
- Making sure that employees know what material is confidential
- Having employees sign an agreement indicating that they will keep trade secret material to which they have access secure and confidential
- Holding exit interviews with departing employees, stressing the inappropriateness of disclosing trade secrets, especially to a new employer
- Sending a follow-up letter to ex-employees reminding them of the confidentiality obligation
- Keeping trade secret documents apart from other documents in a locked and fireproof location
- Making employees sign out files containing trade secret materials
- Labeling trade secret materials as such; consider reproducing them on paper that defeats further copying
- Shredding or otherwise destroying extra copies of materials relating to trade secrets
- Having a sign-out process to trace who uses trade secret files
- Consulting computer and network security professionals to make sure that access to trade secret material in digital form is properly restricted (e.g., with passwords and encryption)—and that materials that are supposed to be deleted from the computer are indeed deleted and can't be recovered!
- Informing customers and licensees of their obligation to maintain confidentiality of trade secrets that they are entitled to use
- Reviewing press releases, trade show speeches, technical articles published by employees, etc., to make sure that trade secrets are not disclosed.

[¶1350] Patents

In a way, the patent is the most absolute form of intellectual property. It is quite possible for two similar works both to qualify for copyright (as long as one does not plagiarize the other), or for two similar trademarks to be granted (as long as they are not confusingly similar). But the grant of a patent requires a patent examiner's determination that the same invention has not already been patented, and that the current invention is not an obvious development of existing public domain or patented inventions.[31]

Although in general monopolies are disapproved of, a patent is a "statutory monopoly," permitting the patentee exclusive use (within the United States) of the invention for a 20-year term, running from the date of filing (35 USC §154).[32] The holder of the patent can prevent unauthorized persons from manufacturing, using, offering to sell, or selling the invention. When a patent expires, the item or process goes into the public domain.

[¶1350.1] Patentable Subject Matter

Any "new and useful process, machine, manufacture or composition of matter, or any new and useful improvement thereof" can be granted a utility patent: 35 USC §101. The invention must be new; useful; and non-obvious to a person who has ordinary skill in "the art" (i.e., the type of technology for which the patent has been issued).

A design patent covers an object's non-functional visual and tactile characteristics (e.g., the shape and decoration of a table lamp, but not the way its wiring or bulb works). The design must be new, original, and ornamental. Novelty is tested on the basis of whether an average observer[33] would consider it a new design; changing finish, color, or workmanship of an existing design is not sufficient. The design patent term (35 USC §171) is 14 years.

Certain subject matter is not entitled to patents, such as laws of nature, natural phenomena or principles, or mathematical algorithms.[34] Although traditionally patents were denied for systems or methods of doing business, several Internet-related patents have been issued for business methods, e.g., "reverse auctions" conducted on-line. There is some concern as to whether such patents were properly issued after adequate review, and whether they are defensible. Certainly, a great deal of litigation will ensue.

A so-called "plant patent," under 35 USC §161 et seq., is issued on a method of asexually reproducing a plant. P.L. 103-349, the Plant Variety Protection Act Amendments of 1994, conforms U.S. law to the International Convention for the Protection of New Varieties of Plants.[35] Also see P.L. 105-289, the Plant Patent Amendments of 1998, protecting the owner of a plant patent against unauthorized sale of parts taken from an illegally reproduced plant.

Invention, for patent purposes, has two phases: conception and reduction to practice. Reduction to practice can be either actual (making a tangible exemplar or embodiment of the invention) or constructive (by setting out a detailed description in the patent application).

[¶1350.1.1] Novelty; Non-Obviousness

In order to be patented, an invention must be novel. 35 USC §102(a) denies patentability to inventions "patented or described in a printed publication in this or a foreign country, before the invention thereof by the application for patent."

35 USC §103 imposes a further requirement of non-obviousness. *Graham v. John Deere Co.*[36] sets out a three-part test for non-obviousness:

- Scope and content of prior art
- Differences between the patent claims and prior art
- Level of ordinary skill in the art found among other potential inventors and practitioners

"Double patenting"—the issuance of multiple patents on the same invention—is barred. An inventor who has patented an invention cannot also patent the means of producing the patented invention. If the inventor later improves on the invention, additional patents can be granted on the improvements.

Although there are no state patent laws, federal preemption of this area is not complete. According to the Federal Circuit[37] a state-law claim of unfair competition against the holder of a patent is not preempted by federal patent law, as long as the defendant could be found liable under state law without actually conflicting with the federal law. Nor does patent law preempt the state law of trade secrets,[38] because the two forms of protection serve different purposes, and patent law revolves around complete disclosure, whereas trade secret law requires complete secrecy.

[¶1350.2] The Patent Application

Substantive legal requirements for patent applications are found in 35 USC §111; the required disclosures are set out in §112. The application is made to the Commissioner of Patents and Trademarks. Requirements appear at 37 CFR §1.51, 1.52, and 1.58. The application must contain:

- The specification, including at least one patentable claim
- The inventor's oath or declaration
- Drawings showing each feature of the invention, if needed to understand the subject matter. (Most applications do require drawings.)

More specifically, the application must include:

- A descriptive title
- Cross-references to any related patent applications
- A brief summary of the invention
- A brief description of the drawings, if any

A 1992 federal statute, the Patent and Plant Variety Protection Remedy Clarification Act, grants the right to sue states for patent infringement, but the Supreme Court found that Congress lacked substantiation of the assertion that patent infringement by states was a significant problem; hence, it lacked authority to enact the statute.

The patent owner also has a cause of action against a party who induces someone else to infringe on the patent, or who contributes to patent infringement. 27 USC §1338(a) gives the federal courts exclusive jurisdiction over patent infringement, and 35 USC §281 grants civil remedies to the patent owner.

[¶1350.7.1] Proof of Infringement
There are two steps in determining whether a patent claim has been infringed:

- Construct the claim and determine its scope and meaning
- Compare the claim to the device or process accused of infringing the patent.

Markman v. Westview Instruments Inc.[43] makes claim construction a matter of law, for the court (so when it is appealed, a de novo standard of review is applied[44]).

In practice, a *Markman* hearing takes place early in the case to determine the scope of the claims. Claims construction requires consideration of the claims; the specification; and the patent's prosecution history. Prosecution history is an especially important factor where there is a great deal of prior art, or the applicant wants to distinguish his or her claim from particular prior art. Wherever possible, claims are construed to be valid over prior art, and to cover at least one embodiment disclosed in the specification.

Under 35 USC §271(a), the occurrence of direct infringement (which, unlike claims construction, is a fact question for the trier of fact) can be literal or under the doctrine of equivalents. The patentee always has the burden of proving infringement. For the mere fact of infringement, the standard is preponderance of the evidence; clear and convincing evidence is required to prove that the infringement was willful (and, perhaps, additional damages are warranted).

[¶1350.7.2] Doctrine of Equivalents
A finding of literal infringement is made after the court has defined the claims that have allegedly been infringed. The finder of fact compares these claims with the allegedly infringing device and determines if they are the same. The "doctrine of equivalents" holds that making a trivial change or slight improvement doesn't prevent a finding of patent infringement, as long as the invention has been misappropriated from its true owner.

This doctrine was upheld in 1997 by the Supreme Court, which applied the doctrine to each element or limitation, not to the patent as a whole. But in practice, "file wrapper estoppel" (also known as prosecution history estoppel) will prevent application of the doctrine in many cases.

A claimant who narrows or abandons part of a claim to meet the examiner's objection, or to get around prior art, can't revive the abandoned claims in an infringement suit. If there is no explanation for a change in claims during the application process, there is a rebuttable presumption that the change is based on reasons related to patentability.[45]

A "pioneer invention"—one which is a major advance in its field—will be given the protection of many equivalents, whereas a narrower scope of protection will be given to more modest inventions.

Infringement can be proved without proof of copying (after all, practitioners of an art are supposed to be familiar with prior art, including the information disclosed in patent applications). The infringer's knowledge of the patent, or even its intent to infringe, are not very relevant to a direct infringement case. However, these are important elements in proving willful infringement that will support additional or treble damages under 35 USC §284.

Direct infringement must be proved before a case of contributory infringement can be made. To prove contributory infringement[46] the patent owner must show:

- The alleged infringer sold, offered for sale, or imported articles for use in the patented invention
- Those articles are a material part of the patented invention
- The infringer knew the articles were especially designed or adapted for use in infringing the patented invention
- Those articles are not a staple of commerce suitable for noninfringing use.

The contributory infringement case requires mere knowledge, not intent.[47]

The cause of action for inducement of infringement also depends on proof of direct infringement. Most courts will not impose liability unless the inducement was knowing and intentional.

[¶1350.7.3] Defenses to Allegations of Infringement

Alleged infringers are entitled to defenses, such as denying that infringement occurred; asserting that their use is non-infringing; and asserting invalidity of the patent.[48] However, under 35 USC §282, an issued patent is presumed to be valid, so the challenger must offer clear and convincing evidence of invalidity.

A patent that is obtained by fraud or inequitable conduct is unenforceable. Patent misuse—extending the patent monopoly past the claims asserted in the patent application as it was granted—does not invalidate the patent, but may prevent a patent owner who has "unclean hands" from obtaining remedies for infringement as long as misuse continues. (In 1988, 35 USC §271(d) was amended to make it clear that mere refusal to use or license any rights to a patent does not constitute patent misuse.)

Patentees are allowed to fix the price at which a licensed manufacturer can sell the patented article; the patentee may not fix the resale price of the patented item once it has been sold. The owner of a license may not combine with another patentee under a cross-license to fix prices under their respective patents. A patent owner is not allowed to condition the grant of one license on the prospective licensee's acceptance of a license on unwanted patents.

Alleged infringers are entitled to assert the affirmative defense of laches. Laches is rebuttably presumed to be present given a six-year delay in filing the infringement suit if the delay materially injured or prejudiced the defendant. However, the defense of laches bars relief only for infringement before the filing of the suit; it is no defense to infringement occurring post-filing. If the patent owner's statements or conduct led the infringer to believe that the owner would not sue, leading to detrimental reliance on the part of the infringer, the owner will be estopped from suing.

[¶1350.7.4] Infringement Remedies

It is unusual for a preliminary injunction to be granted in an infringement action. For one thing, if it is later determined that there was no infringement, the enjoined party would have a good cause of action against the party who obtained the injunction. The case for preliminary injunction (see 35 USC §283) requires proof of irreparable harm if infringement continues; proof beyond a reasonable doubt that the defendant is indeed an infringer; and proof that the patent is clearly valid.

However, if and when infringement is found, the court probably will issue an injunction. The exception might be a case in which the injury to the infringer would exceed the benefit to the patent holder.

The damage standard of 35 USC §284 is damages adequate to compensate for the infringement, but not less than a reasonable royalty for the use made by the infringer. A standard for a reasonable royalty would be set by industry standards or, if there are none, by the price a willing licensor and licensee would agree on.

35 USC §394 permits arbitration of infringement claims. The arbitrator's award is final and binding on parties to the arbitration, but not to others. *Aro Manufacturing Co.*, above, defines infringement damages as the owner's pecuniary loss, without regard to whether the infringer actually profited by the infringement.

The owner's actual post-infringement financial condition is compared to the condition it would have achieved absent infringement. Lost profits can be recovered, including potential sales that went to the infringer instead of the owner; profits lost because competition from the infringer mandated price cuts; and projected lost sales.

Where the owner gives the trier of fact clear and convincing evidence of willful infringement, the court can increase the damages (up to treble). To avoid being held liable for willful infringement, product users have an affirmative duty of care to ascertain whether or not their proposed products infringe on any patents; the duty includes securing competent legal advice.

The prevailing party (plaintiff or defendant) can get an award of attorneys' fees, in an "exceptional" case. Pre-judgment interest and costs can be awarded in a willful infringement case.[49]

A patentee guilty of laches who is denied damages for past infringement is also unable to get an injunction against the future use, maintenance, and repair of products for which the damages are not recoverable—but can get an injunction against the infringer's manufacture, sale, or use of infringing products after the laches has ended.[50]

ENDNOTES

1. A derivative work is a separate work, that can itself be copyrighted, that recasts, transforms, or adapts an underlying work.
2. Note that copyright registration, rather than filing of a UCC-1 statement, is the only manner in which a security interest in the copyright of a film can be registered: *National Peregrine Inc. v. Capitol Federal S&L Ass'n of Denver*, 116 B.R. 194 (C.D. Cal. 1990).
3. 523 U.S. 135 (Sup.Ct.1998).
4. *Tasini v. New York Times*, 972 F.Supp. 804 (S.D.N.Y. 1997) permits publishers of collective works to license the entire compilation for inclusion in an Internet database even without consent of the authors of the underlying works in the compilation, because the license is a permissible revision of the collective work. (In September, 1999, the Second Circuit reversed the S.D.N.Y. #97-9181.)

    However, an online service that took orders for copies of scholarly articles, to be faxed to persons placing orders (and paid fees for second or subsequent uses of an article from a particular publisher) was held to require permission of both author and publisher: *Ryan v. CARL Corp.*, 23 F.Supp.2d 1146 (N.D. Cal. 1998). The court distinguished *Tasini* because it did not deem faxing the articles on request to be a revision of a collective work.
5. *Feist Publishers Inc. v. Rural Telephone Service Co.*, 499 U.S. 340 (Sup.Ct. 1991). Also see *Bell South Advertising & Publishing Corp. v. Donnelley Information Publishing Inc.*, 977 F.2d 1435 (11th Cir. 1993).
6. *Matthew Bender & Co. v. West Publishing Co.*, 158 F.3d 674 (2nd Cir. 1998), cert.denied #98-1500, in conjunction with denial of certiorari in *West Publishing Co. v. HyperLaw*, #98-1519, at the end of the 1999 term. However, the earlier case of *West Publishing Co. v. Mead Data Central Inc.*, 799 F.2d 1219 (8th Cir. 1986) did deem the arrangement and pagination of the cases to be copyrightable.
7. *Recording Industry Association v. Diamond Multimedia Systems,* #9856727 (9th Cir. 6/15/99). There is an Audio Home Recording Act of 1992, which requires audio devices to use a Serial Copy Management System to store information about the source and copyright status of the music files they play, but the Ninth Circuit held that the Rio does not fit the narrow statutory definitions of "recording device" and "recorded music."
8. 490 U.S. 730 (Sup.Ct. #1989).
9. The Copyright Renewal Act of 1992, P.L. 102-307, granted an automatic 47-year renewal of copyrights that came into existence between 1/1/63 and 12/31/77.

    Prior to the '78 Act, when the first 28-year copyright term was completed, the renewal copyright reverted to the author or a specified beneficiary. This renewal feature was dropped other than for works that were in their first term of copyright protection on 1/1/78.

embodiment is built: *Continental Plastic Containers Inc. v. Owens-Brockway Plastic Products Inc.*, 66 LW 1656 (Fed.Cir. 3/31/98).

41. The Bayh-Dole Act, 35 USC §202(c)(7)(B) requires universities and other not-for-profit organizations that receive federal funding to share patent royalties with employee inventors. However, the statute was enacted to regulate the commercial exploitation of federally funded inventions, and only incidentally to benefit the inventors themselves, so it does not provide an implied private right of action for employee-inventors who seek a specific profit percentage: *Platzer v. Sloan-Kettering Inst.*, 983 F.2d 1086 (2nd Cir. 1992), *cert. denied* 507 U.S. 1006.

42. 119 S.Ct. 2199 (Sup.Ct. 1999).

43. 517 U.S. 370 (Sup.Ct. 1996).

44. *Cybor Corp. v. FAS Technologies Inc.*, 138 F.3d 1448 (Fed.Cir. 1998).

45. *Hilton Davis Chemical Co. v. Warner-Jenkinson Co. Inc.*, 520 U.S. 17 (Sup.Ct. 1997). Also see *Roton Barrier Inc. v. Stanley Works*, 79 F.3d 1112 (Fed.Cir. 1996): to prove infringement under the doctrine of equivalents, the plaintiff must prove not only traditional infringement elements, but also that any difference between the products is insubstantial.

46. *Aro Manufacturing Co v. Convertible Top Replacement Co.*, 377 U.S. 476 (Sup.Ct. 1964).

47. *Hewlett-Packard v. Bausch & Lomb*, 909 F.2d 1464 (Fed.Cir. 1990).

48. The patent owner is estopped from asserting the validity of the patent if the patent was earlier declared invalid in a proceeding where the owner had a full and fair opportunity to litigate: *Blonder-Tongue Lab, Inc. v. University of Illinois Foundation*, 402 U.S. 313 (Sup.Ct. 1971). A patent licensee is allowed to assert invalidity as a defense against a claim of infringement, but an assignee is estopped from challenging the validity of the patent.

49. Pre-judgment interest can be awarded in any case of willful infringement; there is no exceptionality requirement: *General Motors Corp. v. Devex Corp.*, 461 U.S. 648 (Sup. Ct. 1983).

50. *Odetics Inc. v. Storage Technology Corp.*, 66 LW 1797 (E.D. Va. 6/5/98).

Insurance Law

[¶1401]

As a result of natural disaster, illness, accident, or the negligence or misconduct of human beings or organizations, people, property, and businesses can suffer various kinds of accident or damage with financial implications. Public policy supports legitimate activities such as operating a business or supporting a family, so insurance is recognized by law and even given favorable tax status (e.g., in many situations, insurance proceeds are not taxable income for income tax purposes; and, as ¶3111 shows, under appropriate circumstances life insurance proceeds can be excluded from the estate of the insured decedent).

Insurance exists to transmute the risk of a large, unpredictable loss into a smaller, more predictable obligation to pay insurance premiums. If and when an insured event occurs, insurance proceeds are available to cushion the financial implications of the event.

However, for various reasons, the insurance is unlikely to remove all financial impact. Most policies do not start paying until a deductible has been satisfied. In many, if not most, situations, the insured will have coinsurance responsibilities: the insurance will pay only a percentage of the loss. Even if there are two or more policies that might potentially provide coverage, they will be "coordinated" so that coverage will not exceed 100% of the loss.

There are many kinds of insurance, and many variations of policy design within each kind. It can be categorized as coverage for individuals or businesses; or coverage of the person (e.g., life and health insurance) versus property insurance. Another division is that between first-party coverage (the insured is reimbursed for his, her, or its own losses) and third-party coverage (the injured person is reimbursed by the insurer of the party responsible for the losses).

Liability insurance includes two important components: reimbursement of the individual's obligations to other people (such as persons injured in automobile accidents caused by the insured) and the insurance company's duty to defend by supplying an attorney or paying the costs of the attorney selected by the defendant-insured.

There are also some important differences between individual and group policies. Technically, the entity buying the group policy is the policyholder; the individuals covered under the plan are "certificate holders." Furthermore, the entity selects the policy and the carrier, and pays part or all of the premium—with the result that it might select provisions that save money for the entity but are not the ones the individual members might have chosen.

Despite the variety of provisions, many insurance policies are organized similarly. The insured person is entitled to the "coverages" specified in the policy, up to policy limits, but is not entitled to coverage under the circumstances specifically excluded by the policy. Coverage does not begin until any deductible is satisfied, and is subject to the insured's copayment responsibilities. It is very common for the exclusions, deductibles, coinsurance, and policy limits to be different for the different coverages.

Insurance law draws a distinction between cancellation and nonrenewal of a policy. The insurer's ability to cancel a policy that has an indefinite duration is quite limited, and usually requires some form of wrongdoing by the insured (such as misrepresentation on the application). But if a policy has a designated term (e.g., five-year term life insurance), the insurer often has the option to deny renewal, even if the insured has complied with all obligations under the policy.

The concept of subrogation applies in most insurance situations. That is, an insurer that pays benefits is likely to be entitled to a share of any contract or tort recovery that compensates the party receiving the benefits for the events causing the injury or damage. For instance, a health insurer that pays hospital bills may be entitled to part of the injured person's recovery against the negligent driver. However, insurers are also subject to any defenses that the defendant can assert against the recipient of the benefits.

Insured parties must notify their insurers whenever an event occurs that affects the policy—usually because the insured claims that policy benefits are due, but sometimes so that the insurer can stay up to date on the insured's financial condition. In addition to prompt notice of claim, the insured must file "proof of claim" (a signed, sworn statement giving details of the incident) within a specified time, such as 60 days.

Some states have enacted "notice-prejudice" statutes, under which an insurer can reject a claim on the basis of late filing if, and only if, the delay actually prejudiced the insurance company financially. A 1999 Supreme Court decision[1] holds that ERISA does not preempt these state laws.

That brings up the question of state versus federal regulation of insurance. By and large, insurance law is state law. However, the federal McCarran-Ferguson Act, 15 USC §1011–1015 exempts "the business of insurance" from antitrust scrutiny[2] and, in some cases, preempts state regulation of insurance.[3] For instance, McCarran-Ferguson protects insurers against state charges that they conspired with foreign insurers to keep foreign coverage off the market.[4]

Applicants for insurance usually have the option of choosing among several insurers, and once one is selected, there are usually a number of related policies or policy options that can be chosen. Nevertheless, insurance policies are sold in forms drafted by the insurer and approved by state licensing authorities. There is little real opportunity for negotiation. Therefore, any ambiguous provision in an insurance policy will be construed in favor of the insured.

[¶1410] Life Insurance

It might seem that life insurance is not really insurance, because everybody is certain to die sooner or later. But a legitimate element of risk shifting is present, because it is not certain that the individual will die while insured by a life insurance policy.

Life insurance companies do business either as "stock" companies which, like conventional corporations, are owned by stockholders, or as "mutual" companies owned by the owners of policies. Mutual companies pay dividends to their policyholders, which can be received in cash, accumulated to earn interest, applied against future premiums, or used to purchase paid-up insurance (i.e., insurance for which no further premiums will be charged).

Congress has granted life insurance extremely favorable tax status. As long as the insured person had no "incidents of ownership" (rights to control the policy) at the time of death, and did not have such incidents during the three years prior to death, and as long as the insurance is payable to a named insured rather than the insured person's estate, the insurance proceeds will not be included in the decedent's estate, no matter how large they are.

Combined with the unlimited marital deduction (see ¶3120.3), this treatment makes it possible for a married person to provide generously for a surviving spouse without estate tax liability in the first estate. (The estate of the surviving spouse, however, may be quite large and generate significant estate tax.)

Life insurance is also significant in corporate planning. Insurance is frequently used to fund buy-sell agreements (¶150.2) under which owners of a partnership or closely-held corporation buy out the interest of a deceased owner.

[¶1410.1] Whole Life, Term, and Investment-Oriented Insurance

"Whole life" insurance can be maintained for an indefinite number of years, as long as the insured or other policy owner continues to pay the premiums. Whole life insurance also has cash value.[5] The general rule is that the premium for a whole life policy remains level as long as the policy is maintained; it does not increase as the insured gets older (and, presumably, is more likely to die). That means that the premium charged is higher than the pure cost of insurance in the early years of the policy, creating cash value that can be borrowed against or used as security for other loans.

A single-premium policy exchanges a sum of money for immediate protection and cash value; the policy remains in force without additional premium payments.

In a conventional whole-life policy, the insurance company controls investment of the premiums paid by insureds. Investment-oriented policies such as variable life, universal life, and the hybrid variable-universal life policy allow the insured to select investment alternatives, similar to mutual funds, for the premium, and sometimes for additional sums deposited by the insured.

The death benefit in a variable life policy is always at least equal to the minimum guaranteed by the contract. If the policyholder's investment decisions work out well, the death benefit can increase. The cash value of the policy also fluctuates, and is not protected by any minimum guarantee.

The death benefit of a universal life policy is guaranteed only for the first month of the contract. Subsequently, a minimum interest rate is guaranteed, but the death benefit fluctuates. The policyholder also has control over the premium payments, and can increase or decrease them, changing the amount of insurance.

[¶1410.2] Term Insurance

In contrast to whole-life insurance, term insurance lasts only for a certain number of years (typically, five). At that point, the coverage expires. If desired, the owner can renew the policy, but most term insurance policies cannot be renewed more than a certain number of times, or after a certain age (e.g., 75). Furthermore, term insurers usually refuse to sell new policies to older individuals. Sometimes the premium remains level during the term; some policies call for annual increases. It is almost certain that the premium for a renewal policy will be higher, based on the insured's increased age.

In addition to term policies whose amount of coverage remains the same, "increasing" and "decreasing" term policies adjust coverage during the term, to cope with anticipated increases or decreases in financial responsibilities.

[¶1410.3] Policy Ownership

The simplest case is for a person to purchase coverage on his or her own life, designating one or more beneficiaries (and preferably designating one or more contingent beneficiaries, in case the original beneficiary predeceases the insured person).

However, anyone who has an "insurable interest" in someone else's life can purchase insurance on that person, or can become the owner by transfer of the insurance. Insurable interest means a reasonable expectation of financial benefit from the policy, or from the person's estate. Thus, a spouse, close relative, or business partner would have an insurable interest, but a stranger would not.

The owner of a policy can name anyone as beneficiary—the beneficiary does not have to have an insurable interest in the life of the insured.

As noted above, good estate planning frequently calls for individuals to avoid owning policies on their own lives, or to transfer the policies and hope to survive the transfer by at least three years. Another possibility is for spouses each to purchase coverage on the spouse's life, rather than on their own.

The "incidents of ownership" of a policy (relevant not only between the insurer and its customers, but in determining whether proceeds should be included in the estate of the insured) include the ability to surrender the policy and receive its cash value (in the form of cash or paid-up insurance), the right to take policy loans, and the right to designate the beneficiary. The owner can also assign the policy, with the result that the assignee and not the original owner can now exercise the incidents of ownership. The general rule is that policies can be assigned to anyone, although some jurisdictions do limit assignment to persons with an insurable interest in the owner's life.

[¶1410.4] Standard Provisions of Life Insurance Policies

Most of these provisions are required by state law, although some of them are choices adopted by insurers seeking to increase the attractiveness of their products:

- Death benefit (or face value): the amount that will be paid to the beneficiary(ies) if the insured person dies when the policy is in force
- Cash value: value built up within a whole life policy; if the policyholder surrenders the policy, he or she will receive the cash value
- Loan value: most whole-life policies set a guaranteed interest rate for loans against the cash value. (Any unpaid loans at the time of the insured's death will be subtracted from the death benefit paid to the beneficiary(ies).
- Designation of beneficiaries and contingent beneficiaries
- Incontestability: Once the policy has been in force for a period (generally two years; sometimes one year), the insurer cannot contest the payability of the death benefit, even if the insured committed suicide or if the original application for the policy was not accurate. An exception is that misrepresentations as to an insurance applicant's age will reduce the death benefit. Suicide while the policy is still contestable will result in return of the premiums paid, but not payment of the full death benefit.
- Misrepresentations: if an applicant misrepresents a material fact (e.g., state of health), the policy is voidable if disclosure of the actual facts would have prevented issuance of the contract at that premium level (e.g., standard rather than the more costly "rated up"). The insurer can rescind the policy based on deliberate concealment by the applicant of a material fact, but minor misrepresentations will not justify rescission. Jurisdictions differ as to whether an insurer can rescind a policy on the basis of material but innocent misrepresentations (if so, the insured is entitled to a refund of the premiums paid). Another factor is that in some jurisdictions, insurers will not be allowed to avoid policies on the basis of obvious misrepresentations, or misrepresentations that would have been discovered pursuant to an adequate investigation.
- Nonforfeiture: Amount of insurance that can be taken in lieu of cash when a policy is surrendered; naturally, this is lower than the amount of insurance that would be available if premium payments continued. States require nonforfeiture provisions because otherwise policy owners could pay premiums for many years and have nothing to show for it if they let the policy lapse during the lifetime of the insured.

[¶1410.5] Riders

In addition to the basic coverage available under the policy chosen, additional benefits can be obtained by supplementing the basic contract with "riders." Some riders are free; others carry a surcharge. Appropriate selection of riders depends on the purchaser's objectives for the insurance.

- Waiver of premium: This rider continues the insurance in full force, without additional premium payments, if the policyholder becomes totally and permanently disabled, and the disability lasts a stipulated period of time (usually six months). The cash value continues to grow while the premium is waived.

- Disability payout: the face amount of the policy is parceled out in a series of continuing payments starting when the policyholder becomes totally disabled
- Disability income: a certain amount of income (typically, 1% of the policy's face value) is paid after a waiting period (e.g., six months) to a totally and permanently disabled insured. Generally speaking, payments continue until age 65, at which point the death benefit is paid out in cash.
- Accidental death benefit: a multiple of the face value of the policy (e.g., "double indemnity") is paid if the policyholder dies as a result of an accident. (Usually, the death must follow the accident by no more than 90 days.) Some policies, especially in the group insurance market, provide additional benefits for accidental death and dismemberment (loss of a body part, or function of a body part).
- Guaranteed insurability: the rider specifies "option dates" at which the insured can purchase additional insurance at standard rates, without proof of continued insurability
- Automatic premium loan: the insurer is given authorization to borrow from the cash value to pay a forgotten premium (or a premium the insured cannot afford), to keep the policy in force so that it does not lapse. State law, or company policy, may call for older insureds to designate an agent who will be notified of possible lapse, and who can pay the premium to keep the policy in force.
- Retirement option: the policy's cash value and accumulated dividends can be paid out as an annuity (for life, joint lives of the insured and spouse, or for a term of years) when the insured person retires.

[¶1410.6] Settlement Options

When an insured person dies and the policy is incontestable, the death benefit must be paid to the beneficiary, or to the contingent beneficiary if the beneficiary predeceased the insured. The basic form of payment is a lump sum, but in some instances the beneficiary does not want the lump sum, or is not capable of administering it.

A settlement option is an arrangement under which the insurance company retains control over the death benefit, making payments of interest and/or principal to the beneficiary, for life or for a term of years. That way, the beneficiary has regular income but is not saddled with a large sum of money that might be wasted or invested improvidently.

It should be noted that lump-sum life insurance proceeds are not taxable income for the recipient. However, the part of a settlement option check that represents interest earned on the funds after the insured's death constitutes taxable income.

[¶1410.7] Viatication and Accelerated Death Benefits

Policy loans are one way to get value out of a life insurance policy prior to the death of the insured. Viatication and accelerated death benefits are other methods.

Viatication is the irrevocable assignment of a policy, usually by a terminally ill person, to a third party who pays a discounted portion of the death benefit to the "viator" (insured). The longer the insured is predicted to live, the deeper the discount, because the investor expects to have to wait longer to collect. Viatication has the same effect as selling the policy to a third party.

Accelerated Death Benefits (ADB), in contrast, are offered by the insurer. The insurer offers ADB as a rider (often without additional premium); the rider contains a schedule of the amount that can be accessed under various conditions. ADB does not have to be repaid, but advances will, of course, reduce the death benefit that is eventually paid to the beneficiary.

Both viatication and ADB offer an additional source of cash for seriously or terminally ill persons who need money (to pay for medical treatment or otherwise). Under Code §§101(g)(1)A) and 7702B, ADB and viatical settlement funds can sometimes be received tax-free. Terminally ill persons can receive the funds (within dollar limits) tax-free no matter how they apply them; chronically ill persons get the tax advantage only if they use the funds for medical care.

[¶1410.8] Insurance Sales by Banks

The National Bank Act, a federal statute, authorizes a national bank doing business in a community with a population of 5,000 or less to act as agent for any insurance company. The Comptroller of the Currency interprets this to mean that insurance can be sold in any town where the population does not exceed 5,000, even if the bank's central office is in a larger city.[6]

[¶1420] Casualty Insurance

The broad rubric of casualty insurance includes many of the types of insurance other than life and health insurance. Liability insurance; burglary and theft insurance; property damage; collision; glass; boiler and machinery; Worker's Compensation policies maintained by employers; credit insurance; and fidelity and surety bonds all are considered casualty insurance. A Comprehensive policy (e.g., for an automobile) combines fire and casualty insurance.

An "all risk" (also called "open perils) policy covers any kind of damage to the covered property that results from any cause that is not specifically excluded by the policy. In contrast, a "specified risk" policy is limited to damage caused by something specifically included in the policy. Fire and collision insurance are issued as specified risk policies.

A "valued" policy stipulates the value of the insured property at the outset, and any insurance payment made during the policy term will be calculated on the basis of this value. This provides the security of knowing in advance how the value will be set, and eliminates disputes, but will not necessarily reflect the actual market value of the property. In contrast, an "open" policy does not set the value in advance; it must be determined if and when loss occurs.

If more than one policy covering the same insured property, interest in the property, and risk is in force at the time the property is damaged or destroyed, the coverage must be coordinated. Some policies have an "other insurance" clause that excludes coverage altogether if other insurance is in force; others declare that they are excess insurance, triggered only if the other policy is exhausted. (If both policies say this, the insured can have problems.) The most common "other insurance" provision is pro rata: that is, the insurer who has issued 2/3 of the insurance has 2/3 of the risk.

Although it usually is purchased and benefits the owner of the covered property, casualty insurance can be assigned to someone who has an economic interest in the property, such as a mortgagee or major creditor.

[¶1430] Property Insurance

Property insurance covers direct loss to tangible property, such as buildings and their contents, suffered as the result of a covered "peril." It usually covers loss of use of damaged property. Consequential loss coverage (loss of use, or reduced value of property that is not actually damaged) can often be added for an additional premium. "Multiple-peril coverage" includes several separate coverages.

Some significant questions arise as to whether there has been an "occurrence" that is covered by the policy; sometimes it is not doubted that damage has taken place, but there is a lively contest as to whether there was any "occurrence" within the meaning of the policy.

Timing is also important. In an "occurrence" policy, coverage is provided when the insured event occurs while insurance is still in force, even if the claim is not made until much later (e.g., ceiling collapses because of undetected slow, persistent water leak). A "claims-made" policy, in contrast, allows the insurer much greater certainty because it covers only claims actually made during the time when the insurance is in force. Claims-made policies are also usually subject to a "retroactive date": even if claims are made while the policy is in force, they will be excluded if they relate to events occurring before the policy became effective.

[¶1430.1] Floater Policies

Floater policies are so-called because they cover property that is not always used or kept in the same place. Floaters are all-risk policies. A personal property floater covers items such as expensive jewelry and camera equipment.

A business floater policy covers all of the company's equipment or inventory, even if it is located off business premises (e.g., at a trade show; in transit). "Block" policies are adapted to all the requirements of a particular business or industry. Block policies have been developed for jewelers, furriers, dealers in cameras and musical instruments, and heavy equipment retailers, for instance.

[¶1430.2] Fire Insurance

Fire insurance covers the perils of direct loss by fire and lightning, plus certain types of smoke damage. However, certain types of smoke damage (e.g., caused by a defective heating apparatus) are excluded. Fire insurance often draws a distinction between "friendly" and "hostile" fire, excluding or limiting claims relating to "friendly" fire such as furnaces and fireplaces, as distinguished from "hostile" fires that start outside the premises or accidentally within the premises.

Fire insurance can be combined with other perils in an "extended coverage" endorsement to the policy. This endorsement insures against windstorm, hail, explosion, riot, civil commotion, aircraft damage, smoke, explosion, and vehicle damage. The "additional extended coverage" endorsement adds coverage for building collapse, explosion of steam or hot water systems, fallen trees, glass breakage, vandalism and malicious mischief, vehicles owned or operated by the insured or insured's tenants, water damage, ice and snow, and freezing.

"Allied lines" coverage is either an endorsement to fire insurance, or written as a separate policy. It covers destruction caused by natural disasters and events such as fire sprinkler leakage.

It is a typical requirement of home mortgages that the mortgagor must carry fire insurance representing at least a certain percentage (e.g., 80%) of the current value of the home. A "co-insurance clause" provides that, if the building is underinsured when a loss incurs, the owner's insurance recovery will be reduced in proportion to the underinsurance.

Assume that a home is worth $250,000 and is subject to an 80% insurance requirement, and that the owner maintains $200,000 worth of insurance. That is deemed adequate, so the owner will be entitled to receive covered losses (subject to the deductible) up to the policy limit.

However, if only $150,000 in insurance had been maintained, then only three-quarters of the loss otherwise recoverable could be recovered, because the insured had only three-quarters of the required amount of insurance.

[¶1440] Automobile Insurance

The no-fault system (see ¶3250.1), although it limits the number and complexity of automobile-related tort suits, certainly does not eliminate the need for automobile insurance, because availability of liability insurance is central to no-fault.

It is a requirement of obtaining or renewing a driver's license that the driver demonstrate "financial responsibility" by having an adequate amount of liability insurance. This is a legal requirement, not a personal decision. Many motorists also choose to protect themselves with first-party coverage. Comprehensive insurance combines liability insurance with first-party property insurance. Collision insurance covers damage to the insured's vehicle. The decision to maintain collision or comprehensive insurance often depends on the age and value of the vehicle; the cost of insuring an older or modest vehicle is often heavy in comparison to the amount of benefits that can be paid after damage.

[¶1450] Business Insurance

In addition to the CGL and EPLI liability policies discussed in ¶¶1460.2 and 1460.5, respectively, there are many kinds of property insurance that are typically owned by businesses rather than by private individuals.

[¶1450.1] Burglary and Theft Insurance

Burglary and theft insurance is written in many variations:

- Open stock burglary policies cover loss by burglary of merchandise, furniture, fixtures and equipment, and damage to the premises during a burglary, but not loss of money, securities, records, or accounts
- Mercantile safe burglary policies cover loss of money, securities, and other property, as well as damage resulting from burglary of a safe
- Mercantile robbery policy covers robbery hazards inside and outside business premises
- Paymaster robbery policies cover the risk of robbery of payroll funds
- Storekeeper's burglary and robbery policies are small-scale package policies
- Office burglary and robbery policies are their counterparts for service businesses and professional offices
- Money and securities broad form policies offer comprehensive coverage for most losses of money and securities, including but not limited to burglary and robbery.

[¶1450.2] Surety and Fidelity Bonds

Suretyship is the relationship between one individual, corporation, or partnership and another to whose obligations it lends its name or credit. For instance, a founder of a start-up corporation might provide a personal guarantee of corporate debts.

Bonding is an important aspect of suretyship. Many transactions are dependent on a bonding company or insurance company issuing a bond that can be used to pay a defaulter's obligations.

- Contract bonds secure satisfactory completion or performance of a major long-term contract; the bond cannot be canceled during the term of the contract
- Performance bonds cover various kinds of contractual performance. A construction contract bond guarantees the contractor's performance when it constructs a building. A completion bond is a variation that runs to the lender who finances the construction project. A labor and material performance bond ensures that, if the contractor fails to pay for labor and materials, the bond will take over. (This could be either a separate policy or a component of a construction contract bond.) A maintenance bond (which, again, can be discrete or part of a construction contract bond) provides coverage if the contractor's product is defective as to workmanship or materials. A supply contract bond guarantees a contract to supply goods or materials.
- Bid bonds are usually required when contractors bid on public works projects, and are sometimes required by private companies letting a contract. The bond guarantees that if the bidder is awarded the contract, it will enter into the contract and provide a performance bond and, if required, a payment bond.

The fidelity bond covers the employer against employee dishonesty that results in loss of money, securities, or other business property. Some bonds insure only named individuals; some cover whoever holds named positions, and some cover all of the firm's employees. (Partners are not considered employees of their partnerships.) Corporate officers are considered employees, and thus are covered by the fidelity bond, but corporate directors are covered only if they are inside directors or officers.

[¶1450.3] Package Policies

A multiple-peril, or package, policy includes many coverages in a single policy. The policy could be written on either an all-risk or a specified basis.

* Manufacturer's output policy: covers the merchandise and other personal property of the manufacturer, such as large stocks of goods in dispersed locations, when the materials are off the manufacturer's premises
* Industrial property policy: all of the personal property of a manufacturer (and perhaps its buildings), plus property of other parties that is on the premises
* Commercial property policy: covers personal property of retailers and wholesalers, on or off the premises. However, this coverage is not sold to jewelers, furriers, or others who can buy block policies
* Office contents policy: covers the personal property located in an office; the building owner and the tenants are eligible to be insured. The building owner's policy is designated as the office package policy.

[¶1450.4] Credit Insurance

In the consumer credit arena, credit insurance is purchased by a mortgagor or person with a large loan. The insurance provides funds to pay the debt in case of the death or disability of the debtor.

In the business arena, credit insurance indemnifies a manufacturer, wholesaler, or jobber for unusual losses caused by customers' failure to pay. Usually, this coverage is not available to retailers, because it is too difficult to assess the creditworthiness of their customers.

A general policy covers all accounts of the insured described in the policy, usually restricted to those of a specified credit rating so that it will not be necessary for the insurer to undertake individual investigation. A specific policy relates only to particular, investigated accounts.

[¶1450.5] Consequential Loss Coverage

Often, a peril will not only cause direct damage (for instance, burning or smoke damage to merchandise) but indirect damage (for instance, water damage caused by firefighters). In fact, a business can suffer economic loss even as a result of perils to others: a retail store that does not receive merchandise it ordered because of a fire at the factory, for example. Many commercial contracts disclaim responsibility for buyers' consequential damages, so first-party coverage for such losses can be especially valuable.

Consequential loss coverage reimburses businesses for the loss of use of damaged or destroyed property, and property loss that is indirectly connected with a hazard.

Business interruption insurance is the best-known form of consequential loss coverage. Coverage could also be available for contingent business interruption (interruption of business of a channel partner, such as a supplier, which has a ripple effect on the insured's business); extra expense coverage (costs of responding to an emergency); rent insurance (issued to a landlord who loses rent revenue because of damage to a building); delayed profits insurance (compensating for profits lost because a project is completed late); leasehold insurance (compensating a tenant for losses attributable to non-renewal of the lease); and profits and commission insurance (used for seasonal goods and individualized manufactures, where finished goods are destroyed and consequently profits are lost).

[¶1460] Liability Insurance

Remember, in a first-party coverage, the insured person (or the insured person's beneficiary) looks to his, her, or its own insurer for coverage of covered perils. But in third-party coverage, the insured has harmed the person or property of someone else in some way covered by the policy. Therefore, the insurer's duty to defend is triggered, and if the insured is found liable to someone else, some or all of that liability will be satisfied or reimbursed by the insurer.

The duty to defend is extremely significant, but not without its problems. The insured may feel that the insurer does not provide top-quality counsel, or that the attorney is more cognizant of the insurer's interests than those of the insured. The insurer could press for a quick settlement, when the insured is more interested in continuing the fight to vindicate its reputation. The insurer may also take the position that a "claim," creating a duty to defend, does not arise until litigation has actually been commenced, while the insured may feel that legal counsel is acutely required during time-consuming, expensive administrative phases (such as investigations by OSHA, the EEOC, or the EPA).

The usual pattern for liability insurance is a division into Coverage A (bodily injury) and Coverage B (damage to property); some policies add Coverage C (advertising injury), if this is suitable for the objectives of the policy.

Certain types of liability may be excluded from liability insurance, or coverage limited, on public policy grounds. For instance, insurance coverage of punitive damages is problematic, because the intended deterrent function would be unavailable if the insurer bore the burden. Coverage of intentional wrongdoing is also likely to be barred for public policy reasons.

However, neither exclusion is absolute, especially since corporations are chargeable with misconduct of individual employees (such as those who commit sexual harassment), and an argument could be made that the corporation itself is a victim of the wrongdoing.

are all considered to have arisen on the date of the first claim, so there will be no gap in coverage and it will not be necessary to figure out whether the initial or the later insurer is responsible.

[¶1470] Health Insurance

The first form of health insurance to emerge was indemnity coverage, permitting the patients to select their own health care providers. Since the 1970s, managed care has become the dominant form of health insurance. There are many kinds of managed care plans; they all involve some degree of "gatekeeper" mechanisms (limitations on which doctors the patient can see) and incentives or requirements that the insured person use health care providers who are part of the plan. See ¶¶345-345.13 for discussion of health insurance as an employee benefit.

Consumer advocates are concerned about the potential of managed care to deny needed, or even life-preserving, care for financial reasons. Several states have already passed laws increasing the liability potential of the managed care entity when managed care patients are dissatisfied with the amount or quality of their care, and it is likely that Congress will pass legislation on this subject.

Health insurance covers "reasonable and medically necessary" services only, and nearly always excludes "experimental" treatment. Therefore, a major litigation issue is determining when a particular treatment has achieved acceptance in the medical profession and can no longer be excluded as experimental.

Pennsylvania's Workers' Compensation Act requires that, once liability is no longer contested, the employer or its insurer must pay for all reasonable or necessary treatment. However, it is permissible to withhold payment for disputed treatment until an independent third party has performed utilization review.

This statute was construed by the Supreme Court in *American Manufacturer Mutual Insurance Co. v. Sullivan.*[10] The *Sullivan* plaintiffs sued state officials, Workers' Compensation insurers, and a self-insured school district, charging that benefits had been withheld without notice, depriving them of a property right.

Their arguments were unsuccessful. The Supreme Court decided that private insurers are not state actors, and therefore their utilization review activities do not raise Due Process issues. Employees do not have a property right until the treatment they seek has been determined to be reasonable and necessary, and therefore there is no right to notice and hearing until that point.

[¶1470.1] Indemnity Insurance

Indemnity[11] plans are often divided into "basic" and "major medical" models. Basic coverage includes payments for surgery, hospitalization, and care rendered by doctors during hospitalization. A major medical plan covers costs excluded by other policies. A comprehensive major medical plan includes both basic and major medical aspects, whereas a supplemental major medical plan is pure excess insurance.

The typical indemnity plan imposes deductibles (either by the year or by family member) and coinsurance. Payment under indemnity plans is often based on a fee schedule of "usual, customary and reasonable" charges for each service, so the insured person will have additional payment responsibilities if the doctor's actual charge is higher than the schedule charge. The plan sets overall limits on yearly coverage or lifetime coverage.

In compensation, most indemnity plans provide a "stop-loss" limit (a maximum out-of-pocket payment any employee will have to make in any year).

Indemnity insurance plans allow insured persons to choose their own health care providers, and do not impose limits on the number of doctor visits or the number or identity of specialists consulted. For these reasons, indemnity insurance premiums can be quite high, and can increase unpredictably from year to year. Understandably, indemnity plans are not very popular with employers who have to pay all or most of the premium for the policies in their Employee Group Health Plans (EGHPs).

[¶1470.2] Managed Care

During World War II, when civilian employees were scarce, the federal government imposed limitations on wage increases civilian employers could use to recruit or retain employees. However, fringe benefits were not frozen, and employers often competed on the basis of the generosity of the health insurance benefits they provided. Thus, an expectation developed among workers that it was normal for employers to provide health insurance, and often to pay its full cost.

In the post-World War II environment, medical care became much more comprehensive, scientifically sophisticated—and expensive. Employers found that paying for health benefits had become a major component of payroll expense. They began to look for ways to reduce health care costs.

The approach they usually took was a shift away from indemnity, and to managed care. The objective of managed care is to reduce the cost of health care by reducing unneeded care. There are two major mechanisms for doing so: gatekeeper mechanisms and provider networks.

The managed care plan includes gatekeeper mechanisms such as utilization review: insured persons cannot get covered care from specialists unless they have been referred by a primary care physician who decides if a specialist is really needed. Non-emergency hospitalization is not covered unless permission has been obtained in advance. Usually, a second opinion will be required before the managed care plan will cover the costs of surgery.

Nearly all managed care plans cover care only if it is provided by a "network provider": i.e., a doctor, hospital, nursing home, testing laboratory, etc. that has a contract with the managed care organization and agrees to accept its rate schedule or capitation rates.

Capitated plans pay the health care provider a flat amount per month or year for each person enrolled, regardless of how much or how little care the person actually uses; this is supposed to discourage the doctor from prescribing unneeded tests or repeat visits.

There are many kinds of managed care entities, but the leading form is the Health Maintenance Organization (HMO). Patients covered by an HMO are expected to get all or most of their care from providers who participate in the HMO. In exchange for this limitation, they are relieved of most out-of-pocket medical expenses (although they may be responsible for small deductibles for prescriptions and visits to the doctor). The HMO concept has variations, such as the "staff model HMO," "group model HMO," and Individual Practice Association (IPA).

A Preferred Provider Organization (PPO) is a company set up by insurers, health care providers, or a coalition. The preferred providers agree to accept the managed care organization's rate schedule, although they are not employees of the managed care organization.

A Point of Service (POS) plan has some features of the HMO, some of the PPO. Patients have a wider choice of health care provider, but their copayment responsibility increases if they choose a non-network health care provider.

[¶1470.3] Health Insurance Renewals

Health insurance policies may fall into five categories of renewability:

- Cancelable policy (least protective for the insured): the insurer can increase premiums whenever and to whatever extent is permitted by state regulators; the insurer can terminate the policy at any time by notifying the insured and returning any premiums paid in advance
- Optionally renewable policy: the premium can be raised for an entire class of insureds, but not for an individual who has made large claims. The policy can be terminated on the date set by the contract (typically, the policy anniversary)
- Conditionally renewable policy: the insurer can terminate this type of policy because of a condition named in the contract (e.g., reaching a particular age), but not because of deterioration in health. Premium increases must be class-wide, not individual
- Guaranteed renewable policies: must be renewed at the insured's option until a specific age (usually 60 or 65), and premium increases must be class-wide
- Noncancelable health policies: quite rare, they continue until the insured reaches age 65 (the age of Medicare eligibility), and the insurer can neither terminate the coverage nor increase its premium.

[¶1470.4] Medigap

Medicare Supplementary (Medigap) insurance supplements the coverage that senior citizens and disabled persons receive under the federal Medicare system. Although Medicare offers fairly extensive benefits for hospitalization and doctor bills, coverage is subject to deductibles and coinsurance. Medigap insurance reimburses policy owners for those deductibles and coinsurance. The Medicare system (at least as currently constituted) does not cover prescription drugs, but some of the more comprehensive Medigap policies include prescription drug coverage.

Medigap insurance is subject to an unusual degree of federal regulation. Except in a few states that have opted to maintain their own system of regulation, Medigap insurance is subject to federal laws that impose uniformity. Only ten basic Medigap policies (Forms A-J) can be sold. All ten are variations on a basic package of coverages.

As a general rule, Medicare beneficiaries who get their care from a Medicare managed care organization don't need and should not pay for a Medigap policy, because they should not have gaps in coverage or out-of-pocket expenses high enough to justify purchase of a policy. However, a person who leaves the Medicare managed care system and returns to conventional fee-for-service Medicare may need to purchase or reinstate Medigap coverage.

[¶1470.5] Long-Term Care Insurance

Although Medicare covers many of the acute health interventions required by senior citizens, the Medicare system excludes custodial care, such as long-term nursing home care or extensive care at home. Many senior citizens suffer from cognitive disabilities, such as Alzheimer's Disease, or from overall frailty, but not from specific diseases that are Medicare-covered.

Long-term care insurance (LTCI) is a specialized health coverage designed to address senior citizen health needs. The basic LTCI policy covers skilled or custodial care in a nursing home; most LTCI policies also cover home care, either as part of the policy or by addition of riders. Some LTCI policies also cover additional innovative benefits such as adult day care and specialized housing for the elderly.

Unlike most policies, LTCI policies do not have a deductible, although many policies have a waiting period (10-100 days) before coverage begins, which serves a similar function. LTCI policies usually pay a certain amount per day (e.g., $100–$250) for nursing home care. The basic amount of home care coverage is half the nursing home amount, but additional home care coverage can be added by rider. LTCI policies are usually written for either two years, three years, four years, five years, or lifetime of the insured.

The Health Insurance Portability and Accountability Act of 1996, P.L. 104-191 (HIPAA) added tax incentives for "qualified" LTCI policies. (Qualification depends on the policy satisfying various administrative and consumer protection standards.) Part of the premium for a qualified policy may be deductible,[12] and policy benefits can be received tax-free (within limits). Non-qualified policies can lawfully be sold, but they do not get the favorable tax treatment. HIPAA makes it clear that LTCI policies are treated like accident and health insurance policies if they are offered by an employer as an employee fringe benefit. However, they cannot be included in either a cafeteria plan or a flexible spending account.

[¶1480] Bad Faith

Although insurance policies are contractual in nature, they involve issues and funds that can be crucial to a business or a family. Therefore, a body of insurance

activity in any billing period in which the customer's account is either debited or credited. All dollar amounts and percentages must be in boldface type. Annual percentage rates and finance charges must not only be bold, they must be in larger type than other terms.

Lenders who use the "model forms" given in an Appendix to Regulation Z are automatically deemed to comply with truth-in-lending requirements. Reg. Z also includes "sample forms." Use of the sample forms—or individually drafted forms that include all of the mandatory disclosures and other mandatory language—is not illegal, but does not carry this degree of protection.

[¶2010.4] TILA Remedies

There is a private right of action for TILA violations, including compensatory and punitive damages, attorneys' fees, and costs. See 15 USC §1640. The creditor is liable to the consumer for twice the finance charge. For closed-end transactions secured by a dwelling or real property, there is a statutory minimum damage award of $200, but damages cannot exceed $2000. Damages in consumer lease transactions range from $100–$1000; there is no minimum or maximum in other individual TILA cases. Damages in a class action are capped at the lesser of $500,000 or 1% of the credit grantor's net worth.

Truth in Lending violations do permit rescission of a mortgage (see 15 USC §1635), but the right of rescission expires three years after the loan closing. *Beach v. Ocwen Federal Bank*, 522 U.S. 912 (Sup.Ct. 1998) holds that the three-year period is not a statute of limitations, but a limitation on the use of the rescission defense.

The Truth in Lending Act statute of limitations is subject to equitable tolling—for instance, if the creditor concealed misrepresentations that were made on a disclosure statement.[4]

[¶2010.5] TILA Exemptions

States can seek exemption from the Federal Reserve Board from certain TILA requirements, if they have consumer credit laws "substantially similar" to TILA, e.g., the Uniform Consumer Credit Code (U3C).

Certain types of transaction are exempt:

- Extensions of credit for business purposes (even small ones)
- Transactions over $25,000 that do not grant a security interest in the borrower's principal residence
- Agricultural transactions over $25,000
- Budget plans for paying for home heating fuel
- Student loans issued or guaranteed by federal agencies
- Some personal property leases that are incident to leases of real property
- Purchase-money second mortgages (i.e., financed by the seller of the home), because the seller is not considered a "creditor" because this is a one-time transaction rather than part of an ongoing business.

TILA amendments passed as part of the Omnibus Consolidated Appropriations Act of 1996, P.L. 104-208 permit TIL coverage to be waived by the Federal Reserve Board, by regulation, for wealthy consumers (annual income over $200,000, or net assets over $1 million), as long as the opulent consumer signs a handwritten assent to the waiver.

¶2010.6 Closed-End Credit

Closed-end credit is a single extension of credit, such as a loan or purchase of an item of property "on time." The rules for closed-end credit are somewhat more stringent than the regulation of open-end credit, such as credit cards (see below).

If a lender offers "loan payment holidays" (the option, in return for a small fee, to skip a payment and add the omitted payment at the end of the term), TILA does not require disclosure of the additional finance charges that result when a consumer debtor accepts the offer. The Sixth Circuit views the payment holiday as a "special occurrence," not a refinancing creating disclosure obligations.[5]

The Seventh Circuit requires a car dealer that assigns its installment contracts at a discount to disclose the amount of the discount, unless the cash price also includes part of this cost.[6] The discount must be disclosed as part of the finance charge, as an amount separately imposed on the consumer; it cannot be treated as a cost of doing business that does not require disclosure.

[¶2010.6.1] Loan Disclosures

The mandated disclosures for a loan are:

- Date of the transaction, or other date on which the finance charge begins to accrue
- Annual percentage rate (APR) of the finance charge[7]
- The number of scheduled payments
- The dollar amount of scheduled payments
- When the payments are due
- The total dollar value of all scheduled payments
- Whether a "balloon" payment (single large payment at the end of the term) is due; if so, its amount
- How late payment charges will be computed
- Identification of any security interest retained by the lender
- Identification of the collateral
- The amount financed (the credit extended: i.e., the amount of credit other than prepaid finance charges)
- Amount of any prepaid finance charges
- Amount of any deposit
- Sum total of prepaid finance charges and deposits
- Total finance charge
- Disclosure of any right of rescission (e.g., loans secured by principal residence).

above the yield of Treasury bills. However, the statute does not cap rates on home equity loans.

Violation of the Home Ownership and Equity Protection Act is punishable by civil liability for statutory damages, actual damages, fees, and costs. The homeowner is given additional rights to rescind the transaction, and state Attorneys General have the power to bring their own proceedings. See 15 USC §1640(a). Purchase money mortgages, reverse equity mortgages, and construction loans are exempt.

The Homeowners Protection Act of 1998, P.L. 105-216 (7/29/98), 12 USC §4901 requires automatic cancellation (and notice of cancellation rights) in transactions where private mortgage insurance is a prerequisite (e.g., the home buyer is permitted to make a smaller down payment on condition of maintaining private insurance that will make good if he or she defaults). It also limits the amount of private mortgage insurance that home buyers can be required to purchase.

[¶2020] Equal Credit Opportunity: Regulation B

The Equal Credit Opportunity Act, 15 USC §1691 et seq., and its implementing Regulation B (12 CFR Part 202), are designed to protect credit-worthy members of traditionally disfavored groups against credit discrimination on the basis of race, national origin, sex, marital status, or age (although positive discrimination in favor of senior citizen borrowers is permissible). Credit discrimination against public assistance recipients is also forbidden.

Although business judgments about creditworthiness do not violate the ECOA, the judgment must be based on objective factors about the applicant, not conclusions about the affluence or reliability of an entire group of people.

A married credit applicant must be allowed to secure credit based only on his or her own income, resources, and credit history, without the necessity of having the other spouse join in or even approve the extension of credit. Creditors are prohibited from asking certain questions (e.g., except in community property states or states in which spouses are responsible for necessaries purchased by their spouses, marital status is not a permissible inquiry on an application filed by only one obligor).

It is forbidden to make an oral or written statement that might have the effect of discouraging a potential borrower from applying for credit. Unless the application states conspicuously that disclosure of such information is optional, the creditor may not inquire about alimony or child support payments unless the applicant lists these as a potential source of income that could support repayment.

When a credit application has been made, the creditor must inform the applicant of its decision on the application within 30 days of receipt of the completed application. When the application is denied, or other adverse action is taken,[15] the creditor must either give a written explanation or disclose the fact of adverse action and give the name of a person who can be contacted for an explanation. (Small-scale creditors who received less than 150 applications in the preceding year can notify unsuccessful applicants orally.)

Regulation B includes model application forms. Their use is not mandatory (and in fact the ECOA does not require the use of written application forms at all), but using the model forms does provide a safe harbor.

ECOA or Regulation B violations can be punished by civil liability of actual damages (without limit) plus punitive damages of up to $10,000. Class-action damages are limited to 1% of the creditor's net worth or $500,000 (whichever is less), plus costs and attorneys' fees.

The normal ECOA statute of limitations is two years from signing of the loan agreement that allegedly violates the debtor's equal credit rights, but the alleged violation can be raised as a defense against collection even after the two years have expired.[16]

Similarly, a spouse who was forced to sign a guarantee that violates the ECOA can use the statute defensively to defeat enforcement of the guarantee, even after the statute of limitations for recovering ECOA damages has expired.[17]

[¶2030] Fair Credit Reporting Act (FCRA)

The Fair Credit Reporting Act, Title VII of TILA, 15 USC §1581-1681T, governs the activities of consumer reporting agencies in collecting, processing, and especially in disseminating information about consumers. The FCRA preempts state laws on credit reporting only to the extent that they are inconsistent with the federal law.

In addition to the consumer and the consumer reporting agency, the FCRA affects the activities of users of consumer reports (e.g., lenders who decide whether or not to grant credit; landlords who decide whether or not to rent an apartment; employers who decide whether or not to extend a job offer). Users of consumer reports must inform consumers when any such denial is made based on a consumer report. The user of the report must identify the reporting agency that is the source of the report.

Any information (oral or written; positive or negative) that bears on a consumer's creditworthiness, credit standing, credit capacity, character, personal characteristics, mode of living, or reputation is treated as a consumer report, if it is collected, used, or expected to be used for a business purpose such as establishing the consumer's eligibility for consumer credit, insurance, or employment.

If credit is denied because of information from any source other than a consumer report, the creditor must inform the consumer of the right to request the nature of the negative information within a 60-day period.

[¶2030.1] 1997 Amendments

Major FCRA amendments, enacted as part of the Omnibus Consolidated Appropriations Act of 1996 (P.L. 104-208), took effect on September 30, 1997:

- Credit bureaus are obligated to resolve consumer complaints about disputed information faster, and must offer more options.
- Employers are limited in their ability to obtain and use credit reports in the hiring process.
- Each credit offer must include toll-free credit bureau numbers, so consumers can have their names removed from the lists used to solicit credit cards and

insurance. Credit bureaus must also provide written forms so consumers can have their names permanently removed from solicitation lists.

- When a consumer complains about information in the file, the credit bureau has an obligation to investigate, review all relevant information,[18] and report inaccuracies and omissions to all other national credit bureaus.

It violates the FCRA for a lawyer to get a credit report about his client's adversary when preparing for a trial that is not directly related to the credit transaction, because researching a litigation opponent is not a "legitimate need" under 15 USC §1681b(3)(E).[19]

An employer can be held liable for FCRA violations committed by employees who have apparent authority to obtain credit information, because their position as agents of the employer facilitates their commission of impropriety, because the transaction appears to be regular and in the course of business.[20]

The states have the power to take enforcement action on behalf of consumers in federal or state court, up to $1,000 per violation; the FTC is empowered to seek up to $2,500 per violation.

[¶2040] Fair Debt Collection Practices Act (FDCPA)

Although all may be fair in love and war, federal law limits the extent to which threats (even threats of lawsuit), harassment, pressure, and humiliation can be used to collect debts from consumers who obtained extensions of credit for personal, family, or household needs.

Applicability of the FDCPA, 15 USC §1692—, depends on the existence of a covered debt, and actions of a debt collector (i.e., a party who regularly rather than casually makes efforts to collect debts).

The creditor itself is not a debt collector subject to the FDCPA, as long as it uses its own name; but FDCPA coverage can occur if the creditor uses an assumed name that suggests the intervention of a third party: according to the Second Circuit, dunning letters sent by the creditor's in-house collection unit, under a different name, could be deceptive to unsophisticated consumers. Therefore, the FDCPA is triggered.[21]

The FDCPA requires debt collectors who collect debts from consumers to provide them with disclosure as to their right to dispute the debt. Debt collectors must disclose whenever the debt they are attempting to collect is in dispute, even if the dispute was stated orally, without creation of a written record.[22]

Consumer debtors are protected against unfair or unconscionable debt collection methods, harassing, oppressive, or abusive conduct, and false, deceptive, and misleading statements in connection with debt collection.[23]

The FDCPA (at 15 USC §1692k(d)) gives state and federal courts concurrent jurisdiction over claims of unfair collection practices. If the FDCPA is violated, consumers are entitled to statutory damages even without proof of actual damages.[24] They can also receive compensatory damages (including damages for emotional distress), costs, and attorneys' fees. The statute of limitations is one year from mailing of the collection letter or filing of an improper legal action. FDCPA class actions are permitted.

[¶2040.1] What is a "Debt"?

The Seventh, Eighth, and Ninth Circuits have ruled that a dishonored check creates a payment obligation, so third-party attempts at collecting bounced checks are subject to the FDCPA.[25] But attempts to collect a tort judgment arising out of an automobile negligence case are not subject to the FDCA, in the Eleventh Circuit's reading, because the FDCPA covers transactions that a consumer enters into on a contractual or consensual basis—hardly a fair description of getting sued.[26]

According to the Seventh and Tenth Circuits, fees owed by a condominium owner to the condo association are debts for FDCPA purposes, but the Florida Court of District Appeals says that maintenance assessments owed to a homeowner's association are not debts.[27]

A state's efforts to collect unemployment insurance contributions are not subject to the FDCPA, because the business' obligation to pay is not primarily for personal, family, or household purposes, even if the employee involved is employed by a family as a nanny.[28] Tax liabilities[29] and child support obligations[30] are not considered debts either.

[¶2040.2] Who is a "Debt Collector"?

A 1995 Supreme Court decision says that attorneys who regularly engage in litigation to collect consumer debts are FDCPA-covered debt collectors: *Heintz v. Jenkins*.[31] However, sending 35 collection letters on one occasion does not make a law firm a debt collector, if this was an isolated, non-recurring incident and not part of regular practice.[32]

A company that buys a portfolio of delinquent debts from the original creditor thereby becomes a debt collector.[33]

[¶2040.3] Verification Requirement

Within five days after its initial communication with the debtor, the debt collector must provide a disclosure statement that has been described as a "civil Miranda warning." See 15 USC §1692g. (The disclosure is not necessary if the information already appeared in the initial communication, or if the debtor has paid the debt before the five days elapse.) The required disclosures are:

- The amount of the debt
- The identity of the creditor
- Warning that the debt is presumed valid unless the consumer disputes[34] all or part of the debt within 30 days of receipt of the notice
- Statement that, if the debt collector receives a written protest within 30 days, it will send the debtor verification of the debt or a copy of the judgment against the debtor

- Disclosure that the debtor has 30 days to make a written request for the name and address of the current creditor, if different from the original creditor with whom the debtor did business

This disclosure statement must be conspicuous, and must not be overshadowed by conflicting statements, e.g., orders to the consumer to pay before the 30 days elapse.[35] A debt collector that threatens to sue within the 30-day period must explain the relation between the creditor's right to sue and the debtor's right to validation of the debt.

[¶2040.4] Forbidden Conduct

The general test of whether a communication violates the FDCPA is whether the least sophisticated consumer would be deceived or would feel threatened.[36]

15 USC §1692e(11) requires disclosure that communications are for debt collection purposes. It is not, for instance, permissible to tell debtors that their work address is needed as part of a survey. Section 1692e(5) makes it unlawful to threaten any illegal action; any action that is not intended to be taken (typically, a lawsuit) or to misstate the debtor's liability for civil damages or multiple penalties. It is also unlawful under this section to collect any amount (including interest) that is not specifically authorized by law or by the underlying contract.

No one who is not an attorney can claim to be one (§1692e(3)) and if an attorney's name or letterhead is used, the attorney must have real involvement in the case.[37] Debt collectors are not allowed to use names or statements that falsely suggest that they are credit reporting agencies or government agencies (§1692e; this section also lists 16 other forms of false, deceptive, or misleading representations that are forbidden).

Collectors are forbidden to use harassment (repeated or anonymous phone calls; obscene or profane language; threats of violence). They are not permitted to communicate with debtors at inconvenient times (times before 8 a.m. and after 9 p.m. are presumed to be inconvenient); at work, if personal communications are forbidden; or at all, if the debtor is represented by counsel. Third parties (persons other than the debtor's spouse) can only be contacted once and then only to get information about the debtor's location. See §§1692b-d and f.

For creditors who undertake their own collection efforts, §1692j bars furnishing forms that are used to deceive the consumer into believing that someone other than the creditor is undertaking the collection.

Under 15 USC §1692f(6)(A), a repossessor is not permitted to threaten non-judicial action without having a present right to the collateral. However, the FDCPA is not violated by imposing a storage charge on items left inside a repossessed vehicle, or by maintaining possession of those items until the storage fees have been paid.[38]

In 1998, the Northern District of Illinois held class certification to be proper in an FDCPA case alleging the use of form letters that were ambiguous or contained false and misleading threats, based on the similarity of claims involving the letters, rather than the similarity of the underlying debts.[39]

[¶2050] Personal Property Leasing

Federal statutory rules about personal property leases lasting four months or more appear beginning at 15 USC §1667–1667e, the Consumer Leasing Act as amended by the Omnibus Consolidated Appropriations Act of 1996, P.L. 104-208.

The implementing regulations found in the Federal Reserve Board's Regulation M, 12 CFR Part 213[40] deal with consumer leasing. UCC Article 2A should also be consulted; it regulates lease transactions, without limitation to consumer leases.

Like most consumer credit regulation, Regulation M is highly disclosure-oriented; it also contains substantive limitations on "balloon payments" (disproportionately large payments at the end of the lease term).

Regulation M applies to leases of personal property for personal, family, or household purposes, as long as the lease lasts at least four months and has a total contractual obligation of $25,000 or less. It does not apply—although general Truth in Lending principles do apply—if the transaction is actually a credit sale (an arrangement where the lease payments are at least as great as the price of the property, and the lessee has an option to purchase the property at a nominal payment).

Regulation M deals with several issues:

- Mandatory disclosure of all material lease terms before the lease agreement is signed
- Limitation on the consumer's liability at the expiration or termination of a lease
- Mandatory, permitted and forbidden expressions in advertisements for consumer leases
- Cause of action for consumers injured by Reg. M violations[41]
- Survival of state laws and regulations that are not inconsistent with Reg. M. The FRB can exempt any class of lease transactions from Reg. M coverage if the transactions are subject to substantially similar state-law regulation.

Credit grantors and their counsel should also consult the Uniform Consumer Sales Practices Act, which identifies factors states can use in determining if a consumer contract is unconscionable (i.e., so unfair that the state will not participate in enforcing it):

- Transaction is unfairly one-sided in the seller's favor
- Unusually vulnerable consumer (aged, ill, illiterate, not fluent in English, etc.)
- Grossly unfair price, as compared to similar goods obtained from other sources
- As of the time of the transaction, it was obvious that the merchandise would be repossessed, because of the impossibility of payment in full
- As of the time of the transaction (with no consideration of later developments) it was impossible for the consumer to receive significant benefits from the transaction

A fraudulent conveyance is not absolutely void, but it can be voided by creditors who are placed at a disadvantage by the conveyance. A preferential transfer (which gives favored creditors a higher percentage of their claim than non-favored creditors who have the same degree of legal priority) can be attacked by the non-favored creditors, but only if it had been made with actual intent to defraud, delay, or hinder the other creditors.

[¶2070] Handling Collection Claims

In addition to complying with all applicable laws, handling collection claims creates various practical problems. Not every claim can economically be recovered by litigation, even in small claims court.

In addition to FDCPA liability, the collector might also be liable for defamation, invasion of privacy, bankruptcy misconduct, or negligent or intentional infliction of mental anguish, and the creditor might have derivative liability. Therefore, it's important to work with collectors who are ethical and aware of their legal responsibilities (and to supervise them to make sure that they maintain good practices).

[¶2070.1] Claims Checklist

- ❏ Debtor's name
- ❏ Debtor's address
- ❏ Was the debtor a minor when the debt was contracted? If so, was the debt reaffirmed post-majority, or for necessities?
- ❏ Debtor's marital status
- ❏ Is the spouse also obligated?
- ❏ Are there any other co-signers or guarantors?
- ❏ Nature of the claim (i.e., for goods, services, installment contract, money lent)
- ❏ Evidence of the claim
- ❏ Security for the claim
- ❏ Evidence of bills sent to the debtor and accepted without protest
- ❏ Past payment history on the claim
- ❏ Defenses (if any) to the claim
- ❏ Lowest settlement the creditor will accept
- ❏ Witness list and other evidence for litigating the claim
- ❏ Is the debtor judgment-proof?
- ❏ Has the debtor filed for bankruptcy protection? If not, is an attempt to enforce the claim likely to trigger a filing?

ENDNOTES

1. See 62 FR 10193 (3/6/97), 63 FR 16669 (4/6/98), and 64 FR 16614 (3/31/99) for Regulation Z amendments and updates. The 1999 update prohibits issuance of unsolicited credit cards and gives guidance for calculation of pay-

ment schedules for transactions involving private mortgage insurance and transactions involving a down payment that combines cash and a trade-in.

2. The Regulation Z provisions for open-end disclosures begin at 12 CFR §226.5; closed-end credit disclosures start at 12 CFR §226.17. Regulation Z Subpart E was added in 1996 (see 61 FR 14952), governing disclosure for home mortgages, including post-consummation disclosures when terms change. Section 226.32 covers closed-end home mortgages, including APR calculations for adjustable rate mortgages; 226.33 deals with reverse mortgages.

3. A national bank is permitted to impose a late charge that is permitted by the state in which the bank is located, even if the actual consumer lives in a state that forbids the fee: *Smiley v. Citibank*, 517 U.S. 735 (Sup.Ct. 1996). The Supreme Court upheld a Commissioner of the Currency interpretation that late fees are a component of interest. The National Bank Act, 12 USC §85, allows banks to impose charges allowed in their home states and preempts inconsistent state laws.

4. *Ellis v. GMAC*, 160 F.3d 703 (11th Cir. 1998).

5. *Begala v. PNC Bank*, 163 F.3d 948 (6th Cir. 12/28/98).

6. *Walker v. Wallace Auto Sales Inc.*, 155 F.3d 927 (7th Cir. 1998).

7. Disclosure is not required of certain very small amounts.

8. Debtors who prepay are also entitled to refund of the unearned portion of any credit insurance premium already paid.

9. *Benion v. Bank One*, 66 LW 1723 (7th Cir. 5/21/98).

10. It is not necessary to send a statement during any billing cycle unless a finance charge was imposed during that cycle, or there was an outstanding credit or debit balance greater than $1 at the end of the cycle.

11. *Dawkins v. Sears Roebuck & Co.*, 109 F.3d 241 (5th Cir. 1997).

12. *Greisz v. Household Bank*, 8 F.Supp.2d 1031 (N.D. Ill. 1998).

13. *Peoples Bank v. Scarpetti*, 1998 Westlaw 61925 (Conn.Super. 1998).

14. Rate adjustments must be made according to a publicly available index that is not controlled by the creditor: 15 USC §1647.

15. ECOA defines an adverse action as a denial or revocation of credit; change in the terms of an existing credit agreement; or refusal to grant credit as requested in the application (as to amount or terms). Refusing to extend additional credit under an existing agreement because the customer is delinquent, or if the additional credit would exceed a pre-set limit, is not deemed an adverse action.

16. *Silverman v. Eastrich Multiple Investor Fund LP*, 51 F.3d 283 (7th Cir. 1997).

17. *Roseman v. Premier Financial Services-East LP*, 66 LW 1223 (E.D. Pa. 9/4/97).

18. Once on notice of incorrect information, the consumer reporting agency has an obligation to go beyond its original sources to verify the consumer's complaint: *Cushman v. TransUnion Corp.*, 115 F.3d 220 (3rd Cir. 1997).

ruptcy case; create, perfect, or enforce liens that secure a claim arising before commencement of the case.

- [In Chapter 13] pursue a civil suit or other action to collect all or part of a consumer debt from a codebtor rather than the principal debtor who is also the bankruptcy filer. This stay ends automatically if the Chapter 13 case is closed, dismissed or converted to Chapter 7 or 11.

Activities undertaken contrary to the automatic stay are void even if the creditor did not have actual knowledge of the stay. Pursuant to §362(f), the court can enjoin violations of the automatic stay, and has discretion to order other statutory and administrative remedies.

The debtor, under §362(h), can recover actual damages, costs, attorneys' fees,[25] even punitive damages in appropriate cases, if any creditor injures the debtor by a willful violation of the automatic stay. In this context, "willful" means "knowing"; malice is not a required element. Refusal to rectify actions taken after notice of the stay is also subject to §362(h). If the enjoined party was aware of the automatic stay, then violation of the stay can constitute contempt of court as well as an actionable wrong against the debtor.

Also note that §366 provides that, for a period of at least 20 days after filing of the petition, public utilities are not permitted to alter, refuse, or discontinue service or discriminate against a debtor solely because there is an unpaid pre-petition debt, or on the grounds that the debtor has filed for bankruptcy protection. However, it is permissible to terminate service if, within 20 days of the filing, the debtor fails to furnish adequate assurance of future payment. This can take the form of a deposit or other security (such as lien on the debtor's property to be executed in case of further delinquency). In many states, regulations limit the size of the deposit that a utility can require in this context.

In addition to the automatic stay, the bankruptcy court has the general injunctive power (under §105) to stay actions that are not subject to the automatic stay.

See IRS Announcement 98-89, 1998-40 IRB 11 (9/25/98), explaining the IRS' efforts to coordinate collection efforts and bankruptcy cases to avoid violating the automatic stay.

[¶2160.1] Exceptions to the Automatic Stay

The automatic stay does not prohibit commencement or continuation of criminal proceedings, even those that are related to the debt: §362(b)(1). Collection of alimony, maintenance, or child support from property that is **not** within the bankruptcy estate is not stayed. Furthermore, §362(b)(2)(A) permits litigation to establish paternity during the automatic stay; litigation to establish or modify a court order requiring payment of alimony, maintenance, or support is also permitted.

UCC filings relating back to the creation of a security interest can be made during the automatic stay (§362(b)(3)), and other actions can be taken to perfect or continue perfection of security interests in property within the bankruptcy estate.

Although Tax Court proceedings are barred, §362(h)(9) allows taxing authorities to audit bankruptcy debtors, issue notices of deficiency against them, and assess taxes, but can only impose liens if the tax is a debt that will not be discharged and the property revests in the debtor. See §362(b)(18) for the extent of the exception for post-petition statutory liens for property taxes.

Creditors can apply for relief by filing motions for termination, annulment, modification, or conditions on the automatic stay: see §362(d) and FRBP 4001(a). At least a preliminary hearing must be held within 30 days of filing of such a motion; the stay terminates by operation of law if there is no hearing (§362(e)). At the hearing, §362(g) places the burden of proof on the party seeking relief from the stay to prove the debtor's equity in the property; on other issues, the burden is on the party opposing the relief.

[¶2170] Assumption or Avoidance of Obligations

Various cases outline the extent to which claims are avoidable or must be assumed.

"To the extent a creditor's lien is avoided, the creditor becomes an unsecured creditor and the lien cannot attach to property that the debtor acquires after the petition is filed"[26] but holders of nondischargeable claims might be able to pursue property acquired after bankruptcy.

State law may grant the power to avoid transfers that are not enforceable against a bona fide purchaser of real estate, and thus may permit the debtor to avoid foreclosure sale transfers that have not been completed by the filing of a deed.[27]

Once a lease is assumed, rent under that lease is treated as a priority administrative expense, even if the debtor later decides to reject the lease.[28]

The "strong arm clause" (Bankruptcy Code §544) gives the trustee the power to avoid transfers governed by state law, such as unrecorded security interests. Also see ¶2185.1 for the trustee's power to avoid improper transfers.

BFP v. Resolution Trust Corp.[29] holds that a regularly conducted, non-collusive foreclosure sale, or a foreclosure sale on behalf of an Article 9 secured creditor, cannot be avoided, but *BFP* is a narrow decision that is inapplicable to tax lien executions and other creditors' remedies that do not include auctions.

Section 545 permits avoidance of certain statutory liens, even if they have already been enforced by sale of the encumbered property: for instance, liens that became effective upon the insolvency of the debtor; liens that could be defeated by a bona fide purchaser; and liens for rent.[30]

If a judicial lien impairs property in which the debtor holds an exempt interest, §522(f)(2)(A) allows avoidance only of the part of the lien needed to prevent impairment, not the entire lien.[31] The trustee has the power, under §549, to avoid many post-petition transfers of the debtor's property, although some protection is afforded to bona fide purchasers.

For Chapter 7, but not for Chapter 13, BCode §724(a) permits avoidance of liens imposed for penalties, fines, and punitive damages imposed on the debtor, to the extent that the amount secured by the lien does **not** represent compensation for

tative spouse, has not been dissolved. A good-faith partner in a bigamous marriage may even be entitled to alimony when the relationship terminates, and children of such a union are considered legitimate. As long as the good-faith belief in the validity of the marriage continues, a putative spouse has the same rights as a legal spouse.

The Social Security Administration has elaborate rules concerning the rights of various kinds of deemed, putative, and quasi-spouses to receive OASDI benefits based on the earnings record of the other partner to the alleged marriage: see 20 CFR Part 440, especially 440.345 and .346.

[¶3010.3] Cohabitation

Although some states still have never-enforced laws forbidding cohabitation, the predominant legal issue is the extent to which cohabitation gives rise to enforceable economic relationships between the partners. An increasing number of corporations make "domestic partner" benefits available to unmarried cohabitants, but this is still a minority position. An unmarried person can be named as beneficiary of an insurance policy, will provision, or pension, but will not be entitled to a share of such assets automatically, by operation of law.

A few cases do permit an economic partnership ("palimony") argument to be made by cohabitants who allegedly had an unwritten understanding that the poorer cohabitant would be supported by the richer one. But there is no body of statutory and case law giving cohabitants the kind of rights (e.g., election against the will) available to participants in a formal marriage.

Therefore, cohabitants who are very concerned about financial issues are often well-advised to enter into a written agreement expressing their financial understanding and the expected consequences on the death of one cohabitant, or the termination of the relationship.

The problem is that, although individuals who happen to cohabit can validly enter into contracts, a "meretricious relationship" does not furnish consideration for a contract. In other words, care must be taken to draft the agreement so that there is no suggestion that one cohabitant is paying the other for sexual services. Safer ground is to premise the support agreement on, e.g., one cohabitant's participation in the other's business, or career opportunities foregone by one cohabitant in order to accompany the other.[2]

In the tax context, see *Reynolds*, TC Memo 1999-62, (3/4/99). When a cohabitation relationship terminated, the Tax Court held that the payment made by the male to the female cohabitant was not taxable compensation for services during the relationship. Instead, it was payment for property previously given to her. There was no gain for the female cohabitant, because the property was now worth less than her basis.

[¶3015] Annulment

Annulment is the retroactive determination by a court that a purported marriage was never valid because it was, e.g., incestuous; bigamous; the product of fraud or duress; or contracted by parties incapable of marrying because of age or mental status. Annulment actions are now comparatively rare, although they were common when the legal barriers to divorce were sturdier and unhappy marriage partners had to prove that their marriage had never validly come into effect. (The Uniform Marriage and Divorce Act uses the term "Declaration of Invalidity" rather than "annulment.")

A distinction should be drawn between marriages that are absolutely void and those that are only voidable. Because a void marriage is contrary to public policy, there is no need for the court system to intervene to declare the marriage invalid. However, a marriage that is merely voidable remains valid until and unless one spouse raises the invalidity of the marriage. Therefore, a voidable marriage can be ratified by the conduct of the "innocent spouse," and if a voidable marriage was not annulled as of the death of the first spouse, the other spouse will have a right of election against the decedent's will.

For a marriage to be annulled on the grounds of fraud, the fraudulent representations must have been made prior to the marriage, not afterwards; must be material; must have been relied on by the innocent party; and must go to the essence of the marriage contract (e.g., a representation to a Catholic fiancee of being a widower rather than divorced).

If a marriage is only voidable, not absolutely void, the spouse who is defending against the annulment action can raise defenses such as estoppel, ratification, and unclean hands. An absolutely void marriage cannot be ratified, although a party's unclean hands will prevent him or her from deriving any benefits from a void marriage.

Many states (Alaska, Connecticut, Delaware, Illinois, Iowa, Michigan, Minnesota, New York, Oregon, Texas, Washington, Wisconsin) allow "equitable distribution" (see ¶3020.2, below) in annulment cases, although if the purported marriage was of short duration, the annulment court may refuse to make a property distribution because of the limited economic impact of the short "marriage."

[¶3020] Divorce

Traditional religious concepts, which were very influential in civil law, considered marriage to be essentially indissoluble. Although on appropriate proof a legal separation (including support payments for the wife) could be granted, such a decree would not permit either spouse to remarry. As the twentieth century went on, divorce became far more socially acceptable, and there was significant demand for liberalization of divorce laws. Eventually, fault-based divorce became more easily accessible to plaintiffs who could prove, e.g., adultery, desertion, or physical or mental cruelty. (In many instances, the "evidence" was collusive or entirely fabricated, on behalf of a couple who simply didn't want to be married to each other any more.)

Over time, a demand arose for "no-fault" divorce, based on a declaration by one or both spouses that the marriage was irretrievably compromised. All of the states have some form of no-fault divorce, but most of them also permit fault divorces. (Divorces generally can be granted more quickly on a fault basis; no-fault divorces often require a period of separation before the decree.) It is also possible that proof of fault will influence property division and spousal support in a no-fault divorce (i.e., the party at fault may have to pay more or receive less, especially if the marital fault itself was not only distressing to the party not at fault, but directly involved family finances).

A no-fault divorce is granted (depending on state law and circumstance) based on proof of irretrievable breakdown of the marriage or incompatibility of the partners. Another approach to no-fault divorce is the "conversion" divorce, finalized after the parties have been living apart for a stated period of time. Some conversion divorce statutes require the separation to have occurred pursuant to a separation agreement or court order.

The property of the spouses can be divided pursuant to a legal separation, and support can be ordered for the poorer spouse, but the parties remain married until such time as the marriage is actually dissolved by divorce.

[¶3020.1] Divorce Instruments

The separation agreement is the central document in the process of divorce. Although only a court can issue a divorce decree (thus formally terminating the marriage), in practice courts generally approve the arrangements already agreed upon by the divorcing spouses and memorialized in the separation agreement.

Under the Uniform Marriage and Divorce Act, the court is bound by the provisions of the proposed agreement that deal with the relationship between the spouses (unless the proposals are unconscionable) but is not bound by provisions dealing with the support and custody of the children of the marriage. In non-UMDA jurisdictions, a separation agreement might be rejected by the court if it is unfair; if the parties failed to make full disclosure during the negotiation of the agreement; or if one party was represented by counsel but the other was denied access to legal advice.

An important issue is whether the separation agreement is intended to survive the divorce decree, or if it is intended to merge with the decree. If it merges (is incorporated) into the decree, then the agreement itself achieves the status of a court judgment. Violations can be punished as contempt of court. But flexibility is sacrificed: the provisions that derive from the separation agreement can only be modified to the extent that the judgment can be modified.

If, in contrast, the separation agreement is incorporated into the decree by reference, but does not merge, then the agreement becomes res judicata between the parties but is not a court judgment. Enforcement is via suit for breach of contract, not contempt of court, and it is unclear if the court even has continuing jurisdiction to hear an application for modification.

[¶3020.2] Property Distributions

Until the 1960s, property distribution worked very differently in the community-property states (Arizona, Georgia, Idaho, Louisiana, Nevada, New Mexico, Texas, Washington, and Wisconsin) and the other ("common-law") states. The community property states deemed the "community property" to belong to both spouses, and therefore it would have to be divided between the spouses incident to a divorce, no matter who formally owned the property, or whose funds had been used to acquire it. Division could be done equally (50% of the community property to each spouse) or using other approaches and formulas.

The common-law states tended to use a title theory: that is, property would be distributed to the spouse in whose name title was held. Usually, this was the husband, so wives often emerged from divorce with little or no property. Theoretically, some of the harshness of this result was ameliorated by the assumption that the husband would be required to pay alimony or other support to the wife, although ordered amounts often proved to be uncollectable in practice.

Since the 1960s, all the states, community and common-law, have been greatly influenced by equitable distribution concepts. The theory behind equitable distribution is that marriage is an economic as well as emotional partnership, and that both spouses make a contribution to the family's economic success. The contribution could be made in non-economic terms (homemaking and child rearing) as well as by earning money or investing the family's income.

Given this postulate, it is equitable to divide the couple's marital property to reflect their respective contributions as well as their financial needs. But that creates a complex system of interrelations between property division and orders for ongoing support. Furthermore, for couples with children, the financial needs of the children are a crucial factor. Because alimony is deductible by its payor and child support is not, there may be an incentive to structure the transaction to favor alimony; naturally the Internal Revenue Code, Regs., and court cases include some disincentives to abusive structures.

A bonus for the court system: the more a couple's financial affairs can be settled by a one-time division of property (especially one that is not subject to modification), the less ongoing supervision is required. A one-time division also greatly reduces the interaction between former spouses, so potential friction, hostility, or even violence becomes less likely.

Depending on circumstances, distribution of assets may direct conveyance of specific assets to one spouse; or it may be necessary to sell certain assets in order to share the value equitably. A court in one state does not have the power to directly affect title to real property located in another state, but the court's personal jurisdiction over the parties is broad enough to order the parties to perform legal acts, such as quitclaiming property to the other spouse.

Many state divorce statutes provide for division of marital liabilities as well as marital assets. Even in the other states, debts related to acquisition of marital property will probably be subtracted when the value of such property is calculated.

Under Bankruptcy Code §523(a)(5), discharge of property settlement obligations is possible, although arrears of payments supposed to be made but not made are not dischargeable. The 1994 reform of the Bankruptcy Code limited dischargeability in situations where the debtor has the ability to satisfy the marital property division obligation, and the financial harm to the other spouse outweighs the debtor spouse's interest in securing a fresh start.

[¶3020.3] Separate vs. Community or Marital Property

However, an essential part of the community property or equitable distribution process is dividing the MARITAL property that belongs to the couple. In most cases, at least some items of property will actually be separate property of one spouse, and thus not subject to equitable distribution. Predictably, the allocation between marital and separate property can become a very contentious issue.

Certain types of property are usually accepted as separate:

- Property acquired before the marriage
- Property inherited by one spouse (unless the bequest was in the form "my niece Alice and her husband Greg")
- Gifts made to one spouse by someone other than the other spouse
- Each spouse's Social Security benefits (although the respective size of each spouse's benefit could affect the spousal support obligation: see ¶3020.6)
- Property subject to an agreement, such as an antenuptial or postnuptial agreement that exempts certain items from equitable distribution; perhaps property covered by a separation agreement

If separate property is mingled with community or marital property, "transmutation" into marital property may occur if it becomes impossible to determine the nature of certain assets.

Certain items are more problematic, and state legislatures and courts in the various states have reached widely varying conclusions:

- Income or appreciation in value accruing during the marriage, on separate property
- Property acquired during marriage, but in exchange for separate property
- Personal injury proceeds received by one spouse; the issue could be whether the injury affected only that spouse, or (to the extent that the injury occurred and/or proceeds were received during the marriage) affected the family's overall financial status

It is also vital to establish a "cutoff date" after which time property items will clearly not be marital, because the marriage has terminated. The cutoff date might be the date of the divorce; the date on which a decree of legal separation was entered; the date of the separation agreement between the parties (which can be much earlier than a litigation-related date, because the parties control the timing of their own agreement, without being bound by court calendars), or the valuation date for the property itself.

[¶3020.3.1] Status of Special Items

If the property is of a type that generates income (e.g., stocks that pay dividends), further issues arise, especially as to the correct relationship between property division and ongoing spousal support. If the income-producing asset is used by one spouse in his or her work, the asset will probably be distributed to him or her. Other factors include which spouse is less financially well-off after the divorce (the poorer spouse is likely to be awarded a higher share of the income-producing property) and whether the income-producing asset is more closely connected to one spouse than the other (e.g., one spouse provided the funds to purchase the asset; if stock was issued as a bonus to an employee spouse).

Most of the states (although not New York, which is certainly the situs of a great many divorces) treat an advanced degree or professional license as the separate property of the spouse who earned it. However, even in states that generally treat the degree or license as separate, a different result might be reached in a case in which there are few other assets (e.g., the divorce occurs shortly after graduation or licensure) and the non-degreed spouse would receive little or no spousal support under the state's rules. Another possibility is that, although the degree or license will be the sole property of the person earning it, the other spouse might be awarded money plus interest as compensation for the investment the non-degreed spouse put into the earning of the degree. (The classic instance is the nurse who puts her husband through medical school, or the secretary who contributes toward her husband's law school tuition.)

In contrast, the goodwill of a business, or even of a professional practice, is commonly treated as a marital asset. Recent cases often add a refinement: the goodwill of a professional practice might be deemed marital only if it could be sold separately as a business asset, and is not dependent on the personal reputation or continued presence within the firm of the divorcing spouse.

Another recent trend is to treat "celebrity status" (which might be interpreted as the goodwill of an "entertainment" or "sports" practice) as a marital asset.

At least four analyses have been applied to Workers' Compensation benefits:

(1) If the claim accrued during marriage, the benefits are marital, even if payments have not begun, and the claim has not been liquidated, as of the time of the divorce

(2) The claim is marital only to the extent that it compensates for injury to the marital estate

(3) Payments received before the cutoff date can be marital, but those received afterwards are separate

(4) Benefits are marital only to the extent that they can be traced either to wages lost during the marriage, or to medical expenses paid for with marital funds

Another issue is that, even if the benefits are considered marital, the underlying injury is likely to affect the injured spouse's economic status and therefore his or her equitable share of marital assets and entitlement to spousal support.

[¶3020.4] Pensions and Divorce

A very common situation is for divorcing couples to have only two significant assets: a family home and pension rights belonging to one spouse, often the husband. If the pension rights are approximately equivalent in value to the home,

The general rule is that the custodial parent will be allowed to move out of the city or state for bona fide reasons (e.g., remarriage; a new job; a military commitment), taking the child(ren) along, even if this makes it more difficult for the non-custodial parent to see the child.[8] But if a move is allowed, it is very likely that the non-custodial parent will be granted longer visits, e.g., weekends or part or all of school holidays.

A court's custody order can be enforced in contempt, and the appropriate remedy for a non-custodial parent who alleges interference with visitation is to apply for a court order. Withholding alimony will probably not be considered appropriate. Withholding child support will certainly not be considered an appropriate self-help measure, because impairing the child's standard of living is hardly a rational response to denial of visitation. (By the same token, custodial parents who allege non-payment of support are supposed to seek enforcement of the support order rather than interfering with visitation.)

As court orders, custody orders are subject to modification. Usually, the standard is whether there has been a change in circumstances such that the best interests of the child would be served by modification. The Uniform Marriage and Divorce Act imposes a stricter standard, however: modification is permitted only if continuation of the original order would pose a serious danger to the child's well-being.

The federal Parental Kidnapping Prevention Act of 1980 (PKPA) gives full faith and credit to custody decrees (unless the issuing court lacked jurisdiction; declines to exercise its jurisdiction; or emergency measures are necessary to protect an at-risk child) and creates remedies for interstate "child snatching" (kidnapping by the non-custodial parent).

Most nations have signed the Hague Convention, which serves a similar role in international cases. Congress has implemented the Hague Convention in the International Child Abduction Remedies Act, 42 U.S.C. §11601 (civil remedies), and has added criminal remedies in the International Parental Kidnapping Crime Act, 18 U.S.C. §1204.

All of the states in the United States have adopted the Uniform Child Custody Jurisdiction Act (UCCJA) or have their own equivalent legislation, under which the court that originally had jurisdiction over the custody case retains jurisdiction even if the children have moved to another state. The UCCJA includes procedures for filing the decree with courts of other states.

Thus, only the original court can modify the decree. For instance, if a New Jersey court issues a decree, a non-custodial parent resident in Mississippi cannot attempt to use "home court advantage" by petitioning the Mississippi family court for custody. However, jurisdiction under the UCCJA could change, if the original state loses all ties with the case. The original court might also decline to exercise its jurisdiction, e.g., in a case in which the petitioner has unclean hands or has intentionally interfered with visitation.

According to the Fifth Circuit,[9] it does not violate the Establishment Clause to order all divorcing couples who have minor children to participate in a divorce education seminar under the auspices of a Roman Catholic charitable organization, in that the seminar served valid secular goals (better parenting) and did not advance the Catholic religion.

[¶3030.2] Child Support

Divorce terminates the status of two adults as one another's spouses, but (at least unless a step-parent adoption occurs), the two adults continue their status as the parents of children born or adopted during the marriage.

Child support continues until:

- The child reaches majority
- The child becomes emancipated (e.g., by marriage, employment, or military enlistment)
- Parental rights are terminated (based on abuse, or when the child is adopted by the new spouse of the custodial parent)
- The child dies
- The payor parent dies. However, the Uniform Marriage and Divorce Act §316(c) holds that the death of the payor parent does NOT terminate the support obligation, although the obligation may be revoked, modified, or commuted to a lump sum if the interests of justice so require.

Usually the child support obligation will end when the child reaches 18, but some divorce courts will order the obligor parent to pay higher education expenses for a child over 18. (This is true even though, in an ongoing marriage, the court would not intervene to require parents to pay college expenses.)

In order to receive federal funding, states are required to have child support guidelines in place, focusing on the payor parent's income level (rather than on the needs of the child), or the combined income of both custodial and non-custodial parent. The result is that a very wealthy child support obligor may be required to make extremely high child support payments. Changes in the financial circumstances and needs of either the child or the payor can lead to modification of the child support obligation.

The Uniform Interstate Family Support Act (UIFSA) has replaced earlier legislation on this topic, the Uniform Support of Dependents Law (USDL), Uniform Reciprocal Enforcement of Support Act (URESA), and Revised Uniform Reciprocal Enforcement of Support Law (RURESA). Although in many instances so-called uniform laws are subject to significant state-to-state differences, UIFSA has been adopted by all the states in more or less the same form. Technically, UIFSA applies to spousal as well as child support, but many of its provisions are drafted with child support in mind. When the custodial parent files a support action in the jurisdiction in which the child lives, the case will then be referred and heard in the jurisdiction in which the allegedly defaulting child support obligor lives.

Long-arm jurisdiction is available under the UIFSA under eight grounds, including personal service within the state; consent; having resided with the child within the state; or even having engaged in sexual relations within the state that could have led to conception of the child requiring support.

The court issuing a UIFSA child support order retains continuing exclusive jurisdiction over the award, and it can be modified by another state (i.e., the state in which the potential payor resides) only under very limited circumstances. Other

non-marital child is entitled to collect Workers' Compensation benefits premised on the death of the father.[25]

Even if the biological father denies this role, it may be possible to determine scientifically (normally, by DNA testing) that he has fathered the child. In a 1987 case,[26] the Supreme Court ruled that it is not unconstitutional to establish paternity by preponderance of evidence rather than beyond a reasonable doubt. Once made, a judicial determination of paternity is entitled to full faith and credit in other jurisdictions.

The Supreme Court has not determined exactly how long a mother or child can wait to establish paternity, but the holding of *Clark v. Jeter*,[27] is that a six-year statute of limitations is too short for this purpose. The federal child support laws have a statute of limitations of at least 18 years (i.e., until the child reaches majority).

Under the Uniform Parentage Act, as enacted in about half the states, if both spouses consent, a child born to a married woman by artificial insemination is deemed to be a child of the marriage, and the husband becomes the child's legal father. The sperm donor has no rights or obligations vis-à-vis the child.

In fact, the presumption that a married woman's child is the child of her husband is a very strong one, and could be used by a husband to block custody of the child by the unmarried biological father.[28] A 1998 Pennsylvania case[29] applies this presumption where the family unit has remained intact for over a year, thus estopping a woman and her estranged husband from bringing a paternity suit even though blood testing established that the husband was not the father of the child.

A child, who is not a party to the paternity action, is not barred by the mother's settlement with the biological father, because the mother has no right unilaterally to terminate the child's right to a relationship with, and support from, the father.[30]

[¶3060] Adoption

Adoption is the creation of a parent-child relationship. Once adopted, a child has the same status as a child born into the family. For instance, the child becomes a distributee of relatives who die intestate.

Children become available for adoption in various ways. The parental relationship may be terminated, e.g., for severe abuse. A child who has no living or identified parents can be made available for adoption. However, the majority of adoptions are stepparent adoptions: i.e., the child legally becomes the child of one biological parent and the biological parent's spouse or new spouse. If the other natural parent is still alive, the adoption requires surrender of parental rights.

Parental rights cannot be surrendered in the abstract: they must either be transferred to an adoption agency, or directly to a stepparent or other potential adoptive parent. A child generally cannot have more than two legal parents, so it is not always possible for a stepparent (or same-sex partner of a biological parent) to adopt a child without the other biological parent surrendering or being deprived of parental rights.[31]

Most adoptions are of infants or young children, but it is generally permissible for one adult to adopt another, e.g., for estate planning purposes. Adoption of an adult requires consent by adoptee, adopter, and adopter's spouse. State law may require consent of the biological parents whose rights are terminated, or proof that the adoption creates a genuine parent-child relationship rather than adding economic rights to a non-marital liaison. A posthumous adoption has even been permitted, so that potential adoptive parents could maintain a wrongful death action against a surgeon who operated on the child they wanted to adopt.[32]

A couple who visited a child for over a year, in anticipation of adopting him, came to stand in loco parentis to the child, and therefore had standing to seek custody or visitation after his birth mother decided not to finalize the adoption.[33]

[¶3060.1] The Placement Process

Traditionally, the adoption process was controlled by adoption agencies. The agencies served as intermediaries and could conceal the identity of women giving birth at a time when non-marital childbirth was viewed as disgraceful. Today, there is much greater acceptance of single parenthood, and potential adopters often prefer to deal directly with biological mothers. Nearly all of the states allow "direct placement" adoptions with no involvement by an agency.

It is allowable for adopters to pay maternity expenses, legal expenses, and incidental living expenses of the biological mother, but it is illegal to make payment of expenses contingent on the mother's consent to the adoption and surrender of parental rights. If improprieties occurred (such as excessive or inappropriate payments), the adoption will probably be allowed to proceed, if it is in the best interests of the child, but other sanctions will be applied.

An adoption proceeding is a legal action. The court will only approve the proposed adoption if a home study, done by a court-appointed investigator, confirms the suitability of the applicants. (This requirement is waived for stepparent adoptions.) Adoptions are not finalized for a period such as three months, six months, or a year, and the court retains ongoing jurisdiction for the protection of the potential adoptee.

Generally, the birth mother will not be allowed to consent to adoption until after the baby's birth, although some states do allow prenatal consent that is affirmed after the child is born. A valid consent to adoption must either be written and witnessed, or made orally before a judge or court-appointed referee.

The Uniform Adoption Act §2-406 requires the consent for direct placement or relinquishment to an adoption agency to provide plain language consent to transfer of legal and physical custody and termination of parental rights. The form must be executed in the birth mother's native language. The document must disclose that consent is final and irrevocable except under circumstances given in the document itself. Under the Uniform Act, there is a period of 192 hours after birth during which prenatal consents can be revoked.

If, as often happens, the birth mother is a minor, a guardian ad litem will be appointed for her, or the adoption court may, on its own motion, develop evidence about the validity of her surrender of parental rights.

If the biological father of the baby is known, he will generally be entitled to notice of the adoption proceeding, and to participate in it, although he will probably not be given outright veto power over the adoption. The rights of an unmarried father whose children are proposed for adoption depend on the nature and extent of the father's relationship with the children. A parent who lived with the child(ren) is entitled to notice and hearing before the adoption[34] but a father who never legitimated the child and provided support only intermittently does not have veto power over the proposed adoption.[35]

In contrast, a father who lived with the children for five years and continued to support them even though no longer living with them was permitted to block a stepparent adoption by the mother's new husband.[36] Some states maintain a Putative Father Registry; in order to contest an adoption, a man must sign the registry and admit paternity (thus rendering himself liable for child support).

There is an increasing trend to permit "open adoptions," in which the biological mother and the adopters are aware of each other's identity. Some laws permit the birth mother the option of visiting the child, and the child is aware of her biological motherhood. In most states, adoptees can get at least some health and genetic information about the birth parents, with identifying information removed. Some states maintain registries that permit birth parents and adoptees to indicate interest in contacting each other or in receiving information.

Several states consider "wrongful adoption"—negligent material misrepresentation of fact about an infant's origin or health history—to be a tort for which compensatory damages can be recovered.[37]

By the late 1980s, all of the states had adopted the Interstate Compact on Placement of Children, to protect children placed across state lines. The "sending agency" is required to transmit a form to the appropriate welfare department official in the receiving state, giving a social and case history of the child and a home study of the applicants for adoption.

The number of people who want to adopt (especially infants) often exceeds the number of healthy adoptable children within the United States. Therefore, many Americans want to adopt children from other countries. They may have humanitarian motives in wanting to adopt a child who otherwise would be unwanted and live in poverty. However, there is a risk that children will be removed from their home countries even though they are not orphans or unwanted.

Several nations—but not the United States—have ratified the Hague Convention on Protection of Children and Cooperation in Respect of Intercountry Adoption (1993). The Convention forbids abduction, sale, or traffic in children under 18. Authorities in the country of origin have an obligation to verify that a child released for adoption is, indeed, adoptable (including valid non-coerced consent from the child's parent or guardian). The ratifying countries have an obligation to supervise the activities of adoption agencies under their jurisdiction. Americans who wish to adopt must submit an official report about their reasons for adoption and suitability as adoptive parents.

[¶3060.2] Foster Parents

Foster parenthood is designed as a temporary arrangement for the protection of children who do not have a safe, appropriate, permanent home.

Foster parents whose relationship with the child has some indicia of permanence (the child had lived with them since infancy, for more than a year; the biological parents' relationship was terminated) have a protected liberty interest in being able to adopt the child, so they are entitled to notice and hearing before the child is removed from their home.[38]

A 1997 federal law, the Adoption and Safe Families Act of 1997, P.L. 105-89, strives to coordinate foster placement with termination of parental rights, with a view toward promoting adoption of children by their foster parents.

[¶3070] Reproductive Technology

Various forms of reproductive technology are used so that fertile women who have infertile male partners, or no male partners at all, can have children, or so that fertile males can have children despite their female partners' inability to conceive or carry a pregnancy to term. These arrangements can create legal problems if they go wrong, or when a relationship is terminated.

It is unlikely that a surrogacy contract (under which a woman is impregnated with sperm of a man who intends to gain custody of the child) will be enforced if the surrogate does not wish to surrender custody after the baby is born,[39] and courts may decline to hear such cases.

Arizona passed a statute, voided on Equal Protection grounds, that allowed a biological father, but not a surrogate mother, to rebut the presumption that the surrogate mother's husband was the parent of the child. A surrogate mother must be given access to a "maternity" proceeding to determine the true parenthood of the child.[40]

A California couple entered into a surrogacy agreement; after the couple's divorce, it was held[41] that the same rules should apply as if the child had been conceived via artificial insemination: i.e., they are both the legal parents of the child, despite the lack of biological relationship.

Under a 1998 Connecticut case,[42] a child born to a man under a surrogacy agreement and never adopted by his wife, is not a "child of the marriage," but the divorce court nevertheless has subject matter jurisdiction over the custody of the child. (The case had dragged on for seven of the 14 years of the child's life.)

Where fertility technology is used by a married couple, questions may arise as to the paternity of the child. The New York case of *Kass v. Kass* has been litigated several times. The Court of Appeals, New York's highest court, decided in mid-1998[43] that fertilized "pre-zygotes" that a couple had frozen during marriage could not be used by the wife to get pregnant over the husband's objections. The consent form they signed, calling for surrender of the pre-zygotes for biological research, prevails over the ex-wife's desire for "sole custody" of the fertilized eggs.

ENDNOTES

1. But see *Brause v. Bureau of Vital Statistics*, 66 LW 1576 (Alaska Super 2/27/98) permitting a male couple to maintain a suit after being denied a marriage license. The court's rationale for allowing the suit is that a statu-

The Taxpayer Relief Act of 1997 added a new §2035(e), stating that transfers of any portion of a trust, made while the decedent had grantor powers as defined by §676, will be attributed to the decedent. The result is that any gifts made out of a revocable trust during the three years preceding the decedent's death will be thrown back into his or her estate.[2]

[¶3105] §2036: Transfers with Retained Life Estate

The §2036 inclusion is popularly known as a transfer subject to a retained life estate. It mandates inclusion of the date-of-death (or alternate valuation date) value of the transferred property, which could be the entire corpus of a trust created by the decedent. Case law also mandates inclusion of income accumulated within the trust if inclusion of the corpus is required. If more than one transferor is involved, only transfers attributable to the decedent are included in his estate.

The most obvious example of a transfer with retained life estate is a family home, whose ownership is transferred to the owners' children, but subject to the parents' right to live in the home for the rest of their joint lives. However, §2036 applies, sometimes in very unexpected ways, to a broader range of transfers than the classical life estate. This section includes in the gross estate interests retained by the decedent for:

- Life
- A period that is not ascertainable without reference to the decedent's death
- A period that does not actually end before the decedent's death (e.g., the decedent retained a 10-year interest in certain property, but in fact died six years after the transfer).

One surprising effect of §2036 is that, if trustees of a trust were required to apply trust income to satisfy the decedent's obligation to support his or her dependents (as distinct from trustees other than the decedent having discretion to do so), the trust corpus could be included in the decedent's estate.

Under §2036(a)(2), the estate includes property over which the decedent retained the right to control who would enjoy the property or its income, even if the decedent could not enjoy the property or income personally. However, as long as a trustee is not related to the transferor, or subordinate to the transferor (as defined by §672(c)), a grantor's power to remove one trustee and substitute another will not result in estate inclusion.

[¶3105.1] The Effect of Control

Ability to direct income to others is sufficient control to place the underlying property in the estate of the person holding such a power. This is even if the power can be exercised only in conjunction with another individual (and even if that other individual's interest is adverse—e.g., a remainderman who is interested in the preservation of trust corpus rather than its dispersion).

However, estate inclusion on this ground can be avoided by drafting the trust so that the consent of all potential beneficiaries is required to direct the income stream. But if the grantor/trustee's ability to direct income is subject to an ascertainable standard, such as the health, education, welfare, and support of the income recipient, §2036 inclusion can be averted except in cases where the distribution of income satisfies the grantor's support obligation.

Because control is the key to §2036 (and many other estate tax provisions), direct or indirect retention of voting rights in a corporation controlled by the decedent will mandate inclusion of the stock in the decedent's estate, even though the decedent no longer holds the actual stock. In this context, control means that the decedent continues to own stock carrying at least 20% of the combined voting power of all classes of the corporation's stock (including stock whose ownership is attributed under §318).

[¶3105.2] Effect of Full Consideration

Transfers will not be subject to §2036 if they are made for "adequate and full consideration." The theory is that there is no real diminution in the potentially taxable amount, because the consideration received by the transferor, plus its investment return between the time of the transfer and the time of death, should replace the transferred amount.

Although the IRS has litigated this issue repeatedly, it is well-accepted that in this context, adequate and full consideration is the actuarial value of the transferred remainder, with no consideration of the retained life estate.[3]

[¶3105.3] Trust Issues

In the numerous cases in which the grantor of a trust also serves as trustee, the trust corpus will probably not be included in the grantor's estate merely because of the retention of typical fiduciary managerial powers (such as selling securities held by the trust and replacing them with others).

Drafters should also be alert to the doctrine of "reciprocal" or "crossed" trusts which applies to §2038 and other transfer-oriented provisions as well as to §2036. The IRS may seek to disregard arrangements under which, for instance, John creates a trust benefiting Mary's family while Mary creates a similar trust benefiting John's family.

If a person who makes a transfer but retains a life estate subsequently decides to transfer the life estate as well, §2035 will bring that transfer back into the estate if it occurs within three years before the decedent's death. But if the transfer is more remote in time, it will not be included in the estate.

[¶3106] §2037: Transfers Taking Effect at Death

Conditional transfers that are not bona fide sales are subject to estate inclusion under §2037, but only if possession or enjoyment of the property is contingent on surviving the transferor, and the transferor retained a meaningful reversionary in-property; the lapse is a gift to whoever would have lost the property if the power had been exercised.

However, if a "5 or 5" power (the power to demand either $5,000 or 5% of trust corpus, whichever is greater) lapses, there are no tax consequences; and if such a power is exercised, only the amount involved greater than "5 or 5" will be taxed: §2041(b)(2). It is also possible to execute a §2518 disclaimer (see ¶3140) to escape the tax consequences of holding an unwanted power of appointment.

[¶3110.3] Gift Tax on Powers of Appointment

In the gift tax context, §2514 governs power of appointment transactions. The definition of "general power of appointment" is the same as in the estate context, so a power is not general if it is subject to an ascertainable standard, or if the creator of the power, a person with an adverse interest, or a potential appointee must join with the holder to exercise the power. Either the exercise or release of a power (other than a 5-or-5 power) is a gift, but disclaimer of a power is not.

[¶3111] §2042: Insurance on the Decedent's Life

Taxation of life insurance on the life of the decedent is subject to §2042; if the decedent owned policies on someone else's life, those might be brought into the decedent's estate by §2033. Included in the decedent's estate is insurance on the decedent's life that is payable to his or her executor, or is payable to a named beneficiary but the decedent had incidents of ownership in the policy at the time of death, or surrendered them within three years of death. (In the community property states, insurance purchased with community funds is only 1/2 in the estate of the decedent, even if payable to the decedent's estate, because it is a community asset.)

More to the point, insurance that is payable to a named beneficiary and is not in any of these categories is not included in the decedent's estate—which opens up many tax-saving possibilities for wealthy people who can easily afford to pay insurance premiums.

A corporation's purchase of insurance on the life of its controlling stockholder does not put the insurance into the shareholder's estate. (The theory is that the estate tax value of his or her shares will reflect the insurance, among other assets.) However, if the insurance is payable to the stockholder's family rather than to the corporation, and the decedent had legal or equitable ownership of 50% or more of the corporation's shares, then corporate incidents of ownership will be attributed to the stockholder.

[¶3120] Calculating and Paying the Federal Estate Tax

Once the gross estate has been calculated, and once the amount of gift tax paid on gifts within the three years before death has been determined (the estate is "grossed up" by adding these taxes), a tentative estate tax can be calculated. In virtually all cases, the tentative tax will be significantly higher than the actual tax, because various deductions and credits are available to reduce or eliminate the estate tax.

The estate tax is the tentative tax on the entire taxable estate and adjusted taxable gifts, reduced by gift taxes payable on gifts made after 1976.

[¶3120.1] §2053, 2054: Debts, Expenses, Taxes, and Losses

A deduction is available under §2053 for funeral expenses and claims against the estate, including the decedent's debts and the actual expenses of administering the estate. Claims against the estate are limited to personal obligations of the decedent that were valid and enforceable as of the time of death, not, for instance, claims on which the statute of limitation had expired.

Administration expenses are actual necessary costs for marshalling and distributing the decedent's property, a category that includes executor's commissions, court costs, and attorneys' fees for services rendered to the estate as distinct from services to individual beneficiaries.

Expenses of the decedent's last illness that were not reimbursed by insurance or otherwise (e.g., Medicare) qualify for an estate tax deduction under §2053(a)(3). Such expenses, if paid by the estate within one year of death, can be claimed as an income tax deduction on the decedent's final return (see ¶3170.4.3 for a discussion of IRD and other issues of the final return), but claiming the income tax deduction requires a statement that the estate tax deduction has not been allowed and has been waived. Also see §642(g) for limits on the extent to which "overlapping" expenses (which might qualify for both estate and income tax deductions) can be claimed on both returns.

Section 2054 provides a deduction for casualty and theft losses of estate property occurring before settlement of the estate. The deduction is limited to amounts not reimbursed by insurance or otherwise, and an election must be made between claiming an income tax or estate tax deduction.

There are no hard and fast rules as to which deduction will be most beneficial. On the one hand, estate tax rates are much higher than income tax rates. On the other hand, virtually everyone is subject to income tax, whereas the interplay of the various deductions and credits eliminates tax on most estates, and greatly reduces the tax that would otherwise be due on large estates.

In a 1999 Tenth Circuit case, an estate paid over $2 million to the decedent's family to settle tort claims involving alleged interference with its inheritance rights. The estate was not permitted to take a tax deduction for this amount, because it was neither a claim against the estate, administrative expense of the estate, nor charitable deduction.[6]

[¶3120.2] §2055: The Estate Tax Charitable Deduction

Although income tax charitable deductions are limited by the concept of a "contribution base" linked to the contributor's income, there is no limit on the estate tax charitable deduction, provided that the bequest is made for "public, charitable and religious uses." In other words, bequests to public charities are not limited, but those to private foundations are.

[¶3120.3] §2056: The Marital Deduction

An unlimited estate tax marital deduction, the counterpart of the unlimited gift tax marital deduction (see ¶3133) is permitted for two kinds of transfers to the surviving spouse: outright bequests, and Qualified Terminable Interests in Property (QTIPs). (In addition to transfers qualifying for the marital deduction, many estate plans make part or all of the credit shelter trust payable to the surviving spouse.)

A marital deduction is available only if, as of the decedent's death, the couple were legally married: it is not available to cohabitants, for instance. Nor is it available to an ex-spouse subsequent to an absolute divorce. However, if local law provides that a couple is married after they have secured an interlocutory but before they have secured a final divorce decree, then they are married and the marital deduction can be used.

To qualify for the marital deduction, the interest passing to the spouse must have been included in the decedent's gross estate (thus, no marital deduction is available for tenancies in common and community property, because they do not pass through the gross estate); must not be deductible under §2053 (e.g., commissions received by the surviving spouse in his or her role as executor of the estate); and must not be a terminable interest other than a QTIP.

[¶3120.3.1] QTIPs

QTIPs are often used so that a person planning an estate can make sure that his or her surviving spouse will have lifetime income, but that after the second spouse's death, the trust corpus will pass as directed by the deed or will of the first spouse to die. For instance, in second-marriage situations, QTIPs are often used to grant income to the spouse, while the corpus eventually goes to the children of the first marriage. QTIPs are also used if the person planning the estate does not believe the surviving spouse will be able to manage a large inheritance, but will be able to manage current income.

QTIPs can be created either inter vivos or by will. The most common form of QTIP is a testamentary trust. An interest is a qualified terminable interest (qualified in the sense that it is eligible for the marital deduction) if the surviving spouse receives all the income from the subject property during his or her life. The trustee can be permitted to invade the QTIP for the benefit of the surviving spouse (but for the benefit of no one else), and the surviving spouse can be given a power of appointment over the property. Whatever property remains as of the surviving spouse's death will be included in his or her estate, notwithstanding the fact that the surviving spouse does not have the power to dispose of the property by will.

Because only 50% of joint property acquired by a married couple by purchase (as distinct from gift or inheritance) is included in the gross estate of the first spouse to die, only 50% qualifies for the marital deduction. Therefore, the surviving spouse gets a stepped-up basis in only 50% of the joint property. For certain marital joint tenancies created before 1977, however, a basis step-up is available in the entire value of the property.

If the surviving spouse is not a U.S. citizen, then QTIP treatment is not available, but a somewhat similar mechanism, the Qualified Domestic Origin Trust (QDOT) is available under §2056A.

[¶3120.4] Valuation Issues

Since the tax depends on the size of the estate, valuation of non-cash property within the estate becomes crucial. It is important for owners of valuable property to maintain current appraisals (which are also needed if, for instance, an outright or split gift of the property is made).

In certain situations, usually involving securities, the property will be valued for gift and/or estate tax purposes at a discount from the fair market value that would obtain in an arm's-length transaction. For example, a minority interest in a closely-held corporation will often be valued at a discount because the owner of such an interest is unable to control corporate policy.

If the stock is subject to transfer restrictions, these restrictions affect marketability and therefore might also give rise to a discount, but see below for the IRC Chapter 14 rules on transfer restrictions. In the opposite situation, a "blockage" discount could apply if selling a large block of stock all at once would have the effect of depressing the price of the shares. It should also be noted that the IRS may seek to impose a valuation **premium** rather than a discount if a transferee or heir acquires the ability to control a corporation.

The problems of valuing an outright gift can be difficult enough; when future interests such as remainders and reversions are involved, the problems multiply. In a common arrangement, the grantor retains the right to receive income for life from a trust, with the remainder going, e.g., to a spouse or child. The gift is valued on the basis of the present interest of the remainder, calculated on the basis of the grantor's life expectancy. Similar considerations come into play for charitable remainder trusts and for more complex transactions.

[¶3120.4.1] Valuation Under Chapter 14

Before Chapter 14 was enacted, donors tried to accomplish several objectives with complex donative transactions. Of course, they wanted to reduce the size of their taxable estates by removing valuable assets from the estate. But, at the same time, they sought to reduce the gift tax cost of making the transfer, by claiming that the remainder interest, the subject of the gift, had a low value whereas the retained interest had a high value. They also wished to assign most or all of the appreciation potential to the remainder interest, with the result that a small gift tax cost would shift an appreciating asset to its donees, with the appreciation itself escaping both gift and estate taxation.

Only intrafamily transactions are subject to Chapter 14, although the definition of *family* is quite broad and includes adoptees, relatives of the half blood, and spouses as well as blood relatives. Under Chapter 14, relatively favorable tax treatment is available for transfers of Qualified Interests (QIs) within the family, but correspondingly harsh treatment is assigned to transfers of interests that do not conform to the QI definition.

For gift tax purposes, a non-QI is assigned a value of zero, so that the entire amount of the transfer is assigned to the remainder and thus is a taxable gift. Although most Chapter 14 transactions involve trusts, the chapter applies to non-trust transactions as well.

It should be noted that Code §6662, which imposes accuracy-related penalties in a number of contexts, also imposes a penalty for serious valuation errors or misconduct on gift and estate tax returns. The penalty is 20% of the tax underpayment attributable to a valuation that is 50% or less of the actual value of the asset; 40% of the underpayment, if the valuation was 25% or less of what it should have been. The penalty is waived if the underpayment attributable to the valuation was under $5,000.

[¶3120.4.2] Qualified Family-Owned Business Interests

In response to concerns about adverse estate taxation of small business, Congress adopted a "QFOBI exclusion" in TRA '97, enacted as new Code §2033A. That is, certain amounts attributable to qualified family-owned business interests could be excluded from the estates of deceased business owners. The exclusion operated reciprocally with the unified credit: the amount potentially excludable was the difference between $1.3 million and the then-prevailing amount that could be sheltered by the unified credit. Thus, the QFOBI would phase down as the unified credit phased up.

As originally enacted, the QFOBI provisions contained some serious ambiguities. TRA '97 did not make it clear whether specific property could be excluded from the estate, or only the value of the property, and this ambiguity made it hard to determine how the QFOBI exclusion would work in conjunction with the marital deduction, the §1014 calculation of basis of property acquired from a decedent, the GST rules, §2032A special use valuation, and §6166's provisions for installment payment of estate tax.

IRSRRA dealt with these problems by changing the QFOBI exclusion under §2033A into an estate tax deduction enacted by a section redesignated as §2057. (The deduction is unavailable in the gift tax and GST contexts.) Section 2057(a)(1) allows a deduction of up to $675,000 for the adjusted value of qualified family-owned business interests that the decedent owned, provided that at least half of the estate consists of the adjusted value of the business, plus certain inter vivos gifts of interests in the business to family members.

[¶3130] Gift Tax

One way to decrease the size of the estate is to spend money. Another way, certainly more palatable to the donees, is to give money away. Theoretically, the unified transfer tax system will capture the transaction either way, taxing the gift at one end (under IRC Chapter 12) and amounts not gifted or expended at the other. However, many gifts are exempt from tax (gifts between spouses; small gifts; certain gifts for minors) and, in any event, the gift tax is applied only to "completed" gifts, so planning advantages can be secured by allowing the donor to retain enough "strings attached" to prevent the completion of the gift.

[¶3130.1] Completed Gifts

A gift is completed when the transferor relinquishes dominion and control over the property that is the subject of the gift. A simple example is giving a person an art object, or mailing a check payable to a person or a charitable organization. A gift of shares of stock becomes complete when the change of ownership is registered; a gift of real property is complete when the deed is recorded.

Conversely, a gift is not complete if the donor has the outright power to revoke it, or has lesser powers nonetheless treated by the IRC as tantamount to power to revoke. Thus, if the grantor has the power to remove a trustee and take the trustee's place, the gift is not complete; nor is it complete if the donor can change the beneficiaries of the gift, even if the donor cannot receive the money or property personally. If the donor can change the time or manner in which a beneficiary can enjoy his or her interest, but not the identity of the beneficiary, that power has estate tax consequences (under Reg. §20.2038-1(a)) but does not make the gift incomplete. Any contingency within the donor's control is ignored in determining whether a gift is complete.

[¶3130.2] Effect of Unified Rates

Until 1976, the gift tax rates were set at only 75% of the estate tax rates, as an incentive to prefer lifetime gifts over bequests. Since then, the taxes have been imposed at the same rates, but are figured differently, so that estate tax can be imposed on the amount of estate tax as well as the amount of the underlying taxable estate. Another complicating factor is that, although most gifts made within three years prior to a decedent's death are removed from his or her estate, the gift tax paid on those gifts is included in the taxable estate.

[¶3130.3] Gift Tax Compliance

The gift tax return, Form 709, is due annually, covering all taxable gifts for the year (i.e., no matter how large the gifts, it is not necessary to file on a gift-by-gift basis). However, the unified credit operates so that individuals who make taxable inter vivos gifts do not have the option of either applying the unified credit to the gifts or paying the tax during life in order to retain the unified credit for use in the estate. The credit must be applied to lifetime gifts, with the result that less or none of the credit will be available subsequent to making large gifts or funding large trusts.

The gift tax statute of limitations is three years from the filing date of any return actually filed, or six years if a return was filed but omitted 25% or more of the value of the gift: see Code §6501(e)(2). There is no statute of limitations, and tax can be assessed at any time, if a necessary return was not filed and transfers subject to §2701 or 2702 (transfers of corporate or partnership interests, or of unitrust or annuity interests) were made, or if a fraudulent return is filed.

One of the many TRA '97 provisions affecting estate planning provides that, as long as a gift was adequately disclosed (on a gift tax return or other notice to the government), the IRS will not be permitted to challenge the valuation placed on the gift once the statute of limitations has expired.

[¶3131] §2503: Taxable Gifts and The Gift Tax Annual Exclusion

Theoretically, the rule is that gifts are taxable unless covered by a specific exemption, but in practical terms, the gift tax exemptions are broad enough to remove most gifting from the transfer tax ambit. Most importantly, §2503(b) creates a per-donee annual exclusion of $10,000 which will be adjusted for inflation over and above 1998 baseline levels. However, because the exclusion must go up in increments of $1,000, the adjustment will not take place until the CPI has increased by 10%.

There is no limit on the number of donees, so it's clear that a systematic gifting program involving several siblings, children, grandchildren, and friends each year can have the effect of removing a significant amount of assets from the potentially taxable estate without incurring any gift tax cost.

A married person whose spouse agrees to join in the gift can "gift split," (see §2513) making gifts of up to $20,000 per year per donee (plus any applicable inflation investment).

[¶3131.1] *Crummey* Powers

However, the annual exclusion is only available for gifts of a present interest, not of a future interest. Thus, writing a check to a nephew qualifies for the annual exclusion; naming the nephew as remainderman of a trust generally would not. The exception is the *Crummey* power, named after *Crummey v. CIR*, 397 F.2d 82 (9th Cir. 1968). A *Crummey* power turns what would otherwise be a future interest into a present interest qualifying for the annual exclusion. The power requires that, for a period of at least 60 days a year, trust beneficiaries must be given the right to demand invasions of trust principal. This power, even if it is never exercised (and, in the real world, it never is), converts the interest to a present interest.

[¶3131.2] §2503(c) Trusts

Section 2503(c) permits a trust gift to a minor to be treated as a gift of a present interest as long as:

- Trust principal and income can be expended by or for the minor until he or she reaches age 21
- Anything not so expended and remaining in the trust when the minor reaches 21 goes to the minor at age 21. (If the minor dies before reaching age 21, the trust corpus goes into the minor's estate or as the minor exercised a gen-

eral power of appointment over the property—even if local law forbids minors to make wills or exercise GPAs.)

However, the property can remain within the trust after the minor reaches age 21, if he or she consents to continuation of the trust.

[¶3131.3] Direct Payments

Under §2503(e), no gift tax is ever assessed on direct payments made to a provider of education or medical services, on behalf of someone other than the payor. In other words, a person can devote any amount, without gift tax, to paying tuition or medical bills for a relative or friend, although giving money directly to the person who needs the services (or that person's parent) would be a taxable gift unless another exemption is available.

[¶3132] §2522: Charitable Deduction

Unlike the income tax charitable deduction (¶4150.8), the gift tax charitable deduction is unlimited, but the amount of the deduction is reduced by the annual gift tax exclusion: see §2524.

The deduction is naturally available for outright gifts. A gift tax charitable deduction is also available for certain split-interest transfers: transfers to a Charitable Remainder Annuity Trust (CRAT), Charitable Remainder Unitrust (CRUT), or pooled fund only (see ¶3152). The deduction is the present value of the interest the charity is expected to receive in the future (calculated on the basis of the IRS actuarial tables). If the split-interest transfer is not a CRAT, CRUT, or pooled fund, the gift tax deduction will not be available, although it is possible that an estate tax deduction will be.

[¶3133] §2523, 2516: Marital Planning

Gifts from one spouse to the other are free of gift tax, regardless of amount. However, the gift must be made subsequent to the marriage (a gift from one engaged person to another is not exempt from gift tax, even if the engaged couple marries and files a joint return in the year of the gift). If a couple divorces, gifts in the year of the divorce but subsequent to the divorce are not deductible either. The gift tax marital deduction is available only when the donee spouse is a U.S. citizen. However, for non-citizen donees, §2523(i) permits a $100,000 annual exclusion for present-interest gifts (as a compromise between the ordinary §2503(b) $10,000 annual exclusion and the unlimited marital deduction permitted for citizen spouses).

Gift tax issues also arise in conjunction with the dissolution of a marriage. There is no gift when one spouse agrees to pay a lump sum to discharge support obligations to the other spouse and the children of the marriage (§2516).

[¶3134] Other Gift Tax Issues

As a result of §2512, gifts are valued as of the date they are completed. In other words, there is no gift tax alternate valuation date. However, control premiums, or discounts for minority interests, lack of marketability, or blockage can be applied in the valuation of gifts.

If a transfer is made for partial value (other than an unsuccessful but arm's-length business deal), §2512(b) provides that the transfer is a part-gift, part-sale.

Transfers involving life estates, income, annuities, remainders, and reversions are valued under §7520, using officially promulgated unisex tables of life expectancies. The tables are used for income, estate, and GST purposes as well as gift tax purposes.

However, the tables cannot be used to value transfers by a terminally ill person. For this purpose, a terminally ill person is defined as having an incurable illness or other deteriorating physical condition, whose probability of death within one year of the death of the person whose estate is being valued is at least 50%. If the "measuring life" survives the decedent by eighteen months, it is then presumed that the measuring life was not terminally ill, unless the terminal condition can be proved by clear and convincing evidence.

[¶3140] §2518: Disclaimers

Although disclaimers appear in the Code with the gift tax provisions, they are perhaps more useful in the estate planning context. A qualified disclaimer, made in writing and no later than nine months after the creation of the interest being disclaimed, prevents an individual from receiving property that would be undesirable for tax or other reasons. Disclaimer of an inheritance must be made within nine months of the death; disclaimer of a gift must be made within nine months of the time that the gift becomes complete.

Before December 31, 1997, there was a difficulty in disclaiming spousal joint tenancies: the interest was sometimes deemed created at the time the tenancy was created, thus rendering untimely a disclaimer after one spouse's death.

T.D. 8744, published on that date, adds Final Regulations under §25.2528-2(c)(4)(i) permitting a surviving spouse to disclaim survivorship interest in a marital joint tenancy at any time within the nine months after the death of the first spouse to die, no matter when the tenancy was created, and whether or not either spouse could have severed the tenancy unilaterally. The effect of a disclaimer is that half of the property can pass under the will of the deceased spouse. This might, for instance, be desirable if the deceased spouse did not have a credit shelter (bypass) trust, and the estate wants to take advantage of the unified credit. The unified credit is not available for amounts already protected by the marital deduction.

T.D. 8744 also clarifies that mere creation of a joint bank or brokerage account is not a completed gift because the creator of the account has the power to remove the contents of the account without consent of the joint tenant (and therefore disclaimers of interests in such accounts are timely within nine months of completion of the gift, not the mere creation of the account).

Certiorari has been granted in the case of *Drye v. U.S.*,[7] on the question of whether an effective disclaimer of an inheritance can be made if the intention is to avoid using the inheritance to pay overdue federal taxes.

[¶3150] Trusts

A trust is an arrangement for dividing the ownership of assets from management of those assets, and it usually also involves a division between income and remainder interests. Trusts serve important practical purposes (continuing professional management of assets; carrying out a complex dispositive plan; managing the assets of an incapacitated person) as well as important tax planning purposes. The settlor, creator, or grantor places funds into trust, to be managed by one or more trustees (who may include the grantor). One broad analytic division is between revocable trusts, whose grantor retains the power to amend or revoke the trust, and irrevocable trusts, where this power has been surrendered. Revocable trust assets are always included in the estate of the grantor, because the retention of the power to revoke subjects the trust to taxation under §2038.

Several factors determine whether or not an irrevocable trust will be included in the estate. Several IRC sections and Regulations, and many cases, deal with the question of which powers on the part of the grantor will be sufficient to make the trust a "grantor" trust (whose income is taxed to the grantor rather than the trust itself or its beneficiaries) and which powers will result in estate inclusion.

During the term of the trust, some or all of its income is paid out to one or more income beneficiaries. A trust is a simple trust in a year in which all trust income is paid out and none is accumulated; it is a complex trust, subject to additional difficulties in tax computations, in a year in which some or all income is retained.

ILITs, or Irrevocable Life Insurance Trusts, are often used to plan for potentially taxable estates. Having a trust purchase a policy, or placing a policy into the trust (in the hope of outliving the three-year period during which transfer of incidents of ownership will result in estate inclusion) makes it possible to create a large fund that can be administered in accordance with the estate plan. The fund can be created by recurring small contributions (premium payments), and perhaps at a discount (if the insured person dies relatively soon after the purchase of the policy).

[¶3150.1] Duration and Termination of a Trust

When the trust's term ends, or when a determinative event happens or fails to happen (e.g., when Person A dies; if Person B fails to receive an M.D. degree from an accredited university), the corpus remaining in the trust will be distributed to remaindermen as prescribed by the terms of the trust. The income beneficiary(ies) and/or remaindermen can be people and/or charitable institutions.

The general rule is that merger will occur, and the trust will be disregarded for legal purposes, if the sole trustee, income beneficiary, and remainderman are all the same person, although some state statutes do grant validity to such "one-person" trusts.

Another general rule is that a charitable trust can be drafted to be perpetual, but that trusts for natural persons are subject to the Rule Against Perpetuities: the trust must end and its corpus be distributed not more than 21 years after the death of the last person named in the trust who was alive when it was created. However, states such as Alaska and Delaware permit perpetual trusts benefiting individuals, and also allow other favorable features (such as allowing self-settled spendthrift trusts).

In many instances, creation of a trust will include at least some element of a completed gift, and therefore at least some gift tax will theoretically be generated. (Except for very wealthy people, gift tax remains theoretical because the unified credit is drawn down first, and no actual cash payment of gift tax will be required until the unified credit is exhausted.) With revocable trusts, the completed gift element is absent, because of the grantor's retained power to revoke the trust. The ability of the grantor's creditors to reach the trust can also prevent completion of the gift.

[¶3151] Grantor Trusts

Most trusts are grantor trusts for income tax purposes: that is, no matter who actually receives the income, the trust grantor is taxed on it. (Charitable remainder trusts and pooled income funds are exempt from the grantor trust rules, which appear at §§671–678.) A trust is treated as a grantor trust because of the extent of control that the grantor exercises, or is permitted to exercise (even if he or she never actually does so) over the trust, its income, and its administration.

The Code contains a number of overlapping provisions, and avoiding grantor trust characterization can be very difficult in drafting one that escapes *all* the grantor trust provisions.

Although grantor trust treatment in one sense appears to be punitive—trusts are usually employed by wealthy individuals who are already in the highest tax bracket, so additional income from the trust will be taxed at their marginal rate—in another sense it is beneficial. Because the grantor pays the tax, the trust itself doesn't, so the trust need not be invaded to pay taxes, and the trust continues to appreciate tax-free. The longer the term of the trust, the more powerful this effect will be. Grantor trust treatment can apply to the entire trust, or only to the trust income.

Reg. §1.671-3 provides that a grantor who is treated as the owner of the entire trust must take all trust income, deductions, and credits into his or her own income, as if the trust did not exist. But if the grantor is treated as an owner only because of a share of trust income, the grantor takes into account only that share of trust tax items that a current income beneficiary would report.

The grantor is the "owner" of the trust if he or she retains the power to revoke, terminate, or amend the trust, or appoint its income or principal: §§671, 676. This is true even if the power is never in fact exercised. But the grantor will not be treated as owner if such a power can only be exercised in conjunction with an adverse party: §676(a).

Under §672(e), a power held by either spouse is attributed to the other, so no tax advantages can be gained by one spouse setting up a trust rather than the other.

[¶3151.1] §674 Grantor Trust Provisions

Section 674(a) makes the grantor the owner of any part of a trust by which the grantor has power to control the beneficial enjoyment of income, corpus, or both. That is, even if the grantor doesn't actually derive financial benefit from the trust, "pulling the strings" to determine who will get the benefits is an ownership power. If the grantor can only exercise this power in conjunction with an adverse party—i.e., someone whose financial interests oppose those of the grantor—then §674(a) will not apply.

But if the consent of someone who is a neutral (non-adverse) party is required, §674(a) does apply. (A non-adverse party is one who has no financial interest in the trust, or whose interest is unaffected by whatever the grantor chooses to do.) If an independent trustee (one who is not subject to the control of the grantor or grantor's spouse) has a "spray" or "sprinkle" power to direct income or corpus within a specified class, this power will **not** make the grantor taxable on the trust. See §674(c).

The grantor will not be treated as the owner of the trust purely by reason of these powers:

- Power to apply income to the support of his or her dependents
- A power exercisable only by will
- Certain powers to distribute corpus
- Power to defer the payment of income
- Power to define a particular payment as income or invasion of principal
- Power to withhold income from a minor or disabled beneficiary.

[¶3151.2] Administrative Powers Under §675

Section 675 details which administrative powers will force ownership treatment:

- Ability to dispose of trust income and/or corpus for less than its fair market value
- Power to borrow from the trust without paying adequate interest or providing adequate security
- Actual borrowing by the grantor or grantor's spouse, unless full repayment (including interest) is made by the beginning of the tax year

Section 675 also makes the trust a grantor trust on the basis of any power of a nonfiduciary (unless supervised by a fiduciary) to vote the trust's stock holdings in a corporation controlled by the grantor; to repurchase trust assets; or control investments to the extent that the trust owns stock in a corporation controlled by the grantor.

funding. A pooled fund is a single fund administered by a charitable organization; it serves trust-like functions for sums of money too small to be administered as separate trusts.

TRA '97 tightened the requirements for qualified CRTs by mandating that the annual non-charitable annuity or unitrust interest cannot exceed 50% of the value of the trust property. Furthermore, the charity's remainder interest must be worth at least 10% of the initial value of the contribution. The interaction of the two provisions means that CRTs cannot be used to achieve very high income for the donor or other recipient of the current income, and the younger the income beneficiary, the smaller the rate of return that can be provided.

[¶3155] Generation Skipping Transfers

A wealthy family with dynastic aspirations could, theoretically, place vast sums of wealth into trusts and keep the funds tied up for generation after generation. There are two limitations on this tactic: first, the Rule Against Perpetuities, which requires the trust corpus to be distributed within lives in being plus 21 years (but which is being eroded by the "Alaska-type" trust statutes discussed in ¶3150.1).

The other is the federal tax on generation-skipping transfers (GST), which is imposed at the highest estate tax flat rate: currently, 55%. The GST is imposed in addition to the estate or gift tax on the transaction, so it is perfectly possible for the tax on a transfer to be larger than the transfer itself! GST is of concern only to the affluent, because each individual is entitled to a $1 million exemption (as indexed for inflation).

A generation-skipping transfer (whether outright gift, in trust, or otherwise) is one made to a close relative of the grandchild's generation or any younger generation, or to a remote relative or non-relative who is 37.5 or more years younger than the transferor. A person's spouse is always deemed to belong to the same generation as that person, whatever the actual age may be, and adopted persons are treated in the same way as blood relatives.

There are three kinds of generation-skipping transfers, each bearing different tax consequences. A "direct skip" is an outright gift. A "taxable distribution" is a distribution from an ongoing trust; a "taxable termination" is a distribution in conjunction with the termination of a trust (e.g., one that calls for income for a period of years to A, then remainder to B, C, and D).

Also note that if a direct skip is a net gift (i.e., the transferor pays the GST, so the skip person receives the intended amount of the gift in full), the GST paid by the donor is considered an additional gift, which gives rise to additional GST liability.

[¶3160] Planning the Estate and Drafting the Will

An estate that is below the amount that can be protected by the unified credit, or one that qualifies for the marital deduction in whole or in large part will not be subject to federal estate taxation (although it may be subject to inheritance taxation in one or more states). Nevertheless, the estate still has to be planned.

A will is an "ambulatory" document, which can theoretically be revoked and replaced at any time. Certainly, wills should be redrafted based on major changes in the law, or major changes in circumstances (such as a marriage, divorce, or significant change in the size or composition of the estate). The difficulty is that clients will not always be conscientious about such matters. They may also lose testamentary capacity before the time that a will change becomes necessary.

Testamentary capacity is a modest standard (ability to understand the nature and approximate size of one's assets, and to recognize one's "natural objects of bounty" such as family members), but nevertheless some people are unable to satisfy it. In arguable cases, some attorneys videotape the execution of the will, so that eventually the probate court will be able to observe the demeanor of the testator. Some very cautious attorneys videotape will executions routinely, so that no inference will be drawn that the capacity of a particular testator was dubious.

The "second estate problem" occurs at the death of a surviving spouse who has not remarried. In many instances, the size of the estate has increased because of investment returns, and it exceeds the amount that can be protected by the unified credit; or it is in one of the higher estate tax brackets. The decedent has no surviving spouse, so the marital deduction is unavailable.

In the smaller estate, use of a credit shelter trust reduces or eliminates the second estate problem. The amount that can be sheltered by the unified credit is placed into a trust, benefiting either the surviving spouse, the testator's children, or other desired beneficiary(ies). The surviving spouse then reduces his or her estate by charitable gifts, a giving program, or expenditures, so that the credit shelter trust can pass intact at his or her death. The balance of the estate, if any, will be subject to estate taxation.

Life insurance or "second to die" insurance (which is purchased when both spouses are alive, but payable only on the second death) can provide liquidity to pay estate taxes without reducing the amount available to heirs. No matter what the source of the funds, the will should clarify the apportionment of estate and other transfer taxes, that is, whether each legacy is reduced by a share (proportionate or otherwise).

The needs of the recipient, not just the testator, should be considered. It is unwise to leave sums of money outright to a person with Alzheimer's disease, or who is otherwise incapable of managing it. In that situation, a disposition in trust might be better. But if the person received Medicaid or other public benefits, even an interest in a trust could impair the availability of benefits. No one should be named as executor or trustee unless he or she can be expected to be physically mobile and mentally alert throughout the entire period that a fiduciary could be expected to be required.

[¶3161] Drafting Structures

It is not quite a truism to say that the function of a properly drafted will is to administer the disposition of exactly 100% of the testator's assets that can pass by will. An improperly drafted will might attempt to dispose of assets that pass by operation of law, assets that no longer form part of the estate, or might make $3 million worth of dispositions of an estate whose actual value is only $1 million!

- Notify the Social Security Administration of the decedent's death; if necessary, assist survivors in applying for Social Security benefits (e.g., as surviving spouse, mother of deceased worker's minor child, etc.)
- Find out if the decedent's estate or survivors are entitled to buy-out of
business interests or stock in closely-held corporations; if required, put
the stock or satisfy the business', partners' or other stockholders' right of
first refusal
- Determine the amount of any transfers made within three years of death that
must be included in the gross estate (e.g., life insurance transfers)
- If necessary, obtain a bond covering services as executor. (Especially if the ex-
ecutor is a family member or friend, the will may call for service without bond.)
- Keep track of administration expenses
- Set up accounting system for the estate, and for any trusts
- Submit the will for probate.

[¶3170.3] Tax Aspects of Estate Administration

The estate itself is capable of earning income (indeed, one of the executor's
duties is to make it productive without violating fiduciary principles), and therefore is capable of becoming a taxpayer. A simple estate is likely to be settled in less
than a year, but more complexity takes more time to work through, and the estate
may have to cope with income tax returns for several years.

[¶3170.3.1] Relief Provisions

Even if two estates are the same size, and contain the same proportion of
property subject to estate tax, the two are not necessarily equal in other respects.
One estate may consist entirely of cash and marketable securities; the other, of
illiquid assets such as hard-to-sell and hard-to-value interests in close corporations. Although no one enjoys paying estate taxes, the hardship on the latter type
of estate is obviously much greater than on the former.

Therefore, the Code contains several provisions that can be interpreted as relief provisions for illiquid estates, including closely-held businesses and family
farms. The provisions are:

- §2032—alternate valuation date; executor's election to value all property
in the gross estate as of six months post mortem, not the date of death; anything disposed of within the six-month period is valued as of the date of disposition
- §2032A—covering up to $750,000, as adjusted for inflation, for farms and
other real estate used in business and constituting a major part of the estate
- §2057—small business interests, and
- §6166—extension of time to pay estate tax in installments, including a preferential interest rate on the installment payments.

A trust or estate is a related party as to its beneficiary, so losses cannot be recognized on distribution of property. However, a trust or estate can make an irrevocable election under §643(e) to recognize **gain** on all distributions during the tax year, as if the property had been sold to the beneficiary for its fair market value as of the time of the distribution.

An estate or trust can take an unlimited charitable deduction for any amount that its governing instrument directs to be paid for a charitable purpose (§642(c)). An estate, but not a trust (other than a pooled income fund), can deduct any amount of gross income permanently set aside (rather than actually paid) for charitable purposes.

The trust is entitled to a deduction for administrative expenses, but only if these expenses are not used to reduce the decedent's estate for estate tax purposes: §642(g). Section 642(b) gives an estate a $600 personal exemption. A simple trust gets a $300 personal exemption, but only $100 for a complex trust. Personal exemptions are not allowed in a trust's or estate's final year. Neither an estate nor a trust gets a standard deduction (§63(c)(6)(E)), but either can claim a net operating loss deduction under §642(c).

Code §6034A obligates beneficiaries to treat items consistently with their treatment by the payor trust or estate. Most trusts and some estates have to make quarterly estimated tax payments, using Form 1041-ES. However, §6654(l)(2) exempts estates and grantor trusts that receive the residue of a probate estate from having to make estimated tax payments for their first two tax years after the decedent's death.

As ¶3107 shows, revocable trusts are included in the gross estate of the deceased grantor. Code §645 tackles a related issue by permitting the trustee and executor (both must join in the election) to elect to have the revocable trust treated as part of the estate for income tax purposes, rather than as a separate trust. Combining the two could be more convenient and less costly than separate tax compliance.

Two or more trusts can be treated for tax purposes as a single trust, pursuant to §643(f), if the multiple trusts were created with tax avoidance as a principal motive, and all the trusts have substantially the same grantor(s) and primary beneficiary(ies). A married couple is treated as one person.

[¶3170.4.2] Tax Issues for Beneficiaries

Section 652(a) provides that the beneficiary of a simple trust is taxed on either his or her proportionate share of the trust's DNI, or trust income required to be distributed to him or her (whether or not it is actually distributed)—whichever is lower. The rules for taxation of beneficiaries of complex trusts, found in §662(a), are beyond the scope of this discussion.

The beneficiary is not taxed on amounts paid as a gift or bequest of a specific sum of money, or specific items of property, as long as the distribution is made in a lump sum or in only two or three installments: §663(a).

The beneficiary's basis in property distributed from the trust or estate depends on whether the trust or estate elected to recognize gain on the distribution. See §643(e), 662(a)(2). The basis computation begins with the adjusted basis that the trust or estate had in the property just before the distribution, adjusted for the gain recognized by the trust or estate on the distribution.

Also see §678, which provides that a beneficiary or trustee can be taxed as the owner of trust income based on a power (including a *Crummey* power) to vest corpus or income in him- or herself, if the power can be exercised alone. This section is broad enough to encompass individuals who have modified or released a power, but who still retain enough control over the trust so that a grantor would be taxed in the same circumstances.

[¶3170.4.3] IRD and Related Issues

An individual's tax year ends with the death of that person. Nearly all decedents will have been cash basis taxpayers, and their final return must include income actually or constructively received prior to death. The estate, or anyone else acquiring rights and obligations related to the decedent, will be required to report such items as Income in Respect of a Decedent (IRD) or post-mortem deductions: §691.

IRD is income (including capital gains) that the decedent had a right to receive but did not actually or constructively receive before death. It includes taxable distributions from qualified plans; a deceased partner's partnership income; and a deceased shareholder's Subchapter S income.

IRD might be reportable on the decedent's final income tax return. If not, it is reported in the tax year of receipt, by the estate (if it received the right to the item from the decedent) or by any non-estate party that received the income. The characterization of the items is the same in the hands of the recipient as it was in the hands of the decedent. The recipient of IRD is permitted, under §691(c), to deduct estate tax and generation-skipping transfer tax attributable to the inclusion of IRD in the gross estate.

[¶3180] Intestate Administration

In the absence of a will, or if it is so clear that a purported will is invalid that there is no proponent to seek its probate, assets will pass by intestacy (the state's dispositive scheme) to "distributees." For a married person, the typical intestacy scheme transfers all or most of the estate to the surviving spouse; if there are children, the spouse's share is often reduced correspondingly. If there is no spouse, the assets are divided among the surviving children; if none, among other relatives.

An appropriate person will receive "letters of administration" to administer the estate, much as an executor would do.

ENDNOTES

1. Current law provides that, as the higher unified credit phases in, the minimum tax rate will also increase (because amounts once subject to the lowest tax rate will be freed of estate tax). For the years 2004–2005, the minimum estate tax rate will be 39%, and it will be 41% for 2006 and later years.
2. This section was enacted to reverse the result in *Estate of Jalkut v. Comm'r*, 96 TC 675 (1991) and the cases following it.

3. See, e.g., *Estate of D'Ambrosio v. Comm'r*, 78 AFTR2d 96-7347 (3rd Cir. 1996); *Wheeler v. U.S.*, 116 F.3d 749 (5th Cir. 1997).
4. 64 FR 23187 (4/30/99); corrections at 64 FR 33194 (6/22/99).
5. *Gallenstein v. U.S.*, 975 F.2d 286 (6th Cir. 1992); *Patten v. U.S.*, 96-1 USTC ¶60,231; *Anderson v. U.S.*, 96-2 USTC ¶60,235; *Hahn*, 110 TC No. 14 (3/4/98).
6. *Lindberg v. U.S.*, 67 LW 1444 (10th Cir. 1/13/99).
7. #98-1101 (below, 82 AFTR2d 98-5821, 8th Cir. 8/17/98).
8. *Estate of Wall v. C.I.R.*, 101 TC 300 (1993).
9. A trust is simple if it must distribute all of its income currently; does not make charitable contributions; and does not make distributions from corpus. Otherwise, the trust is complex.

to satisfy the requisite standard of care. It's important to note that physicians are not required to save every patient or provide a good result in every case—only to act with the necessary knowledge, skill, and care of a physician with comparable training. (Specialists are held to a higher standard than generalists.)

The cause of action requires proof that this failure to manifest due care was the proximate cause of injuries to the plaintiff. Of course, proximate cause is an issue in all tort cases, but it's especially significant in medical malpractice cases because of the need to distinguish between harm caused by negligence and the disease process itself.

Medical malpractice can manifest itself in the context of diagnosis, medical treatment, surgery, and other contacts between provider and recipient of care. At one time, the "locality rule" was extremely significant, with the standard of care measured by other practitioners in the same geographic area. In current practice, and in large part because of improved communications, the extent to which a health care practitioner has specialized is more significant than the locality in which he or she practices.

[¶3220.1] Liable Parties

In traditional medical practice, if nothing else, it was easy to identify the plaintiff, because a single physician commenced and completed treatment. Today, the question is far more difficult. It is very common for a patient to consult an internist or other general physician, who then refers the patient to one or more specialists, and such arrangements create potential for liability.[2]

Sometimes the patient must go through a "gatekeeper" in order to have specialty care reimbursed by his or her HMO or other managed care organization (MCO). That opens up significant questions of whether referrals were properly made or improperly withheld, as well as the evolving jurisprudence about the role of MCOs. It is possible to commit malpractice by not treating, when treatment is required, as well as by mismanaging a course of treatment. Questions of denial of treatment and abandonment are especially salient in the managed care context.[3]

Traditionally, many cases against MCOs were preempted by ERISA, because the patient received care through an employer's group health plan. ERISA preempts state-law causes of action "relating to" a pension or benefit plan.

In the late 1990s, however, ERISA preemption is eroding, and some courts have held MCOs liable for negligent care by MCO doctors, or for failure to notify plan participants of the availability of appeals within the system when coverage is denied.[4] ERISA does not preempt a patient's or survivor's action against an MCO doctor who failed to give the patient a timely referral to an appropriate specialist.[5]

The relationship between patient and care provider is supposed to be a fully voluntary one, based on the patient's informed consent to treatments recommended by the care provider. There is a fiduciary element in the relationship, obligating the doctor to perform in good faith and provide fair dealing. Therefore, failure to warn (as long as the failure was material and would have affected a reasonable person's decision to accept or refrain from treatment) can be an independent ground for malpractice liability, or part of a larger malpractice case.

The patient has a reciprocal responsibility to provide accurate information and inform the doctor of changes during the course of treatment. A patient's failure to do this might be considered contributory negligence, reducing or even eliminating the potential recovery.

The principle of *res ipsa loquitur* (¶3217) is applicable in medical malpractice cases, e.g., when a surgical instrument is found in the abdomen of a person who underwent abdominal surgery. The res ipsa doctrine might also be applied if a part of the body that was not being treated is injured; if an operation is performed on the wrong patient or on the wrong part of the patient's body; or if a patient is burned during treatment. If a foreign object is discovered and removed promptly, the patient's damages would be small, based on the need to undergo a second operation, but with little or no recovery for pain and suffering.

[¶3220.2] Doctor-Patient Relationship

Except in emergencies, doctors have the right to refuse to enter into a doctor-patient relationship (e.g., if the patient is uninsured and unable to pay out-of-pocket, and the doctor is in private practice). But once the relationship is created, the doctor has an obligation to continue treatment as long as it is reasonably required, until the doctor has notified the patient of intent to terminate treatment, until another doctor is substituted as treating physician or the patient withdraws from further treatment. Failing to follow up (e.g., interpreting the results of medical tests ordered by the doctor) can constitute abandonment; so can failing to give the patient information about side effects that must be reported, or how to take medication safely.

However, the relationship is created by the patient's desire to consult the doctor, and the doctor's acceptance of the patient for treatment. Therefore, there is no doctor-patient relationship if someone other than the patient is the actual employer of the physician. (This is distinct from the question of who actually pays for the treatment or reimburses a patient who advances payment for treatment.)

For instance, a doctor who performs an employment physical or examines a Workers' Compensation claimant is working for the employer or Compensation system, not the patient, and thus can disclose medical information about the patient even if the patient does not want the information disclosed.

Depending on the facts and applicable law, more than one party may be involved and named as malpractice defendants. For instance, a hospital may be negligent in permitting certain doctors to have practice privileges. A hospital might also be negligent in supervising its house staff (doctors in training), or in permitting them to undertake procedures that are too sophisticated for their skill levels.

However, if a doctor transfers the care of a patient to a specialist or sends the patient to another health care provider for diagnostic tests or treatment, the negligence of these other providers will probably not be imputed to the first doctor (unless he or she had some reason to know that the other practitioners were not qualified). Similarly, if several doctors are treating a patient for different conditions, negligence will probably not be imputed.

Hospitals are clearly responsible for proper hiring and supervision of physicians who are hospital employees. It has also been held[6] that a hospital has a nondelegable duty to provide adequate Emergency Room services. Therefore, the hospital can be held strictly vicariously liable for ER doctors, even if they are not hospital employees. By soliciting patients, the hospital holds itself out as the single entity that provides integrated medical care.

In the case of a mistake in filling a prescription, giving an injection, or transfusing blood, a nurse or technician might be directly liable for the error, but there may also be vicarious liability of the doctor or hospital that failed to supervise properly. Generally speaking, the intervening or supervening negligence of another person relieves the doctor of malpractice liability. However, if the plaintiff was treated by many doctors and it is impossible to apportion liability (e.g., in a teaching hospital), then all will be liable.

In some instances, someone other than the patient becomes the plaintiff: e.g., when wrongful death is alleged, or when the non-patient suffers emotional distress. States vary in their approach to emotional distress claims. The emotional distress must be reasonably foreseeable. In some jurisdictions, the "zone of danger" rule is applied: i.e., only people physically at risk can bring a claim.[7]

Emotional distress claims are also brought by patients. For instance, a person wrongly diagnosed with cancer or AIDS may seek damages against the physician. Such a claim requires proof that the doctor breached the standard of care in making the diagnosis, and may require physical impact (e.g., weight loss, insomnia).

Except in very limited circumstances, strict liability in tort will not be applied to medical services. Even cases involving pharmaceuticals and, e.g., HIV-infected blood, are often dismissed on the theory that the health care provider offers services rather than products, so warranty and strict liability theories are inapplicable. Furthermore, any products liability claims that are tenable may have to be pursued against the manufacturer or distributor of the product, and not against the doctor or hospital that prescribed or used the product.

[¶3220.3] Duty of Care

Except in an absolute emergency, the duty of due care requires the physician to get a complete medical history, containing elements such as these:

- Patient's chief complaints
- Present symptoms
- Past history
- Hospitalizations
- Prescriptions now being taken
- Family history.

The patient's failure or refusal to provide complete, accurate information can operate as comparative negligence, reducing the potential recovery.

[¶3220.3.1] Medical Tests

After taking the patient's history, the doctor has an obligation to perform a physical examination, including recognized tests to discover the cause of the patient's symptoms. As long as the necessary equipment, and personnel qualified to interpret results, are available, it can violate the standard of care to fail to do tests such as CAT scans and MRIs.

The standard of care requires the performance of appropriate lab tests as required for diagnosis. Misinterpretation of test results also departs from the standard of care, although a non-specialist doctor is entitled to rely on conclusions drawn by a radiologist or other specialist.

"Self-regulatory" standards are an important indication of the duty of care. The malpractice attorney should consult the standards promulgated by the AMA (e.g., Principles of Medical Ethics) and the standards of local medical societies. The medical profession enforces these standards by removing hospital privileges of doctors who fail to meet the standards.

Hospitals have various review committees (tissue review committees that examine tumors and other tissues removed from patients); mortality review committees, and chart review committees. These committees issue reports after investigation of a negative result, or routinely. Committee reports can be important in establishing a doctor's departure from the standard of care, although these reports are often written in very discreet terms just for this reason.

The doctor has a duty to inform the patient how to treat and monitor his or her health condition. In prescribing drugs, doctors have a duty to follow the instructions provided by the drug manufacturer, unless there is some scientifically valid reason to depart from the instructions. It has been held, however that the warnings about particular drugs printed in the Physicians' Desk Reference (PDR) are admissible, but taken by itself, mere failure to follow those warnings is not malpractice. This result was reached because the PDR warnings do not set the standard of care for prescribing physicians.[8]

Information provided by the patient is confidential, and must not be disclosed by the doctor except in appropriate circumstances (e.g., as directed by the patient; in response to a subpoena). However, in some circumstances doctors are actually required to report information that would otherwise be confidential: e.g., when they treat a gunshot or knife wound; if they have reason to believe that a domestic partner or child has been physically or sexually abused.

If the medical profession deems several alternative procedures to be acceptable, a doctor will not be culpable by choosing one acceptable procedure rather than the others.

Continuing practice of medicine implies a duty to keep up with developments in medical care (including discovery of side effects of previously accepted treatments). If a case clearly exceeds a generalist's knowledge and skills, it is malpractice not to make a referral to a specialist. A doctor can be negligent in failing to order further medical tests that are warranted based on clinical observation or the results of earlier tests. Negligence can also be present if the doctor does not test for sensitivity to prescription drugs or fails to warn of the risk of side effects.

[¶3220.3.2] Loss of Chance

Although it is not universally recognized, many jurisdictions permit a "loss of chance" argument to be made, on the theory that incorrect diagnosis leads to incorrect treatment—and, more importantly, to treatment other than treatment that could have saved the patient's life, health, or function.

A possible problem with this theory is that a patient who suffers from a very fast-spreading disease (e.g., ovarian cancer) might not have had a chance of survival even if a correct diagnosis had been made. Loss of chance requires proof that is more likely than not that loss of chance was due to physician's negligence rather than the underlying disease.

[¶3220.4] Tort Reform in Medical Malpractice Cases

States have adopted various tort reform measures to limit the amount of malpractice litigation. These measures include permissive or mandatory arbitration of claims; increases in the plaintiff's burden of proof; requirement that the plaintiff's attorney provide a certificate of merit before a case can be filed; need for an expert witness affidavit or summary of expert testimony as a prerequisite to filing; and caps on damages.

Malpractice panels usually include a judge, an attorney, and a doctor. Some panels have jurisdiction to make awards; some make an initial determination on liability and damages; others are limited to a fact-finding role. However, sometimes the trial itself is a de novo hearing, (practice varies as to whether the panel's decision is admissible) and either side might be given the right to demand a de novo hearing.

If a state has a malpractice panel, resort to the panel is probably obligatory. Failure to do so can deprive the courts of subject-matter jurisdiction. The general rule is that the statute of limitations is tolled after a timely filing with the panel; while the panel is reviewing the claim; and for a prescribed time afterwards. Even if the panel ruled for the plaintiff, its conclusion will not be enough to support a jury verdict; expert testimony will still be required.

Because the patient has little or no opportunity to negotiate the contract, due process claims against mandatory arbitration may be successful. Because the arbitration panels typically include health care providers (doctors, hospital administrators), the panels can also be attacked for bias.

[¶3220.5] Informed Consent

Except in rare cases (e.g., an unconscious patient is brought to a hospital Emergency Room), treatment is not imposed on patients by the medical system. Instead, patients who have the legal right to control their own bodies seek medical assistance, and the health care provider renders services based on the informed consent of the patient. Carrying out medical treatment without the patient's consent (or without the consent of a surrogate decision-maker for a minor or incompetent patient), or carrying out treatment beyond the scope of the consent, could constitute assault and battery.

Although they may seem to be contractual in nature, patients' claims revolving around informed consent are really negligence claims: the patient takes the position that the doctor failed to make a full and accurate disclosure of the material risks inherent in the treatment (such as anesthesia risks in surgery; risks of medication side effects), with the result that the patient consented to procedures that he or she would have refused if given adequate information (or that a reasonable patient would have refused with the same knowledge). Risks are material if they would influence the treatment choice of a reasonable person. In other words, then, the failure to disclose was the cause of the injuries.

Anesthesia risks are especially high, so extensive warnings are required. Patients could aspirate vomit while unconscious; could be allergic to anesthetic agents; could receive an excessively high dose, leading to respiratory suppression and death or brain damage; and could be physically injured by a needle or tube used to induce anesthesia. Explosion of anesthetic gases is also a potential risk.

In special circumstances, the duty to warn might be excused: if the risk of not treating a patient whose consent cannot be obtained in an emergency outweighs the risks of treatment. A patient's emotional state might be such that the disclosure itself would be harmful.

[¶3220.5.1] Exceptions to Informed Consent

Sometimes the patient is unable to consent (is a child; is unconscious; is seriously mentally ill; is developmentally disabled). In such a situation (other than a severe emergency where there is no time to seek consent), informed consent must be obtained from an appropriate surrogate: a parent, court-appointed guardian, or agent serving under a durable power of attorney for health care, for instance.

If no guardian is available, it will often be necessary for the health care provider to bring an emergency guardianship proceeding so that a guardian can be appointed who can consent to the treatment. Guardianship statutes typically provide that a hospital or doctor has standing to file a guardianship petition to ensure that treatment can be provided legitimately—and that reimbursement will be available for the cost of treatment, which was not undertaken on a volunteer basis.

[¶3225] Malpractice Litigation

The question of what was actually done during treatment, and how it compares to what should have been done, is naturally a highly technical question, most aspects of which are beyond the scope of lay testimony. (The plaintiff can, of course, testify as to topics such as pain and limitation of function.)

Therefore, the medical malpractice case is highly dependent on expert testimony, to show what the standard of care was; that the standard was breached; that the breach was the proximate cause of the plaintiff's injuries; and the amount of the damages.

For obvious reasons, defense expert witnesses are easier to find that plaintiffs' witnesses. Many doctors are unwilling to testify against their fellow physicians. Furthermore, since malpractice defense is largely conducted by insurance companies, they have access to a group of experts willing to testify.

One analysis is that invasion of privacy consists of public disclosure of embarrassing facts, so that personal matters are publicized in a way that an ordinary person would find highly offensive, when there is no legitimate public concern over the information.

- Trespass to land: traditionally, this tort was committed by intentional entry on property (whether or not the intent was to trespass), and actual damages did not have to be shown, and at least nominal damages were always awarded when any trespass was proved.

  Today, trespass can be either an intentional or a negligent tort, and liability will probably not be imposed without actual damage, unless the trespasser was reckless or at least negligent. Contemporary trespass damages are all direct harm from the trespass, plus consequential damages (e.g., water damage caused by a faucet that the trespasser turned on but failed to turn off). Depending on the jurisdiction, environmental trespass (such as entry of airborne particles, or contamination of underground water) might be treated as either trespass or nuisance.

- Trespass to chattel and conversion are intentional torts to personal property. Trespass to chattel is intentional interference with the owner's rights, e.g., by destroying or damaging the property, using it without permission, or depriving the owner of possession or control. Trespass to chattel is solely an intentional tort, although wrongful motive is not required; liability will probably not be imposed without actual damage to the chattel.

  Conversion, another purely intentional tort, is severe, aggravated trespass to chattel that permanently deprives the owner of control. In effect, the trespass is so severe that the court forces the tortfeasor to "buy" the chattel, because the measure of damages is the entire value of the chattel plus interest.

  Liability in a trespass to chattel or conversion case depends on factors such as the extent and duration of control exercised by the tortfeasors; extent of assertion of rights inconsistent with the rights of others; the tortfeasor's good or bad faith; the degree of harm to the chattel; and the degree of inconvenience or expense resulting from the harm.

Some jurisdictions treat "spoliation"—intentional or negligent interference with a civil action by destruction of evidence—as a separate tort.[21]

[¶3240.3] Misrepresentation and Fraud

Misrepresentation torts usually occur in a business context. See immediately below for business torts; also see ¶205.6 for a discussion of warranties, 700 for consumer protection law, and 630.1 for securities litigation premised on alleged misreprestation by the issuer company.

Under traditional tort principles, misrepresentation damages were limited to pecuniary harm caused by the misrepresentation to the persons to whom the misrepresentations were made. However, the Restatement (2nd) of Torts §531 position is that misrepresentation liability extends to anyone who could be foreseen to rely on the truth of the representations.

Misrepresentation liability usually requires scienter: the person making the statement must have known that it was false. A representation is not fraudulent if the person making the representation believes it, even if belief is foolish.

Negligent misrepresentation might be actionable if it caused actual physical harm, or if there was some duty (such as fiduciary duty) running from the person making the representation to the recipient of the representation. A negligent misrepresentation could also furnish a defense (if someone who relied on the misrepresentation is sued, e.g., for breach of contract) or a counterclaim.

Misrepresentation is only actionable if reliance on the representation was justifiable. The highest standard is required of factual representations apparently within the speaker's knowledge, that are material[22] to the transaction. Hearers are expected to "discount" statements based on the speaker's obvious interest (e.g., a used-car dealer's description of the cars on the lot).

There may also be a duty to disclose facts discovered after making a representation that was true or believed true, but which has now been rendered untrue or misleading by subsequent events.

Misrepresentation plaintiffs' remedies fall into two categories: keeping the transaction intact and receiving fraud remedies, or undoing part or all of the transaction. Another option is to stop performing on the contract, then raise fraud as a defense to suit for breach of contract.

[¶3240.4] Business Torts

Torts committed in the course of business include:

- Unfair competition, which can be committed, e.g., by confusion of trade identity, palming off (substituting goods other than those ordered); misappropriation of a distinctive characterization; and false advertising
- Copyright infringement
- Trademark infringement
- Trademark dilution
- Patent infringement
- Disparagement or trade libel: i.e., non-privileged statements about the quality of a business' property or products, if the statements are, in fact, false and cause actual damage. In some jurisdictions, disparagement/trade libel causes of action will be cognizable only if the defendant acted with actual malice. Disparagement of someone else's products must be distinguished from "puffing" of one's own products, which is considered permissible as long as it is not tantamount to deception of consumers
- Misappropriation of trade secrets
- Tortious inducement of breach of contract (e.g., inducing a supplier to renege on its contracts to supply a competitor; inducing an individual to abandon an employment contract).

If the defendant's duty arises out of a contractual relationship between the parties, there is no tort liability for any harm caused by breaching the contract by not starting performance in the first place. However, once performance begins, tort liability can be imposed for intentional, reckless, or negligent misperformance, including either misfeasance or nonfeasance.

[¶3240.4.1] Employment Torts

The employment relation can also give rise to tort claims[23]: for instance, that the employer wrongfully terminated an employee, that sexual harassment occurred, or that the employee suffered emotional injury (with or without physical consequences).

In many instances, state-law claims will be preempted by federal laws such as the anti-discrimination laws discussed at ¶350, to the extent that they involve the federal statutes themselves. However, in some instances state tort claims will be permitted: for instance, if the employer company is too small to be covered by the federal statutes.

Employers have the right to dismiss at-will employees for good cause, or for no reason at all, but are not permitted to dismiss them for an improper cause, such as discrimination against a suspect classification (e.g., race, sex, or age discrimination) or retaliation for exercising a legal right (e.g., filing a legitimate Workers' Compensation claim).

In some circumstances, the discharge will be wrongful because it violates public policy. Examples include discharging an employee who serves on a jury, or a "whistleblower" who exposes the employer's unlawful conduct.

[¶3240.5] "Life Torts"

This category includes several controversial related torts. These torts are controversial in that not all jurisdictions recognize them as causes of action, or to the same extent. These torts are easy to confuse, but the potential plaintiff or litigator must distinguish between them based on who is permitted to sue, on what grounds, and for what elements of damages:

- Wrongful pregnancy is the parent's claim that a healthy but unwanted child was born because of the defendant's negligence in prescribing birth control or performing sterilization or abortion. Depending on the jurisdiction, damages may be denied altogether (on the grounds that birth of a healthy child is not a compensable injury); limited to the cost of rearing the child reduced by benefits of having a child; damages including the cost of rearing the child may be granted, or some damages permitted but childrearing expenses excluded
- Wrongful birth is the parent's cause of action alleging that the pregnancy would not have been conceived or carried to term if they had been properly warned of genetic characteristics leading to the child's defect. The elements of damages include the extra expenses of rearing a disabled child and the parents' emotional distress
- Wrongful life is the impaired individual's own cause of action based on grossly poor quality of life due to the defect

- The tort of wrongful survival is closely related to battery: it refers to life-saving or life-sustaining treatment provided contrary to the expressed wishes of the patient.

[¶3250] Automobile-Related Torts and No-Fault

The operation of automobiles can cause physical injury to the occupants of one's own car or other cars, and property damage (to other vehicles as well as other objects). The obvious defendant in an automobile-related case is the driver, but other persons may be liable instead or additionally. The owner of the car may be liable, based on agency concepts or the "family purpose" doctrine (where someone else is allowed to drive the car for the benefit of the owner's family).

A person who allows a minor, incapacitated, or drunken person to drive might be liable for "negligent entrustment." If the driver was an employee acting in the scope of employment, the employer might be liable on agency principles. "Dram-shop" liability is imposed on bars and restaurants (and sometimes on social hosts) for furnishing liquor to an obviously intoxicated person who then drove unsafely.

See ¶1440 for a discussion of automobile insurance and ¶6020.5 for drunk driving offenses.

[¶3250.1] No-Fault

Many of the injuries that the tort system has to cope with are the result of automobile accidents. These accidents differ greatly in the conduct and liability of the drivers. Sometimes both were seriously negligent or even reckless; sometimes neither was in any way culpable—or anything in between. If every automobile case were litigated, the court system, already strained by many other kinds of cases, would be completely unworkable.

Many states have adopted some kind of "no-fault" system to relieve pressure on the court system, reduce insurance premiums, and speed up recoveries that injured persons can use to get medical care, or owners of damaged cars can use to get repairs or new cars. Massachusetts was the first state to adopt no-fault insurance, in 1971. Today, most of the states have adopted some kind of no-fault system, whether in the form of an "add-on" that leaves tort litigation intact, or a fairly comprehensive system under which only very serious injuries can be litigated.

Classic tort litigation is a third-party system. That is, when someone is injured or his or her car is damaged, the tortfeasor (or, more practically, the tortfeasor's insurance company) has to pay. Under a first-party system, the person who suffers injury or property damage looks to his or her own insurer for compensation.

A no-fault system has more first-party than third-party elements. In theory, all persons suffering automobile-related bodily injury or economic loss can get compensated, whether they had any share in causing the accident or not. The system is financed by automobile drivers, via compulsory insurance (rather than public funds or the pool of potential victims). However, the no-fault system does not compensate pain and suffering; such damages are available only if the injured per-

[¶3270.4] Consent

Consent (as long as the plaintiff had capacity to consent)is a defense against most torts. Consent can be manifested by silence and inaction in a situation in which a non-consenting person would be expected to protest. It can also be inferred from custom and usage. Consent is implied in some circumstances: for instance, to give medical treatment in an emergency to an unconscious person. Consent that stems from the plaintiff's ignorance, misunderstanding, or material mistake is nevertheless valid in the tort context, unless the defendant knew of the mistake or induced it through misrepresentation.

The defendant's mistake (even if not negligent) is not necessarily a defense to an intentional tort claim. However, mistake is often relevant to the existence of a privilege that insulates the defendant's actions from liability. Privilege could be asserted based on the defendant's reasonable belief about the state of facts, especially if the plaintiff induced the mistake.

[¶3270.5] Self-Defense

Self-defense is a defense to claims of assault, battery or unlawful imprisonment, if the defendant acted to prevent a threat of unlawful confinement or even negligently caused harm. However, the defendant is justified in using only enough force as immediately necessary for self-protection and the protection of others. Reasonable force can be used in defense of property, but only if actual intrusion has occurred, or there is a threat of immediate interference with the defendant's possession of property.

Accidental injuries caused to third persons in the course of self-defense are analyzed on a negligence standard.

A limited self-help privilege is allowed for immediate forcible retaking of chattels that have been wrongfully taken by force, or that have been obtained by fraud or duress. This is the principle that authorizes reasonable detention of shoplifters and prevents it from constituting unlawful imprisonment.

[¶3280] Tort Damages

The basic elements of tort damages are property damage plus direct medical and surgical costs, plus past and future lost earnings, plus pain and suffering. Sometimes "hedonic" damages (for loss of quality of life) will be available.

In a wrongful death case, the traditional measure of damages was pre-death pain and suffering of the victim,[34] plus income lost by the dependents of the decedent. Originally, lost income was the only recoverable element. Over time, additional elements were added.

Husbands of injured or deceased wives could recover for "consortium" (loss of households and sexual services). The loss-of-consortium action has become unisex, and has been extended to non-economic and non-sexual aspects of family relationships.

There is a trend toward permitting the children of decedents to recover for loss of emotional support and parental guidance, as well as for lost financial support, and parents may be able to recover for loss of companionship and perhaps economic loss when their children are injured or killed. (In some cases, even parents of adults will have a cause of action of this type.)

[¶3280.1] Shared Liability

In many situations involving multiple tortfeasors, liability will be joint and several. That is, the plaintiff has the option of suing any tortfeasor, all of them, or any combination of tortfeasors. Defendants can then bring in other potentially liable parties if they believe that it is unjust for them to stand trial without the others. Furthermore, if a judgment or verdict is granted, it is the plaintiff's option which defendant(s) to pursue for payment, although joint tortfeasors who pay more than their fair share are entitled to contribution from other liable parties in percentages reflecting the liability of the others.

Contribution has to be distinguished from indemnification. Contribution is sharing of the liability among defendants to reflect their relative culpability. Indemnification shifts the entire loss from one tortfeasor to another, because the relieved tortfeasor is entitled to indemnification by law or as a result of a contract. All jurisdictions allow indemnification, although some do not provide for contribution.

The basic rule is that all damages are to be recovered at once, in a single suit, to restore the plaintiff to pre-injury condition.

The "collateral source" rule permits plaintiffs to recover damages for medical expenses and time lost from work, even if the plaintiff did not pay for these out of pocket, and a "collateral source" (such as insurance or professional courtesy) made the actual payment.

The general rule is that tort plaintiffs have an obligation to mitigate damages, such as taking reasonable steps to treat injuries and prevent future harm to property. A minority of jurisdictions impose this requirement in advance of the injury, for instance by wearing a seat belt or helmet. If so, the defendant will not be liable for whatever percentage of the injury is attributable to the plaintiff's failure to take such steps.

Another general rule is that a prevailing party is entitled to receive attorneys' fees and litigation costs as an element of damages only if an applicable statute authorizes such an award. Otherwise, each party remains responsible for its own fees and costs.

[¶3280.2] Structured Settlements

Tort settlements are frequently "structured," especially if the plaintiff is a child or incapacitated person. In a structured settlement, the plaintiff receives a series of annuity-type payments rather than a lump sum.[35] This is preferable for the payor, of course, who can either continue managing the principal sum and make only the required payment each year, or who can purchase an annuity to make the payments. Structuring the settlement benefits a plaintiff who might oth-

Removal is considered a civil rather than a criminal proceeding (even though many removal proceedings in fact involve persons convicted of crimes within the U.S.), so *Miranda* warnings are not required. However, 8 CFR §242.2(b) does require similar warnings to be given at the time of an immigration arrest.

If an alien is taken into custody after an immigration arrest, INA §236(a) says that the alien can be kept in custody; released on bond of at least $1,500; or released on conditional parole. (If the alien was admitted lawfully, but removal is sought due to a conviction for aggravated felony, release on bond requires demonstration of willingness to appear at hearings, and lack of danger to the community; see INA §238(a)(1) for special expedited removal proceedings for convicted aggravated felons.) Usually, aliens who are not security or bail risks will be released on their own recognizance. The bond or parole can be revoked at any time, and the alien re-arrested.

Under 8 CFR §239.1, the removal process is commenced by filing of Notice to Appear issued by an official qualified to issue warrants, based on a prima facie showing that the alien can be removed from the United States.

Removal proceedings, under INA §§239-240, require proper notice to the alien, who has the right to counsel (including appointed counsel) and can offer evidence and cross-examine the witnesses against him or her. Any order of removal must be based on reasonable, substantial, and probative evidence (i.e., not proof beyond a reasonable doubt; once again, this is not a criminal proceeding). If the alien has already been admitted, the INS has the burden of proof (with a clear and convincing evidence standard) of showing removability.

The alien must be given a chance to designate a country where he or she will be sent if removal is ordered; this designation is not an admission that the alien considers removal appropriate (INA §241(b)(2)).

Once removed, INA §212 provides that special permission from the Immigration and Naturalization Service is required for the removed person to re-enter the U.S. at any time within five years of the removal.

[¶3370.1] Grounds for Removal

Pre-IIRIRA law recognized several grounds for excluding potential entrants, e.g., criminal convictions; terrorism; voluntary membership in a Communist or other totalitarian party; becoming a public charge within five years of entry; and a catch-all barring entrance of a person whose entrance would be contrary to U.S. foreign policy. INA §212(a) contains the current list of ten grounds for inadmissibility, e.g., ineligibility for citizenship; health reasons; criminal record; U.S. national security issues; likelihood of becoming a public charge if admitted. IIRIRA added a category of aliens who overstay a visa or otherwise are unlawfully remaining within the U.S.

The applicant for admission has the burden of proof, under INA §240(c)(2)(A), of proving "clearly and beyond doubt" that he or she does not fall into any category of inadmissible persons. The burden then shifts to the INS to prove, by clear and convincing evidence, that removal is appropriate.

See INA §237(a) for the numerous categories of circumstances that will justify removal of a person who has already entered the United States. Persons who are entitled to conditional permanent resident status can be removed unless they convert their status to unconditional permanent resident. Removal for marriage fraud is also provided by §237(a).

Conviction of a criminal offense in the United States is grounds for removal, if a moral turpitude felony[15] is committed within five years of admission (or two moral turpitude crimes at any time). Conviction is defined as a guilty verdict or judicial decision or a guilty or nolo contendere plea, plus some form of punishment, plus a possibility of sanctions for probation violations or failure to comply with a court order.

Other offenses can also be grounds for removal, e.g., violation of any drug law (even if not tantamount to conviction of a moral-turpitude felony) or becoming a drug addict, as well as specific immigration-related offenses such as high-speed flight from an immigration checkpoint or assisting someone else to prepare a false immigration-related document. "Undesirables," including aliens convicted of domestic violence offenses or stalking, are also removable. Because the immigration consequences of a serious conviction are so drastic, the lawyer representing an alien defendant might want to suggest an immediate plea bargain to a misdemeanor or other charge not involving moral turpitude.

Commencement of removal proceedings is by INS Notice to Appear, directing the alien to appear at immigration court to defend against a charge of inadmissibility: see INA §239.

Post-IIRIRA, judicial review of an order of expedited removal is quite limited. INA §242(e)(2) now limits review to a habeas corpus proceeding, involving only four issues: whether the petitioner is an alien; whether his or her removal was ordered under INA §236(b)(1); whether the alien can prove lawful permanent resident status by a preponderance of evidence; and whether asylum or refugee status is available. Also see §242(a)(2)(A), depriving all courts of jurisdiction to review the Attorney General's decision to use expedited removal, or the expedited removal of individual aliens.

An early 1999 Supreme Court decision[16] holds that the IIRIRA limitations on judicial review (8 USC §1252(g)) prevent federal courts from reviewing pre-IIRIRA attempts to deport resident aliens, even if it is alleged that the deportation attempts were discriminatory and premised on the individual's unpopular political views.

Aliens lacking proper documentation when they seek to enter the U.S. can be removed from the U.S. without prior hearing or opportunity for review, unless the alien seeks asylum or expresses a fear of persecution if returned to the home country.

[¶3370.1] Discretionary Relief

Immigration judges have the power to grant discretionary relief at the application of the alien, postponing removal or permitting the alien to remain within the U.S. The alien must prove eligibility for discretionary relief (see 8 CFR §240.8), but it is up to the immigration judge to grant or deny any discretionary relief for which the alien is eligible. IIRIRA bars judicial review of decisions about discretionary relief.

There are seven categories of discretionary relief:

- Voluntary departure
- Cancellation of removal
- Restriction of removal
- Stay of removal
- Adjustment of status
- Asylum
- Other discretionary relief

In rare cases, governmental misconduct will be held to estop removal of an alien (or other negative immigration action).

Voluntary departure is an alien's agreement to leave the U.S., at his or her own expense: INA §240B. An alien who elects voluntary departure can choose his or her next destination, and can attempt to re-enter the U.S. without being subject to the 10-year bar on re-entering the U.S. after removal (20 years after a second removal; the bar is permanent after conviction of an aggravated felony).

Cancellation of removal, governed by INA §240A, means permitting certain long-term residents to remain within the United States if they have not been convicted of crimes, are persons of good moral character, and their removal would create exceptional and extremely unusual hardship to immediate family members (not the alien him- or herself). (See *INS v. Hector*, 479 U.S. 85 (Sup.Ct. 1986).) If cancellation of removal is granted, the alien's status is altered to that of permanent resident, but only 4,000 adjustments to permanent resident status can be made per year on this basis.

[¶3370.2] Appeals

Aliens who have been found removable by an immigration judge can either take administrative or judicial appeal (subject to AEDPA and IIRIRA limitations), or apply for discretionary relief. Relief must be requested before the order of removal is executed. See 8 CFR §3.23 for the motion to reopen or reconsider (using Form I-328).

[¶3370.2.1] Executive Office for Immigration Review

The Executive Office for Immigration Review (EOIR) is an administrative body (not, for Constitutional purposes, a court system), comprising the immigration courts and the Board of Immigration Appeals. It is independent of the INS and provides some degree of review power for INS decisions.

The immigration judges handle the unified removal hearings prescribed by IIRIRA, as well as proceedings to rescind adjustment of status and withdraw approval of schools attended by non-immigrant foreign students. Decisions of immigration judges become final unless appealed to the Board of Immigration Appeals (BIA). The 15-member BIA is divided into five permanent three-judge panels. See 8 CFR §3.1 for the requirements for BIA appeals.

[¶3370.2.2] Judicial Review

Many Constitutional provisions are limited in their applicability to U.S. citizens, or at least to legal residents. Recent legislation has greatly limited the extent to which would-be immigrants and potential deportees can use the court system.

Both AEDPA and IIRIRA have restricted the judicial review of immigration decisions, stating that discretionary decisions of the Attorney General (other than asylum decisions) cannot be judicially reviewed. However, the Ninth Circuit position[17] is that all judicial review cannot be eliminated. Therefore, to the extent that INA §242(g)'s current provisions rule out court review of a final deportation order that is premised on criminal activity, then the alien can use 28 USC §2241, the general habeas corpus statute.

Post-IIRIRA, INA §242 gives an alien 30 days from the date of a final order of removal to file a petition for review by the Court of Appeals. Unless the court issues a stay of removal, even filing the appeal does not stay the removal. The Court of Appeals' sole inquiry is whether the removal proceeding violated Due Process or was conducted in an arbitrary, capricious, or illegal fashion. Only issues raised during the removal hearing and placed on the record can be heard on appeal.

[¶3370.3] Criminal Immigration Offenses

Under INA §275, it is an offense, punishable by a fine and/or up to six months' imprisonment, for an alien to enter or attempt to enter the United States without authorization, by escaping inspection or making a willfully false misrepresentation of material fact. Repeat offenses can be penalized by up to two years' imprisonment. In addition, civil penalties of up to $500 can be imposed for actual or attempted improper entrance.

Section 276 makes it a felony (maximum sentence: two years) for a person to re-enter or attempt to re-enter the United States after removal, except in the rare cases where the Attorney General has authorized the re-entry. Pleading guilty under §275 or 276 will render the individual vulnerable to removal.

Once in the United States for 30 days or more, aliens have a duty to register and be fingerprinted; willful failure to comply carries a fine and up to six months' imprisonment (INA §266(a)), with lesser penalties for failing to provide written notice of change of address. Non-compliance is also grounds for removal. These provisions are seldom enforced.

It is unlawful, with a penalty of a fine and/or up to five years' imprisonment, to smuggle (or attempt to smuggle) aliens into this country: see INA §274(a)(1)(A). A fine and up to a year's imprisonment per transaction can be imposed under §274(a)(2) for bringing or attempting to bring an unauthorized person into the U.S., knowingly or with reckless disregard of the person's immigration status. The sentence can be up to 10 years if §274(a)(2) is violated for commercial gain; the sentence range is five to fifteen years for third or subsequent offenses. Even if the alien never manages to enter U.S. territory, conspiracy to violate §274 is nevertheless illegal.

Also see §274(a)(1)(A)(ii) for penalties for knowing or reckless transportation of an alien within the United States, if such transportation is in furtherance of

¶4100

Personal Income Tax and Tax Planning

Note: This discussion reflects law in effect as of August, 1999. As of that time, both Houses of Congress had passed the Taxpayer Refund and Relief Act of 1999, H.R. 2488, which calls for significant tax cuts, especially for businesses. At press time, the President had announced his intention to veto the bill.

[¶4101]

The much-loathed and despised personal income tax is imposed by §61 on all income other than that specifically exempted. The basic tax computation therefore consists of aggregating all income items; taking certain deductions to compute Adjusted Gross Income (§62); either itemizing other deductions or claiming the standard deduction; and claiming personal and dependency deductions. Taxable income is then determined by using the tax tables (for taxable income under $100,000) or the tax rate schedules (for greater income). Finally, any applicable credits are used to reduce the amount of tax.

For most individuals, withholding during the year will represent the full amount of tax liability, and therefore the taxpayer will have a choice between receiving a refund and applying the excess to the following year's taxes.

Self-employed persons, persons with significant non-employment income (e.g., from investments), and high-income persons (whose employment income is higher than the maximum amount covered by withholding tables) will have to make quarterly estimated tax payments in addition to the annual return. If the quarterly payments are insufficient by more than 20%, they will also have to pay a penalty excise tax in addition to making up the shortfall.

U.S. citizens are subject to income tax on all their income, whether or not it derives from sources within the U.S. More or less the same is true of resident aliens. Non-resident aliens are subject to taxation on U.S. source investment income and income connected with U.S. businesses, even if the actual source of the income is outside the United States.[1]

Certain concepts are sometimes needed to file personal income tax returns, but are more common in the corporate tax context. See, for instance, the discussion of depreciation at ¶453.

[¶4101.1] Obligation to File

Persons with very low incomes are not obligated to file income tax returns; persons over 65 are allowed to have slightly more income than "junior citizens" before a tax return will be required.

Using 1999 figures, a return is required by §6012(a)(1) for a single person who has $7050 in gross income ($8100 if over 65), $12,700 for a married person filing a joint return ($13,550 if one spouse is over 65, $14,400 if both are), only $2750 for a married person filing a separate return, $9100 for a head of household ($10,150 for a senior citizen head of household), and $9950 for a surviving spouse ($10,800 for a surviving spouse over 65).

Some persons with even lower incomes are obligated to file. For example, a person who can be claimed as a dependent on someone else's tax return must file a return if his or her gross income exceeds the standard deduction (see ¶4150.11), or has unearned income over $700. Anyone with net earnings from self-employment over $400 must file, no matter how low his or her gross income. However, a return does not have to be filed for a child subject to "kiddie tax" if the child's parents elect to include the child's income on their own return(s).

[¶4101.2] Tax Brackets

The basic tax brackets are 15%, 28%, 31%, 36%, and 39.6%. The breakpoints between one bracket and another differ based on the taxpayer's filing status [¶4103.3]. The question of tax brackets is complicated for high-income individuals because the applicability of various deductions phases out when income exceeds certain levels. Children under age 14 are subject to the "kiddie tax" [¶4101.3.4] imposed to limit the advantages of shifting income within the family.

[¶4101.3] Filing Status

The basic filing statuses are:

- Single
- Married, filing a joint return
- Married, filing a separate return
- Head of household

In addition, special tax rules apply to children under 14 and widows and widowers for the two years following the death of the spouse. (For the actual year of the spouse's death, the widow/er is permitted to file an ordinary joint return, unless he or she remarries by the end of the year, or unless an executor or administrator is appointed by the end of the year: §6013(a)(2).)

[¶4101.3.1] Marital Status

In most instances, a marital joint return will give the best tax consequences, marital separate returns will give the worst. However, some high-income married couples suffer a "marriage penalty" and in fact pay more than they would if they were unmarried and cohabiting.

Marital status is determined as of the close of the tax year (or as of the date of a spouse's death). In general, two persons are married if they are married under state law, but the federal Defense of Marriage Act, P.L. 104-199 (9/21/96) restricts the definition of marriage to a relationship involving one man and one woman.

Cohabitants are not married for tax purposes unless they have a locally recognized common-law marriage.

Marriage is terminated by a decree of divorce or separate maintenance, but not by mere separation or the granting of an interlocutory decree. The IRS has long ruled that a pattern of end-year divorces, followed by remarriage early in the new year, will not be given effect to avoid the marriage penalty; the divorces will simply be disregarded.[2] For tax purposes, an annulment is treated as if the couple had never been married, so they must file amended returns for pre-annulment years in which they filed joint returns.

[¶4101.3.2] Head of Household Status

Head of household status, which is generally less favorable than married/joint filing, but more favorable than filing as a single person, is available to taxpayers who are unmarried, or married but living apart from their spouses, while maintaining a household in which a qualified person (generally, a child, elderly parent, or other relative) lives for more than half the tax year. See §2(b)(1).

A child of divorced parents is presumed to live with the parent who has legal custody. The presumption can be rebutted if the child actually lives with the parent who does not have legal custody. It is not relevant which parent can claim the dependency deduction.

Head of household status is also available if the taxpayer maintains a household where his or her dependent parents live, even if the taxpayer lives somewhere else. To claim head of household status, the taxpayer must provide at least 50% of the expenses of running the qualifying household. Taxpayers who qualify for head of household status may also qualify for other tax relief provisions, such as the Earned Income Credit and Child Care Credit.

[¶4101.3.3] Tax Status of Surviving Spouse

Although technically a decedent's death ends his or her tax year, the surviving spouse is permitted to file a joint return by §6013(a)(2) for the year of the decedent spouse's death unless the decedent had filed prior to dying; or unless a personal representative has been appointed before the return has been filed (and also before its due date). (Once appointed, the personal representative's duties include filing the final income tax return.)

A decedent's final tax return is still due on the same date it would have been due if he or she had survived and, although the final return is a short-period return, the decedent is entitled to claim the full standard deduction and personal exemption. These need not be prorated for the portion of the year the decedent lived.

A surviving spouse is also entitled, under §1(a)(2), to use joint-return rates for two years following the date of the spouse's death, if he or she has not remarried and maintains (paying at least 50% of the cost) a household for a dependent child. To qualify for this relief, the surviving spouse must have been able to file a joint return in the year of the decedent spouse's death (i.e., must not have been divorced or legally separated).

[¶4101.3.4] Kiddie Tax

The "kiddie tax" is imposed by §1(g) on the unearned income of children under 14. The child is taxed at his or her own rates on the first $1400 of unearned income, but the parent's highest rate is applied to additional unearned income. (However, in the rare case that the child is in a higher bracket than the parent, the child's rate prevails.)

The kiddie tax is reported on Form 8615. If the child's income comes solely from interest and dividends and is between $700 and $1700, the parent can elect on Form 8814 to include the child's gross income in excess of $1400 on the parent's return. If this is done, the child need not file a return.

[¶4105] Forms and Tax Compliance

The basic personal income tax form is the "long-form" 1040, for which many schedules and attachments are available. A shorter form, 1040A, is intended for use by taxpayers with simpler tax situations. An even simpler "postcard" form, the 1040EZ, can be used by taxpayers who do not have multiple sources of income and who do not itemize. However, several common credits cannot be claimed on the 1040EZ, only on one of the longer forms.

[¶4105.1] Electronic Filing

The IRS has permitted various forms of electronic filing for several years (from submission of supporting documentation to filing of an entire form, with a written signature supplied separately). Businesses were supposed to be compelled to file in electronic form, but difficulties with implementing the IRS computer systems have led to several delays in the mandate of electronic filing. See IR 98-28, 3/31/98, deferring from 7/1/98 to 1/1/99 the requirement that business with $50,000 employment tax liability in both 1995 and 1996 would have to use the EFTPS electronic filing system.

A Proposed Rule[3] suggests increasing the threshold for mandatory electronic filing from $50,000 to $200,000 as of January 1, 2000; small businesses will probably not be penalized for filing on paper rather than electronically, as long as their filings are timely.

The IRS Restructuring and Reform Act of 1998 (IRSRRA), P.L. 105-206, reinforces Congress' commitment to moving tax compliance from an all-paper system to a predominantly electronic one. At least 80% of tax filing is supposed to be in electronic form by 2007.

However, under current law (§6061), any taxpayer filing an electronic return must also file the paper Form 8453 containing the taxpayer's written signature. Furthermore, a taxpayer who seeks to have tax return information released (e.g., in connection with litigation or business planning) must make the request on a paper form. The 1040PC program allows tax preparers to file returns on plain-paper sheets generated by a computer, using IRS-approved software; the end results can be scanned by the IRS. The Telefile program allows very simple returns to be filed via touch-tone telephone.

"as an annuity" if it is paid at regular intervals occurring at least once a year after the start date. Lump sums and other withdrawals that are not received in annuity form are taxed to the extent that they exceed the cost of the contract.

The annuitant must compute an "exclusion ratio" to determine what part of each payment is a non-taxable return of capital, and what part is taxable appreciation. The exclusion ratio is simply the cost of the contract divided by its expected return.

For a term annuity (e.g., one that will make payments for 10 years—to the designated beneficiary, if the annuitant is no longer alive), the expected return is just the number of payments times the amount of each payment. For a life or joint life annuity, the expected return equals the payments to be made in one year, times the life expectancy(ies) as measured by official IRS tables.

Once the entire "investment in the contract" (capital; the total premiums paid before the annuity starts, minus any amount received before the start date and not included in income for tax purposes) has been recovered (typically, when the taxpayer reaches his or her actuarially predicted life expectancy), each payment is fully taxable.

If there is no investment in the contract (e.g., the annuity was received as a gift, or is provided by someone else's will), then all payments are 100% taxable. In contrast, if the investment in the contract exceeds the expected return, then no tax is imposed on the payments. The investment in the contract must also be reduced if the annuity has a refund feature, because the annuitant's risk is less and therefore there is more taxable income.

A single-life annuity terminates with the death of the annuitant. If the annuitant dies before his or her predicted life expectancy, the unrecovered investment in the contract can be deducted on the deceased annuitant's final income tax return. See §72(b)(3)(A). Because such an annuity ends when its recipient dies, there is nothing to include in his or her taxable estate: §2039. However, if the annuity is a joint and survivor annuity (payments are made while both annuitants are alive, and continue, often in reduced form, to the survivor), then when one annuitant dies, §2039 requires inclusion in the estate of the decedent the present value of payments that will be made to the SURVIVOR.

The tax code's annuity provisions also require annuity contracts to provide that, if the annuitant dies on or after the start date, with part of the investment in the contract still undistributed, the balance must be distributed to the designated beneficiary at least as rapidly as payments would have been made to the annuitant. Section 72(s)(1) provides that, in case of death before the annuity start date, the entire interest must be distributed within five years; or, if a beneficiary has been designated, the interest can be distributed over the beneficiary's life or a period of years that does not exceed the beneficiary's predicted life expectancy.

[¶4130] Capital Gains Tax

A capital asset is one that is amenable to appreciation (or depreciation) in value, and that is not inventory or stock-in-trade for the taxpayer. For most taxpayers, the two commonly-found categories of capital assets are investment securities (e.g., stocks and bonds) and the family home(s). Long-term capital gains receive more favorable tax treatment than short-term gains.

[¶4130.1] Capital Gain/Loss Calculation

Section 1222 provides a somewhat cumbersome set of rules for calculating an individual's capital gains or losses. First, all short-term transactions are aggregated, to determine the net short-term gain or loss. Next, the same calculation is performed for all long-term transactions. The individual taxpayer's net capital gains consist of the excess of his or her net long gains over net short losses. The taxpayer has capital gain net income, which must be included in gross income, to the extent that capital gains minus capital losses exceed $0. There is no limit on the amount of capital gain a taxpayer may have to recognize—but the capital loss current deduction is subject to strict limits.

Limitations are placed on individual taxpayers' capital loss deductions by §1211(b). The taxpayer can deduct only the net loss (losses minus gains) or $3,000 ($1,500 for a married taxpayer filing a separate return), whichever is lower. Capital losses can be carried forward indefinitely. When items are carried forward, they retain their characterization as short- or long-term.

[¶4130.2] Holding Period

Under TRA '97, the rules originally enacted effective for sales after 5/6/97 defined long-term capital gain as gain deriving from the sale of an asset held at least 18 months. The maximum capital gains tax rate was set at 20%, a significant reduction from the 28% rate imposed by prior law. Furthermore, taxpayers in the minimum (15%) income tax bracket were to be taxed only 10% on their long-term capital gains.[5]

The Tax Technical Corrections Act of 1998, Title VI of the IRSRRA, P.L. 105-206, changed the rules once again, by reinstating the definition of long-term assets as those held for 12 months or more. The change is effective after December 31, 1997. Inherited property is deemed to have been held for 12 months, and thus to be eligible for long-term capital gain treatment.

TRA '97 adds a category that might be called "ultra-long-term capital gains": that is, sales occurring after 12/31/2000, of assets held for at least **five** years, are taxed by §1(h) at 18% (or 8%, for lowest-bracket taxpayers).

As if all that weren't complex enough, §1(h) also imposes a maximum tax rate of 28% on gain recognized on art works and collectable items, if the items were held for over one year.

[¶4130.3] Small Business Stock Provisions

The maximum tax rate is also 28% on §1202 gain: that is, 50% of the gain on qualified small business stock held for five years or more. (The other 50% is excluded from income.) A qualified small business corporation is a C corporation with aggregate gross assets under $50 million.

Section 1244 provides that the original purchaser of such stock from the corporation (but not a transferee of the original purchaser) can benefit in two ways. Gain, if any, on the stock is capital gain, but if a loss occurs, it is an ordinary loss. Section 1244 limits the ordinary loss to the lesser of the actual loss or $50,000 ($100,000 on a joint tax return); any additional loss must be treated as a capital loss. (Remember, an ordinary loss is more valuable to a high-bracket taxpayer than a capital loss, because it reduces ordinary income that would otherwise be taxed at above-capital-gains rates.)

Section 1231 covers another category of "capital gain[6]/ordinary loss" property: real estate; depreciable tangible and intangible personal property used in business, if it was a long-term asset as of the time of its sale, exchange, or involuntary conversion. Inventory does not qualify as §1231 property. Nor does property held for sale to customers in the course of business, or copyrights and artistic creations in the hands of their creators or donees of their creators.

[¶4130.4] Home Sale Gains

Under prior law, the financial importance of the family home in most financial plans was addressed by two tax relief provisions. One of them, which could be used repeatedly, permitted a "rollover" of capital gain when a more expensive residence was purchased (i.e., it was not necessary to pay tax on the theoretical gain on selling one residence if another was purchased shortly before or afterward). The other was a one-time exclusion available only to persons over 55.

In effect, TRA '97 combines the characteristics of both provisions (former §§121 and 1041) in a single new Code §121. An unmarried taxpayer can exclude capital gains on home sales of up to $250,000; up to $500,000 can be excluded on a joint return. Furthermore, the exclusion can be repeated on subsequent sales, but not more often than once every two years.

Timing requirements (how long the residence was owned; how long it operated as the taxpayer's principal residence) must also be met. In general, the property must have been owned and used as the taxpayer's principal residence for two out of the five years preceding the sale. Some newly-married or remarried taxpayers may have to prorate or lose the exclusion. The Tax Technical Corrections Act further liberalized this provision by allowing a prorated exclusion for those unable to satisfy the "2 of 5" test.[7]

[¶4130.5] Basis of Capital Assets

Although the issue is more common for corporations (see ¶453.3), individual taxpayers sometimes encounter basis issues, e.g., when they receive a gift or inheritance including capital assets. Section 1015 states that the basis of property acquired by gift is the same as the donor's adjusted basis. However, if at the date of the gift, the fair market value of the gift property is below the donor's adjusted basis (i.e., the donor is making a gift of depreciated rather than appreciated property), the basis for determining the donee's loss is fair market value at the time of the gift. If the fair market value is greater than the donor's adjusted basis, the donee's basis is also increased by any gift tax paid that can be traced to net appreciation in the value of the gift.

The underlying §1014 rule is that heirs, unlike donees, get what is usually referred to as a "stepped-up" basis: i.e., their basis is the property's value at the date of the decedent's death (or the alternate valuation date, if one is elected: see ¶3170.3.1). More accurately, their basis is calculated as of date of death and not with reference to the decedent's basis; the basis could actually "step down" if the heir receives depreciated property.

[¶4130.6] Fringe Benefits

Fringe benefits offered by employers to their employees are included in the recipient employee's gross income unless there is a specific reason for the exclusion (§61(a)). If a fringe benefit is taxable, the employee's income is the fair market value of the benefit (the price that would be paid for it in an arm's length exchange), minus any amount the employee paid for it and also minus any other exclusion permitted by the Code.

A vehicle provided by the employer is taxed to the employee at the value of a lease of a comparable vehicle (Reg. §1.61-21(d)). Transportation (e.g., car service for those who work overtime) furnished by the employer, pursuant to a written policy, and solely because of unsafe commuting conditions, is valued at the bargain price of $1.50 per employee per trip: Reg. §1.61-21(k)(3).

Section 132 is the main section dealing with fringe benefits, although various other sections may have to be consulted in a particular case. To be excluded from gross income, some fringe benefits must be provided under an employer plan that is non-discriminatory: that is, it must not be limited to highly-compensated employees, and it must not be disproportionately favorable to HCEs.

Fringes that are excluded from income, either because they are too trivial to be worth accounting for, or because the IRC wants to permit them preferential status, include:

- Services that generate no additional cost for the employer, such as use of the employer's extra capacity: §132(a)(1)
- Discounts employees get when they buy the employer's products: §132(a)(2)
- "Working condition fringes" defined by §132(a)(3) that would be deductible if the employee paid out-of-pocket, e.g., business travel, use of corporate vehicles
- De minimis fringes such as occasional meals or transportation home after working late; office parties; meals in an employer-operated facility whose revenues are at least equal to its direct operating costs: §132(a)(4)
- Qualified transportation fringes under §132(a)(5) and (f)(5), such as vanpooling, transit passes, and parking, subject to dollar limits
- Qualified moving expense reimbursement: §132(a)(6)
- Benefits under a cafeteria plan, defined by §125 as a plan that gives employees a choice between taking certain compensation in cash and making their own personal choice of benefits from a "menu." Permissible cafeteria

The taxpayer claiming a large charitable deduction must be able to substantiate it, with the requirements increasing with the size of the claimed deduction. A canceled check would be sufficient for a small cash contribution, but the organization must substantiate donations over $250, and Form 8283 must be filed to substantiate a noncash contribution over $500, and an appraisal is required for donation of items (e.g., artwork) with a claimed value over $5,000. The IRS itself issues Statements of Value for donated artworks valued at over $50,000.

See ¶3152 for a discussion of Charitable Remainder Trusts and Charitable Lead Trusts, mechanisms under which some trust interests go to the charity, others to the grantor or members of the grantor's family.

[¶4150.9] At-Risk and Passive Loss Rules

In the bad old days, personal income tax rates could be extremely high, as high as 70%, so there was a corresponding desire to reduce taxable income. One way to do this was to borrow large sums of money to buy investment properties, generating heavy interest deductions yet the alleged borrowers had little or no real personal liability for the alleged loans. Today, lower tax rates take some of the zest out of the tax-shelter game, but the Code continues to retain limitations (in §465) on the taxpayer's deductions attributable to an activity that does not involve real, personal, financial risk for the taxpayer.

The at-risk rules apply to individuals; to C Corporations that are personal holding companies, personal service companies, or owned 50% or more by one to five individuals. Although the rules do not apply to S Corporations or partnerships at the entity level, they do apply to determine individual partner's or stockholders' ability to deduct or amortize items passed through from the entity.

A taxpayer is deemed to be at risk to the extent of money and the adjusted basis of property contributed to the activity, plus money borrowed from an unrelated party to participate in the activity, to the extent that the taxpayer is personally liable on the loan.

A loss from an activity subject to the at-risk rules (reported on Form 6198) is deductible only to the extent that the taxpayer is at risk: i.e., the excess of deductions otherwise allowable for the activity, minus income earned from the activity. If a taxpayer has a loss that is disallowed under this principle, it can be allocated to the same activity in the next tax year, and deducted up to the limit for that year.

The related concept of "passive activities" comes from §469. Individuals, trusts, estates, publicly traded partnerships, personal service corporations, and some closely held C Corporations are subject to the passive activities rules. These rules also affect the pass-through items of partners and S Corporation shareholders but not the entities themselves.

A passive loss is defined as aggregate losses from all passive activities, minus aggregate income from all passive activities. Losses and credits from passive activities are limited. Passive losses offset income from other passive activities, but not compensation or investment income. Section 469(b) permits passive-activity deductions and credits disallowed in one year to be carried forward to the next year.

A trade or business is considered a passive activity for any taxpayer who does not materially participate in it—i.e., who is not involved in its operations on a regular, continuous, and substantial basis. Spending more than 500 hours a year on an activity would constitute participation; so would spending over 100 hours a year, if no one else devotes more time to the activity. As a general rule, activities involving the rental of real estate are passive for taxpayers who are only real estate investors, but are not passive for real estate professionals. Otherwise, "portfolio" income deriving from investments is not considered passive; nor is income earned in the ordinary course of the taxpayer's business.

[¶4150.10] Tax-Free Exchanges; Non-recognition Transactions

Neither gain nor loss is recognized when a taxpayer exchanges common stock for other common stock, or preferred stock for other preferred stock, of the same corporation (§1036(b)).

Neither gain nor loss is recognized on the sale or exchange of:

- A life insurance policy for another life insurance policy, or for an endowment or annuity contract
- One annuity for another
- An endowment contract for an annuity or another endowment contract with a later beginning date for the payments (§1035).

"Like-kind" exchanges of business or investment property, as defined by §1031, create neither loss nor gain. The exchange must involve only properties, no "boot" (additional cash)(§1031(b)). If the exchange includes boot, then §1031(c) provides that gain can be recognized but loss cannot.

In a related-party transaction, §267(a) denies a loss deduction. Such transactions for individuals include, e.g., transactions between blood relatives (although in-laws are not considered related parties), between a taxpayer and corporation he or she controls, and between an estate and its beneficiaries.

Loss deductions are denied for "wash sales" (§1091): i.e., transactions lacking economic reality, in which the taxpayer sells or otherwise disposes of securities (including options and futures) if the taxpayer enters into a contract or has an option to acquire substantially identical securities in the period starting 30 days before and ending 30 days after the wash sale.

[¶4150.11] Standard Deduction

Taxpayers who do not choose to itemize their deductions, or whose deductions are lower than the standard deduction, claim the standard deduction instead. The basic standard deduction for 1999 is $7200 on a joint return, $6350 for a head of household, $4300 for a single person, and $3600 for a married person filing a separate return.

Additional standard deductions are available to senior citizens (over 65) and blind persons; a blind elderly person can claim two additional standard deductions. The maximum additional standard deduction is $850 for a married person, $1050 for an unmarried person or head of household. A complicating factor is that elderly and blind persons may be dependents of other taxpayers, which limits their standard deduction.

For any taxpayer who could be claimed as someone else's dependent (usually a child, but possibly an elderly parent supported by one or more children), the dependent's standard deduction is limited to the greater of $700, or $250 plus the dependent taxpayer's earned income, but not to exceed the normal standard deduction no matter how much the dependent taxpayer earns.

Non-resident aliens do not get a standard deduction; neither do married persons filing separately whose spouse itemizes deductions.

[¶4150.11.1] Dependent Status

There are five §151 factors determining whether a taxpayer can claim another person as a dependent; the dependency deduction is available only if all five factors are present:

- The dependent must be a relative (defined quite broadly) of the taxpayer, or must reside in the taxpayer's household—e.g., it might be possible for one cohabitant to claim the other as a dependent.
- The dependent's gross income does not exceed the amount of the dependency deduction. This rule is not applied in the case of dependents under age 19, or full-time students under age 24.
- If the dependent is married, he or she cannot file a joint return with his or her spouse.
- At least half of the dependent's support must come from the taxpayer claiming the deduction, unless there is a multiple support agreement under which a number of taxpayers (e.g., an elderly person's children) agree to render support, and also agree that one of them, who personally provides at least 10% of the dependent's support, will be entitled to claim the deduction. In-kind items, such as housing, medical expenses, and education are treated as items of support, but neither alimony nor arrears of child support is deemed to constitute support of the child. If a parent remarries, support provided by the new spouse is deemed to come from the parent: §152(e)(5).
- The dependent is a U.S. citizen; a U.S. national; or a resident of the United States, Canada, or Mexico.

Parents of a child born during the year are entitled to a dependency deduction for the entire year; proration is not required.

A dependent could be the taxpayer's child, grandchild, step-child, sibling, parent, grandparent, brother- or sister-in-law, parent-in-law, uncle or aunt, or nephew or niece. Once a relationship comes into existence, it is not terminated by divorce or death. A legally adopted child, or a child placed for adoption by an authorized agency, is treated as the taxpayer's child. However, a foster child is not a dependent if the taxpayer receives payment for caring for the child.

As a general rule, in case of divorce or separation, the dependency deduction is claimed by the custodial parent, even if the non-custodial parent provides a large fraction of the child's support. (Custody is determined by the most recent court decree, or by the separation agreement, if there is no decree: Reg. §1.152-4(b).)

The rule can be reversed if the couple is subject to a pre-1985 matrimonial decree or separation agreement, or if the custodial parent waives the deduction, using Form 8332 for the purpose. The decision to waive should not be made casually; it has broader implications, because waiver could lead to loss of head of household tax status, ineligibility for the Earned Income Credit, and/or the dependent care credit [see ¶4160 for a discussion of tax credits], with a resulting increase in the tax burden.

[¶4150.12] The Personal Exemption

A personal exemption is granted for the taxpayer, with the exception that persons who could be claimed as a dependent on someone else's tax return (even if they are not actually claimed) are not entitled to a personal exemption.

The basic personal exemption for 1999 is $2750, but taxpayers with AGI over $126,600 (or $189,950 on a joint return) can claim only a limited personal exemption. The personal exemption phases out entirely at AGI of $249,100 (single person), $280,800 (head of household) and $312,450 (married person filing jointly). See §151(d) for application of indexing in later years.

Resident aliens are permitted to claim the personal exemption on their U.S. tax returns (and can also claim dependency deductions).

[¶4160] Tax Credits

A tax credit is more valuable than a tax deduction, because each dollar of deduction merely reduces the overall tax burden by one dollar times the taxpayer's marginal (highest) tax rate, but each dollar of credit eliminates one dollar of tax liability. Furthermore, many tax credits (e.g., the Earned Income Credit) are refundable: that is, if they reduce tax liability below zero, the taxpayer can receive a corresponding refund. Certain other credits (e.g., those for the elderly and disabled and for adoption expenses) are not refundable, but can be carried over from year to year.

In addition to the credits discussed in more detail, individual tax credits are available to individuals who have overpaid FICA taxes (usually because they changed jobs during the year, and had total income greater than the FICA limit—$72,600 for 1999—but income from each job was below the limit, with the result that overwitholding occurred). A credit is also available for tax withheld on wages, pensions, annuities, interest, and dividends.

Code §25(a) provides a credit for post-secondary education expenses of the taxpayer, the taxpayer's spouse, and dependents, as long as the expenses are not

personal exemption, tax-exempt interest, and tax refunds must be added back into the calculation base. Another complex calculation is applied to find the "taxable excess" of AMT-taxable income over an exemption amount.

The tentative minimum tax is 26% of the taxable excess up to $175,000, plus 28% of any additional taxable excess. For married taxpayers filing singly, the AMT is 26% of taxable excess to $87,500, plus 28% of the balance. Yet another level of complexity is added in the calculation of net capital gains for AMT purposes.

Taxpayers who encounter AMT are entitled to claim a "minimum tax credit," using Form 8801, against their ordinary income tax in the year after the year in which the AMT was imposed.

ENDNOTES

1. Under §6013(g) and (h), a U.S. citizen or resident alien and his or her non-resident alien spouse can join in an election to be taxed as U.S. residents, on all income worldwide, for the year of the election.
2. Rev.Rul. 76-255, 1976-2 CB 40.
3. See 64 FR 13940 (3/23/99).
4. But see *Davis v. Comm'r*, TC Memo 1998-248 (7/7/98): punitive damages in a consumer credit abuse case were included in income, but the portion that went to the attorney as part of the attorney's contingent fee was not income. The IRS was wrong in treating it as income reduced by a miscellaneous itemized deduction.
5. There is a special transition rule for sales between 5/6/97 and 7/29/97, when assets held at least 12 months were deemed long-term. For certain post-7/29/97 sales of assets held 12-18 months, an intermediate rate of 28% was imposed.
6. Treated as long-term capital gain.
7. *Gummer v. U.S.*, 66 LW 1701 (Fed.Cl. 4/30/98) , involving the former senior-citizen provision, calls for analysis under all the facts and circumstances, so a taxpayer who lived in a rented apartment was allowed to treat a house that was on the market, where she stored her furniture, and where her grandchildren lived, as her residence.
8. See IRS Publication 502, "Medical & Dental Expenses."
9. Different rules are in place for pre-1985 instruments that have not been modified since then; for such instruments, the distinction is whether the alimony is deemed to be "periodic" or "non-periodic."

¶4300

Tax Enforcement

Note: at press time, both houses of Congress had passed a tax relief bill, then adjourned; President Clinton announced his intention to veto the bill.

[¶4301]

Tax collectors can never expect to be popular, but in the late 1990s, the IRS became the target of significant legislation aimed at restricting the agency's scope of operations. Taxpayer Bills of Rights were passed in 1988 (the Omnibus Taxpayer Bill of Rights, P.L. 100-647), and 1996 (Taxpayer Bill of Rights II, or TBOR II, P.L. 104-168), culminating in the Internal Revenue Service Restructuring and Reform Act of 1998 (IRSRRA), P.L. 105-206.

In this context, "restructuring" means that the IRS was directed to organize itself to concentrate on the type of taxpayer filing a return, or whose return was under examination (individual, small business, corporation, or tax-exempt organization—defined to include employee benefit plans, not just charitable organizations) rather than on the geographic district in which the return was filed. Furthermore, the appeals function must be separated from the operational function, and appeals officers are not supposed to have ex parte discussions with IRS operating personnel.

It should also be noted that, thanks to the IRSRRA, both general and taxpayer-specific advice issued by the IRS' chief counsel is now included in the category of "written determinations" that can be inspected by the public under Code §6110, with all references that could identify the taxpayer removed. (The Code §6110 procedure is the sole means of access to Chief Counsel advice; FOIA requests for this information will not be honored.)

However, Chief Counsel advice is treated on a parity with Private Letter Rulings, Technical Advice Memoranda, and determination letters. That is, although such material can be helpful in identifying IRS thinking on a particular issue or in a particular fact situation, it has no precedential value and cannot be cited by other taxpayers in their struggles with the IRS.

As much as possible, the IRS must assign one particular employee to handle a tax matter from beginning to end. Individual correspondence from the IRS to taxpayers must include the name, telephone number, and ID number of that particular employee whom the taxpayer can contact.

IRSRRA requires the IRS to expand the availability to taxpayers of telephone "help line" service, and Spanish-language service must be offered. The help line cannot offer only pre-recorded messages; any taxpayer who calls during normal business hours must have the option of talking to a person.

Before the IRSRRA, taxpayers who undertook the reasonable option of trying to telephone the local IRS office often found it difficult even to find a telephone number. IRSRRA requires the IRS to include this information in local telephone directories, although if the IRS really wants to wiggle out, it can satisfy the letter of the law by publishing in only one local directory—and not necessarily in an English-language directory.

[¶4310] Examination and Audit of Returns

The U.S. tax system depends on voluntary compliance by taxpayers, but §7602 defines the IRS' responsibilities to include auditing tax returns to see if the taxpayer is in full compliance. Audits can be performed at random, with no individualized suspicion of the taxpayer. It has long been suspected that the executive branch uses IRS audits to discredit or harass political opponents.

Code §7217(a), added by the IRSRRA, forbids any "applicable person" to intervene in an IRS audit, or to seek to influence the IRS to audit any person or organization. Applicable persons are the President, Vice President, employees in their Executive Offices, and cabinet-level officials. Conviction is punishable by a fine of up to $5,000 (plus the costs of prosecution) and/or imprisonment of up to five years.

[¶4310.1] Review of Returns

All tax returns are checked by computer, to find mathematical errors; §6213(b)(1) directs the IRS to notify taxpayers of such mistakes. (The notification is not a deficiency notice, and does not give the taxpayer the right to go to Tax Court.) Returns are also checked against information returns, and if there seems to be a discrepancy, the IRS issues a CP-2000, a computer-generated request for information about the alleged discrepancy. The CP-2000 is not a demand for payment. A taxpayer who disagrees with the notice can challenge it, but has the burden of proof.

The DIF (discriminant function) is used to program the IRS computers to select returns with the highest audit potential (i.e., those that differ significantly from average figures for the same type of return), but fewer than 2% of all returns are audited. Under the IRSRRA, IRS Publication 1, "Your Rights as Taxpayer," must explain the IRS' criteria for choosing returns for examination. IRSRRA also severely limits IRS use of techniques called "financial status examination" or "economic reality examination," under which the taxpayer is interrogated about expenditures and financial lifestyle rather than the return under examination.

[¶4310.2] Audits

Code §7605(a) permits the IRS to set the time and method of examining a possibly improper return, but the agency is required to select a method that is reasonable under the taxpayer's circumstances. In a correspondence audit, the taxpayer is asked to mail written information to the IRS office. In an office audit, the taxpayer is asked to appear at the office, bringing documentation; a field audit takes place in the office of the taxpayer or taxpayer's representative.

tax unless the taxpayer calls it a deposit. But access to Tax Court is possible only if the remittance is treated as a payment (i.e., is **not** identified as a deposit).

Form 843 is used to request abatement of interest pursuant to §6404, in situations where the taxpayer detrimentally relied on IRS actions or advice. IRS has discretion to abate the interest if it results from unreasonable errors or delays by IRS personnel (whether acting in a managerial or ministerial capacity) and where the taxpayer was not also at fault. The Tax Court can be used to litigate IRS refusals to exercise this discretion. Section 6404(f) also provides that the IRS **must** abate penalties and additions to tax resulting from incorrect written advice that the IRS gave to an individual taxpayer, who reasonably relied on the advice and who also gave the IRS sufficient accurate information to enable proper advice.

[¶4390.2] Civil Penalties

It is important to distinguish among the many types of penalties that can be imposed, and to make sure that clients are not subjected to inconsistent or duplicative penalties.

[¶4390.2.1] Failure to File Penalties

For failure to file any required income, estate or gift tax return, a penalty of 5% for the first month, and 5% for each additional month or partial month (up to a limit of 25%) that the non-filing continues, is imposed under §6651. The percentages apply to the amount of unpaid tax that should have been shown on the return.

If an income tax return should have been filed, but remains unfiled for 60 days after the due date as extended, the §6651(a) minimum penalty is the tax that should have been shown on the unfiled return, or $100, whichever is less.

The failure-to-file penalty is abated if there was a reasonable cause for non-filing, and the taxpayer did not willfully neglect the filing obligation. On the other hand, if the failure to file was fraudulent, the penalty increases, to 15% per month or partial month, up to a maximum of 75% (§6651(f)).

[¶4390.2.2] Failure to Pay Penalties

In many instances, failure to file is accompanied by failure to pay. In months in which this occurs, the 1/2% failure to pay penalty reduces the 5% failure to file penalty, but the minimum failure-to-file penalty is still imposed: §6651(c).

The penalty for failure to pay the tax on a return without reasonable cause is 1/2% per month or partial month, up to 25%, or 1% per month or partial month, up to 25%, for failure to pay within 10 days after service of an IRS Notice Of Levy. See §6651(d).

The same penalty is imposed for failure to pay an assessed deficiency by the prescribed payment date. The failure-to-pay penalty applies to taxpayers who get an automatic extension of time to file if the tax is not paid by the extended filing date, or the extended form 1040 shows a payment due greater than 10% of the tax shown on the 1040. (Generally, this means that withholding and prior payments are not at least 90% of the total.)

[¶4390.2.3] Accuracy-Related Penalty

The §6662 "accuracy-related penalty" of 20% of the understatement applies to any portion of the understatement of the tax on a tax return that is not fraudulent,[9] but that can be traced to negligence, disregard of IRS rules, substantial misstatements of income, gift, or estate tax valuation, or overstatements of pension liabilities. This penalty does not apply if the taxpayer had reasonable cause for the understatement—e.g., advice from a CPA.[10]

The definition of negligence includes failure to make a reasonable attempt to comply with the law; failure to keep adequate books and records; failure to substantiate items; and failure to exercise ordinary and reasonable care in preparing tax returns (§6662(i)). The penalty for non-compliance with IRS rules will not be applied when the taxpayer takes a position contrary to a Revenue Ruling or Notice, but the taxpayer's position has a realistic possibility of being sustained on its merits.

To constitute a substantial misstatement as defined by §6662(h), the statement must indeed be highly inaccurate: e.g., a value or adjusted basis on an income tax return that is at least twice the actual figure. The penalty is 20% of the portion of the underpayment traceable to the misstatement, or 40% if the misstatement is "gross" (four times or more the actual figure). This penalty will not apply in tax years in which underpayment attributable to all misstatements is under $5,000 (under $10,000 for a C Corporation). See §6662(e)(2).

The §6662(d) 20% accuracy-related penalty also applies to taxpayers who substantially understate the amount of income tax. A substantial understatement is 10% or more of the tax that should have been shown, or $5,000 ($10,000 for a C Corporation), unless the taxpayer had substantial authority for the tax position, or the facts behind the treatment of the item are disclosed on the return or Form 8275/8275-R. (The former is for opposition to a rule, the latter for opposition to a Regulation.)

Substantial authority, in turn, means that the weight of authorities (Code, other statutes, case law, Regs., TAMs, Notices, tax treaties, and Congressional Legislative History) supporting the taxpayer's position stacks up fairly well to the weight of authority supporting the IRS position. Under §6664(c)(1), penalties will not be imposed on taxpayers who acted in good faith, with reasonable cause.

A very similar penalty of 20% for substantial, 40% gross misstatements that lack substantial authority is imposed by §6662(f) for overstatement of deductible pension liabilities, if income tax is underpaid by at least $1,000. A substantial understatement is twice or more the actual amount. A gross misstatement (penalized by §6662(h)(2)(B) with 40% rather than 20% additional tax) is four times or more the appropriate amount.

Yet another accuracy-related penalty is imposed by §6662(b)(5) and (g) if the value assigned to property on a gift or estate tax return is 50% or less of its actual value. The penalty is 20% of the underpayment of tax attributable to the artificially low value; 40% of the underpayment if the property is valued at 25% or less of its true value. The penalty is waived in cases of understatement resulting in underpayment of tax in an amount under $5,000.

Penalties under §6662 are not cumulated. In other words, a negligent substantial understatement triggers only one accuracy-related penalty, not two.

On a related issue, see §6702, imposing a $500 civil penalty in addition to all other applicable penalties for filing a "frivolous" tax return (e.g., a tax protester's return). A return is frivolous if it fails to provide an accurate self-assessment of taxes, because of a frivolous tax position (e.g., that the entire federal income tax system is unlawful) or a desire to delay or impede federal tax administration.

[¶4390.3] Fraud Penalties

When a taxpayer files a return, but fraudulently fails to pay some of the tax shown on the return, a civil fraud penalty of 75% of the fraud-related portion of the underpayment is imposed by §§6663, 6664. The IRS cannot impose both an accuracy-related penalty and a fraud penalty on the same underpayment or portion of an underpayment. If the IRS can show that any portion of an underpayment is traceable to fraud, the entire underpayment is treated as fraudulent unless the taxpayer can show by a preponderance of the evidence that any portion was not fraudulent. Innocent spouses are not subject to fraud penalties for joint returns.

[¶4390.4] Responsible Person Penalties

For a "trust fund tax" (e.g., FICA), there is at least one "responsible person" in each organization required to collect and remit the tax.[11] Section 6672 imposes a penalty of 100% of the amount that should have been but was not paid, if the responsible person willfully fails to account for, collect, or pay the tax. The IRS must give at least 60 days' notice of its intent to impose the penalty, so that the responsible person can settle the account.

If there is more than one responsible person (a category that includes corporate officers and certain employees, partners, and certain partnership employees), and if one pays more than his or her proportionate share of the tax, he or she can recover the excess from the other responsible persons. The notice requirement is waived where the IRS deems collection of the penalty to be in jeopardy.

[¶4390.5] Non-Taxpayer Penalties

The penalties discussed above are imposed on the taxpayer. In various situations, penalties can be imposed on third parties as well as, or instead of, the taxpayer—for instance, if the non-taxpayer has aided and abetted the taxpayer in failing or refusing to make proper returns and payments.

Code §6701(b) imposes a $1,000 penalty (or a $10,000 penalty, in connection with a corporate return) for preparing, assisting in the preparation of, or advising about any tax return or other tax-related document that understates tax liability or overstates a refund, knowing that if the advice were taken, it would result in an understatement of tax. The wrongful act is preparing the document or giving the advice, even if the document is not used or the advice is not taken. This penalty is clearly applicable to lawyers and accountants. The preparer penalty can only be imposed on a paid preparer; the §6701(b) penalty can be imposed even if the advice was not given in return for a fee.

Penalties for paid preparers are governed by §§6694 and 6695. The penalty is $250 for any return or refund claim prepared for a customer, if the preparer knowingly takes a position that has no realistic possibility of being sustained by the IRS or the courts. (Preparers and other advisors who take unrealistic positions can also be barred from practice before the IRS.) A $1,000 penalty can be imposed per return or claim showing willful understatement by the preparer, or reckless or intentional disregard of IRS rules. However, if both willful understatement and advice leading to understatement penalties are imposed, the $250 offsets the $1,000.

Other incidents of preparer misconduct can lead to §6695 penalties of $50, $100, or $500 per offense (subject to a maximum of $25,000 per type of offense per calendar year): e.g., not signing a return; not providing the preparer's taxpayer ID on a return; improper record management; failure to follow due diligence when claiming the Earned Income Credit.

Thanks to lower tax rates, tax shelters (valid or abusive) have a much lower profile than in the past, but §§6701 continues to impose penalties on organizing, selling, or failing to register potentially abusive tax shelters.[12]

Deficiencies in information reporting by payors (e.g., banks; brokerages; employers who sponsor pension plans) can also generate penalties.: see, e.g., §6721 (failure to file required information return; failure to furnish payees with 1099s or other required statements (§6722); willful failure to furnish a required statement, or furnishing a fraudulent statement (§6674); failure to file annual returns, information returns, or actuarial reports for pension plans, or failure to keep adequate records (§§6652, 6692, 6704). Not only can the IRS penalize deficiencies in information reporting, but someone who is the subject of a fraudulent information return has a cause of action against the reporter, for the greater of $5,000 or actual damages, plus costs: §7434.

[¶4390.6] Criminal Penalties

In practice, the IRS seldom brings criminal charges, other than in the most flagrant cases, because of the comparatively greater difficulty of proving an intent offense versus merely proving failure to satisfy tax obligations. Nevertheless, a variety of criminal penalties are at least hypothetically imposed by §§7201-7207. The criminal tax statute of limitations is three years—six years for willful fraud offenses. See §6531.

Criminal tax evasion (willful evasion of tax due) is a felony, carrying a term of up to five years' imprisonment and/or a $100,000 fine for an individual or $500,000 for a corporate wrongdoer (§7201). Willful assistance in or advice about a materially[13] false or fraudulent tax return or other document is punishable under §7206 by three years and/or $100,000 for an individual, $500,000 for a corporation. Section 7206 also criminalizes the making of a false declaration under penalty of perjury. Willful failure to maintain records, file a return or pay a tax, collect and remit a tax, obey a summons, or willful filing of a false or fraudulent tax return are also criminal acts: see §7203.

Part VI

CIVIL LITIGATION

Federal Civil Procedure

[¶5001]

Federal civil procedure is applied, of course, within the federal court system. For convenience, it is also discussed here as a single system whose basic principles are applied (in however varied form) by the states in their own court systems. This section discusses the maintenance of civil cases in the federal system, trial practice, evidence, and appellate procedure.

[¶5010] The Federal Court System

The federal courts have been created pursuant to Article III of the Constitution; the Judicial Code is contained in Title 28 of the U.S. Code (which also contains the Federal Rules of Evidence). The local rules of the various federal courts, dealing with issues such as admission to the bar; getting a case set down for trial; how to petition for rehearing; and time limits on appellate oral arguments are reprinted as an appendix to Title 28.

The basic federal court system contains three tiers of courts. The 94 District Courts are the trial courts, with original jurisdiction over civil cases dealing with inherently federal issues such as federal tax; bankruptcy; federal questions; diversity cases; patents and copyrights; and unfair competition.

Appeals from decisions of the District Courts go to the thirteen Circuit Courts of Appeals (the First through Eleventh Circuits, the Federal Circuit, and the District of Columbia Circuit) and, in some instances, to the U.S. Supreme Court.

The First through Eleventh Circuits and the District of Columbia Circuit handle cases from particular geographic areas. The Federal Circuit handles specific types of cases. This court replaces the former Court of Customs and Patent Appeals. It has jurisdiction over civil appeals in which the United States is a defendant, and it is the only court that can handle appeals from the Court of Federal Claims and the administrative decisions of the Patent and Trademark Office.

The federal system also includes specialized courts: the U.S. Court of Federal Claims, which has jurisdiction over non-tort claims against the United States (e.g., contract claims; claims based on the Constitution, federal statutes, or federal administrative regulations),[1] and the Tax Court.

The Tax Court has jurisdiction over cases in which a deficiency or overpayment of federal tax is alleged. The general rule (see ¶4360.1) is that if the tax has already been paid, the taxpayer will seek a refund from the District Court; if the tax has not been paid, the Tax Court is the usual forum. Most Tax Court cases are appealable to the Court of Appeals, but the Tax Court has a simplified procedure for small cases (¶4360.1). If the amount in controversy is under $10,000, the taxpayer can elect to use this procedure, but the trade-off is that the Tax Court's decision becomes final and cannot be reviewed by any court.

[¶5020] Jurisdiction

The first hurdle toward getting any matter heard in court is jurisdiction. Clearly, no court can handle a matter over which it lacks jurisdiction. Certain areas of the law and causes of action are completely federal, so state courts have no jurisdiction over them. This could occur because the cause of action arises under a federal statute, and there is no counterpart state statute; or because Congress has preempted the field, expressly or impliedly preventing state law-making on the subject. Federal jurisdiction is exclusive with respect to, e.g.,

- Bankruptcy
- Patents
- Trademarks
- Copyrights
- IRS actions
- Customs
- Admiralty
- Fines and forfeitures imposed under federal law

The scope of exclusive state jurisdiction is much narrower: only probate and certain aspects of family law fall into this category.

[¶5020.1] Federal Question Jurisdiction

Between the two extremes of federal and state exclusive jurisdiction falls a vast group of cases, including diversity cases (involving citizens of different states) and federal question cases. At least theoretically, such cases could be brought in state court (thus foregoing remedies under federal law); brought in state court, then removed to federal court; brought in federal court; or there could be separate proceedings in each system. "Supplemental jurisdiction" (formerly known as pendent and ancillary jurisdiction) is present when the federal court has the option of either hearing or remanding causes of action that could properly be brought in state court.

The federal courts have "subject matter jurisdiction" or "federal question jurisdiction" in cases involving the laws passed by Congress, and the administrative and executive-branch rulings implementing those laws, or arising under federal common law. Cases arising under state laws that incorporate federal law cannot be brought in federal court, because there is no federal question jurisdiction. Under *American National Red Cross v. S.G.*,[2] the basic requisite is that the face of the complaint (not just the defendant's answer or special defenses) must establish federal subject matter jurisdiction.

In a case removed from state court, the District Court must find subject matter jurisdiction before reaching any issues of personal jurisdiction.[3]

or permissible to add further parties and the consideration of new issues to the action. The objective is to prevent what is essentially the same case from being relitigated. At best, relitigation is wasteful of limited resources of the court system; at worst, it creates inconsistent rulings that have to be reconciled via further litigation.

Rule 18(a) allows, but does not require, joinder of all legal or equitable claims against any opposing party. The claims can be added as either independent or alternate claims. Rule 13 covers claims by one party against one or more other parties. Such a claim is treated as a 13(a) compulsory counterclaim if it arises out of the transaction or occurrence that is the subject of the main action, in that it:

- Raises similar issues of law and fact
- Could not be brought as a separate suit if it were not brought as a counterclaim, because res judicata (see ¶5110) would apply
- The same evidence either proves or disproves the claim and the counterclaim
- The claim and the counterclaim are logically related.

Failure to raise a compulsory counterclaim generally prevents the counterclaim from being raised in subsequent litigation, but there are various exceptions to this rule:

- The claim requires the presence of certain third parties over whom the court does not have jurisdiction
- When the complaint was served, the potential counterclaim had not yet matured
- When the action was initiated, the potential counterclaim was part of another pending suit
- The original action involved a property interest, and the court never obtained personal jurisdiction over the party who could have asserted the counterclaim

Under Rule 13(f), either party can secure permission from the court to amend a pleading to add an omitted counterclaim.

Understandably enough, Rule 13(b) classifies all counterclaims that are not compulsory as permissive. Permissive counterclaims are those that do not arise out of the same transaction or occurrence as the main action. (The theory is that if the plaintiff is permitted to join unrelated claims in a single action, the defendant should be granted the same latitude.) A permissive counterclaim must have its own basis for federal jurisdiction (subject matter or diversity). It is up to the discretion of the court to permit or deny the inclusion of permissive counterclaims in a suit. If permission is denied, the defendant can bring an independent lawsuit; those claims are not precluded because they are not related to the original transaction or occurrence.

[¶5080.1] Cross-Claims

A cross-claim, as defined by Rule 13(g), is brought by a party against a co-party who is on the same side in the action. All cross-claims are permissive, not compulsory, so the potential cross-claimant can also become the plaintiff in a suit involving such claims. A cross-claim must either:

- Arise out of the suit's underlying transaction or occurrence
- Arise out of the counterclaim in that action
- Relate to property that is the subject matter of the suit.

The court has discretion, under Rule 13(h), to join additional persons or entities who are not parties to the original action, thus making them parties to a counter- or cross-claim, but only if a claim is asserted against the new party in conjunction with at least one existing party. On the other hand, 13(i) also gives the court discretion to order one or more separate trials with respect to counter- or cross-claims that are unrelated to the main action or involve too many disparate issues.

[¶5080.2] Joinder of Parties

Joinder of parties under Rule 19, like joinder of issues, can be either compulsory or permissive. The rule is that anyone who can be served and joined without depriving the court of its jurisdiction (e.g., a non-diverse party in a pure diversity suit) should be joined, if the result of non-joinder would be that the existing parties would not be able to secure relief, or if their absence could impair the interest that the potentially joined party claims in the subject property. Rule 19(b) provides that if it is impossible to join a person or entity who should be joined, the court must decide whether to proceed without that party, or dismiss the case.

Permissive joinder is governed by Rule 20. Subject to the discretion of the court, anyone who asserts or defends against joint, several, or alternative claims that arise out of the same transaction or occurrence as the suit can be joined in the action, as long as at least some common questions of law or fact apply to all the parties joined. But if joinder would not promote justice, 20(b) authorizes the court to order separate trials or make other orders needed to prevent prejudice or delay to the parties.

Rule 21 provides that actions cannot be dismissed for misjoinder of parties; as long as the parties are not prejudiced, parties can be dropped or new parties added in response to a motion by a litigant, or sua sponte on the court's own motion. The court also has the power to order severance if venue is proper for some defendants but not others. Also see Rule 25, governing substitution of parties (e.g., when a party dies or becomes incapacitated; when an official sued in official capacity is replaced by a new office-holder).

[¶5080.3] Third-Party Practice

Impleader, under Rule 14, also known as third-party practice, allows a defending party to a suit (a defendant; a plaintiff subject to a counterclaim; someone already brought in as a third-party defendant) to implead (i.e., bring in) a non-party who may be liable to that party on any pending claim. Thus, it differs from counterclaims and cross-claims, because those involve persons and entities who are already parties to the suit.

Impleader is generally a right of defending parties, because the plaintiff could have sued the potential third-party defendant initially, or could have amended the complaint to add a new defendant. However, Rule 14(b) provides that a counterclaim asserted against a plaintiff will have the effect of making the plaintiff a defendant with respect to the counterclaim, thus entitling the plaintiff to bring in a non-party who is or might be liable to the plaintiff on the counterclaim.

Once the defending party has served the necessary responsive pleading, he, she, or it can serve a third-party complaint seeking impleader without leave of court, for a ten-day period. After the ten days elapse, the court has discretion to allow service of a third-party complaint, but only through a motion made on notice to all parties.

Third-party claims are usually heard under the court's supplemental jurisdiction, so it is not necessary for independent grounds for jurisdiction to be present. However, in a diversity case where the diverse defendant is no longer a party, leaving no one but the plaintiff and a non-diverse third-party defendant, the case must be dismissed.

[¶5080.4] Interpleader

Rule 22 interpleader is sort of the reverse of a "whodunnit." Interpleader actions are brought by stakeholders, who have possession of sums of money they acknowledge really belong to someone else; but the stakeholders are unsure who the true owners are. Without interpleader, the stakeholder might have to face multiple suits brought by multiple claimants—and a significant portion of the fund might be consumed by these suits! Instead, Rule 22 permits the stakeholder to join all the claimants as defendants, in cases where a limited fund is at risk of excessive, expensive, or multiple litigation.

Interpleader is available to both plaintiffs and defendants, but there is a prerequisite to interpleader brought by defendants: at least one interpleaded party must already be a party to the action. Rule 22 supplements but does not supplant joinder under Rule 20, so in some cases it will be a strategic decision which will work better.

[¶5080.5] Class Actions

One representative, or a small group, may be able to bring a Rule 23 class action to resolve claims involving a large group having a common interest. It can be a close question whether a case should be handled by Rule 19 joinder or via class action; class actions are clearly preferable if joinder of all parties would be impossible or at least unwieldy.

Rule 23(a), which contains two implied and four express prerequisites, determines whether a case can be brought as a class action at all. The implied prerequisites are that there must be a definable class that can be certified; and that the would-be plaintiffs must be members of this class. All four of the express requirements must be met:

(1)   Numerosity (there are too many class members to join all of them)
(2)   Commonality (the class members are united by common issues of law or fact[12])
(3)   Typicality (the would-be representatives' claims and defenses are typical of the class)
(4)   Adequacy (they fairly and adequately protect the interests of the class)

When representation is inadequate but a class action would otherwise be proper, the court has discretion to dismiss the case; let the suit go forward but as an individual action; limit the class to those for whom the applicants would be suitable representatives; or add more representatives until the interests of the class are handled satisfactorily.

If the class action is based on a federal statute, the specific jurisdictional requirements of the statute must be met. If diversity jurisdiction is sought, then all named representatives must be diverse from all defendants, and the $75,000 minimum amount in controversy must be present. The claims of various class members can be aggregated if a single right is being enforced; yet many class actions will be deemed to involve several claims, thus preventing aggregation.

Once the requirements of Rule 23(a) have been met, the potential class action must satisfy the requirements of Rule 23(b)(1), (2), or (3). Many class actions satisfy two or all three sets of requirements; if so, the case will be classified as a (b)(1) or (b)(2) rather than a (b)(3) class action, because the class members' power to opt out of a (b)(3) class action (see below) opens up a risk of duplicative litigation.

A (b)(1) class action is one where separate suits by or against individual class members are undesirable because there might be inconsistent or varying adjudications (with the result that it would be impossible for the defendant(s) to be in full compliance), or nonparty class members might be brought in, impairing their ability to protect their own interests.

In a (b)(2) class action, the opposing party has acted or refused to act in a way that affects the whole class, and injunctive or declaratory relief is required to determine the legality of such conduct. This provision was enacted to permit civil rights class actions in the 1960s; even to this day, it is usually used in cases asserting Constitutional rights.

A (b)(3) class action is permissible if common questions of law or fact predominate over the individual issues, and a class action is procedurally the best way to achieve a fair and efficient adjudication of the controversy. Factors in the decision include:

- Whether individual class members have an interest in controlling their own litigation
- If a test case or other mechanism would explicate or protect class rights just as well as a class action
- The number and nature of suits already pending against or by class members

related in the two suits. But collateral estoppel can also be used by outsiders, if the estopped party was a party in the previous suit and it is inappropriate to re-litigate the issue.

[¶5200] Commencement of the Federal Case; Service of Process

Under FRCP 3, a federal case is commenced when the complaint is filed. Rule 4 provides that the clerk of the court must immediately issue a summons as soon as the complaint is filed. The plaintiff decides whether the summons should be issued against all defendants, or whether each should receive a separate summons.

The usual federal practice is to serve the summons by mail. The party served receives a notice and acknowledgment form, which is to be returned to prove that service has been completed. Rule 4 allows service by first-class mail; it is not necessary to use, e.g., registered or certified mail. The pleadings must be accompanied by two copies of the notice and acknowledgment form (which must be prepared in accordance with Rule 18A) and by a postpaid return envelope, addressed to the plaintiff or plaintiff's attorney.

However, if mail service is unsuccessful for some reason, and the acknowledgment form has not been returned 20 days after the summons was mailed, almost any person over 18 who is not a party to the suit can perform personal service. The person effecting service must complete an affidavit of service. (Under prior law, all summonses had to be served by the U.S. Marshal's office, but this requirement has been abrogated.)

Furthermore, in most federal suits, service can be made by any method approved by the state courts of the state in which the District Court is located. (It should be noted that in a diversity case, the statute of limitations is not tolled by the filing of the complaint in federal court if state law requires actual service of the complaint.) Unless good cause is shown, the case is dismissed without prejudice if the plaintiff is unable to complete service of the complaint within 120 days of commencement of the action.

[¶5200.1] Service by Type of Party Served

Under Rule 4(d), service on a corporation, partnership, or unincorporated association that can be sued under a common name is performed by serving an officer or managing or general agent who has express or implied authority to be served. Service can also be made on any other agent appointed or authorized by law. (It may also be necessary to mail a copy of the summons and complaint to the defendant.) In situations in which the federal government has waived sovereign immunity, service against the United States is performed by delivering a copy of the summons and complaint to the U.S. Attorney or Assistant U.S. Attorney.

Rule 45, not Rule 4, governs service of subpoenas, including territorial rules. Other forms of federal process continue to be served by the U.S. Marshal or by a specially appointed person. Federal process other than subpoenas can always be served within the limits of the state in which the District Court is sitting.

If the person to be served cannot be found in that state, all is not necessarily lost: many federal statutes authorize nationwide service of process in suits to enforce the statutes.

Another possibility is that, if additional parties must be brought in under Rules 14 or 19, Rule 4(f) permits service outside the state but inside the United States, at any place within 100 miles of the place where the action was commenced or will be tried. See rule 4(i) for service in a foreign country if the party is not an inhabitant of, or found within, the state in which the District Court is located.

The service of papers other than the complaint comes under Rule 5. Unless the District Court excuses it when there are numerous defendants, copies of all subsequent pleadings must be served on each party. Service is made on the attorney of a represented party, unless the court orders service of the party him- or herself.

[¶5210] Federal Pleadings

The intention of the FRCP is to adopt "notice pleading" and to eliminate technical pleading requirements; to reduce the number and variety of pleadings; and to encourage "short, plain statements" in the surviving pleadings. Amendments and supplements are available as needed, but under FRCP 7(a), the only permissible pleadings are:

- The plaintiff's complaint
- The defendant's answer
- Third-party complaint
- Third-party answer
- The plaintiff's answer to a counterclaim asserted by the defendant
- A co-defendant's answer to a cross-claim

All pleadings must contain a caption giving the court (the District, and the Division, if any); the title of the action; its file number; its designation (e.g., complaint, answer, etc.); and the names of the parties. Local rules may require additional information, such as the judge's name.

Note that Rule 19(c) requires the pleader of any complaint, counterclaim, cross-claim, or third-party claim to identify all persons known to the pleader to be necessary for "just adjudication" of the matter but who have not, in fact, been joined. The pleader must explain why joinder is not feasible. (Rule 23 class actions are exempt from this requirement, so it is not necessary to join all class members, explain their non-joinder, or even provide a list of all of them. See ¶5080.5 for a discussion of class actions.)

Rule 15 gives a party who has served a pleading the right to amend it once before the responsive pleading is served. (A motion is not considered a responsive pleading for this purpose.) In a situation in which no responsive pleading is permitted, the pleading can be amended within 20 days of serving it, as long as it has not yet been placed on the trial calendar. But once the responsive pleading has been served, written consent from the adverse party or leave of court is required to amend. (Leave to amend is supposed to be granted freely in the interest of justice.)

The general rule is that when a pleading has been amended, the opposing party must respond to the amended version within the remaining response time for the original pleading, or within ten days after service of the amended pleading, whichever is later. However, the court can order a different timetable. Rule 15(d) permits a party to make a motion for service of a supplemental pleading. Unlike an amended pleading, a supplemental pleading deals with transactions, occurrences, and events after the date of the prior pleading.

[¶5210.1] The Complaint

As noted above, filing of the complaint commences a federal action, and the summons and complaint must be served together.

The complaint must be organized into separate numbered paragraphs that set out the facts and legal claims under which relief is sought. The complaint should contain:

- The general nature of the claim(s)
- The name and state citizenship of all parties
- A brief statement of the involvement of each party in the controversy
- The sections of the Judicial Code (28 USC) supporting jurisdiction and venue
- If there is a jurisdictional amount (e.g., in a diversity case), a statement that the damages (exclusive of costs and interest) equal or exceed the jurisdictional amount
- Background facts needed to understand the claim
- An identifying heading for each Cause of Action, plus material required to set out a cognizable claim for relief under that cause of action (all necessary facts; the legal theory asserted in connection with those facts; the injury alleged; and the relief sought, e.g., damages, injunction, declaratory judgment[17])
- A summary of the relief sought for all Causes of Action and a request for "such other and further relief as to the Court may appear just."

The complaint must be signed by the plaintiff's counsel (thus bringing it within the ambit of Rule 11: see ¶7040). Any exhibits referred to in the complaint must be attached. Like all pleadings, the complaint must have a back conforming to local practice. It must be served pursuant to Rule 4 and must be filed with the Clerk of Court.

[¶5210.2] The Answer

The answer is the responsive pleading that the defendant uses to respond to the allegations raised by the complaint. Rule 8(b) provides that the answer is used to raise affirmative defenses and assert counterclaims and cross-claims. The basic time frame for answering the complaint is 20 days, although an additional three days are allowed if (as usually happens) the complaint is served by mail. (The United States as defendant is given 60 days to answer.)

The answer should consist of separate, numbered paragraphs responding to each of the allegations of the complaint. Any allegation that is not addressed is deemed admitted. Every allegation must be admitted; admitted in specified part and denied as to the rest; or the defendant can claim lack of knowledge or information sufficient to form a belief as to the truth of the allegation.

Rule 8(e)(2) allows two or more statements of claim or defense to be made alternatively or hypothetically. The defendant's attorney must sign the answer, so Rule 11 applies. As long as Rule 11 is not violated, inconsistent statements are permitted in pleadings.

[¶5210.2.1] Available Defenses

Defenses (including affirmative defenses) that can be raised in an answer include:

- Failure to state a claim on which relief can be based
- Plaintiff's lack of standing to sue
- Court's lack of subject-matter jurisdiction over the action
- Court's lack of personal jurisdiction over the defendant
- Defective service of process
- Defenses contained in the relevant statute
- Preclusion by res judicata or collateral estoppel
- Equitable defenses (laches, unclean hands)

Any valid defense can be raised in the answer. Certain defenses that go to the very heart of the action (e.g., failure to state a claim on which relief can be based; lack of jurisdiction or venue) can also be raised by a 12(b) motion to dismiss.

Rule 8(c) holds that failure to plead an affirmative defense waives that defense, unless the court grants the right to amend. Affirmative defenses include accord and satisfaction, payment, or release; arbitration and award; assumption of risk; contributory negligence of the plaintiff, or negligence of a fellow-servant; discharge in bankruptcy; duress; estoppel; fraud; illegality; laches; lack of consideration; res judicata; lack of written agreement in a situation subject to the Statute of Frauds; claims that are time-barred because the statute of limitations has expired; and waiver.

The answer can also include properly labeled counter- and cross-claims (e.g., First Counterclaim; First Counterclaim Against X and Y). Such claims follow the format of a complaint: they identify the parties, state the bases for jurisdiction and venue, and set out the facts, legal claims, and relief sought. The proper responsive pleadings are a Reply, filed by a plaintiff who becomes the subject of a counterclaim, and an Answer for co-defendants served with cross-claims.

[¶5210.3] Third-Party Pleadings

If it is necessary to bring a party into the action who is not already involved (i.e., is not already a plaintiff or defendant), the defendant can use Rule 14's third-party complaint procedure. The defendant becomes the plaintiff as against the new

All or part of a deposition can be offered in evidence, to the extent that it is admissible under the Federal Rules of Evidence: Rule 32. The testimony is treated as if the deponent were present and testifying. The admissible evidence from the deposition can be used against any party who was present when the deposition was taken; was represented at the deposition; or had reasonable notice of the deposition (and thus could have been present or represented).

[¶5330.4.1] Deposition Technique

Because most cases are settled before trial, the deposition is absolutely crucial to successful resolution of the matter. The size of the settlement obtained for, or exacted from, the attorney's client depends in large part on the facts adduced by depositions, and the degree to which each side's witnesses are articulate, credible, and well-prepared.

Questions can be asked at a deposition that are not admissible in evidence, as long as they are reasonably calculated to lead to evidence. Although it is usually a mistake to ask a trial witness "Why?" such a question is often useful in a deposition. It is also often a good idea to ask witnesses if anything else happened or if they are aware of any additional facts.

If a deposition contains vital material, but the witness is inarticulate or unattractive, it may be more effective to admit the deposition rather than have the witness testify at the trial.

[¶5330.5] Other Discovery Devices

Rule 34 governs requests that a party produce materials for inspection. The demanding party can measure, sample, test, and photograph those materials. Rule 45 implements a somewhat similar procedure when the person or entity in control of those materials is not a party to the action; in this situation, leave of court is required.

A physical or mental examination of a person can be compelled under Rule 35, if those issues (e.g., blood group) are in controversy in a suit. The person doing the examination must have any required licenses; and the requesting party must demonstrate good cause for the request.

Any party can request any other party to admit the truth of any matter that comes within the scope of Rule 26(b): see Rule 36. The requester serves a request for admission of specific items; if there is no response, the items are deemed admitted unless the served party files an objection.

Even if there is an objection, the court can order that the objection is invalid and the admissions must be made. An uncooperative party can be sanctioned, and can be ordered to pay the cost of proving items whose truth should have been admitted. Admitted facts are conclusively established for the case at bar, but can't be used in other cases.

Rule 26 permits a party to use interrogatories to require another party to disclose the expert witnesses scheduled to be called at trial; what they will testify about, and a summary of the facts and opinions they are expected to express and the grounds for such statements of fact and opinion.

If a showing of exceptional circumstances and inability to get the information otherwise is made, discovery can be obtained from experts hired by another party but who will NOT testify at trial. There is no mechanism for discovery from experts who are informally consulted but not retained.

[¶5330.6] Limitations on Discovery

The discovery process gives rise to many motions. Proponents of discovery can move to compel answers or sanction non-compliance with discovery orders. Opponents of discovery can object to discovery requests or seek protective orders, but they should be aware that Rule 26 requires discovery of all material that is not privileged. Federal Rules of Evidence 501 holds that state law of privilege applies if the rule of decision comes from state law (as, for instance, in a diversity case or a case in which the federal court exercises supplemental jurisdiction over a state claim). In all other cases, the federal common law of privilege governs. Most discovery orders are not appealable, because they are not "final orders" in the sense of resolving litigation or even an independent phase of litigation.

Rule 26(b)(3) codifies the "work product" doctrine enunciated in *Hickman v. Taylor*, 329 U.S. 495 (Sup.Ct. 1947). Work product consists of documents and other items prepared in anticipation of litigation. It is discoverable only if the requester shows a substantial need of the material to prepare the case for its own side, and only if it is impossible to secure the same information without substantial hardship.

Rule 26(f) provides for a discovery conference, in which the court (sua sponte or on motion of a party) brings the attorneys in to discuss the schedule for discovery and the allowable scope. For instance, limits might be set on the number of depositions or interrogatories; or the number of questions permitted in an interrogatory (50 is standard).

Discovery does carry with it the potential for abuse, so Rule 26 allows the court to limit the use of discovery if:

* The discovery sought merely duplicates other sources of information
* Discovery is more burdensome than other means to acquire the same information (e.g., doing research; hiring a private investigator)
* Discovery is more expensive than other means
* The party seeking discovery already had a full opportunity to acquire the information now sought in discovery
* Discovery is excessively burdensome when considered in the context of its importance to the suit

[¶5330.7] Subpoenas

A subpoena is not required to make a party give a deposition, but usually is required to compel the deposition of a non-party.

Rule 45 provides that subpoenas, whether ad testificandum or duces tecum (i.e., for testimony or for production of documents) are issued from the court where testimony or production is required. The subpoena must give the name of

lic record, the only possible objection is to the relevancy of the document, not its admissibility.

Under Rule 1006, a summary of voluminous records is admissible, when the writings, recordings, photographs, or other materials cannot conveniently be produced. The party seeking to present a summary must give advance notice to the opposing party. The judge can, however, direct production of the underlying materials.

See ¶5500 for a fuller discussion of evidentiary issues under the Federal Rules of Evidence.

[¶5400.5.3] Expert Testimony

The optimum expert not only has impressive technical qualifications, but is able to instruct the jury about his or her technical area, can express conclusions in plain English, and is viewed by the jury as a credible and likeable person. If several expert witnesses are available, often the best choice will be the one with the best communications skills.

The expert witness should make it clear that the expert is being paid to testify, and should bring out occasions in the past when the expert has testified—preferably instances in which the expert has represented plaintiffs rather than defendants (or vice versa), or has reached conclusions opposite to those he or she is testifying about currently. Such testimony rebuts the common perception that expert witnesses are merely hired guns who always reach whatever conclusion is favorable to the paying party's position.

Effective expert testimony often is divided into "sound bites"—brief, easily understood units. Use follow-up questions to bring out the meaning of technical terms used but not defined by the expert.

[¶5400.5.4] Cross-Examination

It is not necessarily valid strategy to cross-examine every witness. If testimony is not genuinely damaging to your case, it may be better to avoid cross-examination, especially if the witness seems sympathetic or vulnerable. But the jury will be surprised, or even suspicious, if major witnesses are not cross-examined.

Major points in cross-examination should be raised at the beginning and end of the cross, when jurors are at their most attentive.

Federal Rules of Evidence 607 allows any party to impeach any witness; it can be helpful to anticipate problems by bringing out potentially dangerous areas on direct examination. Nevertheless, attempts at impeachment usually occur during cross-examination. There are seven major sources of impeachment:

(1) The witness' bias in favor of, or prejudice against, a person or position; the witness' own ability to benefit from or suffer detriment from the case
(2) Prior convictions
(3) Prior bad acts
(4) Prior inconsistent statements. The prior inconsistent statements of an opposing party are always admissible; prior inconsistent statements are not hearsay when used for the limited purpose of impeaching a non-party witness

(5) Contradictory facts
(6) The witness' poor reputation for truthfulness
(7) Accepted treatises that disagree with the position expressed by an expert witness.

[¶5400.5.5] Closing Argument

Generally speaking, the party having the burden of proof makes the last closing argument. If there are multiple parties to a case, each can make a closing argument, or they can consolidate and offer a single closing.

Usually, closing arguments should be brief (15–20 minutes), and should parallel the structure of argument used in the opening argument and case in chief. The closing argument is the attorney's last chance to stress the strengths of the case and rebut challenges to it. It can be useful to re-use some key exhibits to refresh the jurors' recollection, or to create a summary chart that is not independent evidence but that aids argument.

Closing argument topics include:

* Identification of the parties and issues
* Relevant evidence and exhibits
* Deficiencies in the case presented by the opponent
* Challenges to the credibility of opposing witnesses
* Applicable law
* Jury instructions requested by the attorney
* Proposed damages.

[¶5400.6] Dismissal of Actions

Under Rule 41, dismissal of an action can either be voluntary (from the plaintiff's viewpoint) or involuntary. Voluntary dismissals come under 41(a), and can be handled by either notice of discontinuance or stipulation. The plaintiff is only permitted to file a notice of discontinuance at a very early stage in litigation, before the defendant files its answer or serves a motion for summary judgment. The dismissal automatically becomes effective when the notice of discontinuance is filed with the court clerk; the participation of the adverse party is not required. Rule 41(a) cannot be used in class actions or cases in which a receiver has been appointed, because in such cases the court's permission is required to discontinue the action.

After the complaint has been answered, or a summary judgment motion has been filed, the case can be dismissed voluntarily by stipulation, which ends the action. It is not necessary for the settlement agreement between the parties to be filed with the court.

There are some rare circumstances in which the plaintiff wants to dismiss the case, but the defendant is unwilling—probably because a counterclaim is involved. In such situations, the plaintiff must move to the court for dismissal, but the case cannot be dismissed if there is a counterclaim unless the counterclaim can be maintained on the basis of its own independent jurisdictional status (i.e., it presents a federal question or diversity is present).

The general rule is that, unless the notice of discontinuance or stipulation is to the contrary, voluntary dismissals occur without prejudice, but 41(a)(1) provides that the dismissal operates as an adjudication on the merits if the notice or stipulation is filed by a plaintiff who has already dismissed an action based on or including the same claim in any state or federal court.

Involuntary dismissal on motion by the defendant, or the court's own motion, comes under 41(b). It can be sought if the plaintiff fails to prosecute the action; fails to obey a court order; or fails to comply with the Federal Rules of Civil Procedure. Unless the order of dismissal is to the contrary, a Rule 41(b) dismissal is an adjudication on the merits that has res judicata effect.

Rule 50(a) governs motions for judgment as a matter of law—what used to be known as motions for a directed verdict. The judge rules on the merits of the claim as a matter of law; the jury never receives any issue decided by the judge in this manner. Judgment as a matter of law can be granted on any claim, counterclaim, cross-claim, or third-party claim as to which a party has been fully heard, if it would be impossible for a reasonable jury to find for that party.

[¶5400.7] Jury Instructions

At the close of the evidence (or at an earlier point as directed by the judge), any party can make a written request to have the court instruct the jury on the law. The judge responds to the attorneys' requests before their closing arguments. If one side objects to the other side's proposed instructions, or the instructions actually given by the judge, the objection must be raised before the jury retires. Failure to raise the objection on time prevents assignment of error on appeal (absent a gross miscarriage of justice).

[¶5400.8] Verdicts and Decisions

A general verdict, signed by all the jurors, simply indicates in which party's favor the jury has found. A special verdict (also known as special interrogatories) is more detailed, setting out answers to questions posed by the judge. Under Rule 49(a), the judge can direct the jury to return a special verdict, including special written findings on each issue of fact. The court can provide three types of guidelines to the jury:

- Written questions that can be answered briefly
- Several special findings that the jury could make, based on the pleadings and the evidence offered
- Whatever the court deems appropriate.

That is, in the federal system, use of a special verdict is discretionary at the judge's option. States vary in their practice: some mandate special verdicts, whereas others leave it up to the judge.

It is permissible, under Rule 49(b), before a general verdict is rendered, for the judge to give the jury general verdict forms and written interrogatories dealing with issues of fact that must be decided in order to render a verdict, with necessary explanations and instructions that the jury will need to answer the interrogatories and render the verdict.

In cases in which there is no jury (or only an advisory jury), the court must make findings of fact and conclusions of law before entering final judgment (pursuant to Rule 58) granting or denying relief. If the judge's decision is appealed, the appellate court is not bound by conclusions of law, but almost always upholds findings of fact (which are assessed by a "clear error" standard).

Depending on local rules, the judge either may or is obligated to ask the attorneys to prepare their proposed findings and conclusions for the court to consider. Usually the plaintiff submits first, but the court can order simultaneous submissions. Proposed findings are usually drafted in separate numbered paragraphs that give a simple statement of the facts the party relies on to support each claim or defense. Conclusions of law and supporting authorities should be provided in separate numbered paragraphs for jurisdiction, venue, and each element of a claim or defense asserted by the party.

Unless the parties stipulate to the contrary, the verdict of a federal jury must be unanimous and must be rendered by at least six jurors. Rule 47(b) provides that alternate jurors are not empanelled in the federal courts. Rule 48 says that as long as at least six jurors remain, or if the parties accept the lesser number, the loss of a juror does not require declaration of a mistrial. The judge has discretion to excuse a juror who becomes ill, is needed in an emergency, or has committed misconduct that would justify a mistrial. However, jurors cannot be excused because they refuse to join in an otherwise unanimous verdict.

[¶5400.8.1] Judgment of the Court

In a court trial, Rule 52(c) provides that the court may enter judgment as a matter of law against a party who has been fully heard on an issue, as to any claim that is contingent on a favorable ruling on the issue.

In either a court or a jury trial, Rule 54(a) governs decrees and court orders that may be subject to appeal: i.e., the judgment itself, but not the judge's written opinion. Rule 54(c) provides that (other than for default judgments), a final judgment granting relief must grant all relief to which the party is entitled—including elements of relief that were not requested in the pleadings. But default judgments are limited to relief prayed for in the pleadings.

In federal practice, the clerk of the court prepares the judgment form, unless the court specifically asks the prevailing attorney to do so. In contrast, the practice of many states is to have the attorney prepare the judgment and give it to the clerk for entry.

[¶5400.8.2] Enforcement of Judgments

The enforcement of money judgments rendered in federal civil cases falls under Rule 69. Unless the court directs otherwise, enforcement occurs via writ of execution. The writ is issued by the court that handed down the judgment. It is served by the U.S. Marshal or designate. However, Rule 69(a) provides that a writ of execution for a private party can be executed only in the state in which the District Court sits.

[¶5400.8.3] Prison Litigation

The Prison Litigation Reform Act, P.L 104-134 (1996) seeks to discourage prisoners from filing suits about prison conditions by limiting the available relief to the minimum necessary to vindicate federal rights. If an inmate is awarded any monetary relief, the statute requires notice to be given to the victims so they can seek restitution from the award. Judges are encouraged to screen prison petitions[23] and dismiss frivolous cases. An inmate who makes repeated frivolous claims, or any malicious claims, can be deprived of "good time" that would otherwise be used to reduce the sentence.

[¶5500] Evidence

The Federal Rules of Evidence (FRE) govern testimony in trials held in federal courts. However, the FRE does not apply to preliminary questions of fact or preliminary examinations; Grand Jury proceedings; bail hearings; sentencing; or matters relating to probation or revocation of probation. In effect, the rules apply at the main trial, not at preliminary or subsequent court proceedings. The Fourth Amendment applies to searches and seizures in the civil context.[24]

The rules take a balancing approach to admissibility. That is, evidence is considered relevant and admissible if it tends to prove a matter of consequence, thus helping to resolve a factual dispute—and also if at its introduction is not unduly prejudicial, misleading, or time-consuming. Admission of evidence is favored if the risks can be minimized. The federal judge is given significant discretion over admission and exclusion of evidence.

Rule 105 allows a party to request that evidence be admitted only as to one party or as to specific issues; the jury must be instructed on the implications of such limited admission.

[¶5500.1] Admissibility

In general, evidence is admissible in either a civil or criminal context if it resolves facts necessary to the question, decided by preponderance of the evidence. Certain relevant evidence must be excluded for Constitutional reasons—for instance, if it is the product of an unlawful search or improper custodial interrogation.

The standard the federal Court of Appeals uses to review evidentiary rulings of the District Court is abuse of discretion.[25] Where the District Court has discretion to accept or exclude evidence, the appeals court will reverse a ruling only if it is manifestly erroneous.

Rule 103(a) says that no error can be assigned unless a substantial right of a party is affected and:

- (If evidence was admitted) the record includes a timely objection or motion to strike
- (If excluded) the substance of the evidence was offered to the court or was apparent from the context.

Error in reception of evidence is harmless if it did not influence the jury or change the outcome.

[¶5500.2] Structure of the FRE

The Federal Rules of Evidence cover ten substantive topics:

- General matters
- Judicial notice
- Presumptions
- Relevancy
- Privilege
- Competency, examination, and impeachment of witnesses
- Opinion and expert testimony
- Hearsay
- Authentication of exhibits
- Originals and copies of evidence

For reversal, trial-court error with respect to evidence must affect substantial rights, and a timely objection, stating specific grounds, must have been made. But FRE 103(d) codifies the doctrine of plain error: in egregious circumstances, the appeals court can reverse even in the absence of a timely objection.

When evidence is excluded, the losing party must make an offer of proof stating the evidence that would have been offered, in order to augment the record for appeal. The offer of proof is usually made at sidebar, so the jury can't hear; or the jury would be excused if proceedings would take more than a few minutes.

In most circumstances, the federal jury is the trier of facts, but FRE 104 provides that the judge determines certain preliminary questions in both court and jury trials—i.e., admissibility in general; competency; privilege; and the availability of a presumption. Hearings on such matters are usually held while the jury is excused.

If a party introduces only part of a writing (or a recorded statement), Rule 106 permits the opponent to put that material in context by introducing other parts of that writing or statement—or even related materials—to prevent unfairness.

[¶5500.3] Judicial Notice

Judicial notice can be taken (under rule 201), by either a trial or appellate court, of "adjudicative facts"—facts that are not subject to reasonable dispute because they are generally known in the geographic area where the court is located, or are readily and accurately determined from sources of unquestionable accuracy.

The court, in its discretion, can take judicial notice of any matter. The court must take judicial notice of anything that is the subject of a request by a party who furnishes the necessary proof of the matter. Judicial notice can be taken of scientific theories (e.g., the laws of thermodynamics) that are firmly enough established to be granted the status of scientific laws.

Rule 201(g) requires the jurors in a civil trial to accept all facts of which judicial notice has been taken. But in federal criminal cases, the jury is instructed that they may but need not accept judicially noticed facts. Judicial notice can be taken at any stage of the proceeding, including appeal, as long as there is no unfairness to any party, and the trial court's fact-finding authority is not undermined.[26]

[¶5500.4] Presumptions

Under the Federal Rules of Evidence, presumptions apply only to the burden of going forward (introducing at least some evidence to rebut the presumed point). The ultimate burden of proof still remains upon whatever party would have carried it without the presumption (Rule 301).

Rule 302 permits state-law presumptions to apply in cases in which the decision on the merits depends on state law, with respect to facts that constitute elements of any state-law cause of action or defense. This rule comes into play in diversity cases and certain supplemental jurisdiction claims.

[¶5500.5] Relevancy

Evidence is relevant, under Rule 401, if it makes a fact of consequence to the case either more or less probable. Irrelevant evidence is never admissible. Rule 403 permits exclusion of even relevant evidence whose probative value is less than the prejudice, delay, confusion, or repetition that would ensue if the evidence were admitted. Rule 403 doesn't apply in trials to the court, because the rule's specific purpose is to prevent juries from hearing improper evidence.[27]

There is no full, clear definition of "prejudice" in the FRE, but the definition is approximately material that seeks to create an irrational perception in the jurors' minds of a person because of that person's intrinsic characteristics; by association with an unpopular group; or by exciting the jury's rage or desire for revenge (e.g., by showing inflammatory photographs of a crime scene, even though the brutality of a crime does not prove that the defendant committed it).

Rule 403 does not exclude otherwise relevant evidence on the ground of surprise. In the federal system, the remedy is not exclusion of the evidence, but continuance of the trial for the opposing party to deal with the new evidence.

The trial court must act as "gatekeeper" to make sure that all expert testimony is relevant and reliable, with respect to expert testimony based on any form of technical or specialized knowledge, not just scientific testimony: *Kumho Tire Co. v. Carmichael*, 119 S.Ct. 1167 (Sup.Ct. 3/23/99).

[¶5500.6] Character Evidence

Under Rule 404, character traits are generally not admissible to prove that someone acted in conformity with those traits. There is an important exception with regard to the character of the accused. In a case involving death, the reputation of the deceased for peaceful conduct (or the opposite) is admissible on the question of whether the deceased was actually the aggressor in the incident leading to death.

Evidence of character takes the form of reputation and opinion (Rule 405). Character can be proved by testimony as to reputation; the witnesses' own opinion; and proof of specific conduct where character or a character trait is an essential element of a charge, claim, or defense, or cross-examination of a character witness.

Testimony about specific acts, crimes, or wrongdoing is not admissible to prove that the subject of the testimony would act the same way on another occasion, but might be admissible as to other matters (such as motive, opportunity, intent, plan, or identity). Evidence of specific acts can also be introduced if it constitutes an essential element of a claim, defense, or cross-examination. For instance, if the defendant asserts an insanity defense, other acts could show awareness of the world and ability to plot and carry out crimes, thus rebutting the defense.

If specific-acts evidence is going to be introduced in a criminal trial, the defendant can request the prosecution to give reasonable notice of the general nature of the evidence (unless the judge excuses compliance with this requirement). In response, the defendant should consider filing a motion in limine to exclude the evidence under Rule 403, on the grounds that potential prejudice exceeds the probative value.

Rule 404(b) provides that acts, crimes, or wrongs not charged in the current indictment are admissible only if the jury could find, by a preponderance of the evidence, that the defendant committed those acts. The other acts must be close in time to the charged offense (although they can have occurred either before or after it); must relate to a material issue in the indictment; and must have probative value, not mere possible worth.

The character of witnesses is covered by Rules 607-609 (see below). Note, however, that although the character of a person is generally inadmissible, the habit or a person or the routine practice of an organization CAN be admitted under Rule 406, to prove that conduct on a given occasion conformed to the habit or practice.

[¶5500.7] Witnesses

Rule 601 makes everyone competent to testify unless specifically ruled out for some reason. The judge has the power, under Rule 611, to control the questioning of witnesses to lead to the truth, prevent delay, and prevent attorneys from harassing witnesses.

The Federal Rules follow the so-called "American rule": i.e., the scope of cross-examination is limited to the subject matter of the direct examination, unless the court exercises its discretion to widen the scope. FRE 607 allows anyone to impeach a witness—even the lawyer who called the witness in the first place.

[¶5500.7.1] Impeachment

The character of a witness can be attacked to impeach his or her testimony only on the basis of testimony about the witness' reputation for truthfulness, or the opinion that another witness holds as to the first witness' truthfulness. Rule 608 permits this to be done only if the witness' credibility has been attacked. Extrinsic evidence cannot be used to prove that the witness is untruthful by proving the existence of acts that have been denied by the witness, even though this might seem more probative as to the witness' credibility than his or her reputation.

A witness can be impeached (in either a civil or criminal trial) by evidence of conviction of a crime involving dishonesty. A felony conviction of any type can be introduced if the court finds that its probative value exceeds its potential for prejudice. But convictions more than 10 years in the past can be admitted only at the discretion of the court: see Rule 609. Under *James v. Illinois*,[28] illegally obtained evidence that is subject to the exclusionary rule can be used for impeachment of the defendant—but cannot be used to impeach defense witnesses.

Witnesses can be asked leading questions on direct as well as cross-examination, with respect to preliminary or uncontested matters. An attorney can also lead hostile witnesses (as established by their demeanor) or adverse witnesses (as determined by their party alignment).

[¶5500.7.2] Opinion Evidence

Rule 701 allows a lay witness to give an opinion based on his or her perceptions where this would assist the trier of fact—e.g., how fast a car was going at a particular time. By and large, however, opinion testimony is the province of expert witnesses, and such testimony is governed by Rule 702.

An expert is a person who is qualified in an area of scientific, technical, or specialized knowledge, and whose knowledge assists the trier of fact in deciding issues or interpreting other testimony (see Rule 104(a)).

Rule 703 permits experts to base their conclusions on facts that are independently admissible, and/or facts of a type commonly used by experts in the same field. If a neutral opinion is required to supplement the opinions offered by the expert(s) for one or both sides, Rule 706 gives federal judges the power to appoint experts and order their compensation.

The test, under *Daubert*[29] is whether the reasoning or methodology behind the proposed testimony is scientifically valid; and whether it is proper to apply it to the facts at issue. The *Kumho* case extends *Daubert* to all expert witness testimony, rather than limiting it to scientific evidence.

A judge or juror cannot testify in any trial where he or she acts as such (Rules 605, 606). In fact, jurors are forbidden to testify orally or by affidavit about the deliberations leading up to an indictment or verdict. Even if a collateral or post-verdict attack on a verdict is made, the jurors are permitted to testify only about extraneous prejudicial information that was considered in the deliberations.

[¶5500.8] Public Policy Exclusions

The FRE renders inadmissible some categories of evidence that might be useful to the trier of fact, because public policy requires that certain activities be encouraged, rather than discouraged by their impact on potential future litigation.

Under Rule 407, subsequent remedial measures taken by a party (e.g., repairing a machine; changing the specifications of a manufactured product) are not admissible to show that the party was negligent in the first place. However, testimony about the remedial measures can be admitted for other purposes, e.g., for impeachment or to rebut a contention that remediation was impossible. Should evidence of remedial measures be improperly admitted, the District Court has discretion either to declare a mistrial, or to instruct the jurors that the improper evidence is not relevant to liability.

Rule 407's application is limited: it covers only remedial measures taken by the defendant, not a third party. Furthermore, not all steps taken by the defendant after an accident are remedial—they might, for instance, be investigative, and thus admissible. In a strict liability diversity case, Rule 407 is a procedural rule, so it (rather than conflicting state rules) will be applied.[30] Similarly, the fact that a defendant had or did not have liability insurance is rendered inadmissible as to the issue of negligence by Rule 411. Paying or agreeing to pay a plaintiff's medical expenses is not admissible as to the defendant's liability for the injury (Rule 409).

When negotiations occur as to entry of a plea of guilty or nolo contendere, but the plea is withdrawn, statements made during those negotiations are in general inadmissible in a civil or criminal proceeding. However, Rule 410 makes an exception (understandably) for perjury prosecutions, or if another statement made in the course of the same plea negotiation has been admitted, and must be put into context.

A criminal defendant's agreement to waive the FRE 410/Federal Rules of Criminal Procedure 11(e)(6) exclusion is enforceable absent proof that the waiver agreement was not knowing and voluntary: *U.S. v. Mezzanatto*, 513 U.S. 196 (Sup.Ct.1995).

[¶5500.8.1] Evidence of Sexual Behavior

In general, Rule 412(a) makes other sexual behavior of an alleged victim of a sex crime, or the alleged victim's sexual predisposition, inadmissible in a civil or criminal proceeding that charges a defendant with sexual misconduct. However, certain otherwise admissible evidence can be admitted under 412(b):

- Specific sexual behavior by the alleged victim proving that someone other than the defendant was the source of physical evidence (including semen and physical injury to the alleged victim)
- Specific sexual behavior involving the defendant, rather than other persons, to prove consent or when offered by the prosecution
- Evidence whose exclusion would violate the defendant's Constitutional rights.

In a civil case, otherwise admissible testimony as to the alleged victim's sexual behavior or predispositions can only be admitted if its probative value exceeds its potential for prejudice. The alleged victim's reputation is admissible only if it is raised by the victim.

[¶5500.8.2] Similar Acts Evidence

Rules 413-415 permit admission of evidence that the defendant committed other sexual assaults or acts of child molestation, in either a prosecution or a civil case involving sexual assault or child molestation. Such evidence can be considered for its bearing on any matter to which it is relevant. However, the prosecu-

A claim for benefits under an ERISA plan involves a federal question, so the privilege rules come from the federal common law, where doctor-patient privilege is unavailable.[41] In a federal-question case, state grand jury proceedings are entitled to the same protection against discovery in a civil suit as federal grand jury proceedings.[42]

In a case involving state law, where there is a conflict of laws between the state laws that might apply, the District Court must follow the law of privilege of whichever state the state's courts would apply using its own conflict-of-law rules.

In the federal system, some privilege and cognate rules are found outside the FRE. For instance, FRCP 26(b)(3) grants attorney work product a qualified immunity from discovery (which is not the same thing as attorney-client privilege at trial; see below).[43]

FRCP 26(c)(7) privileges trade secrets and confidential commercial information. Privileges are also available under FRCrimP 6(b) for grand jury materials, and 12.2(c) for statements made by the defendant in the course of a court-ordered psychiatric examination.

The claimant of privilege, rather than the proponent of the evidence, has the burden of proof with respect to issues relating to privilege.

Privilege can be waived by failing to object at the appropriate point of discovery or trial, or by making voluntary disclosure of matter that is alleged to be privileged.

[¶5500.11.1] Attorney-Client Privilege

In order to ensure that persons facing criminal charges or civil litigation can be adequately represented, communications between attorneys and clients are privileged. However, the privilege is subject to various limitations and qualifications. The privilege is deemed to operate for the benefit of the client, not the attorney. If the court is informed of a genuine need for disclosure, and there are no special circumstances present, the identity of a client and information about the fees is not protected, even if the substance of matters confided by the client is privileged.

For attorney-client privilege to be available, the information as to which privilege is asserted must have been imparted to the attorney in the context of legal representation, not other situations, and in order to secure legal advice not for other purposes (e.g., preparation of a tax return, which is a public document and therefore cannot be privileged[44]).

Disclosure of the information to a third party (other than one whose presence is indispensable—e.g., a stenographer taking notes) terminates the privilege. The privilege runs to the law firm, not the individual attorney, so waiving the privilege as to one attorney (for instance, by testifying about a confidential communication; putting the attorney-client relationship directly at issue; asserting reliance on an attorney's advice as an element of a claim or defense) waives it as to everyone in the firm.

Even if the final version of a document is published, earlier drafts can qualify for attorney-client privilege if they were intended to be confidential and they communicate legal advice to a client.[45]

The so-called "crime-fraud" exception applies to communications that do not serve the permissible objective of obtaining legal advice about past actions already taken, but those that involve advice about crimes or frauds that the client contemplates committing in the future.

The crime-fraud exception applies to client communications in furtherance of contemplated or ongoing criminal, fraudulent, or wrongful conduct. The exception is triggered on the basis of the client's motives; it doesn't matter whether or not the attorney was aware of impropriety.

The party seeking to introduce a client confidence on this basis must make a prima facie showing, by competent evidence, that the consultation was undertaken to further improper activity. It's not enough to show that the client was involved in contemporaneous criminal activity.

U.S. v. Zolin,[46] holds that a party raising the crime-fraud exception to the attorney-client privilege can request in camera review of the applicability of the privilege. Before granting review, the judge should require a showing of facts that would induce a reasonable person to believe in good faith that reviewing the disputed material would demonstrate the applicability of the crime-fraud exception. (In chambers disclosure of material for the limited purpose of assessing whether the privilege applies does not terminate the privilege.)

Not only are attorneys immune from being required to disclose client confidences; the attorney-client privilege prevents the government from forcing a suspect to instruct his or her attorney to disclose a confidential communication.[47]

It should be noted that §7525 of the Internal Revenue Service Restructuring and Reform Act broadens the "attorney-client" privilege, for tax purposes to cover communications engaged in to obtain tax advice from a CPA, enrolled agent, or enrolled actuary. However, the privilege is limited to non-criminal tax matters before the IRS and in federal court.

[¶5500.11.2] Doctor-Patient Privilege

The doctor-patient privilege is recognized in the evidence rules of most states, but does not exist as such in the FRE. In 1996, the Supreme Court applied a balancing test to recognize the validity of a psychotherapist-patient privilege, which extends to confidential communications made to licensed social workers (not just psychiatrists and psychologists) in the course of psychotherapy.[48]

[¶5500.11.3] Marital Privilege

In the federal system, marital privilege falls into two categories: a privilege against giving testimony adverse to one's spouse; and privilege against disclosure of confidential marital communications. (There is no privilege unless the testimony is genuinely adverse to the spouse's interests.)

Neither category is the same as the traditional rule of making one spouse incompetent to testify against the other. The witness spouse decides whether the privilege will apply: he or she can neither be forced to testify unwillingly, nor precluded from testifying should he or she wish to do so. The marital privilege is terminated by divorce (although it probably survives as to confidential communications made during the marriage), and is applicable only to persons who are considered married under the laws of the jurisdiction. The presence of third parties when communication occurs—even the couple's children—renders the privilege unavailable.

[¶5500.11.4] Clergy-Penitent Privilege

Under Catholic doctrine, confidences given in the confessional are sacred, and cannot be revealed by the priest without the consent of the penitent. This concept has been adopted in secular law, in religious contexts broader than ritual confession.

The clergy-communicant privilege has been held[49] to protect communications made to a member of the clergy, who was acting in a spiritual or professional capacity (not merely as a friend), by a penitent who seeks spiritual counseling and reasonably expects that the communication will remain confidential. The privilege is not vitiated by the presence of a third party who was essential to and in furtherance of the communication.

A clergymember does not have to disclose, in a civil action, documents containing the substance of the information divulged by the penitent.[50] A non-confessional communication to church officials, made for the purpose of receiving church counseling and ecclesiastical advice, is immune from disclosure in an abuse suit brought by the adoptive daughter of the person making the communications.[51]

[¶5500.11.5] Journalist's Privilege

A qualified privilege is available to journalists, so they are not generally required to divulge their confidential sources or disclose unpublished information acquired in the course of news-gathering activities. However, because the privilege is qualified rather than absolute, it may have to yield, e.g., if the journalist possesses highly material and relevant information, otherwise unobtainable, that is critical to a claim.[52]

See the Privacy Protection Act, 42 USC §2000aa-(6), creating a federal District Court cause of action for anyone aggrieved by search for or seizure of journalists' work product. The plaintiff is entitled to recover actual damages (but in any event, the liquidated damages of $1,000 provided by the statute), plus fees and costs as awarded by the court.

However, according to the Second Circuit, journalists do not have a First Amendment privilege with respect to nonconfidential information, and they must disclose it in civil suits.[53]

[¶5500.11.6] Governmental Privilege

Privilege is recognized in:

- State secrets of military or diplomatic significance
- Executive privilege for official information, including inter- and intra-agency communications dealing with policy- and decision-making functions
- Reports on ongoing investigations
- Communications about investigative techniques, including the identity of informants
- Judicial communications

The privilege for investigative techniques gives way if the defendant can show significant need for information (e.g., location of surveillance cameras). There is no privilege for the identity of informants if their identity has already been disclosed. A defendant who seeks disclosure of an informant's identity must show a concrete need for the information greater than mere suspicion or speculation; the question is usually resolved at an in-camera hearing.

[¶5500.11.7] Critical Self-Analysis

Some courts recognize a qualified privilege for a company's "critical self-analysis" (e.g., analysis of the business' success in achieving equal employment opportunity goals). To the extent that the privilege is recognized, it applies to subjective or evaluative material (but not hard data) prepared for a mandatory government report, where the policy reasons for exclusion (e.g., encouraging candor so organizations will improve their performance) clearly exceed the other party's need for the information.

Reports prepared for use by a hospital peer review committee have been deemed confidential, and can't even be released to the trial judge. In this reading, it's better for peer reviewers to be able to speak candidly than for litigants to have access to additional information.[54]

[¶5600] Appeals

Appellate courts serve two major functions: redressing errors committed by lower courts, and furthering the progress of the law by adopting new principles.

The decision to appeal involves several related determinations: that there is a right to appeal, or that the case will be attractive to a court that selects the cases it will review; that there is a meaningful probability that the appellate court will rule favorably; and that the benefits of the appeal are likely to exceed its costs in delay, money, and effort.

On the other hand, delay can be favorable to a litigant: for instance, a defendant ordered to pay a large sum may be willing to appeal simply in order to be able to earn interest on the amount of the judgment for several more years. Taking—or threatening—such an appeal can be a potent weapon to induce a successful plaintiff to settle post-trial for less than the amount awarded by the trier of fact.

In 1997 the Supreme Court withdrew former Federal Rules of Appellate Procedure (FRAP) 74-76, which contained an optional appeals procedure for civil cases in which both sides consented to trial before a Magistrate Judge. With the termination of the optional procedure, the surviving form of appeal is appeal to the Court of Appeals from a final judgment (FRAP 3).

[¶5605] Standard of Review

Depending on the type of case and the nature of the ruling appealed from, the appellate court may either be entitled to review the case de novo (i.e., as if the earlier ruling did not exist), or will merely examine the prior decision for obvious error or abuse of discretion.

It is very common for habeas proceedings to be maintained *in forma pauperis*, so the rules of 28 USC §1915 and FRAP 24 must be consulted.

Under *O'Sullivan v. Boerckel*,[69] state prisoners must exhaust their state-court remedies before seeking federal habeas relief. They must seek discretionary review in the state's highest court, if that is part of the ordinary appellate procedure.

[¶5650] Certiorari

Except in the very rare cases in which Supreme Court review is obtainable as of right, cases reach the Supreme Court only based on the discretionary grant of certiorari. See P.L. 100-352.

The Supreme Court has never been able to consider more than a fraction of the cases in which certiorari is sought, and in recent years, the Court has taken on a smaller-than-usual caseload. Denial of certiorari is not an opinion about the merits of the case.[70]

Certiorari jurisdiction over state court decisions is granted by 28 USC §1257(3). Review is available only if a federal question is directly ruled on or necessarily decided by the state court. To be reviewable by the Supreme Court, a state court judgment must be "final"[71]—that is, no other state tribunal can have the power to review or correct it. The judgment must effectively determine the litigation, not just an intermediate or interlocutory step.

Furthermore, a federal claim in a petition for certiorari can be considered only if it was addressed by or properly presented to the state court that rendered the decision the Supreme Court is being asked to review.[72] If the highest state court is silent on an issue, the aggrieved party has to overcome presumption that the issue was not properly presented below, and thus the state court did not have a chance to address it.

[¶5650.1] Role of Precedent

The Supreme Court is not obligated to adhere to a statutory precedent merely because Congress did not repeal it. In this context, non-action is not probative.[73]

The Supreme Court presumes that Courts of Appeals decide questions of state law correctly, but that presumption is inapplicable if the Court of Appeals was "plainly wrong."[74]

The Supreme Court's own precedents will usually be stare decisis and not reconsidered, because it is deemed that the integrity of judicial process usually requires reliance. This rule is subject to various exceptions[75]:

- Since the case was decided, it has turned out to be a solitary departure from established law
- The policy behind stare decisis not applicable
- The majority of courts won't follow it
- The case deals with interpretation of the Constitution, so it can only be altered by an amendment to the Constitution or change in the Supreme Court's position.

When the Supreme Court applies a new legal rule to a case, the rule becomes retroactive and applies to all pending cases, even those involving events before the Supreme Court decision was rendered.[76]

[¶5650.3] Rule Changes

Several changes in the Supreme Court rules took effect May 3, 1999 (see 67 LW 4064). A respondent/appellee who supports a petitioner/appellant is subject to the same time schedule for filing documents. Respondents or appellants who support other respondents or appellants are granted the right to file a reply brief. As a general rule, documents filed with the Supreme Court must be 6 $^1/_8$" x 9 $^1/_4$" booklets, typeset, conforming to the length limits and physical production standards of Rule 33.1.

ENDNOTES

1. Originally, this court was known as the U.S. Court of Claims. The Federal Courts Improvement Act of 1982 created the U.S. Claims Court. The court was redesignated again, as the U.S. Court of Federal Claims, by the Federal Courts Admin. Act of 1992, P.L. 102-572.
2. 505 U.S. 249 (Sup.Ct. 1992).
3. *Marathon Oil & Gas v. A.G. Ruhrgas,* 145 F.3d 211 (5th Cir. 1998).
4. Nor can multiple punitive damage claims be aggregated to reach the necessary level: *Ard v. Transcontinental Gas Pipeline*, 139 F.3d 596 (5th Cir. 1998).
5. 519 U.S. 611 (Sup.Ct. 1996)
6. *Leonhardt v. Western Sugar Co.*, 160 F.3d 631 (10th Cir. 1998); *Meritcare Inc. v. St. Paul Mercury Insurance Co.*, 166 F.3d 214 (3rd Cir. 1999).
7. *Free v. Abbott Labs*, 51 F.3d 524 (5th Cir. 1995); *In re Brand Name Prescription Drugs Antitrust Litigation*, 123 F.3d 599 (7th Cir. 1997).
8. E.g., *Bennett v. Spear*, 520 U.S. 154 (Sup.Ct. 1997) and *Lujan v. Defenders of Wildlife*, 504 U.S. 555 (Sup.Ct. 1992).
9. Under *United Food & Commercial Workers v. Brown Group, Inc.*, 116 S.Ct. 1529 (Sup.Ct. 1996).
10. See *Arizonans for Official English v. Arizona*, 520 U.S. 43 (Sup.Ct.1997).
11. *Calderon v. Moore*, 518 U.S. 149 (Sup.Ct. 1996).
12. According to *Barnes v. American Tobacco Co.*, 161 F.3d 127 (3rd Cir. 1998), a class of Pennsylvania smokers seeking a mandatory injunction creating a medical monitoring program cannot be certified, because of the need for individual inquiry as to when they started smoking and how much they smoked.
13. *Williams v. G.E. Capital Auto Lease Inc.*, 159 F.3d 266 (7th Cir. 1998).
14. *Thomas v. Albright*, 139 F.3d 227 (D.C. Cir. 1998).
15. *Matsushita Electric Industries Co. v. Epstein*, 516 U.S. 367 (Sup.Ct. 1996).
16. *California Public Employees' Retirement System v. Felzen*, #97-1732, 67 LW 4090 (1/20/99), affirming (without opinion) the Court of Appeals decision.

Part VII

CRIMINAL LAW

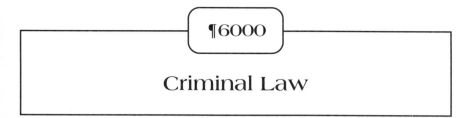

¶6000

Criminal Law

[¶6001]

This discussion is divided into two parts. The first deals with the concepts of substantive criminal law, including elements of offenses; elements of proof; and defenses. The second deals with Constitutional and other issues of criminal procedure, such as search and seizure, right to counsel, conduct of a jury trial, and remedies for persons convicted of a crime.

[¶6002] Substantive Criminal Law

A crime is wrongful conduct that is penalized by the state, in contrast to breach of contract or tort, which are conduct penalized by private parties. In many instances, the same conduct is both criminal and tortious. The general rule is that an offense penalized by a fine and/or less than one year of imprisonment is a misdemeanor; the offense is a felony if a conviction can result in imprisonment for more than a year.[1]

Society has many objectives in enacting criminal law, and there is high potential for conflict among the objectives. Society attempts to deter wrongdoing in general, and to deter particular individuals from engaging in crime. Imprisonment serves a restraint function (placing convicted individuals in a situation where they cannot harm the general public), but a retributive function and a rehabilitative function are also sought.

[¶6002.1] General Elements of a Crime

Several elements must be present in order to have a crime:

- Generally, a wrongful act, although sometimes omission can be a crime if there is a duty to act
- Mens rea: wrongful or "evil" state of mind
- Corpus delicti: Harmful effect of the activity (although sometimes attempts are penalized even if no one is harmed); the prosecution case requires proof that the harm was caused by criminality rather than accident, and any confession must be corroborated by proof of corpus delicti
- Prescribed punishment; if no punishment is prescribed, there is no crime.

Some subtle problems are raised by "inchoate offenses" such as attempt, conspiracy and solicitation. Both mens rea and actus reus (evil act) are required for proof. There must be a direct connection between the defendant's conduct and the harmful result.

Criminal statutes also differentiate among degrees of offenses, typically divided into first, second, and third (or even fourth and greater) degrees, depending on the number of elements of crime that can be proved and how serious each element is. The degree of an offense can be enhanced by aggravating factors and reduced by mitigating factors.

One offense is a lesser included offense of another if it is necessary to commit that offense in the course of committing a more serious offense. For instance, it is necessary to deliberately set a fire as part of the more serious offense of committing arson for profit at a time when the premises were occupied. The defendant is entitled to a jury instruction on the lesser included offense if, but only if, the evidence could reasonably be construed to mean that the defendant committed the lesser but not the more serious offense.

[¶6002.2] Burden Of Proof

In a criminal case, the prosecution is required to prove, beyond a reasonable doubt, all facts needed to establish the guilt of the defendant. Due Process is violated by a jury instruction that raises the standard of reasonable doubt to "grave uncertainty" or "actual substantial doubt."[2] Such an error is not harmless, so a conviction based on such an instruction would have to be reversed.[3]

There are two aspects: the burden of producing evidence, and that of persuading the trier of fact. To avoid a directed verdict, the prosecution must produce evidence of each element of the crime and convince the trier of fact as to each. If additional elements are present that enhance punishment (e.g., recidivism), the prosecution must prove those as well.

The burden of proof can be placed on the defendant to establish the affirmative defense of extreme emotional disturbance.[4] Indeed, because affirmative defenses are unusual factors, the defendant is required to prove them rather than the prosecution having to rule them out.

Sometimes the prosecution is entitled to rebuttable presumptions: for instance, that if a defendant has no explanation for possession of stolen property, that he or she stole it; that if a victim is shot at point-blank range, intent to kill was present.

There is no such thing as a directed verdict of guilty in a criminal case, no matter how strong the evidence. In fact, the judge can't even direct the jury to find for the prosecution on uncontested issues.

In contrast, verdict of acquittal can be directed, on the defendant's motion or the court's own motion, if the evidence is insufficient to support a conviction (e.g., not enough proof of corpus delicti; lack of connection between the defendant and the offenses charged). However, the defendant is not entitled to a directed verdict based on introduction of uncontradicted testimony that establishes a defense, because the trier of fact has the option of doubting the witness' credibility, even if the witness was not impeached.

[¶6002.3] Intent and State Of Mind

Criminal culpability can exist based on several states of mind:

factors such as the disability or restraint imposed by the sanction; whether it was historically regarded as punishment; if imposing the sanction requires a finding of scienter; whether it is excessive vis-à-vis its claimed purpose; whether it is intended to provide deterrence or retribution on behalf of society.[16]

In most instances, civil forfeitures are remedial and not punitive in nature, so there is no double jeopardy bar to both imprisoning an individual and declaring that person's property subject to forfeiture.[17]

The double jeopardy challenge might fail if concurrent criminal and civil proceedings are considered part of a single, coordinated prosecution or because the forfeiture requires different elements of proof.

Prison disciplinary proceedings (e.g., for escape) don't bar federal criminal charges; nor do administrative probation or parole revocation hearings. Confinement under a sexual predator statute is defined as treatment-oriented, not punitive, and thus not subject to double jeopardy arguments.[18]

Debarment from government contracting isn't double jeopardy unless it is overwhelmingly disproportionate to the contractor's improper conduct. Administrative suspension of a driver's license for driving under the influence of alcohol or drugs is remedial, not punitive.

Failure to contest an administrative forfeiture means it never becomes a judicial forfeiture, so jeopardy does not attach.[19] Jeopardy didn't attach in forfeiture if criminal proceedings were completed before forfeiture proceedings began.

It constitutes double jeopardy to prosecute a person both for an offense and for lesser included offenses of that offense. The basic rule comes from *Blockburger v. U.S.*,[20] which defines double jeopardy as a successive prosecution where the second or later offense contains elements identical to, or contained within, the first offense charged. If a single act violates more than one statute, the double jeopardy test is whether each provision requires proof of facts that the other does not.[21]

Simultaneous possession of different drugs can constitute different offenses. Two conspiracies are different if primary objects of the conspiracy are different, and each includes at least one element not present in the other. After a conviction has been reversed on appeal, the defendant can be prosecuted for conspiring to commit the act for which the conviction has been reversed. Both conspiracy and CCE (continuing criminal enterprise) can be charged for essentially the same conduct, as long as the sentences run concurrently, not consecutively.

The holding of *Witte* is that not only does the double jeopardy doctrine forbid more than one punishment for the same offense, but that ordinarily, prosecutors cannot get more than one trial to impose the single punishment. Sentencing a defendant within the range permitted by the Guidelines (see ¶6080) is not deemed to be multiple punishment even if the sentence includes consideration of uncharged conduct. It would be double jeopardy to sentence a defendant to two consecutive prison terms for a single violation of a statute.[22] A "three-strike" statute is not double jeopardy because it punishes the current crime more heavily when priors are taken into account; it is not additional punishment for the earlier convictions.[23] In a three-strike sentence enhancement proceeding it is not double jeopardy to retry an allegation of prior conviction,[24] although this rule is limited to non-capital cases; post-trial proceedings cannot be used to obtain a death sentence that was rejected by the trial jury.[25]

In another group of cases, the defendant has waived the double jeopardy defense—e.g., by applying for, or even consenting to, a mistrial. In essence, double jeopardy bars successive trials after one completed, fair trial; incomplete or unfair trials creating a manifest necessity for retrial do not necessarily have double jeopardy consequences.

The defendant has the initial burden of making a prima facie case on double jeopardy, but once this is done, the government has the burden of producing a preponderance of evidence that double jeopardy should not bar prosecution.[26] Unlike exclusionary rule claims (which are waived if not asserted before trial), a double jeopardy claim can be raised on appeal even if this argument was not presented to the District Court.[27]

[¶6007.1] Collateral Estoppel

The doctrine of collateral estoppel is related, but not identical, to double jeopardy. Collateral estoppel can be asserted to prevent repeat litigation, between the same parties, of an issue which has already been determined by a valid and final judgment. In the criminal context, the parties must be so closely related that they are considered to be the same. Such a determination would probably be made involving a District Attorney's office and a Department of Parole, but probably not in the case of a District Attorney's and U.S. Attorney's offices.

Collateral estoppel or issue preclusion is an issue of ultimate fact that has already been determined by a valid final judgment and thus cannot be re-litigated by the same parties.[28] The collateral estoppel component of the Double Jeopardy clause doesn't necessarily exclude otherwise admissible, relevant, and probative evidence because it relates to charges of which the defendant was acquitted.[29]

[¶6007.2] State and Federal Prosecution

The "dual sovereignty" doctrine allows successive prosecutions by state and federal authorities, if the governmental entities maintain the cases separately; see *Koon v. U.S.*[30] A contrary result would create problems if a state prosecution for a comparatively minor offense derailed a major federal prosecution.

However, a valid double jeopardy argument might exist if the federal prosecution is merely a sham to make up for a failed state prosecution. Under the so-called "Petite policy," the federal government refrains from prosecuting defendants who have already been tried in state courts for acts that could generate federal charges. However, this is merely a policy, not a substantive right upon which defendants can rely to block a federal prosecution.

About half the states have adopted the Model Penal Code view, that a federal prosecution (whether it results in acquittal or conviction) bars a subsequent state prosecution whenever the federal case involves the same conduct as the state case, unless:

- The federal and state statutes are aimed at different harms or evils
- Different proof is required
- The state offense had not been consummated as of the beginning of the federal trial.

State prosecution is also barred by a federal resolution in favor of the defendant, in a manner inconsistent with proving facts required to establish the state case.

If a federal statute supports two plausible interpretations, the one that does not alter the balance of power between state and federal governments will be preferred.[31] However, such analysis will only be undertaken if the statute is ambiguous.[32]

The federal Assimilative Crimes Act prevents a state conviction of second-degree murder and a state-law life sentence, given that there is a federal statute penalizing murder and a Guidelines sentence of 168-210 months.[33]

[¶6007.3] Ex Post Facto

The Constitution forbids Congress to make any "ex post facto law." The ex post facto concept applies to criminal legislation only, not to civil legislation or court decisions. An ex post facto law imposes a criminal penalty on an action that was legal at the time it was committed; aggravates the degree of the offense; increases its punishment; or changes the applicable evidentiary rules. (Ex post facto reductions in punishment are permissible, because they do not have negative consequences for defendants.)

Lowering the maximum punishment for an offense but raising the minimum sentence is considered an increase. A rule that permits additional kinds of evidence is acceptable if its effect is to allow defendants in general to present additional evidence of innocence even if it also permits more evidence of the guilt of a particular defendant.

Procedural changes that do not involve evidence (for example, changes in rules of jurisdiction or venue; number of peremptory challenges available during jury selection) are only ex post facto if they impair a substantial right that was available to the defendant at the time of the alleged offense.

The common-law rule is that outright repeal of a statute that does not have a savings clause prevents prosecutions (pending or not instituted before the repeal) for earlier violations. However, any conviction that was finalized before repeal remains valid. Furthermore, most statutes are drafted with a savings clause precisely to eliminate this line of defense.

A decision that is reached after a petitioner's conviction is final (i.e., after all direct appeals have been completed) that creates a new Constitutional rule of criminal procedure, will not be applied retroactively.[34]

[¶6007.4] Entrapment

The defense of entrapment does not dispute that the defendant performed the actions alleged in the indictment or information—only that the actions were performed with the requisite criminal intent, in that the defendant responded to the government agent's provocation but lacked the predisposition to commit the crime without government involvement. Factors in determining the defendant's predisposition include, e.g.,

- Character and reputation
- If the initial suggestion of criminal activity came from the government agent
- If the defendant exhibited reluctance that had to be overcome by the government agent
- The nature of the persuasion or inducement provided by the government agent.

Assertion of an entrapment defense can open the door to introduction of testimony about the defendant's lack of prior arrests or convictions, under Federal Rules of Evidence 404(b) and 405(b), because character is an essential part of the defense.[35]

Inconsistent defenses can be asserted in federal court, so a defendant who denies one or more elements of the offense can still get a jury instruction on entrapment if this is supported by the facts of the case.[36]

[¶6007.5] Duress

The defense of duress takes the position that the individual lacked mens rea, and committed the crime not out of personal intention or for personal advantage, but because forced to commit it by someone else: e.g., that someone else threatened to harm the defendant or someone close to the defendant unless the defendant committed the crime. Such a defense requires proof of force or a threat of a nature such that a reasonable person in the defendant's situation would have been unable to resist.

[¶6007.6] Necessity

The necessity defense depends on circumstances rather than the act of another person. For instance, a prison escape might be excused if the prison were burning at the time of the escape. A necessity defense might be asserted by a cancer or glaucoma patient who uses marijuana for symptom relief, or by an ideologically motivated person who attacks a missile base or abortion clinic. However, it is far from certain that a necessity defense will succeed in such cases.

[¶6007.7] Alibi

A defendant who asserts an alibi claims that he or she was somewhere other than at the scene of the crime at the relevant time. In some jurisdictions, alibi is an affirmative defense (i.e., the defendant must prove it). In others, however, when an alibi is asserted, it is merely an additional part of the prosecution case to prove that the defendant was indeed present.

Generally, the sale of printed pornography depicting adults, to adults, is not a law enforcement priority. However, issues involving pornography on the Internet, especially child pornography, are significant, especially in light of the difficulty of controlling who gains access to a particular Web site.

[¶6020.4] Arson

Arson is the crime of intentionally creating a fire or explosion involving a building or vehicle. Degrees of enhancement include the extent of the damage to the building or vehicle; using explosive devices; arson for profit (e.g., burning down a building of limited worth but with significant insurance coverage); committing arson when the perpetrator knew or should have known of the presence of people; and actual harm to people.

P.L. 104-155, the Church Arson Prevention Act of 1996, enacted at 18 USC §247, making it a federal crime intentionally to deface, damage, or destroy religious real property because of the race, color, or ethnicity of the congregation associated with the property.

[¶6020.5] Drunk Driving and Vehicular Offenses

A high percentage of arrests are made for driving while under the influence of alcohol or controlled substances, so these cases make up a large part of the criminal lawyer's caseload. They may also make up part of the caseload of the general practitioner, because individuals (or their relatives) who do not otherwise come within police jurisdiction may do so because of an allegation of DUI (driving under the influence) or DWI (driving while intoxicated). The offense consists of having a BAC (blood alcohol concentration) higher than the statutory limit: typically, .08% or .10% of alcohol in the blood.

Depending on the jurisdiction and the facts of the case, an accused drunk driver might also be charged with reckless driving, vehicular assault, vehicular homicide,[41] manslaughter, or even "depraved-heart" murder.

DUI/DWI cases comprise both criminal and administrative elements, because it is very likely that a convicted drunk driver will face suspension of his or her driver's license. There may also be consequences for automobile insurance: for instance, the person may be denied insurance other than limited, high-cost coverage under the assigned risk pool. Conviction of, or guilty or no contest plea to, a drunk driving offense is likely to have negative consequences if the driver is sued for injuring another person or harming property.

Especially for first offenses and persons with strong ties in the community, attendance at "DWI School" (a program of alcohol education and remedial driving education), or entrance into an alcohol rehabilitation program,[42] may result in pretrial diversion or an Adjournment in Contemplation of Dismissal. Sometimes limited driving privileges will be permitted so a person can continue to work. Sometimes sentences involving incarceration can be suspended, or served on weekends, so the driver can maintain employment and family responsibilities.

[¶6020.5.1] Intoxication Testing

Usually, when the police stop[43] a person who is suspected of impaired driving, they will ask him or her to perform simple tests such as walking a straight line or reciting the alphabet backwards. Some states use a "horizontal gaze nystagmus" test to see if the driver's eyes track normally[44]; other states do not consider this a scientifically valid test of intoxication.

The next step is usually an "intoxilyzer" breath test. The premise of breath testing is that there will be a predictable ratio between alcohol in the breath and alcohol in the blood. Some cases have successfully challenged treating the ratio as a conclusive, irrebuttable presumption.[45]

Sometimes a successful challenge can be posed to the validity of the police stop; the accuracy of the testing instrument; or the validity of a borderline result.

A *Miranda* warning is required before custodial interrogation by the police (see ¶6035.1), but not before collection of non-testimonial information. Videotaped evidence of an arrested person's slurred speech and lack of coordination is non-testimonial, and therefore does not require a warning, but asking an arrested person the date of his or her sixth birthday is testimonial and requires a *Miranda* warning.[46]

According to the Ninth Circuit, if there is probable cause to suspect DUI, the police have a reasonable belief that an emergency threatens the destruction of evidence, and a reasonable testing procedure is used, a blood sample can be taken prior to arrest even over the objections of the alleged drunk driver.[47]

BAC test results are medical records that qualify for the medical records hearsay exception in a civil suit. Neither the chain of custody nor the reliability of BAC testing has to be established.[48]

[¶6020.5.2] Implied Consent Laws

Surrendering a breath, blood or urine sample for BAC testing is inherently self-incriminatory, yet there is an important public policy in deterring and punishing drunk driving. Most states have adopted "implied consent" laws that hold that the act of driving a car constitutes consent to BAC testing incident to any arrest made by the police on reasonable cause to believe the driver is intoxicated.

Refusal to submit to testing can result in immediate confiscation of the driver's license, which can only be returned after an administrative hearing on the reasonableness of the police action.[49] On the other hand, a person who is tested and found to have an excessive BAC is very likely to be convicted of drunk driving and to undergo license revocation or suspension.

A license suspension hearing is an administrative hearing, but carries a right to counsel, right to confrontation, and cross-examination of the arresting officer. Some states also penalize failure to submit to BAC testing as an offense independent of drunk driving.

The general rule is that suspending or revoking a driver's license for failure or refusal to be tested is not punitive in nature. Since it is not punitive, it cannot constitute double jeopardy to suspend or revoke the license and also punish the individual for drunk driving.[50]

[¶6020.6] Firearms Offenses

The typical state criminal code sets out requirements (such as applying in advance so a records check can be performed) for getting a license or permit to own firearms. An additional permit, or special circumstances (such as carrying bank deposits or valuable merchandise) is usually required to carry a weapon outside one's home or place or business, or to carry a concealed weapon. Certain types of weapons, such as machine guns and assault weapons, are banned or restricted.

In the federal system, 18 USC §924(c)(1) imposes a five-year mandatory sentence for "carrying" a firearm "during and in relation to" a drug trafficking crime. Conviction does not depend on the defendant's carrying the firearm on his or her person; the statute s satisfied by having the firearm in a locked trunk or glove compartment during a drug deal.[51] "Use" of a firearm under §924(c) is defined to require active employment, not mere possession, of the firearm.[52]

Possession of firearms by convicted felons is unlawful under 18 USC §922(g)(1), and §924(e) imposes extra penalties on three-time convictees found to possess firearms. If the civil rights of a felon are restored, but he or she is allowed to possess certain kinds of firearms but forbidden to possess others, §§922(g)(1) and 924(e) are triggered by any firearm possession, not just the forbidden types.[53]

"Willful" violations of license requirements for selling firearms violate §924(a)(1)(D). In general, proof of a willful act requires proof that the defendant knew the conduct was illegal as well as bad, but a §924(a)(1)(D) conviction can be obtained by proof that the defendant knew that selling the firearms was illegal. It is not necessary that he knew and flouted the federal licensing requirements.[54]

The Northern District of Texas ruled[55] that 18 USC §922(g)(8), which makes it a federal crime for the subject of a domestic violence protection order to possess a firearm, is unconstitutional. In this analysis, the statute does not give proper notice, and violates the Second Amendment, which is read to provide an individual right rather than being limited to the creation of militias.

[¶6020.7] Drug Offenses

All of the states ban the use, sale, transportation, or even possession of "controlled substances": i.e., illegal drugs, or legal drugs that are not the subject of a lawful prescription. The degree of the offense depends on the nature of the drug (some jurisdictions have decriminalized or reduced penalties for possession of small amounts of marijuana) and, critically, on the amount involved. An inference is often drawn that possession of a large amount of a controlled substance shows intent to sell, not just intent to use the substance personally. Drug offenses may carry mandatory prison sentences, or longer prison sentences than non-drug felonies of the same degree.

In prosecutions for drug conspiracies under 21 USC §848 (Continuing Criminal Enterprise, or CCE), a mid-1999 Supreme Court decision[56] holds that the jury must be unanimous as to which specific violations are part of the continuing series of violations to be penalized.

A person convicted of a dual object drug conspiracy, (21 USC §841, 846) involving both cocaine and cocaine base, can be sentenced based on the guidelines covering all the drugs involved in the same course of conduct.[57]

[¶6020.8] Larceny and Fraud Offenses

Theft offenses, both violent and non-violent, are very common, and are criminalized under many headings and in various degrees, depending on factors such as the degree of force used (if any), the degree of risk to victims, and the amount stolen. Larceny consists of taking other people's money or property without their consent, and with intent to keep it (rather than, for instance, joyriding, which consists of taking a car without permission but with intent to return it).

Larceny also includes obtaining property with the consent of its owner, if the consent was obtained by improper means such as deception, or by "paying" for merchandise with a check known to be fraudulent.

[¶6020.8.1] Robbery

Robbery, one of the most serious larceny offenses because of the potential for harm to the victim, consists of forcible theft by use or threatened use of physical force to prevent or overcome the victim's resistance, or to induce the victim to surrender the property that is the subject of the offense.

Carjacking is a particular type of robbery: forcibly stealing a vehicle from the owner who is entering, exiting, or operating it. It is a federal crime. Conditional intent to kill or harm (i.e., if the victim refused to surrender the vehicle) satisfies the intent requirement of 18 USC §2119.[58] Under §2119, serious bodily injury or death of the victim are elements of the highest level of the offense, not mere sentencing factors.[59]

[¶6020.8.2] Criminal Trespass and Burglary

The lowest degree, criminal trespass, involves entering a building that is not open to the public. If "breaking and entering" rather than just entering is involved, the offense is likely to constitute burglary. The offense is enhanced if the building is a dwelling; if entry or remaining in the building is unlawful; if there is an intent to steal or commit another crime; if the theft or other crime actually occurs; if entry occurs at night rather than in the daytime.

Related offenses include possession of burglar's tools and possession of stolen property.

[¶6020.8.3] Fraud

Fraud involves obtaining money or property by deception or by false promise (an express or implied representation that the fraudfeasor or a third party will do something desired by the victim of the fraud). Forgery involves the creation of false documents, or affixing an unauthorized signature to a document.

In a prosecution for bank, wire, or mail fraud, the prosecution must prove that the allegedly fraudulent act affected the outcome of a transaction.[60] In a tax

- Tangible materials seized during an unlawful search
- Testimony about knowledge acquired during an unlawful search
- Tangible or testimonial evidence deriving from an unlawful search.

Recent decisions are far more restrictive as to the scope of the exclusionary rule than earlier decisions. Compare *California v. Acevedo*,[74] and *Minnesota v. Dickerson*,[75] [searches and seizures outside the judicial process, without prior approval, are per se unreasonable under the Fourth Amendment unless they fall into a few specific well-defined categories of exceptions] with *Vernonia School District v. Acton*[76] [the Fourth Amendment doesn't require a warrant to establish the reasonableness of all government searches, and probable cause is not inevitably required when a warrant is not necessary].

State Constitutions and state statutes may be either more or less protective of individuals than the U.S. Constitution. A state Constitutional amendment that eliminates the exclusionary rule with respect to evidence seized contrary to state—but not federal—law does not violate the Due Process clause.[77]

The exclusionary rule does not apply to illegally seized evidence (e.g., weapons found in a parolee's home) used in parole revocation hearings, because allowing the evidence to be used in the limited context of parole revocation hearings does not significantly encourage police misconduct.[78]

Courts differ on the application (if any) of the exclusionary rule to civil cases. The decision depends on whether the court believes that exclusion will deter improper police conduct. In general, the exclusionary rule is not applicable in Grand Jury proceedings[79] or to proceedings where a prisoner's supervised release might be revoked.[80]

The exclusionary rule does not require exclusion of evidence obtained pursuant to an arrest that was based on erroneous information,[81] nor evidence that would have inevitably been discovered through an independent source that is free of the taint of the unlawful search.[82]

Chambers v. Maroney, 399 U.S. 42 (Sup.Ct. 1970) and *Fahy v. Connecticut*, 375 U.S. 84 (Sup.Ct. 1963) hold that admission of evidence that was unreasonably seized can be harmless error, if the defendant could not have been prejudiced by the admission—i.e., it did not contribute to the conviction. But if it was contributory, reversal is required even if there was enough other evidence to justify the conviction.

Evidence that, because of the exclusionary rule, cannot be admitted in the case in chief can be used to impeach the testimony of a defendant who testifies,[83] but not the testimony of defense witnesses[84] because a defendant who chooses to testify assumes an obligation of truthfulness.

[¶6030.4] What is a Search?

The question is not trivial, because if no "search" has occurred, clearly there has been no unreasonable search. *Maryland v. Macon*,[85] defines a search as an infringement of what society considers an expectation of privacy. Looking at items in plain sight—even if a device such as a flashlight or binoculars is used—does not constitute a search. See, e.g., *Coolidge v. New Hampshire*.[86]

The "plain view" doctrine of *Minnesota v. Dickerson*,[87] authorizes a seizure if the police were lawfully in the position from which they observed an object whose incriminating nature was immediately apparent, and if they had lawful access to the object.

Dickerson also authorizes "plain touch," seizure of an object whose suspicious outline or mass became apparent during a pat-down for weapons during a *Terry* stop. However, "plain touch" does not excuse a warrantless seizure of a small bag of crack cocaine, whose outline made it obvious that it could not be a weapon.

Inspecting "open fields" is not a search, but a distinction is drawn between "curtilage"—the fields, yard, etc. surrounding a building—and "open fields." The distinction depends on factors such as the perception of the occupants; how close the alleged curtilage is to the house; whether it is enclosed or screened from view; and if its use is primarily residential.

Various results have been reached about garbage placed outside a home for collection, and other abandoned items.[88]

The Fourth Amendment governs the conduct of police and their agents, so it is generally inapplicable to a search performed by a private individual with no police participation. The individual (even if he or she wishes to cooperate with a police investigation) must not be acting at the order, request, or suggestion of the police for this exception to apply: *Coolidge v. New Hampshire*.[89]

The protection of the Fourth Amendment runs to persons, not places, so ownership of property has some relevance, but the real test is the invasion of a person's legitimate right of privacy in the place that has been invaded.[90]

[¶6030.4.1] Reasonable Expectation of Privacy

Some expectation of privacy is recognized in business and commercial premises, but to a lesser degree than in a residence,[91] but there is no expectation of privacy in a prison cell.[92]

Someone who pays a short visit to a home for commercial purposes (in this case, the none-too-lawful commercial purpose of bagging cocaine) does not have a reasonable expectation of privacy within the home.[93]

A reasonable expectation of privacy has been deemed to exist in a hotel room[94] and in a taxi.[95] Searches of schoolchildren are analyzed for their reasonableness under all the circumstances, and probable cause is not required to search a student's gym locker.[96]

There doesn't have to be a tangible place for these issues to emerge. It has been held that there is no reasonable expectation of privacy in chat room communications or e-mails, so seizure of messages dealing with child pornography did not violate the Fourth Amendment.[97]

[¶6030.5] Search Warrants

Although certain exceptions apply,[98] the basic search-and-seizure rules revolve around the issuance of a warrant by a neutral and detached magistrate. According to *Michigan v. Summers*,[99] a search warrant implies a power of reasonable detention of occupants of the place being searched, while the search continues. However, absent exigent circumstances or a valid consent, it is not permitted to search for the subject of an arrest warrant in another person's house.[100] Once a search has been made pursuant to a warrant, the general rule is that the police may not return to make a further, warrantless search.[101]

The trial court has discretion to interview the officer/affiant in camera to test the accuracy of assertions relating to confidential informants, but probably will not do so unless the defendant has raised significant doubt as to the credibility of the affiant.[102]

Franks[103] permits the defendant to seek suppression of evidence on the grounds that the police officer/affiant lied on the warrant application; included misinformation; or omitted information with reckless disregard for truth. However, the falsehood or omission must be material. The defendant must furnish evidence to support the claim of falsehood in order for the court to grant a "Franks hearing." *Franks* applies only if the affiant, not someone else (e.g., the informant) was lying, and the lie or misstatement must be material, not trivial.

Questions about the competency of evidence produced by an allegedly illegal search or seizure are questions of law, to be determined by the judge—especially questions as to the validity of a warrant.

Analysis of the conditions of entry pursuant to a "no-knock" warrant involve considerations such as whether the police reasonably believed that announcing their entry would lead to danger, futility or impairment of the investigation. It is not relevant whether or not property was destroyed.[104]

If a warrant is invalid in whole or in part, the doctrine of redaction provides that only evidence obtained under the invalid part of the warrant need be suppressed. Furthermore, two 1984 cases[105] take the position that the exclusionary rule exists to deter knowing misconduct by the police Therefore, if the police rely in good faith on an invalid warrant, exclusion is not required because there has been no knowing misconduct.[106]

Generally, evidence will **not** be suppressed on the grounds of noncompliance with a rule of procedure, e.g., failure to give the suspect a copy of the warrant attachments.

On a related issue, a prosecutor who makes false factual statements in the affidavit that is part of the application for an arrest warrant can be sued for civil rights damages under 42 USC §1983, because absolute prosecutorial immunity does not extend to falsehoods.[107]

[¶6030.6] Searches Incident to a Lawful Arrest

In the course of a lawful arrest, the police can search the arrestee's person and the area within his or her immediate reach.[108] An arrest is always proper when made pursuant to a valid arrest warrant. It can also be proper in exigent circumstances, e.g., when the police officer has actually observed a crime in progress or observed suspicious behavior (such as the exchange of money for glassine envelopes or vials), or has enough reasonable information (including hearsay) to conclude that the suspect committed a felony.[109] When a lawful arrest is made, the arresting officers are permitted to make a search incident to the arrest, to prevent destruction of evidence and to remove weapons that could be used to injure the arresting officer.

However, exceeding the permitted scope of search incident to arrest violates the Fourth Amendment, so any evidence so obtained must be excluded.[110] The permissible scope is limited to the person of the arrestee and the areas within his or her immediate control. The search cannot precede the arrest and also be used to justify the arrest if contraband is discovered.[111]

Officers executing an arrest warrant who have a reasonable belief that the suspect is in a building can enter that building and search places where a person could hide; but once the arrest is made, it is not legitimate to use the pretext of looking for the person to search the other rooms of the building.[112]

When a person is arrested at home, a precautionary search can be made, without a warrant, probable cause, or even reasonable suspicion, provided that it is limited to places immediately adjoining the place of the arrest from which an attack could be launched. The police are permitted to make a protective sweep, based on reasonable suspicion that a dangerous person could be hiding in the places to be inspected.

The Tenth Circuit has ruled[113] that the Fourth Amendment justifies a search of the covered area of a sports utility vehicle (covered by a built-in vinyl cover) incident to the arrest of the driver.

[¶6030.7] Vehicle Searches

Many, many cases involve an automobile that is stopped for a traffic offense, and in which contraband is discovered. *Whren v. U.S.*,[114] holds that the Fourth Amendment's test for reasonableness of an automobile stop is probable cause to believe that a traffic violation occurred, not whether a reasonable officer would have made the stop. In other words, the officers' actual motivation, not a reasonableness test, is the issue.

Reasonable suspicion for automobile stops and probable cause for warrantless search are fluid concepts,[115] involving determination of historical facts leading up to the stop or search, involving mixed questions of law and fact (whether a reasonable officer would be suspicious or find probable cause for the search).

Nevertheless, if a police officer stops a car based on probable cause to believe that a traffic offense occurred, and the police officer issues a citation for the traffic offense, there has not been an "arrest" that will justify a search, because the police are at much less risk than if there had been an arrest and the suspect faced incarceration rather than a mere traffic fine.[116]

If there is probable cause to believe that the vehicle contains contraband, the vehicle can be searched without a warrant,[117] given the high mobility of vehicles and the diminished expectation of privacy resulting from heavy regulation of vehicles and driving. *Maryland v. Dyson*[118] permits a warrantless search of a car (even if there is enough time to get a warrant) if the police have a tip or other reasonable belief that there are illegal drugs in the car.

[¶6035.2.1] Undercover Agents

The Supreme Court has held that an undercover police agent placed in a cell with a suspect is not required to give a *Miranda* warning before asking the suspect if he had ever killed anyone.[146]

[¶6035.3] Testimonial vs. Non-Testimonial Conduct

Although the Fifth Amendment precludes anyone from being forced to incriminate him- or herself, there is a range of issues that overlaps the Fourth and Fifth Amendments. Causing a suspect to exhibit physical characteristics is not testimonial in nature, and therefore is not self-incriminatory, an argument that permits warrantless examinations and testing incident to an arrest, especially in circumstances where delaying the test until a warrant is obtained makes the test results less useful (e.g., the alcohol content of blood diminishes over time).[147]

A suspect can be required to submit to photographing and fingerprinting, and can be required to give voice exemplars and handwriting samples[148]—in other words, painless and reasonably non-intrusive demands. But it is an unreasonable search to require a defendant to submit to surgery that is expected to remove an incriminating bullet.[149]

[¶6040] Sixth Amendment Issues

The Sixth Amendment governs the right to counsel; various issues of identifications and their admissibility; confrontation of accusers[150] and public trials; and guarantees a "speedy" trial—the latter very much a term of art.

[¶6040.1] Identification Issues

In the Sixth Amendment context, identification of a suspect can be challenged on the grounds of impermissible suggestiveness. Challenges may succeed, for instance, if the identification was made at the crime scene, when the victim or other witness is emotionally stressed. Due Process forbids unduly suggestive police identification procedures that create a serious risk of misidentification by witnesses.

The bedrock case on identification is *U.S. v. Wade*, 388 U.S. 218 (Sup.Ct. 1967). *Wade* requires lineups to be conducted under reasonable conditions (although it is not necessary for the "fillers" other than the suspect to look like the suspect's clones), and bans one-person "show-ups" (the police ask the witness if the suspect is the person they saw commit the crime) as unduly suggestive. The prosecution must give notice to the defense that out-of-court identification evidence will be introduced. Such notice entitles the defense to a "*Wade* hearing" on the admissibility of the testimony.

Under *Wade*, if the pretrial identification was improper, an in-court identification of the defendant may still be admissible, but first it must be validated as an independent recollection.

A lineup is considered superior, because it involves human beings rather than pictures, but asking a witness to view a photo array is not necessarily improper. Identification of photographs may be challenged[151] if there are not enough photographs to make a valid array; if they do not bear a close enough resemblance to the suspect to create a valid identification (i.e., if only one dark-skinned or light-skinned person, or only one with long hair, is included, the suspect may be identified purely on the basis of this one characteristic, rather than a true resemblance). However, an impermissible photo identification can be rehabilitated by an in-court identification.

Some eyewitnesses are not particularly observant or do not have very good memories, so their testimony can be challenged on these bases. Observing a crime is a brief event, and conditions of observation are typically poor, but it is also a memorable event—so attempts to challenge eyewitness testimony may backfire, if the jury is firmly convinced that the victim or other witness is accurate and truthful.

The test of either out-of-court or in-court identification is its reliability. But where the pretrial identification procedures were not unduly suggestive, challenge of an in-court identification goes to weight rather than admissibility.[152]

[¶6040.2] Attachment of the Right to Counsel

The Sixth Amendment provides a right to counsel, applicable to both the federal government and the states, in all criminal prosecutions.[153]

There are four interrelated elements in the Sixth Amendment right to counsel: the simple right to counsel; the right to counsel of one's own choice; to effective counsel (see ¶6087.2.1); and for the attorney to have a long enough period of preparation to render an effective defense. The right to counsel applies to state courts on the same terms as to federal courts.

Incriminating statements uttered during custodial interrogation are inadmissible if the suspect was denied access to an attorney.[154] Interrogation must stop when the suspect makes an unequivocal demand for counsel, but can resume without counsel if the suspect voluntarily re-initiates contact with police.[155] After charges have been filed, law enforcement officials are not permitted to deliberately elicit incriminating information from a defendant unless the attorney is present or the defendant has waived the presence of the attorney—whether or not the defendant is in custody.[156]

The Supreme Court's position is that the right to counsel is specific to a particular offense; interrogation without a lawyer on Offense B is permissible even if the suspect is represented by counsel on Offense A.[157]

Although the police must not impair the right to consult an attorney (if the suspect wants one), there is no affirmative duty for the police to have lawyers available in case they are requested by suspects.[158]

A suspect can invoke the right to counsel conditionally, for instance, "If I take a polygraph test, I want a lawyer"; in such a case, it would be permissible to question the suspect with no attorney present as long as there is no polygraph test.

[¶6040.3] Critical Stages

The right to counsel attaches at "critical stages" in the law enforcement process, as soon as an individual becomes the subject of adversary criminal proceedings (and is no longer a mere subject of investigation). A stage of the prosecution is critical if the lack of counsel could impair the right to a fair trial.[159]

According to *Wade*, there is no right to counsel at lineup before the suspect has been accused of a crime, but there is at the preliminary hearing, or at any identification of the defendant at of after initiation of adversary judicial proceedings.[160]

FRCrimP Rule 44(a) requires appointment of counsel for an indigent defendant at every stage of the proceedings, unless the right is waived and the defendant chooses to appear pro se (see ¶6040.4).

The defendant's ability to choose counsel is not infinite. The District Court judge has discretion to either grant or deny a continuance to a defendant who wants to substitute counsel. Factors in the decision include possible prejudice if the continuance is denied; who will be inconvenienced if it is granted; and whether the defendant is using the motion for substitution as a delaying tactic.

[¶6040.4] Defendants Proceeding Pro Se

An accused person can waive the right to counsel, as long as the waiver is intelligent, knowing, and voluntary. The state has the burden of establishing that the right to counsel has been waived.[161]

A defendant can choose to represent him- or herself pro se, but the judge must inquire if the defendant is capable of self-representation. The request must be clear, unequivocal, and timely (e.g., made before the trial begins). The court can appoint stand-by counsel for a pro se defendant, even if the defendant objects.[162]

In a felony (but not necessarily a misdemeanor) case, the Sixth Circuit requires indigent accused persons to be offered appointed counsel unless the right to counsel is knowingly and intelligently waived.[163] However, neither the Sixth Amendment, the Criminal Justice Act, nor 18 USC §3006A requires appointment of counsel for a corporation.[164]

Once a law firm has entered an appearance for a defendant, the District Court has the power to order the firm to remain as standby counsel for a defendant who elects to proceed pro se. The extent of the firm's commitment depends on factors such as the complexity of case, the detriment to the firm of continued representation, and the impact of the defendant's pro se election on co-defendants and the speedy trial process.[165]

[¶6040.5] Confrontation Clause and Public Trial

The Sixth Amendment gives the defendant the right to confront his or her accusers, and to have a public trial—not a secret proceeding. However, these rights are not absolute: in some instances, the courtroom can be closed, and a witness permitted to testify other than in open court, if a sufficient showing of danger to witnesses, informants, or undercover police officers is made.

The courtroom can be closed only if:

- The party seeking closing advances an overriding interest that is at risk of being prejudiced
- The closure is only as broad as necessary
- The court considers reasonable alternatives to closing the proceedings to the public
- Closing the court is supported by adequate findings by the judge.

A defendant is not entitled, under the Sixth Amendment or the due process clause, to be present at sidebar or in camera conferences, so it is not an error to exclude the defendant.[166]

[¶6040.6] Forfeiture and the Right to Counsel

21 USC §853, the Comprehensive Forfeiture Act of 1984, permits forfeiture of the assets of a person convicted of certain drug offenses. It also authorizes a pretrial restraining order freezing assets that would be subject to forfeiture if the defendant were convicted. Forfeiture provisions are also included in RICO, at 18 USC §3006A.

The Supreme Court has ruled that the freeze does not violate the Sixth Amendment, although the practical difficulties of paying an attorney when one's assets have been frozen are significant.[167]

Also see *Florida v. White*[168]: probable cause to believe that a car is property linked to a crime, and therefore subject to forfeiture, justifies warrantless seizure of the car from a public place.

[¶6040.7] Timing of the Trial; Speedy Trial Issues

The Sixth Amendment[169] guarantees the accused a "speedy" trial—a factor that is particularly important when the defendant has been denied bail, or has been unable to post bail, and thus is incarcerated prior to trial.

There are four factors in determining whether a delay violates the guarantee of a speedy trial: the length of the delay; reasons for it; whether the defendant raised the issue (e.g., by pretrial motion); and the extent to which the defense was prejudiced by delay.[170]

The right of speedy trial attaches only with arrest or indictment; defendants are not prejudiced by any indictment brought within the statute of limitations.[171] With respect to pre-indictment delay, as long as the statute of limitations has not run, dismissal for delay requires not only proof of actual, substantial prejudice, but proof that the prosecutor intentionally delayed for an improper purpose.[172]

A guilty plea waives claims of violations of the right to a speedy trial.[173]

The statute of limitations, not the Speedy Trial Act, determines when an indicted defendant can be charged with additional crimes via a superseding indictment.[174]

[¶6050.3] Selection of Grand Jurors

A Grand Jury panel usually consists of 12-23 people. In the federal system, the size of the panel ranges from 16-23 (FRCrimP 6(a)), with a quorum of 16. The Grand Jury term could be anywhere from 10 days to 18 months (with extensions to finish cases in progress). Provisions are made for replacing Grand Jurors during the term.

Although attorneys play a major role in selecting petit jurors, they have little to do with selection of federal Grand Jurors. Peremptory challenges are unavailable. Potential jurors may be examined briefly by the impaneling court to determine whether they meet the rather minimal requirements for Grand Jury service (e.g., adult U.S. citizens[195] who can read and write English and have not been convicted of a felony), but extensive voir dire is not conducted. 28 USC §1863(b) outlines individuals who are ineligible to serve, or who are entitled to an exemption from service.

In the federal system, and in some states, Grand Jurors are selected randomly from lists such as voter registration lists. Some states still use a "key-man" system under which judges or jury commissioners are given discretion to select suitable Grand Jurors.

The Fifth Amendment requires Grand Juries to be drawn from a representative cross-section of the community, as does the Jury Selection and Service Act, 28 USC §1861, and about one-third of the states. The analysis requires proof of a distinct or cognizable group within the community (e.g., women; black people), and that representation of that group on the Grand Jury panel is not fair and reasonable as compared with the size of that group within the community.

A white defendant is allowed to place a due process/equal protection challenge to the underrepresentation of black people on Grand Juries,[196] including their access to service as foreperson of the Grand Jury.

FRCrimP 6(b)(2) holds that a juror's lack of legal qualifications may make the indictment invalid. All jurisdictions allow a challenge to the array (the entire Grand Jury panel) on Constitutional grounds; each jurisdiction has its own rules as to permissible non-Constitutional grounds for challenge (for instance, a major deviation from the normal process of selecting Grand Jurors). Note that states usually have strict time limits for posing such challenges.

However, unlike petit jurors, Grand Jurors cannot be disqualified based on prior knowledge of the case, because they can still perform their function of determining whether an indictment should issue. In fact, even bias probably will not disqualify a Grand Juror or invalidate the indictment. *U.S. v. Mechanik*,[197] holds that violations of FRCrimP 6(d) cannot be raised on appeal to challenge a conviction because the error, if any, must be harmless because the petit jury convicted the defendant based on the evidence presented at trial.

[¶6050.4] The Indictment

In the federal system, or in a state that retains the requirement of a Grand Jury indictment, serious crimes can only be charged in an indictment. A proper indictment gives adequate notice of the charges against the accused. If a statute describes multiple ways in which a single offense can be committed, FRCrimP 7(c)(1) authorizes a single count that alleges that the defendant committed the offense by one or more specified means.

Improper "multiplicity" occurs if a single offense is divided into two or more counts of the indictment, because the defendant therefore is at risk of being punished more than once for the same offense—and a susceptible jury may feel that the defendant must be guilty of something if so many charges are brought against him or her. However, there is no multiplicity in charging separate counts if the offenses require different proof.

After trial, variation between the charges and the proof is a legitimate ground for challenging a verdict. If the indictment was "constructively amended" in that the prosecution case, plus the jury instructions, modified the essential elements of the offense to the point that the defendant was convicted of something other than the crime(s) charged in the indictment, the defendant may be entitled to relief.

A defendant can move to strike surplusage from an indictment. Such motions are disfavored, and are granted only if the indictment includes highly inflammatory, prejudicial allegations that are not relevant to the charge.

In general, factors relating only to sentencing are not elements of the criminal offense and don't have to be stated in the indictment. Trial on the merits can be had if an indictment that is valid on its face is returned by a legally constituted and unbiased Grand Jury—even if some of the evidence they considered was inaccurate, untruthful, or inadmissible under the rules of evidence. (Otherwise, everyone who was indicted would get another trial first, to test the validity of the indictment.)

[¶6050.5] Investigative Grand Juries

The Grand Jury can play another role, investigating crime, especially organized crime, white-collar crime, and political corruption.[198] An investigative Grand Jury determines whether crimes have been committed, and if so by whom, but issues a written statement addressed to the court that impaneled the Grand Jury, rather than a formal written accusation charging a specific person with a specific offense.

The Organized Crime Control Act of 1970, P.L. 91-452, authorizes special Grand Juries that can submit reports on organized crime in the area, then investigate and issue indictments. See 18 USC §3333 for reports of such special Grand Juries.

[¶6055] Pretrial Discovery

"Trial by ambush" is even less acceptable in the criminal than in the civil context, and U.S. law requires the prosecution not only to apprise the defense of the strength of the prosecution case but also of its weaknesses.

The prosecution's Constitutional duty to disclose favorable material evidence[199]—that is, exculpatory or potentially exculpatory material relevant either to guilt or punishment—requires the presence of favorable but undisclosed evidence. Materiality is measured by a reasonable probability that the outcome would be different if disclosure were made. The prosecutor is only obligated to disclose material favorable to the defendant and material either to guilt or punishment.

Failure to produce such material violates the defendant's Constitutional rights, and a new trial may be required. There is no violation if the undisclosed information was already known to the defendant, or could have been determined with reasonable diligence (e.g., by reading a transcript). Furthermore, failure to produce potentially exculpatory material before trial might be cured by disclosure at trial, giving the defense a reasonable opportunity to cross-examine.

The prosecution is under no obligation to investigate and seek out exculpatory material not already in its possession.[200] Unless law enforcement officials act in bad faith, Due Process is not violated by failure to preserve items that might, arguably, have been exculpatory if preserved and tested.[201]

The defense can inspect and copy government-held documents and materials that are either scheduled for use in the prosecution case in chief, or material to the defense: FRCrimP Rule 16(a)(1)(C). It does not create a broader right to discover documents that are material to a claim of selective prosecution, because that would allow defendants to discover all government work product merely by claiming selective prosecution.[202]

Rule 16(a)(1)(D) permits the defense to inspect photographs, reports of mental and physical examinations, and scientific tests in the prosecution's possession. Rule 16(a)(1)(E) permits pretrial disclosure of expert opinions that are scheduled to be introduced by the prosecution. However, the prosecution's witness list need only be disclosed if the court so orders, based on a specific showing that the information is material to preparation of the defense.

In addition to general rules about providing exculpatory matter to the defense, certain specific discovery issues are addressed by federal rules. FRE 404(b) requires the prosecution to provide reasonable pretrial notice of the general nature of evidence it will introduce about other acts committed by the defendant.

FRCrimP 12.2(a) obligates the defense to inform the government of its intention to rely on an insanity defense. Rule 12.2(b) governs defense expert testimony on the defendant's mental condition not tantamount to an insanity defense. On the motion of the prosecution, Rule 12.2(c) authorizes the court to order a mental examination of a defendant who has not announced the intention to present an insanity defense.

[¶6055.1] ABA Standards for Criminal Justice

ABA Standard 11-2.1 requires that, within a specified and reasonable time pretrial, the prosecution should disclose the following to the defense. Disclosure includes allowing the defense to inspect, copy, test, and photograph these materials:

- All written and oral statements made by defendant[203] and co-defendants relating to the "subject matter of the offense charged" and "any documents

relating to the acquisition of such statements." A "written statement" that may
be discoverable is not attorney work product unless, for instance, the defense puts counsel notes at issue by using them to impeach witnesses
- Names and addresses of everyone the prosecution knows "to have information concerning the offense charged" plus any written statements the
  prosecution has regarding the subject matter of the offense charged
- Names of witnesses the prosecution plans to call at trial; relationship between the prosecution and witness (including any incentives to testify)
- Reports, written statements by experts, including scientific tests and results
  of physical, mental exams; for experts to be called at trial, curriculum vitae
  of each and written description of the expert's proposed testimony, the expert's opinion, and basis for the opinion
- Tangible objects which pertain to the case or were obtained for or belong to
  the defendant—and which ones the prosecution intends to offer at trial
- Prior convictions, pending charges, probation status of the defendant, co-defendants, and witnesses, that could be used for impeachment by either side
- Materials, documents, information about lineups, showups, picture or voice
  identification
- Any exculpatory evidence or evidence "which would tend to reduce the punishment of the defendant"
- Intent to use, and substance of information regarding character, reputation,
  or other acts evidence
- The fact of any electronic surveillance (including wiretapping) of the defendant's conversations or premises. Information, documents, or other material dealing with the search and seizure of any tangible object.

The prosecution is required to give the defense access to the material, but not
necessarily to deliver it. Prosecutors have no possession or control over, and therefore no responsibilities with respect to, materials held by the court, private corporations, or unrelated agencies. Nor can states be deemed to control materials
held by federal agencies, and vice versa.

As you would expect, the defense's disclosure burden (under Standard 11-
2.2) is lower:

- Names and addresses, of all non-defendant witnesses; all written statements
  that the defense has relating to subject matter of witness' testimony, but dis-
  closure of the identity and statements of rebuttal witnesses is not required
  until after the relevant prosecution witness testifies
- Reports and written statements of expert witnesses to be called, with their
  CV and summary of proposed testimony
- Tangible objects to be introduced at trial
- Intention (if any) to introduce the character and reputation of the defendant,
  and the substance of such evidence
- Names of any supporting witnesses to affirmative defenses of alibi or insanity

A person indicted for a capital crime is entitled, under 18 USC §3005, to appointment of two attorneys, at least one of whom is "learned in the law applicable to capital cases," and the attorneys have free access to the accused at all reasonable hours. See 21 USC §848(q)(10) for counsel fees in capital cases and entitlement to expenses, including investigative expenses. The right to appointed counsel in a capital habeas petition does not depend on the merits of the claim.[266]

Proportionality is an important issue in capital sentencing. It has been held that the death penalty is disproportionate for the rape of an adult victim[267] and for a person convicted of felony murder who neither committed the actual killing nor intended that lethal force be used in the crime.[268]

States that allow capital punishment are divided into "weighing" and "nonweighing" states. In the former, when the defendant is found guilty of a potentially capital offense, the jury sets the sentence by balancing aggravating against mitigating factors. In the latter, it is permissible but not mandatory to impose the death penalty when at least one valid aggravating factor is present, whether or not mitigating factors also exist.

An "aggravating factors" capital statute, listing factors justifying death sentence, is not void for vagueness, because its function is to guide sentencing, not warn criminals of offenses that could carry the death penalty.[269]

Even Constitutional errors in jury instructions in capital cases can be harmless, if they did not affect the final result, and thus do not necessarily result in overturning the sentence.[270]

Setting the execution date is ministerial, not a critical part of the sentencing process, so in the view of the Fifth Circuit the defendant need not be present.[271]

[¶6087] Post-Conviction Remedies

A confusing variety of channels, presenting a confusing variety of Constitutional and practical issues, can be used by a convicted person to challenge the conviction or the sentence, especially a death sentence.

A person convicted in a state court has various appellate options within the state system: some appeals of right, some discretionary with the state appellate courts. The writ of habeas corpus can also be used, within limits, to collaterally attack a state conviction. "Habeas corpus" is Latin for "produce the body": i.e., the state system surrenders custody of the prisoner so the federal court can inquire into whether such custody is valid.

Although there are some exceptions (involving technical issues beyond the scope of this book[272]), the most common post-conviction remedy for federal prisoners is not habeas corpus, but a motion to vacate sentence, brought under 18 USC §2255. Non-Constitutional errors are not cognizable in a §2555 proceeding, and even errors of Constitutional dimension (e.g., invalid search and seizure) are relevant only if they were not harmless and actually prejudiced the defendant.[273]

A large part of the Supreme Court docket consists of criminal cases in which discretion was exercised to grant certiorari although, of course, the vast majority of criminal certiorari petitions are denied.

[¶6087.1] Habeas Corpus

Habeas petitions are filed only after the completion of many earlier steps in the criminal process:

- Trial
- Sentencing hearing
- Motion for a new trial
- First state appeal as of right
- Discretionary state appeal
- Petition for certiorari
- State post-conviction proceedings on any state or federal claims that are available but have not yet been fully litigated
- State post-conviction appeals
- Petition for certiorari to review the state post-conviction appeals.

Fourth Amendment claims cannot be raised in a habeas proceeding if the petitioner has already had full and fair opportunity to litigate those claims in state court.[274] According to the Eleventh Circuit,[275] a federal habeas court won't hear new evidence in support of a claim unless the petitioner shows both cause for the failure to bring out the facts in state court, and actual prejudice from the failure.

Habeas can be used to pursue a claim of actual innocence if it can be shown that an innocent person was convicted, and a Constitutional violation "probably occurred." It is not required that the habeas petition show by clear and convincing evidence that, but for the error, no reasonable jury would have convicted the defendant[276]—but see the AEDPA discussion, below.

Habeas relief was granted in a 1998 Eighth Circuit murder case[277] because of a juror's failure to disclose that the juror's brother had been a homicide victim and other family members were also crime victims. The non-disclosure undermined the validity of the conviction and death sentence. Although the juror was not biased in fact against the defendant, bias has to be presumed if deception is used to get onto a jury.

Evidentiary hearings are probably not required in habeas proceedings.

Even if the habeas court agrees that an aggravating factor considered in imposing a capital sentence is invalid, it must perform harmless error analysis (did the error have a substantial and injurious influence on the verdict?) before granting habeas relief.[278]

[¶6087.1.1] AEDPA

The Anti-Terrorism and Effective Death Penalty Act of 1996 (AEDPA), P.L. 104-132, has two main focuses.[279] First, it limits the number of habeas challenges that can be brought to a conviction. Second, it permits a federal court to overturn a state conviction only if an egregious mistake was made by the state court.

The post-AEDPA text of 18 USC §2254(b) provides that, before applying for federal habeas relief, the defendant must show that state remedies have been

- In general, retrial after grant of a new trial must begin not more than 70 days from the finality of the act that made a new trial necessary: 18 USC §3161(e), although the court can extend this to 180 days if the witnesses become unavailable.
- A habeas petition must be filed within 180 days after final state affirmance of the conviction: 28 USC §2263.
- Federal Rules of Appellate Procedure 4(b) requires a defendant's notice of appeal as of right to be filed within 10 days of entry of judgment or motion for a new trial; the prosecution has 30 days to appeal. A 30-day extension can be granted on a showing of excusable neglect.
- FRAP 5(a) requires a petition for permissive appeal of an interlocutory order to be filed within 10 days of entry of the order.
- The appellant must order the transcript within 10 days after filing notice of appeal: FRAP 10(b).
- A petition for rehearing can be filed within 14 days of entry of judgment (unless the local rule is different): FRAP 40(a).
- The appellant's brief must be filed within 40 days of the date the record is filed, giving the appellee 30 days from the service of the appellant's brief to file its own brief. Then the appellant's reply brief is due 14 days from the date of the appellee's brief, but it must be filed at least three days before the scheduled date for argument: FRAP 31(a).

[¶6087.2.3] Ineffective Assistance of Counsel

The right to counsel implies the right to effective counsel, although not necessarily the counsel of the defendant's choice.[294] The attorney has a duty to represent clients "zealously," while also serving as an officer of the court. The latter role forbids knowing introduction of perjured testimony. The attorney may be sanctionable for abusive litigation tactics, but is also at fault for failing to utilize appropriate tactics.

Actual conflict of interest when an attorney represents multiple defendants can constitute ineffective assistance. If error occurs on this issue, it is never harmless,[295] but joint representation is not a per se violation of the right to effective assistance, if there is no actual conflict or significant possibility of conflict (such as would occur if the co-defendants blamed each other).[296]

Even if a defendant shows that the lawyer failed to satisfy minimal standards of professional skill and competence, to be entitled to relief the defendant still must show prejudice from the lawyer's inadequate performance.[297]

The Sixth Amendment right to counsel is only violated by ineffective assistance of counsel if the challenged conduct affects the reliability of the trial process, so both defective performance and prejudice, resulting in an unreliable or fundamentally unfair trial, are required. Mere proof that the result of the trial would have been different but for inadequate advocacy is not necessarily enough.[298]

A defendant who alleges ineffective assistance of counsel must identify specific acts or omissions on the attorney's part, not merely make conclusory allegations of ineffective assistance.

Issues that may justify a finding of ineffective assistance of counsel:

- Conflict of interest, such as past representation of a prosecution witness
- Failure to undertake a reasonable investigation to locate witnesses whose testimony would be helpful at trial (although it can be a reasonable strategic decision not to call convicted felons whose testimony is subject to impeachment)
- Failure to use jury challenges appropriately
- Failure to assert meritorious defenses
- Failure to file the appropriate motions[299]
- Failure to object to improper questions or prejudicial or inflammatory testimony
- Failure to make an adequate record for appeal
- Failure to apply for mistrial, where appropriate
- Failure to request cautionary jury instructions
- Failure to raise meritorious issues that could result in a sentence reduction
- Failure to file a timely notice of appeal, raising all appropriate issues.

The effective attorney should call witnesses about potentially exculpatory physical evidence, even if the defendant has confessed, because it is possible that the confession could be excluded from evidence.

Effective assistance of counsel can be provided without undertaking every possible legal action. The defense attorney can make a valid strategic decision not to introduce evidence that is likely to backfire (e.g., by opening the door to cross-examination or impeachment). An attorney is not necessarily ineffective merely for failing to raise an insanity defense absent reason to believe it would have been successful.[300] Where the defendant is, in fact, fit to stand trial, not requesting a fitness hearing can be harmless.[301] Recommending a guilty plea is not ineffective, if there is a mass of evidence against the defendant, although the attorney must discuss the ramifications of a plea bargain.

It may actually be better for the attorney to refrain from doing an investigation into the defendant's background before the sentencing hearing, if the investigation would only elicit information harmful to the defendant. Failure to object to misapplication of the Sentencing Guidelines could constitute ineffective assistance,[302] but the attorney is not obligated to seek a downward departure from the Guidelines that there is no reason to believe would be granted.

[¶6087.3] Standard of Review

Motions to suppress are generally reviewed de novo, as a mixed question of law and fact. Findings of fact are reviewed to see if the trial court's position was clearly erroneous, but the application of law to those facts is reviewed on a de novo basis. The "plain error" doctrine permits the appellate court to take notice of plain errors or defects affecting substantial rights, even if they were not raised before the lower court.

Convictions solely or primarily based on illegally obtained evidence must be reversed[303] (but this rule is inapplicable if evidence of guilt is overwhelming even without the tainted evidence).

Harmless error does not require reversal and retrial. Harmless error is error that did not change the result of the trial: e.g., a trial in which the other evidence was strong enough to make conviction virtually inevitable. However, some errors are so egregious that they can never be harmless, such as total deprivation of the right to counsel or right to public trial, or exclusion of the defendant's race from the Grand Jury.[304]

Rule 9(a), not general equitable principles, is used to analyze first petitions for federal review. The rule is the sole source for determining whether the state is prejudiced by delay.[305]

When a Court of Appeals reviews a District Court's decision on a habeas corpus petition, the Court of Appeals has no duty to raise, sua sponte, procedural errors made by the petitioner but not raised by the state.[306]

[¶6090] Prison Litigation

The Prison Litigation Reform Act (PLRA) is found at 28 USC §1915—. It forbids prisoners to bring civil actions or appeal civil judgments if, on three or more earlier occasions and while incarcerated, the prisoner brought suits that were dismissed as frivolous, malicious, or failing to state a cause of action. (A prisoner in imminent danger of serious physical injury is permitted to sue, despite earlier inappropriate litigation.) Because PLRA proceedings are civil suits, also see ¶5400.8.3 (in the Federal Civil Procedure chapter) for consideration of the PLRA.

The PLRA calls for maximizing use of technology, including videoconferencing, and an inmate's civil claim can be tried entirely via videoconference, without moving the inmate from the prison where he or she is confined.[307]

42 USC §1997e(a) requires prisoners to exhaust administrative remedies before bringing suit about prison conditions. Exhaustion of remedies is mandatory, even if the administrative remedies are inadequate or using them is futile.[308] A 1999 Supreme Court decision[309] prevents prison litigants from raising issues in federal court that were not brought before the state's highest court, even if raising the claims was almost certain to be futile.

Prison litigants are required to pay the filing fees for their cases, although §1915(a) permits filing of an affidavit of poverty so that they can pay the fees in installments rather than all at once. Filing fees are waived for habeas proceedings.[310]

If an indigent PLRA litigant requests appointed counsel, he or she must file a statement with the court showing reasonable but unsuccessful attempts to secure representation, addressing the merits of the claim; ability to investigate and present the case pro se; and any need for counsel to deal with, e.g., complex legal or factual issues.[311]

28 USC §1915A requires the court to review prisoners' civil complaints against the government or government employees as soon as possible (preferably before the case has been docketed) to see if the complaint is frivolous or malicious; fails to state a claim; or seeks damages against a party that is immune.

ENDNOTES

1. The felony/misdemeanor distinction has other implications as well. For instance, the prevailing evidence rules may allow impeachment of a witness by showing felony, but not misdemeanor, convictions. In the federal system, and in some state systems, prosecution of a felony requires a Grand Jury indictment, whereas this is not required for misdemeanor prosecutions.
2. *Cave v. Louisiana*, 498 U.S. 39 (Sup.Ct.1990).
3. *Sullivan v. Louisiana*, 508 U.S. 275 (Sup.Ct. 1993).
4. *Patterson v. N.Y.*, 432 U.S. 197 (Sup.Ct. 1997).
5. *Bryan v. U.S.*, 514 U.S. 184 (Sup.Ct.1998).
6. 511 U.S. 513 (Sup.Ct.1994).
7. *U.S. v. Cheek*, 498 U.S. 192 (Sup.Ct.1991).
8. *Mullaney v. Wilbur*, 421 U.S. 684 (Sup.Ct.1975).
9. See *Medina v. California*, 505 U.S. 437 (Sup.Ct.1992).
10. 517 U.S. 348 (Sup.Ct.1996).
11. 509 U.S. 389 (Sup.Ct.1993).
12. *McDonald v. Bowersox*, 101 F3d 588 (8th Cir. 1996). But see *Stewart v. Gramley*, 74 F.3d 132 (7th Cir. 1996), holding that not appointing a psychiatrist did not constitute reversible error, since evaluations done after the defendant was sentenced to death showed understandable anxiety but no psychosis.
13. *Daniels v. State*, 538 A.2d 1104 (Delaware 1988).
14. *Kansas v. Hendricks*, 521 U.S. 346 (Sup.Ct. 1997). However, Washington's Code §710.09 [indefinite post-sentence civil commitment of convicted sexually violent predators] was invalidated on Due Process grounds because commitment and indefinite incarceration could occur without proof that the committed person is mentally ill: *Young v. Weston*, 898 F.Supp. 744 (W.D. Wash. 1995).
15. 511 U.S. 767 (Sup.Ct.1994).
16. *Hudson v. U.S.*, 522 U.S. 93 (Sup.Ct.1997).
17. *U.S. v. Ursery*, 518 U.S. 267 (Sup.Ct.1996). Under *U.S. v. Alt*, 83 F.3d 779 (6th Cir. 1996), IRS civil penalties are not punishment, so the IRS can impose interest and collect back taxes from a person convicted of tax fraud.
18. *Kansas v. Hendricks*, 521 U.S. 346 (Sup.Ct.1997).
19. *U.S. v Clark*, 84 F.3d 378 (10th Cir. 1996); *U.S. v. Branham*, 97 F.3d 835 (6th Cir 1996); *U.S. v. Morgan*, 84 F.3d 765 (5th Cir 1996).
20. 284 U.S. 299 (Sup.Ct.1932).
21. *Witte v. U.S.*, 515 U.S. 389 (Sup.Ct.1995); *Rutledge v. U.S.*, 517 U.S. 292 (Sup.Ct.1996).
22. *U.S. v. Gonzalez*, 520 U.S. 1 (Sup.Ct.1997), but *U.S. v. Watts*, 519 U.S. 148 (Sup.Ct. 1997) holds that sentence enhancements merely, and permissibly, punish the defendant for the manner in which the crime was committed; they do not punish the defendant for offenses for which there was no conviction.
23. *U.S. v. Farmer*, 73 F.3d 836 (8th Cir. 1996).

24. *Monge v. California*, 524 U.S. 721 (Sup.Ct. 1998).
25. *Bullington v. Missouri*, 451 U.S.430 (Sup.Ct. 1981).
26. *U.S. v. Schinnell*, 80 F.3d 1064 (5th Cir. 1996).
27. *U.S. v. Hardwell*, 80 F.3d 1471 (10th Cir. 1996).
28. *Schiro v. Farley*, 510 U.S. 222 (Sup.Ct. 1994).
29. *Dowling v. U.S.*, 493 U.S. 342 (Sup.Ct. 1990).
30. 518 U.S. 81 (Sup.Ct.1996).
31. *Gregory v. Ashcroft*, 501 U.S. 452 (Sup.Ct.1991).
32. *U.S. v. Lopez*, 514 U.S. 549 (Sup.Ct.1995); *Salinas v. U.S.*, 522 U.S. 52 (Sup.Ct.1997).
33. *Lewis v. U.S.*, 523 U.S. 155 (Sup.Ct. 1998).
34. *Teague v Lane*, 489 U.S. 288 (Sup.Ct.1989).
35. *U.S. v. Thomas*, 134 F.3d 975 (9th Cir. 1998).
36. *Mathews v. U.S.*, 485 U.S. 58 (Sup.Ct.1988).
37. *Chicago v. Morales*, 119 S.Ct. 1849 (Sup.Ct. 6/10/99).
38. *Martin v. Ohio*, 480 U.S. 228 (Sup.Ct. 1987).
39. *Montana v. Egelhoff*, 518 U.S. 37 (Sup.Ct. 1996).
40. *Smallwood v. Maryland*, 680 A.2d 512 (Md.App. 1996).
41. Proof of voluntary driving while intoxicated, and death of another person, is sufficient for a conviction of vehicular homicide. It is not necessary to prove that drinking rather than excessive speed proximately caused the death: *Colorado v. Gamer*, 781 P.2d 87 (Colo.Sup. 1989).
42. But see *Warner v. Orange County Department of Probation*, 870 F.Supp. 69 (2nd Cir. 1996) finding an unconstitutional establishment of religion to force a convicted drunk driver to attend Alcoholics Anonymous meetings (which involve invocation of a "higher power"). *O'Connor v. California*, 855 F.Supp. 303 (C.D. Cal. 1994) permits giving the convicted person a choice between attending AA meetings and participating in a sobriety program without spiritual content.
43. The Supreme Court has upheld the practice of placing sobriety checkpoints on the highway, where all motorists can be detained briefly even without individualized suspicion: *Michigan Department of State Police v. Sitz*, 496 U.S. 444 (Sup.Ct. 1990).
44. *Oregon v. O'Key*, 899 P.2d 663 (Ore.Sup. 1995).
45. E.g., *California v. McDonald*, 206 Cal.App.3d 877 (Cal.App. 1988); *South Dakota v. McCarty*, 434 N.W.2d 67 (S.D. Sup. 1988).
46. *Pennsylvania v. Muniz*, 496 U.S. 582 (Sup.Ct. 1990).
47. *U.S. v. Chapel*, 55 F.3d 1416 (9th Cir. 1995); *on remand*, 61 F.3d 913.
    Fink v. Ryan, 673 N.E.2d 281 (Ill.Supp. 1996) finds that an arrestee who was involved in a serious accident is already under police control, so a "special needs" exception to the Fourth Amendment permits blood testing for the presence of alcohol and drugs.
48. *Judd v. Louisiana*, 663 So.2d 690 (La.Sup. 1995).
49. This procedure is Constitutional: *Mackey v. Montrim*, 443 U.S. 1 (Sup.Ct. 1979).

50. See, e.g., *Maryland v. Jones,* 340 Md. 235 (App. 1996); *Hawaii v. Toyomura,* 904 P.2d 893 (Haw. 1995); *Matter of Smith, N.Y.L.J.* 11/6/96 p. 25 col. 3 (A.D. 3d Dept.)
51. *Muscarella v. U.S.,* 524 U.S. 125 (Sup.Ct. 1998).
52. *Bailey v. U.S.,* 516 U.S. 137 (Sup.Ct. 1995). On the retroactivity of *Bailey,* see *Bousley v. U.S.,* 523 U.S. 614 (Sup.Ct. 1998). The five-year sentence under §924(c) must run consecutively with all other state and federal sentences: *U.S. v. Gonzalez,* 520 U.S. 1 (Sup.Ct. 1997).
53. *Caron v. U.S.,* 524 U.S. 308 (Sup.Ct. 1998).
54. *Bryan v. U.S.,* 524 U.S. 184 (Sup.Ct. 1998).
55. *U.S. v. Emerson,* 67 LW 1631 (N.D. Tex. 4/7/99).
56. *Richardson v. U.S.,* 119 S.Ct. 1707 (Sup.Ct.1999). Also see *U.S. v. Shabani,* 513 U.S. 10 (Sup.Ct. 1994):it is not necessary to prove an overt act to get a conviction under 21 USC §846, the drug conspiracy statute. Conspiracy to distribute controlled substances is a lesser included offense of Continuing Criminal Enterprise, so a defendant cannot be sentenced to life imprisonment on each count, even if the terms are concurrent rather than consecutive: *Rutledge v. U.S.,* 517 U.S. 292 (Sup.Ct. 1996).
57. *Edwards v. U.S.,* 523 U.S. 511 (Sup.Ct. 1998).
58. *Holloway v. U.S.,* 526 U.S. 1 (Sup.Ct. 1999).
59. 526 U.S. 227 (Sup.Ct. 1999).
60. *Neder v. U.S.,* 119 S.Ct. 1827 (Sup.Ct.1999)
61. *Bates v. U.S.,* 522 U.S. 285 (Sup.Ct. 1997).
62. *U.S. v. Wells,* #95-1228, 65 LW 4146 (Sup.Ct. 2/26/97).
63. 119 S.Ct. 1402 (Sup.Ct. 1999).
64. *U.S. v. Lundwall,* 66 LW 1629 (S.D.N.Y. 4/1/98).
65. *Hubbard v. U.S.,* 514 U.S. 695 (Sup.Ct. 1995).
66. *Brogan v. U.S.,* 522 U.S. 398 (Sup.Ct. 1998).
67. *U.S. v. Bonanno Organized Crime Family,* 879 F.2d 20 (2nd Cir. 1989).
68. At least two predicate acts must have been committed after RICO's effective date, and not more than ten years apart.
69. *Salinas v. U.S.,* 522 U.S. 52 (Sup.Ct. 1997). This case also holds that a person can be convicted under 18 USC §666 (local official of a federally funded agency accepts a bribe) with or without proof that the bribe had an effect on federal funds.
70. *Alderman v. U.S.,* 394 U.S. 165 (1969); *Brown v. U.S.,* 411 U.S. 223 (1973).
71. See *Mancusi v. DeForte,* 392 U.S. 364 (1968).
72. *City of West Covina v. Perkins,* 119 S.Ct. 678 (Sup.Ct. 1999).
73. 487 U.S. 533 (Sup.Ct.1988)
74. 500 U.S. 565 (Sup.Ct.1992).
75. 508 U.S. 366 (Sup.Ct.1993)
76. 515 U.S. 646 (Sup.Ct.1995)
77. *California v. Greenwood,* 486 U.S. 35 (1986). Also see *US v Chavez-Vernaza,* 844 F.2d 1368 (9th Cir. 1987): evidence seized by state officers in compliance with federal law is admissible in federal prosecution without regard to state law.

South Carolina, Tennessee, Texas, Virginia, West Virginia. In Florida, Louisiana, Minnesota, and Rhode Island, a Grand Jury indictment is required in cases that could result in the death penalty or life imprisonment, but not for other serious charges.
See Sara Sun Beale, William C. Bryson, James E. Felman, Michael J. Elston, *Grand Jury Law and Practice* (2nd edition), Westgroup 1997/1998 supplement.

184. Although news media sought access to proceedings or documents ancillary to Grand Jury proceedings in the Starr investigation of Paula Jones' case against President Clinton, access was denied. The proceedings remained secret, and First Amendment, common law and local-rules arguments were disregarded: *In re Dow Jones & Co.*, 66 LW 1697 (D.C. Cir. 5/5/98).

185. The Fourteenth Amendment is not violated by searching attorneys, even if its purpose and effect is to prevent attorneys from advising clients appearing before a Grand Jury: *Conn v. Gabbert*, 119 S.Ct. 1292 (Sup.Ct. 1999).

186. Via amendments approved by the Supreme Court on April 26, 1999; see 67 LW 2651.

187. *U.S. v. Bagley,* 473 U.S. 667 (Sup.Ct. 1985).

188. *U.S. v. Calandra*, 414 U.S. 338 (Sup.Ct. 1974) and *U.S. v Williams*, 504 U.S. 36 (Sup.Ct. 1992).

189. *LaChance v. Erickson*, 522 U.S. 262 (Sup.Ct. 1998).

190. *U.S. v Mandujano*, 425 U.S. 564 (Sup.Ct. 1976).

191. *Butterworth v. Smith*, 494 U.S. 624 (Sup.Ct. 1990).

192. *Finn v. Schiller*, 72 F.3d 1182 (4th Cir. 1996). Also see *U.S. v. Smith*, 66 LW 1520 (D.N.J. 2/4/98): Internet posting of a sentencing memorandum that contained Grand Jury information, without consent of the court, violated FRCrimP 6(e) and 32.

193. The Jencks Act, 18 USC §3500, mandates production of relevant prior statements of government witnesses at trial, and a 1970 amendment makes it clear that Grand Jury testimony is considered a prior statement for this purpose. Government agents have no duty to record witness interviews or take notes that would not otherwise be kept, merely to disclose them. Furthermore, statements that do not relate to the same subject matter as the testimony cannot be used to impeach the witness, and therefore need not be disclosed.

194. *U.S. v. Sells Engineering Inc.*, 463 U.S. 418 (Sup.Ct.1983).

195. *Perkins v. Smith*, 426 U.S. 913 (Sup.Ct. 1976) holds the citizenship requirement to be Constitutional.

196. *Campbell v. Louisiana*, 523 U.S. 392 (Sup.Ct. 1998).

197. 475 U.S. 661 (Sup.Ct. 1986).

198. In California, Maine, Michigan, New Mexico, New York, Oklahoma, and Utah, a Grand Jury is empowered to start proceedings to remove a public employee or official.

199. Under, e.g., *Brady v. Maryland*, 373 U.S. 87 (Sup.Ct.1963) and *Kyles v. Whitley*, 514 U.S. 419 (Sup.Ct.1995). Evidence that tends to impeach prosecution witnesses' testimony is *Brady* material: *U.S. v. Bagley*, 473 U.S. 667 (Sup.Ct. 1985).

200. *California v. Trombetta*, 467 U.S. 479 (Sup.Ct. 1984).
201. *Arizona v. Youngblood*, 488 U.S. 51 (Sup.Ct. 1988). *Youngblood* also holds that the prosecution does not have a duty to perform all tests that the defense claims might be exculpatory.
202. *U.S. v. Armstrong*, 517 U.S. 456 (Sup.Ct.1996).
203. *Jackson v. Denno*, 378 U.S. 368 (Sup.Ct. 1964) requires pretrial disclosure of admissions allegedly made by the defendant, so the defense can raise the issue of whether or not the admissions were made voluntarily. It applies only to admissions that the prosecution plans to use in its case in chief, not admissions that will be used only for impeachment. Also see FRCrimP 12(a)(1)(A), disclosure of relevant written or recorded statements of the defendant.
204. But not necessarily whether the federal sentence will be served consecutively or concurrently with the state sentence: *U.S. v. Parkins*, 25 F.3d 114 (2nd Cir. 1994).
205. A plea induced by threats is not voluntary and thus is void: *Machibroda v. U.S.*, 368 U.S. 487 (Sup.Ct. 1962).
206. *Parke v. Raley*, 506 U.S. 20 (Sup.Ct.1992).
207. *U.S. v. Olano,* 507 U.S. 725 (Sup.Ct.1993).
208. 400 U.S. 25 (Sup.Ct.1970).
209. *Mabry v. Johnson*, 467 U.S. 504 (Sup.Ct. 1984).
210. *U.S. v. Raynor*, 66 LW 1511 (D.D.C. 12/29/97).
211. *U.S. v. Bunner*, 134 F.3d 1000 (10th Cir. 1998).
212. 516 U.S. 29 (Sup.Ct.1995).
213. 1993 U.S. Claims LEXIS 28 (Fed.Cl. 1993).
214. *U.S. v. Bazzi*, 94 F.3d 1025 (6th Cir 1996).
215. *U.S. v. Carrington*, 96 F.3d 1 (1st Cir 1996).
216. But see *Lewis v. U.S.*, 518 U.S. 322 (Sup.Ct. 1996): right to jury trial is not triggered by multiple petty offenses punishable by under 6 months imprisonment each, even if the aggregate is over 6 months.
217. *U.S. v. Gaudin*, 515 U.S. 506 (Sup.Ct.1995).
218. *Estelle v. McGuire*, 502 U.S. 62 (Sup.Ct. 1991).
219. See, e.g., *U.S. v. Upton*, 91 F.3d 677 (5th Cir 1996). *U.S. v. Brazel*, 102 F.3d 1120 (11th Cir 1996).
220. *Shannon v. U.S.*, 512 U.S. 573 (1994), interpreting the Insanity Defense Reform Act of 1984.
221. 508 U.S. 275 (Sup.Ct.1993).
222. *Lowenfeld v. Phelps*, 481 U.S. 231 (Sup.Ct. 1988).
223. 96 F.3d 698 (3rd Cir 1996).
224. *U.S. v. McClinton*, 135 F.3d 1178 (7th Cir. 1998).
225. But see *U.S. v. Cabrales*, 524 U.S. 1 (Sup.Ct. 1998): in a money laundering case, venue is not proper in the state where the crime whose proceeds were laundered was committed, if the money laundering defendant did not participate in that crime or transport funds from that state. In a prosecution under 18 USC §924(c)(1) [using or carrying a firearm during and in relation to a violent crime], venue is appropriate in any state in which a violent crime

was committed, even if the gun was carried in only one state of a multi-state series of crimes: *U.S. v. Rodriguez-Moreno*, 119 S.Ct. 1239 (Sup.Ct. 1999).
226. *Zafiro v. U.S.*, 506 U.S. 534 (Sup.Ct. 1993).
227. *U.S. v. Palomba*, 31 F.3d 1456 (9th Cir. 1994).
228. 28 USC §636(b)(1)(A) allows the judge to refer motions to suppress to a magistrate, but if a party objects to the magistrate's report, the judge must make a de novo decision on the portions of the report objected to.
229. *Waller v. Georgia*, 467 U.S. 39 (Sup.Ct.1984).
230. *U.S. v. Enjady*, 66 LW 1470 (10th Cir. 1/20/98).
231. *U.S. v. Castillo*, 66 LW 1666 (10th Cir. 4/6/98).
232. *U.S. v. Saenz*, 134 F.3d 697 (5th Cir. 1998). Also see *U.S. v. Tilghman*, 134 F.3d 414 (D.C. Cir. 1998): reversal is required if the questioning creates the impression that the judge doesn't believe the defendant's testimony.
233. *U.S. v. Burch*, 156 F.3d 1315 (D.C. Cir. 1998).
234. 391 U.S. 123 (Sup.Ct. 1968). But see *Gray v. Maryland*, 523 U.S. 185 (Sup.Ct. 1998): redaction is inadequate if it permits a reasonable inference by the jury that the defendant is one of the persons named in the confession.
235. *Richardson v. Marsh*, 481 U.S. 200 (Sup.Ct. 1987). *Bruton* does not apply to a bench trial: *Lee v. Illinois*, 476 U.S. 530 (Sup.Ct. 1986), nor to a co-defendant's confession introduced to rebut a claim by the defendant, rather than as part of the case in chief, because the confession is not hearsay when used for rebuttal: *Tennessee v. Street*, 471 U.S. 409 (Sup.Ct. 1985).
236. 119 S.Ct. 1998 (Sup.Ct. 1999).
237. The Guidelines also cover supervised release; fines, forfeiture and restitution; and home detention, community service, and other non-custodial sentences.
An Adjournment in Contemplation of Dismissal (ACD) is an indefinite adjournment of a case, with the expectation that the case will be dismissed if the defendant stays out of trouble (or serious trouble) until the adjourned date. ACDs are discretionary with the court (the defendant never has an absolute right to an ACD) and can only be granted with the consent of the prosecution.
238. 28 USC §994(b)(2) restricts the range between the highest and lowest guideline sentence to 25% or six months difference (whichever is greater).
239. *U.S. v Adu*, 82 F.3d 119 (6th Cir. 1996), *U.S. v. Ajugino*, 82 F.3d 925 (9th Cir. 1996), *U.S. v. Vernes*, 103 F.3d 108 (10th Cir. 1996).
240. *Harmelin v. Michigan*, 501 U.S. 957 (Sup.Ct. 1991).
241. *U.S. v. Iversen*, 90 F.3d 1340 (8th Cir 1996).
242. *Wisconsin v. Mitchell*, 508 U.S. 476 (Sup.Ct. 1993).
243. *Doe v. Poritz*, 662 A.2d 367 (N.J.Sup. 1995). But see *Kansas v. Scott*, 947 P.2d 466 (Kan.App. 1997), finding the state's sex offender notification provision to violate the state Constitution's ban on cruel and unusual punishment, if the registrant is not in danger of re-offending, public access to the information is expansive, and the ten-year notice period is disproportionate to the sentence.
244. See 67 LW 2651.

245. *U.S. v. Medina,* 90 F.3d 459 (11th Cir 1996).
246. *Mitchell v. U.S.,* 119 S.Ct. 1307 (Sup.Ct. 1999).
247. *Harvey v. Shillinger,* 76 F.3d 1528 (10th Cir. 1996).
248. *Peguero v. U.S.,* 119 S.Ct. 961 (Sup.Ct. 1999).
249. *U.S. v. Rhodes,* 145 F.3d 1375 (D.C. Cir. 1998).
250. *U.S. v. Bingham,* 81 F.3d 617 (6th Cir. 1996).
251. *U.S. v. Navarro,* 67 LW 1565 (5th Cir. 3/8/99).
252. Expressed in *U.S. v. Marmolejo,* 139 F.3d 328 (5th Cir. 1998).
253. *California v. Superior Court of San Diego County,* 37 Cal.Rptr.2d 364 (Cal.App. 1995).
254. *California Department of Corrections v. Morales,* 514 U.S. 499 (Sup.Ct. 1995).
255. *Young v. Harper,* 65 LW 4197 (Sup.Ct. 1997).
256. However, the Ninth Circuit has ruled that execution by gas chamber constitutes cruel and unusual punishment, although execution by lethal injection is permissible: *Fierro v. Gomez,* 77 F.3d 301 (9th Cir. 1996).
257. 428 U.S. 153 (Sup.Ct. 1976); the Texas and Florida capital punishment statutes were also found Constitutionally acceptable in that year, in *Jurek v. Texas,* 428 U.S. 262 (Sup.Ct. 1976); *Proffitt v. Florida,* 428 U.S. 242 (Sup.Ct. 1976).
258. *Lockett v. Ohio,* 438 U.S. 586 (Sup.Ct. 1978); *Roberts v. Louisiana,* 431 U.S. 633 (Sup.Ct. 1977); *Wooden v. North Carolina,* 428 U.S. 280 (Sup.Ct. 1976).
259. Generally speaking, capital punishment is imposed by a jury, but a 1995 Colorado statute, which was not actually applied until Spring, 1999, delegates capital sentencing to a panel of judges. See "A First Test on Executions for Judges in Colorado" (no by-line), *New York Times* 4/18/88 p. A23.
The judicial panel system is also used in Nebraska; seven other states permit a single judge to impose a death sentence.
260. *Buchanan v. Angelone,* 522 U.S. 269 (Sup.Ct.1998).
261. *Jones v. U.S.,* 526 U.S. 227 (Sup.Ct. 1999).
262. *Delo v. Lashley,* 507 U.S. 272 (Sup.Ct.1993).
263. *Ford v. Wainwright,* 477 U.S. 399 (Sup.Ct.1986).
264. *Thompson v. Oklahoma,* 487 U.S. 815 (Sup.Ct.1988).
265. *Penry v. Lynaugh,* 492 U.S. 302 (Sup.Ct.1989).
266. *Weeks v. Jones,* 100 F.3d 124 (11th Cir 1996).
267. *Coker v. Georgia,* 433 U.S. 584 (Sup.Ct. 1977).
268. *Enmund v. Florida,* 458 U.S. 782 (Sup.Ct. 1982).
269. *Poland v. Stewart,* 92 F.3d 881 (9th Cir 1996).
270. *Calderon v. Coleman,* 525 U.S. 141 (Sup.Ct. 1999).
271. *Belyea v Johnson,* 82 F.3d 613 (5th Cir 1996).
272. For discussion see, e.g., James S. Liebman and Randy Hertz, *Federal Habeas Corpus Practice and Procedure* (3rd ed.), Lexis Law Publishing 1998; Larry W. Yackle, *Postconviction Remedies,* WestGroup 1991/1999 supplement.
273. *Kaufman v. U.S.,* 394 U.S. 217 (Sup.Ct. 1969).
274. *Stone v. Powell,* 428 U.S. 465 (Sup.Ct.1976).
275. *Williams v. Turpin,* 87 F.3d 1204 (11th Cir 1996).

attorney represents the client. Clients must be given enough information to make reasonable decisions about the matter.

Alaska Supreme Court Order #1239 (1/15/99; see 67 LW 2422) requires attorneys to inform their clients if they lack the minimum required amount of malpractice insurance ($100,000 per claimant, $300,000 total).

[¶7010.5] Rule 1.5 Fees

See ¶7060 for computation of attorneys' fee awards. Even in the context of negotiated attorneys' fees, the fees are required to be reasonable. The reasonableness factors are quite similar to the "lodestar" factors used to set fee awards:

- Amount of time devoted to the work
- Local fee scale for comparable work
- Opportunity cost—the extent to which other work was ruled out
- Attorney's success in obtaining a result for the client
- Attorney's ability, experience, and reputation
- Whether the fee was fixed or contingent; the risk element in contingent fees justifies a larger payment

The best practice is for all fees to be set out in a written contract; contingent-fee arrangements must be in writing. Contingent fees are considered unethical in domestic relations matters (other than outright collection of past-due sums) and criminal cases.

If the attorney withdraws from the case, or is fired, before there is a resolution that generates a fund from which a contingent fee could be paid, then the attorney is not entitled to the contingency fee, but is entitled to sue on a *quantum meruit* basis—i.e., for the fair value of work done prior to termination of representation.

Taking a retainer in advance of providing services is acceptable, but any unearned portion of the retainer will have to be returned when representation is terminated.

As a general rule, attorneys are not permitted to split fees with attorneys outside their own firm. However, if the total fee is reasonable; the client is notified and does not object; and the fee is divided based on the respective shares of the work performed by the attorneys (or pursuant to a written agreement with the client), fee-splitting is permissible. A contract to split fees is not necessarily invalid if it fails to comply with Rule 1.5(e). It depends on the facts; relative culpability of the attorneys; the presence of good or bad faith; and whether some of the funds should have been rebated to the client.[3]

Double billing is forbidden: that is, if a lawyer works on a matter for one client while traveling on behalf of another client, it is improper to bill both of them for the same time.

If a third party (e.g., a family member) pays the fee, the attorney's ethical duties continue to run to the client (the person for whom the services are rendered), not the person who pays the fee.

[¶7010.6] Rule 1.6 Attorney-Client Confidences

As a general rule, attorneys are not permitted to disclose any confidential information imparted in the course of legal representation, unless the client permits disclosure. The dramatic exception to the general rule is that confidential information can be disclosed if the attorney believes disclosure is vital to prevent a homicide or infliction of serious bodily injury.

Disclosure is also permitted if it is essential for the attorney to defend him- or herself in a suit brought by a former client.

An attorney-client relationship is created when someone who seeks legal advice discusses a situation with an attorney; it is not necessary for payment to be made.

Attorney-client privilege can survive the death of the client.[4]

Documents become work product if they are prepared in anticipation of litigation (whether or not litigation actually ensues). The work-product privilege is not limited to materials that relate to a specific claim.[5] However, documents and communications generated by an attorney who prepares a tax return (even if an audit is involved) are not privileged, on the theory that documents used in return preparation are not privileged when created by an accountant or other non-lawyer.[6] When an attorney seeks a motion for protection from discovery, covering documents that are alleged to be privileged and to be work product, the District Court's order denying the motion is a collateral order and thus immediately appealable.[7]

Attorney-client privilege is not available for in-house counsel's work in negotiating contracts and reporting to management on negotiations, in that this work is business advice, not the traditional confidential functions of an attorney.[8]

A criminal defense attorney is required to complete the IRS Form 8300 currency transactions report (cash payments over $10,000), even if this requirement is adverse to the interests of a client accused of money laundering.[9]

Even if the lawyer and not the clients is the target of an IRS investigation, the IRS can properly serve the lawyer with a summons requiring disclosure of the names of clients not reported on Form 8300. Court authorization is not required, because client identity and the nature of fee arrangements are not privileged—especially if the lawyer is the actual target of the investigation.[10]

States vary in the way they treat attorney-client confidences; this is one area in which departures from the Rules and Canons are quite common. Some states require that attorneys disclose that their clients have committed or intend to commit perjury; other states forbid the same disclosure.

Sometimes the line is drawn between information about past crimes (confidential) and future crimes (in which case disclosure may be permitted or required; the nature and seriousness of the crime may also be an important factor).

The ABA Standing Committee on Ethics and Professional Responsibility's Formal Opinion 98-411 (released in October, 1998) requires an attorney who asks another lawyer for advice to take extra steps to protect the confidentiality of client information, and the consulted attorney must avoid conflicts of interest with his or her own client. Naturally, the attorney seeking advice should check first to see if there are any conflicts. It is not required, under Model Rule 1.6, to get the client's permission before consulting another attorney, if the lawyer who asks for assistance reasonably believes the consultation will be to the client's benefit.

The client's real name or identifiable facts should not be disclosed in the consultation. Don't identify the real client or the real situation—make it anonymous or hypothetical; if absolutely necessary, disclose the minimum amount of client information to allow answering the question.

[¶7010.7] Rule 1.7 Conflict of Interest

This is not a problem for corporate counsel, who represent the company they work for (or at least is not a problem until they change jobs). But a law firm or sole practitioner may not be able to accept certain clients, because representing them would be a conflict of interest with current or past clients. Representation that would otherwise be improper is permissible if all the clients involved are fully informed of the potential conflict, and consent to have the attorney continue to represent them.

The clearest case of conflict is where the second client's interests are directly adverse to those of the first client, but conflicts can also arise on other bases, such as the potential for one client to sue another. In particular, mergers (either of law firms or of client companies) have a significant potential for generating conflict.

Where conflict arises after the second client relationship is created, the attorney is obligated to withdraw from representing one of the clients (unless both consent).

Rule 1.5 states that the beneficiary of the services, not a third-party payor, is treated as the client. Rule 1.7 enlarges on this by providing that third-party payment is acceptable if the client is informed of the payment; agrees to it; the payment does not weaken the attorney's loyalty to the client; and the third party has no rights in the attorney-client relationship.

An entire firm may have to be disqualified based on a conflict of any attorney (i.e., a past attorney-client relationship that created an obligation of confidentiality). Mergers between law firms—or between client businesses—can also create conflicts. If two corporations merge, a law firm that has represented either is also deemed to have represented the other.

Whether a law firm has to be disqualified from representing a client because of a newly-hired attorney's conflict of interest depends on factors such as:

- Whether there is a substantial relationship between the past and current representation
- The attorney's role in the past representation, especially the degree to which confidences were given
- Whether the attorney has imparted any of those confidences to the new firm; if so, it is disqualified.[11]

Where the past and current matters are both litigation, a substantial relationship exists if the same facts give rise to a material issue in both cases. If the current representation is litigation and the past representation involved non-litigation, background legal work, there is a substantial relationship if facts pertinent to the past representation are also relevant to the litigation.

The presumption of shared confidences is rebuttable. For instance, a large firm may include attorneys who never speak or share files; a firm may have formal provisions to prevent improper interchange of information; and attorneys may limit their practice to a particular field of law, thus will not encounter unrelated matters.

According to the Southern District of New York,[12] a law firm is barred from representing an employment discrimination defendant after one of the firm's lawyers acted as a mediator with respect to the same discrimination complaint. Mediators must be neutral, so it appears improper for the mediator's law firm to take a partisan stand.

The presumption that confidences are shared within a law firm does not apply to a situation in which separate firms act as co-counsel on a matter. Nor is it presumed that married couples, both of whom are attorneys, will necessarily share confidences and thus be disqualified from representing adverse clients.

[¶7010.8] Rule 1.8 Prohibited Transactions

This is something of an omnibus rule, covering several related situations. Attorneys are not allowed to enter into transactions with a client, or to obtain a business or financial interest that the attorney knows is adverse to the client. Transactions can be insulated by the client's written consent, if the transaction is inherently reasonable and fair, and if the client has been given the chance to seek independent counsel.

It is unethical for an attorney to engage in personal financial transactions on the basis of confidential information obtained from a client, if the attorney's action is detrimental to the client (with an exception for situations in which the client gives fully informed consent). Canon DR 4-101(B)(3) also prohibits the attorney from using the confidence for the benefit of a third party without the client's informed consent.

The "draftsman's rule" prohibits an attorney from drafting any document (e.g., a will) that transfers property to the attorney or a close family member of the attorney, unless the transferor is also a relative.

During the pendency of any case, the attorney is forbidden to get any publication or other media rights from the client.

It is unethical for an attorney to give financial assistance to a client, with two exceptions. The attorney can pay court costs and expenses for an indigent client. In a contingent-fee case, the attorney can advance the court costs, but the client will have to repay the attorney out of the proceeds. It is unethical for an attorney to have an ownership interest in litigation, other than a contingent fee or a lien to ensure payment of attorneys' fees.

Rule 1.8 once again returns to the subject of third-party payment for legal services. Payment from non-clients is permitted only if the client gives knowing consent, the attorney-client relationship is not impaired, and attorney-client confidences are not disclosed.

as well as substantive legal, factors is appropriate. Both favorable and unfavorable facts should be discussed with the client.

[¶7010.19] Rule 2.2 Intermediary Role

It is permissible for an attorney to act as intermediary between two or more clients—e.g., if the clients are contemplating a business transaction, or the property of an estate has to be distributed. All clients must consent to the intermediary role. The attorney must withdraw if any of the clients so direct, or if it becomes impossible to satisfy ethical obligations. The attorney can only serve as intermediary based on a good-faith belief that he or she can be impartial and act without prejudice to the interests of any client.

[¶7010.20] Rule 2.3 Evaluation for Third Party

On the request of a non-client, an attorney can evaluate a matter that affects a client, based on the client's informed consent and the attorney's belief that rendering the evaluation is consistent with effective representation of the client. It is also permissible for the client to instruct the attorney to prepare the evaluation. Normal rules of attorney-client confidentiality continue to apply.

[¶7010.21] Rule 3.1 Meritorious Claims

The attorney's role as advocate requires the attorney to use the tools of the legal system to their fullest, for the benefit of the client—but not to raise or defend frivolous issues or to abuse the legal system or harass an opponent. (Legitimate measures that have the incidental effect of annoying an opponent are permissible.) However, in a criminal case, certain additional latitude is permissible—for instance, the attorney can require that each element of the charges be proved beyond a reasonable doubt, even though the attorney is aware that the evidence against the client is strong or even overwhelming.

See ¶7040 below for a discussion of sanctions imposed for maintaining baseless complaints or frivolous claims.

[¶7010.22] Rule 3.2 Expedience

In this context, "expedience" does not have a Machiavellian connotation. It refers to expediting litigation as much as possible, consistent with the client's best interests. Cases must not be delayed for financial reasons (even if the client benefits financially by the delay), and in particular, cases may not be delayed or over-litigated merely in order to increase the fee.

[¶7010.23] Rule 3.3 Candor

As long as representation continues, this Rule forbids knowing misstatements (including misrepresentations as to the law) to a court. In fact, if the opponent has failed to raise a statute or case adverse to the client's position, the lawyer has a duty to raise it him- or herself. The attorney must disclose factual information adverse to the client's position if it is unknown to the adversary.

The attorney is not permitted to offer false evidence, even at the client's direction. However, attorneys do not vouch for the truthfulness of evidence. They cannot offer evidence that they know to be false, but they are not insurers. It violates both this rule and Rule 3.4 to knowingly destroy evidence in present or potential litigation.

One of the toughest ethical issues is balancing this duty of candor against the duty to represent the client zealously and preserve confidences. After all, many clients have engaged in conduct that could be penalized criminally or civilly.

Rule 3.3 requires attorneys to report their client's perjury to the court. Other options are allowed, however. The attorney can ask to withdraw based on the presence of a fraud on the court; or can apply for permission to have the client testify as a narrative rather than in response to questioning, so that the attorney will not become a party to the perjury.

A late-1998 opinion by the ABA Standing Committee on Ethics and Professional Responsibility[16] covers the situation of an attorney who discovers that a client has violated a civil court order not to dispose of assets. The lawyer is obligated to correct any misconceptions the court has about the status of the assets, including those arising out of the attorney's lack of knowledge about the client's treatment of the assets. It may be permissible to withdraw earlier material statements about the assets.

As for statements made or to be made by the client, the attorney must attempt to persuade the client not to make false representations. For statements already made, if necessary to prevent fraud on the tribunal, the attorney may have to disclose what the client has done.

[¶7010.24] Rule 3.4 Fairness to Party Opponents

General duties as an officer to the court, and duties to the opponent, overlap to a significant degree. Rule 3.4 forbids destruction of evidence or concealing evidence or obstructing the opponent's access to it, as well as falsifying evidence or testimony, or knowingly disobeying a court order or rule. Rule 3.4 also forbids refusal to comply with appropriate discovery requests as well as making improper and unreasonable discovery requests of the opponent. At trial, Rule 3.4 forbids raising irrelevant matters.

With certain exceptions, the Rule forbids any attempt to prevent a witness who has relevant information from coming forward. The exceptions are employees and relatives of the client, in situations in which the other party will not be prejudiced by the failure of disclosure.

[¶7010.25] Rule 3.5 Impartial Tribunal

Rule 3.5 forbids not only intentional disruption of courtroom proceedings, but also ex parte contacts that are not permitted by law, and attempts to influence officials, judges, jurors, and prospective jurors.

[¶7010.34] Rule 5.1 Responsibilities Of Firm Partners/Supervisors

Partners and supervising attorneys are obligated to make all reasonable efforts to ensure that colleagues follow the Rules of Professional Conduct. They will be vicariously liable for Rules violations by other attorneys if they order, specifically ratify, or know of the conduct. Reasonable remedial action is required for conduct that can be avoided or mitigated—e.g., removing an attorney from a case where a violation has occurred; giving notice to opposing parties; or reporting the violator to the local ethics committee.

[¶7010.35] Rule 5.2 Responsibilities Of Subordinate Attorneys

An attorney's subordinate position does not relieve him or her from abiding by the ethics rules, but in certain instances, a subordinate attorney might be permitted to rely on a supervising attorney's reasonable interpretation of the ethical rules. Subordination might also be held to negate a wrongful state of mind on the part of the attorney.

[¶7010.36] Rule 5.3 Responsibilities of Non-Attorneys

A law firm's non-attorney employees, such as paralegals, secretaries, and law clerks are still subject to the Rules of Professional Conduct. Law firm partners and supervisors are required to make reasonable efforts to supervise such compliance. Attorneys are vicariously liable for Rules violations by non-attorneys if they order, ratify, or know of the conduct and fail to take reasonable steps to prevent or mitigate the improprieties.

The Pennsylvania Bar Commission on Legal Ethics and Professional Responsibility's Formal Opinion #98-75 (12/4/98; discussed at 67 LW 2469) says that non-lawyer assistants must be warned to observe client confidentiality. The lawyers who employ them must be sure that non-lawyers do not perform specifically legal tasks such as taking depositions, appearing in court, or handling real estate closings.

[¶7010.37] Rule 5.4 Attorney Independence

Under current rules, attorneys can form partnerships with other attorneys—but not with anyone else. That could change in the future, because there is a good deal of interest in Multi-Disciplinary Practice (MDP)—e.g., a business practice that combines attorneys, CPAs, MBAs, and investment bankers. Another aspect of MDP is employment of attorneys by CPA and consulting firms.

On June 8, 1999, the ABA's Commission on Multidisciplinary Practice recommended unanimously that attorneys should be able to form partnerships with other professionals, as long as those professionals are willing to abide by attorneys' rules of professional conduct.

Non-attorneys (except for executors or other estate representatives of deceased attorneys) cannot own interests in law practice P.C.s. Non-lawyers cannot serve as officers or directors of law P.C.s. Non-lawyers (other than clients) are not permitted to control legal matters or regulate practice by attorneys.

Other than payments to decedent attorneys' estates, and referral fees to nonprofit referral organizations, attorneys are not allowed to share their legal fees.

[¶7010.38] Rule 5.5 Unauthorized Practice of Law

Although this Rule forbids attorneys to practice in jurisdictions where they have not been admitted, its main focus is on practice by non-attorneys. The Rule forbids attorneys to delegate practice tasks to non-lawyers. It also forbids non-lawyers to render legal advice to others for pay. (Non-lawyers can appear pro se if they so choose.)

Searching real estate records is considered factual, not practice of law, so non-attorneys have not committed unauthorized practice of law by doing so.[18]

[¶7010.39] Rule 5.6 Restrictions on Practice

Another area in which a balance must be struck: the law firm's desire to hold on to its clients, versus the right of an attorney who departs from a firm to continue to practice law. Law firm employment agreements and partnership agreements must not restrict the right to practice law after the agreement ends. (If an improper agreement is signed, only the offeror of the agreement is guilty of a Rules violation. The signing attorney, who presumably had less negotiating power, is not in violation.) However, retirement-related agreements are allowed to restrict future practice of law.

Clients have a right to choose their own attorneys, so an attorney can legitimately retain his or her clients after departing from a law firm, if the clients prefer to follow the attorney rather than remain with the firm.

A somewhat anomalous result was reached in *Fred Siegel Co. v. Arter & Hadden*, 67 LW 1628 (Ohio 4/7/99). A law firm and its newly hired associate were held liable to the firm where the associate had previously worked, for tortious interference with contract and misappropriation of trade secrets. The associate wrote to her clients explaining that she would be changing firms; the new firm publicized that the new associate would be coming on board. The court's view is that clients have the right to change lawyers, but lawyers do not have a right to entice them to do so.

[¶7010.40] Rule 5.7 Law-Related Services

In a sense, this rule is the mirror image of Rule 5.3. That deals with non-attorneys doing things that might be construed as the practice of law; this deals with attorneys doing things other than practicing law. Law-related services are things like accounting, social work, financial planning, and real estate work, that have a reasonable relation to legal services but could lawfully be performed by a non-attorney.

Rule 5.7 permits attorneys to undertake any lawful work—but they become subject to the Rules of Professional Conduct if they do legal work in the course of the job, or indicate that they are acting as the client's attorney. In particular, the attorney is responsible for informing the client that attorney-client privilege is not available in the case of law-related services.

In 1994, the Supreme Court struck down a Florida rule that forbade attorneys from identifying themselves as CPAs or certified financial planners on their letterheads, business cards, and advertisements. Such identification, if accurate and non-deceptive, is protected as commercial speech.[19]

[¶7010.41] Rule 6.1 Pro Bono

Although there is no disciplinary requirement of pro bono services under the Model Rules of Professional Conduct, the ABA recommends that all attorneys should do at least 50 hours of pro bono work each year. For this purpose, pro bono work is defined as free or reduced-cost work for people of limited means; organizations that assist the poor; or civil rights/civil liberties organizations that do not have the capacity to pay market-rate fees. Pro bono work must be intended to be gratuitous from the outset—unpaid fees don't render services retroactively pro bono.

Seeking to improve the legal profession (e.g., by lobbying, providing training, or serving on bar association committees) also counts as pro bono work.

The ABA endorses financial contributions by attorneys to legal services organizations, even if the attorney also does pro bono work.

The Florida Bar's "aspirational goal" is 20 hours of pro bono work, or a $350 payment to a legal aid organization, per year. It is a disciplinary offense to fail to report compliance with this requirement on the annual dues statement, a requirement that was upheld by the Eleventh Circuit. A Due Process challenge failed, given the state's clear interest in having pro bono work performed, and the status of reporting as a rational mechanism for monitoring the success of the system.[20]

[¶7010.42] Rule 6.2 Appointments

Much of the legal work for persons entitled to representation, but who cannot afford to pay privately, is done by court-appointed attorneys. Rule 6.2 says that attorneys must accept appointments unless they have good cause to decline the appointment—e.g., the appointment creates a conflict of interest with current clients; the attorney would suffer an unreasonable financial burden if forced to accept the appointment; or the client or client's actions are so offensive to the particular attorney as to preclude maintenance of an attorney-client relationship.

In 1990, Florida granted a petition to amend the state rules, so that attorneys have a duty to provide legal services when they are court-appointed. The court did not accept opposing arguments that court appointments are a "taking" or involuntary servitude.[21]

[¶7010.43] Rule 6.3 Membership In Legal Services Organizations

Attorneys are allowed to administer legal services organizations, although this Rule forbids the attorney from engaging in conduct for the legal services organization that is in conflict with his or her other clients.

[¶7010.44] Rule 6.4 Law Reform Activities

It is permissible for an attorney to advocate changes in the law, even if those changes affect the attorney's clients. If the change would be beneficial to a client, the attorney has a duty to disclose that the change benefits a client, but disclosure of the client's identity is not required. Disclosure is not required if the reform would be detrimental to a client(s).

[¶7010.45] Rule 7.1 Communication

Rule 7.1 forbids false or misleading statements, or statements that create false or misleading implications, about the services the attorney can render. It is unethical to make unsubstantiated comparisons of the attorney with other attorneys; to make statements that are false or materially incomplete; to provide unsupported guarantees; or to imply that the attorney will exercise undue influence on the legal process.

[¶7010.46] Rule 7.2 Advertising

Traditionally, attorney advertising was deemed unethical. It is now permitted (as commercial speech protected by the First Amendment), but is strictly regulated. Telephone directory advertisements, print ads, and broadcast (radio, television, Internet) ads are permissible, within limits.

The advertisements can give the name of the firm; its address; names of its attorneys (including the name of at least one attorney who is responsible for the content of the ad); phone numbers; areas of practice; and fees. The names of clients can be disclosed, with their consent, but celebrity endorsements are permitted only if the celebrity actually is a current client. The advertiser must keep a copy of the actual advertisement on file for at least two years.

The Rule is violated by giving any thing of value to a person who recommends the attorney, with three exceptions. Advertisements can be purchased at reasonable cost; payments can be made to buy a law practice, as permitted by Rule 1.17; and not-for-profit attorney referral services can be paid their usual fee.

An Ohio ethics ruling forbids advertisements about contingent fees to say "No fee without recovery" or "no charge unless we win." The advertiser must disclose the client's liability for costs and expenses and explain how the actual fee is calculated.[22]

Early in 1998, the Eleventh Circuit struck down a Georgia statute requiring advertising by Worker's Compensation lawyers to warn that filing false Comp claims is a crime. In the court's view, the requirement was not necessary in truthful, non-misleading advertising, and there was no evidence that television advertising is particularly appealing to fraudulent claimants. It would be unduly burdensome to make lawyers devote part of their expensive air time to the warning![23]

[¶7010.47] Rule 7.3 Contacting Prospective Clients

This is the rule concerned with solicitation of potential clients. As a general rule, attorneys are not permitted to make direct solicitations (as distinct from generalized advertising) of potential clients. (Exceptions are made for family members or those with whom the attorney already has a professional relationship, and for potential pro bono clients.) Coercive or harassing solicitations are banned, as are solictations of persons who have indicated that they don't want to hear from the attorney.

Solicitation materials must be labeled as advertising material. This disclosure must be on the front of the envelope of mailed material, or repeated at the beginning and end of a broadcast announcement.

The Supreme Court upheld a Florida statute forbidding direct-mail solicitation of accident victims within 30 days of the accident, on the grounds that the state has a legitimate interest in protecting the privacy of accident victims and their families that is broad enough to justify some limitation on commercial speech.[24]

The Eleventh Circuit has upheld a Georgia law that forbids in-person solicitation, against a First Amendment challenge.[25]

[¶7010.48] Rule 7.4 Communicating Fields of Practice

There is no real counterpart in the legal profession of "board certified" medical specialties, although there are numerous organizations of attorneys within a particular specialty field of practice. Clients often prefer to hire an attorney who concentrates on a particular area of practice and has developed relevant skill and knowledge. Therefore, lawyers have an incentive to hold themselves out as specialists in a particular field, and clients are at risk of inaccurate claims of specialized knowledge.

The balance struck by Rule 7.4 is that, in general, attorneys are allowed to indicate that they practice in particular areas of the law (or that their practice is limited to a particular area or that they do not practice in other areas), but by and large they are not allowed to claim that they "specialize" in a particular area.

This rule is subject to some important exceptions. Attorneys admitted to practice before the U.S. Patent and Trademark Office are permitted to describe themselves as patent attorneys, and admiralty lawyers can describe themselves as such.

ABA-granted specialties and certifications can be advertised. In states where specialty certifications are granted, attorneys certified by the appropriate authority can advertise that fact. Certifications from other organizations must disclose the lack of state authority (or that authorization was denied). If the state does not have a certification or specialty process, this must be communicated by any attorney claiming certification or specialty.

[¶7010.49] Rule 7.5 Firm Name and Letterhead

Firm names and letterheads must not be false or deceptive. Artificial trade names are allowed, as long as they do not falsely imply connection to a government agency or public organizations. Only firms that really are partnerships can describe themselves as such. The names of attorneys currently holding public office can be included on the firm's letterhead only if the attorney is a current, active participant in the firm's practice.

If the firm has offices in more than one jurisdiction, it can use the same firm name in all of them, but the letterhead must make it clear which attorneys are admitted in which jurisdictions.

[¶7010.50] Rule 8.1 Admission to the Bar

Each state's highest court has the exclusive right to regulate Bar membership, including admission and discipline (in the federal system, the Supreme Court has this role). Rule 8.1 imposes similar duties in the context of both admission and bar discipline.

The Rule forbids knowing false statements; knowing failure to disclose facts needed to correct an error; or failure to provide information sought by an admitting or disciplinary board, except to the extent that the information is privileged (as defined by Rule 1.6), or that a Fifth Amendment privilege can be asserted.[26]

Admission to the bar of a Court of Appeals, as stated by Federal Rules of Appellate Procedure 46, requires the attorney to be of good moral and professional character. He or she must already be admitted to the bar of the highest court of a state; the U.S. Supreme Court; another Court of Appeals; or a District Court. The attorney must apply for admission and swear or affirm to act as an "attorney and counselor of this court, uprightly and according to law" and to support the Constitution of the United States. Suspension or disbarment from the Court of Appeals bar is a consequence of being suspended or disbarred elsewhere, or being guilty of "conduct unbecoming a member of the court's bar."

A non-resident member of a bar can be required to maintain an office and attend CLE programs in the state given the state's legitimate interest in encouraging full-time practice of law and well-informed attorneys. The requirements were found to be equal for residents and non-residents, and not unduly burdensome, hence acceptable despite a possible burden on interstate commerce.[27]

According to the Fourth Circuit, a state can maintain a rule conditioning *pro haec vice* admission on sponsorship by a local lawyer who has an office and practices daily within the state. In this reading, practicing law is a fundamental right subject to the Privileges and Immunities clause, but sponsoring the provisional admission of other attorneys is not a fundamental part of law practice. But the Eleventh Circuit held that for a District Court to deny a *pro haec vice* application

Amendment, so suspending the attorney was inappropriate. Statements about a judge's integrity (other than statements susceptible of factual proof) are protected under the First Amendment.[48]

Criticism of an attorney's conduct, where there is no official sanction order and monetary sanctions have been vacated, is not appealable,[49] but there is a split in authority as to whether sanctions can be appealed immediately: yes, in the Second, Seventh, Eighth, Ninth, and Eleventh Circuits, no in the First, Third, Fifth, Sixth, Tenth and Federal Circuits.[50]

The Private Securities Litigation Reform Act of 1995 (see ¶690.1) imposes sanctions for ungrounded securities actions and allegations in complaints.

[¶7050] Regulation of Law Firms and Associations

Most law firms operate as partnerships; professional corporations; or partnerships that include one or more professional corporations in their membership. Generally speaking, creation of a law firm is a voluntary event, but "partnership by estoppel" may occur based on office sharing, letterheads, or other manifestations that lead others to believe that the attorneys practice jointly in a law firm. If other people justifiably rely on the appearance of partnership, to their detriment, a partnership by estoppel is created. Furthermore, a partnership by estoppel creates the same obligations with respect to conflict of interest as an explicit partnership.

A branch of a multi-office law firm must be careful that its letterhead accurately represents the composition of the firm and the jurisdictions in which attorneys are admitted to practice. State rules will probably require at least one partner of the firm (not just an associate) to be admitted in state.

As a general rule, clients can fire their attorneys at any time. However, a group of lawyers who left corporate employment and set up a firm based on a retainer agreement could maintain a breach of contract claim based on their detrimental reliance.[51]

Employing a member of a law firm is treated as employment of the entire firm—for instance, in determining whether a conflict of interest has occurred or is a risk.

[¶7050.1] Law Firm Partnerships

A law firm partnership shares most characteristics of business partnerships (see ¶110), including unlimited liability and tax characterization. Each partner is a fiduciary to the other partners.

A law firm partner can become liable for the acts or omissions of other partners if the other partners acted in the ordinary course of partnership business or with the actual or apparent authority of the other partners. Partners are jointly and severally liable for negligence of other partners. Failure to provide proper supervision to associates can also constitute malpractice.

Common law and the Uniform Partnership Act are in agreement that a partnership is not an entity that can be sued for malpractice, but several states have enacted statutes to permit such suits.

Traditionally, all law firm partners were on an equal footing, much like general partners in a business partnership. Associates were given a certain number of years to earn promotion to partnership; those who were not promoted were generally fired. Today, many firms have a two- or multi-tier partnership arrangement, with equity partners at the top and with non-equity partners, counsel, or permanent associates between partners and associates.

Non-equity, income, or junior partners do not contribute capital to the firm, and they are not liable for the firm's financial liabilities. In most instances, they will not have voting rights within the firm, Technically, they are salaried employees of the firm, probably compensated with salary and bonuses (which may reflect a share of firm profits).

A two-track partnership system can increase the profits available to equity partners; permit retention of attorneys who are a profit center for the firm but for some reason do not merit promotion to equity partner; and can permit demotion of equity partners instead of expelling them for mediocre performance. Demotion can also be used as a transition to retirement for older partners.

[¶7050.1.1] Partnership Agreements

Although not legally requisite, law firm partnership agreements are useful in planning the strategy the firm will use, and in avoiding (if possible) and otherwise resolving conflicts among partners. A typical partnership agreement obligates its attorneys to devote full time to work for the partnership, and determines matters such as:

- Capital contributions to be made by partners
- Management of capital and income accounts for each partner
- Regular draw each partner can take against his/her share of the firm's profits for the year
- Percentage of profit and loss allocated to each partner; or formula for calculating each partner's share
- Fiscal year for the partnership
- Provisions for admitting new partners; whether a unanimous vote of partners is required
- Whether all partners will be full equity partners or whether a two-tier system will be implemented
- Formulas for compensation of associates, including salary; bonuses based on firm profits; bonuses based on exceptional performance by the associate; and bonuses based on new business brought in by the associate
- Whether a partnership vote is needed to take on new cases or retainer clients
- Buy-out of the partnership interest of a disabled, retiring, or deceased partner; typically, the firm will re-purchase the interest at its book value. The estate of a deceased partner is entitled to an accounting from the firm, and the estate is entitled to the partner's interest in all partnership assets, including pending files in contingent fee cases.
- Expulsion of a partner. Clearly, a partner must be expelled for a criminal conviction, disbarment, or serious ethical violation, but there are more con-

tentious issues about whether expulsion is justified based on a change in the practice or relative lack of productivity

[¶7050.1.2] Compensation of Partners

Law firm partnerships have evolved many methods of allocating compensation other than simple equal division of post-expense net revenues. For instance, there may be a formula under which each partner is responsible for a certain portion of expenses, and is entitled to receive a certain percentage of the profits—but the two percentages need not be equal, and need not be the same as those assigned to other partners. Various pools of funds may be created, and divided according to formulas that reflect individual partners' hours worked, rainmaking ability, results obtained, etc.

[¶7050.2] Law Firm Management

A very small firm does not require a formal management structure, but as a firm grows, it becomes more important to tackle current questions and make plans for the future in areas such as:

- Marketing the firm
- Adding or changing areas of practice
- Malpractice insurance
- Maintaining appropriate computers, networks, and other communications equipment
- Maintaining the office; moving or expanding as necessary; re-decorating and buying new furniture
- Recruiting attorneys
- Promoting attorneys to partnership; using forms such as two-tiered partnership and "of counsel" arrangements
- Docketing and calendar control
- Management of documents, discovery, and litigation
- Hiring and supervising non-attorney employees
- Setting compensation policy for the firm

Depending on preferences and circumstances, a law firm might have a single managing partner or a management committee. Many management tasks can be delegated to a non-attorney administrator, working under the supervision of one or more partners.

Law firm management requires planning, not just attention to daily obligations. The manager(s) should analyze various measures of profitability, to see if they are increasing or decreasing. Revenue can be measured by lawyer or by partner; so can expenses and overhead. The number of billable hours, net income per partner, and speed of collecting fees can all be tracked. If profits are declining, the firm may be able to shift to more profitable areas of practice; add more clients through better marketing; shift to more profitable clients; change billings methods; improve speed of collection; or improve efficiency.

[¶7050.3] Dissolution of a Partnership

Unless the partnership agreement is to the contrary, a partnership is dissolved by the departure of any partner (whether by resignation, retirement, disability, termination, or death). On dissolution, the partnership has to finish ongoing work for its clients, or give them the opportunity to obtain other representation. The affairs of the partnership cannot be wound up until all client matters are completed or other counsel has been obtained.

When a firm dissolves, many questions have to be resolved, including:

- Who gets to keep the office
- Who gets to keep the telephone number—not a trivial matter when it may appear in hundreds of influential Rolodexes! Soon, ability to keep the address of the Web site will be almost as important
- Who can keep the file of forms that the firm has developed over time
- How the firm's pending bills will be divided among attorneys.

[¶7050.4] Professional Corporations and LLPs

Lawyers can also associate to practice in professional corporation (PC) form.

Some states allow Limited Liability Partnerships (LLPs), a form that permits some limitation of liability for firm debts and tort liability related to actions of other attorneys who were not supervised by that particular attorney-partner.

[¶7060] Attorneys' Fees

The basic American rule[52] is that each party is responsible for its own attorneys' fees, unless there is a statute that calls for shifting of fees, or unless there has been some form of litigation abuse that justifies fee-shifting. Another exception is that a prevailing party who secures a common trust fund for others, or preserves a common fund that benefits a class, is entitled to attorneys' fees.

There are, in fact, about 100 federal statutes under which a prevailing party (or only a prevailing plaintiff) can recover fees. However, it is much more likely that a prevailing plaintiff will be entitled to recover fees as an element of damages than that a prevailing defendant will be entitled to recover damages. In general, defendants get damage awards only if the plaintiff abused the litigation process—not if the plaintiff advanced a theory in good faith but without impressing the trier of fact.[53]

The Equal Access to Justice Act, 28 USC §2412 provides fee awards to private parties who sue or are sued by the federal government, and prevail against it, if the government's position was not substantially justified.

The Civil Rights Attorneys' Fee Awards Act, 42 USC §1988, makes a fee award almost automatic for prevailing plaintiffs in civil rights and civil liberties actions, although the District Court has discretion to determine what fee is reasonable.[54] Other federal fee-shifting statutes include the Freedom of Information Act; Bankruptcy Act; Clayton Antitrust Act; Fair Credit Billing and Reporting Acts; ERISA; and the Federal Tort Claims Act.

[¶7060.1] Prevailing Party

A party need not succeed as to every count in the complaint to have the status of a prevailing party. Mere success on procedural issues is not enough—concrete substantive rights must be gained,[55] either in the courtroom or via consent decree.[56] Success on any significant issue, resulting in some of the benefits for which the suit was brought, is sufficient.[57] A party also prevails by acting as a catalyst for voluntary action by the defendant that also achieves objectives of the plaintiff.

If only nominal damages are awarded, the plaintiff has indeed prevailed—but such a limited degree of success will be a potent factor in determining the fee![58]

In the view of the Second Circuit, shareholders have created a common benefit supporting a fee award if they win an action under '34 Act Rule 14a-8, resulting in the inclusion of a shareholder proposal in a proxy statement—even if the proposal is heavily defeated.[59]

[¶7060.2] Attorneys' Fee Awards Under FRCP Rule 54

In a case brought under a federal statute that lacks a fee provision, Federal Rules of Civil Procedure Rule 54 governs the motion applying for an award of fees and costs.

Such a motion must be made within 14 days of entry of judgment. The motion papers must give a fair estimate of the fee the attorney expects to be able to prove. However, any party or class member has the right to make an adversary submission with respect to fees. The fee application can be referred to a Rule 53 master (there is no need to prove or even assert that the matter is particularly complex). The court will consider the facts and circumstances and enter a judgment as to attorneys' fees.

As a general rule, attorneys' fee awards will be calculated based on the forum in which the case was litigated but the D.C. Circuit found an exception where most of the work was done away from the forum, in a jurisdiction where prevailing fees are much lower.[60] In other words, attorneys can't get a windfall by litigating away from home.

The Prison Litigation Reform Act (PLRA), 42 USC §1997e, limits attorneys' fee awards in prison litigation to those incurred in proving an actual violation of prisoners' rights. The hourly rate cannot exceed 150% of the fee paid to appointed counsel. However, the fee cap applies only to services performed after the effective date of the PLRA.[61]

[¶7060.3] Fee Calculations and the Lodestar

Statutory fee calculations depend on the "lodestar": a somewhat flexible standard based on a list of factors such as time expended on a case, results obtained for the client, novelty and difficulty of issues raised, and prevailing local fees. Upward deviations from the lodestar are possible, but the Supreme Court treats them as exceptional.[62]

According to the Third Circuit, application of the lodestar process is mandatory; it is improper for the court to make each side submit a figure and then pick one of them.[63]

The Seventh Circuit held that the District Court should not have upheld a bankruptcy court's fee award in a Chapter 13 case that used an $800 base fee that was established a decade earlier as presumptively reasonable. The presumptively reasonable fee requires periodic review and updating.[64]

U.S. v. Chapman, 146 F.3d 1166 (9th Cir. 1998) holds that the United States, but not a private party, can recover reasonable attorneys' fees as CERCLA response costs for prosecuting a cost recovery action. Attorneys' fees as response costs were denied to private parties by the Supreme Court in 1994.[65]

[¶7060.4] Tax Deductibility of Fees

An individual can deduct legal fees related to gain-seeking activities, but not those relating to their personal affairs. (Collecting alimony is deemed to be a gain-seeking activity, so related legal fees are deductible.) Fees expended in connection with the determination, collection, or refund of any tax can be deducted under Code §212.

A business' legal fees (or the salary of in-house counsel) are deductible under §162 if they are ordinary and necessary business expenses, but expenses for defending or perfecting title to property are capital expenditures that must be written off over a period of years, not in the year they are incurred (§263).

The retainer for an attorney applied to legal expenses for acquisition of a business must be capitalized.[66]

[¶7070] Law Practice in the Internet Era

Two 1999 ethics opinions state that it is not an unethical breach of confidentiality for an attorney to communicate via unencrypted e-mail[67] (as long as the recipient is a proper person to get the information, of course!).

The ABA says that the client's consent is not necessary before sending e-mail about the client's matter, unless the information is so sensitive that special security measures are required. E-mail could be intercepted by a hacker, but it's also true that phones can be tapped and documents can be stolen.

In mid-1998, the State Bar of Texas proposed innovative rules for integrating an Internet presence into law practice. Under the rules, law firm Web sites are governed by advertising rules, and are subject to review by the bar's Advertising Review Committee. E-mail solicitations would have to include the word "Advertisement" in the subject line.[68]

At about the same time, the ABA Commission on Advertising released a paper, "A Re-Examination of the ABA Model Rules of Professional Conduct Pertaining to Client Development in Light of Emerging Technologies."[69] Using the Internet for marketing creates problems that did not have to be confronted in a paper-based world—such as how to treat payments for maintaining a Web site, doing broadcast e-mail, or placing banner ads. Contact with potential clients can

47. *Sussman v. Bank of Israel*, 56 F.3d 450 (2nd Cir. 1995).
48. *Standing Committee on Discipline v. Yagman*, 55 F.3d 1430 (9th Cir. 1995).
49. *Williams v. U.S.*, 156 F.3d 86 (1st Cir. 1998).
50. This issue is discussed in *Starcher v. Correctional Medical Systems Inc.*, 66 LW 1799 (6th Cir. 5/21/98).
51. *Atkins & O'Brien LLP v. ISS International Service System Inc.*, 678 N.Y.S.2d 596 (N.Y.A.D. 1998).
52. Upheld, as the normal rule in U.S. litigation, by *Alyeska Pipeline Service Co. v. Wilderness Society*, 421 U.S. 240 (Sup.Ct. 1975).
53. For instance, the standard under which a prevailing Title VII defendant can receive attorneys' fees, under *Christiansburg Garment Co. v. EEOC*, 434 U.S. 412 (Sup.Ct. 1978) is whether the plaintiff's claim was unreasonable, frivolous, or groundless; or whether litigation was maintained after the groundlessness of the claim became evident. A prevailing defendant who is awarded attorneys' fees is also entitled to be reimbursed for the necessary expenses of collecting the award: *Vudakinovich v. McCarthy*, 59 F.3d 58 (7th Cir. 1995).
54. See, e.g., *Pino v. Locascio*, 101 F.3d 235 (2nd Cir. 1996); *Luciano v. Olsten*, 109 F.3d 111 (2nd Cir. 1997).
55. *Hanrahan v. Hampton*, 446 U.S. 754 (Sup.Ct. 1980).
56. *Maher v. Gagne*, 448 U.S. 122 (Sup.Ct. 1980).
57. *Hensley v. Eckerhart*, 461 U.S. 424 (Sup.Ct. 1983).
58. *Farrar v. Hobby*, 506 U.S. 103 (Sup.Ct. 1992).
59. *Amalgamated Clothing & Textile Workers Union v. Wal-Mart Stores*, 54 F.3d 69 (2nd Cir. 1995).
60. *Davis County Solid Waste Management & Energy Recovery District v. EPA*, 67 LW 1532 (D.C. Cir. 2/26/99).
61. *Martin v. Hadix*, 119 S.Ct. 1998 (Sup.Ct. 1999)
62. *Blum v. Stenson*, 465 U.S. 996 (Sup.Ct. 1984).
63. *Pennsylvania Environmental Defense Foundation v. Canon-McMillan School District*, 152 F.3d 228 (3rd Cir. 1998).
64. In re Kindhart, 160 F.3d 1176 (7th Cir. 1998).
65. *Key Tronic Corp. v. U.S.*, 511 U.S. 809(Sup.Ct. 1994).
66. *Dana Corp. v. Comm'r*, 83 AFTR2d 98-5031 (Fed.Cir. 4/7/99).
67. ABA Standing Committee Formal Opinion 99-413 (3/10/99); Ohio Supreme Court Board of Commissioners on Grievances and Discipline Opinion 99-2 (4/9/99); see 67 LW 2645-2646.
68. See Kate Thomas, "Texas Bar Proposes Internet Regulations," *Nat.L.J.* 7/2098 p. A5.
69. The white paper is available at http://www.abanet.org/legalserv/advertis-ing.html, and is discussed at 67 LW 2150 (9/22/98).
70. Philadelphia Bar Association Professional Guidance Committee Op 98-6 (3/98); 66 LW 2613.
71. Discussed in George Relles and Richard Solomon, "Electronic Research Poses Billing Dilemma," *Nat.L.J.* 7/13/98 p. B7.

¶7500

Computers and the Law

[¶7501]

In earlier editions and supplements of this work, computers were discussed in two aspects: the computers themselves might be found in law offices, and the legal consequences of computing, especially software. By now, computers (desktop, laptop, networked) are an essential part of the law office environment. Computers make a firm's support staff much more productive—or, in fact, replace most or all of the support staff. Even lawyers who are allergic to keyboarding can get into the act with speech recognition software.

Computers are used for litigation management, time management, and billing. Researching on-line and communicating by e-mail are an important part of the lawyer's day. Courts are moving toward acceptance of electronically filed documents and CD-ROM briefs.

However, the legal system doesn't always "get it" when it comes to software, and especially the Internet and electronic commerce. See ¶215 for proposals to add electronic commerce and software licensing provisions to the UCC.

[¶7510] The Office Network

In the pre-computer era, the typical legal document was drafted by an attorney who hand-wrote research results (usually on yellow legal pads), hand-wrote drafts, had those drafts typed by a secretary, revised the drafts by hand, had them re-typed, and so on through many iterations.

Under current practice, (and as long as the attorney can learn to type and use the software!) the attorney can assemble the document entirely electronically, with little or no support staff assistance. Documents can be completed much faster, with greater accuracy. Instead of consulting a printed form book, or forms file assembled by the firm, the attorney can select and customize clauses from a document assembly database of suitable clauses.

A sole practitioner who doesn't have a secretary will probably want to have at least one computer, and perhaps two or more: a desktop computer and a laptop, plus other communications devices such as a pager or hand-held device.

A very small firm may be able to operate with stand-alone computers, with files exchanged by "sneakernet" (i.e., walking over and giving a disk to the person who needs to use it). But a sophisticated small firm, or a larger firm, is far more likely to connect its computers into a network, for sharing data and for applications such as scheduling and collaboration. If collaboration software is used, it's especially important to keep track of the various versions and see who has made which revisions.

Therefore, the hardware and software for the office should be chosen with attention to their network-friendliness. Additional steps will have to be taken for stability (so that one machine's crash will not destroy data on the entire network); for routine backup of the entire system as well as backups by individuals of files currently in use (and perhaps for remote storage of backups, in case there is damage to the physical plant); and for confidentiality and security (making sure that only authorized persons can view confidential or sensitive files; preventing intrusion by hackers; preventing data loss).

For the purposes of law office computing, "client" means something quite different from what it does in general legal parlance. A "server" is a powerful central computer that runs a network; a "client" is an individual workstation within the network. Computers within a network are also known as "nodes" of the network. A small network (up to about six computers) can be set up as a "peer-to-peer" network, where the computers are interconnected but there is no central server. A larger network will require at least one server.

[¶7510.1] Typical Law Office Hardware

A suggested minimum system would give each attorney a desktop computer with a hard drive capacity of at least 4.5 gigabytes (GB). The computer should have Random Access Memory (RAM) of 32 megabytes (MB) or more. The computer should have an internal modem (for connecting to the Internet) at the fastest available speed, unless the firm has a faster Internet connection using ISDN, a T-1 line, or one of the varieties of DSL. Each lawyer should either have a printer, or have network access to a laser printer that prints at least 600 dots per inch (the more dots, the finer the resolution of the printed material), and prints 8-10 pages per minute (ppm).

Scanners with OCR (Optical Character Recognition) and automatic document feeders should also be available, although not necessarily one per attorney.

It will usually be helpful for at least some of the attorneys to have laptop computers in addition to their desktop computers, although laptop computers are significantly more expensive than their less-mobile counterparts, and using both laptop and desktop computers requires efforts to synchronize the files used on both.

The firm will have to communicate in other media, too. Telephone service is mandatory, whether POTS (Plain Old Telephone Service) or additional features such as call forwarding, call waiting, and Caller ID. Answering machines and/or voice mail will be of critical significance. Although eventually fax and e-mail will probably merge into a single Internet-based system, the ability to send and receive faxes (whether through the computer or through a stand-alone fax machine) is currently very important.

Lawyers who have to be reached when they are outside the office may want to carry beepers, and usage of portable phones is close to universal.

[¶7510.2] Typical Law Office Applications

Although not all law offices will use all of these applications, this is a list of potential applications:

- Word processing
- Document drafting
- Scanning printed documents into the computer system, so they will not have to be re-keyed
- "Burning" CDs containing large amounts of information
- E-mail for communications within and outside the firm (with due attention to security and confidentiality). Both ABA and Ohio ethics committees have ruled that sending unencrypted e-mail that discusses client matters is not per se an unethical breach of confidentiality. The client's consent is only required for the use of e-mail if the information is sensitive enough to require special security measures.[1]
- Time management and planning
- Calendaring and scheduling
- Tickler systems, so that, for instance, preparation of a motion begins a certain number of days before the motion has to be filed
- Project management and coordination
- Checks for conflict of interest
- Billing
- Legal research (commercial services such as Lexis and Westlaw; servers operated by courts, government units, and administrative agencies)
- Dictation and speech synthesis, to reduce or eliminate the need to "type"
- Continuing legal education
- Litigation management (preparation of a searchable database of documents related to a case, so the information can be correlated and will be available for trial preparation and at trial).

To an increasing extent, communications with courts (including scheduling meetings and court appearances and filing documents) will be done electronically rather than in person or via telephone.

In order to use the World Wide Web (Web or WWW), the firm must have both the necessary connections and a relationship with an Internet Service Provider (ISP) or proprietary service such as America Online (AOL). There are many ways to connect with the Internet,[2] and new ways are emerging. A modem is a piece of equipment (either inside the individual computer or connected to it) that uses telephone lines to link the computer to the Web. Although modems are inexpensive, they do not allow high-speed Web access.

Other methods include cable modems, special fast telephone connections (ISDN, DSL), satellite connections, and leasing or sharing a fast, full-time connection to the Web (a full or fractional T-1 or T-3 line—there's no such thing as a T-2 line). Although price is important, it is not the only factor in selecting a connection method. The firm will want to select a stable technology, that can be installed without too long a waiting period. The provider must offer close to 100% "uptime." Another factor is the ability of the provider to survive in a competitive environment: many law firms (and other businesses and individuals) have seen a satisfactory service provider go out of business.

The subject of law firm telecommunications in general is a complex one, and either an economically and technologically sophisticated firm employee, or an outside consultant, will be needed to advise the firm of its options for telephone service, Internet service, and Internet connections.

A further complication: many law firms will want to maintain their own Web site. This will require creating a design (either in-house or by hiring a design firm), adding content to the site, handling routine site operations and maintenance in-house or by contract with an outside service provider ("hosting"), and adding new content to keep the site fresh.

Steps must be taken to publicize the Web site and attract the attention of clients, potential clients, and other attorneys. Steps must also be taken to segregate confidential client matters communicated electronically from the Web site that is available to the public. One way to do this is with password protection "firewalls" that limit access to authorized users. Sensitive material can be placed on a limited "intranet" system that is not publicly available, rather than on a Web site.

[¶7520] E-Commerce

From the seller's perspective, having an on-line "store" on a Web site instead of, or in addition to, a conventional bricks-and-mortar store can be an excellent way to serve new customers at low cost. From the buyer's perspective, on-line shopping can be convenient and permits unparalleled access to price comparisons and auctions. However, commercial law—which evolved in a nineteenth century mixed agricultural and manufacturing economy—has some difficulties in catching up to electronic commerce.

[¶7520.1] Commerce Issues in Cyberspace

One of the most serious issues that commercial law faces is what can be considered a "writing" or "signature" for transactions that occur electronically. As of early 1999, states had adopted three models:

- "Absolute grant of authority" (e.g., Florida law)—i.e., "writing" includes any electronic information that can be retrieved in perceivable form; any electronic symbol that is intended to authenticate a document will be accorded the status of a signature. However, there is no provision for notarization or admission of electronic documents into evidence, and the possibilities of biometric identification (e.g., through fingerprints or retina prints), or authentication by a third-party "trusted intermediary" are not dealt with.
- Statutory franchise (e.g., Utah): a franchise is granted to certain intermediaries to handle certification; these statutes imply the use of cryptography to protect commerce documents.
- Uniform Electronic Transactions Act's flexible standards, including permissive standards for what will be accepted as a signature, but with higher standards for negotiable instruments and with a provision that electronic documents will be admissible in court.[3]

An "electronic signature," as defined by the National Conference of Commissioners on Uniform State Laws, is "an electronic sound, symbol or process attached to or logically connected with an electronic record," that has been executed or adopted with intention to sign. See http://www.webcom.com/legaled/ETAForum. Also see the Final Report of the Commission on Electronic Commerce and Crime, http://www.mbc.com with information about an infrastructure for secure e-commerce, including digital signatures and secure certificates.

The proposed Uniform Electronic Transactions Act (UETA) is designed to defer to the UCC if there are conflicting provisions. The proposed Uniform Act applies to "electronic records and electronic signatures that relate to any transaction." See http://www.law.upenn.edu/library/ulc/ulc.htm. On July 29, 1999, the National Conference of Commissioners on Uniform State Laws approved the UETA, paving the way for state legislators to take it up.[4]

In a mid-1998 Notice, the FTC took the not-surprising position that most of its rules and guidelines apply to transactional electronic media such as the Internet, e-mail, and CD-ROM. The proposal (see 63 FR 2693) treats regulatory references to "written" material as including information that can be preserved in any readable tangible form, not just print. Guidance for making mandatory disclosures online is also given.

[¶7520.2] Prevention of Fraud

The Internet offers a form of instantaneous, inexpensive, widespread communication, where it is easy to conceal or misrepresent the origin of the message. Anyone who has a computer and modem can engage in active trading in stock and other securities. The potential for securities fraud is obvious. For the SEC's response, see the GAO Report, "Securities Fraud: The Internet Poses Challenges to Regulators and Investors," GAO/T-GGD-99-34 (3/22/99), available from the U.S. government information Web site (http://www.access.gpo.gov).

[¶7530] Jurisdiction in Cyberspace

Data appearing on a Web site can give rise to litigation for various reasons. It might be alleged to be libelous or fraudulent, for example. The operation of the site itself may give rise to claims.

The very nature of the Internet is that any site can be accessed by any Internet-ready computer anywhere in the world. This is a very long arm indeed, so conventional notions of jurisdiction are hard to apply. There have only been a few years in which a jurisprudence of Internet jurisdiction could have emerged, so this discipline is still in its infancy.

Personal jurisdiction requires at least minimum contacts with the forum[5]; otherwise, it would not be fair to force the party to litigate in a remote forum. The defendant must deliberately have taken advantage of the opportunity to contact potential customers within the forum.

Merely posting a Web site will not create personal jurisdiction everywhere in the world, and probably not even everywhere the site is in fact accessed. Courts usually look for "something extra," such as creation of a contract, choice of law provisions in the contract, purposive contacts directed specifically at residents of a particular jurisdiction, or intent to extort (by cybersquatting) in order to find personal jurisdiction.[6] By analogy to "old media," states tend to treat material on the Web in much the same light as an advertisement in a periodical sent to the jurisdiction; if the advertisement would give rise to personal jurisdiction, probably so would the site.

[¶7530.1] ISP Safe Harbor

It should be noted that a provision of the Communications Decency Act that has survived the Supreme Court *Reno v. ACLU* decision (see ¶7550), 47 USC §223(e), is a safe harbor provision for Internet Service Providers (ISPs) and others who provide Internet access. The service provider is not liable for criminal penalties for transmission of obscene matter, if the matter is transmitted by subscribers who are not under the control of the access provider. The defense is not available if the access provider is involved in providing the content.

The fact that an ISP or other access provider undertakes screening to see if obscene material is present will not, in itself, make the access provider civilly liable as a publisher of the obscene material, because 47 USC §223(e) also contains a "good Samaritan" provision that insulates it against liability.

The Digital Millennium Copyright Act (see ¶1310.6) enacts a new 17 USC §512, indemnifying ISPs against copyright liability when users who are not under the control of the ISP use Internet access provided by the ISP to transmit infringing materials.

[¶7540] Domain Names

Every Web site must have a domain name, a combination of up to 22 letters and numbers ending in a period and the name of the top level domain (TLD).[7] The most common TLD is the familiar "com," for a commercial Web site. The other current TLDs in the United States are .gov, for government sites,.org for organizations, .edu for educational institutions, .net for networks such as Internet Service Providers, and .mil for military sites. Other domain names, such as .uk for United Kingdom and .de for German (Deutschland) indicate sites originating outside the United States.

So far, there is no requirement for domain name registrars to ascertain whether applicants for .com, .org, or .net registrations really fit into those categories (although only actual government and military units can get .gov or .mil domain names). Some trademark attorneys suggest registering trademarks in all the top level domains (including new ones as they are added) to prevent others from registering the same name in other TLDs.

[¶7540.1] Assignment of Domain Names

At first, all domain names were assigned by a single entity, the Internet Assigned Number Authority (IANA), which delegated the process to a private corporation called Network Solutions, Inc. (NSI). The Department of Commerce issued two statements, the "green paper" (January, 1998) and the "white paper" (June, 1998) calling for expansion and adding more domain name registrars. In 1999, the transition from a monopoly to a competitive system began. A not-for-profit corporation called ICANN (Internet Corporation for Assigned Names) was created to supervise the addition of dozens of new registrars.[8]

[¶7540.2] Misuse of Domain Names

Most of the litigation has arisen in the context of "cybersquatting"—registering a domain name including the name of a famous company or product, for the purpose of getting the owner of the company or product to pay for the domain name. Other forms of deception are possible in the Internet context. See ¶1330.1 for a discussion of trademark infringement and trademark dilution in general.

"Metatags" are descriptions of a Web site and its content. They are not visible to ordinary users, but are used to index the site. Using someone else's trademark in metatags without permission is also wrongful. Using a domain name and metatags that are likely to create confusion with someone else's trademark constitutes trademark infringement that can be enjoined by the senior trademark owner.[9]

A domain name that would be an "intuitive" choice for a competitor's site is considered confusing to consumers, and hence inappropriate.[10] Registering as domain names proper names that are part of someone else's trademark, then licensing the names for use in e-mail addresses, is unlawful trademark dilution.[11]

Internet domain names are property, and therefore can be garnished by a judgment creditor. A cybersquatter can be forced to surrender all domain names, not merely the ones that a particular proceeding has determined to be infringing.[12]

Most of these cases involve clear, intentional trademark abuse and intent to confuse. In the future, however, we will see many more cases involving individuals and businesses using trademarks and service marks in good faith, and seeking to extend them to the Internet, coming into conflict with other individuals who arrived at the same or similar marks independently.

[¶7550] Pornography

Although a vast variety of pornographic materials depicting most imaginable forms of sexual activity can be found on the Internet, legislation and court cases concentrate on two related issues: the ability of children to access pornography, and the ability of anyone to access pornography depicting children.[13]

In 1996, the Communications Decency Act, part of P.L. 104-104, was enacted. The CDA imposed federal criminal penalties for making "obscene, indecent and patently offensive materials" accessible to minors via commercial online services or other means of Internet access. These provisions of the CDA were found unconstitutional by the Supreme Court in July, 1997.[14]

Congress attempted to draft a bill that would pass Constitutional scrutiny, and the Child Online Protection Act (COPA; P.L. 105-277) was signed on 10/21/98, forbidding the online dissemination of material that is "harmful to minors." However, this bill was no more successful in court than its predecessor.

In late 1998, the Eastern District of Pennsylvania granted a TRO against enforcement of the Child Online Protection Act, given the likelihood of determination of its unconstitutionality.[15] In this reading, the COPA is not narrowly tailored to protect minors. The affirmative defense of maintaining a site that requires users to verify their age or give a credit card number is technologically impractical, and without that possibility for affirmative defense, COPA unconstitutionally prohibits speech that is authorized for adults.

To the Eastern District of Virginia, the First Amendment is violated by a public library's use of a filter to block access to material deemed harmful to minors. The court viewed this as not narrowly tailored to protect children, but an impermissible prior restraint on speech.[16]

The CDA criminal provision, 47 USC §223(a), barring transmissions that are "obscene, lewd, lascivious, filthy, or indecent, with intent to annoy, abuse, threaten or harass" was upheld.[17] The provision survives a First Amendment challenge as long as it is read narrowly enough to apply only to obscene communications.

[¶7555] SPAM

Spam—unsolicited e-mail—is often annoying to recipients, and often poses a tremendous problem to Internet Service Providers (ISPs) who find their servers clogged with such messages.

The Eastern District of Virginia has held the transmitter of "spam" liable to AOL, because the spammer violated state and federal computer fraud law by falsely designating the origin of the e-mail messages. AOL's trademark and service mark were also diluted by the spam, violating the Lanham Act.[18] Other theories that have succeeded include trespass to chattel—i.e., improperly occupying an Internet server with a barrage of unsolicited messages.[19]

[¶7560] Privacy Issues

A certain amount of information can be gathered about a computer user merely by observing the sites that he or she connects to. If the individual registers at a site, additional information will be generated. If he or she makes purchases on-line, information about purchasing habits (as well as address, addresses of persons to whom gifts are sent, and credit card numbers) becomes available. Once gathered, information can be harvested or re-sold in various ways, so protection of the privacy of Web users is a salient issue.

In July, 1999, the Federal Trade Commission reported to Congress about privacy issues online. The FTC's position as of that time is that, in general, industry can perform effective self-regulation (despite some problem areas), and privacy legislation is not currently needed. The report, "Self-Regulation and Privacy Online: A Report to Congress," can be downloaded from http://www.ftc.gov.

Children are especially vulnerable to appeals for information, and misuse of that information, leading to the passage of the Children's Online Privacy

Protection Act of 1998 (COPPA; P.L. 105-277). The COPPA defines a child as a person under age 13. "Personal information" means name; address; e-mail address; telephone number; Social Security number; or other identifying information. "Disclosure" means any release of personal information disclosed by a child, including making the information available on the Internet (e.g., e-mail, message boards, and chat rooms).

The FTC has proposed a COPPA implementing rule, available at http://www.ftc.gov/opa/1999/9904/childrensonlineprivacy.pdf. The proposal requires commercial sites to post a notice on the site disclosing how they handle personal information about children. The site must have a procedure for getting consent from a parent before collecting, using, or disclosing personal information from children. The parent could gain access to information about his or her own children, and could halt further use or collection of personal information about the child or could permit its disclosure to third parties.

In practical terms, e-mail is the equivalent of a post card, offering little privacy. It is not a violation of an employee's right to privacy for an employer company to examine e-mails sent and received on the corporate computer network,[20] and employers do have an incentive to do so, because, for instance, e-mails can be introduced as evidence of a hostile work environment or antitrust conspiracy.

[¶7570] Linking and Framing

It is technologically possible to place hyperlinks leading from any Web site to any other file that is accessible on the Web. Free availability of links is considered part of the Web culture. However, in some instances, linking will result in unauthorized duplication of copyrighted text, images, and multimedia files. If those files are altered, an unauthorized derivative work can be created.

In addition to the practice of linking—where it is evident that the user has left one Web site and moved to another—"framing" is the practice of placing material from one site inside another site. Not only is there potential for confusion, but the framing might be done in such a way as to limit exposure of Web users to advertisements on the "linked" site. Although this may be seen as a boon by consumers, it is less attractive to the advertisers who have paid to place the advertisements.

Although to date few U.S. cases have been filed, and those few cases have settled,[21] it seems to be better practice to avoid framing, and to make sure that links are permitted by the originating site.

[¶7575] Y2K Liability

The Y2K problem. or Millennium Bug, is caused by the inability of most computer systems to represent dates with four rather than two figures. The result is an inability to differentiate between twentieth and twenty-first century dates: for instances, 1902 and 2002 would both be represented by "02."

This book went to press in the summer of 1999, so it was unclear to what extent businesses would be able to make their computer systems "Y2K compliant" before 1/1/00, and what kinds and amounts of damage would be suffered from inability to do so.

In addition to the federal lawmaking described immediately below, several states have also passed bills limiting Y2K suits against agencies of state government: e.g., Nevada, Florida, Georgia, and Virginia.[22]

[¶7575.1] Federal Statutes

Four federal laws deal with Y2K issues in the private sector. The first is P.L. 105-164, the Year 2000 Readiness Act, centering on the readiness of financial institutions to handle the Y2K problem. Federal banking regulators are directed to provide seminars for the banking institutions under their jurisdiction, to train them in project management and vendor relations for Y2K upgrades.

[¶7575.1.1] Disclosure Act

Next out of the box was P.L. 105-271, the Year 2000 Information and Readiness Disclosure Act. It provides that corporate statements[23] about the degree of their Y2K readiness will not be admissible in state or federal civil suits against the disclosing company to prove the accuracy or truth of the statement, unless the disclosure was fraudulent, made in bad faith, or was otherwise unreasonable; or except to support a claim for anticipatory breach or repudiation. In general, Year 2000 statements will not amend or alter contracts or warranties.

The disclosing company is not liable for false, inaccurate, or misleading disclosure statements unless the plaintiff can prove that the statement was knowingly false or deceptive, or without notice of the maker's lack of direct knowledge of the validity of the statement. If the suit is for defamation or trade disparagement, liability will lie for the statement only if the statement is false, inaccurate, or misleading, unless the plaintiff proves that the statement was knowingly false or made with reckless disregard of its truth or falsity.

P.L. 105-271 exempts businesses from antitrust liability for Y2K-related communications, disclosures, or attempts to resolve problems. In other words, collaborative efforts and standards will not be deemed anticompetitive or collusive.

[¶7575.1.2] Small Business Loans]

The Small Business Y2K Readiness Act is enacted by P.L. 106-8. It requires the federal government to designate eligible lenders for a short-term[24] program of small-business loans, backed by federal guarantees, so small businesses can upgrade their computer systems. The bill also aims to relieve substantial economic injury incurred by small businesses because of their own Y2K problems or problems of their service providers and suppliers, to the extent that the injury is not covered by insurance.

[¶7575.1.3] The Y2K Act

Congress' major Y2K measure of 1999 is P.L. 106-37, the Y2K Act, (signed July 20, 1999). Congress indicated that business should spend the rest of 1999 upgrading systems for Y2K readiness, rather than suing other businesses for actual or anticipated Y2K problems. The law is intended to encourage informal alternatives, such as mediation, in lieu of litigation. The law is supposed to establish uniform legal standards for Y2K compliance.

P.L. 106-37 defines a "Y2K failure" as failure of a computer device, system, or software to display 21st century dates properly. A "Y2K action" is a civil suit or administrative proceeding where the plaintiff alleges harm or injury from an actual or potential Y2K failure. The Act does not create any new causes of action, and it does not apply to personal injury or wrongful death claims. Inconsistent state laws are preempted. Contract defenses based on impossibility and commercial impracticability can still be asserted, using the law in existence on January 1, 1999.

The Y2K Act applies to any Y2K action brought after 1/1/99 for Y2K failure that occurred before 1/1/2003, or a potential Y2K failure that could occur or has allegedly caused harm or injury before 1/1/2003.

In Y2K actions, written contract terms, including warranty disclaimers and exclusions or limitations of liability, will be strictly enforced, unless an applicable state law in effect on January 1, 1999 forbids strict enforcement. Any Y2K plaintiff who seeks damages must file with the complaint a "statement of specific information as to the nature and amount of each element of damages and the factual basis for the damages calculation." A similar statement must be filed when the plaintiff alleges a material defect in a product or service, as to the manifestations of the material defects and the facts behind the claim of materiality. A statement of facts giving rise to a "strong inference" of the defendant's state of mind must be filed with the complaint for any cause of action where the defendant's state of mind is relevant.

Would-be plaintiffs in Y2K-related cases (other than those who seek only injunctive relief) are obligated to provide prelitigation notice by certified mail to each prospective defendant's registered agent, CEO, or person designated to receive such notices.[25] The notice must disclose, in detail:

- The harm or loss allegedly suffered by the would-be plaintiff
- Manifestations of any material defect alleged to have caused the problem
- The prospective plaintiff's grounds for relief
- What the prospective plaintiff would like done to resolve the problem
- Name, title, address, and telephone number of someone who can negotiate dispute resolution for the prospective plaintiff.

The prospective defendant has 30 days to give the plaintiff a written statement (also sent by certified mail) describing its existing and planned future actions to resolve the plaintiff's problem, including willingess to use alternative dispute resolution (ADR) measures. The defendant's statement is not admissible in evidence if a lawsuit eventually ensues.

If the potential defendant fails to respond, the prospective plaintiff can immediately bring suit. The potential defendant's response starts a 60-day "cooling off" period during which the potential plaintiff is barred from suing, to give the potential defendant time to implement corrective measures.

On the other hand, if the potential plaintiff does not provide prelitigation notice before filing suit, the defendant can elect to treat the complaint as prelitigation notice, in which case discovery will be stayed and time periods will be tolled to give the defendant a chance to put corrective measures into place.

Y2K damages are subject to the plaintiff's duty to mitigate based on available information about coping with Y2K risks. In contract actions, damages will be awarded only as allowed by the express terms of the contract, or by operation of the state or federal law in existence at the time of contract creation.

In Y2K tort cases, other than claims of intentional tort arising independent of any contract, the plaintiff is not entitled to economic loss damages (e.g., business interruption; lost sales or lost profits) unless the plaintiff was a party to a contract providing such damages, or applicable state or federal law awards damages for tangible property damaged by the Y2K failure. Damages for "bystanders" (plaintiffs not in substantial privity with a manufacturer, seller, service providers, or distributor defendant) are also limited.

Punitive damages can be imposed in Y2K-related actions only if the plaintiff proves the availability of such damages by "clear and convincing evidence." Furthermore, if the defendant is an individual with net worth under $500,000, or a small business (under 50 employees), punitive damages are capped at three times the amount of compensatory damages, or $250,000—whichever is less. But the cap does not apply if the plaintiff can establish the defendant's specific intent to injure the plaintiff. (Here, again, the evidentiary standard is clear and convincing evidence.)

In a multiple-defendant Y2K case (other than a contract case), each defendant is liable only for its own relative and proportionate responsibility for the damages, as established by special interrogatories to the jury (or by specific findings in a court trial). That is, liability is not joint and several, unless a finding is made of knowing fraud or specific intent to injure the plaintiff. Another exception to the general rule relates to a consumer suing as an individual, not in a class action, who sues for a Y2K-related consumer product defect. In this case, defendants are jointly and severally liable for the "uncollectible share" of damages (e.g., any damages attributable to an entity that no longer exists, or that is judgment-proof). State laws that give defendants even greater protection against liability are **not** preempted by this Act.

Businesses can assert a defense of "Y2K upset" when sued by government entities, if they experienced a temporary period of exceptional noncompliance with federal requirements because of a Y2K problem. Y2K upset is a complete defense to the imposition of a penalty for failure to satisfy federal measurement, monitoring, or reporting requirements. But the defense applies only to an upset of 15 days or less, unless the regulatory authority grants specific relief for a longer period; and only upsets occurring before June 30, 2000 qualify for relief.

The statute also includes consumer relief provisions. A consumer's residential mortgage can't be foreclosed on the basis of a Y2K failure that prevented the mortgage payment transaction from being recorded.

ENDNOTES

1. ABA Standing Committee on Ethics and the Profession Formal Opinion 399-413 (3/10/99), 67 LW 2645; Ohio Supreme Court Board of Comm'rs on Grievances and Discipline Op 99-2 (4/9/99), 67 LW 2646.
2. Technically, the Internet is a system of connections between computers that can communicate using a standardized protocol. The Web is the part of the Internet—by now, the largest and fastest-growing part—that uses a graphical user interface (GUI) for the convenience of users, rather than older menu-based command systems.
3. The Utah law is discussed in Richard Raysman and Peter Brown, "Legislation on Digital Signatures," *N.Y.L.J.* 4/13/99 p. 3, and the Illinois Electronic Commerce Security Act (8/14/98) is discussed at 67 LW 2112.
4. See 67 LW 2069.
5. *Plus System, Inc. v. New England Network, Inc.*, 804 F.Supp. 11 (D.Colo. 1992) is an early statement that the minimum contacts can be electronic in nature.
6. The classic statement is *Panavision International LP v. Toeppen*, 141 F.3d 1316 (9th Cir. 1998). In contrast, a very early case,, *Inset Systems Inc. v. Instruction Set Inc.*, 937 F.Supp. 161 (D.Conn. 1996) does permit very expansive personal jurisdiction over Web sites. See Wendy Liebowitz, "Courts Struggling With Cyberspace Jurisdiction," *N.Y.L.J.* 1/26/99 p. 5.
7. See 66 LW 2563.
8. See 67 LW 2205 and Richard Raysman and Peter Brown, "Developments in Trademark and Domain-Name Disputes," *N.Y.L.J.* 3/9/99 p. 3; John Simons, "Monopoly on Web Addresses is Broken as Network Solutions Gets Five Rivals," *Wall Street Journal* 4/22/99 p. B10. Although international developments are beyond the scope of this volume, their relevance to the Internet is obvious. Attorneys with an interest in these issues should follow developments in the European Union and the World Intellectual Property Organization (WIPO). See, e.g., Jeri Clausing, "United Nations Group Issues Report on Internet Addresses," *New York Times* 5/3/99 p. C2.
9. *Brookfield Communications Inc. v. West Coast Entertainment Corp.*, 67 LW 1654 (9th Cir. 4/22/99). *Planned Parenthood Federation v. Bucci*, 66 LW 1528 (2nd Cir. 2/9/98) is a summary order affirming an injunction granted against the use of a deceptive domain name registered by an anti-abortion activist.

The Playboy trademark is quite valuable, especially in light of the large amount of sexual content on the Web, and therefore several cases have been brought by Playboy Enterprises Inc. to protect its trademarks. A pornography site wrongfully entitled "Playboy's Private Collection" was liable to Playboy for trademark infringement, trademark dilution, and counterfeiting: *Playboy Enterprises Inc. v. Universal Tel-a-Talk Inc.*, 67 LW 1320 (E.D. Pa. 11/4/98).

Hong Kong defendants who created a false association by using "Playboy" as a metatag for an unauthorized site were subject to jurisdiction in Virginia, because of tortious injury caused to Playboy and regular solicitation of business in the state: *Playboy Enterprises v. Asia Focus Inc.*, 66 LW 1704 (E.D. Va. 4/10/98).

However, a one-time Playboy Playmate was entitled to a Lanham Act fair use defense for using "Playmate" as a metatag for her personal site, because it was an accurate description of herself; use of the Playmate title was not contractually restricted; and she did not deceive consumers into believing that her site was authorized by Playboy: *Playboy Enterprises Inc. v. Welles*, 66 LW 1686 (S.D. Cal. 4/22/98).

Earlier Playboy cases involve copyright violations in distributing photographs copyrighted by Playboy over the Web: *Playboy Enterprises v. Sanfilippo*, 46 USPQ 2d 1350 (C.D. Cal. 1998); *Playboy Enterprises, Inc. v. WebbWorld, Inc.*, 991 F.Supp. 543 (N.D. Tex. 1997).

Trademark/domain name interactions are discussed in Carl Oppedahl, "Pursuing Domain Name Registrants Can Backfire," *National Law Journal* 4/26/99 p. B6, pointing out that domain names do not always operate as trademarks, and litigation can actually have the effect of weakening a trademark by establishing the challenger's superior claim.

Attempts to use initials as a trademark or domain name create particular difficulties, in light of the numerous other businesses with the same initials. See, e.g., *C.D. Solutions Inc. v. Tooker*, 15 F.Supp.2d 986 (D.Ore.1998); *Data Concepts Inc. v. Digital Consulting Inc.*, 150 F.3d 620 (6th Cir. 1998).

10. *Washington Speakers Bureau Inc. v. Leading Authorities Inc.*, 67 LW 1528 (E.D. Va. 2/2/99).
11. *Avery Dennison Corp. v. Sumpton*, 66 LW 1608 (C.D. Cal. 3/19/98).
12. *Umbro Int'l Inc. v. 3263851 Canada Inc.*, 67 LW 1576 (Va.Cir.Ct. 2/3/99).
13. *U.S. v. Charbonneau*, 979 F.Supp. 1177 (S.D. Oh. 1997) holds that there is no reasonable expectation of privacy when using a public e-mail system to transmit child pornography.
14. *Reno v. ACLU*, 521 U.S. 844 (Sup.Ct. 1997).
15. *ACLU v. Reno*, 67 LW 1336 (E.D. Pa. 11/19/98).
16. *Mainstream Loudon v. Board of Trustees of Loudon County Library*, 24 F.Supp.2d 552 (E.D. Va. 1998).
17. *Apollo Media Corp. v. Reno*, 19 F.Supp.2d 1081 (N.D. Cal. 1998), aff'd without opinion, #98-933 (Sup.Ct. 4/19/99).
18. *AOL v. LGCM, Inc.*, 67 LW 1416 (E.D. Va. 11/10/98). Also see *AOL v. Prime Data Systems Inc.*, also 67 LW 1416 (E.D. Va. 12/20/98), a federal magistrate's recommendation of over $400,000 in compensatory and punitive damages for AOL because of trademark violations resulting from spam, and misappropriation of AOL member lists to send them the unwanted messages.
    Earlier anti-spam cases include *Hotmail v. Van$Money Pie, Inc.*, 47 USPQ 2d 1020 (N.D. Cal. 1998) and *CompuServe, Inc. v. CyberPromotions, Inc.*, 962 F.Supp. 1015 (S.D. Oh. 1997).

19. Such theories are discussed by Richard Raysman and Peter Brown, *"Conversion, Trespass and Other New Litigation Issues," N.Y.L.J.* 5/11/99 p. 3.

20. See, e.g., *Restuccia v. Burk Technology, Inc.*, #95-2125 (Mass..Super.Ct. 1996); *Smyth v. Pillsbury Co.*, 914 F.Supp. 97 (E.D. Pa. 1996). Possibly, this principle is limited to an internal e-mail system rather than a public one: see, e.g., *Andersen Consulting v. UPON and Bickel & Brewer*, #97 C 5501, 1998 U.S. Dist. Lexis 1016 (D.Ill.1/23/98) and *Bourke v. Nissan Motor Corp.*, 3B068705 (Cal.App. 7/26/98).

    Additional issues arise in the unionized workplace, where using the e-mail system to complain about working conditions might constitute protected concerted activity, e.g., *Timekeeping Systems Inc. v. Leinweber*, 323 NLRB No. 30 (1997).

21. See, e.g., Bob Tedeschi, "Ticketmaster and Microsoft Settle Suit on Internet Linking," *New York Times* 2/15/99 p. C6.

22. Margaret A. Jacobs, "Whose Problem Is It Anyway? States Tackle Y2K Liability Issue," *Wall Street Journal* 1/15/99 p. B3.

23. The Act applies to Year 2000 statements made between 7/14/98 and 7/14/2001, and Year 2000 readiness disclosures made before 7/14/2001.

24. Expiring 12/31/2000.

25. In a class action, only the named plaintiff has to satisfy these requirements. In addition to the normal federal class action requirements, a Y2K class action must involve a product or service defect that is material for the majority of class members, and each class member is entitled to notification of the class counsel's fees in addition to normal class action notification.

INDEX

Note: All references are to paragraph numbers, not pages.